British Civil Aircraft

1919–1972: Volume III

British European Airways' Vickers Viking 1B G-AJBR 'Sir Bertram Ramsey', flying over Chatham Dockyard in the Corporation's Admiral Class livery in 1951. *(B.E.A.)*

British Civil Aircraft

1919–1972: Volume III

A J Jackson

BY THE SAME AUTHOR

De Havilland Aircraft since 1909

Avro Aircraft since 1908

Blackburn Aircraft since 1909

First published in 1959 as *British Civil Aircraft since 1919* as a two-volume study, this work was updated and republished in 1973. Due to the death of the author it has not been possible to bring this title up to date but R. T. Jackson has made amendments to his father's second edition so that this major reference book can once more be available. Its publication now is offered as a tribute to A. J. Jackson's many years of research.

ISBN 0 85177 818 6
Printed in Great Britain at
the University Printing House, Oxford
for
Putnam, an imprint of
Conway Maritime Press Ltd.
24 Bride Lane, Fleet Street,
London EC4Y 8DR
First Published 1960
Second Edition 1974
Reprinted with corrections 1988

Contents

Foreword

This third volume of *British Civil Aircraft 1919–1972* is uniform in layout with the first two and completes the detailed description, illustration and listing of all transport aircraft, light aeroplanes, home-builts, civil registered military types and helicopters constructed in Britain, or imported for British operators, from 1919 to 1972.

Commencing with the highly successful Hawker Siddeley H.S.748 propeller-turbine medium transport, it covers the entire output of other well known British manufacturers such as Hunting Percival, Martinsyde, Miles, Percival, Saunders-Roe, Scottish Aviation, Short, Slingsby, Spartan, Supermarine, Vickers and Westland. It recalls epic long distance flights and brilliant racing successes by the classic Miles and Percival monoplanes of the 1930s; tells of the revolution in air transport and the new standards of passenger comfort set by Short's immortal Empire Flying Boats on the world trunk routes of Imperial Airways and B.O.A.C.; and begins the story of the company's modern Skyvan.

The activities of pre-1939 light aeroplanes built by Parnall, Redwing, Westland and others are discussed along with modern equivalents such as the Nipper; Rollason's well known free enterprise Condor; and the Popular Flying Association's ever-growing family of home-builts.

Examination of the extensive contents list for this volume shows that the later part of the alphabet includes a considerable number of British and foreign designers and constructors, all of whom had at least one aircraft perpetuated in the pages of the register of British civil aircraft which qualified for inclusion in this book.

Current names are used for airports and airfields, but for nostalgic reasons, and for uniformity with the first edition, the famous Kentish Customs airport of Ashford, whose hallowed turf is mentioned so often in the annals of aviation history, is referred to in all three volumes by its ancient name of Lympne.

The author again acknowledges with gratitude contributions so willingly provided by many individuals and organisations during the compilation of this volume. He wishes, in particular, to thank Edgar W. Percival, managing director of Percival Aircraft Ltd., for his painstaking assistance during the reshaping and correcting of chapters on Percival aeroplanes. The author also expresses regret for any embarrassment caused, or harm done to Edgar W. Percival's reputation, by erroneous statements concerning the aircraft he designed, which, derived from other sources, found their way into the 1960 edition of this book.

Further sincere thanks are extended to Ann Tilbury, photographic librarian of *Flight International*; and to the following editors—David Dorrell,

Air Pictorial; F. G. Swanborough, *Air Enthusiast*; M. J. Hooks, *Air-Britain Digest*; J. W. R. Taylor, *Jane's All the World's Aircraft*; B. N. Stainer, *Aviation Photo News*; P. W. Moss, compiler of *Impressments Log*; and the editors of *Air-Britain News* and *Anglia Aeronews*. Also to A. W. L. Nayler, librarian, Royal Aeronautical Society; the staff of *Lloyds List and Shipping Gazette*; the B.E.A. Photographic Department; and to L. E. Bradford for the enlivening selection of new and updated three view drawings in his own inimitable style.

John Goring has again assisted with the preparation and updating of chapters concerned with transport aircraft; David Roberts double checked all factual data; and my wife Marjorie, at whose feat of endurance one can only marvel, has typed all three volumes.

Satisfactory completion of the book would not have been possible without the notable assistance of D. J. Penn-Smith; N. H. Ellison, Slingsby Sailplanes Ltd.; Harry Holmes, Hawker Siddeley Aviation Ltd., Manchester; Michael Jones, Rollason Aircraft and Engines Ltd.; J. D. Oughton, British Aircraft Corporation Ltd., Filton; Wg. Cdr. K. H. Wallis, Wallis Autogyros Ltd.; K. Ellis, Merseyside Aviation Society; G. Riley and R. P. Smith, Midland Aircraft Preservation Society; David Reid, Prestwick Airport Aviation Group; of long term associates C. H. Barnes, D. L. Brown, M. D. N. Fisher, Leslie Hunt, J. O. Isaacs, P. M. Jarrett, G. A. Jenks, W. L. Lewis, S. MacConnacher, Ann and Roy Procter, Richard Riding, Monsieur G. Saillot, and of the numerous friends who have assisted in other ways.

Leigh-on-Sea
October 1973

A. J. J.

Hawker Siddeley H.S.748 Series 2 G-ATMI flying from Luton in Autair International Airways' colours, 1966. It was twice leased to L.I.A.T. as VP-LIU and to British Air Ferries, Ltd., Southend in 1971.

Hawker Siddeley H.S.748

In 1957 A. V. Roe and Co. Ltd. decided to re-enter the civil market with a turbine powered Dakota replacement, rugged, economic and capable of operating from primitive grass airfields or 'hot and high' aerodromes overseas. A design team led by J. R. Ewans explored several layouts and in January 1959 work began at Chadderton on four prototypes of the chosen Avro 748 design, two for flight trials and two for static tests. The first of these, G-APZV, flew at Woodford on 24 June 1960 piloted by chief test pilot J. G. Harrison.

The 748 all-metal, pressurised, low-wing monoplane was of Avro fail-safe construction accommodating up to 44 passengers. To ensure sufficient airscrew ground clearance and avoid cut-outs in the spars, 1,740 e.s.h.p. Dart R.Da.7 Mk.514 engines were mounted with their jet pipes over the wing with the undercarriage retracting forward into a bulbous compartment ahead of the leading edge. This gave the nacelle a cranked appearance reminiscent of the A.T.L. 90 Accountant.

The second prototype, G-ARAY, first flew on 10 April 1961 and in the following July went to Cyprus for hot weather trials and to Madrid for high altitude tests. It then returned to the factory to be converted into the first Avro 748 Series 2 with 1,910 e.s.h.p. Dart R.Da.7 Mk.531s which imparted better all-round performance. Thus powered G-ARAY first flew on 6 November 1961.

A manufacturing agreement signed with the Indian Government for the assembly of Avro 748s from British-built components at Kanpur by Hindustan Aircraft Ltd. bore fruit on 1 November 1961 with the first flight of the first Indian Air Force Series 1, BH572 'Subroto', while the first Series 2, BH576, flew on 28 January 1964. The first civil Series 2, VT-DUO, entered service with the Indian Airlines Corporation on 8 August 1967 and by 1972 had been joined by at least VT-DXF to 'XR and VT-EAT to VT-EBC.

G-ARMV, first of three Series 1 aircraft for Skyways Coach Air Ltd., flew at Woodford on 31 August 1961, appeared at the Farnborough S.B.A.C.

Show, toured Jordan and Syria, and completed 160 hours of route proving between Lympne, Beauvais, Lyons and Montpellier before entering service on the Skyways Lympne–Beauvais shuttle on 1 April 1962.

The excellent performance of the Series 2 prototype, G-ARAY, during tests from deeply rutted surfaces at Martlesham in February 1962 led to an order from R.A.F. Transport (later Air Support) Command for the Avro 780 strengthened military version with rear loading doors and 'kneeling' undercarriage. This type entered R.A.F. service as the Andover C.Mk.1 but four standard Series 2 aircraft, XS791 to XS794, for ferrying senior officers, and two more, XS789 and XS790, for the Queen's Flight at Benson were designated Andover C.C.Mk.2. To speed certification of the first Avro 780, the prototype 748 Series 1, G-APZV, returned to Chadderton on 2 August 1962 for conversion to this standard as the Avro 748MF and first flew as G-ARRV on 21 December 1963.

LV-PIZ, first of nine Series 1 aircraft for Aerolineas Argentinas, flown on 10 December 1961, was ferried 11,300 miles to Buenos Aires via the North Atlantic route in 8 days by test pilot Colin Allen. On arrival it was christened 'Ciudad de Bahia Blanca' and became LV-HGW. The Aerolineas fleet was increased to 12 in 1963 and operated almost entirely from rough provincial airstrips although two international routes, to Montevideo in Uruguay and to Ascuncion in Paraguay, occasionally took them to paved runways.

Following an extensive sales tour of Europe, Africa, India and the Far East by J. G. Harrison in G-ARAY between March and May 1963, a number of aviation's great companies were re-shuffled to form Hawker Siddeley Aviation Ltd. and the aircraft changed its name to H.S.748 overnight. Another sales expedition made to the Caribbean, South America and Canada early in 1964 brought G-ARAY's mileage for the two trips to 91,263 in $413\frac{1}{2}$ flying hours. It was then loaned to Linea Aeropostal Venezolana (LAV) in February 1965 as YV-C-AMC; to VARIG (Brazil) in December 1965 as PP-VJQ; to Leeward Islands Air Transport (LIAT), Antigua, in April 1966 as VP-LIO; and to Philippine Air Lines in February 1967 as PI-C784 before actual sale to Falcks Flyvetjeneste (Denmark) in the following year as OY-DFV. It returned to Gatwick for service with Dan-Air as G-ARAY in May 1971.

H.S.748 Series 2 G-ATEJ, one of four purchased by Southend-based Channel Airways Ltd. 1965–66. (*Aviation Photo News*)

The policy of encouraging customer evaluation paid off and orders built up from all over the world, making the 748 Britain's best selling medium transport. Six were supplied to the Brazilian Air Force in 1963, initially for the Brasilia–Rio de Janeiro shuttle; three for Thai Airways' domestic services and one for Air Ceylon in 1964; plus six to LAV and two to LIAT in 1965–66.

The maximum permissible take-off weight of the Series 2, increased to 43,500 lb. in August 1963, was further raised to 44,495 lb. in October 1965, enabling G-ATEH, 'EI, 'EJ and 'EK, supplied to Channel Airways Ltd. at Southend, to be equipped as 62 seaters. Airline orders followed from Bahamas Airways (4); LAN-Chile (9); VARIG of Brazil (10); and Philippine Air Lines (8) but the 748 was in such demand that British operators leased aircraft abroad during off-peak months, as for example Skyways' G-ARMW to LIAT in January 1965 as VP-LII; the B.K.S. G-ATAM to Aerotaxi (Mexico) in July 1966 as XA-SEI and to Philippine Air Lines in August 1967 as PI-C1020; Channel Airways' G-ATEH to COPA (Panama) in October 1965 as HP-416 followed by G-ATEI to LIAT in December 1965 as VP-LIN; and Autair's G-ATMI and 'MJ to LIAT and Jamaica Air Services in December 1967 as VP-LIU and 6Y-JFJ respectively. In 1971 this pair went into service on British Air Ferries cross-Channel routes out of Southend. The first instance of a re-imported 748 occurred in 1970 when Skyways acquired OE-LHS 'Franz Lehar' which, with OE-LHT 'Anton Bruckner', had operated over Austrian Airlines' mountainous routes since 1966. It went into service on the Beauvais shuttle as G-AXVG in January 1970.

V.I.P. versions of the H.S.748 were supplied not only to the Queen's Flight but to the King of Thailand, to the Presidents of Argentina, Brazil, Ecuador, Venezuela and Zambia, the Sultan of Brunei, and to No. 34 Squadron R.A.A.F., Fairburn, for Government use. Eight navigation trainers were also supplied to the R.A.A.F. as flying classrooms, the first, A10-601, flown on 21 February 1968, being registered briefly as G-AVZD for certification trials of the Dart R.Da.8 engine.

Two special aircraft, G-AVXI and 'XJ, were used by the Civil Aviation Flying Unit, Stansted, for radio calibration work and D-AFSD was supplied to the Bundesanstalt für Flugsicherung for the same purpose in West Germany. Other aircraft ordered included ZK-CWJ for Mount Cook Airways Ltd., the New Zealand scenic airline much used by ski enthusiasts, and two for even higher altitude work with Royal Nepal Airlines. The first of these was 9N-AAU which flew as G-AXVZ during certification flights in 1970.

A new version, the H.S.748 Series 2A with R.Da.7 Mk.532 engines, was announced in June 1967 and although this type was first ordered by Avianca of Columbia, the first delivery of a Series 2A was made to VARIG Airlines whose last two aircraft were brought up to this standard while under construction, the Series 2s already delivered to VARIG being converted later.

Hawker Siddeley's Series 2A demonstrator, G-AVRR, first flown on 5 September 1967, spent much of its life on lease to potential purchasers just as G-ARAY had done and went to SATA, Azores, in February 1969; to Transair, Canada, in April 1969 as CF-YQD; to Olympic Airways, Greece, in June 1969; to Air Cape and Suidwes Lugdiens in South Africa in the following December as ZS-IGI; to Zambia Airways in March 1970 as 9J-ABM and then to South African Airways as ZS-HSI. From January to June 1971 it

First flown at Woodford on 12 October 1967, PP-VDN was first of a fleet of eight H.S.748 Series 2s and two Series 2As supplied to the Brazilian airline VARIG, 1967–68.

H.S.748 Series 2A 5W-FAN, first for Polynesian Airlines, Samoa.

was in Indonesia with Merpati Nusantara Airlines, and in the following October was leased to Transgabon as TR-LQJ until they purchased it outright in August 1972.

G-AZJH, a convertible passenger/freight version with an additional door adjacent to the existing passenger door to give a cargo entry width of 8 ft. 9 in., first flew at Woodford on 31 December 1971. Late in 1972 it was camouflaged for demonstration to the Royal Malaysian Air Force and the Belgian Air Force.

By the end of 1972 further deliveries to Fiji Airways for its longer inter-island routes to the New Hebrides and the Solomons; to Air Gaspé, Chevron Standard Oil and Midwest Airlines, Canada; B.F.S., Germany; Botswana, Ghana, South African and Zambian Airways; COPA, Panama; SAESA, Mexico; Air Malawi; Bouraq Airlines and Merpati Nusantara Airlines, Indonesia; Rousseau Aviation, Dinard; Thai Airways; and the air forces of Columbia, Ecuador and Zambia, plus two special electronics trainer versions for the Royal Australian Navy, brought the total number of H.S.748s ordered, including those built for the R.A.F. and in India, to 264.

SPECIFICATION

Manufacturers: A. V. Roe and Co. Ltd., Greengate, Middleton, Manchester and Woodford Aerodrome, Cheshire (style changed to Hawker Siddeley Aviation Ltd. in 1964).
The Indian Air Force Maintenance Base, Kanpur, India.

Power Plants: (Series 1) Two 1,740 e.s.h.p. Rolls-Royce Dart 514.
(Series 2) Two 2,105 e.s.h.p. Rolls-Royce Dart 531.
(Series 2A) Two 2,290 e.s.h.p. Rolls-Royce Dart 532.

	Prototypes	Series 1	Series 2	Series 2A
Span	95 ft. 0 in.	98 ft. 6 in.	98 ft. 6 in.	98 ft. 6 in.
Length	67 ft. 0 in.	67 ft. 0 in.	67 ft. 0 in.	67 ft. 0 in.
Height	24 ft. 10 in.	24 ft. 10 in.	24 ft. 10 in.	24 ft. 10 in.
Wing area	795 sq. ft.	811 sq. ft.	811 sq. ft.	811 sq. ft.
Tare weight	19,444 lb.	22,614 lb.	25,600 lb.	26,000 lb.
All-up weight	33,000 lb.	38,000 lb.	44,495 lb.	44,495 lb.
Max. cruise	264 m.p.h.	270 m.p.h.	273 m.p.h.	280 m.p.h.
Maximum range	1,630 n.m.	1,565 n.m.	1,695 n.m.	1,840 n.m.

Production: (a) H.S.748 Series 1

Two prototypes, six others British registered and the following for export: (c/n 1539) LV-PIZ/LV-HGW; (1540) LV-PJA/LV-HHB; (1541) LV-PJR/LV-HHC; (1542) LV-PJS/LV-HHD; (1543) LV-PUC/LV-HHE; (1544) LV-PUM/LV-HHF; (1545) LV-PUP/LV-HHG; (1546) LV-PVH/LV-HHH; (1547) LV-PVI/LV-HHI; (1556) LV-PXD/LV-IDV; (1557) LV-PXH/LV-IEE; (1558) LV-PXP/LV-IEV.

(b) H.S.748 Series 2

Seven British registered and the following for export or the R.A.F. (excluding H.S.780 Andover C.Mk.1s which did not have constructor's numbers): (c/n 1550-1555) Brazilian Air Force C91-2500 to C91-2505; (1561) XS789; (1562) XS790; (1563-1566) XS791 to XS794; (1567) HS-THA; (1568) HS-THB; (1569) HS-THC; (1570) HS-TAF/HS-R-TAF/11-111; (1571) 4R-RCJ; (1572-1575) XS594 to XS597; (1577) YV-C-AME; (1578) YV-C-AMI; (1579) YV-C-AMO; (1580) YV-C-AMY; (1581) YV-C-AMF; (1582) YV-C-AMC; (1583) VP-LIK; (1584) VP-LIP; (1589) OE-LHS, later G-AXVG; (1590) OE-LHT; (1591) Venezuelan Ministry of Defence 0111; (1594) HP-432; (1595–1596) R.A.A.F. A10-595 and A10-596; (1597) LV-PGG/Presidential T-01; (1598) XA-SEV; (1599) XA-SEY; (1600) Zambian Air Force AF-601; (1601–1608) R.A.A.F. A10-601/G-AVZD to A10-608; (1609) VP-BCJ, later PI-C1027; (1610) VP-BCK, later PK-RHQ; (1611) VP-BCL, later CF-INE; (1612) VP-BCM, later G-AZSU; (1613) VQ-FAL; (1614–1622) CC-CEC to CC-CEK; (1625–1632) PP-VDN to PP-VDU; (1636–1643) PI-C1014 to PI-C1022; (1644) HS-THD; (1645) HS-THE; (1646) HS-THF; (1648–1655) Argentine Air Force; (1659) PI-C1023; (1660) PI-C1024; (1662) HP-484; (1663) PI-C1025; (1664) PI-C1026; (1670) VP-LAA; (1673) XA-SAB; (1674) XA-SAC; (1675) XA-SAF.

(c) H.S.748 Series 2A

Eight British registered aircraft and the following for export: (c/n 1633) PP-VDV; (1634) PP-VDX; (1647) ZK-CWJ; (1656) D-AFSD; (1657) HK-1408; (1658) HK-1409;

(1661) VQ-FBH; (1665) VQ-FBK; (1666) 7Q-YKA; (1667) 7Q-YKB; (1668) CF-MAK; (1669) CF-AMO; (1671) 9N-AAU/G-AXVZ; (1672) 9N-AAV; (1676) 9J-ABJ; (1677) 9J-ABK; (1680) 9J-ABW; (1682) Ecuadorian Air Force FAE.682; (1683) FAE.683, later HC-AUF; (1684) FAE.684; (1685) 9G-ABW; (1686) 9G-ABX; (1688) Zambian Air Force AF-602; (1689) ZK-DES; (1690) ZS-SBU; (1691) A2-ZFT; (1692) ZS-SBV; (1693) HS-THG; (1694) Brunei Air Force AMDB-110; (1696) PK-MHR; (1699) G-11-6/CF-AGI; (1702–1705) G-11-1/Colombian Air Force (Satena) FAC.1101 to G-11-4/FAC.1104; (1706) G-11-5/A2-ZGF; (1707) HS-THH; (1708) HS-THI; (1709) Royal Australian Navy N15-709; (1710) N15-710; (1711) D-AFSE; (1712–1713) awaiting sale 1973; (1714) 5W-FAO; (1715) HS-TAF; (1717) awaiting sale 1.73.

(d) Indian-built

Approximately 30 aircraft by 1972: (c/n HAL/K/748/501) Indian Air Force BH572 'Subroto'; (502) BH573 'Jumbo'; (503) BH574; (504) BH1047; (505) BH1048; (506) BH1010; (507) VT-DUO 'Taj Mahal'; (508–510) BH1011 to BH1013; (511) H913; (512) VT-DXF 'Ajanta'; (513) VT-DXG 'Sauchi', crashed at Madurai, India 9.12.71; (514) VT-DXH 'Somnath'; (515) VT-DXI 'Amber'; (516) VT-DXJ 'Rameswaram'; (517) H914; (518) H915; (519) VT-DXK 'Ellora'; (520) VT-DXL 'Konark'; (521) VT-DXM 'Khajuraho'; (522) VT-DXN 'Sarnath'; (523) VT-DXO 'Martund'; (524) VT-DXP 'Partapgurh'; (525) VT-DXQ 'Pushkar'; (526) VT-DXR 'Mahabali'; also VT-EAT to VT-EBC, including (544) VT-EAX 'Chittaurgarh'.

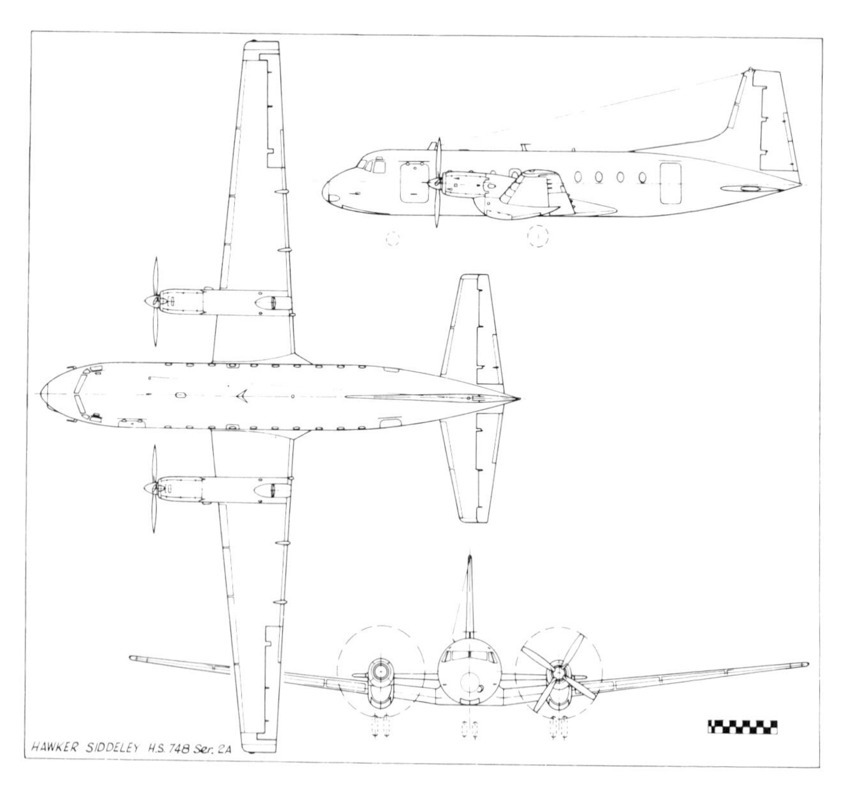

G-AEHJ, last of the three Gipsy VI Series I engined Phoenix monoplanes. (*Aeroplane*)

Heston Type 1 Phoenix

The Heston Type 1 Phoenix five seat commercial or private owner aircraft was, as the name implies, the first product of the Heston Aircraft Co. Ltd. formed in 1934 to take over the assets of Comper Aircraft Ltd. Designed by Mr. George Cornwall, it was of wooden construction, the plywood-covered fuselage consisting of a large, rectangular-section, cabin terminated by an elliptical section semi-monocoque rear portion. All flying surfaces, including the unflapped mainplane, were of orthodox design, fabric covered with plywood leading edges. Its most revolutionary feature was the Dowty hydraulically operated inward-retracting undercarriage, the first fitted to a British high-wing monoplane. The wheels retracted into a thickened lower stub wing which swept gracefully upward to maintain the line of the rigid N-type wing-bracing struts.

The prototype, G-ADAD, made its first flight at Heston on 18 August 1935 piloted by E. G. Hordern and proved to be 7 m.p.h. faster than the designed top speed. With five occupants, 100 lb. of luggage and fuel for 500 miles, it cruised at 125 m.p.h. on the 200 h.p. of one Gipsy VI. It was particularly notable, not only for the generous leg room and quietness in the cabin but also because no important modifications were recommended after official Martlesham trials.

The registration of the second Phoenix, VH-AJM, included the initials of C. J. (Jimmy) Melrose who bought it to start an 'Adelaide to Anywhere' air taxi service in South Australia. The words 'South Australian Centenary Flight from London' were painted along the fuselage and its name, 'Billing', was in honour of Melrose's uncle, N. Pemberton Billing, founder of the Supermarine Aviation Works. Leaving Lympne on 9 April 1936, he reached Adelaide on 25 April and completed a trip to Brisbane, Sydney, Launceston and Hobart in May and a number of charter flights in June. On 5 July he left Melbourne on the first leg of a charter to Darwin but covered only 30 miles in rough weather when the Phoenix crashed out of control with the loss of both occupants at Glenelg, South Australia. The prototype was sold to a Greek air taxi firm, and a second demonstrator, the blue and silver G-AEHJ, appeared at the Heathrow Garden Party of the Royal Aeronautical Society on 10 May 1936 and the Hatfield S.B.A.C. Show two months later.

The fourth Phoenix, G-AEMT, resplendent in silver and red, was the first of three improved models fitted with the Gipsy VI Series II engine driving a de Havilland constant speed airscrew.

The next Phoenix was the yellow G-AESV delivered to Standard Telephones and Cables Ltd. at Hatfield in March 1937 as a flying laboratory for the demonstration and development of their aircraft radio installations. This particular Phoenix was exhibited at the Heathrow R.Ae.S. Garden Party on 9 May 1937, but the type did not find a ready market, and only one other, G-AEYX, was built and sold to joint private owners C. Randrup and S. T. Worth at Heston in May 1939. The two earlier machines 'HJ and 'MT, unsold but with a two-year record of flying on hire, were also disposed of in 1939, the first to British American Air Services Ltd. of Heston and the other to the Luton Flying Club. Both did a considerable amount of charter flying just prior to the war until 'HJ was damaged beyond repair in an accident.

The three survivors, all with Gipsy VI Series II motors, were impressed in March 1940 for R.A.F. communications duties. The Luton Flying Club's G-AEMT went to No.24 Squadron, Hendon as X9393, served with No.4(C) Ferry Pilot Pool at Cardiff and after postings to Honeybourne and Lyneham, was ferried back to Luton on 17 March 1942 and attached to the Napier factory until scrapped a year later.

G-AEYX, re-registered to Allflight Ltd., Heston in March 1939, followed 'MT to Cardiff as X9338 but served with No.116 Squadron, Hatfield during 1941, No.24 Squadron and Boscombe Down in 1942, and No.6 (R.C.A.F.) Group Communications Flight, Dishforth from February 1943 until scrapped in the following year. The former Standard Telephones aircraft, G-AESV, went directly to No.24 Squadron as X2891; to the A. & A.E.E., Boscombe Down in December 1941 for trials with Blind Approach equipment; to Scottish Aviation Ltd., Prestwick in 1942; and the Air Fighting Development Unit, Wittering in 1943.

Unlike its brethren, 'SV survived to be sold back to Heston Aircraft Ltd. at the famous disposals sale at Kemble in 1946. In March 1950 it was acquired by A. R. Pilgrim who kept it at Elstree but in 1951 it spent some time

Standard Telephones' Heston Phoenix II with constant speed airscrew. (*W. K. Kilsby*)

joyriding at Bembridge and elsewhere. In April 1952 the veteran Phoenix crashed in the French Alps and the type became extinct.

SPECIFICATION

Manufacturers: The Heston Aircraft Co. Ltd., Heston Airport, Hounslow, Middlesex.
Power Plant: One 200 h.p. de Havilland Gipsy VI Series I.
One 205 h.p. de Havilland Gipsy VI Series II.
Dimensions: Span, 40 ft. 4 in. Length, 30 ft. 2 in. Height, 8 ft. 7 in. Wing area, 260 sq. ft.

	Gipsy VI Series I	Gipsy VI Series II
Tare weight	2,000 lb.	2,150 lb.
All-up weight	3,300 lb.	3,300 lb.
Maximum speed	145 m.p.h.	150 m.p.h.
Cruising speed	135 m.p.h.	135 m.p.h.
Initial climb	650 ft./min.	850 ft./min.
Ceiling	14,000 ft.	20,000 ft.
Range	500 miles	500 miles

Production: Five British registered aircraft and VH-AJM (c/n 1/2) for C. J. Melrose.

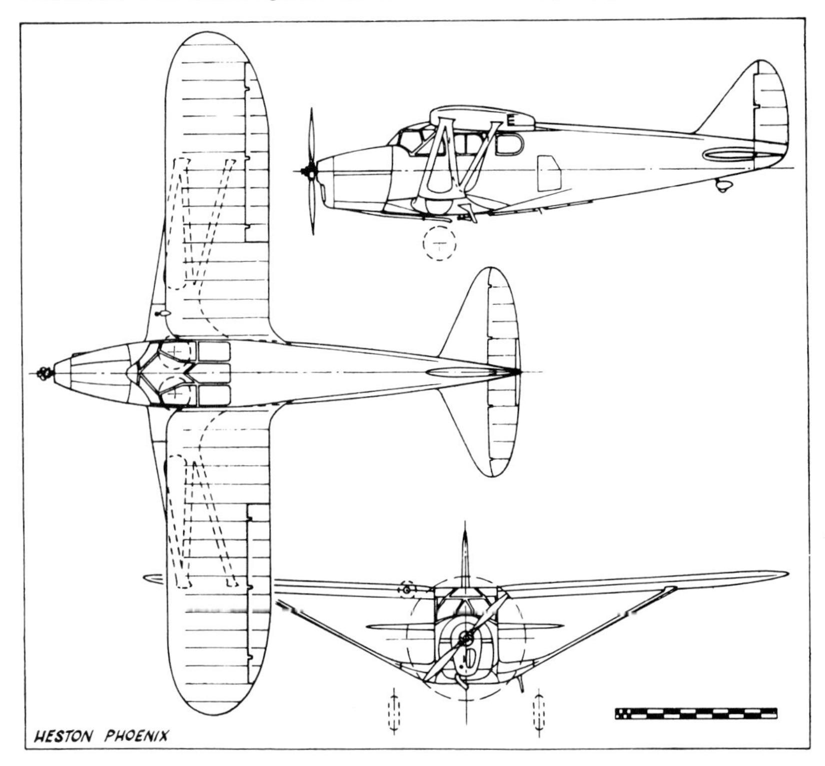

One of the fleet of Hillson Pragas used by the Northern School of Aviation at Barton in 1937. (*J. G. Ellison*)

Hillson Praga

Designed by M. Slechta and built at Karlin, a suburb of Prague, Czechoslovakia, the Praga E.114 light aeroplane first flew in 1934. On 15 August 1935, the second prototype, OK-PGB, landed at Heston, where test pilot Kostalek gave demonstrations. These resulted in the woodworking firm of F. Hills and Sons Ltd. acquiring a licence to build the type in their Trafford Park, Manchester, works. Of all-wood construction with plywood covering throughout, the diminutive Praga cantilever monoplane offered cabin comfort for two passengers side by side. Entry was effected by folding back the leading edge of the centre wing (to which was attached the cabin top) and lowering the side windscreens. The engine, also Czech, was a Praga B two cylinder, horizontally opposed, 36 h.p. unit.

In November 1935 an early production Praga E.114 was imported from Czechoslovakia by Messrs. Comper and Walker as a pre-production specimen. Doped a vivid yellow over all, with British markings G-ADXL, it was loaned to C. W. A. Scott's Flying Display at the beginning of the 1936 season, but on 6 May left Lympne en route to South Africa piloted by H. L. Brook. He reached the Cape in 16 days 4½ hours, bettering the 23 day trip made by David Llewellyn in Aeronca C-3 G-AEAC three months earlier. In spite of considerable optimism, South African markets did not materialise for these ultra lights, although 'XL was sold locally. After the 1939–45 war it was converted into a glider, and in 1953 was still in existence at Youngsfield Aerodrome, Cape Town.

Production of the British model, known as the Hillson Praga, began at Manchester in 1936, the Praga B engine being built under licence by Jowett

Cars Ltd. The first completed aircraft was shipped to Australia, where it was eventually destroyed in a hangar fire at Broken Hill, N.S.W. on 16 April 1945, and the second, G-AEEU, became the firm's demonstrator. Piloted by R. F. Hall, it won the Manx Air Derby on 1 June 1936, covering three circuits of the Isle of Man at an average speed of 89·5 m.p.h. but aviation on 36 h.p. had little appeal for the British private pilot and the Praga experienced the same sales resistance suffered by its contemporary, the Aeronca 100.

Thirty-five were laid down, 10 of which were sold to the Northern Aviation School and Club Ltd., formed at Barton in 1937 to operate Pragas for instructional purposes. Five others were used by Straight controlled flying clubs at Ipswich, Ramsgate and Weston-super-Mare, whence all fled when war became imminent. First to go into service was the silver and green G-AEUP which arrived at Ipswich on 1 September 1937, but trouble was experienced with the Praga motors, and all five were fitted with 40 h.p. Aeronca J.A.P. J-99 Mk.1A two cylinder engines during 1938. In the following year, in the Straight blue and red colour scheme, they were flown intensively by the Civil Air Guard. Only four other Pragas were sold in Britain: G-AELK to Messrs. Jagger, Waugh and Kenworthy, a Barton private ownership group; 'PK to Midland Aircraft Repair Ltd. for use by the North Staffordshire Aero Club at Meir, Stoke-on-Trent; and 'EV to R. J. Pattinson at Sherburn-in-Elmet. En route from Barton to Yeadon in June 1937, 'LK was forced down at Chorley by bad weather and wrecked by striking a wall in the ensuing take off. The syndicate then successfully operated G-AEOL until the outbreak of war.

In 1937 two were shipped to D. McArthur Onslow in Australia where they were registered VH-UXQ and 'XR and operated until 'XR crashed at Melbourne on 11 September 1943 and 'XQ was destroyed in a hangar fire on 19 November 1944.

The little Pragas were not suitable for R.A.F. impressment and were stored until space could no longer be spared and then scrapped. Five managed to survive, 'EU and 'UT at Hooton, 'UP at Perth, 'OL at Barton and 'EV at Doncaster. Two of these, 'UP and 'UT, were overhauled to fly again with Praga B motors replacing the original Aeronca J.A.P.s but were both destroyed in crashes far from home. First to go, G-AEUP, was burned out in the Turkish mountains while being flown to the Near East by Flt. Lt. F. Bosworth in July 1946. The other, serviced at Hooton by the cannibalisation of 'EU, was stored until acquired by Lt. Cdr. G. A. J. Goodhart R.N. and flown to Portsmouth in 1950. It was subsequently owned by V. H. Hallam at Abingdon and finally by Mr. and Mrs. C. M. Roberts at Croydon in 1956. Its end came during an Italian tour in 1957, a forced landing while en route from Peretola to Naples resulting in a destructive collision with trees. The fourth survivor 'EV was acquired by R. Fowler of Hatfield Motor Wreckers near Doncaster in 1945, and for 10 years kept company with the famous Blackburn Dart skeleton until burned at Yeadon in 1955. G-AEOL, overhauled by Astral Aviation Ltd. at Greatham, Co. Durham, in 1947, was not re-erected and did not fly again.

SPECIFICATION

Manufacturers: F. Hills and Sons Ltd., Trafford Park, Manchester.
Power Plants: One 36 h.p. Praga B.
One 40 h.p. Aeronca J.A.P. J-99 Mk.1A.
Dimensions: Span, 36 ft. 0 in. Length, 21 ft. 6 in. Height, 5 ft. 6 in. Wing area, 152 sq. ft.
Weights: Tare weight, 584 lb. All-up weight, 1,080 lb.
Performance: Maximum speed, 93·3 m.p.h. Cruising speed, 79·6 m.p.h. Initial climb, 350 ft./min. Range, 280 miles.

Production: Twenty-five British registered aircraft and the following for Australia: (c/n H.A.1) VH-UVP; (H.A.21) VH-UXQ; (H.A.22) VH-UXR. Seven additional aircraft, (H.A.40–H.A.46), allotted British registrations G-AEYN to 'YU, were not completed.

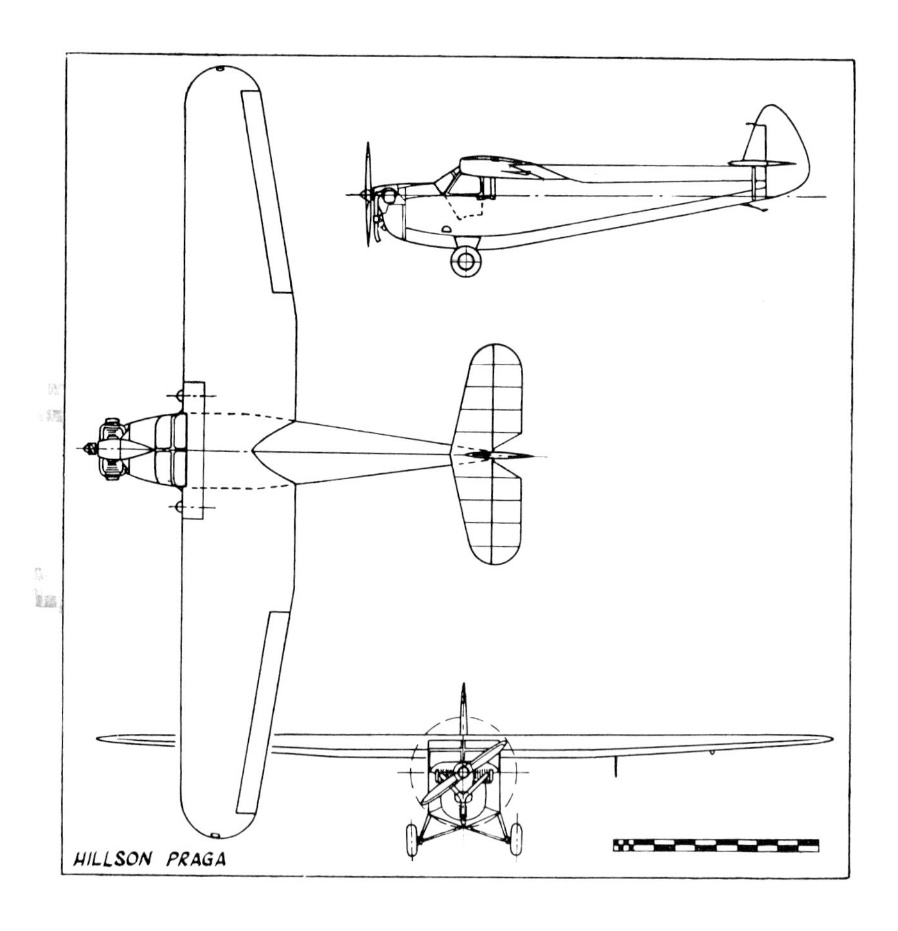

David Spall landing at Sywell in his Aeronca-J.A.P. powered L.A.4A Minor, G-AXGR, after the long flight from Scotland, 11 July 1970. (*Air Portraits*)

Luton L.A.4 Minor

This single-seat ultra-light of spruce, ply and fabric construction powered by a 35 h.p. Anzani inverted Vee air-cooled engine, was designed by C. H. Latimer-Needham (creator of the famous Halton light aeroplanes) and built by Luton Aircraft Ltd. at Barton-in-the-Clay, Beds. in 1936. The prototype, G-AEPD, designated Luton L.A.3, used the fuselage and other components of the experimental L.A.2 tandem-wing aircraft, also registered G-AEPD, which the designer had earlier produced to take the place of the Pou du Ciel. Authorisation to Fly was issued to the L.A.3 in March 1937 and two years later it was sold to A. J. Cook of Anstruther, Fife, who stored it at Macmerry Aerodrome, Edinburgh 1939-45. After the war a car backed into, and destroyed, the fuselage so that when Macmerry closed in the 1950s, the engine was sold and the wings stored in a barn.

G-AEPD flew so convincingly on low power that the airframe was redesigned for home construction as the L.A.4 with strutted undercarriage incorporating rubber shock absorbers, parallel wing struts and single, in place of double, front centre section struts. First of the new type, G-AFBP (first aircraft to be built in the company's new Phoenix Works at Gerrards Cross, Bucks.) was fitted with a 40 h.p. A.B.C. Scorpion two cylinder horizontally opposed engine but thereafter all Luton Minors were home-built from plans supplied by the company.

The first of these, G-AFIR, constructed by J. S. Squires at Rearsby 1937–38, was followed by G-AFRC completed by J. E. Carine in the front room of his home at Douglas, Isle of Man 1938–39 and flown quite intensively from Hall Caine's private aerodrome in the north of the island. While flying locally on 2 September 1939 the Anzani engine failed and 'RC fell undamaged into trees during an attempted approach to R.A.F. Jurby. As the pilot extricated himself it fell to the ground and was irreparably damaged, finally succumbing to vandals during storage at the nearby Andreas airfield.

C. F. Parker's G-AFIU (also known as the Parker C.A.4) and W. S. Henry's G-AFUG were never completed, but L. R. Miller's, third and last of the pre-war Luton Minors, was superbly finished at Seaton, Devon, fitted with a 40 h.p. Aeronca J.A.P. J-99 and registered G-AGEP in September 1942. This and the Anzani engined G-AFIR somehow survived the war, the latter being entirely rebuilt at Pinner, Middlesex by A. W. J. G. Ord-Hume who fitted first a French-built 38 h.p. Menguin and finally a 40 h.p. Aeronca J.A.P. J-99. Following a crash and further rebuild, this famous aeroplane was still airworthy at Fairoaks more than 20 years later with a considerable list of enthusiastic owners in its log books.

Although Luton Aircraft Ltd. no longer existed and the Phoenix Works had been burned down in 1943, there was considerable post war interest in the Minor and four more aircraft were laid down: G-AHMO, Aeronca J.A.P.,

Running up the Anzani engine of the first-ever Luton Minor, G-AEPD, at Barton-in-the-Clay in 1936. (*Aeroplane*)

G-AFIR, first home-built Luton Minor, the familiar performer of the 1970s, as it was when new in 1938. (*A. R. Weyl*)

J. R. Coates' well known and much travelled G-AMAW, 32 h.p. Bristol Cherub, on a visit to Sywell in July 1970 at the age of 21. (*Air Portraits*)

Built by W. C. Hymas at Corringham, Essex, and first flown with Aeronca-J.A.P. engine in 1965, G-ARXP was re-engined with a 62 h.p. Walter Mikron III at Rochester in 1967. (*John Goring*)

The cabin Minor G-AVLX, built at Belfast by N. F. O'Neill and R. S. Parke and first flown at Newtownards in 1968. (*G. J. R. Skillen*)

by R. S. Finch at Darwen, Lancs; G-ALUZ, 25 h.p. Scott Squirrel, by D. E. Felce at Hinckley, Leics.; G-AMAW 'Sunbury', 32 h.p. Bristol Cherub III, built at R.A.F. Bassingbourne, completed at Oakington and first flown at Waterbeach in 1949 by Flt. Lt. J. R. Coates; and G-AMUW by W. Petrie at St. Margaret's Hope, Orkney. G-AMAW flew the length and breadth of the country for many years and G-AHMO was completed by T. G. Thomas at R.A.F. Cottesmore in 1966 but the others did not materialise.

To foster and satisfy renewed interest in home construction C. H. Latimer-Needham and A. W. J. G. Ord-Hume founded a new company in March 1958, known appropriately as Phoenix Aircraft Ltd. to acquire the Luton design rights. With supplies of traditional vintage engines exhausted, Phoenix completely restressed the airframe to permit the installation of modern lightweight four cylinder horizontally opposed engines such as the 55 h.p. Lycoming and to permit an increase in all-up weight from 620 lb. to 750 lb. The updated version, designated L.A.4A was fitted with fin and horn balanced rudder and was thus easily distinguishable from the earlier L.A.4.

Drawings and materials were sold all over the world, among the first to fly being three Australians: VH-RPH built by R. Pearman and H. Nash, first flown at Montmorency, Vic. on 14 October 1962; R. D. Meares' VH-AYP, first flown at Caringbah, N.S.W. on 8 March 1964 and R. F. Tilley's VH-RFT, first flown at Launceston, Tasmania six days later. The first Canadian Minor, CF-OVZ, constructed by G. Fryer at Calgary, flew in September 1963 and the first American, N4762T, was built by R. Ryburn at Atwood, Illinois in 1966 and fitted with the American-type 36 h.p. Aeronca E.113C engine.

By 1972 a further 25 had been registered in Britain alone and a great many others were under construction in garages, lofts and lounges all over the country under the vigilant eye of Popular Flying Association inspectors. Reference to Appendix E will show both Phoenix (PAL) and PFA constructors numbers. The Aeronca J.A.P. engined G-ASCY, built by the Cornelis Bros., which flew a great deal at Norwich and Grimsby, was the first to be exported when it was sold to B. A. Carpenter at Coonagh, Ireland as EI-ATP in February 1970, and the long distance capability of this diminutive aeroplane was amply demonstrated by David Spall, who, with the aid of his father, built G-AXGR at Longniddry, East Lothian 1969–70. By landing at Sywell in his Aeronca J.A.P. powered machine just before dusk on 11 July 1970 at the end of a 300 mile flight in a journey time of 12 hours, he won the 'Most Commendable Flight' award at the Air League's Flying for Fun Rally.

At least eight different types of engine were fitted to Minors and one aircraft, G-ATFW, built at Mexborough Grammar School, Yorks, by the headmaster, Mr. G. W. Shield, initially boasted a three bladed airscrew but airframe modifications were confined to a cockpit canopy on G-AVDY and two widely differing cabin versions. The first, G-AVLX, was a standard Minor with cabin added, built at Belfast 1966–68, which came to grief at Newtownards on 27 October 1968 during preliminary trials. The second, G-ARIF, registered in June 1960 as a Luton L.A.4C, was an entirely new design by A. W. J. G. Ord-Hume which used only the standard metal fittings of the L.A.4A. It was redesignated OH-7 when his partnership with Phoenix was dissolved and construction began at Sandown Airport in 1965 with completion expected in 1973.

SPECIFICATION

Designers:	Luton Aircraft Ltd., Barton-in-the-Clay, Beds.; later Phoenix Works, Gerrards Cross, Bucks.
	Phoenix Aircraft Ltd., St. James Place, Cranleigh, Surrey.
Power plants:	One 25 h.p. Scott Squirrel.
	One 34 h.p. Ardem 4CO2-1
	One 35 h.p. Anzani.
	One 36 h.p. Aeronca E.113C.
	One 40 h.p. Aeronca J.A.P. J-99.
	One 55 h.p. Lycoming O-145-A2 or B2.
	One 62 h.p. Walter Mikron III.
	One 65 h.p. Continental C65-8F.
Dimensions:	Span, 25 ft. 0 in. Length, 20 ft. 0 in. Height, 6 ft. 3 in. Wing area, 125 sq. ft.
**Weights:*	Tare weight, 450 lb. All-up weight, 750 lb.
**Performance:*	Maximum speed, 85 m.p.h. Cruising speed, 75 m.p.h. Initial climb, 450 ft./min. Range, 180 miles.

* Luton L.A.4A Minor with 40 h.p. Aeronca J.A.P. J-99.

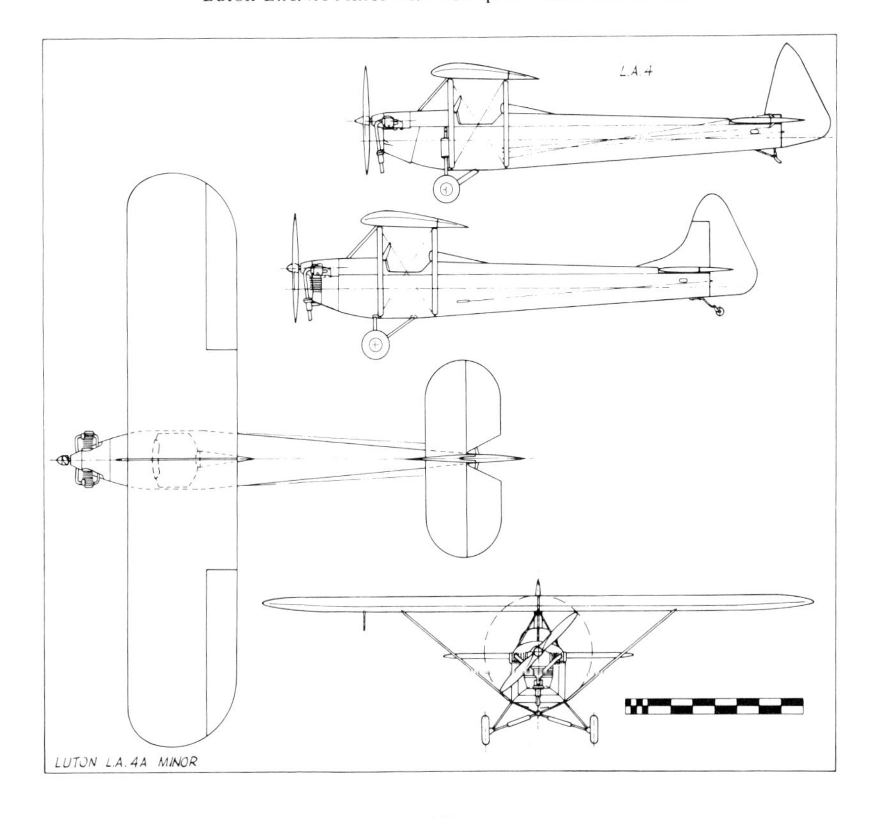

F. P. Raynham taking off from Croydon in the single seat Viper engined Martinsyde F.6 G-EBDK at the start of the 1922 King's Cup Race. (*Flight Photo 2055*)

The Martinsydes

Immediately after the 1914–18 war, Martinsyde Ltd. produced several civil types, most of which were derived from the F.4 single seat fighter, a fabric covered, wooden biplane designed by G. H. Handasyde, with wire braced, box girder fuselage and two spar, single bay wings. Some 280 were constructed, of which only about 50 were delivered to the R.A.F., the remainder, brand new, being stored at the firm's Brooklands works. Their unusually deep and capacious fuselages and relatively high cruising speed made them eminently suitable for civil adaptation as a means of keeping Martinsyde Ltd. in business during peace-time. Piloted by R. H. Nisbet, K-152, the first demilitarised F.4, powered by a 275 h.p. Rolls-Royce Falcon III, gained second place in the Aerial Derby at Hendon on 21 June 1919, at an average speed of 124·61 m.p.h. It was followed by four standard F.4 fighters G-EANM, 'UX, 'YK and 'YP, which received temporary civil status for overseas demonstration. The first left Brooklands piloted by F. P. Raynham on 6 October 1919, performed in Madrid, and on arrival at Lisbon on 11 November was named 'Vasco da Gama' to become the first British aircraft ever to fly in Portugal and the first of a number of F.4s supplied to its air force.

Although incorporating many F.4 components, the Falcon powered Martinsyde Type A Mk.I long-range two seater G-EAMR was a two bay biplane considerably larger than its predecessor, built in 1919 to compete for the Australian Government's £10,000 prize for the first England–Australia flight. It fared no better than F. P. Raynham's unregistered Martinsyde Raymor, an essentially similar Falcon III powered machine which had crashed in Newfoundland on 17 July 1919 while he was taking-off for an attempted transatlantic flight. Capt. C. E. Howell and his navigator, Cpl. G. H. Fraser, left Hounslow in G-EAMR on 12 December 1919 but after making good progress were drowned when forced down off the west coast of Corfu five days later.

Fitted with floats the Type A became the Type AS, two of which, G-CAAX and 'DG, were acquired by Price Bros. Ltd., Quebec in July 1920 for timber survey and fire patrol work but their careers were brief for 'AX crashed at Lake Onatchiway on 18 August and 'DG at Chicoutimi on 30 May 1921.

A second version, seating four passengers in side-by-side pairs in a glazed cabin ahead of the pilot, was designated Type A Mk.II. No market existed at

K-152, the Falcon engined Martinsyde F.4 at Hendon on Aerial Derby day 1919. (*Flight Photo 287*)

A standard F.4 fighter in civil guise at Croydon, just before leaving for Warsaw, 29 January 1921. (*The Aircraft Disposal Co. Ltd.*)

The Semiquaver fitted with 20 ft. 2 in. wings for the 1920 Aerial Derby.

The ill-fated Martinsyde Type A Mk.I leaving Hounslow for Australia, 12 December 1919. (*Flight Photo*)

The Martinsyde Type A Mk.II commercial seaplane G-CAEA on the Saguenay River, P.Q., Canada in 1921. (*K. M. Molson*)

home and only the first of the four built, G-EATY, was of British registry. All were exported, the first, with C. of A. issued to R. H. Nisbet on 27 May 1921 for shipment to Price Bros. Ltd. as G-CAEA to replace 'DG, spun in at Chicoutimi on 12 July 1923 while in service with the Dominion Aerial Exploration Co. Ltd., Toronto. G-EATY and an unregistered example were sold to F. S. Cotton's Aerial Survey Co., equipped with radio, cameras and interchangeable ski undercarriages for seal spotting in Newfoundland. One took part in the gold rush at Stag Bay, Labrador, in 1921. The final Martinsyde Type A Mk.II, also unregistered, christened 'The Big Fella' and delivered from Brooklands to Baldonnel for the Irish Air Corps on 16 June 1922, remained in service until 1927.

A racing machine, G-EAPX, resembling a scaled-down F.4 and known as the Semiquaver, was also constructed. Flown by F. P. Raynham, it set up a British record of 161·43 m.p.h. over a measured kilometre during Martlesham trials on 21 March 1920. It was later exhibited at the Olympia Aero Show, London, and in the hands of F. T. Courtney won the Aerial Derby at Hendon on 28 July 1920 at 153·45 m.p.h. but turned over on landing at the end of the race. Wings of reduced span were then fitted and F. P. Raynham towed it from Brooklands to Etampes behind a car for participation in the Gordon Bennett Race on 28 September and in the following year it became a monoplane with the experimental Alula wing (Volume 1, page 284).

Although the Semiquaver was the last new Martinsyde design, several F.4 variants were devised and flown. First came the F.4A tourer with cockpit for a second occupant ahead of the pilot, four of which were produced, the second machine G-EAPP carrying Sqn. Ldr. T. O'B. Hubbard into 8th place in the 1920 Aerial Derby. The F.6 version, two of which were built initially, had heavily staggered centre section struts, vertical in front elevation instead of splayed out as on the F.4 and F.4A. The undercarriage was also raked forward and strengthened.

Martinsyde pilot R. H. Nesbit was 6th in the 1920 Aerial Derby in the first F.6, G-EAPI, before it was sold to the Canadian Government and taken on charge at Camp Borden for No.3 Squadron, R.C.A.F. on 9 October 1922 as G-CYEQ. The second F.6, G-EATQ, was almost certainly the aircraft sold to

G-EAPI, first of the Martinsyde F.6 two seaters. *(Martinsyde Ltd.)*

The Jaguar engined Martinsyde A.D.C.I. (*Flight Photo*)

H. H. Perry leaving Hendon in the Nimbus Martinsyde G-EBOJ at the start of the King's Cup Race, 9 July 1926. (*Flight Photo*)

Amherst Villiers' Martinsyde A.V.1 'Blue Print' at Brooklands in 1931.

Bishop-Barker Aeroplanes Ltd., Toronto and flown by Lt. Col. W. A. Bishop V.C. who was uninjured when it crashed at Armour Heights Aerodrome, Toronto, on 25 October 1920 before it had been allotted a Canadian registration.

Despite the sale of many F.4s to foreign air forces, by 1921 Martinsyde Ltd. found itself in difficulties, a victim of the post-war slump. Its last aeroplane was a low powered F.6, built for F. P. Raynham and fitted with a 200 h.p. Wolseley Viper for more economical private use. First flown at Brooklands on 29 September 1921, the machine later became G-EBDK and was converted into a single seater for racing purposes, coming second in the King's Cup Race of 8–9 September 1922, and competing in the 1924 race piloted by J. King. Its subsequent owners, all well known, were L. C. G. M. Le Champion of Brooklands 1924–25, Leslie Hamilton of Croydon 1925–26 and Major J. C. Savage, Hendon 1927. This famous aircraft was dismantled in Dudley Watt's shed at Brooklands in April 1930 and its remains lingered there for several years.

The final chapter in F.4 history opened in 1921, when Martinsyde Ltd. went into liquidation. All surviving airframes were then acquired by the Handley Page controlled Aircraft Disposal Co. Ltd. and went by road to Croydon to join the surplus R.A.F. F.4s already held by the company. Four of the latter had lately become civil aircraft in the usual racing and demonstration roles, G-EAXB and 'TD being flown by Major E. L. Foote and R. H. Stocken in the 1921 and 1922 Aerial Derbys respectively. By 1927 a considerable proportion of the F.4 stock had been sold to foreign air forces, 41 going abroad with civil Cs. of A. and two more, G-EBDM and 'FA, in civil marks. To G-EBMI, one of the last to be made airworthy, fell the honour of becoming the only privately owned F.4, property of E. D. A. Biggs at Woodley in March 1930. It crashed a few months later due to failure of the tailplane spar, with the loss of instructor S. W. 'Pat' Giddy.

In 1924 John Kenworthy modernised the F.4 for the Aircraft Disposal Co. Ltd., redesigning the front fuselage to carry a 395 h.p. Armstrong Siddeley Jaguar radial and thereby putting the top speed up to 160 m.p.h. The prototype, G-EBKL, designated Martinsyde A.D.C.I, was first flown at Croydon by the company's test pilot H. H. Perry on 11 October 1924, and competed in the 1925 and 1926 King's Cup Races piloted by W. H. Longton and Sqn. Ldr. H. W. G. Jones respectively. Just as all Martinsydes were affectionately known as 'Tinsydes', 'KL was inevitably dubbed the 'Disposalsyde', forerunner of eight sold to the Latvian Air Force in June 1926. A further redesign with 300 h.p. A.D.C. Nimbus appeared in 1926 as the Nimbus Martinsyde and G-EBOJ and 'OL, the only machines of the type, were flown in the 1926 King's Cup Race by H. H. Perry and F. T. Courtney respectively. In the following year, 'OJ, fitted with cylinder head and undercarriage fairings, was re-styled Boreas and won the High Powered Handicap at Hucknall on 1 August 1927, at 141·2 m.p.h. piloted by Sqn. Ldr. H. W. G. Jones. When the Aircraft Disposal Co. Ltd. ceased operations in 1930, all three A.D.C. prototypes were dismantled and burned.

The very last civil Martinsyde was G-ABKH, a two seater known as the Martinsyde A.V.1, erected at Croydon in 1931 by A.D.C. Aircraft Ltd., successors to the disposal company. Externally identical to an F.4A, it embodied many airframe and engine modifications devised by the owner, engine designer C. Amherst Villiers, whose initials it bore. Resplendent in two vivid shades of blue, it was kept at Brooklands until sold to C. B. Field in October 1932. Following an accident at Bekesbourne in February 1933, it lay derelict at the owner's private aerodrome, Kingswood Knoll, Surrey, until scrapped in 1935.

SPECIFICATION

Manufacturers: Martinsyde Ltd., Maybury Hill, Woking, and Brooklands Aerodrome, Byfleet, Surrey; The Aircraft Disposal Co. Ltd., Regent House, Kingsway, W.C.2, and Croydon Aerodrome, Surrey.

Power Plants:

(Martinsyde F.4)	One 275 h.p. Rolls-Royce Falcon III. One 300 h.p. Hispano-Suiza.
(Martinsyde F.4A and A.V.1)	One 300 h.p. Hispano-Suiza.
(Martinsyde F.6)	One 300 h.p. Hispano-Suiza. One 200 h.p. Wolseley Viper.
(Martinsyde Type A Mk.I)	One 275 h.p. Rolls-Royce Falcon III.
(Martinsyde Type A Mk.II)	One 300 h.p. Hispano-Suiza.
(Semiquaver)	One 300 h.p. Hispano-Suiza.
(Martinsyde A.D.C.I)	One 395 h.p. derated Armstrong Siddeley Jaguar III.
(Nimbus Martinsyde)	One 300 h.p. A.D.C. Nimbus.

	F.4 and F.4A	F.6	Type A Mk.I and Mk.II
Span	32 ft. 9⅜ in.	31 ft. 11¼ in.	43 ft. 4 in.
Length	25 ft. 5⅝ in.	24 ft. 6 in.	29 ft. 1¼ in.
Height	9 ft. 6 in.	9 ft. 1¼ in.	10 ft. 6 in.
Wing area	328·5 sq. ft.	320 sq. ft.	512 sq. ft.
Tare weight	1,811 lb.	–	1,800 lb.
All-up weight	2,300 lb.	2,300 lb.	4,600 lb.
Maximum speed	145 m.p.h.	–	125 m.p.h.*
Cruising speed	–	–	100 m.p.h.
Initial climb	1,600 ft./min.	–	650 ft./min.
Ceiling	24,000 ft.	–	16,000 ft.
Duration	3 hours	3 hours	5 hours

	Semiquaver	A.D.C.I.	Nimbus
Span	20 ft. 2 in.	32 ft. 9⅜ in.	32 ft. 9⅜ in.
Length	19 ft. 3 in.	25 ft. 0 in.	26 ft. 10 in.
Height	–	9 ft. 6 in.	9 ft. 6 in.
Wing area	–	320 sq. ft.	320 sq. ft.
Tare weight	–	1,865 lb.	2,014 lb.
All-up weight	2,025 lb.	2,650 lb.	2,665 lb.
Maximum speed	165 m.p.h.	163 m.p.h.	150 m.p.h.
Cruising speed	–	–	131 m.p.h.
Initial climb	–	2,250 ft./min.	1,350 ft./min.
Ceiling	–	27,000 ft.	23,500 ft.
Duration	2·5 hours	3 hours	2·5 hours

* Mk.II 115 m.p.h.

Production: (a) Martinsyde F.4

Eleven British civil conversions and 29 reworked for export to foreign air forces with Cs. of A. 24.9.23 (17 aircraft for Finland); 7.10.23 (4); 2.2.24 (1); 15.10.24 (5); 4.3.27 (2).

(b) Martinsyde F.4A

Five British registered aircraft shown in Appendix E.

(c) Martinsyde F.6

Three British registered aircraft shown in Appendix E.

(d) Martinsyde Type A

Four Mk.I aircraft only: (c/n E4-500*) G-EAMR; (15/1) G-CAAX; (15/2) G-CADG; (E4-500*) G-EAPN.

Four Mk.II aircraft only: (c/n 215) Cotton, Newfoundland; (216) G-CAEA; (217) Irish Air Corps 'The Big Fella', believed reworked version of Type A Mk.I G-EAPN; (218) G-EATY.

(e) A.D.C.I and Nimbus

Nine A.D.C.I aircraft: (c/n 501) G-EBKL; (502) G-EBMH; (503-509) Latvian Air Force. Two A.D.C. Nimbus aircraft only: (K.1001) G-EBOJ; (K.1002) G-EBOL.

* As documented. Not the same aircraft.

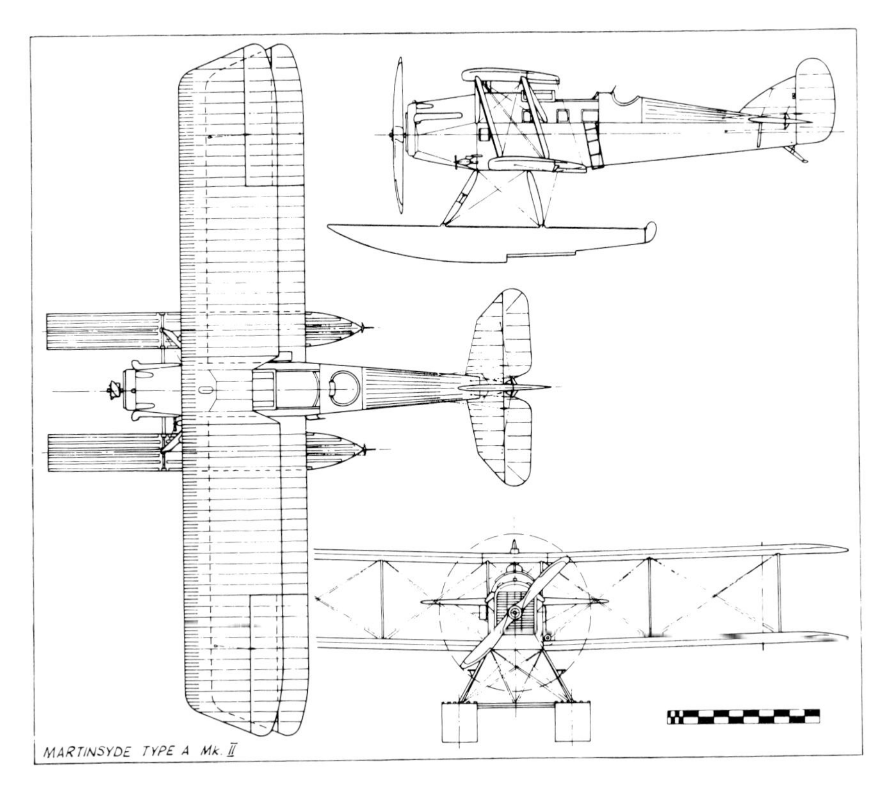

S. V. Appleby with G-ADMH, first British-built Pou du Ciel to be completed, at Heston in July 1935. (*Aeroplane*)

Mignet H.M.14 Pou du Ciel

In 1933 the French inventor M. Mignet succeeded in flying an aircraft of his own design and construction, afterwards describing it in a best seller entitled 'Le Sport de l'Air'. Aptly named Pou du Ciel, or Sky Louse, it comprised a plywood fuselage carrying rudder, engine, wheels and the lower and smaller of two upswept tandem wings. The upper mainplane was pivoted about the front spar and tilted for longitudinal control. There were no ailerons, turns being made on the rudder, operated by sideways movement of the control column and Mignet claimed that anyone who could make a packing case could build a Pou and then teach himself to fly it.

The first British Pou du Ciel, G-ADMH, promptly dubbed Flying Flea, was built at Heston by S. V. Appleby and flown for the first time on 14 July 1935, powered by a Carden-Ford unit. Others followed rapidly. G-ADME with Aubier et Dunne engine was built for Air Commodore J. A. Chamier of the Air League, publishers of an English translation of Mignet's book; Cyril Brook coaxed his Scott Squirrel engined G-ADPP into the air at Sherburn-in-Elmet and National Aviation Day Displays Ltd. bought two French built Fleas which cavorted with Cobham's Circus as G-ADSC and 'SD. On 25 July S. V. Appleby turned 'MH over on its back at Heston, thus giving the well-known sailplane designer L. E. Baynes an opportunity of analysing and remedying defects in the design. He rebuilt the main wing with stouter spars and 5 ft. greater span, the pivot point being moved forward relative to the chord. The front fuselage was also redesigned, totally enclosing engine and radiator.

C. F. Rae Griffin, who assisted in the construction of his G-ADSE 'Winnie the Pou' from approved materials in the workshops of Messrs. Zander and Weyl at Dunstable, used the Bristol Cherub III once fitted to the Avro Avis G-EBKP (and later to the Supermarine Sparrow G-EBJP), and the wheels and axle from the defunct Gadfly monoplane G-AAEY.

Amateur-built models emerged all over the country to be exhibited in motor showrooms, marvelled at in church halls and to make their pathetic hops and occasional circuits from adjacent fields. Overnight they created new problems in certification and insurance, so that the Permit to Fly was created to legalise their activities, No. 1 being issued to Appleby's 'MH on 24 July 1935. By April 1936, some 81 Fleas were complete or under construction, many by groups such as the Glasgow Tramways Flying Club, which built G-AEFP.

Attempts were also made to build the Flea commercially. F. Hills and Sons Ltd. experimented with G-ADOU at Barton, disliked it and built no more. E. G. Perman and Co. Ltd. constructed 11, G-ADOV, 'PU–'PY, 'ZG, 'ZW and G-AECK–'CM, in mews off Grays Inn Road, London, and fitted a variety of engines, including the Scott Squirrel and the firm's own Perman-Ford conversion. One, G-ADPW, Anzani engined, flew with Campbell Black's Circus piloted by the owner R. G. Doig. S. V. Appleby established Puttnam Aircraft Co. Ltd., which constructed a number of Fleas embodying L. E. Bayne's modifications but only one, G-AEEC, flew at Heston. In the Southend area, C. L. Storey built the Squirrel engined G-ADXS 'Fleeing Fly' and a syndicate produced the gold-painted G-AEDN with A.B.C. Scorpion. The latter had a particularly lively performance, ably demonstrated at the Aero 8 Club Flying Flea Rally held in a field at nearby Ashingdon on 6 April 1936. S. V. Appleby attended in 'EC, flown from Heston, and F. W. Broughton flew 'MH, fresh from a recent cross-Channel flight. The others present were C. E. Mercer's Squirrel powered G-AEFV built at West Malling, C. M. Cooper's Surbiton built and Austin Seven engined G-AEEI and the Aero 8 Club's Douglas engined Pou variant 'FW.

At the height of the Flea hysteria came the predicted disaster. On 20 April R. H. Paterson was killed instantly when, soon after take off from Renfrew in

C. L. Storey seated in his Scott Squirrel powered Pou at Southend, December 1935. (*Richard Hall Spence*)

G-AEHM 'Blue Finch', built by H. J. Dolman with A.B.C. Scorpion engine at Bristol in 1936, on show at Hendon in July 1951. (*A. J. Jackson*)

G-ADVL, a nose-down attitude gradually developed into a high-speed dive into the ground. Nine more Fleas were built during the next few weeks, but on 5 May Flt. Lt. Cowell was killed in G-AEEW in exactly similar circumstances at Penshurst, Kent. A fortnight later, on 21 May, Sqn. Ldr. C. R. Davidson met the same fate at Digby in the Squirrel engined G-AEBS he had built himself, but blind enthusiasm chose to overlook these grim happenings. E. D. Abbott Ltd. built three examples, G-AEGD, 'JC and 'JD, of a strut-braced, push-rod-controlled model designed by L. E. Baynes. Known as Cantilever Poux, they were flown at Heston alongside several privately owned Fleas. 'JC and 'JD competed in the world's only Flea race at Ramsgate on 3 August in which four French and four British machines dashed four times to Manston and back. Edouard Bret won the trophy, but S. V. Appleby made fastest time at 59·5 m.p.h. in his 'veteran' 'MH. The highlight of the meeting was designer Mignet's fighter-like performance in the new H.M.18 cabin Pou fitted with a small elevator in the trailing edge of the rear wing and powered by a Menguin flat twin. It was sold to Appleby in the following month and flew back to France as G-AENV for exhibition at the Paris Aero Show.

Matters came to a head on 20 September when James Goodall was killed at Dyce in his home-built G-ADXY. On the Air League's initiative G-AEFV was tested in the wind tunnel at Farnborough, where the results of French experiments were confirmed. At angles of incidence in excess of -15 degrees and with the stick hard back, there was insufficient pitching moment to raise the nose. Inevitably the Flea was banned, after 118 had been built or projected, 83 of which had received permits to fly, the last issued on 1 May 1939, to G-AFUL built at Derby by T. H. Fouldes.

In 1973 a few still survived as curios, notably G-AEHM built at Bristol by

H. J. Dolman in 1936, stored at Hayes, Middlesex, with other Science Museum aircraft; G-AEJX 'The Angus Flea' built at Brechin by Small and Hardie in June 1936, stored at Perth; C. L. Storey's 1935 G-ADXS housed in the Southend Historic Aircraft Museum; G-AEGV and 'OH kept for exhibition by the Midland Aircraft Preservation Society, Coventry; and G-AEBB, built by K. W. Owen at Southampton in 1936 and restored to taxying condition by the Shuttleworth Trust in 1968.

Additionally several of the many unregistered examples came to light in the 1950s and '60s, including one built by A. W. Troop, Wellingore, Lincs. using the Scott Squirrel engine from G-AEBS; another built at Rishworth,

The Carden-Ford powered Pou G-AEFK, with enlarged rudder, which advertised a familiar brand of confectionery during the 1936 season with Scott's Circus.

The first cantilever Pou, showing the revised bracing and control system.

The Aero 8 Club's 'high speed' Pou G-AEFW, boasted a streamlined fuselage, normal cockpit, divided undercarriage and Douglas Sprite engine. It crashed south of Gravesend during an attempted flight to France by Claud Oscroft in the summer of 1936.

The H.M.18 cabin Pou, later registered G-AENV. (*R. P. Howard*)

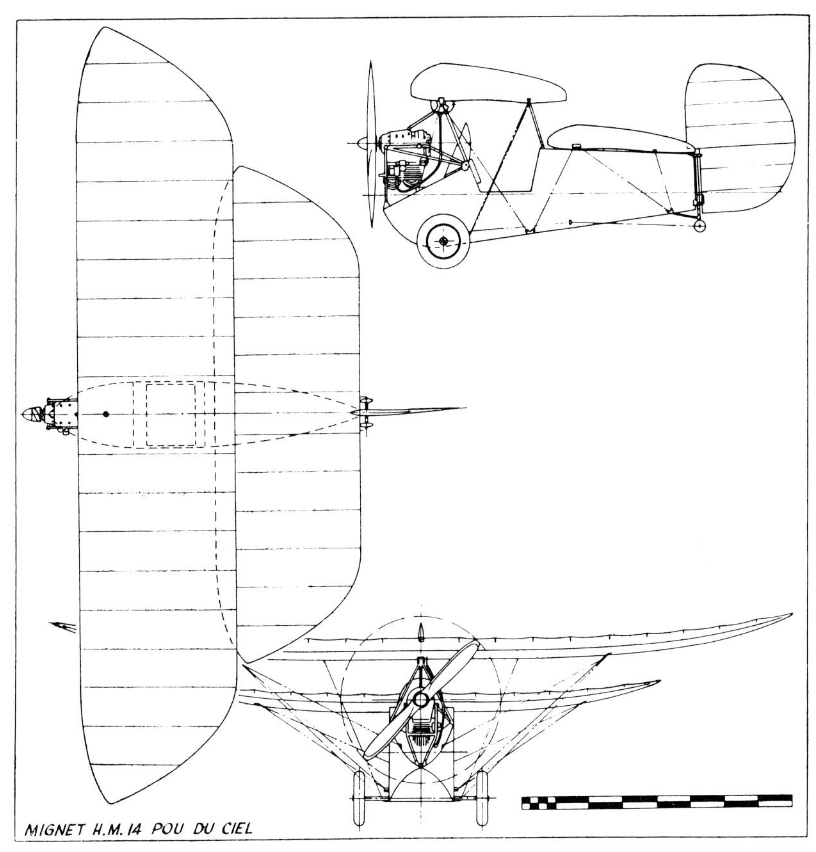

Yorks. by S. O. White 1935–36 and now one of two in the care of the Northern Aircraft Preservation Society; and finally the well known Squirrel engined Pou built by W. Millom at Horton Kirby, Kent 1936–37 and acquired in June 1969 by Messrs. D. Collyer and R. R. Mitchell, who, for realism, painted it up as G-AEOF, a registration from the Pou era that had never been allotted.

Despite prewar disasters, development of Henri Mignet's tandem wing principles continued in France after the war, culminating in a more reliable single seater designated H.M.293, one British registered example G-AXPG (1,300 cc. Volkswagen) being built near Chelmsford 1969–70 by W. H. Cole and flown at his Purleigh, Essex, airstrip in 1971.

SPECIFICATION

Manufacturers: F. Hills and Sons Ltd., Trafford Park, Manchester; E. G. Perman and Co. Ltd., 24 Brownlow Mews, Guildford Street, Grays Inn Road, W.C.1; Puttnam Aircraft Co. Ltd., Victory Works, 407–9 Hornsey Road, London, N.19; E. D. Abbott Ltd., Wrecclesham, Farnham, Surrey; also built in large numbers by home constructors.

Power Plants	Example		
One 35 h.p. A.B.C. Scorpion	G-ADZS	R. R. Little	Bekesbourne
One 35 h.p. Anzani	G-AEEY	R. Butler	Lympne
One 22 h.p. Aubier et Dunne	G-ADME	J. A. Chamier	Hendon
One 847 cc. Austin Seven	G-AEEI	C. M. Cooper	Surbiton
One 1,300 cc. Henderson	G-ADZT	S. S. Miles	Bedford
One 32 h.p. Bristol Cherub III	G-ADSE	R. Griffin	Dunstable
One 30 h.p. Carden-Ford	G-AEIP	G. Oscroft	Ashingdon
One 23 h.p. Douglas Sprite	G-AEFW	Aero 8 Club	Ashingdon
One 38 h.p. Menguin	G-AENV	S. V. Appleby	Heston
One 30 h.p. Perman-Ford	G-AECM	J. E. Foster	Ashingdon
One 25 h.p. Poinsard	G-ADSC	N.A.D. Ltd.	Ford
One 36 h.p. Praga B	G-AEAD	E. W. Kendrew	Leeming
One 25 h.p. Scott Squirrel	G-ADWR	A. U. Tomkins	Brooklands

	Abbott Pou*	Cantilever Pou*	H.M.18†	H.M.293
Span	22 ft. 0 in.	22 ft. 0 in.	17 ft. 0 in.	18 ft. $1\frac{3}{4}$ in.
Length	13 ft. 0 in.	12 ft. $3\frac{1}{2}$ in.	–	12 ft. 6 in.
Height	5 ft. 6 in.	5 ft. 6 in.	–	5 ft. $7\frac{1}{4}$ in.
Wing area	140 sq. ft.	137 sq. ft.	–	108 sq. ft.
Tare weight	350 lb.	327 lb.	250 lb.	421 lb.
All-up weight	550 lb.	550 lb.	–	643 lb.
Maximum speed	70 m.p.h.	–	100 m.p.h.	91 m.p.h.
Cruising speed	60 m.p.h.	–	–	80 m.p.h.
Initial climb	300 ft./min.	–	1,200 ft./min.	–
Range	200 miles	–	–	320 miles

* Carden-Ford. † Menguin.

The modernised H.M.293 Pou du Ciel G-AXPG, built at Purleigh, Essex by W. H. Cole, making its first public appearance at the Flying For Fun Rally at Sywell on 17 July 1971. (*M. F. Jerram*)

A standard M.2 Hawk, G-ACHK, owned by Germ Lubricants Ltd. in 1933 (*Aeroplane*)

Miles M.2 Hawk

The Hawk two seat, low-wing, cantilever monoplane was designed in 1933 by F. G. Miles, and although a structurally orthodox light aeroplane with plywood covered two spar wing and box-built fuselage, excited comment in the heyday of the biplane because its cantilever wing was also designed to fold. Powered by a 95 h.p. A.D.C. Cirrus IIIA, the prototype, G-ACGH, was built at Woodley, Reading, in the workshops of Phillips and Powis Ltd. Piloted by its designer, 'GH made its first flight on the evening of 29 March 1933, and proved so viceless that 53 pilots, mainly inexperienced, flew it within a week.

Without the rigging problems of the biplane and at the attractive price of £395 made possible by the acquisition of new Cirrus engines from a liquidated company in Canada, the Hawk sold without difficulty and in fifteen months, 47 had been supplied to British owners alone. The first production Hawk G-ACHJ was built for Wing Cdr. H. M. Probyn in time for the King's Cup Race of 8 July 1933. Unlike the prototype, which had an undercarriage built from Avro Avian components, 'HJ's was taller and embodied Dowty struts with low pressure wheels. It was flown as a single seater, but forced landed at East Harling with tappet trouble and returned to its base at Farnborough. A fortnight later, the same aircraft and pilot won the Cinque Ports Wakefield Cup Race at an average speed of 115·5 m.p.h., the second production Hawk G-ACHK, belonging to Germ Lubricants Ltd., also competing.

First of four Hawk variants, the Hawk M.2A, a Gipsy III powered cabin version, was built for S. B. Cliff to fly in the Egyptian Oases Rally of January 1934. It was the only one of its kind, and after a couple of years of air taxi work was destroyed in a hangar fire at Brooklands in 1936. Also built to special order, the solitary M.2B VT-AES was a long-range single seater with Fox Moth sliding hood and Hermes IV inverted engine for an attempt on the England–Cape record by Man Mohan Singh, chief pilot to the Maharajah of Patiala. This aircraft was cleared for a maximum take-off weight of 2,200 lb. and when fully loaded carried more than its own weight of fuel but was forced down by an oil leak in darkness at Carcomb (Vaucluse), south of Paris, early on the morning of 20 January 1934 and the flight was abandoned. A second Hawk M.2, c/n 21, certificated in the name of the same pilot on 15 January 1934, and possibly intended for the Maharajah, was never registered in India.

The one example of the M.2C, a standard Hawk with 120 h.p. Gipsy III engine, appeared at about the same time but left Woodley almost immediately in French markings as F-AMZW.

Itinerant air displays were also at the height of their popularity in 1934 and Miles produced two three-seat Hawks, G-ACPC and 'PD, which went on tour with British Hospitals Air Pageants Ltd. Four others followed, one of which, G-ACSX, lasted only a month in private ownership, and two others, G-ACSC and 'VR, were used for joyriding at Skegness. They were superficially similar to the standard Hawk but had an enlarged rear cockpit for two passengers. The same outer wing panels were used, but the centre section was increased in span by 2 ft. and the undercarriage radius rods were repositioned immediately behind the compression struts.

Several Hawks were sold overseas, one of the first being G-ACJC which H. R. A. Edwards flew from Woodley to Baghdad in 47 hours flying time on delivery to its owner Mrs. B. Macdonald; VT-AFD followed for Messrs. Tozer, Kemsley and Millbourne in February 1934; SX-AAB and 'AD certificated in July and November 1934 respectively in the names of D. E. Melton and J. M. Libas, were afterwards based at Athens by Nicholas Efstratou and Stephen Pesinalsoglu; and an unregistered example, c/n 125, to the Kuala Lumpur Flying Club, also in November 1934.

G-ACGH, first of all the Miles Hawks. (*C. A. Nepean Bishop*)

The M.2A Hawk was fitted with a cabin for two passengers in tandem. (*Flight Photo 13736*)

Man Mohan Singh's Hermes powered M.2B Hawk, VT-AES, for which registration G-ACKW was reserved but never used. (*Flight Photo 13747*)

The prototype M.2D Hawk three seater. (*Flight Photo 10304S*)

A special single-seat Colonial-type Hawk, G-ACKX, was sold to the Sourabaya Aero Club as PK-SAL; G-ACTO was exhibited at the Geneva International Aero Show as CH-380 in May 1934; G-ACMX was flown to Dublin by F. R. Hill to become EI-ABQ; while 'NX was acquired by Everson Flying Services, also of Dublin, as EI-AAX. The last mentioned returned in 1935 and, after a succession of owners, crashed at Malmesbury on 12 April 1935, through striking a tree on the approach to a field. After reconstruction and sale to the North Staffordshire Aero Club at Meir, Stoke-on-Trent, it joined the Colonial-type Hawk G-ACTN. Like that supplied to Sourabaya, this was strengthened internally and provided with additional cowling louvres and equipment at an increased tare weight of 1,035 lb. During a snowstorm at Meir on 15 December 1935, 'TN was also involved in a fatal collision with a tree and coincidentally a violent snowstorm also accounted for the destruction of G-ACSD with its owner at Royston, Herts, on 4 April 1935.

As an instructional machine the Hawk was used by the Kent Flying Club, whose yellow G-ACHZ, G-ADBK and 'GI were based at Bekesbourne; by the Ipswich Aero Club with G-ACZD; and by the Phillips and Powis School of Flying at Woodley. One Hawk, G-ACOP, employed by the latter, carried the initials of Mr. C. O. Powis. Another, G-ADVR, was a frustrated Rumanian export which had languished at Woodley as YR-ITR before assuming British nationality. The Hawk G-ACTO eventually returned from Switzerland to be operated in turn by the Ely Aero Club, Cambridgeshire Flying Services and in 1939 by the Kent Flying Club. The last British owned Hawk, G-ADGR, flown at Woodley in 1935 by the Reading Aero Club, carried the initials 'GR in memory of Gerald Royle, killed at Scarborough shortly before. Later sold to the Insurance Flying Club and later still to Julian Rowntree, its career ended on 18 July 1937, in a fatal landing crash at Brussels when returning from a holiday trip to Frankfurt.

Accidents, mainly serious, had accounted for many of the original Hawks, so that by 1939 the only others in existence were G-ACHL of Southern Aircraft (Gatwick) Ltd., 'IZ of W. S. Martin at Tollerton, E. W. Brockhouse's 'MM keeping company at Meir with the rebuilt 'NX, Viscount Clive's G-ACRT at Hanworth, C. G. M. Alington's 'TI at Hatfield and S. B. Wilmot's 'YA at Hooton. The third production Hawk 'HL was sold to Messrs. P. Steinberg and A. Schrechterman at Tel Aviv early in the war, and three others, G-ACNX, G-ACTO and G-ADGI, were impressed by the R.A.F. 1940–41 but only the first served any useful purpose and then only as an instructional airframe, 2617M, with No.1211 A.T.C. Squadron at Swadlincote, Derbyshire. By 1960 the last remaining Hawk M.2 was G-ACRT which had lain semi-derelict at Kidlington since 1946.

SPECIFICATION

Manufacturers: Phillips and Powis Ltd., Woodley Aerodrome, Reading, Berks.
Power Plants: (M.2) One 95 h.p. A.D.C. Cirrus IIIA.
(M.2A) One 120 h.p. de Havilland Gipsy III.
(M.2B) One 120 h.p. A.D.C. Cirrus Hermes IV.
(M.2C) One 120 h.p. de Havilland Gipsy III.
(M.2D) One 95 h.p. A.D.C. Cirrus IIIA.

Dimensions: Span, 33 ft. 0 in. (M.2D), 35 ft. 0 in. Length, 24 ft. 0 in. Height, 6 ft. 8 in. Wing area, 169 sq. ft.

	M.2	M.2A	M.2B	M.2D
Tare weight	1,014 lb.	–	–	1,045 lb.
All-up weight	1,800 lb.	1,800 lb.	2,200 lb.	1,800 lb.
Maximum speed	115 m.p.h.	140 m.p.h.	160 m.p.h.	114 m.p.h.
Cruising speed	100 m.p.h.	125 m.p.h.	140 m.p.h.	98 m.p.h.
Initial climb	860 ft./min.	–	–	860 ft./min.
Ceiling	16,000 ft.	–	–	18,000 ft.
Range	450 miles	1,000 miles	2,000 miles	450 miles

Production: (a) Miles M.2 Hawk

Forty British registered aircraft and the following for test or export: (c/n 2) unfinished, possibly test airframe; (21) Man Mohan Singh, unregistered; (22) VT-AFD; (40) SX-AAB; (42) untraced; (125) Kuala Lumpur Flying Club; (127) SX-AAD; (212) VH-UGQ.

(b) Variants

One each M.2A, M.2B and M.2C followed by six M.2D three seaters, all British registered.

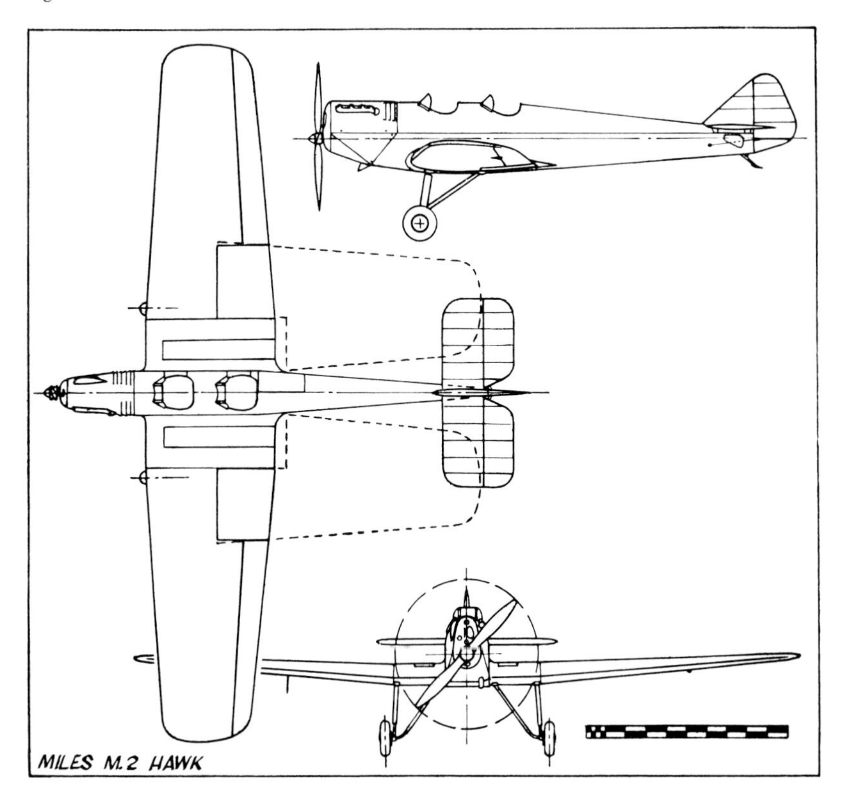

F. G. Miles flying the Hawk Major M.2F G-ACTD near Woodley, July 1934.
(*Flight Photo 14411*)

Miles Hawk Major and Speed Six

The popularity of the M.2 Hawk and the approaching end of limited supplies of Cirrus IIIA engines, compelled the design of a successor which appeared in time to be proved, in traditional style, over the 1934 King's Cup course. Like the M.2C Hawk, it was Gipsy III powered but with metal, instead of wooden engine mounting, and a cantilever, trousered undercarriage. The prototype, G-ACTD, designated the Miles M.2F Hawk Major, temporarily a single seater and flown by Tommy Rose, began the long line of pre-war Miles racing honours by finishing second at an average speed of 147·78 m.p.h. A special single seat variant, G-ACTE, powered by a 200 h.p. Gipsy Six was entered and flown by Sir Charles Rose, who forced landed at Northolt with ignition trouble. The extra weight of the engine replaced that of a passenger, so that standard characteristics were retained, but with a considerable increase in top speed. This model, only one of which was built, was known as the M.2E Gipsy Six Hawk.

Production Hawk Majors were fitted with Gipsy Major engines and sold in quantity, mainly to private owners. They found their way all over the world, the most famous of them all being ZK-ADJ, otherwise G-ACXU, flown by Sqn. Ldr. M. MacGregor and H. Walker, in the 1934 MacRobertson Race from Mildenhall to Melbourne. This Hawk Major not only averaged 105 m.p.h. to finish 5th in the handicap section but also continued to New Zealand by sea to join the Manawatu Aero Club. Two others, G-ACWV and G-ADGA, were fitted with Savage smoke producing gear by the British Instrument Co. Ltd. at Hendon and became a familiar sight in British skies during their skywriting sorties.

The designation M.2G was given to G-ACYB, a three seat cabin version of the Hawk Major built for the Club George Chazez in Switzerland, where it became well known as HB-OAS. In November 1934 a trailing edge flap was added to the standard aircraft to create the M.2H. This model, with its steepened glide and slow landing, largely replaced the M.2F on the Woodley production line. By the time the flag fell at the start of the King's Cup Race of 7 September 1935, 57 Hawk Majors had been delivered to British owners. Seven of these, including the cleaned-up M.2H machines G-ADGE, 'LA, 'LB and 'MW, were flown in the race by A. H. Cook, Mrs. Elise Battye, O. Cathcart Jones and A. C. W. Norman.

Although the M.2F and M.2H were the versions built in quantity, their important contribution to amateur sporting flying was largely overshadowed by that of the variants. The Hawk Major de Luxe G-ADLN, flown into 2nd place at 157·49 m.p.h. by H. R. A. Edwards, was known as the M.2R, while the designation M.2T was applied to the two long-range, single seat, Cirrus Major powered entries. The first, G-ADNJ, piloted by Alex Henshaw, was ditched with engine trouble 6 miles off Malin Head during the race, and the wreck was later brought ashore at Ardrossan. F. D. Bradbrooke flying the other M.2T, G-ADNK, almost suffered a similar fate, but just reached the coast to forced land near Blackpool.

Gipsy Six Hawk G-ACTE, with sliding hood, rechristened Hawk Speed Six and flown by its new owner W. Humble, was placed 13th at 177·79 m.p.h. The two other Hawk Speed Six aircraft unsuccessfully competing with it were the M.2L G-ADGP of Luis Fontes and the M.2U G-ADOD flown by his sister Miss Ruth Fontes. Both these machines had flaps, wide-track undercarriages and increased dihedral, but differed slightly in cockpit canopy detail and in the fact that a Gipsy Six R high-compression engine was fitted to 'OD. The three Speed Sixes met for the last time in the 1936 Race, in which Tommy Rose averaged 160·5 m.p.h. in 'OD to come 2nd. Later in the year (the then) Flt. Lt. A. E. Clouston flew it in the Schlesinger Race to Johannesburg. Leaving Portsmouth at 06.34 hours on 29 September 1936, he reached Khartoum at 01.45 hours the next day, but engine trouble and a series of forced landings ended the race and the career of 'OD in a crash at Gwelo, 130 miles S.W. of Salisbury, Southern Rhodesia. An equally spectacular write-off also occurred a few months earlier when, on 8 June, the airscrew fractured

Mlle. Smoranda Braescu at Woodley with her enclosed single-seat Hawk Major YR-ADB 'Jurel Vlaicu', July 1935. (*Flight Photo 11497S*)

Portuguese private owner Señor Rabello's Hawk Major M.2H G-ADEN in service with General Franco's Nationalist Air Force in Spain 1936. (*Royal Aero Club*)

and the engine fell out of Major R. H. Thornton's M.2H G-ADIG while flying from Budapest to Hamburg. Fortunately the ensuing spin was flat enough to do little damage to the occupants. Another standard M.2H, G-ADEN, purchased by Señor Jose Rabello, was flown to Portugal by the owner and the Reading Aero Club instructor J. F. Lawn and later saw service in the Spanish Civil War.

Production lists are incomplete and it is impossible to say whether untraced aircraft were Hawk Majors or Miles' next design, the M.3 Falcon, a production line for which was in full swing at Woodley. It is evident that many were to foreign order and several for Air Ministry use included Hawk Major K8626, Falcon K5924 and M.6 Hawcon K5925.

Aircraft certificated in Britain 1934–35 before overseas delivery, eleven in number, were: SU-AAP for Prince Omar Salim, Egypt; a special, unregistered, M.2K for the Royal Singapore Flying Club; VT-AGH for H. Mehta & Co., India (later shipped to New Zealand as ZK-AFK); YR-ADB, a single seater with cockpit canopy for Mlle. Smoranda Braescu, Budapest; VH-UAI for the Aero Club of South Australia; HB-ERI for Rudolf Hertzig, Switzerland; OY-DEK for Aage Rasmussen, Denmark; EC-W44 (later EC-ABI) for the Aero Club de Valencia; two more for Rumania–YR-BOB for Spiridon Varnox and YR-ITB for Interprinderila Technica Romana; and a special M.2M, LN-BAH 'Fefor', seating two passengers under a glazed canopy behind the pilot's open cockpit, for C. F. Walther, hotel owner of Vinstra, Norway. This machine crashed and burned at Kjeller on 10 December 1935.

Hawk Major variants ran consecutively from M.2E to M.2U (excepting I and N), three others in this range which appeared in British marks being J. E. D. Houlder's M.2M G-ADCV which resembled LN-BAH; the Cardiff Aeroplane Club's G-ADDK and the Airwork Flying School's G-ADLO, which were of the dual control M.2P type with wider cockpits and 1 ft. greater span; and G-ADLH, the long range, Gipsy Major powered M.2S built in 1935 for J. H. Van of Broxbourne. Two years later this was bought for an Atlantic flight by the Indian pilot G. P. Nair with monies subscribed by his compatriots in Britain. After permission to take off over the North Atlantic had been refused, he decided on a world tour, but was killed near Rouen on 28 October 1937, two hours after leaving Croydon, through stalling on the approach to a field.

One other M.2P, VP-KBT, flown from Woodley to Nairobi by Brig. Gen. A. C. Lewin in November 1935, and back again to Woodley in the following August, was eventually replaced by a Miles M.11A Whitney Straight and sold in New Zealand as ZK-AFJ. Then followed the M.2R, also with increased span and all-up weight, the first, G-ADLN, coming second in the 1935 King's Cup Race piloted by Flt. Lt. H. R. A. Edwards. It afterwards became flying test bed for the American-built Menasco Pirate C.4 engine and a second M.2R, the single-seat, long range CC-FBB 'Saturno', was shipped to Chile in December 1935 for Señor Franco Bianco who made several notable long distance flights through the formidable weather and over the difficult terrain to the north of Cape Horn. Starting from Magellanes before dawn on 7 June 1936, he crossed the Andes at 12,000 ft. and flew 1,150 miles non-stop to Punto Montt in 9 hr. 55 min., completing the trip to Santiago in 6 hr. on 9 June. He afterwards recrossed the Andes and returned to Magellanes via Buenos Aires.

In 1938–39 the Reading Aero Club was operating 'LN alongside the M.2Hs G-AEGP and 'NS, all three eventually suffering wartime impressment as DG664, DP851 and DP848 respectively; as did the North Staffs G-ACXT (DG577), the Cotswold Aero Club G-ADIT (X5125), the Portsmouth Aero

J. E. D. Houlder's three seat Hawk Major M.2M at Heathrow in July 1935. (*A. J. Jackson*)

Flg. Off. A. E. Clouston running up the Hawk Speed Six M.2U prior to the Portsmouth–Johannesburg Race of September 1936 (*Aeroplane*)

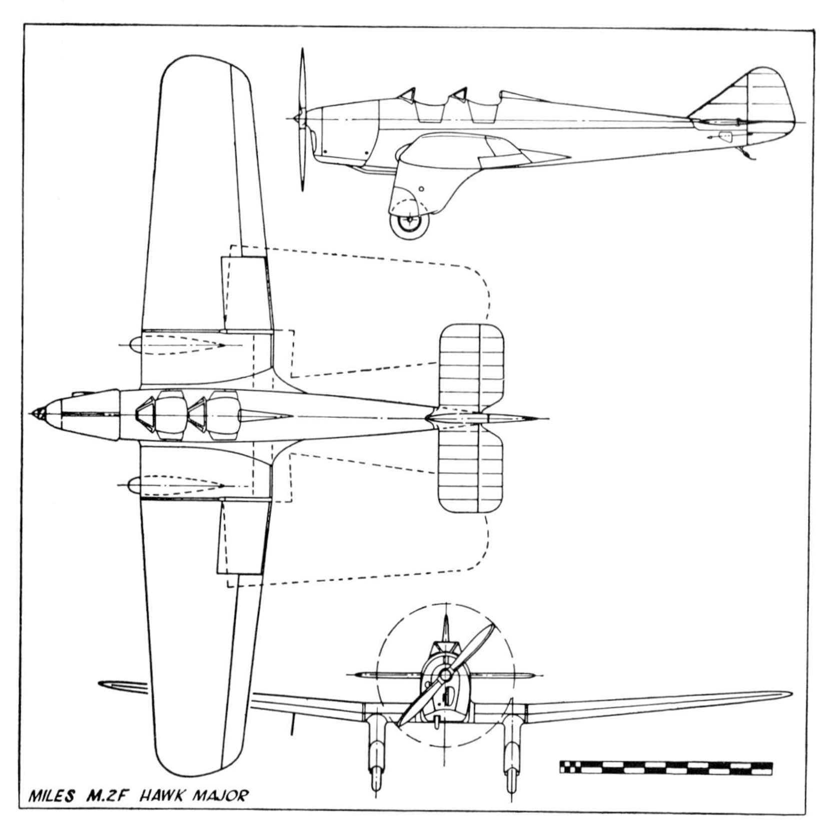

Club G-ADMW (DG590) and the Cardiff Aeroplane Club's G-ADDK (BD180). The total of 10 impressed Hawk Majors was completed by O. F. H. Atkey's de luxe G-AEGE (HL538), F. W. Griffith's G-ACWY (NF748) and Dr. Miles Bickerton's G-ACYO (NF752). Only four survived the war: G-ACYO, restored to the Reading Aero Club in 1947 and winner of the 1954 Air League Challenge Cup at 138 m.p.h., piloted by Miss Freydis Leaf; G-ACYX, serviced at Heston and flown at Broxbourne before sale to France as F-BCEX in 1946; the three seat G-ADCV, denuded of its canopy, flown from Poona to Hamble between 17 November and 14 December 1947, by Lt.-Col. G. H. Wotton, but destroyed at Croydon when a wall collapsed on 4 February 1950; and G-ADMW, flown by several owners after restoration in 1946 but grounded in July 1965 and eventually restored to wartime camouflage and yellow as DG590 for all-time preservation at the R.A.F. Museum, Hendon.

Four others rediscovered were: the prototype, 'TD, involved in a crash at Doncaster Airport on 31 August 1936, and used as a target for Lincoln bombers at York in 1951; G-ADAB and 'BT derelict at Walsall and Blackbushe respectively, and G-AEGE used as an instructional airframe by the College of Aeronautical Engineering at Redhill.

A major contribution to post-war sporting flying was made by R. R. Paine's Hawk Speed Six, G-ADGP, modified almost to M.2U standard, fitted with a Gipsy Six 1F and an enormous bubble hood. Each year after 1949 the veteran fought its private duel with the surviving Mew Gull in the National and other air races, and had a habit of making fastest time, and today still holds the 100 km. closed-circuit record in Class C.16 at 192·83 m.p.h. In 1971 it was completely reconstructed at Derby for new owner David Hood, and on 15 July 1972 came second in the King's Cup Race at Booker, flown once again by R. R. Paine.

SPECIFICATION

Manufacturers: Phillips and Powis Aircraft Ltd., Woodley Aerodrome, Reading, Berks.

Power Plants:

(M.2E)	One 200 h.p. de Havilland Gipsy Six.
(M.2F, H, M, P, R)	One 130 h.p. de Havilland Gipsy Major.
(M.2L)	One 200 h.p. de Havilland Gipsy Six 1F.
(M.2S)	One 150 h.p. Blackburn Cirrus Major.
(M.2U)	One 200 h.p. de Havilland Gipsy Six R.

	M.2E, L, U	M.2F, H, M	M.2P, R
Span	33 ft. 0 in.	33 ft. 0 in.	34 ft. 0 in.
Length	24 ft. 0 in.	24 ft. 0 in.	24 ft. 0 in.
Height	6 ft. 8 in.	6 ft. 8 in.	6 ft. 8 in.
Wing area	169 sq. ft.	169 sq. ft.	174 sq. ft.
Tare weight	1,355 lb.	1,150 lb.	–
All-up weight	1,900 lb.	1,800 lb.	1,900 lb.
Maximum speed	185 m.p.h.	150 m.p.h.	150 m.p.h.
Cruising speed	160 m.p.h.	135 m.p.h.	135 m.p.h.
Initial climb	1,450 ft./min.	1,000 ft./min.	–
Ceiling	–	20,000 ft.	–
Range	–	560 miles	–

Production: (a) Miles M.2F Hawk Major

Seventeen British registered aircraft and two for export: (c/n 126) SU-AAP; (170) OY-DEK

(b) Miles M.2H Hawk Major

Thirty-nine British registered aircraft and at least the following for export: (c/n 144) VT-AGH/ZK-AFK; (150) YR-ADB; (155) VH-UAI; (159) HB-ERI; (172) EC-W44/EC-ABI; (174) YR-BOB; (182) YR-ITB

(c) Miles Hawk Major (other variants)

Eleven aircraft: (c/n 120) M.2G/G-ACYB; (128) M.2M/LN-BAH; (133) M.2K/unregistered for Royal Singapore Flying Club; (156) M.2M/G-ADCV; (190) M.2P/G-ADDK; (194) M.2S/G-ADLH; (203) M.2T/G-ADNJ; (211) M.2R/G-ADLN; (220) M.2P/G-ADLO; (222) M.2T/G-ADNK; (251) M.2P/VP-KBT; (257) M.2R/CC-FBB

(d) Miles Hawk Speed Six

Three aircraft only: (c/n 43) M.2E/G-ACTE; (160) M.2L/G-ADGP; (195) M.2U/G-ADOD.

Edward Eves flying his immaculately restored Miles M.3A Falcon near Baginton in 1970. (*Air Portraits*)

Miles M.3 Falcon and M.4 Merlin

Structurally similar to, and retaining the handling qualities of the Hawk Major, the Falcon was built on more generous lines to accommodate two passengers side by side behind the pilot in a glazed cabin. The split trailing edge flaps were retained and the dihedral increased from $3\frac{1}{2}$ to 5 degrees to improve stability and lessen pilot fatigue on long flights. The prototype U-3/G-ACTM, designated the M.3, was completed in time for H. L. Brook to fly it, with a passenger, in the MacRobertson Race of October 1934. The engine was the veteran Gipsy Major salvaged from Mr. Brook's ex Mollison Puss Moth 'Heart's Content' (see Volume 2, page 109). Ill luck delayed the Falcon, however, and nearly 27 days were taken to reach Darwin. Flying solo and with extra tanks to give a 2,000 mile range, Brook left Darwin again on 23 March 1935, and reached Lympne in the record time of 7 days 19 hours 15 minutes. During one magnificent stage, the 1,700 miles from Jodhpur to Basra was covered non-stop.

The fuselage of the first production aircraft G-ADBF, first flown at Woodley in January 1935, was not only wider to give comfortable seating for four persons but had a modified cabin top and the more familiar forward-sloping windscreen, estimated to add 4 m.p.h. to the top speed. Designated the M.3A, 'BF went to Tripoli in the following June, temporarily becoming I-ZENA to win the Raduno Sahariano piloted by Signor Parodi. Returning to Woodley in the following year, it was sold in Switzerland but after only a brief stay, went north to Macmerry, Edinburgh, owned by Capt. N. A. B. Haddington-Newson. Nine other M.3A Falcons were delivered to British order during 1935, including G-ADER to Maddox Airways Ltd., Brooklands; G-ADHH to D. W. Gumbley of Heston and last heard of in Lydda in 1940;

G-ADFH to E. D. Spratt of Air Service Training Ltd., Hamble, and G-ADIU to the Leicestershire Aero Club, Ratcliffe. G-ADHC was supplied via Galbraith Pembroke and Co. Ltd. to Italy as a second I-ZENA when 'BF returned home.

Like its predecessor, the Falcon was stressed to take engines of higher power, and a Gipsy Six engined M.3B Falcon Six G-ADLC was built in time for the King's Cup Race of 7 September 1935. With Tommy Rose at the controls, the Falcon Six won handsomely at 176·28 m.p.h. and with Hawk Majors 2nd and 3rd, brought the Miles team complete victory. Also competing was the M.3C Falcon Six G-ADLS flown by S. Harris and L. Lipton, who averaged 166·88 m.p.h. to come 5th. Whereas the M.3B was a three seater with the pilot placed centrally, the M.3C held four, with full dual control in the front two seats. It was the only British example, and a year later went to Abbotsinch to remain in the possession of A. D. Farquhar until the war claimed it. At dawn on 6 February 1936, Tommy Rose left Lympne in the King's Cup winner 'LC and succeeded in reducing the Cape record to 3 days 17 hours 37 minutes, leaving again on 3 March to reach Croydon in 6 days 7 hours.

The last four British registered specimens of the M.3A, retrospectively named the Falcon Major, were delivered in 1936. All were used by Phillips and Powis Ltd. at Woodley for club and taxi work, including G-AEFB flown in the 1936 King's Cup Race by Flt. Lt. A. E. Clouston. Another, G-AENG, flew in the 1937 race, but Wing Cdrs. E. G. Hilton and P. Sherren lost their lives when the former was thrown out by violent turbulence at the Scarborough Castle turn. Before Falcon production ceased in 1936, eight more Gipsy Six models were built to British order, including G-AEKK based at Castle Bromwich by the Dunlop Rubber Co. Ltd.; G-ADTD and 'ZL, communications aircraft of Vickers and Faireys respectively and E. G. H. Forsyth's G-AEDL. Two others, G-AFAY and 'BF, acquired by Airwork Ltd. from the Austrian and German owners Leopold Block-Bauer and Karl Roechling in part exchange for newer aircraft, were operated respectively by Brian Allen Aviation Ltd., Croydon and Birkett Air Services Ltd., Heston. Piloted by C. G. M. Alington and carrying two passengers, 'AY flew to Kenya

H. L. Brook's record breaking M.3 Falcon prototype at the Brooklands Flying Club 'At Home' on 20 June 1936. (*R. P. Howard*)

Birkett Air Services' Miles M.4A Merlin at Heston in July 1935. (*E. J. Riding*)

and back early in 1939.

Henri Deterding's G-AEAG and A. N. T. Rankin's G-AECC embodied a number of detail strengthenings permitting an increase in all-up weight to 2,650 lb. with a change in designation to M.3D. Another version, the M.3E G-AFCP, also appeared briefly in November 1937 but was not certificated and it was dismantled after a few months.

At least three Falcon Majors and five Falcon Sixes were built to overseas order for use in Austria, Germany, Hong Kong, New Zealand, South Africa and Spain and two special Falcon Sixes were supplied to the R.A.E., Farnborough for experimental work. K5924 delivered in 1935 with three different sets of Piercy laminar flow mainplanes and L9705 (the 'Gillette Falcon') delivered in 1938 with three sets of mainplanes for research into the behaviour of heavily tapered wings, were followed by a third, R4071, also with Gipsy VI and redesignated M.3F, for spoiler trials. This was originally G-AEAO brought back from Holland where it had spent three years with K. van den Heuvel as PH-EAO. In 1945 it was used for tests in connection with the Miles M.52 supersonic project but was re-civilianised in 1946 for export to Belgium as G-AGZX by Southern Aircraft (Gatwick) Ltd. After a brief stay as OO-FLY it went to France as F-BBCN which, in 1972, still languished at Lognes airfield, France alongside the remains of G-AFBF, acquired as spares in 1954.

Falcon Major G-ADLI and Falcon Sixes G-ADTD and G-AFAY contrived to remain civil communications aircraft throughout the war, but six others were impressed by the Air Ministry. Six survived in 1946, one of which, G-AFAY, beyond restoration, was scrapped at Heston. Those that flew again included two Falcon Majors; G-ADFH based at White Waltham and raced for a few seasons until scrapped at Croydon in 1956; and G-ADLI kept at Panshanger by J. W. Haggas until wrecked when taking off from Elstree in 1952. The other three, Gipsy Six powered, comprised M.3B G-AFBF restored to Southampton Air Services in 1946 but sold in the following year to Cunliffe Owen Aircraft Ltd.; G-ADTD, modified to M.3D standard and winner of the 1956 S.B.A.C. Challenge Trophy at 169 m.p.h. piloted by Geoffrey Marler; and finally, G-AECC, raced for nearly a decade by James Rush of Woolsington and winner of the 1950 Norton Griffiths Trophy at 165·5 m.p.h. In 1957 Crop Culture (Aerial) Ltd. acquired it for communication work, in the course of which it was lost at sea between Bembridge and Exeter on 8 May 1959.

G-ADTD crashed into the sea off Angmering, Sussex with the loss of owner Geoffrey Marler on 21 September 1962 so that in 1972 only two Falcons remained airworthy, pride of place going to M.3A G-AEEG which had been sold in Sweden in 1936 as SE-AFN, was used by the Swedish Air Force as '7001', and returned to Shoreham in July 1961. On 5 July 1962 it was ferried to White Waltham to be stripped and reconditioned by D. E. Bianchi before sale in 1964 to vintage aeroplane connoisseur Edward Eves who thereafter maintained it in mint condition at Baginton. The other airworthy M.3A, VH-AAT and formerly G-ADHG, survived R.A.A.F. impressment as A37-3 and was based at Waikerie airfield, South Australia.

The M.4 Merlin, an enlarged five-seat version of the Falcon with a cabin 6 ft. 7 in. in length and 4 ft. 1 in. wide, was built early in 1935 to the joint requirements of Birkett Air Services Ltd., the Heston air taxi firm, and Tata Air Lines Ltd. of Bombay. The prototype, G-ADFE, first flown at Woodley

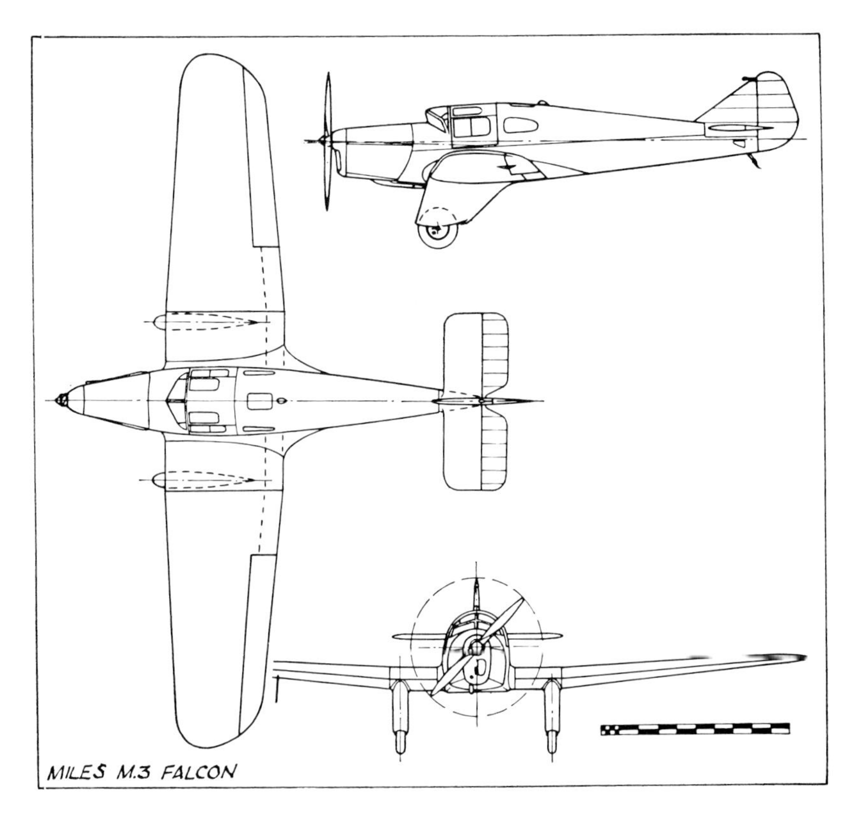
MILES M.3 FALCON

as U-8 by F. G. Miles on 11 May 1935, was delivered to Birkett a week later and made many long distance charter trips, notably several times to Addis Ababa with press men covering the Abyssinian war 1935–36. It roamed Europe until the outbreak of war in 1939 when all trace of it was lost and it is possible that it was destroyed by enemy bombing in 1940.

Only three other Merlins were built and like the prototype were designated M.4A rather than M.4 due to the non-availability of the Ratier v.p. airscrews for which they were originally designed. VT-AGP and 'HC were shipped to India 1935–36 and after erection at Yervada aerodrome, Poona, were used on the Tata route between Karachi and Madras, replacing Puss Moths which could not cover the distance in a single day. The final Merlin, VH-UXN, supplied to Capt. Eric Chaseling for the Melbourne-Hay service of Victorian and Interstate Airways Ltd., was impressed by the R.A.A.F. in 1940 as A37-2.

SPECIFICATION

Manufacturers: Phillips and Powis Aircraft Ltd., Woodley Aerodrome, Reading, Berks.

Power Plants: (M.3 and M.3A) One 130 h.p. de Havilland Gipsy Major.
(M.3B to M.3F) One 200 h.p. de Havilland Gipsy Six.
(M.4A Merlin) One 200 h.p. de Havilland Gipsy Six.

Dimensions, weights and performance:

	M.3 Falcon	M.3A Falcon	M.3B Falcon	M.4A Merlin
Span	35 ft. 0 in.	35 ft. 0 in.	35 ft. 0 in.	37 ft. 0 in.
Length	25 ft. 0 in.	25 ft. 0 in.	25 ft. 0 in.	25 ft. 10 in.
Height	6 ft. 6 in.	6 ft. 6 in.	6 ft. 6 in.	7 ft. 5½ in.
Wing area	174·3 sq. ft.	174·3 sq. ft.	174·3 sq. ft.	196 sq. ft.
Tare weight	1,270 lb.	1,300 lb.	1,550 lb.	1,700 lb.
All-up weight	2,000 lb.	2,200 lb.	2,350 lb.	3,000 lb.
Maximum speed	148 m.p.h.	145 m.p.h.	180 m.p.h.	155 m.p.h.
Cruising speed	130 m.p.h.	125 m.p.h.	160 m.p.h.	140 m.p.h.
Initial climb	–	750 ft./min.	1,000 ft./min.	900 ft./min.
Range	–	615 miles	560 miles	–

Production: (a) Miles M.3A Falcon Major

One prototype M.3, fifteen British registered M.3A, and at least the following for export: (c/n 149) Far East Aviation Co. Ltd., Hong Kong VR-HCV; (197) Rafael de Magarredo, Madrid EC-W48/EC-BDD; (201) Aero Club of Andalusia EC-W45/EC-DBB.

(b) Miles M.3B Falcon Six

Six British registered initially, K5924 for the R.A.E., and at least the following for export: (c/n 232) A. van Hengel, Vienna OE-DVH; (233) Leopold Block-Bauer, Vienna OE-DBB, later G-AFAY; (247) Union Airways of New Zealand Ltd. ZK-AEI; (256) Karl Theodore Roechling D-EGYV, later G-AFBF; (268) African Air Transport Ltd. ZS-AFW.

(c) Miles M.3C to M.3F Falcon Six

Five British registered aircraft and L9705 for the R.A.E.

(d) Miles M.4A Merlin

Four aircraft only: (c/n 141) Tata Air Lines VT-AGP; (151) Birkett Air Services G-ADFE; (272) Capt. Eric Chaseling VH-UXN; (274) Tata Air Lines VT-AHC.

The prototype Miles M.5 Sparrowhawk flying near Woodley in 1935. (*Aeroplane*)

Miles M.5 Sparrowhawk

The prototype Sparrowhawk G-ADNL was built from standard Hawk components as a mount for F. G. Miles in the King's Cup Race of 7 September 1935, and was, of course, a single seater. A standard fuselage was shortened by 12 in. and the top decking lowered as much as possible, the pilot sitting practically on the floor with his legs over the front spar. The centre section was cut to fuselage width and the wings were attached directly to it, reducing the span by 5 ft. The undercarriage track was widened, and a special Gipsy Major high compression engine was fed from a long range tank. By covering the 953 mile course round Britain at an average speed of 163·64 m.p.h. the Sparrowhawk won the speed prize but came 11th in the final. A constant but unspectacular performer, it came 9th at 165·74 m.p.h. piloted by P. H. Maxwell in 1936 and 7th at 172·5 m.p.h. in the hands of Wing Cdr. F. W. Stent in 1937. Four other Sparrowhawks built in 1936 with specially designed (as opposed to modified Hawk Major) fuselages were designated M.5A. The first, G-ADWW, was J. H. G. McArthur's mount for the King's Cup, and the second, G-AELT, Victor Smith's in the Schlesinger Race to Johannesburg which started at Portsmouth on 29 September 1936. These promising entries shared a common fate, McArthur's was disqualified and Smith's retired at Cairo with oil trouble. Both were then sold abroad, 'WW in the U.S.A. where it survived until 1959 and 'LT in South Africa, there to be fitted with a raised decking and cabin top and in 1940 impressed by the S.A.A.F. The next Sparrowhawk, G-AFGA, built to the order of L. E. R. Bellairs, was not certificated until raced for the 1938 King's Cup by W. Humble, but was no more successful than the others, coming 7th at 169·4 m.p.h.

The final Sparrowhawks had more useful, if less spectacular careers. Although built in June 1936, they were stored at Woodley until a wartime requirement by Miles Aircraft Ltd. for experimental aircraft resulted in their assembly and first flights in February 1940. The first flew under B conditions at the R.A.E., Farnborough for high-lift flap research as U-3 but in the December of 1941 reverted to standard and became a camouflaged civil aeroplane, G-AGDL, for communication duties between the firm's Woodley and South Marston factories. At first fitted with a standard Gipsy Major I, it later acquired a high compression Gipsy Major 2 (not to be confused with the Gipsy Major series 2, which was intended for variable pitch airscrews). On 1 June 1946, in new cream and red dope, it gave an aerobatic display, piloted by K. H. F. Waller, at the Woodley Garden Party of the Royal Aeronautical Society but two years later was destroyed in a take-off crash at Tollerton while in service with the Nottingham Flying Club.

The second experimental Sparrowhawk, U-5, had short span wings and wide chord flaps running on rollers and flew without undercarriage fairings. Its true identity is not known but might have been c/n 277, an unidentified airframe following U-3/G-AGDL, or a conversion of G-AFGA.

In 1938 the prototype Sparrowhawk 'NL had passed into the possession of Miss Joan Parsons, and after the 1939–45 war reappeared at Elmdon as the personal aircraft of test pilot C. G. M. Alington. During the early post-war years it was frequently a competitor in major air races and, like its predecessors, constantly averaged 165–170 m.p.h. and although winner of the 1950 race round the Isle of Wight, did not achieve real success.

In December 1950 the aircraft returned to F. G. Miles at Redhill to be remodelled as a jet-powered racing mount for Mr. Fred Dunkerley. An entirely new front fuselage and tail unit were built, and after the firm's move to Shoreham in 1952 modifications were carried out on the wing to house a Turboméca Palas gas turbine in each root end. The aircraft was redesignated the Miles M.77 Sparrowjet and made its first flight at Shoreham piloted by G. H. Miles on 14 December 1953. Although initially dogged by ill luck, the aircraft won the S.B.A.C. Challenge Cup at Yeadon on 21 May 1956, at an average speed of 197·5 m.p.h. Ambition was finally satisfied at Baginton on 13 July 1957, when, after 20 years and a major reconstruction, G-ADNL was brought to victory in the King's Cup Race by Fred Dunkerley at the incredible average speed of 228 m.p.h.

The aircraft was afterwards presented to the Royal Aeronautical Society and housed for a time at the B.E.A. engineering base, Heathrow but was later taken to R.A.F. Upavon where it was destroyed in a hangar fire in July 1964.

Fred Dunkerley taking off in the Sparrowjet at Shoreham in 1954.
(Flight Photo 30473S)

SPECIFICATION

Manufacturers: Phillips and Powis Aircraft Ltd., Woodley Aerodrome, Reading, Berks.
Power Plants: (Sparrowhawk) One 147 h.p. de Havilland Gipsy Major h.c.
One 130 h.p. de Havilland Gipsy Major I.
One 145 h.p. de Havilland Gipsy Major II.
(Sparrowjet) Two 330 lb. s.t. Turboméca Palas.

	Sparrowhawk	Sparrowjet
Span	28 ft. 0 in.	28 ft. 6 in.
Length	23 ft. 6 in.	30 ft. 9½ in.
Height	5 ft. 7 in.	7 ft. 2 in.
Wing area	138 sq. ft.	156 sq. ft.
Tare weight	1,080 lb.	1,578 lb.
All-up weight	1,750 lb.	2,400 lb.
Maximum speed	180 m.p.h.*	228 m.p.h.
Cruising speed	155 m.p.h.*	–
Initial climb	–	2,100 ft./min.
Range	415 miles	270·5 miles

* With Gipsy Major high compression engine.

Production: Five British registered aircraft and one research machine flown as U-5.

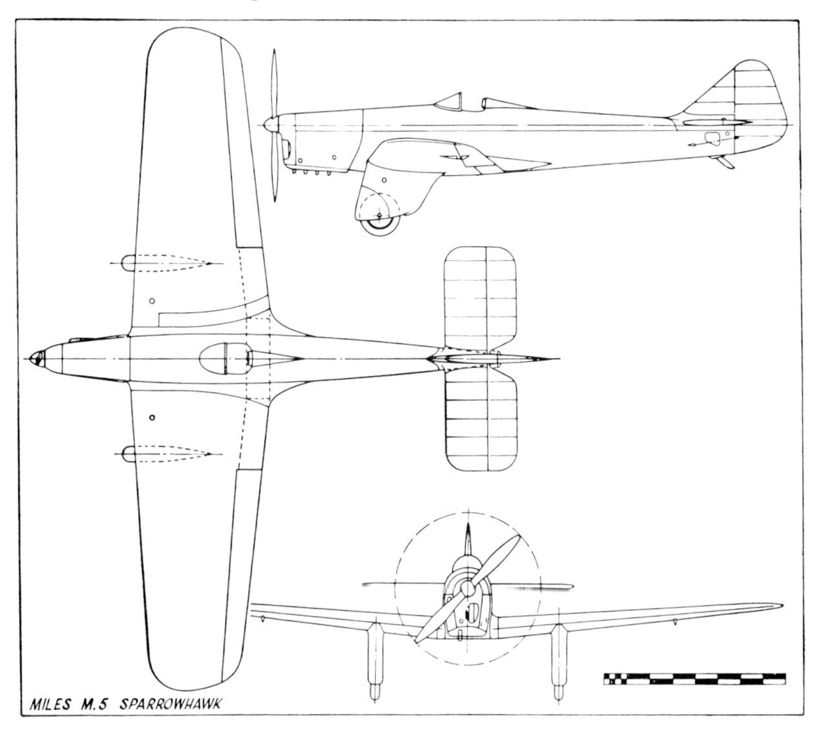

Miles M.11A Whitney Straight G-AERV, flown pre-1939 and post-1945 by H. W. H. Moore.

Miles M.11A Whitney Straight

In 1935 Whitney Straight, then operating a chain of flying clubs in Southern England, laid his conception of a general-purpose light aeroplane before F. G. Miles. The result, first flown in the spring of 1936, afterwards made public debuts at the Heathrow Garden Party of the Royal Aeronautical Society on 10 May and the Hatfield S.B.A.C. Show on 28 June. It was a spruce and plywood, low-wing, cantilever monoplane seating two occupants side by side in cabin comfort and provided with generous luggage space in the rear. Designated the Miles M.11 and inevitably bearing the type name Whitney Straight, the prototype G-AECT was reminiscent of a scaled down Falcon, power being supplied by a Gipsy Major. By virtue of its two position, vacuum operated, trailing edge flaps, it could be pulled steeply off the ground at 50 m.p.h. and was fitted with a very robust undercarriage so that if desired it could be landed heavily at low speeds.

Early in the following year production Whitney Straights were already emerging at Woodley but were designated M.11A due to their revised undercarriage detail and one-piece, seamless windscreen in place of the built-up unit of the prototype. The green and silver first production aircraft G-AENH was publicly demonstrated by F. G. Miles with two others at Heston on 22 January 1937. These were Airwork Ltd.'s demonstrator G-AERS; and G-AERC, acquired by Amherst and Mrs. Maya Villiers and redesignated M.11B as test bed for their 135 h.p. Amherst Villiers Maya I four cylinder inverted engine, first flown in the B.A. Eagle G-ADJS a year previously.

Before private flying was halted by the 1939–45 war, 50 Whitney Straights had been built, including four for New Zealand; two for Swiss private owners; five for France; VH-UZA for the Royal Victorian Aero Club, Australia; OO-UMK for Camille Gutt, Brussels; D-EKTR for Karl Theodore Roechling of Voelkingen, replacing Falcon D-EGYV; YR-MZM for Michael

Marmesco, Bucharest; and VR-SBB for the Royal Singapore Flying Club. Several of the 31 sold on the home market eventually found their way overseas but many became the prized mounts of enthusiastic private owners and aircraft firms.

They were remarkable for docility rather than spectacular achievement, and included H. W. H. Moore's G-AERV; Hawker's 'UJ; the Rolls-Royce 'UZ; the Earl of Ronaldshay's 'WA; J. A. H. Parke's 'VM, kept at a private field at Hambledon near Godalming; and G-AFCC flown for many years at Magellanes, Chile, by T. Saunders. Capt. A. V. Harvey flew 'VH into 4th place in the 1937 King's Cup Race, but the 63-year-old Brig. Gen. A. C. Lewin did better, coming 2nd in 'ZO at an average speed of 144·5 m.p.h. Less than a month later, on 9 October 1937, 'ZO ran out of fuel while heading south over the Sudan en route to Kenya and was wrecked in a forced landing in the Nile swamp, south of Malakal. The combined efforts of the Imperial Airways flying-boat 'Cassiopeia', No. 47 Squadron R.A.F. and the Sudanese, were necessary to extricate the Brigadier and his wife. G-AERS, on the other hand, had a distinguished overseas career with Army officer R. King Clarke, who

The Miles M.11 G-AECT showing the prototype undercarriage and windscreen. (*Flight Photo*)

flew it back and forth to Ismailia, Egypt, in 1937–38 and later based it at Semakh, Palestine, before flying it to Singapore and back.

Another much travelled machine was Whitney Straight's own G-AEWT, sold to Pierre Genin at St. Didier, France, in August 1937 and flown to French Indo China and back by Mme. Genin later the same year. It was hidden during the war but reappeared in 1947 and Genin repurchased it in 1951, passing it on to the Aero Club du Rhone et Sud-Est at Lyons in March 1954. Four months later it was destroyed in a fatal crash at St. Didier.

Instructional usage was confined to 'RC, fitted with a Gipsy Major in May 1938 for the Ipswich Aero Club; 'VH, sold to the Reading Aero Club in the same month; 'XJ, with Air Service Training Ltd. at Hamble, and G-AFBV, which was shared by the Ipswich and Thanet Aero Clubs until it collided fatally with a windsock.

A fourth and final variant, the M.11C G-AEYI, also appeared, fitted with a Gipsy Major Series II driving a variable-pitch airscrew. First flown in May 1937, its take-off and climb were quite remarkable, but the aircraft crashed at Harefield, Berks, on 28 June, killing Phillips and Powis test pilot Wing Cdr. F. W. Stent.

Believed to be the last Whitney Straight built, G-AFGK was sold in April 1938 to Miss Rosemary Rees (later of A.T.A.). It served as a civil communications aircraft with Airwork Ltd. throughout the war, and in 1972 was flying at Panshanger with a Gipsy Major 10 Mk.2 engine. Only the Hawker and Rolls-Royce 'hacks' enjoyed civil lives during war-time. Even the Phillips and Powis machine U-0227, otherwise G-AFZY, was taken over by the R.A.F., along with 20 others. Several reappeared in 1946 when 'RV returned to its pre-war owner, 'UX was flown to Kenya by Wing Cdr. H. M. Probyn, and two others were shipped to New Zealand. One aircraft, G-AETS, which had been impressed in 1941 as DR611 and flew mis-painted as DR617 throughout the war, was bought by the Straight Corporation at Weston-super-Mare in 1946 but although restored as G-AITM was in too poor a condition to fly again. G-AEVG, used by the Andover Station Flight as DP854 and restored for the use of Air Service Training Ltd. in 1947, was later

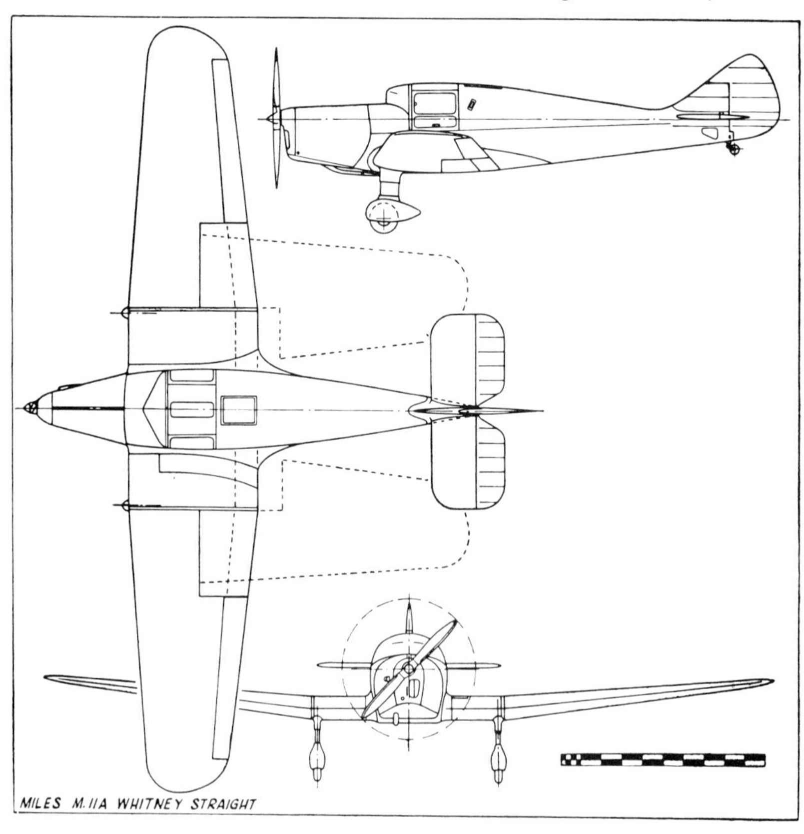
MILES M.11A WHITNEY STRAIGHT

sold to W. A. Strauss who fitted a long range tank and flew it to Australia, arriving at Moorabbin, Victoria on 16 October 1954.

In addition to G-AFGK only five others remained airworthy in 1972 viz. G-AENH/ZK-AXN, ZK-AFH and G-AFJX/ZK-AUK in New Zealand; HB-EPI at Basle; and C. H. Parker's Hurn based G-AEUJ. One other, G-AERV, was at that time on show in the Belfast Transport Museum.

Whitney Straight G-AEVG after re-registration in Australia and carrying the inscription '1954 England–Australia' on the rudder.

SPECIFICATION

Manufacturers: Phillips and Powis Aircraft Ltd., Woodley Aerodrome, Berks.

Power Plants: (M.11 and M.11A) One 130 h.p. de Havilland Gipsy Major I.
(M.11B) One 135 h.p. Amherst Villiers Maya I.
(M.11C) One 145 h.p. de Havilland Gipsy Major II.

Dimensions: Span, 35 ft. 8 in. Length, 25 ft. 0 in. Height, 6 ft. 6 in. Wing area, 178 sq. ft.

Weights: (M.11A) Tare weight, 1,250 lb. All-up weight, 2,000 lb.

Performance: (M.11A) Maximum speed, 145 m.p.h. Cruising speed, 130 m.p.h. Initial climb, 850 ft./min. Ceiling, 18,500 ft. Range, 570 miles.
(M.11B) Maximum speed, 155 m.p.h. Cruising speed, 136 m.p.h. Initial climb, 1,050 ft./min.

Production: One M.11 prototype G-AECT; one M.11B test bed G-AERC; one M.11C trials machine G-AEYI; 31 British registered M.11As initially and the following for export: (c/n 306) OO-UMK, later G-AFJJ; (308) ZK-AEO, later NZ576 and ZK-AJF; (311) ZK-AFH; (323) ZK-AFG, later NZ579 and ZK-AJZ; (327) YR-MZM; (344) HB-URO; (345) F-AQMA; (348) F-AQIK; (349) HB-EPI; (350) VH-UZA; (496) F-AQCZ; (498) D-EKTR; (503) ZK-AGB, later NZ577 and ZK-ALE; (504) VR-SBB; (505) F-AQLX; (508) F-AREQ

G-ADZC, fourth Miles M.2X Hawk Trainer delivered to No.8 E.R.F.T.S., was used also by the Reading Aero Club 1936–37. (*Aeroplane*)

Miles Hawk Trainers

An improved version of the Hawk Major was built in 1935 to supplement the Tiger Moths then in use at Woodley with No. 8 Elementary and Reserve Flying Training School. They were fitted with dual control, full blind flying equipment, vacuum operated flaps and Gipsy Major engines and were known as Hawk Trainers under the designation M.2W. Only four, G-ADVF and 'WT–'WV, were delivered, nine others built in 1936 having horn-balanced rudders of greater area which amended the type to M.2X. Two others, G-ADZD and G-AEAY, outwardly identical, were registered as M.2Y. Two of the batch, G-ADZC and G-AEAX, were released to the Reading Aero Club in May 1939 and G-ADWT later became the mount of test pilot C. G. M. Alington at Castle Bromwich. With the exception of 'WT and three which met with accidents, all continued in use until impressed en bloc in March 1941.

Ten M.2Y Hawk Trainers were given temporary British registrations G-AEHP to 'HZ for delivery by air to the Rumanian Air Force during 1936 and one other, ZK-AEQ, was shipped to the Wellington Aero Club in New Zealand. In 1937 the ultimate development of the Hawk Major appeared as the Miles M.14, produced to Air Ministry specification T.40/36 and at a time when the R.A.F. was saying farewell to the biplane era, was named the Magister and ordered in quantity to teach the new monoplane techniques. Structurally identical to its predecessors, the M.14 had slightly less span, a wide track, spatted undercarriage, anti-spinning strakes and the type of rudder then being fitted to the Monarch. A few were built for civil purposes, with the type name Hawk Trainer Mk.III, the first two flying on test under British marks before despatch to New Zealand in February 1937. VR-SAY for the Royal Singapore Flying Club followed in July 1937; c/n 480 was shipped to the Arcos organisation in Russia; three more went to New Zealand; ZS-ALT to South African Airways for blind flying training; ZS-AMR to 'MW to the Witwatersrand Technical College; ZS-AMY to the Rand Flying

Club; c/n 510 to Aircraft Industries (Pty.) Ltd. who were interested in building the type in Australia; 14 to the Egyptian Air Force; 10 to the Irish Air Corps; and one each to the Estonian Air Force and King Ghazi of Iraq.

G-AEZP, registered as an M.14B Hawk Trainer Mk.II, went to Brough as test bed for the Blackburn Cirrus Major 2 engine and was flown by E. C. T. Edwards in the 1937 King's Cup Race. In the 1938 event J. M. Barwick started first in his red Hawk Trainer Mk.III G-AEZR, but finished last at an average speed of 130·5 m.p.h. Three others, G-AEZS, G-AFBS and 'DB, joined the Woodley E.R.F.T.S., and four more, G-AFET–'EW, were allotted to the Straight Corporation's flying clubs at Ipswich, Ramsgate, Exeter and Plymouth respectively. This, the only bona fide civil order, received low priority due to the intensity of military production (1,293 Magisters were built). Consequently the aircraft were delivered by air in red undercoat with chalked registrations. During 1938, taller rudders of greater area were fitted to assist recovery from the spin, and the Hawk Trainer Mk.III thereafter assumed the designation M.14A. Except for the Thanet Aero Club's G-AFEU,

One of the original Miles M.14 Hawk Trainer Mk.III aircraft showing the increase in depth of the rear fuselage and change in rudder shape. (*C. A. Nepean Bishop*)

Hawk Trainer Mk.III YI-GFH, equipped with blind flying hood for delivery to H.M. King Ghazi of Iraq in October 1938.

G-AHYL, one of three Hawk Trainer Mk.3s converted at Ringway for the Fairey Flying Club, and seen flying near White Waltham in 1947. (*E. J. Riding*)

lost at sea off Cliftonville with two crew in July 1938, all the M.14s were eventually fitted with the new rudder. Pre-war civil deliveries ended with the addition of M.14Bs G-AFTR, 'TS and M.14As G-AFWY, 'XA and 'XB to the Woodley school in 1939, four later aircraft being engulfed by R.A.F. demands. Impressment was inevitable, although, for a time, many flew as civil aircraft in full R.A.F. training camouflage.

Only one of the original Hawk Trainers, G-ADWT, survived the war and was flown by the Reading Aero Club in 1947 with an M.2X type rudder, but when the R.A.F. Magisters were declared obsolete and sold, two more pre-war machines appeared, G-AFBS to fly with the Airways Aero Club and Denham Flying Club for a further 12 years and 'XA, overhauled at Croydon but scrapped in 1956. The first Magister of purely military origin civilianised as a Hawk Trainer Mk.III was P6380, certificated on 19 November 1945 as G-AGVW. Following an inauspicious start when 'VW collided with an Auster J-1 and fell into the sea off Copenhagen on 21 April 1946, the Hawk Trainer Mk.III settled down to a distinguished post-war career as a club and sporting aircraft. The chief exponents were the Darlington and District, Wiltshire, Rochester, Redhill, Weston, Loch Leven, Scottish, Derby, Elstree, Denham, Fairey and Airways flying clubs and schools.

One of a batch of Magisters acquired by the Herts and Essex Aero Club (1946) Ltd. for civil conversion in 1947, proved to be the Cirrus Major 3 engined prototype L6913. Although fully overhauled and in the club's smart silver and green colours as G-AKNA, it failed to obtain a C. of A. because no such variant had existed pre-war. No designation existed to cover it, and in 1956, it was reduced to spares at Speke. The export market and the ravages of old age inevitably thinned the ranks but for over a decade every flying function was ensured of a strong contingent of Hawk Trainer Mk.3s (the 3 having become Arabic).

Miles Aircraft Ltd. also refurbished some 300 Magisters for direct export commencing with 15 for Chile, shipped in 1945, followed by some 150 for the Argentine, some of which carried civil markings. Others were delivered to Australia, Belgium, Denmark, Egypt, France, Iceland, Ireland, Lebanon, Morocco, New Zealand, Portugal, Switzerland and Thailand.

For racing purposes several interesting local modifications included the fairing in of front or rear seats. The 1950 King's Cup Race, in which eight Hawk Trainer Mk.3s competed, was won at Wolverhampton by E. Day in a cabin version G-AKRV 'Judith Anne' at 138·5 m.p.h. This modification, later fitted to the Rochester Flying Club's G-AKRW and the Redhill Club's G-AJRT, originated during the war when 'RV, then Magister T9876, was converted at an R.A.F. station for officer transport. G-AIDF, flown by W. J. Twitchell in the Hurn to Herne Bay Race on 20 September 1950, had both cockpits covered, the pilot's head projecting into a Perspex D.F. loop fairing screwed to the rear cover. His mean speed was 147 m.p.h. One example, G-ALGK, was modified for ground radar co-operation by Short Bros. and Harland Ltd. at Rochester and commissioned in March 1949. The pilot sat in the front seat under a sliding hood, while the completely covered rear cockpit housed Ekco CE217/12 V.H.F. radio. Its East Anglian patrols came to an end in the water off Burnham-on-Crouch on 21 January 1951.

In 1973 the surviving Hawk Trainers included M.2W G-ADMW whose post-war owners included No.47 Squadron Flying Club before it was sold in 1961 to R.C.A.F. padre Father J. MacGillivray serving at Soellingen, Germany. He

The Blackburn Cirrus Major 3 powered Hawk Trainer Mk.2 G-AKNA in the silver and green of the Herts & Essex Aero Club, Broxbourne in 1947.

Hawk Trainer Coupé G-AKRW at Rochester 1951. Entry was via a hinged roof. *(A. J. Jackson)*

shipped it to Canada in 1964 where it became CF-NXT and attended all the long distance fly-ins in North America. Also active was G-AJDR owned by Air Commodore A. H. Wheeler on behalf of the Shuttleworth Trust and flown in camouflage as T9976. Among non-flying examples were G-AHUJ stored at Strathallan, Perthshire; G-AFBS at the Skyfame Museum, Staverton; the Newark Air Museum's G-AKAT; G-AKKR repainted as T9707 and housed in the R.A.F. Museum, Hendon; G-AIUA under reconstruction at Felthorpe; and one each in Belgium, France, New Zealand and Morocco.

SPECIFICATION

Manufacturers: Phillips and Powis Aircraft Ltd., Woodley Aerodrome, Reading, Berks.

Power Plants: (M.2W, X and Y) One 130 h.p. de Havilland Gipsy Major.
(M.14) One 130 h.p. de Havilland Gipsy Major I.
(M.14A) One 130 h.p. de Havilland Gipsy Major I.
One 155 h.p. Blackburn Cirrus Major 3.
(M.14B) One 135 h.p. Blackburn Cirrus Major 2.

	M.2W, X, Y	M.14, M.14A
Span	34 ft. 0 in.	33 ft. 10 in.
Length	24 ft. 0 in.	24 ft. 7½ in.
Height	6 ft. 8 in.	6 ft. 8 in.
Wing area	176 sq. ft.	172 sq. ft.
Tare weight	1,210 lb.	1,286 lb.
All-up weight	1,720 lb.	1,900 lb.
Maximum speed	150 m.p.h.	132 m.p.h.
Cruising speed	135 m.p.h.	123 m.p.h.
Initial climb	1,300 ft./min.	850 ft./min.
Ceiling	18,000 ft.	18,000 ft.
Range	400 miles	380 miles

Production: (a) Miles M.2W Hawk Trainer

Four British registered aircraft and one spare fuselage (c/n 484).

(b) Miles M.2X Hawk Trainer

Nine British registered aircraft.

(c) Miles M.2Y Hawk Trainer

Twelve British registered aircraft and one for export: (c/n 302) ZK-AEQ.

(d) Miles M.14 and M.14A Hawk Trainer Mk.III (pre-war)

Seventeen British registered aircraft, one mock-up (c/n 329), one other (c/n 333) modified as Magister prototype L5912, and the following for export: (c/n 365) VR-SAY; (480) Arcos, Russia; (486) ZK-AEZ, later NZ585; (487) ZK-AFA; (488–489) New Zealand; (490) ZS-AMR, later S.A.A.F. 1476; (491) ZS-AMS/1479; (492) ZS-AMT/1505; (493) ZS-AMU/1448; (510) Australia; (511) ZS-AMW/1483; (512) ZS-AMY/1485; (513) ZS-AMV; (514) ZS-ALT; (543–546) Egyptian L203, L204, L206, L205; (633–635) Egyptian L207–L209; (637) L210; (639) Estonian 159; (797) YI-GFH; (798) L220; (812–820) L211–L219; (1025–1029) N5389–N5393 diverted to Irish Air Corps as '31'–'35'; (1036–1040) N5400–N5404 diverted as '36'–'40'

(e) Miles M.14B Hawk Trainer Mk.II

Three British civil aircraft and five for the R.A.F.: (c/n 530–534) L6909–L6913 (L6913 registered G-AKNA post-war)

(f) Miles M.14A Magister

1,293 aircraft for the R.A.F., 148 civil registered in Britain post-war and at least the following civil exports by Miles Aircraft Ltd.: (c/n 403) L5971/OO-MIC; (409) L5977/LV-XSJ; (415) L5983/LR-AAL; (431) L5999/HB-EEB; (570) L8061/LV-XSF; (571) L8062/LR-AAK; (572) L8063/LV-XMI; (577) L8068/F-OAAQ; (581) L8072/LV-XMW; (586) L8077/F-BDPJ; (597) L8088/Portuguese Air Force/CS-AFM; (600) L8091/F-BDPP; (673) L8206/LV-XNF; (682) L8215/LV-XNH; (686) L8219/LV-XOM; (696) L8229/LV-XQQ; (706) L8250/LV-XRT; (712) L8256/F-BDPK; (717) L8261/F-BDPE; (721) L8265/F-BDPO; (745) L8289/LV-XOI; (783) L8357/ZK-ANJ; (784) L8358/F-BDPL; (811) L8150/LV-XOL; (850) N3802/F-BCDU; (867) N3821/TF-BLU; (873) N3827/LV-XSG; (894) N3848/F-BDPF; (935) N3894/ZK-ANK; (946) N3905/LV-XPW; (963) N3925/F-BDPC; (978) N3940/F-BDPM; (1002) N3969/F-BDPB; (1005) N3972/LV-XPN; (1051) N5415/LV-XMM; (1723) P6355/LV-RUX; (1735) P6367/F-BDPH; (1778) P6423/F-BDPD; (1783) P6439/F-BDPG; (1785) P6441/F-BDPA; (1801) P6457/LV-XRP; (1808) P6464/LV-XPT; (1816) R1815/LV-XPZ; (1848) R1847/F-BDPN; (1889) R1903/LV-XQR; (1946) R1975/OY-DNI; (1962) T9675/LV-XRJ; (1979) T9692/TF-REX; (1981) T9694/LV-XMG; (1992) T9705/OO-NIC; (2026) T9759/OY-ABI, later SE-CGF; (2041) T9804/F-BDPI; (2084) T9847/LV-XPF; (2156) T9963/LV-XSH; (2213) V1040/LV-XSD; (2216) V1063/LV-XMR; (2338) V1085/LV-XQT

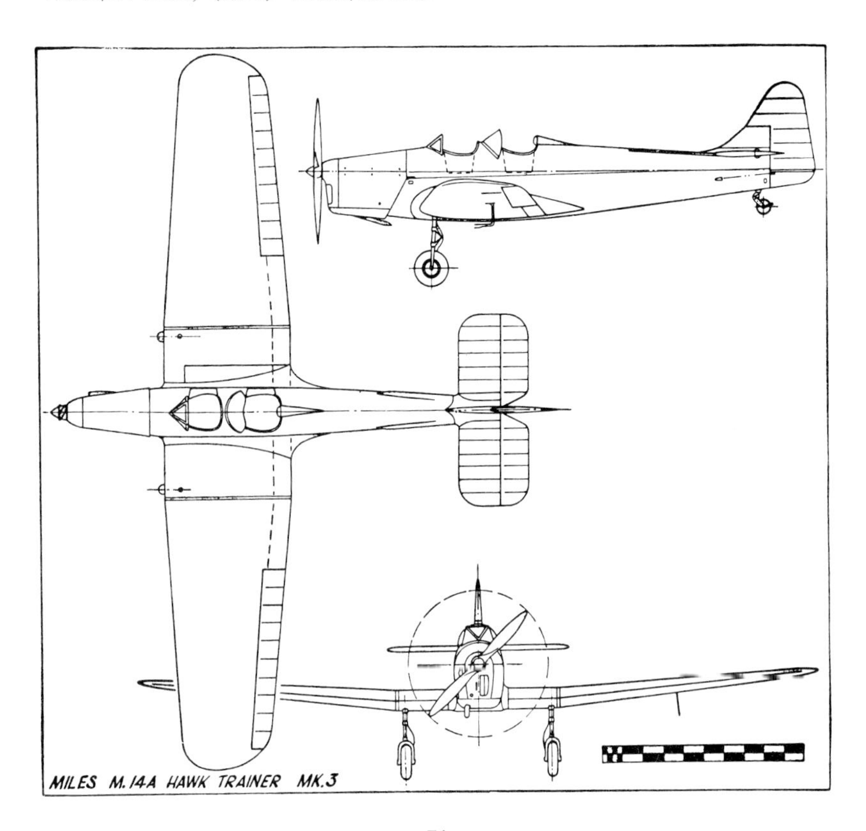
MILES M.14A HAWK TRAINER MK.3

Rex Coates flying his superbly maintained 1938 Miles Monarch near Blackbushe in 1970. (*Air Portraits*)

Miles M.17 Monarch

Phillips and Powis productive effort in 1937 was almost entirely centred on the Magister contract, and little thought could be spared for the civil market. Only one more private owner type was therefore built at Woodley before the 1939–45 war, an enlarged three seat version of the Whitney Straight known as the Monarch. It was the first Miles aeroplane for which the designer's younger brother G. H. Miles was entirely responsible, and the prototype G-AFCR flew for the first time on 21 February 1938, piloted by H. W. C. Skinner. The fuselage was deeper and roomier than that of its predecessor, the third occupant sitting centrally in part of the luggage space. He was also provided with a window in the starboard but not the port side. Standard Magister outer wing panels were used and a novel interconnected throttle and flap lever provided an appreciable measure of automatic glide control.

Eleven aircraft, including the prototype, were constructed during 1938–39, six to British order. G-AFGL and 'TX were based at Heston by Airwork Ltd. and W. H. Whitbread respectively before being sold abroad in 1939; 'JU was acquired by Sir V. A. G. Warrender; 'JZ went to Blackpool with E. O. Liebert; 'LW to Rolls-Royce Ltd., Hucknall and 'RZ to Lord Malcolm Douglas Hamilton. The fate of this select company paralleled that of the Whitney Straights. The Rolls-Royce machine remained in camouflaged civilian use throughout the war, and the remainder were impressed very early in the conflict.

In August 1938 a Belgian private pilot M. Camille Gutt had traded his Whitney Straight OO-UMK to Airwork Ltd. in part exchange for a Monarch. The older machine became G-AFJJ, while the new assumed its predecessor's markings. When the Low Countries were overrun in May 1940 the Monarch escaped and returned to Woodley where it was promptly put to good use by Phillips and Powis Aircraft Ltd., first under B registry as U-0226 and later as G-AGFW. Although returned to M. Gutt's possession in 1944, he was not permitted to fly it in civilian markings, so it went to Hendon to join the Belgian section of the Metropolitan Communications Squadron and in March 1945 became TP819. It returned to Brussels in September 1946 and was restored as OO-UMK but crashed and burned near St. Denis-Westrem airfield, Ghent, on 22 November 1960.

Remaining Monarch production comprised OY-DIO delivered to Dr. Hans Christian Hagedorn at Kastrup in August 1938; ZS-AOY shipped to Aero Services (Pty.) Ltd. in November 1938 which crashed near Cape Town a year later; and PH-ATP flown to Schiphol as a trainer with the Nationale Luchvaart School in April 1939 only to be destroyed on 10 May 1940 during the German obliteration bombing.

E. O. Liebert's G-AFJZ, which had been sold to G. E. Wallace in July 1939, was the only Monarch which failed to return from war service. The others all reappeared in 1946 when the prototype was overhauled for Air Schools Ltd., Burnaston, and 'JU for Lt. Cdr. H. R. A. Kidston. Rolls-Royce Ltd. were still using the faithful 'LW, but when 'RZ came up for civilian disposal its pre-war identity was overlooked so that it became G-AIDE instead. After overhaul at Christchurch it was flown by B. G. Heron for several years, but at some time in its career the aircraft had acquired a window in the port as well as the starboard side and was the only Monarch so fitted. The well-known sporting pilot W. P. Bowles bought it in 1956 and was successful in winning the Goodyear Trophy at Baginton on 13 July 1957, at an average speed of 131·5 m.p.h. later coming 3rd in the King's Cup Race. In 1958 he again tuned the Monarch successfully, winning the Norton Griffiths Trophy at Baginton on 12 July at 136·16 m.p.h., afterwards coming 2nd in the Osram Cup Race. J. E. Fricker kept it at Stapleford 1962–64 after which it went to J. H. Steven's strip at Charing, Kent, until sold to C. D. Cyster and flown over to his strip near Rye.

With the exception of the prototype, lost in a forced landing in gathering darkness near Venice while touring in its 20th year, the surviving Monarchs had long but often undistinguished careers. G-AFJU, veteran of ten post-war owners, saw industrial service with Furzehill Laboratories Ltd., Elstree and S. Smith and Sons (England) Ltd. at Staverton, suffered 'circuits and bumps'

Monarch G-AIDE/G-AFRZ newly released from wartime impressment at Christchurch in 1947. (*E. J. Riding*)

with the Cotswold Aero Club 1955 and the Cambridge Private Flying Group 1962-64, and was eventually dismantled at Staverton in 1964.

The Rolls-Royce 'hack' G-AFLW finally left their employ in 1958 and after instructional use by Blackpool and Fylde Aero Club, Squires Gate, was flown privately from Leicester East by owners A. F. Jarman and M. F. Kirk until sold to R. E. Coates of the P.F.A. Vintage Aircraft Group, Blackbushe in 1968.

SPECIFICATION

Manufacturers: Phillips and Powis Aircraft Ltd., Woodley Aerodrome, Reading, Berks.

Power Plant: One 130 h.p. de Havilland Gipsy Major I.

Dimensions: Span, 35 ft. 7 in. Length, 25 ft. 11¾ in. Height, 8 ft. 9¼ in. Wing area, 180 sq. ft.

Weights: Tare weight, 1,390 lb. All-up weight, 2,200 lb.

Performance: Maximum speed, 145 m.p.h. Cruising speed, 130 m.p.h. Initial climb, 850 ft./min. Ceiling, 17,400 ft. Range, 600 miles.

Production: Eleven aircraft, seven British registered initially and the following for export: (c/n 787) OO-UMK, later G-AGFW; (788) OY-DIO; (791) ZS-AOY; (794) PH-ATP.

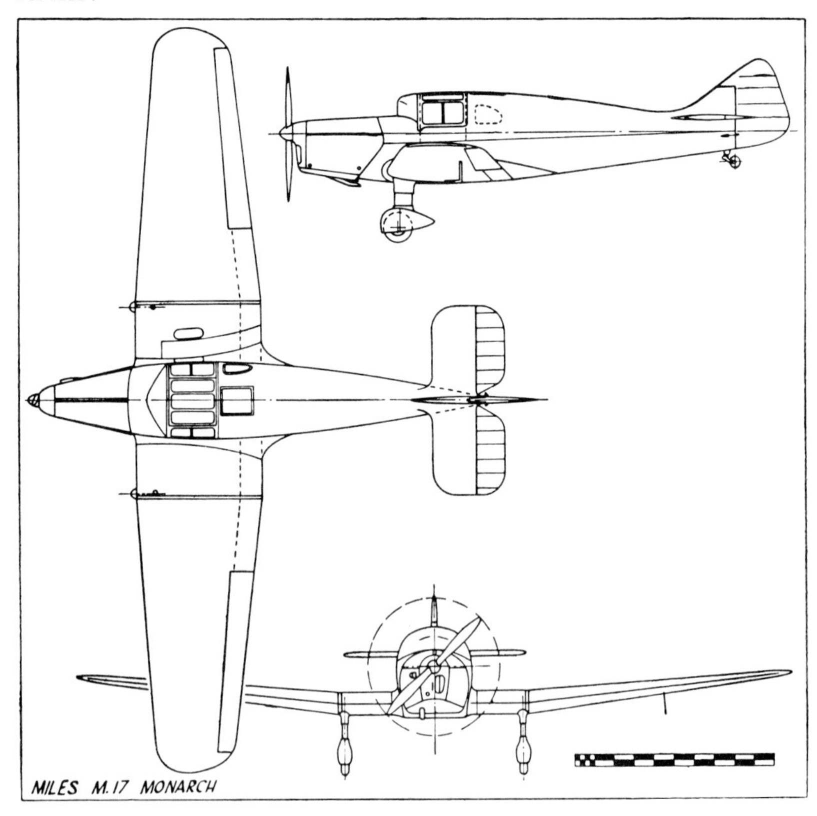

A standard Miles M.38 Messenger 2A showing the characteristic rear window, auxiliary flap and triple rudders. (*Charles E. Brown*)

Miles M.38 Messenger

Built during the 1939–45 war for light liaison duties, the four seat Messenger handsomely fulfilled an Army specification for a robust aircraft with exceptional slow speed characteristics needing only casual maintenance from unskilled labour. The prototype U-0223, converted from the prototype Miles M.28 Mercury, first flew at Woodley on 12 September 1942. The fuselage, built up from longerons, stringers and U frames, was covered with a plastic-bonded plywood skin, through which passed the twin box spars of the one-piece, plywood covered mainplane. Miles non-retractable auxiliary aerofoil flaps were fitted behind and below the trailing edge, three fins and rudders were fitted to ensure maximum control right down to the stall, and an elementary form of single strut undercarriage was devised to withstand deliberate heavy landings.

Messenger I aircraft with Gipsy Major 1D engines were built in small numbers for the R.A.F., but their potential as private aircraft was obvious. After the war production continued to civil standards, and in 1946 a former Messenger I, G-AHFP, was the first Miles demonstrator, later becoming a joyriding and taxi aircraft with Airwork Ltd. at Gatwick and Croydon. The civil Messenger 2A, identified by the oval instead of square rear window, was powered by a Cirrus Major 3, the test bed for which, a three seat Messenger 2B G-AGPX, was supplied to Blackburn Aircraft Ltd. in June 1945. One three seat Messenger 2C, G-AGUW, with Gipsy Major 1D and oval rear window, was built for export to South Africa and left Woodley on 8 March 1946, piloted by Alex Henshaw.

Late in the war a second prototype Messenger, known as the M.48, had been built with fully retractable flaps and flown under B conditions as U-0247. This aircraft was registered to Miles Aircraft Ltd. in June 1945 as G-AGOY with the revised designation M.38 Messenger 3. On its return, in 1948, from two years with Aerotaxi A.G. in Zürich, it became well known in private flying circles and in 1971 was still stored in Ireland, where it had been sold as EI-AGE in 1953.

Production Messenger 2As were built at Newtownards and flown to Woodley for final spraying and when production ceased in January 1948, nine had been exported direct to Argentina, Belgium, the Congo, Chile, Egypt, Iran and South Africa and 58 had been sold on the home market, the first, G-AHZS being acquired by Air Kruise (Kent) Ltd., Lympne.

Later other variants appeared and a Mk.4, Gipsy Major 10, for the Regent of Iraq, left for Baghdad on 5 May 1946, with the British marks G-AHGE. After its loss in an accident, a successor, Messenger 2B G-AHXR, served in Iraq as YI-HRH, returning in 1948 to become British owned. A second

The Miles M.48/M.38 Messenger 3 was fitted with retractable flaps, and unlike other marks, had dual control.

Messenger 4, G-AIRY, built to special order later in 1946, was used for several years by the British Aviation Insurance Co. Ltd. and G-AILI, personal aircraft of G. H. Miles, was temporarily fitted and flown in July 1947 with a Praga E flat six engine. Best known of all Messengers, however, was Mk.4 G-AKKG, originally built to Swiss order, which from 1948 to 1957 was flown on Shell business by Mr. Vivian Varcoe and hardly ever missed an aviation meeting.

When the R.A.F. Messenger I with Gipsy Major 1D engine was declared redundant in 1948, almost the entire military production batch was offered for civilian disposal in relatively new condition. Carrying the new designation Messenger 4A, 18 became private, racing and executive aircraft of distinction, as shown in Appendix E. Messenger I RH420, handed over to Blackburn and General Aircraft Ltd. as a test bed for their Bombardier 702 motor, was flown for a considerable time as the Messenger 5 G-2-1. Its first public

The Bombardier engined Messenger 5 at Shoreham, a few hours before it was written off. *(A. J. Jackson)*

appearance, as G-ALAC, in the *Daily Express* South Coast Air Race at Shoreham on 22 September 1951, was also its last, test pilot P. G. Lawrence making a forced landing near Faversham in which 'AC was damaged beyond repair.

For over a decade assorted Messengers found great favour for touring purposes. While thus engaged on 28 June 1947, G-AJEY, subject of the heading photograph, lost its engine near Bait, S.E. France. Boulton Paul chief test pilot R. Lindsay Neale thereupon brought off his historic forced landing by crowding his passengers forward over the dashboard. Although many were raced, honours were few. Blackburn test pilot Harold Wood won the 1954 King's Cup in Messenger 2A G-AKBO at 133 m.p.h. and A. J. Spiller the 1952 Siddeley Trophy in G-AKIN at 129 m.p.h. W. P. Bowles, for whom the last Messenger 2A, G-AJYZ, was erected from stock components by Handley Page (Reading) Ltd. in 1950–51, won the Norton Griffiths Trophy consecutively at Woolsington in 1952 and Southend in 1953.

In 1972 sixteen Messengers were still registered in Britain, the oldest flying being the Biggin Hill-based G-AHZT. G-ALAH was stored at Blackpool awaiting restoration as RH377 for the R.A.F. Museum, Hendon and VH-AVQ, formerly G-AJKG, was on exhibition at Moorabbin Airport, Melbourne, Australia.

SPECIFICATION

Manufacturers: Phillips and Powis Aircraft Ltd., Woodley Aerodrome, Reading, Berks. Name changed to Miles Aircraft Ltd. in October 1943, production by Miles Aircraft (N.I.) Ltd., Ards Airport, Newtownards, Co. Down, N.I.

Power Plants:
(Messenger 2A, 2B, 3) One 155 h.p. Blackburn Cirrus Major 3.
(Messenger 2C and 4A) One 145 h.p. de Havilland Gipsy Major 1D.
(Messenger 4 and 4B) One 145 h.p. de Havilland Gipsy Major 10.
(Messenger 5) One 180 h.p. Blackburn Bombardier 702.

Dimensions: Span, 36 ft. 2 in. Length, 24 ft. 0 in. Height, 7 ft. 6 in. Wing area, 191 sq. ft.

	Messenger 2A, 2B, 3	Messenger 2C, 4, 4A
Tare weight	1,450 lb.	1,360 lb.
All-up weight	2,400 lb.	2,400 lb.
Maximum speed	135 m.p.h.	115 m.p.h.
Cruising speed	124 m.p.h.	100 m.p.h.
Initial climb	950 ft./min.	1,100 ft./min.
Ceiling	16,000 ft.	17,000 ft.
Range	460 miles	460 miles

Production: (a) Messenger 2A

Fifty-five British registered aircraft (including G-AJYZ erected 1950 by Handley Page Ltd.) and the following for export: (c/n 6342) OO-CCN; (6344) CC-ECA; (6345) CC-ECB, later LV-RUJ; (6361) LV-RNL; (6368) ZS-AVY; (6708) OO-SIX; (6711) SU-AGQ; (6715) SU-AGP; (6723) EP-ACE.

(b) Messenger 4

Three British registered aircraft and one for export: (c/n 6700) HB-EEC.

(c) Messenger 4A

Twenty-one ex R.A.F. Messenger 1s: (c/n 4691) RG327; (4697) RG333; RH368–RH378; RH420–RH424 and (c/n 6350–6354) RH425–RH429. All civilianised as Mk.4As except RG333 and RH373–RH375.

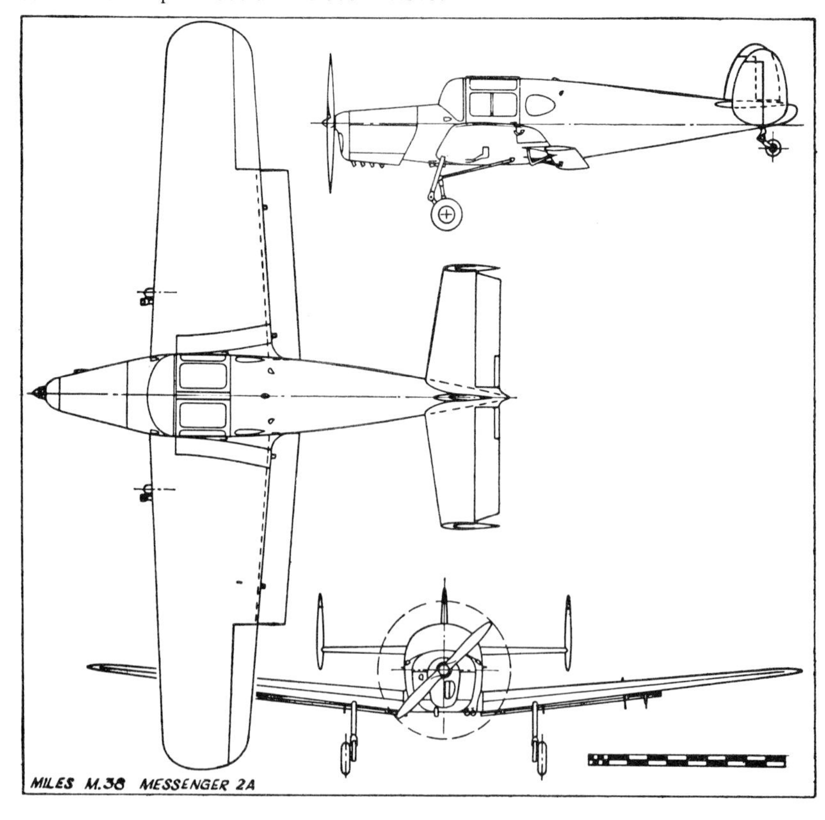

Ken Waller flying the Aerovan 1 at Woodley in November 1945.

Miles M.57 Aerovan

Designed by G. H. Miles in 1944 for the short haul transport of bulky loads, the Aerovan contrived to add beauty of line to its unorthodox utilitarian airframe. The short but capacious fuselage of 530 cu. ft. capacity was of plastic bonded wooden construction with the rear portion hinged to form a door large enough for the entry of a small car. Miles auxiliary aerofoil flaps were fitted to the one-piece cantilever wooden mainplane and the triple tail unit was supported on a metal boom. On the 310 h.p. of two Cirrus Major 3 engines the Aerovan would carry a ton of freight or eight passengers for 450 miles at 110–115 m.p.h. The prototype Aerovan 1 was first flown as U-0248 at Woodley by Tommy Rose on 26 January 1945, thereafter appearing at all the early post-war displays as G-AGOZ. In October 1945 it flew to Switzerland with 5,000 ball point pens, and in the following April toured Denmark piloted by Hugh Kendall. In 1947 it flew with a scale mock-up of a Mamba nacelle outboard of the starboard engine in readiness for the Miles M.69 Marathon 2. A second prototype of lower structural weight, the Aerovan 2 G-AGWO, which first flew in March 1946 piloted by K. H. F. Waller, was fitted to carry 10 passengers. The front fuselage was extended 18 in., five round instead of four rectangular windows were provided in each side and the outboard rudders were no longer horn balanced. A season of demonstration ended in November 1946 when 'WO went to Newtownards, base of its purchaser Lord Londonderry.

Seven production Aerovan 3s, built during 1946, were outwardly identical to the Aerovan 2 except for a heavy duty door lock under the rear fuselage. Five were employed by Air Contractors Ltd. of Blackbushe for the cross-Channel mixed freight traffic, and a sixth, G-AIIG, for passenger charter by Skytravel Ltd. of Speke. When replaced by Dakotas in 1949 the four survivors went to Beirut, Lebanon, in service with the Arab Contracting and Trading Co. Ltd. They ranged all over the Near East, calling at the landing grounds of the Iraq Petroleum Transport Co. Ltd. in the Syrian Desert, and at Kuwait, Bahrein, Qatar and all along the Trucial coast of Oman. One, G-AHXH, brought up to Aerovan 4 standard, returned to the United Kingdom in 1956.

Main production centred round the Aerovan 4, identified by its four circular windows, and forty-three were built before the market was satisfied at the end of 1947. All but four were of British registry, two, G-AIDJ and G-AKHG, joining the Aerovan 3s in Beirut. Air Contractors Ltd. acquired G-AIKV and 'SI, the first of which made sensational headlines when washed out to sea after a successful forced landing on the coast near Cherbourg on 12 January 1947. Four were ferried to Aerotechnica S.A. in Madrid as G-AILB–'LE and subsequently did a great deal of flying in Spain as EC-ACP, 'ABA, 'ABB and 'ACQ respectively. Others were acquired for charter work or joyriding by Air Transport (Charter) (C.I.) Ltd., Jersey; Lockwood Flying Services Ltd., Speeton; British Nederland Air Services Ltd.; East Anglian Flying Services Ltd., Southend; North Sea Air Transport Ltd., Brough (later handed over to Universal Flying Services Ltd., Fairoaks); and Kenning Aviation Ltd., Burnaston. G-AJZR, operated for a few months by Skyfreight Ltd., was sold to Turkish State Airlines in January 1949 and became, appropriately, TC-VAN. Several wore elaborate livery and were named. Patrick Aviation Ltd. of Elmdon operated G-AJKP 'County of Stafford' and G-AJOF 'County of Derby', Culliford Airlines Ltd. of Squires Gate had G-AJZG 'Comatas' and Sivewright Airways Ltd., Ringway, G-AJOI 'Oldhamia'. The largest fleet, that of Ulster Aviation Ltd. of Newtownards, comprising G-AJKJ, 'KU, 'OB, 'TD and G-AKHD, was employed in 1947–49 on the Isle of Man tourist traffic and a freight run to Woodley with Ards-built Messenger and Gemini assemblies.

The last centre of Aerovan activity was the Channel Islands, whither G-AILF, 'SF, G-AJKP and 'OF gravitated in secondhand condition in

An Aerovan 3 of Air Contractors Ltd.

The prototype Aerovan with Mamba nacelle mock-up. (*Miles Aircraft Ltd.*)

The Lycoming engined Aerovan 6, showing the enlarged tail surfaces. (*A. J. Jackson*)

1950–52. They then spent their time on minor charter operations and joyriding among the Islands and to Dinard. G-AJOF had previously achieved distinction by competing in the *Daily Express* Hurn to Herne Bay Race of 16 September 1950, but owner/pilot E. C. Cathels forced landed at Eastbourne. Two others, 'SF and 'KP, later returned to the fold at Shoreham to commence aerial photography in the colours of Meridian Air Maps Ltd. but crashed fatally at Ringway and Oldbury respectively in 1957. The components of two others, for which registrations G-AMYA and 'YC were reserved by Mrs. O. J. Marmol in 1952, were stored at Elstree for some years.

Early in Aerovan production, Gipsy Major 10 engines were fitted into G-AISJ, thus creating the sole Aerovan 5, later destroyed at Woodley during trials. In 1948 the Aerovan 6 appeared with Lycoming O-435-A motors and the enlarged tail surfaces from the dismantled Miles M.68 prototype. Named 'Northern Exporter', it saw limited service carrying lobsters between Kirkwall and the mainland for Air Cargo Distributors Ltd., afterwards appearing at

The Miles H.D.M.105 G-AHDM flying near the cliffs of Dover. (*Flight Photo 37125S*)

many air displays piloted by Ian Forbes. The final and most important variant appeared a year later, when G-AJOF emerged from the Miles works rebuilt with Aerovan 6 tail surfaces and a high aspect ratio metal wing designed by Hurel-Dubois of Villacoublay, France. In this form it was renamed the Miles H.D.M.105, flying for the first time on 30 March 1957, as G-35-3 until the very appropriate markings G-AHDM were transferred from a dead Halifax. After serving as a test bed for larger projects it was damaged beyond repair when landing at Shoreham in June 1958.

Total Aerovan production was 54 aircraft, 48 registered in Britain and a further six for export in foreign marks, the first of which was Aerovan 3 OO-HOM for a Brussels-based charter company, certificated in the name of Paul de Kelvers on 1 October 1946 only to crash at Hadbjaerg, Denmark six days later. The five export Aerovan 4s comprised C-602 for Transaerea Ltda., Bogota, Colombia; HB-AAA for Aerotaxi S.A., Zürich; YI-ABW for the Iraq Aeroplane Society, Baghdad; and two for the Royal New Zealand Air Force erected by Handley Page (Reading) Ltd. in 1950 and first flown as G-21-4 and G-21-3 respectively.

They were delivered to the R.N.Z.A.F. Research and Development Flight at Whenapui in October 1949 as NZ1751 and NZ1752, the former for aerial topdressing trials and the latter for airborne magnetometer survey work. Their tasks complete, they were sold in 1951—NZ1751 to Southland Aerial Fertilising Co. Ltd. (later Hewett Aviation Ltd.) of Mossburn in the southern tip of South Island as ZK-AWW; and NZ1752 to Airwork (N.Z.) Ltd. for a Christchurch—Auckland freight service.

SPECIFICATION

Manufacturers:	Miles Aircraft Ltd., Woodley Aerodrome, Reading, Berks.	
Power Plants:	(Aerovan 1, 2, 3, 4)	Two 155 h.p. Blackburn Cirrus Major 3.
	(Aerovan 5)	Two 145 h.p. de Havilland Gipsy Major 10.
	(Aerovan 6)	Two 195 h.p. Lycoming O-435-A.
	(H.D.M.105)	Two 155 h.p. Blackburn Cirrus Major 3.

	Aerovan 1	Aerovan 2, 3, 4	H.D.M.105
Span	50 ft. 0 in.	50 ft. 0 in.	75 ft. 4 in.
Length	36 ft. 0 in.	36 ft. 0 in.	34 ft. 4 in.
Height	13 ft. 6 in.	13 ft. 6 in.	13 ft. 11 in.
Wing area	390 sq. ft.	390 sq. ft.	388 sq. ft.
Tare weight	3,410 lb.	3,000 lb.	3,219 lb.
All-up weight	5,900 lb.	5,800 lb.	6,170 lb.
Maximum speed	130 m.p.h.	127 m.p.h.	133 m.p.h.
Cruising speed	110 m.p.h.	112 m.p.h.	116 m.p.h.
Initial climb	–	620 ft./min.	650 ft./min.
Ceiling	–	13,250 ft.	18,350 ft.
Range	450 miles	400 miles	–

Production: One Mk.1 G-AGOZ; One Mk.2 G-AGWO; six British registered Mk.3 and (c/n 6381) OO-HOM; thirty-eight British registered Mk.4 and the following for export: (c/n 6390) C-602/HK-602-P; (6419) HB-AAA; (6426) YI-ABW; (6427) G-21-4/NZ1752/ZK-AWW; (6428) G-21-3/NZ1751/ZK-AWV.

Also one Mk.5 G-AISJ, one Mk.6 G-AKHF and one H.D.M.105 G-AHDM converted from (c/n 6403) G-AJOF.

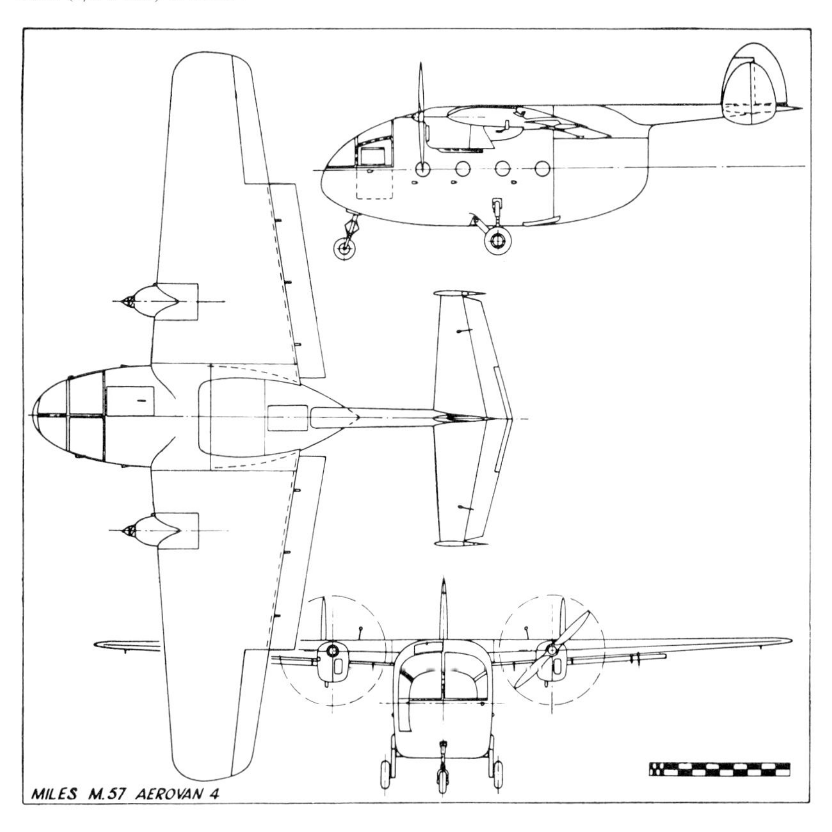

Grp. Capt. Bandidt in Gemini 1A G-AILK just before leaving for Australia in 1946. (*Miles Aircraft Ltd.*)

Miles M.65 Gemini

The Gemini brought twin engined reliability to the Falcon-Mercury-Messenger family and was the last aeroplane built in quantity at Woodley by Miles Aircraft Ltd. Plastic bonded plywood construction, with cantilever wing and auxiliary aerofoil flaps, was retained, the one-piece, moulded windscreen completing the family likeness. The cream and red Gemini 1 prototype G-AGUS, powered by Cirrus Minor 2 engines, first flown at Woodley by G. H. Miles on 26 October 1945, was demonstrated a few days later to United Nations delegates at Radlett. Although designed with a cantilever undercarriage retracting backward into the engine nacelles, first flight trials were advanced by fitting a temporary fixed undercarriage. During 1946 'US toured Europe and performed at every major British air show, and later flew with the mock-up of a third, central engine.

Large-scale production began at once, G-AIDO, the first demonstration machine with retractable undercarriage, being certificated on 30 August 1946, under the designation Gemini 1A. Five others followed quickly, G-AIHM for Lord Londonderry at Newtownards, G-AIDG International Airways Ltd. at Croydon, G-AIHI exhibited at the November 1946 Paris Salon, G-AHKL for G. W. Harben of Elstree and G-AILK, which left immediately for Australia piloted by Grp. Capt. A. F. 'Bush' Bandidt. His arrival at Truscott, N.T., on 7 January 1947, marked the completion of the first post-war solo flight from the United Kingdom. An unsuccessful attempt to secure a Canadian market was made by shipping G-AJKS on a Canadian aircraft carrier and flying it off on arrival. The aircraft returned to the United Kingdom after demonstration and was sold to Edward Day at Rochester.

Approximately 130 Geminis were built within a year, although the last 10 or so remained unsold and were not immediately assembled. Inevitably the overseas market took toll of these desirable four seaters, two-thirds of the British registered examples eventually joining the 28 exported direct. In the 26 years during which Geminis have been permanent features of British civil aerodromes, they have enjoyed outstanding executive, instructional, commercial and private careers. Examples of the first were G-AFLT of 'Flight', G-AKGE of the Goodyear Tyre and Rubber Co. Ltd. and G-AJWC for many years owned by Derek Crouch (Contractors) Ltd. The prototype, G-AGUS, acquired by Walter Instruments Ltd. of Redhill in October 1949, was re-engined with Continental C-125-2 flat six engines as the Gemini 2. Two years service in this condition ended in July 1952, when it was sold in Sweden as SE-BUY. Three, G-AKFW, 'HA and 'HS, were used in the Near East by J. Howard and Co. Ltd. working on oilfield installations and G-AKEG in the Lebanon by the Arab Contracting and Trading Co. Ltd. Another, G-AKZK, was used by the Missionary Aviation Fellowship until it crashed in the Belgian Congo on 10 July 1948.

One of the export machines, VP-RAU, was flown 5,761 miles from Lympne to Lusaka, Northern Rhodesia by Lt. Col. M. J. Muspratt-Williams between 1 and 6 October 1947 in a flying time of 44 hours, and in the following $3\frac{1}{2}$ years completed 1,000 hr. of trouble free flying all over Central, South and East Africa.

The Herts and Essex Aero Club employed a Gemini 1A for many years, their last, G-AIHM, being successor to G-AJEX and G-AKHB. At Roborough G-AKHW 'City of Plymouth' was veteran of a decade in club and taxi service and still wore the dark blue livery of British Overseas Airways Corporation, the original owners. The Ministry of Civil Aviation employed two Gemini 1As G-AKDD and G-AIRS for licence testing and radio calibration from 1947 to 1950, after which 'DD went to Aviation Traders Ltd. to maintain communications between Southend and Stansted and to play a leading part as a taxi aircraft in the mass movement of Prentices in 1956–57. 'RS also went to Southend to join the Municipal Flying School, while G-AJTL was used for the same purpose at Elstree.

As a private aircraft the Gemini, with its high gloss finish and luxury accommodation, was the pride and joy of many private owners, for both air racing and touring. Prince Bira, the racing motorist, owned G-AJWH 'City of Bangkok' for many years, keeping it at Ramsgate when not on Continental trips. Major air races from 1948 always attracted Gemini owners to the

The Continental engined Gemini 2, with the revised front windscreen fitted in 1952. *(A. J. Jackson)*

starting-line, but real success came only to Fred Dunkerley and J. N. 'Nat' Somers. The former's highly polished dark blue G-AKKB, wearing the Lancashire Aero Club's red rose on the fin, became famous as the winner of the Siddeley Trophy in 1949 and 1950, the Kemsley Trophy 1950 and the Air League Challenge Cup 1957. His speeds continually approached 160 m.p.h., a great performance for a standard aircraft. The Somers Gemini, a version with Gipsy Major 1C engines, known as the Gemini 3, was devised in 1949 at a time when well-known types were no longer beating the handicappers. After flight tests as U-23 and later as G-21-2, it became G-AKDC to win the 1949 King's Cup handsomely at 164·25 m.p.h. Gipsy Major 10s were then fitted, changing the designation to Gemini 3C, and it went on to win the 1953 Siddeley, the 1954 Kemsley and the 1955 Goodyear Trophies. Although it has long since been sold in Kenya, it left in its wake a number of similar variants. First of these was G-ALCS, built as a Gemini 3A for J. M. Houlder of the Elstree Flying Club but later fitted with Gipsy Major 10 Mk.2 engines to become a Gemini 3C. Two other Geminis of this mark were also created, E. Crabtree's G-AKEG and M. B. Rose's G-AKGE, both formerly standard 1As, and several other private owners also availed themselves of the opportunity to improve their mounts.

The last eight Geminis were of particular interest, all having been

Gemini 3B G-AJTG with flaps retracted. (*A. J. Jackson*)

The Miles M.75 Aries operated by Pasolds Ltd. (*A. J. Jackson*)

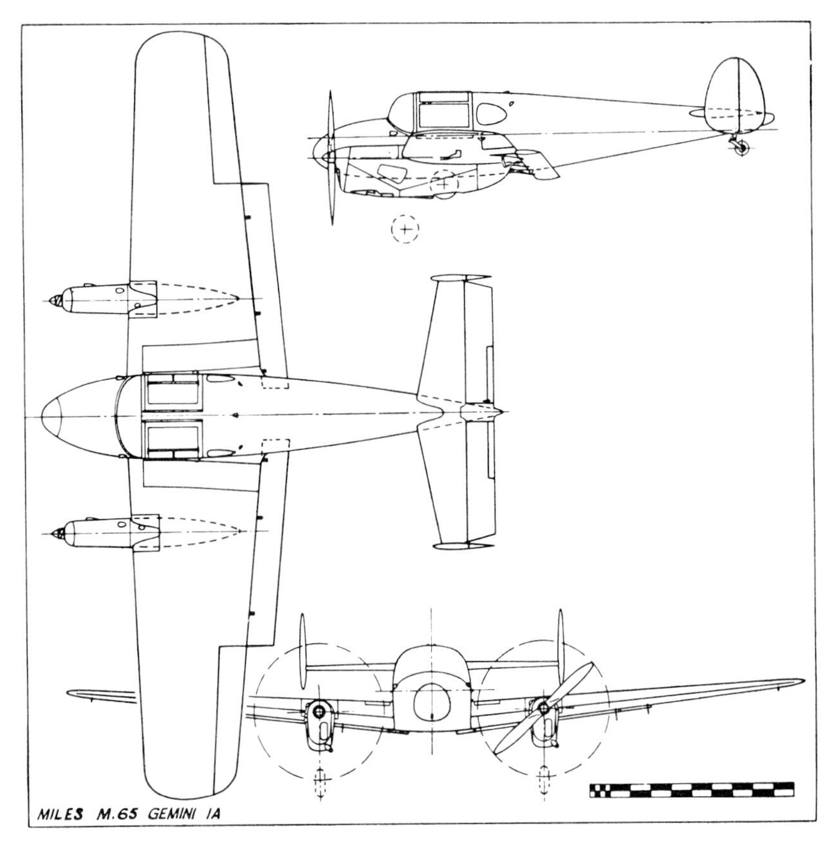

constructed from components left over from the main Woodley production. Two erected in 1950 by Handley Page (Reading) Ltd., Gemini 3C G-ALZG and Gemini 1A G-AMEJ, were delivered to Percy Blamire of Baginton and B. K. S. Engineering Ltd. at Southend. Another, G-AMBH, was erected at Redhill by F. G. Miles Ltd. The rest were Gemini 3As, completed to special order by Wolverhampton Aviation Ltd. in 1951. Aerodynamic refinement was confined to the sole Gemini 1B G-AJTG built with retractable flaps for the Hon. Max Aitken in 1950. A succession of owners ended with Edward Day, for whom it was re-equipped with Gipsy Major 10 Mk.1–3 engines for the 1951 King's Cup Race and redesignated Gemini 3B. One Gemini 4 ambulance, G-AKKE, obtained a C. of A. on 14 January 1948, and Gemini 1A G-AKHU, sold in Australia in 1950 was fitted with Lycoming engines by W. E. James at Bankstown, Sydney, and flew under his initials as VH-WEJ.

At the Fifty Years of Flying Exhibition at Hendon in July 1951, F. G. Miles exhibited the ultimate Gemini development, the M.75 Aries, first flown at Redhill in the previous February. The structure was strengthened to meet the improved performance imparted by two Cirrus Major 3 engines, and redesigned tail surfaces were fitted to increase directional stability during single engine flying. The prototype, G-35-1, later demonstrated as G-AMDJ, was sold to the Hon. M. A. R. Cayzer and then shipped to Australia. It attracted but one order, from Pasolds Ltd., who used G-AOGA for business trips in Europe. Three former Geminis were also raised by modification as near Aries standard as possible, two with Gipsy Major 10 Mk.2 engines as Gemini 7s for Shell-Mex and B.P. Ltd. and one with Cirrus Major 3s as a Gemini 8 for L. R. Snook of Portsmouth. The Shell machines G-AKHZ and G-AMGF flown respectively by Vivian Varcoe and Grp. Capt. Douglas Bader, were distinguishable from the Gemini 8 G-AKFX by their shorter engine naçelles.

By 1972 age had taken its toll and only 12 Geminis remained active on the British civil register.

SPECIFICATION

Manufacturers: Miles Aircraft Ltd., Woodley Aerodrome, Reading, Berks. A number later assembled by Handley Page (Reading) Ltd., Woodley Aerodrome; Wolverhampton Aviation Ltd., Wolverhampton Airport and F. G. Miles Ltd., Redhill Aerodrome.

Power Plants:
(Gemini 1, 1A, 1B, 4) Two 100 h.p. Blackburn Cirrus Minor 2.
(Gemini 1A Special) Two 130 h.p. Lycoming O-290-3/1.
(Gemini 2) Two 125 h.p. Continental C-125-2.
(Gemini 3) Two 145 h.p. de Havilland Gipsy Major 1C.
(Gemini 3A) Two 145 h.p. de Havilland Gipsy Major 10 Mk.1.
(Gemini 3B) Two 145 h.p. de Havilland Gipsy Major 10 Mk.1–3
(Gemini 3C, 7) Two 145 h.p. de Havilland Gipsy Major 10 Mk.2.
(Gemini 8) Two 155 h.p. Blackburn Cirrus Major 3.
(Aries) Two 155 h.p. Blackburn Cirrus Major 3.

Dimensions: Span, 36 ft. 2 in. Length, 22 ft. 3 in. Height, 7 ft. 6 in. Wing area, 191 sq. ft.

	Gemini 1	Gemini 1A	Aries
Tare weight	1,896 lb.	1,910 lb.	2,350 lb.
All-up weight	3,000 lb.	3,000 lb.	3,475 lb.
Maximum speed	140 m.p.h.	145 m.p.h.	172 m.p.h.
Cruising speed	125 m.p.h.	135 m.p.h.	150 m.p.h.
Initial climb	550 ft./min.	650 ft./min.	1,300 ft./min.
Ceiling	13,500 ft.	13,500 ft.	20,000 ft.
Range	820 miles	820 miles	675 miles.

Production: By Miles Aircraft Ltd., Woodley

Ninety-seven British registered aircraft and the following for direct export: (c/n 6301) ZS-BRV; (6313) VR-GGG/VR-RGG/VR-SDJ later G-AMRG; (6314) VR-DCA; (6316) Argentine; (6318) LV-RGH; (6320) EI-ACW later G-ALUG; (6322) ZK-ANT; (6458) HB-EKS; (6463) VP-RAU; (6464) YI-ABC; (6471) ZK-ANU; (6472) ZK-AQO; (6475) OO-NAV/F-BDAJ; (6478) VP-UAZ/VP-KFJ later G-AOXW; (6479) OO-CDO later G-AKKH; (6480) OO-CDP; (6481) OO-CDV; (6497) VH-AKV; (6498) CR-GAD; (6499–6500) Argentine; (6505) SU-ADY/SE-AYA; (6506) SU-AEL; (6520) EI-ADM later G-AFLT; (6529) untraced; (6530) SU-AHF; (6533) untraced; (6535-6536) untraced.

The prototype two seat Hendy 3308 Heck with retractable undercarriage. (*W. K. Kilsby*)

Parnall Heck

The Heck originated as the Hendy 3308, designed by Basil B. Henderson to the requirements of Whitney Straight, who specified fast cruising coupled with unusually low landing speed. The prototype, built at Yeovil by the Westland Aircraft Works, was a tandem, two seat, low-wing, cabin monoplane, built of spruce with plywood covering throughout. An aerodynamically clean airframe, a Gipsy Six engine and a manually operated, outward retracting undercarriage, ensured a high cruising speed, the second design requirement being met by using camber changing flaps in conjunction with Handley Page leading edge slots. The Heck first flew in July 1934 in red undercoat with the Westland Class B marking P. Unfortunately damage resulting from a collision with a cow in a forced landing en route to Martlesham prevented the completion of airworthiness trials in time for the King's Cup Race. Although in 1934 its speed range, 170–44·8 m.p.h., was a sensation and handsomely filled the customer's wishes, the aircraft was never used by Whitney Straight.

Parnall Aircraft Ltd. was formed in May 1935 by the amalgamation of George Parnall and Company, the Hendy Aircraft Company and the armament engineering firm of Nash and Thompson Ltd. When, therefore, the prototype went to Hanworth for public demonstration in black and gold as G-ACTC, it had already been restyled the Parnall Heck. Aircraft Exchange and Mart Ltd. prepared to handle sales, and their pilot Flt. Lt. R. Duncanson demonstrated the Heck at the Hendon S.B.A.C. Show on 1 July 1935. A wheels-up landing at Hanworth in the following month again prevented a King's Cup appearance, but on 8 October it left Hanworth to attack the Cape record piloted by David Llewellyn and Mrs. Jill Wyndham. Forced landings and minor damage en route ruined the attempt, and Cape Town was not reached until the 29th, but on the return journey they beat the previous best time, landing at Lympne on 11 November, 6 days 8 hours 27 minutes after leaving Cape Town. On 10 July 1936, 'TC contrived at last to fly in the

King's Cup Race piloted by J. D. Kirwan, but the port undercarriage collapsed when taxying at Whitchurch. It reappeared after repair with the undercarriage permanently locked down and enclosed in trouser type fairings.

A small production line of six Heck 2C aircraft was then laid down by Parnall Aircraft Ltd. at Yate, Gloucestershire. These were three seaters with cabin door, reduced glazing and fixed spatted undercarriages. Five were registered G-AEGH to 'GL, the first of which was decorated in the light and dark blue of Aircraft Exchange and Mart Ltd. and delivered to Hanworth for demonstration in September 1936. None were sold, and with the R.A.F. expansion gathering momentum, 'GH, 'GI and 'GJ were painted dark grey to become communications machines which flew a total of 1,000 miles daily to the squadrons in connection with Parnall's armament interests. A brief respite was granted on 2 July 1938, to allow test pilots H. S. Broad and J. A. C. Warren, in 'GH and 'GI, to compete for the King's Cup. Although their lap speeds averaged 159 m.p.h., they were placed 14th and 10th respectively.

G-AEGI, second production Heck 2C, showing the revised cabin and fixed undercarriage. (*A. J. Jackson*)

The Parnall 382 open cockpit trainer. (*Flight Photo 16840S*)

The experimental Heck 2C, K8853, believed to have been G-AEGL, flying on wartime communications near Heston in 1940. (*Aeroplane*)

Through a clerical error, the letters G-AEGK were not used and the fourth aircraft joined the communications team in 1939 as G-AEMR. When war came, they were camouflaged to continue their normal usage as civil aeroplanes.

The fifth and sixth aircraft, one of which was to have been G-AEGL, were used for the trial installation of the 225 h.p. Wolseley Aries radial and for armament experiments. One, in R.A.F. colours as K8853, with further cabin revision and fitted with a Gipsy VI Series II driving a variable-pitch airscrew, was the development vehicle for the gun sight installation in the Hurricane and Spitfire. With war imminent, a two seat, open-cockpit, dual control trainer version known as the Parnall 382, or Heck 3, appeared in February 1939. Using the power plant, tail unit, undercarriage and outer wing panels of its predecessor, the Parnall 382 was the first primary trainer to be fitted with interconnected slots and flaps, and could be flown at 43 m.p.h. No military contract was secured, and only the prototype, G-AFKF, flown under B conditions as J-1, was built. Later in its career the rear cockpit was fitted with a coupé top.

G-AEGJ was cannibalised at C. of A. expiry in September 1939 but in March 1943 G-AEGH was impressed by the R.A.F. as NF749 and flown to Turnhouse for No.17 Group Communications Flight until it went to Kemble to be struck off charge in 1944. The other two spent the war with the British Parachute Co. Ltd., at Cardiff, where 'MR was scrapped in 1948. October 1946 found 'GI back at Hanworth to be overhauled and fitted with a Gipsy Queen 3 for Lt. Cdr. J. G. Crammond, afterwards going to a new home base at Rochester. It was the owner's intention to compete annually against the remaining fast vintage aircraft and at Elmdon on 29 July 1949, came 13th in the King's Cup Race at an average speed of 145·5 m.p.h. In the following June, at Wolverhampton, 'GI reproduced its 1938 form to finish 7th at 159 m.p.h., but after the race its rear end was demolished by the civil Spitfire G-AISU, which struck it when landing. Attempts at reconstruction with spares from 'MR failed and the aircraft was broken up in 1953.

SPECIFICATION

Manufacturers:	(Prototype)	Westland Aircraft Works, Yeovil, Somerset.
	(Production)	Parnall Aircraft Ltd., Yate Aerodrome, Gloucestershire.
Power Plants:	One 200 h.p. de Havilland Gipsy Six.	
	One 200 h.p. de Havilland Gipsy Queen 3.	

	Prototype	Heck 2C	Parnall 382
Span	31 ft. 6 in.	31 ft. 6 in.	33 ft. 6 in.
Length	26 ft. $1\frac{1}{2}$ in.	26 ft. $1\frac{1}{2}$ in.	28 ft. 8 in.
Height	8 ft. 6 in.	8 ft. 6 in.	7 ft. 9 in.
Wing area	105·2 sq. ft.	105·2 sq. ft.	155 sq. ft.
Tare weight	1,811 lb.	1,750 lb.	1,655 lb.
All-up weight	2,600 lb.	2,700 lb.	2,450 lb.
Maximum speed	170 m.p.h.	185 m.p.h.	155 m.p.h.
Cruising speed	155 m.p.h.	160 m.p.h.	135 m.p.h.
Initial climb	–	1,100 ft./min.	–
Ceiling	–	16,700 ft.	–
Range	600 miles	605 miles	–

Production: One prototype, G-ACTC, by the Westland Aircraft Works, Yeovil; six Heck Mk.2C by Parnall Aircraft Ltd., Yate; one Parnall 382 Heck 3 prototype J-1/G-AFKF.

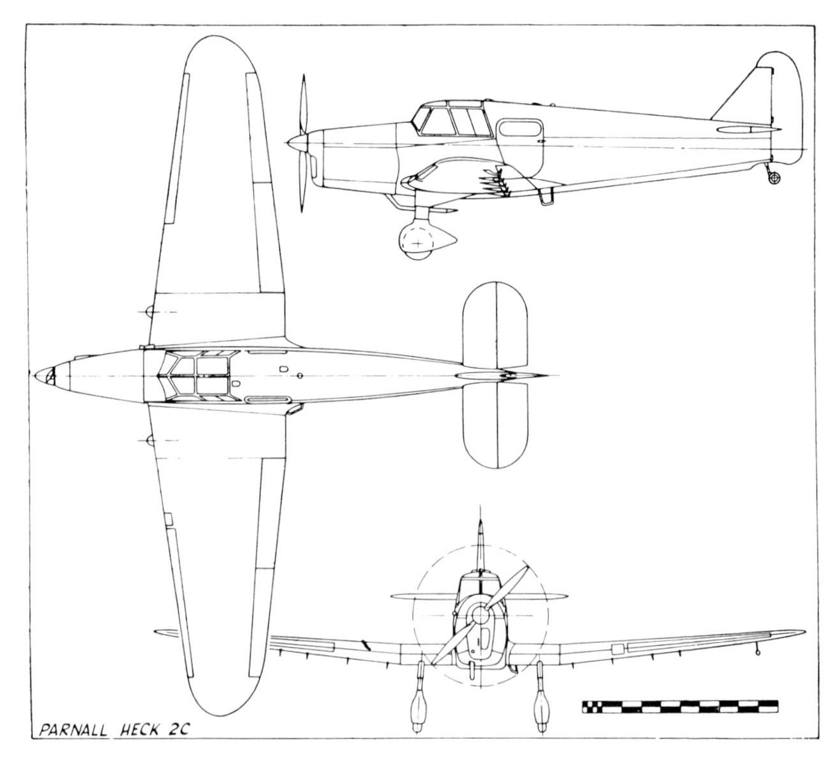

The prototype Gull G-ABUR during early trials. (*Percival Aircraft Ltd.*)

Percival Gull

The Percival Gull was a three seat, all-wood, low-wing monoplane with folding wing, and the prototype, G-ABUR, powered by a 130 h.p. Cirrus Hermes IV, was built in 1932 by E. W. Percival and his team in a small workshop at Maidstone, Kent, used previously by C. H. Lowe Wylde for constructing gliders. Contrary to erroneous statements made in the first edition of this book, the Gull was designed solely by Edgar W. Percival, chief designer of Percival Aircraft Ltd., and not by, or with the assistance of others. He not only designed it and supervised its construction, but also test flew the aircraft and piloted it in the round-Britain King's Cup Race of 8–9 July 1932 at an average speed of 142·73 m.p.h.

The system of P numbers attributed to Percival aeroplanes built before 1945, although widely published, has no basis in fact, having been evolved by others purely for publicity purposes in 1947. They are not, therefore, used in this book, the true designation of the Hermes powered Gull being Percival Type D.1. It was the first low-wing cantilever monoplane to be put into production in the Commonwealth and, according to the Everling formula, its all-round efficiency was greater even than that of the Schneider Trophy aircraft.

In 1933, when temporarily re-engined with a 160 h.p. Napier Javelin III, G-ABUR had a top speed superior to many contemporary fighters. Fitted with a Gipsy Major it was well known all over Europe until written off in Northern Rhodesia during Man Mohan Singh's 1935 Cape record attempt.

The first production batch of 24 Gulls was built at Yate, Gloucestershire, by George Parnall and Company under sub-contract to the Percival Aircraft Co. Ltd., newly formed by E. W. Percival and Lt. Cdr. E. W. B. Leake. As shown in Appendix E, these were powered by a variety of four cylinder engines, those with the 130 h.p. de Havilland Gipsy Major or 160 h.p. Napier Javelin III being designated Percival Type D.2. Generally referred to as Gull Fours, they included G-ABUV, Surrey Flying Services' charter and photographic aircraft 1933–35; and G-ACFY, works communication machine for A. V. Roe and Co. Ltd., Woodford. Private owners Sir Philip Sassoon and W. Lindsay Everard M.P. specified the Javelin III engine for their respective Gulls G-ACGR and G-ACAL 'Leicestershire Fox' but the latter was sold to the British Air Navigation Co. Ltd., Heston, who also acquired the Gipsy Major powered G-ACHM later in 1933. Both aircraft were used for fast newspaper work but the company's chief pilot, A. J. Styran, and manager I. C. MacGilchrist, were killed when G-ACAL crashed in bad weather when returning from the scene of the airship R.101 disaster near Beauvais.

Gull Fours satisfied a lively market and were sold as far afield as Brazil and Japan, while on 11 October 1933 Sir Charles Kingsford Smith arrived at Wyndham, Australia, in G-ACJV 'Miss Southern Cross' after a record breaking flight from Lympne in 7 days 4 hours 44 minutes. Two others, G-ACIS and 'LG, originally supplied to Air Service Training Ltd. and the Hon. Loel Guinness respectively, were sold to Indian National Airways in 1935.

In 1934 the Percival Aircraft Co. Ltd. established its own works at Gravesend Airport, Kent, where G-ACUL was built with a new-type single strut undercarriage, revised cabin top and side entrance doors, features which then became standard. Three similar aircraft, G-ACHA, 'PA and 'XY, were fitted with 200 h.p. Gipsy Six engines as the first three of a new variant designated Percival Type D.3, or Gull Six.

Twenty-two Gulls were built at Gravesend before the company moved to Luton in 1936, including G-ADGK for Mrs. E. M. Highfield of Heston; and G-ADOE which the North Sea Aerial and General Transport Co. Ltd., Brough, acquired as test bed for the Blackburn Cirrus Major engines. This was raced in most major events by C. S. Napier. The Gull Six, with overload cabin tank and a 2,000 mile range, also made an ideal mount for long distance pilots of that great record breaking age, E. W. Percival's dash from Gravesend to Oran, Algeria, and back in one day in 1935 in G-ADEP, being followed by Jean Batten's Britannia Trophy winning flight to Brazil in G-ADPR which included a 13 hours 15 minute crossing of the South Atlantic. On 5 October 1936 she again left Lympne, reached Darwin in the record time of 5 days 21 hours 3 minutes, lowered the time for the Tasman crossing, and completed the first-ever flight from England to New Zealand in a time of 11 days 45 minutes. Three weeks later her fellow New Zealander, L. Ernle Clark, flew

Jean Batten's Gull Six showing the single strut undercarriage fitted to production aircraft. (*Hunting Percival Aircraft Ltd.*)

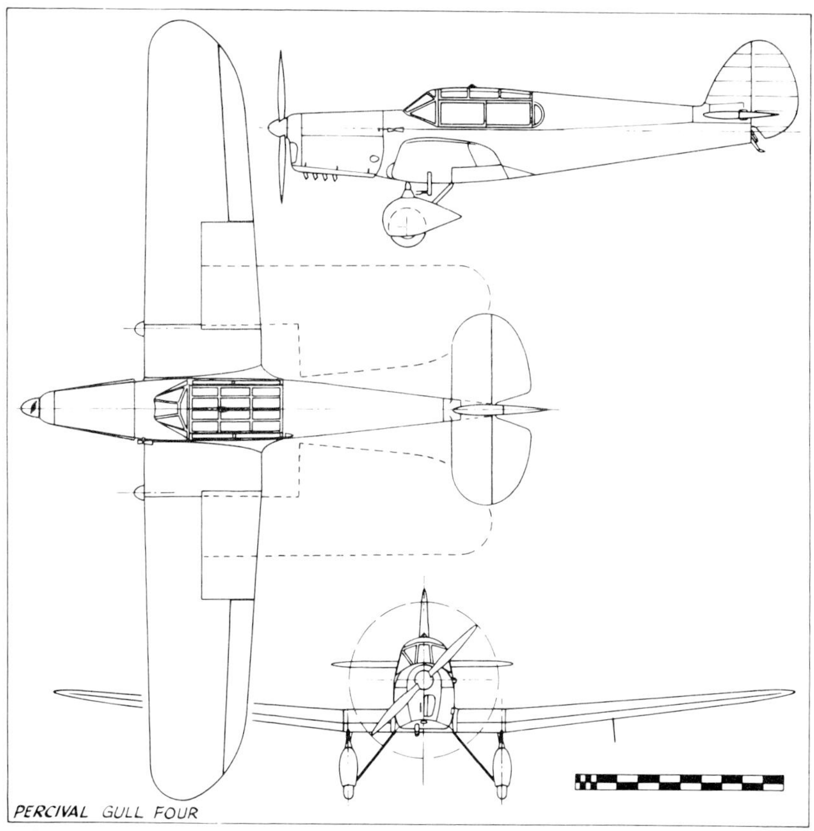

solo along the same route in Gull Four G-ACUL and reached Wigram on 15 November, having been airborne for 12 hours over the Tasman Sea.

The last British registered Gull Six, G-ADZO, was flown by Amy Mollison for her out-and-home record to the Cape in 7 days 22 hours 45 minutes between 4 and 12 May 1936; and by H. L. Brook in May 1937 for his flight from the Cape to Heston in 4 days 18 minutes.

During the Italo-Abyssinian war of 1935 the fast Gulls operated by Brian Allen Aviation Ltd. were obvious mounts for enterprising newspaper men and G-ACHM and G-ADPA were away many months, piloted by C. F. French and Brian Allen, but the original Gull Six, G-ACPA, was lost in an accident at Avignon, France, en route. Other Gull Six aircraft were used executively and privately, G-ACUP by Miss Diana Williams and later by S. K. Davies at Cardiff; G-ADFA by Charles Gardner who won the 1935 Siddeley Trophy with it at 170·08 m.p.h.; G-ADKX by the Shell Company of Egypt Ltd. and later by Lt. Col. Blandford-Newson at Almaza; and G-ADSG by the Duchess of Bedford. The Maharajah of Patiala received G-ACYS in 1935 and a special, one-off, open cockpit version was flown to India by A. F. Muir on delivery to the Maharajah of Jodhpur.

Secondhand Gulls found ready buyers in Australia, Brazil, France, Holland

and India but among new aircraft exported was the Gipsy Major powered VH-UVH in which C. J. Melrose averaged 143·97 m.p.h. during the King's Cup Race of 6–7 September 1935. He left Croydon on 2 November in company with H. F. Broadbent who was ferrying Gull Six VH-UVA for P. G. (later Sir Gordon) Taylor, but on arrival VH-UVH was destroyed in a crash at Goulburn, N.S.W. on 3 December and the registration was reallotted to a Porterfield 35/70. The last production Gull, ZS-AKI, delivered to the Shell Company of South Africa Ltd. on 18 October 1937, was impressed by the S.A.A.F. in 1940 as '1430', a fate which also overtook VT-AGY and 'LT in India. These became HX794 and MA927 respectively.

Jean Batten's 'Jean', G-ADPR, impressed during the war as AX866, was bought back by Percival Aircraft Ltd., Luton, in 1946 and frequently appeared at air shows until ferried to Old Warden on 25 April 1961 to be handed over to the Shuttleworth Trust, by whom it was thereafter maintained in airworthy condition. In Continental Europe the last surviving Gull Six was HB-OFU, delivered to Switzerland in January 1937 and still active in 1970. One other remaining was S. K. Davies's G-ACUP which went to Australia as VH-ACM in 1939, was re-registered VH-CCM in 1949 and won the Warana Air Race at Archerfield, Brisbane, on 6 October 1968.

SPECIFICATION

Manufacturers: The Percival Aircraft Co. Ltd., Gravesend Airport, Kent (moved to Luton Airport, Beds. in 1936); the first 24 aircraft under sub-contract by George Parnall and Company, Yate Aerodrome, Glos.

Power Plants:
Type D.1 One 130 h.p. Cirrus Hermes IV.
Type D.2 One 130 h.p. de Havilland Gipsy Major.
One 160 h.p. Napier Javelin III.
Type D.3 One 200 h.p. de Havilland Gipsy Six.

Dimensions: Span, 36 ft. 2 in. Length, 24 ft. 9 in. Height, 7 ft. 4½ in. Wing area, 169 sq. ft.

	Hermes IV	Javelin III	Gipsy Major and Cirrus Major I	Gipsy Six
Tare weight	1,170 lb.	1,170 lb.	1,290 lb.	1,500 lb.
All-up weight	2,050 lb.	2,250 lb.	2,300 lb.	2,450 lb.
Maximum speed	145 m.p.h.	160 m.p.h.	155 m.p.h.	178 m.p.h.
Cruising speed	125 m.p.h.	140 m.p.h.	133 m.p.h.	160 m.p.h.
Initial climb	850 ft./min.	–	–	–
Ceiling	16,000 ft.	–	18,000 ft.	20,000 ft.
Range	700 miles	700 miles	745 miles	640 miles

Production: (a) Percival Types D.1 and D.2 Gull Four

Twenty-nine aircraft, mainly of British registry but including (c/n D.41 and D.43) untraced; (D.57) VH-UVH.

(b) Percival Type D.3 Gull Six

Eighteen aircraft, mainly of British registry but including (c/n D.60) VH-UVA; (D.61 and D.62) untraced; (D.64) ZS-AHD; (D.65) HB-OFU; (D.66) untraced; (D.67) ZS-AKI.

(c) Percival Type D.3 Gull Six (open cockpit)

One aircraft only: (c/n D.56) VT-AGV.

Edgar Percival flying Mew Gull G-AFAA. (*Flight Photo 17400S*)

Percival Mew Gull

The remarkable career of the Gull, built for touring but already famous as racer and record breaker, made it easy to visualise the success which might come to a specially built racer from the same stable. Edgar W. Percival therefore designed and built the now historic Mew Gull single seater in a few months at the Gravesend works, but it should be noted that the original Mew Gull, and the subsequent models, were designed solely by Edgar W. Percival and not by, or with the assistance of, others as wrongly stated in the first edition of this book. Furthermore, the widely publicised system of P numbers allocated to Mew Gulls, was not devised until 1947 and therefore find no place here because they were non-existent during the lifetime of these aeroplanes. The true designation of the Mew Gull prototype G-ACND was Percival Type E.1.

It was an unusually small low-wing monoplane with spatted, strutted undercarriage, powered by a 165 h.p. Napier Javelin IA with Fairey-Reed metal airscrew, and first flown by E. W. Percival in March 1934. A cantilever undercarriage and 200 h.p. Gipsy Six were fitted for its competition flying debut in the King's Cup Race at Hatfield on 13 July 1934, in which it lapped at 191 m.p.h. It was destroyed near Angoulême, France, at the end of October 1935 after Comte Guy de Chateaubrun parachuted from the aircraft in fog while flying the Bordeaux–Orly leg of the Coupe Michelin event.

Its successor, the Percival Type E.2, was an entirely new aeroplane, also registered G-ACND, which had a longer fuselage, redesigned undercarriage and tail surfaces, trailing edge flaps and Gipsy Six engine. After appearing at the Hendon S.B.A.C. Show on 1 July 1935, it was rapidly and temporarily engined with a French 180 h.p. Regnier of less than 8 litres capacity, to qualify for entry in the Coupe Armand Esders. Over a 1,046 mile course from Deauville to Cannes and back, Comte Guy de Chateaubrun, Percival agent in France, averaged 188 m.p.h. to win the premier award. On its return the Gipsy Six was replaced and, flown by E. W. Percival, it came 6th at 208·9 m.p.h. in the King's Cup Race and was the first aircraft ever to exceed 200 m.p.h. in that annual event. It also came 3rd at 198·5 m.p.h. in the

Folkestone Trophy Race and scored its first success by winning the Heston–Cardiff Race at an average speed of 218 m.p.h.

The next Mew Gull, G-AEKL, was flown by E. W. Percival in the 1936 King's Cup and Folkestone Trophy Races and then sold to Air Publicity Ltd. at Heston. It was then fitted with additional fuselage tanks and Gipsy Six Series II engine with constant speed airscrew, as mount for Tom Campbell Black in the Schlesinger Race to Johannesburg. On 19 September 1936 however 'KL went to Speke to be named 'Miss Liverpool', but collided on the ground with an R.A.F. Hawker Hart with mortal injuries to its illustrious pilot.

Two exactly similar Mew Gulls which took-off from Portsmouth 10 days later to race to Johannesburg, were ZS-AHM 'The Golden City' and ZS-AHO 'Baragwanath', built for the veteran South African pilots Maj. A. M. Miller and Capt. S. S. Halse. The latter's aircraft, temporarily G-AEMO prior to the race, made a meteoric dash southward but made a forced landing near Salisbury, Southern Rhodesia, struck a large ant hill and went over on its back. Miller ran out of fuel, made a dead stick landing almost within sight of the first control at Belgrade, flew in on low grade spirit, retired and returned to England.

The sixth and last Mew Gull, Percival Type E.3H G-AFAA, a completely new design with smaller wing, narrower fuselage, smaller tail areas and Gipsy Six Series II, built for the new racing season, was first flown by E. W. Percival in 1937. The tragic 'KL was also rebuilt for Charles Gardner, while Alex Henshaw acquired Maj. Miller's aircraft, now fitted with a standard Gipsy Six and carrying the British label G-AEXF. During the season Gardner won the Newcastle Race at 221 m.p.h. and Henshaw the Folkestone Trophy at 210 m.p.h. Later all three Mew Gulls faced the King's Cup starter, Gardner winning handsomely at 233·7 m.p.h., with Percival making fastest time in third place at 238·7 m.p.h.

In the following year 'KL was raced by Giles Guthrie, and 'XF went to Gravesend where Essex Aero Ltd. fitted a Gipsy Six R engine with French Ratier v.p. airscrew from the D.H.88 Comet racer G-ACSS. They fought a duel in the Isle of Man Races and met Percival's 'AA in the King's Cup. G-AEXF now had a de Havilland c.s. airscrew on a short extension shaft, with

The first Mew Gull, G-ACND, with Napier Javelin engine. (*Fox*)

G-AEXF at Middleton St. George on 6 August 1965 just before the forced landing which ended its career. (*R. W. Cranham*)

resultant changes in nose and spinner shape. The cowling was also flattened, giving the aircraft a somewhat wicked look because Essex Aero Ltd. had also remodelled the whole decking above the top longerons, lowered the canopy 4 in. and seated the pilot on the floor. It won the 1938 King's Cup at an average speed of 236·25 m.p.h. with Guthrie second and Percival sixth.

'XF then retired to Gravesend to be groomed for Alex Henshaw's phenomenal out-and-home Cape record. Fitted with Gipsy Six Series II, radio and long range tanks, and cleared for a take-off weight of 2,350 lb., it left Gravesend on 5 February 1939 and arrived back 4 days 10 hours 16 minutes later. It was sold in France in the following July but survived storage north of Lyons during the 1939–45 war and was rediscovered by H. E. Scrope 11 years later. With no previous Mew Gull experience and with the engine misfiring, he flew non-stop from Bron to Blackbushe on 2 July 1950.

Following a landing accident at Shoreham in August 1951, D. E. Bianchi rebuilt it with an enlarged cockpit canopy, and in this form it was raced for the Kemsley Trophy at Southend by J. N. Somers in June 1953. In 1954 the canopy was raised still further by Adie Aviation Ltd. at Croydon and won the King's Cup on 20 August 1955 at 213·5 m.p.h., flown by Peter Clifford on behalf of the owner, Fred Dunkerley.

After years in store at Barton, 'XF was flown to Yeadon on 29 October 1962, to be re-engined by J. E. G. Appleyard with the Gipsy Queen 2 from Proctor 3 G-ALFX. Another new canopy was devised, and following a ground accident in May 1963, the Proctor undercarriage was also fitted. Flown by E. Crabtree, the veteran monoplane made its last appearances in the 1965 National Air Races but during practice flying on 6 August, was damaged beyond immediate repair in a forced landing at Catterick, Yorks. Thereafter it passed to the preservationists but was mutilated by vandals at Squires Gate during 1970. Nevertheless, early in 1972 it was acquired by Tiger Club members Martin Barraclough and Tom Storey for eventual restoration to flying condition.

SPECIFICATION

Manufacturers: Percival Aircraft Ltd., Gravesend Airport, Kent; moved to Luton Airport, Beds. in 1936.

Power Plants:	Type E.1	One 165 h.p. Napier Javelin IA.
		One 180 h.p. Regnier.
		One 200 h.p. de Havilland Gipsy Six.
	Type E.2	One 200 h.p. de Havilland Gipsy Six.
		One 205 h.p. de Havilland Gipsy Six Series II.
		One 230 h.p. de Havilland Gipsy Six R.
	Type E.3H	One 205 h.p. de Havilland Gipsy Six Series II.

	Type E.1	Type E.2		Type E.3H
	Javelin	Gipsy Six	Gipsy Six II	Gipsy Six II
Span	24 ft. 0 in.	24 ft. 0 in.	24 ft. 0 in.	22 ft. 9 in.
Length	18 ft. 3 in.	20 ft. 3 in.	20 ft. 3 in.	20 ft. 3 in.
Height	6 ft. 10 in.	6 ft. 10 in.	6 ft. 10 in.	6 ft. 10 in.
Wing area	88 sq. ft.	88 sq. ft.	88 sq. ft.	75 sq. ft.
Tare weight	996 lb.	1,080 lb.	1,150 lb.	1,150 lb.
All-up weight	1,460 lb.	1,800 lb.	2,125 lb.	2,125 lb.
Maximum speed	195 m.p.h.	225 m.p.h.	230 m.p.h.	235 m.p.h.
Cruising speed	175 m.p.h.	190 m.p.h.	205 m.p.h.	232 m.p.h.
Initial climb	–	1,400 ft./min.	1,700 ft./min.	1,800 ft./min.
Ceiling	–	–	21,000 ft.	21,000 ft.
Range	550 miles	575 miles	800 miles	875 miles

Production: Type E.1: (c/n E.20) G-ACND. Type E.2: (E.20A) G-ACND; (E.21) G-AEKL; (E.22) ZS-AHM/G-AEXF; (E.23) G-AEMO/ZS-AHO. Type E.3H; (E.24) G-AFAA.

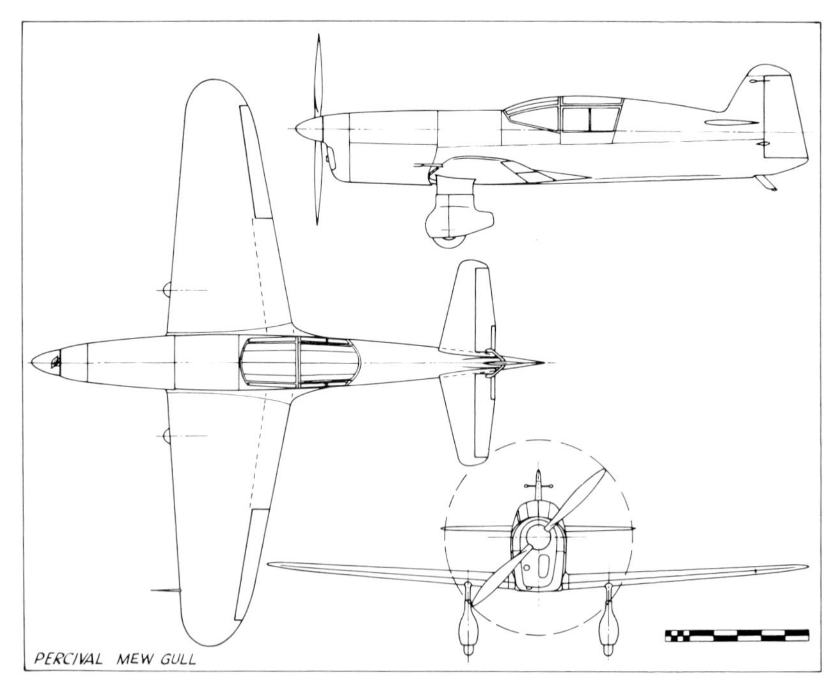

The prototype Vega Gull G-AEAB on an early flight with the final registration letter incorrectly painted as D. (*Percival Aircraft Ltd.*)

Percival Vega Gull

The next type in the Percival range was the Gipsy Six powered Vega Gull which seated four persons in side-by-side pairs, and was equipped with dual control and split trailing edge flaps. It was designed solely by Edgar W. Percival and not by, or with the assistance of, others as wrongly stated in the first edition of this book. Designated Percival Type K.1, its high all-round performance soon made it well known as a fast touring or charter aircraft, and the prototype, G-AEAB, initially mispainted as G-AEAD, was first flown by Edgar Percival at Gravesend in November 1935.

Four Vega Gulls comprising the prototype; G-AEKD; Sir Connop Guthrie's 'KE; and W. Lindsay Everard's 'LE 'Leicestershire Fox IV'; flown respectively by Misri Chand, Lt. P. Randolph, Charles Gardner and P. Q. Reiss, fought a private duel with the Miles team in the King's Cup Race of 10–11 July 1936. Fitted with long range tanks in the cabin and centre section for the 1,224 mile eliminating race, Gardner's was the winner at an average speed of 164·47 m.p.h. After the race, G-AEKE and the prototype, similarly tanked, were fitted with Gipsy Six Series II engines with D. H. Hamilton v.p. metal airscrews for entry in the Schlesinger Race to Johannesburg. Flown by C. W. A. Scott and the owner's son, Giles Guthrie, 'KE was the only finisher, landing at Rand Airport on 1 October 1936, 52 hours 56 minutes 48 seconds out from Portsmouth. Amid the glare of resulting publicity, the Percival works transferred to larger premises at Luton. Here a Vega Gull production line prospered until the 90th, and final, aircraft took-off on 27 July 1939, late production machines having a rounded windscreen.

G AEEM, built initially for Sir Charles Rose, was similarly modified in May 1939 for export to Sweden, where, two years later it was shot down by a German fighter. Of the 44 Vega Gulls delivered to the home market, the following were used commercially: G-AEJJ by Commercial Air Hire Ltd., Heston; 'LW the Anglo American Oil Co. Ltd., Heston; 'RL Air Service Training Ltd., Hamble; 'TF the de Havilland Aircraft Co. Ltd., Hatfield;

'WS European Air Communications Ltd., Gatwick; 'XV Air Commerce Ltd., Heston; G-AFAV Air Hire Ltd., Castle Bromwich; 'IE Smiths Aircraft Instruments Ltd., Hatfield.

Overseas sales included four to Australia, one in Canada, 11 in France, five in India, one to King Ghazi of Iraq, one in Japan and four in Kenya, including VP-KCC 'The Messenger', the Vega Gull flown from Abingdon, England, to Cape Breton Island, Nova Scotia, in 21 hours on 4–5 September 1936 by Mrs. Beryl Markham.

Resulting from demonstrations by E. W. Percival at Gravesend and Martlesham before members of the Fleet Air Arm, R.A.F. and Air Ministry, a number of Vega Gulls were supplied for military communications 1938–39 and two of these, L7272 and P5992, were given civil markings in June 1939 as G-AFWG and 'VI respectively as personal aircraft of the Air Attachés in Buenos Aires and Lisbon. A third Vega Gull, G-AFBO, which had earlier been commissioned for the use of the Air Attaché in Berlin, was seized by the Germans at the outbreak of the 1939–45 war, together with Mrs. H. M. Russell-Cooke's G-AFIM which had been stranded in France.

By March 1940 nineteen British owned Vega Gulls had been impressed for communications work as shown in Appendix E. This sadly thinned their

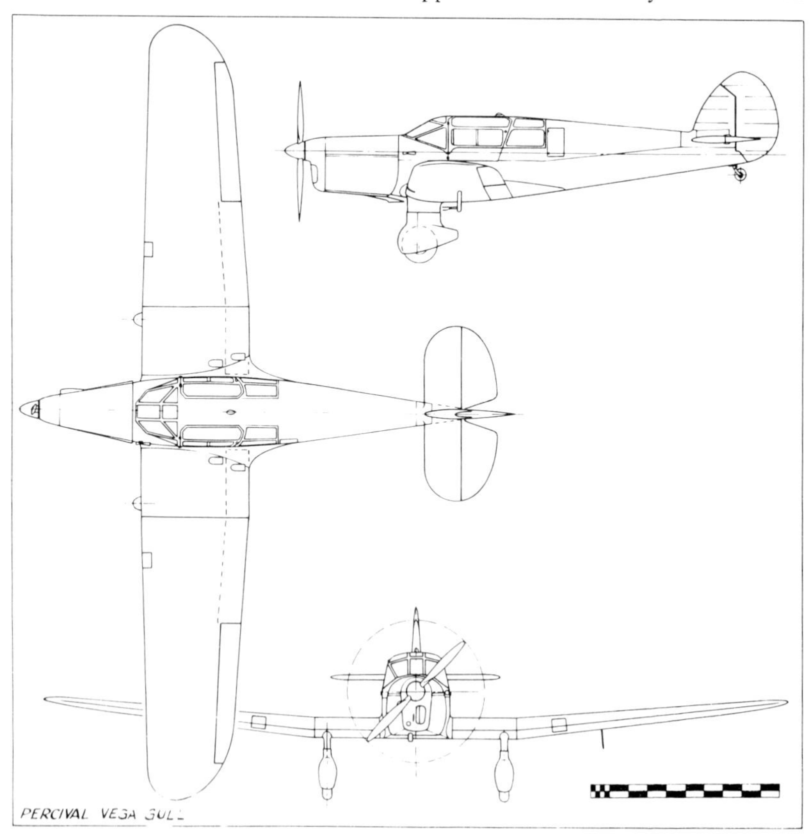

ranks, many served overseas, including W. L. Runciman's G-AEXU at Aboukir in 1943, and only six survived the war.

By 1972 the only complete Vega Gull extant was SE-ALA at Visby Airport in Sweden but its origins remained obscure.

Percival Vega Gull G-AEXV in the colours of British and Continental Airways, 1947, showing the rounded windscreen. (*A. J. Jackson*)

SPECIFICATION

Manufacturers: Percival Aircraft Ltd., Gravesend Airport, Kent, moved to Luton Airport, Beds., 1936.

Power Plants: One 200 h.p. de Havilland Gipsy Six.
One 205 h.p. de Havilland Gipsy Six Series II.

Dimensions: Span, 39 ft. 6 in. Length, 25 ft. 6 in. Height, 7 ft. 4 in. Wing area, 184 sq. ft.

	Gipsy Six	Gipsy Six Series II
Tare weight	1,575 lb.	1,740 lb.
All-up weight	2,750 lb.	3,250 lb.
Maximum speed	170 m.p.h.	174 m.p.h.
Cruising speed	160 m.p.h.	150 m.p.h.
Initial climb	–	1,020 ft./min.
Ceiling	18,000 ft.	17,000 ft.
Range	620 miles	660 miles

Production: Ninety aircraft, mainly British registered but the following for the R.A.F. or export: (c/n K.34) VP-KCC; (K.35) CF-BAR; (K.36) VH-UVG; (K.37) F-APEX; (K.38) F-APIG; (K.39) VP-KCD; (K.40) F-APIL; (K.43) F-APHX; (K.44) VP-KCE; (K.50) F-APOL; (K.53) F-APXA; (K.54) Japan; (K.55) VP-KCH; (K.58) VH-UZH; (K.61) F-AQBV; (K.62) VT-AIQ; (K.63) ZK-AFI; (K.64) HB-OMO; (K.68) F-AQIR; (K.71) L7272, later G-AFWG; (K.72) VT-AID; (K.73) VT-AIV; (K.74) VT-AIW; (K.77) F-AQIG; (K.78) VT-AJQ; (K.80) VT-AJR; (K.81) F-AQEN; (K.83) VH-ABS; (K.85) YI-CPF; (K.86) P1749; (K.87) P5986; (K.88) P5987; (K.94-K.97) P1750 to P1753; (K.98) VH-ACA; (K.101) F-ARAU; (K.102) P1754; (K.103) P5988; (K.104) Rebuild of K.68/F-AQIR; (K.105) P5989, later G-AHET; (K.106) P5990; (K.107) P5993; (K.108) P5991; (K.109) P5992, later G-AFVI.

E. W. Percival flying the turquoise and silver prototype Q.6 near Luton in 1937. (*Aeroplane*)

Percival Q.6

Designed in 1936, the Percival Type Q marked the company's entry into the twin engined market. Designed solely by Edgar W. Percival and not by, or with the assistance of, others as wrongly stated in the first edition of this book, it was in two versions, the Q.4 with Gipsy Majors for pilot and up to four passengers; and the Q.6 with Gipsy Sixes for pilot and five or six passengers according to the cabin layout. The Q.4 was never built but work went ahead on the larger machine whose sole designation was Percival Q.6. It was never known by the P number that was once widely published.

The fuselage was a plywood box faired with fabric over external frames and stringers, and the cantilever wing consisted of two wooden box spars with spruce ribs and plywood skin. Percival split trailing edge flaps were fitted, all control surfaces were fabric-covered and the nacelles, integrated with the trousered undercarriage, housed Gipsy Six Series II engines driving de Havilland variable pitch airscrews. The prototype, G-AEYE, was first flown at Luton by the designer on 14 September 1937 and construction of production aircraft commenced in 1938.

Sir Philip Sasson took delivery of G-AFFD, the grey and silver first production aircraft, at Lympne on 2 March 1938. During the next 12 months G-AFFE went to H. B. Legge and Sons Ltd. at Warlingham; 'HG to Lord Londonderry, Newtownards; 'IW to Vickers Aviation Ltd. at Brooklands; 'GX to Intava; 'KG to L. A. Hordern, Hatfield; and 'KC to Almaza, Cairo, for Lt.-Col. E. T. Peel. A retractable undercarriage was optional but only four had it, first being VH-ABL built to the order of the famous Australian pilot and navigator Capt. P. G. Taylor. This particular Q.6 went to Martlesham for undercarriage trials in June 1938, but was not delivered in Australia. It went instead to Vickers-Armstrongs Ltd. as G-AFMT. The second, G-AFIX, delivered to W. A. Burnside at Croydon on 12 December 1938, carried the red and blue livery of Western Airways Ltd. and flew on the Castle

Bromwich–Whitchurch–Weston–Cardiff route during the summer of 1939.

Among the small but important export sales were YI-ROH 'Bird of Eden' to King Ghazi I of Iraq; LY-SOA and LY-SOB to the Lithuanian Ministry of Communications; VT-AKU to Tata Ltd., Bombay, for internal services in India; VT-AKR to the Hyderabad State Railway; and two to the Egyptian Government in military camouflage as Q601 and Q602.

With one exception the civil Q.6s all served in the R.A.F. during the 1939–45 war, the process starting when the prototype flew away from Luton on 6 March 1940 repainted as X9328. Three days later P5640, last of seven Q.6s built to Air Ministry Contract, was delivered to No.36 M.U., Sealand for R.A.F. communications duties. Impressment came to an end in May 1940, when G-AFVC, flown since the previous September in an all yellow colour scheme with small black markings on the rear fuselage, departed from Weston to become AX860. The Vickers 'hack' 'IW retained its civil status throughout hostilities.

The first Percival Q.6 with retractable undercarriage, VH-ABL, which later became G-AFMT for Vickers-Armstrongs Ltd. (*Flight Photo 17023S*)

The return of peace witnessed the reappearance of four other Percival Q.6s, including the prototype, restored by Southern Aircraft (Gatwick) Ltd. and named 'Southernaire'; G-AFFD operated by the Yorkshire Aeroplane Club at Sherburn-in-Elmet until sold in April 1952 to Walter Instruments Ltd., Redhill; and 'IX demobilised with a fixed undercarriage. The last was used mainly by Fremantle Overseas Radio Ltd., but ended its career in 1949 as a taxi and joyriding aircraft with Starways Ltd. at Speke. Not unexpectedly, three R.A.F. aircraft also survived to be converted for civilian use by Whitney Straight Ltd. at Weston-super-Mare in 1946. One, formerly P5637 of the Woodley Communications Flight, originally delivered on 18 August 1939, went to Denham as G-AHOM and carried out several long-distance charters to Italy and North Africa piloted by A. R. Lewis of Airways Individual Reservations Ltd. Following a crash landing at Jury's Gap, Dungeness, when flying from Le Bourget to Lympne in bad visibility on Christmas Eve 1946, it returned to Weston for reconstruction. It then went on to enjoy a useful life with the Yellow Air Taxi Co. (Midlands) Ltd. at Elmdon in 1947, with Ductile Steels Ltd., Wolverhampton, and with its originator, E. W. Percival, during the E.P.9 production in 1956.

SPECIFICATION

Manufacturers: Percival Aircraft Ltd., Luton Airport, Luton, Beds.
Power Plants: Two 205 h.p. de Havilland Gipsy Six Series II.
Dimensions: Span, 46 ft. 8 in. Length, 32 ft. 3 in. Height, 9 ft. 9 in. Wing area, 278 sq. ft.
Weights: Tare weight (Prototype), 3,100 lb. (Production), 3,500 lb.
All-up weight (Prototype), 5,250 lb. (Production), 5,500 lb.
Performance: Maximum speed, 195 m.p.h.* Cruise, 175 m.p.h.* Initial climb, 1,150 ft./min. Ceiling, 21,000 ft. Range, 750 miles.

* 206 m.p.h. and 188 m.p.h. respectively with undercarriage retracted.

Production: One prototype and 26 production aircraft including the following for export or the R.A.F.: (c/n Q.22) YI-ROH; (Q.24) F-AQOK, later G-AFVC; (Q.25) VH-ABL, later G-AFMT; (Q.28) LY-SOA; (Q.29) LY-SOB; (Q.34) P5638; (Q.35) VH-ABY; (Q.36) VT-AKU; (Q.38) VT-AKR; (Q.39) P5634, later G-AHTB; (Q.40) P5635; (Q.41) P5636; (Q.42) P5637, later G-AHOM; (Q.43) Q601; (Q.44) Q602; (Q.45) P5639; (Q.46) P5640, later G-AHTA.

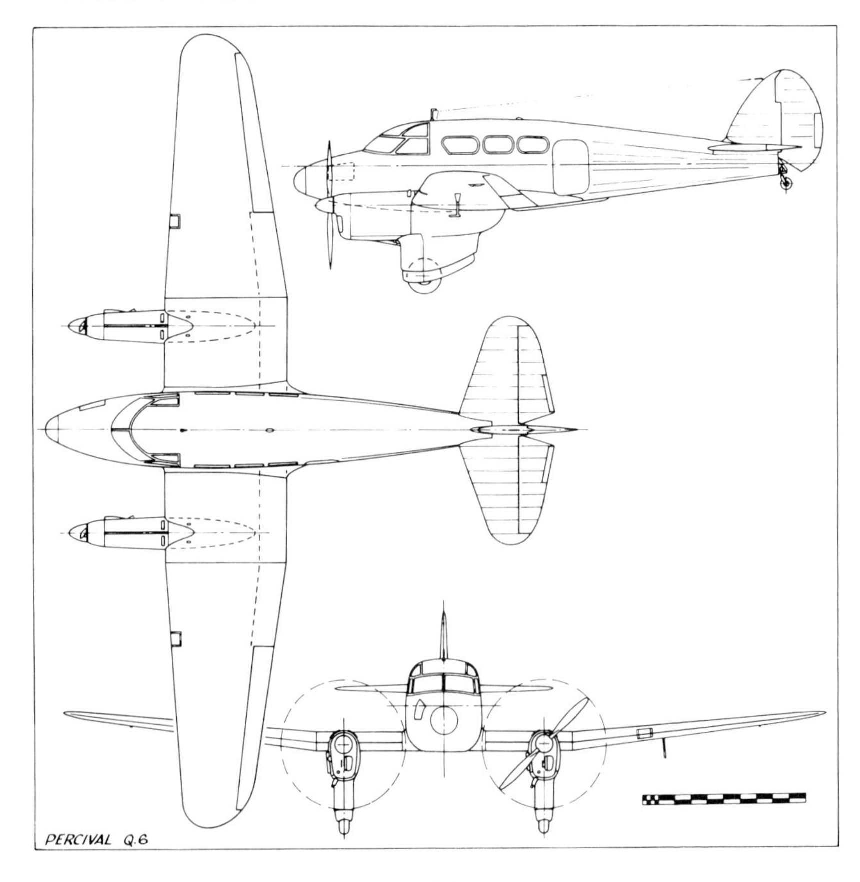

Proctor 5 G-AHBD flying near Baginton in March 1962 while in use by the Armstrong Whitworth Flying Group. (*Whitworth Gloster Aircraft Ltd.*)

Percival Proctor

The Percival Proctor I communications aircraft was the standard Vega Gull built to Air Ministry order with seating reduced from four to three and a small square window replacing the usual type of rear cabin glazing. The first production Proctor I, P5998, first flown at Luton on 8 October 1939, was followed by 246 production aircraft, 25 of which were built under sub-contract by F. Hills and Sons Ltd. at Manchester. Further R.A.F. deliveries totalled 196 Proctor IIs and 436 Proctor IIIs, both radio trainers without dual control, indistinguishable from the earlier mark and nearly all built at Manchester.

In October 1944 a Proctor III, DX198, was earmarked to be G-AGLC, replacement for the Air Attaché's Vega Gull G-AFWG in Buenos Aires. The scheme fell through, and the same Proctor was used after the war as G-ALUJ by J. M. S. Procter at Yeadon. The first active civil Proctor was a Mk.III LZ599 used, initially in camouflage, by the Ministry of Civil Aviation as G-AGLJ for licence testing from 1944 to 1950. Concurrently HM460 was in similar employ at Almaza as G-AGOG, and HM397 became G-AGTH 'Star Pixie', first and smallest aircraft of British South American Airways. Another Proctor 3 (Arabic mark numbers replaced Roman in 1948) served the Air Attachés in Berne and Prague. This was LZ734, civil as G-AGWB from 1946 to 1951 and later employed as the radio test vehicle of Avionics Ltd., Biggin Hill.

After the war some 225 surplus Proctors 1, 2 and 3 were denuded of military equipment for club and charter work. The first conversion was made to Proctor I P6197 at Weston-super-Mare in March 1946, and as G-AGWV the machine made a few runs on the Western Airways service to Cardiff prior to six years in private ownership. The Cardiff–Whitchurch route was later operated by Cambrian Air Services' Proctor 1s G-AHEU 'Montgomery' and

'EV 'Denbigh'. Many post-war charter firms commenced operations with Proctors, notably Air Taxis (Croydon) Ltd. with G-AGYA and 'YB.

A large number of civil Proctors were sold overseas. Many of these were ferried in the early post-war years by servicemen going home, as in the case of W/O J. Dyer, R.A.A.F., who left Hanworth for Australia in G-AHTN on 20 July 1946, a few days before Flt. Lt. J. Dalton in G-AHMG 'Dominion Lass' and Flt. Lt. F. Ogden in G-AHFX 'Yorkshire Lass'. In the following November G-AIEI 'Baby Baroda', piloted by F. James, was the first to reach the Cape. LZ804, first flown on 2 December 1943, and the last Proctor 3 constructed, was also one of the last delivered by air to Australia, leaving Croydon as G-ANGC in December 1957.

As a private aircraft the early Proctors chiefly found favour with sporting pilots such as A. S. K. 'Buster' Paine, whose red G-AHNA 'Nannie Ann', probably best known of all Proctors, won the Kemsley Trophy at Southend on 20 June 1953 at 149 m.p.h. and the Air League Challenge Trophy at Baginton on 21 July 1956 at 153·5 m.p.h. Other memorable Proctor successes included N. W. Chorlton's victory in G-AHUZ 'Nicodemus' in the Hurn to Herne Bay Race of 16 September 1950; the dead heat for the Osram Cup at Baginton on 21 July 1956, between T. G. Knox in G-AMBS and A. Barker in G-ANWY; and Sqn. Ldr. W. I. Lashbrooke's win in G-AIHD in the Air League Challenge Trophy Race at Yeadon on 22 July 1950.

In 1943 the Proctor fuselage was lengthened, deepened and provided with large rear windows with sliding panels. Internally it reverted to Vega Gull layout to accommodate four in side-by-side pairs as well as operational-type radio equipment. In this form it satisfied Air Ministry Specification T.9/41 and was named Proctor IV (Proctor 4 in 1948). Eight pre-production aircraft constructed at Luton were followed by 250 others built at Manchester.

In June 1945 a Proctor 4, RM161, was released to the Ministry of Civil Aviation as G-AGPA and after conversion at Luton went to Gatwick on radio

Proctor 3 G-AKWV, formerly HM350, was first used by the Cinque Ports Flying Club at Lympne. (*Skyfotos Ltd.*)

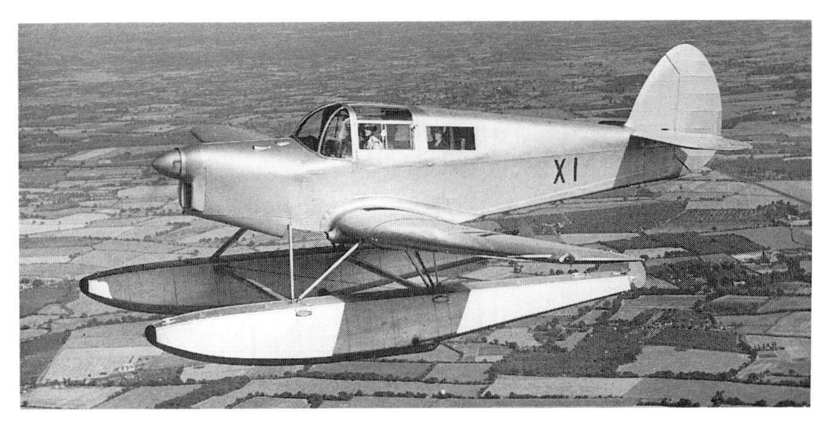

The Hudson's Bay Company's one-off Proctor 6 floatplane CF-EHF flying near the famous Ashford railway, Kent, while on test from Rochester as X-1 in June 1946.

calibration duties. A few others were declared surplus to R.A.F. requirements in 1947, a batch of 16, G-AJMH–'MX, being civilianised at Tollerton and Croydon by Field Aircraft Services Ltd., who exhibited 'MP at that year's Radlett S.B.A.C. Show. 'MH became well known at Redhill in the hands of private owner E. Williams, 'MW and 'MX operated the Rochester Air Charter Service of Short Bros. Ltd. and several were sold abroad. 'MU, named 'Thursday's Child', was fitted with extra tanks for a world flight by Mrs. R. Morrow-Tait with M. Townsend navigating. Leaving Croydon in August 1948, it flew via India, Japan and a 1,730 mile North Pacific crossing, only to be damaged beyond repair in a forced landing on the Alaskan Highway on 21 November. Six others civilianised at Squires Gate as G-AKLB–'LD and 'YI–'YK, went into charter service at Yeadon in the red and green of Lancashire Aircraft Corporation Ltd. One of the few British examples of structural failure in the air occurred on 19 August 1949, when 'LC was destroyed at Shipley, Yorks. Two others, G-AKWL and 'LEO, served the flying schools at Southend and Thruxton for a number of years.

Early in 1955 the R.A.F. declared obsolete all its remaining Proctor 4s, approximately 60 being acquired by civilian firms. Few saw any real service, although G-ANGM flew with East Anglian Flying Services Ltd. at Ipswich; 'XR on communications with Folland Aircraft Ltd., Hamble; 'YP with the Wiltshire School of Flying; 'YV as the camera ship of Film Aviation Services Ltd. and G-AOAR 'The Instrument Rater' used by the Airways Aero Club. The rest were flown mainly under temporary civil marks to Panshanger, White Waltham and elsewhere to be scrapped after the removal of valuable engines and instruments. These included the second prototype, LA589, ferried to Exeter by C. E. Harper and Co. Ltd. as G-ANXI.

When the Proctor 4 contract was terminated by the end of hostilities in 1945, three new aircraft RM193, 196 and 197 went to Luton to become prototypes of a purely civil version, the Proctor 5. Registered G-AGSW–'SY as demonstrators, the first and third went by sea to Canada and Australia respectively. The other, together with 'SZ, was handed over to the associate company Hunting Air Travel Ltd. and on 1 January 1946, the inaugural day of post-war civil flying, made an initial return charter flight from Luton to Croydon piloted by former Imperial Airways pilot W. Rogers. Series production of 150 Proctor 5s then began at Luton, 89 of which were of British registry, and one, G-AGTA, fitted with long-range tanks, made a delivery flight to Brazil piloted by J. A. Mollison, who left St. Mawgan, Cornwall, on 28 January 1946. The flying time of 37½ hours for the 4,640 mile flight included a 15 hour crossing of the South Atlantic.

The Proctor 5, fastest of post-war four seaters, was used executively by the Dunlop Rubber Co. Ltd. with G-AHBA, Helliwells Ltd. 'GT, Shell 'WU, Intava 'ZY, and D. Napier and Son Ltd. 'WV. It saw charter service with Island Air Services Ltd., Marshalls Flying School Ltd., Butlins Ltd., Kenning Aviation Ltd., Atlas Aviation Ltd., Kearsley Airways Ltd., Blue Line Airways Ltd., Skytravel Ltd., International Airways Ltd., Somerton Airways Ltd. and Northern Air Charter Ltd. The last, operating at Woolsington for a short time in 1946, employed two Proctor 5s, G-AGTD and G-AHTK, specially fitted with rounded rear windows.

Outstanding examples of personal Proctor 5s were G-AHGL owned and flown for 13 years by E. S. Davis; G-AIET which became the sole Mk.5A with Gipsy Queen 30-2 engine as J. J. Dyke's Eastleigh-based 'Fourflusher' (but

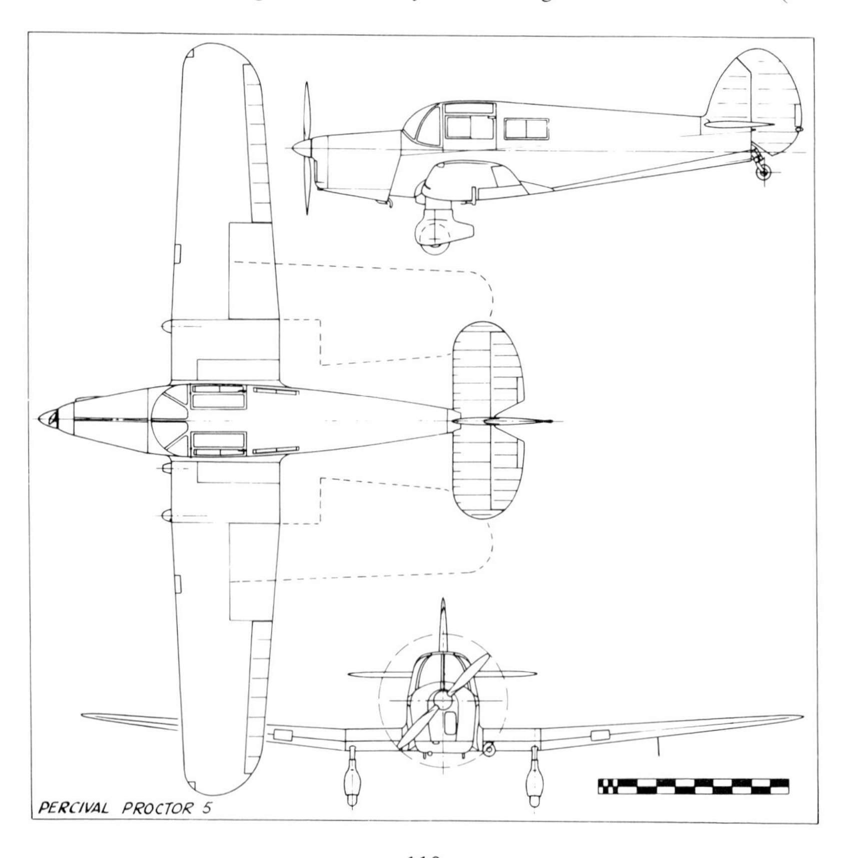

previously one of the 'Windmill Girl' series); and G-AHGN commissioned by the M.C.A. in 1946 for the Civil Air Attaché, Washington, but later flown in the Bahamas under American marks as N558E. Many long distance flights were made, including those of N. S. Norway to Australia in G-AKIW 1949 and A. J. Bradshaw to New Zealand in G-AHWW 'Kiwi Wanderer' 1951.

In true Vega Gull tradition, the 92nd–95th production aircraft were delivered to the R.A.F. in September 1946 for Air Attaché duties in Rome and other European capitals as VN895–8. VN896 did not survive, but in September 1953 the others came up for disposal and were civilianised at Croydon, Squires Gate and Eastleigh respectively as G-ANAT, 'MD and 'GG.

In 1966 Proctor 3 G-AGWB was repainted in immaculate wartime camouflage as LZ734 but forced landed on fire and was destroyed during the National Air Races at Tees-side on 5 August 1967 with injuries to pilot Mrs. Dawn Turley and Flt. Lt. Alan Turley. In the following year Mk.1 G-AIEY, Mk.3 G-ALOK and Mk.5 G-AIAE were remodelled with cranked wings and flew in German markings to impersonate Junkers Ju 87s in the film 'Battle of Britain'.

SPECIFICATION

Manufacturers: Percival Aircraft Ltd., Luton Airport, Beds., sub-contracted by F. Hills and Sons Ltd., Trafford Park, Manchester.

Power Plant: One 210 h.p. de Havilland Gipsy Queen 2.

Dimensions: Span, 39 ft. 6 in. Length (Proctor 3), 25 ft. 10 in. (Proctor 4/5), 28 ft. 2 in. Height, 7 ft. 3 in. Wing area (Proctor 3), 197 sq. ft. (Proctor 4/5), 202 sq. ft.

Weights: (Proctor 3) Tare weight, 1,875 lb. All-up weight, 3,250 lb.
(Proctor 4/5) Tare weight, 2,340 lb. All-up weight, 3,500 lb.

Performance: (Proctor 3) Maximum speed, 165 m.p.h. Cruising speed, 150 m.p.h. Initial Climb, 1,020 ft./min. Range, 660 miles.
(Proctor 4/5) Maximum speed, 157 m.p.h. Cruising speed, 135 m.p.h. Initial climb, 700 ft./min. Range, 500 miles.

Production: (a) Proctor 1, 2, 3 and 4

A large number of civil conversions made in Britain, and others were converted locally in Denmark, France, India, New Zealand and South Africa.

(b) Proctor 5

One hundred and fifty-four aircraft including the following for export: (c/n Ae.1) CS-ADN; (Ae.1a) SE-API; (Ae.4) OO-CAZ; (Ae.5) ZS-ATX; (Ae.6) CC-PEB; (Ae.7) Chile; (Ae.11) ZS-ATY; (Ae.12) ZS-ATZ; (Ae.13) VH-AIE; (Ae.15) VP-RAM; (Ae.19) OO-CCE; (Ae.21) Brazil; (Ae.22) to spares; (Ae.29) VT-CGH; (Ae.30) VT-CIO; (Ae.33) LV-NDI; (Ae.34) VT-CIP; (Ae.35) Argentine; (Ae.40) LV-NCO; (Ae.46) OO-CCH; (Ae.50) ZK-AQJ; (Ae.52) LV-NEJ; (Ae.53) LV-NGH; (Ae.54) LV-NVM; (Ae.63) Syrian SR-A.1; (Ae.64) SR-A.2; (Ae.65) SU-ACH, later G-AKPB; (Ae.76) SR-A.3; (Ae.79) ZK-AQK; (Ae.89) SR-A.4; (Ae.91) VH-BJY; (Ae.92–95) to R.A.F. as VN895-VN898, (VN895, VN897, VN898 later G-ANAT, 'MD, 'GG); (Ae.107) PP-DCQ; (Ae.109) OO-DED; (Ae.110) F-BCJB; (Ae.111) F-BCJC; (Ae.118) unsold; (Ae.120) unsold; (Ae.123) TJ-AAL; (Ae.125) ZS-BSR; (Ae.126) ZK-APH; (Ae.132) TJ-AAM; (Ae.133–137) not completed; (Ae.140) CF-EHF; (Ae.141) TJ-AAO; (Ae.142) not completed; (Ae.143) ZK-AQZ; (Ae.144–149) not completed.

The first production Prince after conversion to Mk.2 with sloping windscreen. (*Percival Aircraft Ltd.*)

Percival P.50 Prince

After the war Percival Aircraft Ltd. produced the five seat P.48 Merganser, which was of all-metal, stressed skin construction with fabric covered control surfaces. It was built primarily for passenger appeal and a high-wing layout was chosen to give the best possible view. An exceptionally roomy fuselage mounted on a retractable tricycle undercarriage gave a low, level floor for ease of entry. The fuselage was completed in November 1946 and immediately despatched by train ferry to the Paris Aero Show. Non-availability of the production Gipsy Queen 51 or suitable alternatives had already doomed the Merganser to extinction, but two such engines were loaned from the Ministry of Supply development order. With these, the first flight took place at Luton on 9 May 1947, the aircraft carrying the Class B marking X-2 in place of its allotted G-AHMH. Extensive flight trials culminated in its appearance at the Radlett S.B.A.C. Show in the following September and in data which speeded the production of a larger type, the P.50 Prince.

This medium range transport, fitted with Alvis Leonides nine cylinder radials, inaugurated an era of fruitful co-operation between Percivals and Alvis Ltd. in which engine development made possible the full exploitation of the basic airframe. The prototype Prince, G-23-1, later G-ALCM, flown for the first time at Luton on 13 May 1948, by Wing Cdr. H. P. Powell, shared the robust single engined performance of its predecessor and the addition of a small dorsal fin was the only major modification found necessary. Outwardly resembling the Merganser, its heavy duty, fork-mounted mainwheels and fluted, metal clad control surfaces were the only visible concessions to the increased weight and speed.

An initial batch of 10 Princes, laid down during prototype trials, benefited from further wind tunnel tests at Toulouse in September 1948. In the following March Capt. R. W. Hornall took off from Luton in the first production Prince 1, G-ALFZ, on a 25,000 mile proving flight to the Cape, carrying out tropical trials at Khartoum, Nairobi and Accra en route. The next machine, G-ALJA, made a demonstration tour to Bombay via the Near East, flying continuously to simulated airline schedules. G-ALRY, a survey version built for Percival's associate company, Hunting Aerosurveys Ltd., and designated P.54, was exhibited at the Farnborough S.B.A.C. Show in September 1949. Operated by a crew of three, it had an observer's station in a lengthened nose as well as vertical and oblique camera hatches. Piloted by J. H. Saffery, it left via Bovingdon on 2 February 1950, on the 3,200 mile positioning flight to Sharjah on the Persian Gulf for a four month oil prospecting contract, first of several carried out in Persia, Turkey, Siam and Kuwait. From May 1956 to January 1959 it was seconded to the firm's East African branch at Nairobi.

Survey Princes VR-TBC 'Prince Charles' and VR-TBD were also supplied to the Tanganyika Government and HB-HOF to the Swiss survey organisation Eidgenössischen Vermessungsdirektion.

The sloping front windscreen, an aesthetic and aerodynamic refinement incorporated in the survey version, was also fitted to the Prince 1s 'FZ and 'JA in April 1950. This and main spar modifications permitting an increase in all-up weight to 11,000 lb., created the Prince 2. A contract for 10 passenger Prince 2s for Transportes Aereos Norte do Brasil resulted in the passage of 'FZ through Prestwick on 7 August 1950. Carrying a 100 gallon overload fuel tank in the cabin, the delivery flight was made via Keflavik, Bluie West One,

The Merganser prototype, G-AHMH, showing the single front and double rear doors. (*Flight*)

The P.54 Survey Prince G-ALRY in service with Société Protection Aéroportée as F-BJAJ for radar calibration duties in 1960. (*John Goring*)

Goose Bay, Dorval, Miami and Jamaica, a route already flown by the Shell Company's Prince 2s G-ALWG and 'WH. Fitted as six seat executive and eight seat convertible freighter respectively, these had arrived at Maracaibo, Venezuela, on 18 April 1950, having covered the 6,500 miles from Luton in 14 days.

Development of the Leonides engine resulting in the 550 h.p. series 502/4 driving de Havilland constant speed, feathering and reversing airscrews made possible the presentation of the much improved Prince 3 G-AMMB at the 1952 S.B.A.C. Show. Operating at higher economical cruising speed at an all-up weight of 11,500 lb., the demonstrator was equipped for six seat executive use and later sold to the South African Iron and Steel Industrial Corporation. Of the five ordered by the Shell Refining and Marketing Co. Ltd., G-AMKK and 'LX went to Borneo, G-AMLW and 'LY to Venezuela, 'LZ being based in Britain. A special executive model, G-AMPR, designated Prince 3E, was delivered to the Standard Motor Co. Ltd. at Baginton, but the appearance of series 502/5 engines then created the Prince 3B. Three of these, G-AMKW–'KY, were equipped with radar nose, astrodome and the necessary equipment for calibrating airfield radio, radar and navigational aids by the M.T.C.A. Flight at Stansted. Progressive engine development resulted in their upgrading to Prince 4B in November 1956 and to Prince 6B in July 1958.

Although a number of Prince 3s were sold overseas, only one, a long-nosed survey model, G-AMNT, designated Prince 3A, was ferried in British marks. Later, in Thai Air Force colours, it carried out survey work for the Mapping Organisation of the Ministry of Defence. Another survey machine, G-AMOT, specially equipped with airborne magnetometer equipment for use in Canada by Hunting Aerosurveys Ltd., was designated Prince 3D. On its return in the following year it was upgraded to Prince 4D and transferred to the uranium survey in Kenya, where it was destroyed in a wheels-up landing in the jungle in 1958. Similar work was carried on in Australia by the one-time Shell Prince 3, 'LW, which returned from Venezuela for modification to Prince 4 before being flown from Elstree to Mascot by R. Keeling in December 1954 and handed over to Hunting Adastra Geophysics Ltd. It flew with appropriate and phonetic Australian marks until its return to Luton in February 1959. In the

President EC-APA, first of three ordered 1957 by TAE, Bilbao, for internal services in Spain and the Balearic Islands. It remained at Luton until sold to the Sudanese Air Force in 1960. (*Hunting Percival Aircraft Ltd.*)

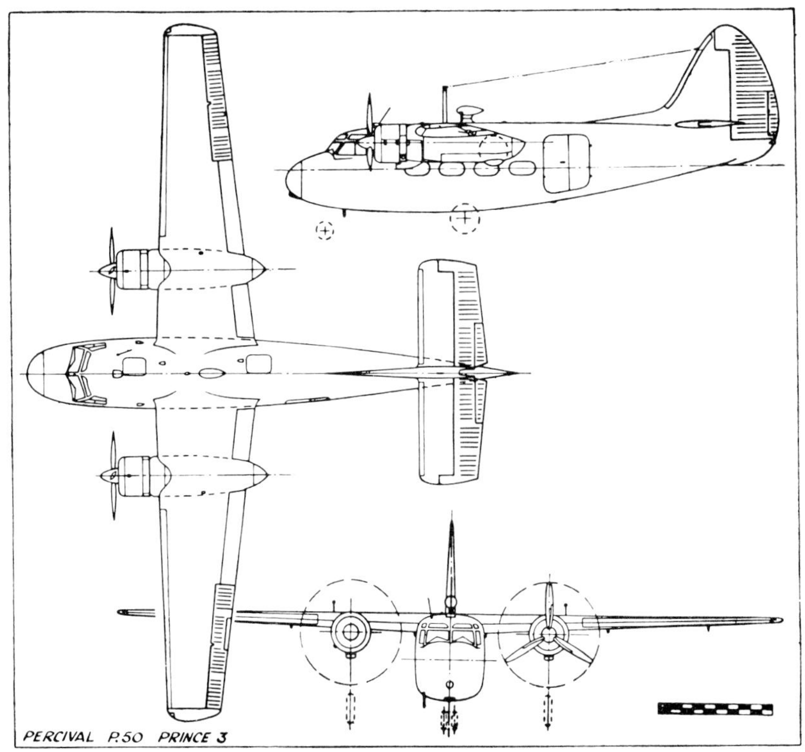

following month it was sold, with Hunting's G-ALRY, to Société Protection Aéroportée, Le Bourget, for airfield radar calibration duties.

Large military contracts for the wide span P.66 Pembroke ended Prince production in 1953 but led to a demand for secondhand specimens. G-ALWH was flown home from South America and sold to the Sperry Gyroscope Co. Ltd. as a test and demonstration vehicle. G-AMLY followed suit for executive use by Martin-Baker Aircraft Ltd. in 1955, but after upgrading to Prince 4 passed through Bahrein on 3 September 1958, en route to the British Malayan Petroleum Co. Ltd. in Borneo. Fitted with series 503/4 engines, the executive Prince 3E G-AMPR became the sole Prince 4E, prior to sale to the Tanganyika Government as VR-TBN 'Prince Hal' in February 1956. In February 1962 this aircraft and VR-TBD were ferried from Dar-es-Salaam to Samoa for Polynesian Airways as ZK-BYN and ZK-BYO respectively.

The ultimate development of the type, G-AOJG, initially the Prince 5 but later known as the President 1, first flew at Luton on 26 August 1956, differing externally from the Pembroke only in the shape of the nacelles, modified at the rear to improve single engined handling. It was shown at the 1956 S.B.A.C. Show as an executive six seater and left Luton on 29 April 1957, for a European sales tour which resulted in an order for three Presidents EC-APA to 'PC for a Spanish airline. These were never delivered and the first went to the Sudanese Air Force with serial number '10' via Southend on 28 January 1959, followed by the other two as '11' and '12' on

3 March 1960. The first one returned in May 1960, eventually to become G-ARCN as communications aircraft for Bristol Aircraft Ltd. at Filton.

One R.A.F. Pembroke was delivered from the Empire Test Pilots' School, Farnborough to the Air Navigation and Trading Co. Ltd., Squires Gate on 29 June 1958 for civil conversion as G-APNL.

SPECIFICATION

Manufacturers: Percival Aircraft Ltd., Luton Airport, Beds., name changed to Hunting Percival Aircraft Ltd. 26 April 1954, further changed to Hunting Aircraft Ltd., 5 December 1957.

Power Plants:

(Merganser)	Two 296 h.p. de Havilland Gipsy Queen 51.
(Prince 1 and 2)	Two 520 h.p. Alvis Leonides 501/4.
(P.54)	Two 520 h.p. Alvis Leonides 501/4.
(Prince 3, 3A, 3E)	Two 550 h.p. Alvis Leonides 502/4.
(Prince 3B and 3D)	Two 560 h.p. Alvis Leonides 502/5.
(Prince 4 and 4E)	Two 550 h.p. Alvis Leonides 503/4.
(Prince 4B and 4D)	Two 550 h.p. Alvis Leonides 503/5.
(Prince 6B)	Two 540 h.p. Alvis Leonides 504/5A.
(President 1)	Two 520 h.p. Alvis Leonides 503/5A.
	Two 540 h.p. Alvis Leonides 504/5A.
(President 2)	Two 560 h.p. Alvis Leonides 514/5A.
(Pembroke)	Two 550 h.p. Alvis Leonides 127.

	Merganser	Prince 1 and 2	P.54	Prince 3, 4, 6	President 1, 2 and Pembroke
Span	47 ft. 9 in.	56 ft. 0 in.	56 ft. 0 in.	56 ft. 0 in.	64 ft. 6 in.
Length	40 ft. 8 in.	42 ft. 10 in.	45 ft. 3½ in.	42 ft. 10 in.†	46 ft. 4 in.
Height	13 ft. 9 in.	16 ft. 1 in.	16 ft. 1 in.	16 ft. 1 in.	16 ft. 0 in.
Wing area	319 sq. ft.	365 sq. ft.	365 sq. ft.	365 sq. ft.	400 sq. ft.
Tare weight	5,300 lb.	7,364 lb.	7,607 lb.	8,038 lb.	9,136 lb.
All-up weight	7,300 lb.	10,659 lb.*	11,000 lb.	11,000 lb.‡	13,500 lb.
Maximum speed	193 m.p.h.	216 m.p.h.	202 m.p.h.	229 m.p.h.	212 m.p.h.
Cruising speed	160 m.p.h.	179 m.p.h.	168 m.p.h.	197 m.p.h.	164 m.p.h.
Initial climb	1,010 ft./min.	1,110 ft./min.	1,100 ft./min.	1,650 ft./min.	1,500 ft./min.
Ceiling	24,000 ft.	23,500 ft.	23,000 ft.	23,400 ft.	22,000 ft.
Range	800 miles	940 miles	1,300 miles	894 miles	1,075 miles

* Prince 2 A.U.W. 11,000 lb.
† Prince 3A length 45 ft. 3½ in.
‡ Improved braking on Prince 4 and 6, permitting A.U.W. of 11,500 lb. and 11,800 lb. respectively.

Production: (a) P.50 Prince and variants

Twenty-four aircraft for civil operators including 19 British registered and (c/n P.50/9) test airframe; (P.50/15) PP-NBG/PT-ASY; (P.54/22) VR-TBC; (P.54/25) VR-TBD/ZK-AYO; (P.54/42) HB-HOF.

(b) P.66 President and variants

At least seven aircraft including (c/n 13) WV710/G-APNL; (79) G-AOJG; (108) EC-APB/Sudanese Air Force '11'; (114) EC-APC/G-APVJ/Sudanese '12'; (1040) EC-APA/Sudanese '10'/G-ARCN; (1071) G-APMO.

G-ABDO, first of the Genet engined Redwing II aircraft. (*Flight Photo 9799*)

Robinson Redwing

The Redwing side-by-side two seater appeared in May 1930 at the height of the new popular enthusiasm for light aeroplanes. Designed by John Kenworthy and built in a workshop near Croydon by the Robinson Aircraft Co. Ltd., newly founded by Capt. P. G. Robinson, the prototype G-AAUO was powered by a 75 h.p. A.B.C. Hornet flat four engine. Its plywood-covered fuselage was supported on a wide-track, split-axle undercarriage, the shock legs of which were attached to the top longerons. As the name suggested, the Redwing's folding mainplanes were doped red overall and were of generous proportions to give easy flying and slow landing characteristics. In the light of early trials, the Genet IIA five cylinder radial was chosen as a more suitable engine and powered the Redwing II prototype G-ABDO which first flew in October 1930. The firm was then financially reorganised as Redwing Aircraft Ltd. and larger premises were obtained in one of the former A.D.C. hangars at Croydon Aerodrome, enabling work to begin on a small batch of production aircraft.

Both prototypes were used by clubs, the Redwing I G-AAUO by the Scarborough Aeroplane Club, and the Redwing II by the newly formed London General Omnibus Company Flying Club at Broxbourne where Flt. Lt. N. M. S. Russell, test pilot to the manufacturers, became the busmen's first instructor. By the end of 1931, eight more Redwings had been completed, two of which, G-ABLA and 'MF, were for the Wiltshire School of Flying Ltd. at High Post. Another, G-ABMJ, was used by the Scarborough Aeroplane Club from July 1931 until it returned to the Redwing Flying School at Gatwick in October 1932. It was then fitted with a Fairey-Reed metal airscrew and increased tankage to give six hours endurance for a number of long European flights by its next owner, Miss Delphine Reynolds. In 1934 it was acquired by Miss Rosalind Norman and kept at Heston until sold in Ireland later in the year.

Redwing Aircraft Ltd. vacated its historic Croydon premises in March 1932 when the works transferred to Blue Barns Aerodrome, Colchester, where Redwings G-ABMU and 'NP could be serviced for the Colchester branch of the Eastern Counties Aeroplane Club Ltd., Ipswich. The official opening of Blue Barns on 10 March was followed by a similar ceremony at Gatwick on 1 July when the firm also took over the Surrey Aero Club and added Redwings G-ABMJ and 'OK to its fleet, eight Redwings being lined up on the aerodrome for the occasion. The firm had again been reconstituted and now numbered designer John Kenworthy and the Junkers concessionaire H. R. Trost among its directors.

G-ABMV, delivered new to the L.G.O.C. Flying Club, Broxbourne in July 1931, was repurchased by the Redwing Co. late in 1932 for export to New Zealand. It was overhauled at Blue Barns and fitted with low pressure wheels and increased tankage to give a range of 500 miles, repainted as ZK-ADD and crated for shipment. It left London Docks on 24 April 1933, was first flown on 30 June after erection at Wigram, and delivered to H. T. Parry at Hokitika on 5 August. It was loaned to the West Coast United Aero Club during August 1935 and last heard of in 1942 as instructional airframe INST.112 with the Invercargill A.T.C. Squadron.

Only two more Redwings, G-ABRM and 'RN, were built, the second being the sole Redwing III which used the same fuselage, empennage and engine installation but the wing span was much reduced and a more streamlined

The Hornet engined prototype Redwing I. (*Flight Photo 8893*)

undercarriage fitted to give higher cruising speeds on cross country flights. It was delivered from the Colchester factory to Gatwick on 11 May 1933 but was not found to be particularly successful and gained no C. of A. until it reverted to Mk.II with standard wings in 1934. Leaving Croydon for Cape Town on 4 January 1935, piloted by Mrs. Keith Miller, 'RL crossed the Sahara and reached Gao on the 24th. A few days later it made a forced landing 10 miles from Kotonu, Dahomey, and was wrecked through striking a tree in swerving to avoid some villagers.

The Redwing III sesquiplane. (*Flight Photo 13067*)

G-ABRM was delivered to the Eastern Counties Aeroplane Club in February 1933 but, the Colchester branch having closed down, went to Ipswich to join their surviving Redwing II G-ABNP. Both continued in service until 1934 but frequent breakages of the top longerons at the main undercarriage leg attachment points, coupled with shortage of spares, resulted in cannibalisation and the eventual emergence of 'RM, re-erected with most of the major assemblies of 'NP. It remained on the club's strength until wrecked in a forced landing at Frinton in the autumn of 1935.

In 1973 the only surviving Redwing was G-ABNX, originally flown by C. P. Hunter at Hooton 1933–35. After a period at Macmerry, Edinburgh, with S. Reid, it was acquired by C. W. Morrison and reappeared in dismantled condition at Elstree in 1945. It was sent by road to the College of Aeronautical Engineering at Redhill on 16 April 1951 and superficially reconditioned for the Fifty Years of Flying Exhibition at Hendon in the following July. After several years at Panshanger awaiting airframe and engine overhaul, it was stored at Heath End, near Farnham, Surrey, until acquired by John Pothecary and E. H. Gould and taken to Christchurch on 18 December 1959 for painstaking overhaul and reconstruction which was rewarded when 'NX took-off on 3 April 1962 for the first time in 22 years. Thereafter it was maintained with expert care by John Pothecary who based it later at his Slinfold strip in Surrey.

SPECIFICATION

Manufacturers: The Robinson Aircraft Co. Ltd., Stafford Road, Wallington, Surrey. Name changed to Redwing Aircraft Ltd. April 1931, works moved to Blue Barns Aerodrome, Colchester, 10 March 1932. Registered office moved to Gatwick Airport, Horley, Surrey, 1 July 1932.

Power Plants: (Redwing I) One 75 h.p. A.B.C. Hornet.
(Redwing II and III) One 80 h.p. Armstrong Siddeley Genet IIA.

	Redwing I	Redwing II	Redwing III
Span	30 ft. 6 in.	30 ft. 6 in.	24 ft. 0 in.
Length	22 ft. 3 in.	22 ft. 8 in.	22 ft. 8 in.
Height	8 ft. 7 in.	8 ft. 7 in.	–
Wing area	250 sq. ft.	250 sq. ft.	154 sq. ft.
Tare weight	860 lb.	870 lb.	850 lb.
All-up weight	1,325 lb.	1,450 lb.*	1,500 lb.
Maximum speed	92 m.p.h.	95 m.p.h.	–
Cruising speed	84 m.p.h.	85 m.p.h.	90 m.p.h.
Initial climb	650 ft./min.	800 ft./min.	–
Range	–	275 miles	550 miles

* Increased to 1,500 lb. in 1938.

Production: (a) Redwing I

One aircraft only: G-AAUO.

(b) Redwing II

Ten aircraft initially: G-ABDO, 'LA, 'MF, 'MJ, 'MU, 'MV, 'NP, 'NX, 'OK and 'RM.

(c) Redwing III

One aircraft only: G-ABRL, later converted to Redwing II.

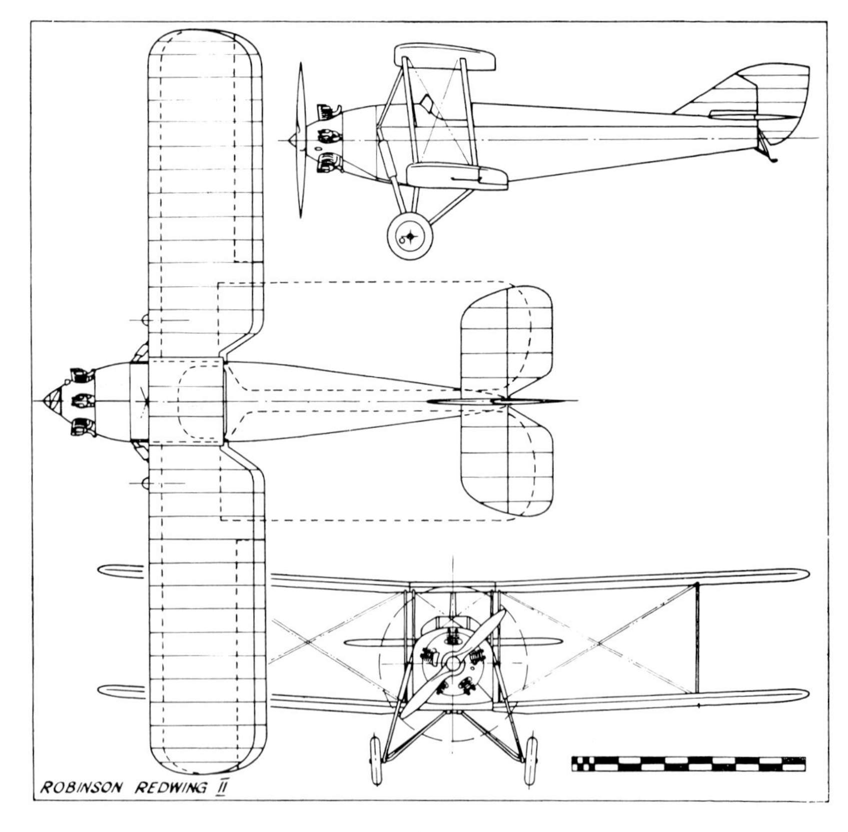

G-ACDP, an Air Service Training Cutty Sark with Genet Major engines, taking off from Southampton Water. (*W. K. Kilsby*)

Saro A.17 Cutty Sark

In 1928 Sir Alliott Verdon Roe joined forces with Mr. John Lord and acquired a controlling interest in S. E. Saunders Ltd., flying-boat builders of Cowes, Isle of Wight. The firm was then reconstituted as Saunders-Roe Ltd., its first product being the twin engined, four seat, Cutty Sark cabin flying-boat. The Avro-Fokker, watertight, plywood-covered, cantilever wing was bolted directly to the gunwales of the corrosion-resisting Alclad hull. The prototype first flew at Cowes on 4 July 1929 piloted by Flg. Off. Chilton and after its public presentation at the Olympia Aero Show as G-AAIP, the same pilot flew it to the La Baule Seaplane Rally on 14 September 1929 carrying the Director of Civil Aviation, Sir Sefton Brancker. A wide track, retractable amphibian undercarriage was then fitted and the machine sold to Norman Holden, for whom it was flown from its base at Selsey Bill by E. G. Hordern but shortly afterwards it was acquired by Messrs. Kirston and Mace for a passenger service between Woolston, Southampton, and St. Helier Harbour, Jersey.

In the following year the aircraft's performance was considerably improved by replacing the original 105 h.p. A.D.C. Cirrus Hermes Is with closely cowled 120 h.p. Gipsy II engines and between 26 March and 23 April 1931, the manufacturers' chief test pilot S. D. Scott made a 3,000 mile sales tour to Dubrovnik, Belgrade and Budapest and also to the Stockholm Exhibition in June.

Early in 1932 G-AAIP was sold to Capt. Campbell Shaw and Flt. Lt. Tommy Rose who formed Isle of Man Air Services and carried passengers between Liverpool and the Isle of Man in competition with British Amphibious Air Lines Ltd. who based the fifth production machine, G-ABBC 'Progress', at Squires Gate but picked up passengers on the foreshore at Blackpool. Both Cutty Sarks alighted in Douglas Harbour, or at Ronaldsway Aerodrome if the sea was rough.

VH-UNV, second of the 12 Cutty Sarks constructed, was first flown with Class B marking L-1 and shipped to Australia in 1930 for the Matthews Aviation Co.'s Melbourne–Flinders Island service, and the third, serialled '3', was delivered to R.N.Z.A.F. station Hobsonville for the use of the Governor General until retired as an instructional airframe in 1937. The sixth Cutty Sark was handed over to the Seaplane Training Flight at R.A.F. Calshot as S1575 in December 1930.

G-AAVX, originally built as a flying-boat for the Hon. A. E. Guinness and launched in May 1930, spent several years under tropical conditions on club and taxi work as an amphibian with the Royal Singapore Flying Club, until the plywood wing became so warped that the aircraft was scrapped in 1935. The ninth aircraft, allotted British marks G-ABVF for test flying at Cowes, was a pure flying-boat to the order of a Japanese pilot Yoshihara for a flight from San Francisco to Japan. Long-range tanks and blind-flying equipment were fitted and 'VF, powered by a 240 h.p. Lynx radial, was unique as the only single engined Cutty Sark.

The remaining aircraft were powered by 140 h.p. Genet Major seven-cylinder radials. Two were shipped to Hong Kong, one for instructional use by the Far East Flying School as VR-HAY and the other for sale in China. Another, G-ADAF, was exported to the island of San Domingo in the West Indies by R. H. Kulka Ltd. The remaining two, G-ACDP and 'DR, delivered

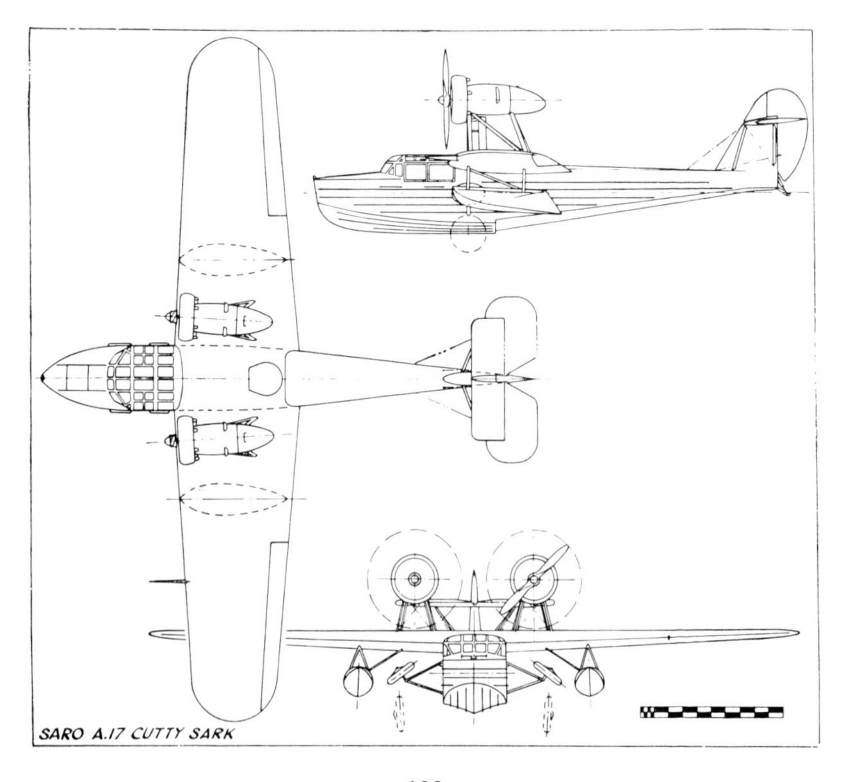

The long range single engined Cutty Sark G-ABVF, built to Japanese order. (*Saunders-Roe Ltd.*)

to Air Service Training Ltd., Hamble, were the best known of all Cutty Sarks, familiar sights in the Solent from 1933 to 1938 on their instructional, navigational and seamanship sorties. In 1937 they were joined by G-AETI, the machine which had lain unused at Hong Kong after the sale to the Kwangsi Air Force in China had fallen through five years previously.

SPECIFICATION

Manufacturers: Saunders-Roe Ltd., East Cowes, Isle of Wight.

Power Plants: Two 105 h.p. A.D.C. Cirrus Hermes I.
Two 120 h.p. de Havilland Gipsy II.
Two 130 h.p. de Havilland Gipsy III.
Two 140 h.p. Armstrong Siddeley Genet Major I.
One 240 h.p. Armstrong Siddeley Lynx IVC.

Dimensions: Span, 45 ft. 0 in. Length, 34 ft. 4 in. Height, 11 ft. 2 in. Wing area, 320 sq. ft.

	As flying-boat	As amphibian	
	Hermes I	Gipsy II	Genet Major
Tare weight	2,375 lb.	2,670 lb.	2,725 lb.
All-up weight	3,500 lb.	3,850 lb.	3,900 lb.
Maximum speed	105 m.p.h.	103 m.p.h.	107 m.p.h.
Cruising speed	85 m.p.h.	85 m.p.h.	90 m.p.h.
Initial climb	600 ft./min.	550 ft./min.	500 ft./min.
Ceiling	9,500 ft.	9,000 ft.	9,000 ft.
Range	340 miles	300 miles	315 miles

Production: Twelve aircraft, seven British registered initially, and the following for export or the R.A.F.: (c/n 2) L-1/VH-UNV; (3) R.N.Z.A.F. '3'; (6) S1575; (7) VR-HAY; (8) unregistered to Hong Kong, later G-AETI.

The prototype Pioneer flying slowly with slats and flaps extended.
(*Flight Photo 26354S*)

Scottish Aviation Prestwick Pioneer

First aircraft produced by Scottish Aviation Ltd., the Prestwick Pioneer I was designed by Robert McIntyre to meet an Air Ministry requirement for a communications aircraft capable of operating into, and out of, confined spaces. It was a strut-braced, high-wing cabin monoplane of all-metal, stressed-skin construction powered by a 240 h.p. Gipsy Queen 32. Full span, controllable leading edge slats and Fowler type trailing edge flaps of generous area imparted sensational take-off, landing and slow flying characteristics. Adequate trimming and control at forward speeds of the order of 30 m.p.h. were achieved by the use of an electrically operated, variable incidence tailplane and an unusually large rudder and elevator. The pilot sat centrally with maximum view, three passengers and luggage being accommodated behind.

VL515, the first prototype, made its debut at the Radlett S.B.A.C. Show in September 1947, but when no military contract was awarded, development continued for civil purposes. Trials proceeded throughout 1948 in the hands of test pilots N. J. Capper and R. C. W. Ellison, the aircraft, re-engined with a Gipsy Queen 34, flying under B conditions as G-31-1. It was exhibited as such at the 1948 S.B.A.C. Show, even though already registered G-AKBF. A decision to increase the passenger seats to four and improve the performance called for the installation of a more powerful engine. A number of power plants were considered, including the Pratt & Whitney Wasp R-1340, several of which were available following the dismantling of the company's Fokker F.XXII G-AFZP. Choice fell on the Alvis Leonides nine cylinder radial, the reworked prototype making its first flight as the Pioneer 2 in June 1950. Steep take off and short landing demonstrations by N. J. Capper at the 1950, 1951 and 1952 S.B.A.C. Shows drew attention, not only to its improved military potential and civil applications in the light transport, ambulance or agricultural roles but also to its docility. With the port half of the elevator torn away in a steep take off at the 1952 Show, the Pioneer continued its circuit to make an uneventful landing. The issue of an unrestricted C. of A. in May 1952, followed by helicopter style landings on 100 yard strips on the Hebridean islands of Mull and Iona, rounded off the development of Scotland's first commercial design and Britain's first STOL* transport.

The adoption of the Pioneer for casualty evacuation in the Malayan jungles by the R.A.F. necessitated a production line at Prestwick, and when production ceased at the end of 1961, fifty-nine aircraft had been completed, including four for the Royal Ceylon Air Force and nine for the Royal Malayan Air Force.

* STOL.–Short Take Off and Landing.

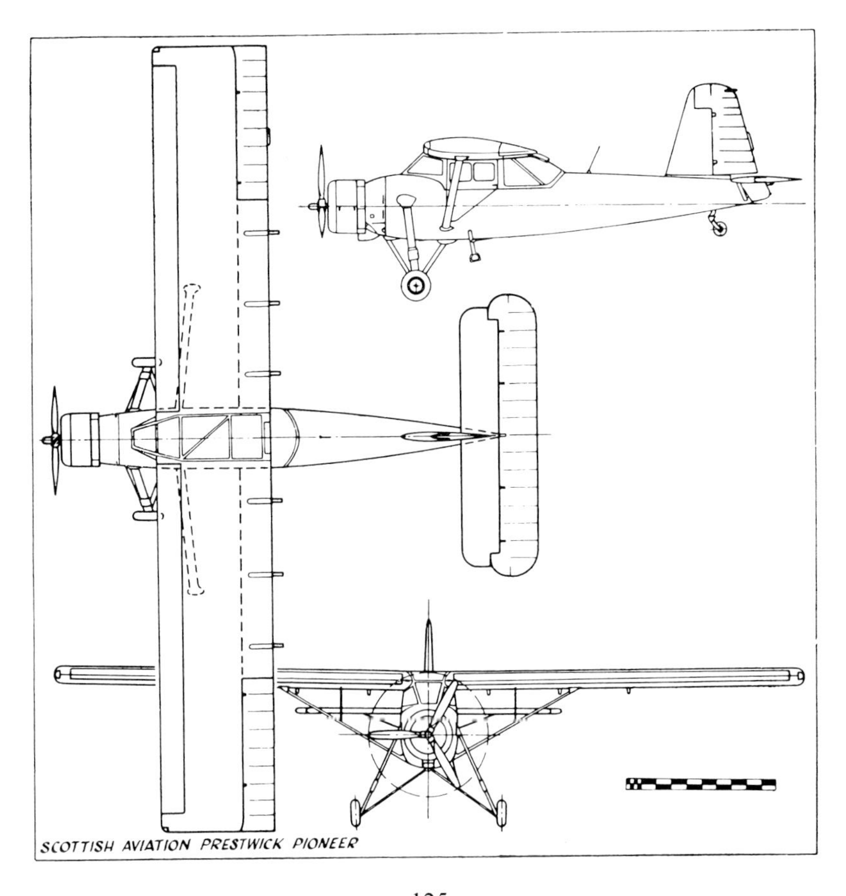

During this period six aircraft were employed by the manufacturers as temporary civil demonstrators, the third R.A.F. aircraft becoming G-ANAZ for a few days in September 1953 purely for ferrying to, and exhibition at, the Farnborough S.B.A.C. Show. The fifth aircraft appeared in the following year as G-ANRG and afterwards appeared in R.A.F. markings as XH469 for participation in Exercise Royal Battle and the Battle of Britain display at Hendon. It was despatched to the Far East in the following June but during demonstration flights at Rangoon on 23 July 1955 was seriously damaged and shipped home for repair, the Far East sales tour being completed by a new demonstrator G-AODZ. This was leased to Film Aviation Services Ltd. early in 1958 and went on location in French Equatorial Africa, piloted by Capt. K. E. Sissons, during the filming of 'Roots of Heaven' but returned to Prestwick for overhaul before leaving for a sales tour of Israel on 24 August 1958.

European sales tours had been undertaken with G-AOGF and 'GK in 1956, the year in which G-AOUE went to the U.S.A. for evaluation by the American authorities but nosed over when taking off on loose sand from Fort Bragg, North Carolina on 6 November, returning as U.S.A.F. air freight to Prestwick, where it was deemed irrepairable and scrapped.

To avoid confusion with the Twin Pioneer, production of which was increasing, the civil Prestwick Pioneer 2 was redesignated Pioneer 1 in March 1957. Demonstrators G-AOGF and 'GK were eventually sold and left Prestwick together on 2 March 1958, at the commencement of their delivery flight to the Iranian Customs Authority which employed them for anti-smuggling patrols. Two others, test flown during the following summer under civil marks as G-APNW and 'NX, were crated and despatched to the Royal Ceylon Air Force.

SPECIFICATION

Manufacturers: Scottish Aviation Ltd., Prestwick Airport, Ayrshire, Scotland.

Power Plants: (Pioneer 1) One 240 h.p. de Havilland Gipsy Queen 32.
One 250 h.p. de Havilland Gipsy Queen 34.
(Pioneer 2*) One 520 h.p. Alvis Leonides 501/3.
One 520 h.p. Alvis Leonides 501/4.
One 560 h.p. Alvis Leonides 502/4.
One 560 h.p. Alvis Leonides 502/7.

Dimensions: Span, 49 ft. 9 in. Length, 34 ft. 9 in. Height, 10 ft. 2½ in. Wing area, 390 sq. ft.

	Pioneer I	Pioneer 2*
Tare weight	3,215 lb.	3,900 lb.
All-up weight	4,250 lb.	5,800 lb.
Maximum speed	126 m.p.h.	162 m.p.h.
Cruising speed	114 m.p.h.	121 m.p.h.
Initial climb	900 ft./min.	880 ft./min.
Ceiling	14,500 ft.	23,000 ft.
Range	500 miles	420 miles

* Redesignated Pioneer 1 in March 1957.

Borneo Airways' Twin Pioneer Series 3 9M-ANO, shown at Kuala Lumpur in 1964, first flew as G-APLW in 1958. (*Aviation Photo News*)

Scottish Aviation Twin Pioneer

The prototype Twin Pioneer G-ANTP, first flown at Prestwick on 25 June 1955, was a twin Leonides powered STOL transport of rugged aspect, carrying 16 passengers and two crew. It incorporated many of the well-proven features of its single engined predecessor, used identical outer wing panels, the same type of all-metal, stressed skin construction, leading edge slats and Fowler flaps. A long travel undercarriage and generous triple tail surfaces guaranteed viceless behaviour when landing slowly in confined spaces. Flight trials proved its outstanding short run take off and landing ability, and the aircraft was presented at the 1955 Farnborough S.B.A.C. Show by Capt. Roy Smith. Three pre-production Twin Pioneers, G-AOEN, 'EO and 'EP, built and flown during 1956, embodied two important modifications. Leading edge slats inboard of the engines were found unnecessary and deleted. Ailerons which originally extended to the wing tips were clipped and full-chord tip fairings fitted. G-AOEN and 'EO made their appearance at the 1956 S.B.A.C. Show painted respectively in the colour schemes of Swissair and the K.L.M. New Guinea subsidiary, de Kroonduif.

Convinced that the Twin Pioneer had a high sales potential, Scottish Aviation Ltd. laid plans for the production of 200 aircraft and instituted a world-wide sales campaign. In January 1957 'EO was despatched to St. Moritz for a three month evaluation on Swissair's mountain ski traffic; 'EP, flown by Capt. Smith, left for demonstrations in the Far East and Australia, while 'EN crossed the Atlantic by the Northern route for a tour of Central and South America. Both 'EP and 'EN carried spares for six months, in which time they covered 46,000 miles in 500 flying hours and 'EN crossed the Andes three times. It also gave full-load demonstrations at La Paz (13,404 ft.) and spent two years in Central America and the Caribbean, during which its annual C. of A. overhauls took place in Mexico. A fourth aircraft, G-AOER, was sold to Rio Tinto Finance and Exploration Ltd., but remained in the factory until 1959 for the installation of airborne magnetometer equipment in special wing tip containers for a 19,300 square mile survey of Mexico and

Lower California in 1962–63. Two others, OE-BHV and HB-HOX, were fitted with floor-mounted cameras for the Austrian and Swiss Government survey departments in 1957 and 1959 respectively.

Trials with the prototype at Aden and Asmara confirmed the calculated performance under tropical conditions and in June 1957 'EO excited considerable comment by flying a passenger service from Issy heliport to the Paris Aero Show at Le Bourget in competition with two Vertol helicopters. It left Prestwick for a South African sales sortie in the following December and was demonstrated en route to the oil companies at Tripoli, Libya. Here it suffered fatigue failure of a structural member in the port wing and crashed with the loss of the firm's managing director D. F. McIntyre, Capt. Smith and the engineer officer. Modifications having already been incorporated in subsequent aircraft, the production programme was not seriously affected and continued until the completion of the 85th aircraft in 1962.

G-APLW, the 32nd aircraft, became the firm's demonstrator in succession to 'EO and spent June 1958 visiting the Near East, the Sudan and Italy, King Hussein of Jordan and the Sudanese Prime Minister being among those who flew in it. With one exception, the remaining British aircraft received civil status for delivery to distant operational bases, G-APHX and 'HY to the Kuwait Oil Company in October 1957, and during 1958 G-APIR and 'PH left for Umm Said in the Qatar Peninsula to transport freight and personnel to new drilling sites of the Iraq Petroleum Co. Ltd. G-APLM and 'LN went to Nigeria for similar transport duties in connection with the oil prospecting contract of Fison-Airwork Ltd. G-APJT 'Lang Rajawali' (King Eagle) left Prestwick on 31 March 1958, to make the long flight to Singapore, where it became the first aircraft of the newly formed Malayan Air Force. One other export, G-APMT, flew to Iran in July of the same year, where it carried out many mercy flights for the Red Lion and Sun Organisation to areas affected by the earthquake.

In 1958 the 33rd aircraft was registered G-APPW as prototype Twin Pioneer Series 2 for A.R.B. and C.A.A. certification with 600 h.p. Pratt & Whitney R-1340 radials in readiness for delivery of five similarly powered machines to Philippine Air Lines. Later when long stroke Leonides 531 engines became available, prototype G-ANTP was re-engined as the Series 3, or 1959 model. G-AOEN which at last returned to Prestwick from Central

The Rio Tinto company's Twin Pioneer Series 1 geophysical survey aircraft G-AOER with fibreglass wing tip pods housing transmitting and receiving coils.

Philippine Air Lines' Twin Pioneer Series 2 PI-C434 showing the large diameter Pratt & Whitney engines of this variant. (*Aviation Photo News*)

America piloted by Beverley Snook on 1 May 1959, was modified to Series 3 standard, leaving again on 21 July for an African sales tour. This ended in a forced landing on an island in the Zambesi, near Luabo, Mozambique on 12 December. Two other Twin Pioneer 3s went overseas in October 1959, 'RS to Fison-Airwork Ltd. and 'UM to the Iraq Petroleum Transport Co. Ltd.

Thirty-nine Twin Pioneers were built for the R.A.F. 1958–59 for use in difficult country around Aden and in the Far East where 12 served with the Royal Malayan Air Force and four with Borneo Airways (later Malaysia-Singapore Airlines). Three supplied to de Kroonduif were taken over by Garuda Indonesian Airways in 1963 and later disposed of to Bird Bros. of Bangkok. They are believed to have seen service in Vietnam.

After seven years with the Royal Flying Club of Iran, EP-AGA, 'GB and 'GC were purchased by Keegan Aviation Ltd. and returned to Panshanger in 1963. After overhaul at Shoreham, 'GA was delivered to Björn Pallson in Iceland as TF-LOA but in 1966 was sold to North Coast Air Services, Prince Rupert, B.C. as CF-STX. EP-AGB went to Ecuador as G-ASHN/HC-AHT and 'GC to Fjellfly, at Skien, Norway as G-ASJS/LN-BFK.

G-APHX and 'HY, which returned in 1969 from long years of service with the Kuwait Oil Company, were overhauled for service with the new Portsmouth-based J. F. Airlines Ltd. and in 1972 two former R.A.F. aircraft were civilianised by Flight One Ltd. at Staverton for aerial survey duties as G-AYFA and G-AZHJ.

SPECIFICATION

Manufacturers: Scottish Aviation Ltd., Prestwick Airport, Ayrshire, Scotland.

Power Plants: (Prototype) Two 540 h.p. Alvis Leonides 503/8.
(Series 1) Two 560 h.p. Alvis Leonides 514/8.
Two 560 h.p. Alvis Leonides 514/8A.
(Series 2) Two 600 h.p. Pratt & Whitney Wasp R-1340-S1H1-G.
(Series 3) Two 640 h.p. Alvis Leonides 531.

Dimensions: Span, 76 ft. 6 in. Length, 45 ft. 3 in. Height, 12 ft. 3 in. Wing area, 670 sq. ft.

	Series 1	Series 2	Series 3
Tare weight	9,969 lb.	10,900 lb.	10,200 lb.
All-up weight	14,000 lb.	14,000 lb.	14,600 lb.
Maximum speed	186·5 m.p.h.	186·5 m.p.h.	186·5 m.p.h.
Cruising speed	117·5 m.p.h.	122 m.p.h.	131·25 m.p.h.
Initial climb	750 ft./min.	600 ft./min.	880 ft./min.
Ceiling	17,000 ft.	15,800 ft.	18,000 ft.
Range	670 miles	670 miles	700 miles.

Production: Eighty-seven aircraft comprising 19 initially of British registry, 39 for the R.A.F. and the following for export: (c/n 509) JZ-PPX; (510) JZ-PPY, later PK-GTA; (511) JZ-PPZ, later PK-GTB; (512) OE-BHV, later LN-BFO; (513) EP-AGB, later G-ASHN; (515) EP-AGC, later G-ASJS; (516) EP-AGA, later TF-LOA and CF-STX; (517) VR-OAE; (519) VR-OAF, later 9M-ANC; (556) R.M.A.F. FM1002; (562) PI-C430; (563) FM1004; (564) PI-C431, later XW-PBJ; (565) PI-C432, later XW-PBN; (566) PI-C433, later G-APXL and XW-PBO; (567) PI-C434, later XW-PBP; (568) FM1003; (570) HB-HOX; (578) FM1061; (579) JZ-PPW, later PK-GTC; (580) FM1062; (581) FM1063; (582) FM1071; (583) FM1064; (584) FM1065; (586–590) FM1066–FM1070. Note: (506) test airframe; (569, 585, 591–598) not used.

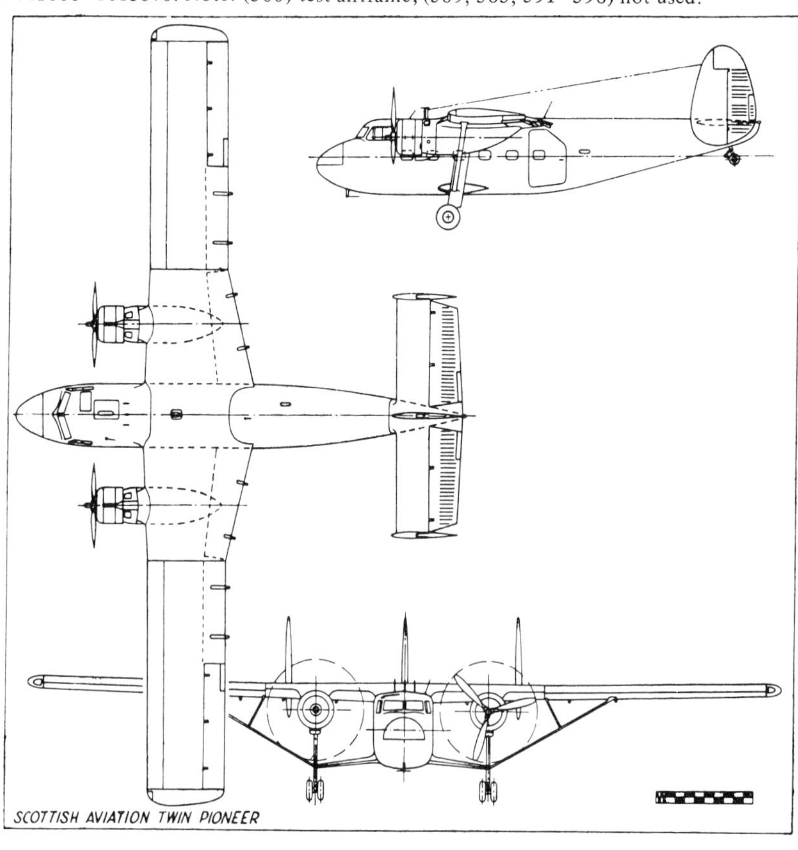
SCOTTISH AVIATION TWIN PIONEER

E. E. Stammers taking off in Mrs. Elliott Lynn's S.E.5A at the start of the Bournemouth Killjoy Trophy Race, 18 April 1927. (*Flight Photo*)

S.E.5A

Designed in 1916 at the Royal Aircraft Factory, Farnborough by H. P. Folland, the S.E.5A was structurally typical of the period with spruce primary structure braced with piano wire and fabric covered, a large proportion of the main production being powered by the 200 h.p. Wolseley Viper engine cooled by a car-type radiator in the nose. A basic design requirement was for the aircraft to be inherently stable and capable of being flown by relatively inexperienced pilots, so that after the 1914–18 war, when vast quantities of S.E.5A airframes, spares and engines were taken over by the Aircraft Disposal Co. Ltd. at Croydon to be reconditioned for sale to foreign air forces, the company also saw it as a potential private or sporting aircraft. Thus in May 1920 the S.E.5A F9022 was stripped of armament, registered G-EATE, and offered for civil use at £700. Eight more, G-EAXQ to 'XX, were then erected and six of them loaned to the Royal Aero Club for the one and only Oxford *v.* Cambridge Air Race, won by Cambridge at Hendon on 16 July 1921.

The first privately owned specimen was G-EAZT fitted with a 90 h.p. R.A.F. IA air-cooled engine for Dr. E. D. Whitehead Reid of Canterbury, who flew from Bekesbourne to land in convenient fields when visiting outlying patients. Underpowered to a degree, it proved very slow, and its short life ended when it stood on its nose and destroyed the front fuselage early in 1923. Its replacement, G-EBCA, secured in time for participation in the Grosvenor Trophy Race at Lympne on 23 June 1923, had a venerable 80 h.p. Renault engine imparting a top speed of some 65 m.p.h.

In civil form the S.E.5A will be associated forever with Major J. C. Savage and skywriting, his first aircraft G-EATE being used by Cyril Turner for the first public demonstration of black smoke writing on 30 May 1922. Smoke producing chemicals were carried in a specially installed tank in the fuselage and could be fed at will into the hot exhaust gases. The smoke was led through a special pipe under the fuselage and the starboard elevator fabric was partly removed to prevent charring but this system was soon superseded by white smoke led through lengthened exhaust pipes to a Y junction at the sternpost. Such pilots as Turner, L. R. Tait-Cox, M. L. Bramson and Sidney St. Barbe, legendary perfectionists in the art of mirror writing in smoke, learned at Hendon by riding the letter shapes in reverse on a bicycle. The advertising value of a word in the sky, often visible over a 50 mile radius, was so immense that to satisfy the demand, which included *Daily Mail*, Players, Ronuk, Persil and Buick contracts, batches G-EBFF to 'FI, 'GJ to 'GM and 'IA to 'IF were converted at Hendon. Eight S.E.5As were shipped to America, where they wrote 'Hello, New York' over the city and were then chartered for a million dollar contract with the American Tobacco Company. They operated as the Skywriting Corporation of America whose fleet eventually numbered 11, five of which were later Americanised with underslung radiators and streamlined, spin polished cowlings. In this form they continued to write 'Lucky Strike' until the end of 1924, when they passed into local ownership and were allotted new constructor's and licence numbers 1–5, NC2677-81 respectively.

The Hendon-based S.E.5As ranged far and wide over the British Isles, G-EBQB and 'QC spent much of their time in Germany, while two others, G-EBQA 'Virgini' and 'VB, were shipped to Melbourne. 'Lux' was written over the city a few times during July 1928 but the venture failed and the S.E.5As were shipped home.

By 1929 the heyday of smoke writing was over and the fleet of tired S.E.5As then dispersed, five to Gesellschaft für Himmelschrift und Wolkenprojektion m.b.H. at Düsseldorf and others to demolition in Coley and Atkinson's yard in Hounslow. The one survivor, G-EBVB, gave itinerant aerobatic displays until 1934.

With the exception of his first machine, Major Savage used only aircraft which had been obtained in new condition from Vickers, Austin and Wolseley, three of the many S.E.5A sub-contractors. Ten other S.E.5As sold by the Aircraft Disposal Co. Ltd. had seen R.A.F. service before entering private ownership, and included Dudley Watt's G-EBOG, Mrs. S. C. Elliott Lynn's 'PA, A. H. Wheeler's 'QM, K. Hunter's 'QK, 1929 Schneider Trophy

Rear view of the original civil S.E.5A G-EATE with prototype skywriting modifications, including underslung smoke stack and cut away elevator fabric. (*Aerofilms Ltd.*)

H. A. Francis (Cambridge) watching A. K. Boeree (Oxford) starting S.E.5A G-EAXV prior to the Oxford and Cambridge Air Race, July 1921. (*O. J. Tapper*)

Short exhaust pipes were retained on S.E.5As reworked for skywriting in the U.S.A. The identity mark G-EBGL is faintly visible on the under fin. (*Real Photographs Company*)

winner H. R. D. Waghorn's 'PD, and G-EBQQ in which Lt. Gwynne Maddocks spun in and was killed at Brooklands on 9 November 1928. Nearly all appeared at the various race meetings held in 1926–27, Flg. Off. A. F. Scroggs winning the Sherburn Private Owners Handicap in 'QK on 1 October 1927, at 113 m.p.h. and Mrs. S. C. Elliott Lynn the Wattle Handicap at the same meeting at 116 m.p.h.

Dudley Watt flew 'OG to victory in the Hotels Handicap at Bournemouth on 18 April 1927, at 114·2 m.p.h. and afterwards rebuilt it as the D.W.1 powered by a 300 h.p. Hispano-Suiza enclosed in a streamlined cowling and cooled by underslung radiators. The rear fuselage decking was also redesigned and built up to form a streamlined headrest. Work on the D.W.1 was done in a shed at Brooklands near the Henderson School of Flying hangars in which two non-standard S.E.5As with air-cooled engines driving four bladed airscrews were erected in 1927. First of these, G-EBTK, belonged to L. R. Oldmeadows and was powered by a 90 h.p. R.A.F. IA. In July 1930 'TK was acquired by Kent Aircraft Services and went to Kingsdown, Kent, and lay dismantled until sold to C. B. Field at Kingswood Knoll, Surrey, in August 1932, but never flew again. The other, 'TO, built for comedian Will Hay, was fitted with a 120 h.p. Airdisco motor and flew from Shoreham until January 1929, when it was purchased by W. L. Handley and moved north to Castle Bromwich.

Today three S.E.5As of the former Savage Skywriting Co. Ltd. are the only survivors. G-EBIA, found hanging fabricless from the roof of the Armstrong Whitworth flight shed at Whitley in 1955, was reconstructed for the Shuttleworth Trust by Farnborough apprentices and staff 1957–59 and flew again on 4 August 1959 in silver as D7000 piloted by Air Commodore

Dr. E. D. Whitehead Reid seated in his Renault engined S.E.5A before the start of the 1923 Grosvenor Trophy Race at Lympne. (*Flight Photo*)

Dudley Watt, wearing his famous black and yellow check helmet, seated in the D.W.1 at Whitchurch, 1930. (*W. K. Kilsby*)

The R.A.F. IA engined S.E.5A built at Brooklands for L. R. Oldmeadows in 1927.

F. G. Miles (centre) with the second S.E.5A replica G-ATGW at Shoreham in August 1965. (*B. P. Lewis*)

A. H. Wheeler. The engine was a 200 h.p. Hispano-Suiza retrieved from the Science Museum store and the aircraft was later camouflaged and given its correct serial F904. G-EBIB, last flown in 1914–18 camouflage at the 1937 Hendon R.A.F. Display by Flt. Lt. R. C. Jonas, now hangs from the roof of the South Kensington Science Museum as F937; and the third, 'IC, repainted as B4563 (later corrected to F938), is exhibited at the R.A.F. Museum, Hendon.

In 1965 two S.E.5A replicas, G-ATGV and 'GW, with steel tube fuselages and 200 h.p. de Havilland Gipsy Queen 30s, were designed, built and flown at Shoreham for the film 'Blue Max' by Miles Marine and Structural Plastics Ltd. under the supervision of F. G. Miles, owner of the genuine G-EBPA back in 1929. For the description of six ·83 scale S.E.5A replicas built by Slingsby for a later film, see Volume 2 page 37.

SPECIFICATION

Manufacturers: (1) The Royal Aircraft Factory, Farnborough, Hants. (2) The Austin Motor Co. (1914) Ltd., Northfield, Birmingham. (3) The Air Navigation and Engineering Co. Ltd., Addlestone, Surrey. (4) Martinsyde Ltd., Brooklands, Byfleet, Surrey. (5) Vickers Ltd., Crayford and Weybridge. (6) Wolseley Motors Ltd., Adderley Park, Birmingham. *(The numbers in parentheses form the key to manufacturers in Appendix E.)*

Power Plants: One 200 h.p. Wolseley Viper.
One 300 h.p. Hispano-Suiza.
One 120 h.p. Airdisco.
One 90 h.p. R.A.F. IA.
One 80 h.p. Renault.

Dimensions: Span, 26 ft. 7½ in. Length, 20 ft. 11 in. Height, 9 ft. 6 in. Wing area, 244 sq. ft.

Weights: (Viper) Tare weight, 1,322 lb. All-up weight, 2,052 lb.
(R.A.F. IA) Tare weight, 1,630 lb. All-up weight 2,050 lb.
(Renault) Tare weight, 1,241 lb. All-up weight 1,829 lb.

**Performance:* Maximum speed, 137 m.p.h. Cruising speed, 100 m.p.h. Initial climb, 1,175 ft./min. Ceiling, 19,500 ft. Range, 250 miles.

* With Wolseley Viper engine.

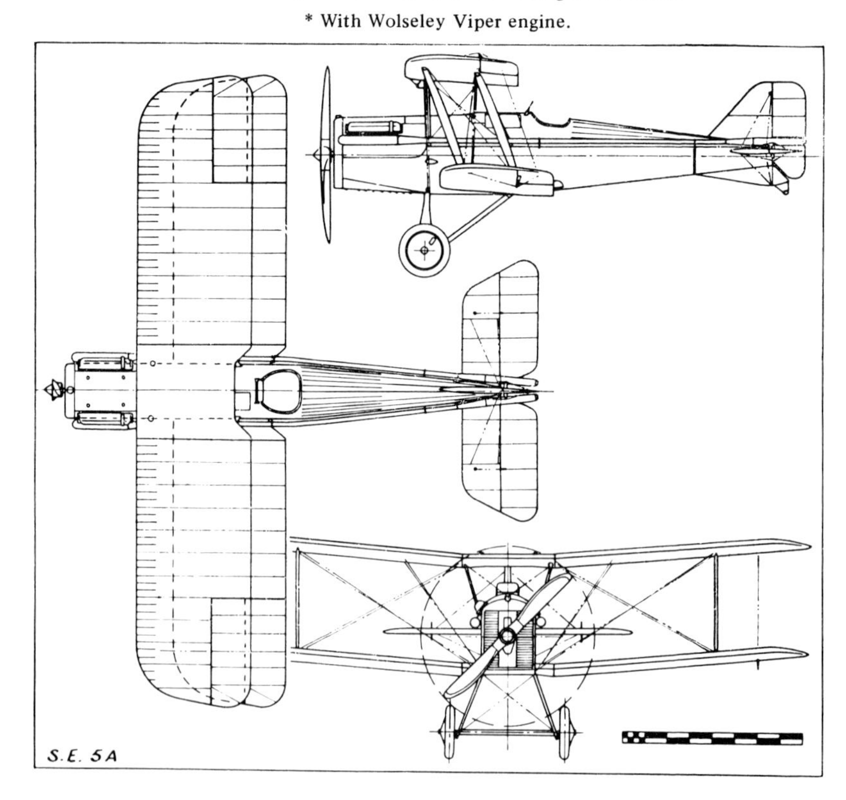

The prototype Calcutta flying with the emergency aerial masts in position on the upper mainplane. (*Flight Photo 5575*)

Short S.8 Calcutta and S.17 Kent

The Calcutta was historically important as the first flying-boat with stressed skin metal hull to go into commercial service, being designed in 1927 by Arthur Gouge for the Mediterranean section of the Imperial Airways route to India, in the light of experience gained with the Singapore I and the metal hulled F.5 of 1924–25. With the exception of certain stainless steel fittings and the fabric covering of flying and control surfaces, the entire structure was of duralumin. Three Jupiter radials gave multi-engined safety and the fuel tanks were located in the upper mainplane to enable smoking to be permitted in the cabin. Comfortable accommodation was provided for 15 passengers, a steward served hot or cold meals from a buffet, and supplementary freight and mail was carried in the rear of the hull.

G-EBVG, first of two aircraft ordered, was first flown by chief test pilot J. Lankester Parker on 21 February 1928, from the Medway outside Short's works at Rochester. After air and seaworthiness tests at the M.A.E.E., Felixstowe, and acceptance tests by the Imperial Airways air superintendent H. G. Brackley, 'VG was flown to London, landing on the Thames at Westminster on 1 August 1928. A three day visit enabled Members of Parliament to inspect an aircraft destined to forge important links in Empire communications. Proving and crew training flights were made to Guernsey on 5 August, Jersey on the 21st, and to Cherbourg on the 27th. The second Calcutta, 'VH, delivered from Rochester to Southampton on 12 September 1928, left two days later on a tour to Stranraer and Liverpool, carrying the Imperial Airways chairman, Sir Eric Geddes. After operating a daily service between Liverpool and Belfast for one week, it joined 'VG in a number of scheduled runs to Jersey over the route formerly operated with Supermarine Sea Eagles.

On 16 April 1929, 'VG left for Genoa to inaugurate the Mediterranean service. Passengers for India flew from Croydon to Basle by A. W. Argosy, thence by sleeping car express to Genoa, continuing by Short Calcutta to Alexandria via Rome, Naples, Corfu, Athens, Suda Bay and Tobruk. The final stage to Karachi was flown by D.H.66 Hercules, the whole service operating to a seven day schedule. A third Calcutta, G-AADN 'City of Rome', was commissioned in March 1929, the originals being allotted the names 'City of Alexandria' and 'City of Athens' respectively, but in the following October 'DN was forced down off Spezia in a gale and foundered with all hands, including the pilot, Capt. Birt.

Four other Calcuttas were also constructed–G-AASJ for Imperial Airways Ltd.; F-AJDB for the Breguet company; an unmarked example for the French Navy; and G-AATZ (replacing G-AADN) which was named 'City of Salonika' following the transference of the flying boat terminal to that port as a result of political unrest in Italy. This differed from the others in having 555 h.p. supercharged Jupiter XFBMs. Brave attempts to fly Argosies to Salonika were defeated by weather and terrain, but eventually the Calcuttas returned to their Italian terminal at Genoa, after a short period at Brindisi. In 1931 the schedule was cut to six days by rerouting via Athens, Haifa and the Sea of Galilee to Baghdad.

G-EBVG at Rochester in September 1935, re-engined with Armstrong Siddeley Tiger VIs as a trainer for Empire Boat pilots. (*Short Bros. Ltd.*)

The Short Kent 'Scipio' at Rochester in February 1931. The large Calcutta and Kent rudders were actuated by small servo units. (*Flight Photo 9846A*)

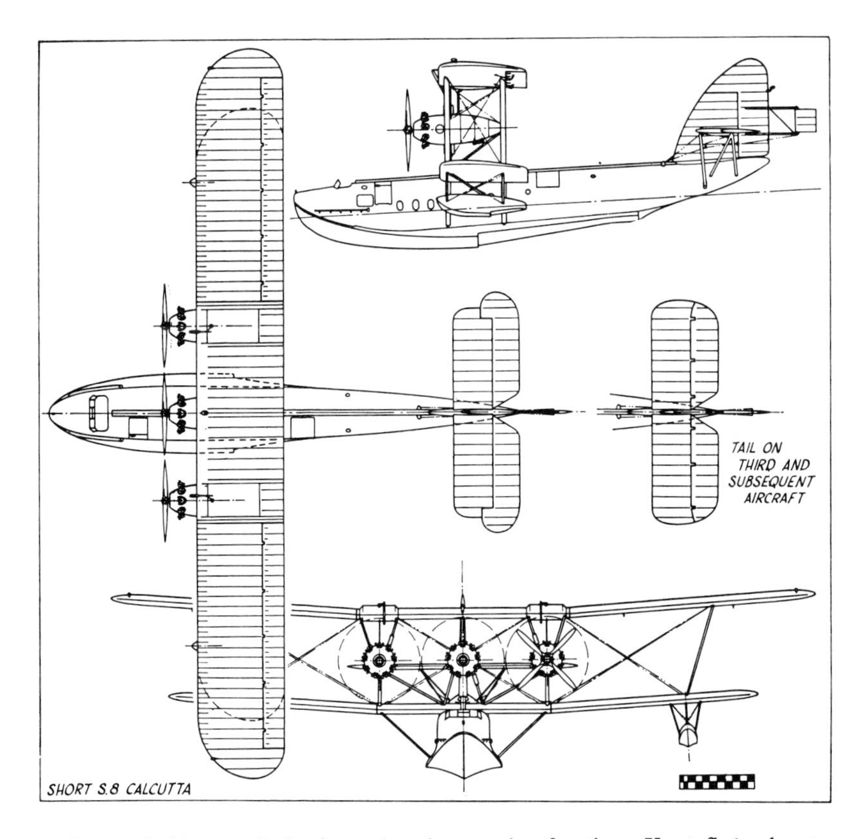

Imperial Airways Ltd. then placed an order for three Kent flying-boats, which were enlarged four engined developments of the Calcutta. Their lower mainplanes were approximately equal in span to the upper mainplanes of their predecessors, the crew was housed in an enclosed cockpit, and 16 passengers enjoyed Pullman comfort in four rows of seats with folding tables. They were considered the most comfortable transports of their age, with room for walking about and a galley for preparing hot meals in the air. The prototype, G-ABFA 'Scipio', made its first flight from the Medway piloted by J. Lankester Parker on 24 February 1931, and it was Short's proud boast that scarcely a single modification was found necessary. After routine trials, 'Scipio' was ferried to the Mediterranean on 5 May 1931, followed 10 days later by 'FB 'Sylvanus'. The third Kent, 'FC 'Satyrus', delivered on 26 May, gained wide publicity by carrying H.R.H. The Prince of Wales on a tour of the Solent area.

As forecast by the name 'City of Khartoum' allotted to Calcutta 'SJ, the difficult Khartoum–Kisumu section of the route to South Africa, opened in January 1932, was operated by Calcuttas released from the Mediterranean by Kents. Their enforced open air life, often in the tropics, had literally no effect on their rugged structures, and by mid-1932 Calcuttas had completed 308,000 miles over the Mediterranean and 186,000 miles along the Upper

Nile. By August 1932 the three Kents had flown 98,270, 90,565 and 77,484 miles respectively on the Brindisi–Alexandria run without a single mechanical breakdown. The combined fleet of seven flying-boats gave uninterrupted service until brought low by a series of tragedies three years later. 'Sylvanus' was set on fire at her moorings at Brindisi by an Italian in November 1935, and a month later Calcutta 'SJ ran out of fuel and made a sudden forced landing from 500 ft. in darkness, and foundered just outside the harbour breakwater at Alexandria. Capt. V. G. Wilson escaped from the open cockpit, but 12 passengers were killed. Eight months later 'Scipio' crashed on alighting at Mirabella, Crete, in exceptionally bad weather, but Capt. A. S. Wilcockson, crew, and all but two passengers escaped.

In September 1935, after more than seven years in the Mediterranean, Calcuttas 'VG and 'TZ were flown to Rochester for conversion to trainers in readiness for the commissioning of the Empire Boats. Flying 'TZ, long ago renamed 'City of Swanage', H. G. Brackley made a number of experimental landings on reservoirs, lakes and rivers in France on the way home, reaching Southampton Water on 1 October 1935.

The prototype, G-EBVG, was re-engined with Tiger radials and spent part of the last year of its flying life with Air Pilots Training Ltd. at Hamble, joining its sister ship 'TZ and a Short S.8/8 Rangoon G-AEIM. The last was externally similar to a Calcutta but equipped with an enclosed cockpit and aft gun positions. First flown in August 1930 as S1433, it had been the first of six Rangoons built for R.A.F. use at Basra on the Persian Gulf. Flown out by R. L. Ragg (later Air Vice Marshal) in February 1931, it returned to Rochester for trainer conversion alongside its civil relatives four years later.

SPECIFICATION

Manufacturers: Short Bros. (Rochester and Bedford) Ltd., Rochester, Kent.

Power Plants: (Calcutta) Three 540 h.p. Bristol Jupiter XIF.
Three 840 h.p. Armstrong Siddeley Tiger VI.
(Rangoon) Three 540 h.p. Bristol Jupiter XIF.
(Kent) Four 555 h.p. Bristol Jupiter XFBM.

	S.8 Calcutta	S.8/8 Rangoon	S.17 Kent
Span	93 ft. 0 in.	93 ft. 0 in.	113 ft. 0 in.
Length	66 ft. 9 in.	66 ft. 9½ in.	78 ft. 5 in.
Height	23 ft. 9 in.	23 ft. 9 in.	28 ft. 0 in.
Wing area	1,825 sq. ft.	1,828 sq. ft.	2,640 sq. ft.
Tare weight	13,845 lb.	14,000 lb.	20,460 lb.
All-up weight	22,500 lb.	22,500 lb.	32,000 lb.
Cruising speed	97 m.p.h.	92 m.p.h.	105 m.p.h.
Initial climb	750 ft./min.	550 ft./min.	840 ft./min.
Ceiling	13,500 ft.	12,000 ft.	17,500 ft.
Range	650 miles	650 miles	450 miles

Production: Thirteen aircraft comprising five for Imperial Airways Ltd. and the following for export or for the R.A.F. under type name Rangoon: (S.751) F-AJDB; (S.755) S1434; (S.756) S1435; (S.757) S1433, later G-AEIM; (S.762) French Navy; (S.764) K2134; (S.765) K2809; (S.780) K3678.

Scion 2 G-ADDN at Southend in 1935. (*A. J. Jackson*)

Short S.16 Scion

In the 1930s the name Short was synonymous with marine aircraft, so that the Scion twin engined cantilever monoplane was a break with tradition. Designed by Arthur Gouge for feeder-line work, it featured a welded steel fuselage and single-spar, fabric-covered metal wing, pilot and five passengers being carried on the power of two uncowled 75 h.p. Pobjoy R radials. The prototype, G-ACJI, first flown at Gravesend by test pilot J. Lankester Parker on 18 August 1933, had a flat top to the rear fuselage, but during the following month a large curved decking was added and became standard. Completion of the first production aircraft, G-ACUV, powered by closely cowled 90 h.p. Pobjoy Niagara Is, was rushed through in time for the same pilot to demonstrate its remarkable quietness at the Hendon S.B.A.C. Show on 1 July 1934. Three others, G-ACUW–'UY, completed in the seaplane works later in 1934, included 'UX equipped with twin floats for export to Port Moresby, Papua. Its long and active life came to an end as a landplane with Marshall Airways, giving pleasure flights at Sydney in 1954.

Well planned flight trials with the early Scions, including 1,082 scheduled flights by the prototype from Rochester to Southend between June and September 1934, led to a 1935 model known as the Scion 2. The nacelles were raised to bring the thrust line level with the leading edge of the wing, a sixth passenger seat was added and considerable improvements were made to cockpit and cabin glazing. The first Scion 2, G-ACUZ, sold to Nottingham Airport Ltd. via Airwork Ltd., was followed by a batch of 15 constructed in the company's new works at Rochester Airport.

During 1935–36 an hourly service between Southend and Rochester was operated jointly by Shorts with Scion 1 G-ACUY and Southend Flying Services Ltd. with Scion 2 G-ADDN. G-ADDO was based at Shoreham by Olley Air Service Ltd. for pleasure flights and occasional jockey transport, and 'DS was sold to Adelaide Airways in South Australia. In the North, 'DP served West of Scotland Airways Ltd. on a route from Renfrew to the Island of Mull, the first Scion 1, 'UV, operated in the Orkneys with Aberdeen Airways Ltd. and the prototype, 'JI, settled down at Yeadon with Yorkshire

Airways Ltd., after a season's joyriding with C. W. A. Scott's Air Display piloted by L. J. Rimmer. The last of the batch of Scion 2s, G-ADDV and 'DX, were operated respectively by Ramsgate and Plymouth Airports Ltd., giving pleasure flights to thousands of holidaymakers in their day. In 1938 'DV went to Ipswich and ran a daily service to Clacton and the Scottish 'DP went to Squires Gate for joyriding with Williams and Company.

Two more Scion 2s were delivered to Adelaide Airways 1935–36 in Australian marks as VH-UVQ and 'TV but whereas the first was withdrawn from use in December 1939, 'TV survived a crash at Meekathara, W.A., on 17 January 1951 and was rebuilt with 90 h.p. D.H. Gipsy Minor in-line engines at Alice Springs by Connellan Airways Ltd. with whom it was still flying in 1965. In 1973 it was stored at the Cliff Douglas Museum in Queensland.

The sole long distance flight by a Scion began at Croydon on 21 January 1936, when C. E. Gardner left for India in the Pobjoy company's machine 'DT. Before its return on 13 March, 15,932 miles were covered, including 1,500 miles at full throttle to come 6th in the Viceroy's Cup Race at Delhi on 14 February. The aircraft then went on tour with Campbell Black's Air Display.

Gouge trailing edge flaps designed for the new Short Empire Boats were air tested in 1935 on the Scion 2 G-ADDR fitted with a tapered wooden wing and flown under B conditions as M-3 but preoccupation with the Empire

The prototype Scion in its original condition without rear decking. (*Short Bros. Ltd.*)

Scion 1 floatplane G-ACUX of Papuan Concessions Ltd. flying over the Medway, February 1935. (*Short Bros. Ltd.*)

Connellan Airways' Scion 2 VH-UTV in service with 90 h.p. de Havilland Gipsy Minors in 1965. (*A. E. Flanders*)

Boat contract finally resulted in Scion production being handed over to the Pobjoy company, which built the last six aircraft. These were near-identical with the Short-built machines, but carried the amended type number S.16/1. Two were exported to Palestine Airways Ltd., but the others were of British registry, the first, G-AEIL, going to Khormaksar, Aden, for service with Arabian Airways Ltd. Here it joined the company's first Scion, G-AEOY, which had been built from the crashed remains of that exported to Adelaide Airways two years previously. The second Pobjoy Scion, G-AEJN, entered private ownership at Gatwick, initially with C. G. M. Alington and in 1939 with E. D. Spratt. The final Scion, G-AEZF, went to Freetown, Sierra Leone, to operate on floats with Elders Colonial Airways Ltd. Returning by sea, it became a civil communications aircraft with No. 24 E.F.T.S. at Barton-in-the-Clay, Beds., in November 1941, continuing in the same employ until demobilised at Sealand in 1945. After a brief period of post-war activity at Exeter and elsewhere, 'ZF lapsed into unserviceability at Croydon and was eventually dismantled at Redhill before being sent by road to Southend on 2 June 1959 where it was allowed to lapse into dereliction.

From April 1935 a daily passenger and mail service was operated between Barnstaple and Lundy Island by Lundy and Atlantic Coast Air Lines Ltd. with Scion 1 G-ACUW. Four years later it was joined by Pobjoy Scion G-AETT and the service continued until the latter crashed in February 1940. The survivor, in common with the majority of Scions, was then impressed for R.A.F. war service. A number were overhauled at Gatwick during the war, and 'JN eventually became an instructional airframe at Kemble, but thereafter all but 'ZF faded into obscurity.

SPECIFICATION

Manufacturers: Short Bros. (Rochester and Bedford) Ltd., Seaplane Works, Rochester, and Rochester Airport, Kent; Pobjoy Airmotors and Aircraft Ltd., Rochester Airport, Kent.

Power Plants:
(Prototype) Two 75 h.p. Pobjoy R.
(Scion 1) Two 85 h.p. Pobjoy Niagara I or II.
(Scion 2) Two 90 h.p. Pobjoy Niagara III.
Two 90 h.p. de Havilland Gipsy Minor.

Dimensions: Span, 42 ft. 0 in. Length, 31 ft. 6 in. Height, 10 ft. $4\frac{1}{2}$ in. Wing area, 255·3 sq. ft.

	Prototype	Scion 1	Scion 2
Tare weight	1,700 lb.	1,710 lb.	1,770 lb.
All-up weight	3,000 lb.	3,050 lb.	3,200 lb.
Maximum speed	117 m.p.h.	125 m.p.h.	128 m.p.h.*
Cruising speed	90 m.p.h.	102 m.p.h.	116 m.p.h.
Initial climb	600 ft./min.	600 ft./min.	625 ft./min.
Ceiling	11,500 ft.	13,000 ft.	13,000 ft.
Range	360 miles	380 miles	390 miles

* Floatplane 117 m.p.h.

Production: (a) Short-built

Prototype and four Scion 1s, nine British registered Scion 2s and the following for export: (c/n S.791) VH-UVQ; (S.793) VH-UTV.

(b) Pobjoy-built

Four British registered aircraft and the following for export: (c/n PA.1001) VQ-PAA; (PA.1002) VQ-PAB. Note: c/n PA.1006 and PA.1007 were allotted to naval spotter projects which were not built.

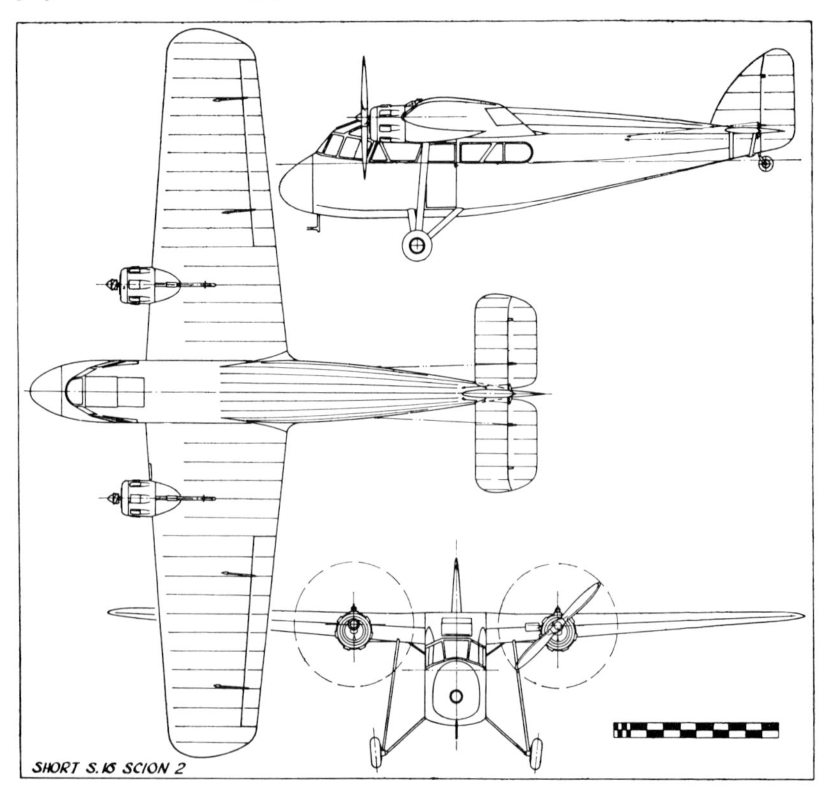

Short S.23 Empire Flying Boat 'Cavalier' moored at Baltimore in 1938.
(via C. H. Barnes)

Short S.23 Empire Flying Boat

A British Government decision made in 1934, to carry all mail without surcharge by air within the Empire, called for a fleet of fast aircraft capable of handling vastly increased loads. Short's team, led by Arthur Gouge, was designing an all-metal flying-boat with monocoque hull of considerable beauty of line, mounting a metal-clad, tapered, cantilever wing carrying four Bristol Pegasus XC radials driving three bladed de Havilland variable-pitch airscrews. Electrically operated Gouge retractable trailing edge flaps were incorporated to improve take-off and to reduce the landing speed by some 12 m.p.h., and the 3½ ton payload included 1½ tons of mail and 24 day passengers, with alternative 16 sleeping berth layout, while on long flights passengers were able to stroll into a promenade lounge. Traditional pilots' cockpits disappeared in favour of a spacious crew cabin for captain, first officer, navigator and flight clerk, and a steward's pantry was situated amidships.

It was a remarkable design, far ahead of its day, and Imperial Airways Ltd. took the unprecedented step of ordering 28 straight from the drawing-board. This far sighted decision was fully vindicated on 4 July 1936, when test pilot J. Lankester Parker took the prototype, 'Canopus', C Class flagship, on a trouble-free maiden flight at Rochester. Empire Boats were, without question, the most famous and successful of all pre-war civil transports, due to Short's carefully planned tank, wind tunnel and practical flying tests. Scale model Gouge trailing edge flaps had been flight tested on a Scion, while the handling qualities had been reproduced in advance with the four motor Scion Senior, aerodynamically a half scale Empire Boat.

'Canopus' was ferried to Genoa by H. G. Brackley on 22 October 1936, and went into service over the Mediterranean on the 31st, the rest of the fleet following at an average rate of two per month. From 4 February 1937, regular services on the Empire routes began at Hythe, the last of the old overland schedules terminating at Croydon on 4 March. In conjunction with Qantas Empire Airways, the Empire Boats flew right through to Sydney and from 28 June 1937, superseded the miscellaneous aircraft operating in

Africa when 'Centaurus', Capt. F. L. Bailey, opened a through service to Durban. The fourth boat, 'Cavalier', was shipped to Bermuda and there assembled for the service to New York which opened on 25 May 1937. By 1938 Empire Boats were flying seven services a week to Egypt, four to India, three to East Africa and two each to South Africa, Malaya, Hong Kong and Australia. Increases in mail reduced the passengers carried to 17, an extra half ton of mail occupying the forward cabin.

Government plans for a transatlantic mail service led to the completion of the second boat 'Caledonia' with long range tanks and strengthened for operation at an all-up weight of 45,000 lb. Capts. W. N. Cumming and A. S. Wilcockson took it from Hythe to Alexandria on 18 December 1936, and flew back to Marseilles, a distance of 1,700 miles, nonstop in $11\frac{1}{4}$ hours. Experimental long distance trials continued with 2,300 mile non-stop flights on 17 February and 4 March 1937, between Hythe and Alexandria and back, a distance 400 miles greater than from Ireland to Newfoundland. The first ocean crossing without payload was made from Foynes to Botwood by Capt. A. S. Wilcockson on the night of 5–6 July 1937, arriving at New York three days later. A second long range boat, 'Cambria', made similar survey flights on 29 July and 27 August, 'Caledonia' completing the series with crossings on 15 August and 13 September.

Three additional Empire Boats, initially of British registry, G-AFBJ to 'BL, were delivered to Qantas Empire Airways at the beginning of 1938, joining three others, G-AEUG–'UI, which, after initial transfer to Qantas in August 1937, returned temporarily to Imperial Airways Ltd. in January 1938 before finally settling down under Australian ownership six months later. The close ties between the joint operators were further emphasised in September 1939 when two Australian boats 'Corio' and 'Coorong' reverted to British marks in exchange for 'Centaurus' and 'Calypso'. The Australian deliveries brought the final total of S.23 boats to 31, but in the first two years of operation the ranks were sadly depleted by the loss of 'Capricornus', 'Courtier', 'Cygnus', 'Calpurnia', 'Capella', 'Challenger', 'Cavalier' and 'Centurion' in major fatal crashes. Shortest lived of all Empire Boats, 'Capricornus', Capt. Paterson, crashed in the Beaujolais Mountains in France on 24 March 1937, soon after leaving Hythe on its maiden service flight.

The long range Short S.30 flying boat 'Cabot' taking off at Rochester on its maiden flight, 27 November 1938. (*Short Bros. Ltd.*)

Short S.30 flying boat G-AEUI 'Coorong' on the Nile in B.O.A.C. wartime livery. (*B.O.A.C.*)

Short S.30 G-AFCZ at Hythe, July 1939, bearing its original name 'Australia'. (*B.O.A.C.*)

Eight S.30 boats powered by Bristol Perseus XIIC sleeve valve radials and strengthened for operation at an all-up weight of 48,000 lb. were delivered in 1938–39. The first four, intended for transatlantic services, were fitted for flight refuelling and cleared for flight, and later take-off, at a maximum weight of 53,000 lb. 'Connemara', lost in a refuelling fire at Hythe a few weeks after delivery, was replaced by 'Cathay' in the following year. The S.30s 'Cabot' and 'Caribou' inaugurated the North Atlantic mail route on 8 August 1939, completing eight round trips before war intervened, additional fuel being taken on from Harrow tankers over Foynes and Botwood (see Volume 2, page 343). Together with Capts. Gordon Store, S. G. Long and crews, they were impressed in October 1939 and worked with No. 119 Squadron from Invergordon and Islay on early A.S.V. radar trials. Both were attacked and sunk by German aircraft at Bodø, Norway, in May 1940 while disembarking an R.A.F. radar unit. Their replacements were the S.23 boats 'Clio' and 'Cordelia', which, equipped with four dorsal radar masts, tail and dorsal gun turrets at Belfast, were redesignated S.23M and spent 1941 patrolling between Loch Indail and Iceland.

Three S.30 boats, laid down as 'Captain Cook', 'Canterbury' and 'Cumberland', were sold before completion to Tasman Empire Airways Ltd. Two, renamed 'Awarua' and 'Aotearoa', operated on the Auckland–Sydney route for 7½ years with over 90% regularity, the first service being flown by Capt. J. W. Burgess in 'Aotearoa' on 30 April 1940. The third boat 'Australia', eventually retained by Imperial Airways, was seriously damaged on take-off from Basra on 9 August 1939, returned to England, was renamed 'Clare' and fitted with long range tanks. 'Clyde', originally built to replace the ill-fated 'Cavalier' on the New York–Bermuda route, then joined 'Clare', six return crossings of the Atlantic with passengers being made in 1940. Italy's entry into the war closed the Mediterranean and the majority of boats were transferred to Durban including 'Corsair', which had been forced down by fuel shortage and bad weather on a small river at Faraje in the Belgian Congo in March 1939. Holed by a rock, it required an epic of engineering skill to repair it and dam the river, before Capt. J. C. Kelly Rogers brought it out of the jungle on 6 January 1940. The fleet also included 'Clifton' and 'Cleopatra', the last Empire Boats to be built. Carrying the type number S.33, they were hybrids with Pegasus XC engines and hulls strengthened for a maximum take-off weight of 53,000 lb.

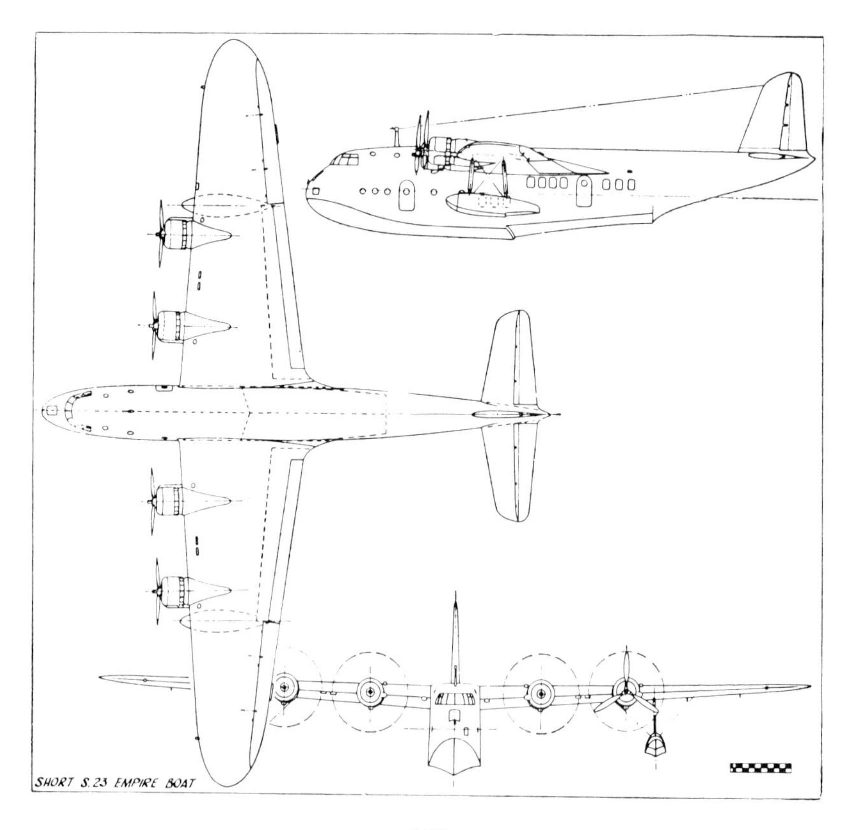
SHORT S.23 EMPIRE BOAT

From this new base at Durban, the Horseshoe Route was operated through East Africa, India and Malaya to Australia. Promenade decks and luxury equipment were removed, seating was increased to 29 and the maximum take-off weight of the S.23s increased to 43,500 lb. 'Champion', 'Clare' and 'Cathay' remained at Poole, and during 1941 worked the Poole–Foynes shuttle; to West Africa; and between October 1941 and March 1942 on the hazardous Gibraltar–Malta–Cairo lifeline. The fleet of Empire Boats was irrevocably split by the Japanese occupation of Malaya in 1942, and the story of those marooned in Antipodean waters, told in graphic detail in E. Bennett Bremner's *'Frontline Airline'*, is one of supreme sacrifice by man and machine under appalling conditions. Ten of these noble craft, including three loaned to the R.A.A.F., fell victim of Japanese attack. Nearer home, 'Cambria' and 'Coorong' evacuated 469 British troops from Crete to Alexandria in 1941.

Thirteen S.23, S.30 and S.33 boats survived the war, having been fitted, for spares economy, with 1,010 h.p. Pegasus XXII radials similar to those fitted to the Corporation's newer Sunderlands. Their useful lives were, however, drawing to a close. 'Castor', stripped of camouflage, flew the last Karachi–Cairo Horseshoe Service on 15 January 1947, and the Hythe–Durban route closed down at the end of the year. As Cs. of A. expired, the veterans were broken up on Southampton Water, one of the first to go being the mighty 'Canopus' herself. At the end of 1947 the same fate overtook her sister craft in the Antipodes. 'Aotearoa' made its 442nd and final Tasman crossing on 29 October and retired in Auckland as a coffee bar, and 'Coriolanus' was broken up at Rose Bay, Sydney, after her last scheduled flight on the Fiji–Sydney route of Qantas on 23 December. In 11 years of service the Empire Boats flew a grand total of 37,779,242 miles, over two million of which were flown by 'Canopus'.

SPECIFICATION

Manufacturers: Short Bros. (Rochester and Bedford) Ltd., Seaplane Works, Rochester, Kent.

Power Plants:
(S.23) Four 920 h.p. Bristol Pegasus XC.
Four 1,010 h.p. Bristol Pegasus XXII.
(S.30) Four 890 h.p. Bristol Perseus XII.
(S.33) Four 920 h.p. Bristol Pegasus XC.
Four 1,010 h.p. Bristol Pegasus XXII.

Dimensions: Span, 114 ft. 0 in. Length, 88 ft. 0 in. Height, 31 ft. $9\frac{3}{4}$ in. Wing area, 1,500 sq. ft.

Weights:
(S.23) Tare weight, 23,500 lb. All-up weight, 40,500 lb.*
(S.30) Tare weight, 27,180 lb. All-up weight, 48,000 lb.†
(S.33) Tare weight, 27,180 lb. All-up weight, 53,000 lb.

Performance: Maximum speed, 200 m.p.h. Cruising speed, 165 m.p.h. Initial climb, 950 ft./min. Ceiling, 20,000 ft. Range (S.23 and S.33), 760 miles; (S.30), 1,300 miles; ('Caledonia' and 'Cambria'), 3,300 miles; ('Cavalier'), 1,500 miles; ('Cabot' and 'Caribou'), 2,500 miles.

* Later 43,500 lb.
† 'Cabot' and 'Caribou' 53,000 lb. airborne.

Production: Thirty-one S.23; nine S.30; three S.33 (only two completed).

'Golden Hind' taking off on its maiden flight, piloted by J. Lankester Parker, June 1939. (*Flight Photo 17529S*)

Short S.26

'Golden Hind', launched in June 1939, was the first of three Short S.26 G Class flying-boats ordered by Imperial Airways Ltd. for non-stop mail services across the Atlantic. The second and third boats, laid down as 'Grenville' and 'Grenadier', were completed as G-AFCJ 'Golden Fleece' and G-AFCK 'Golden Horn'. Although developed from, and superficially resembling an Empire Boat, the S.26 was considerably larger and embodied the four-crew control cabin and modified rear step of the Sunderland I. Power was supplied by four Bristol Hercules IV sleeve valve engines driving three bladed de Havilland constant speed airscrews, and normal tankage gave a cruising range of over 3,000 miles.

When war brought transatlantic aspirations to an end, the three S.26 boats and their crews were commandeered as X8275, X8274 and X8273 respectively for long range reconnaissance duties with No. 119 Squadron, based first at Invergordon and later in Islay and West Africa. Military modifications, carried out at Rochester, included tail and dorsal Boulton and Paul gun turret installations, internal depth charge housing and full camouflage after which the boats were ferried to Blackburn Aircraft Ltd. at Dumbarton for radar installation.

'Golden Fleece', which had been launched as X8274, having carried civil marking G-AFCJ only during assembly, was lost in a forced alighting off Finisterre in August 1941 when two motors failed together, the surviving crew being picked up by an enemy submarine.

Only two S.26s therefore returned to civil life under B.O.A.C. ownership when the squadron disbanded at Pembroke Dock at the end of the year and these were reconditioned and fitted for the carriage of 40 passengers, receiving civil certificates of airworthiness for the first time in 1942. Tail cones removed during military conversion had been lost, and both boats retained the rear gun-turret housing. Based at Poole, they reinforced the service operating through Lisbon, Bathurst, Accra and Freetown to Lagos, the long range S.26 being particularly suited to the 13-hour Lisbon–Bathurst stage.

During a test flight after an engine change at Lisbon on 9 January 1943, 'Golden Horn' suffered an engine fire and crashed into the Tagus with the loss of 13 occupants, including Capt. J. H. Lock, pioneer Hillman, Imperial Airways and Railway Air Services pilot. 'Golden Hind' was then relegated to the Poole–Foynes shuttle until it emerged from a third conversion at Hythe in 1944, equipped to full airline standard for 38 passengers and seven crew. Capt. Mollard then flew it to Durban for operation between Mombasa, Madagascar, Seychelles and Ceylon. After the war it was fitted with Hercules XIV motors at Belfast as conversion SH.42C and ended its airline days on the occasional Poole–Athens–Cairo service which it inaugurated on 30 September 1946 flown by Capt. Dudley Travers.

'Golden Horn' being launched at Lisbon after wing-tip float repairs, January 1943. Note the disused rear gun turret.

On retirement at the end of 1947, the ageing 'Golden Hind' was ferried to Rochester and passed first into the hands of F. J. Cork of Gillingham, Kent, and later to Buchan Marine Services Ltd. 'Golden Hind' remained at her moorings outside the former seaplane works for five years, maintained in serviceable condition with a watchman aboard. Plans to use her on tourist flights abroad came to nought, and in October 1953 the old aircraft was sold to F. C. Bettison and towed away for overhaul at Hamble. The tow ended in the Swale at Harty Ferry, where 'Golden Hind', last of the pre-1940 flying-boats, was sunk in a gale in May 1954.

SPECIFICATION

Manufacturers: Short Bros. (Rochester and Bedford) Ltd., Seaplane Works, Rochester, Kent.

Power Plants: Four 1,380 h.p. Bristol Hercules IV.
Four 1,380 h.p. Bristol Hercules XIV.

Dimensions: Span, 134 ft. 4 in. Length, 101 ft. 4 in. Height, 37 ft. 7 in. Wing area, 2,160 sq. ft.

Weights: Tare weight, 37,700 lb. All-up weight, 73,500 lb.

Performance: Maximum speed, 209 m.p.h. Cruising speed, 180 m.p.h. Range, 3,200 miles.

Production: Three aircraft only: (c/n S.871) G-AFCI; (S.872) G-AFCJ; (S.873) G-AFCK.

A Sunderland 3, later 'Hamilton', in wartime civil colours, at moorings, Lagos 1943. (*B.O.A.C.*)

Short S.25 Sunderland 3 and Sandringham

R.A.F. Sunderland 3 flying-boats powered by four Pegasus XVIII motors, carrying priority passengers and mail on joint B.O.A.C. and Transport Command routes in 1942, were stripped of all armament and fitted with bench-type seats. Gun turrets were replaced by bulbous fairings, the nose fairing being retractable for mooring purposes. From January 1943 they gradually assumed civil markings and went into B.O.A.C. service between Poole and West Africa, and late in the following year a 5,039-mile proving flight, carrying seven passengers and freight, was made to Karachi in 28 hours flying time. It marked the beginning of B.O.A.C. research into the aircraft's flying attitude and power output which eventually halved England–India flight times. After VE Day the Sunderlands were stripped of camouflage, engines were upgraded to Pegasus 38 (later 48), and the interiors modified for the carriage of 24 day or 16 night passengers and 6,500 lb. of mail. They were then known as the Hythe Class, 18 being converted by B.O.A.C. at Hythe and four by Shorts at Belfast in readiness for the reopening of the Empire routes. The Singapore service was reintroduced on 31 January 1946, and on 22 February 'Hythe' arrived at Sydney in the record time of 54 hours and continued to Auckland with V.I.P. passengers. A Poole–Calcutta Sunderland service was withdrawn on 12 May 1946, and replaced by the first post-war through service to Sydney. Inaugural east- and west-bound flights were made by B.O.A.C. and Qantas crews in 'Hudson' and 'Henley' respectively, operating to a 5½-day schedule. A memorable year of Sunderland achievement included the reopening of the Dragon route from Poole to Hong Kong by 'Hamilton' on 24 August.

Simple conversion of military airframes was not sufficient to exploit fully the Sunderland's commercial potential, and in 1945 'Himalaya' returned to Rochester for extensive remodelling by Shorts. It emerged as the Sandringham 1 with S.26 type nose and tail and the whole interior reconstructed with two decks, dining-saloon, cocktail bar and accommodation for 24 day or 16 night passengers. Initially flown in Transport Command markings as OQZF/ML788, its public debut before returning to B.O.A.C. was made as

G-AGKX at the Victory Air Pageant, Eastleigh, on 22 June 1946, and at Farnborough a week later. It was the only Sandringham 1, but a considerable number of similar conversions were made to Twin Wasp engined Sunderland 5s by Short Bros. and Harland Ltd. at Belfast 1945–48.

'Argentina', 'Uruguay' and 'Paraguay', designated Short S.25/V Sandringham 2, built to the order of the Argentine operator Dodero, carried 45 day passengers with cocktail bar on the upper deck. They were ferried under British marks by B.O.A.C. crews, 'Argentina', Capt. Dudley Travers, reaching Buenos Aires on 25 November 1945, after covering the 7,330 miles from Poole in 45 hours 47 minutes flying time. Two similar boats, 'Brazil' and 'Ingleterra', also flown out, were Sandringham 3s with dining saloon and galley on the upper deck and 21 passenger seats on the lower. G-AGWW and 'WX, delivered by air early in 1946 to the Uruguayan airline CAUSA and the Argentine ALFA respectively, were Sunderland 3s with Sandringham interiors, but were without special designation.

The South American boats were joined in 1946 by a Sandringham 2, G-AHRE 'Paraguay' (later LV-ACT) for Dodero; a Sunderland 5, CX-AKR 'Capitan Bosio Lanza', for CAUSA; and two further Sunderland 5s, LV-AHG 'Uruguay' and 'HH 'Rio de la Plata', for Aerolineas Argentinas which had taken over the Dodero fleet.

In the same year four Sandringham 4s, ZK-AMB 'Tasman'; ZK-AMD 'Australia'; ZK-AME 'New Zealand'; and ZK-AMH 'Auckland', were equipped to carry 30 day passengers to replace the aged Empire Flying Boats of Tasman Empire Airways Ltd. and in 1947 New Zealand National Airways Ltd. converted three R.N.Z.A.F. Sunderlands, NZ4102–NZ4104, as ZK-AMF, 'MG and 'MK for scheduled services between Auckland and Fiji. A route between Sydney and Lord Howe Island was operated by Trans-Oceanic Airways Ltd. with three ex R.A.A.F. Sunderland 3s, A26-2/ML731, A26-4/ML733, and A26-5/ML734, which served as VH-BKQ 'Pacific Star', 'KO 'Australia', and 'KP 'Tahiti Star' respectively until 1952.

Three Sandringham 6s (37 day passengers and radar) LN-IAU 'Bamse Brakar'; 'AV 'Kvitbjørn', and 'AW 'Bukken Bruse' delivered to the Norwegian airline D.N.L. in 1948 for their Oslo-Tromsø service and later lost in crashes, were replaced by LN-LAI 'Jutulen' and LN-LMK 'Polarbjørn', the latter being sold to Aerolineas Argentinas in 1955 as LV-AHM 'Almirante Zar'.

CX-AKR, the Sunderland 5 for CAUSA, being launched at Belfast in 1948.
(via C. H. Barnes)

B.O.A.C. took delivery of nine Twin Wasp powered Sandringham 5s during 1947. These were known as the Plymouth Class and carried 22 day or 16 night passengers. The second aircraft, G-AHYZ 'Perth', damaged beyond repair during conversion at Belfast, was replaced by G-AJMZ with the same

'Helmsdale', final B.O.A.C. Sunderland 3, was a freighter which retained the wartime bomb doors and had only two additional windows. (*E. J. Riding*)

The second Dodero Sandringham 2 'Uruguay' on Belfast Lough in December 1945. (*Short Bros. and Harland Ltd.*)

British Overseas Airways Corporation's Sandringham 5 'Portmarnock'. (*E. J. Riding*)

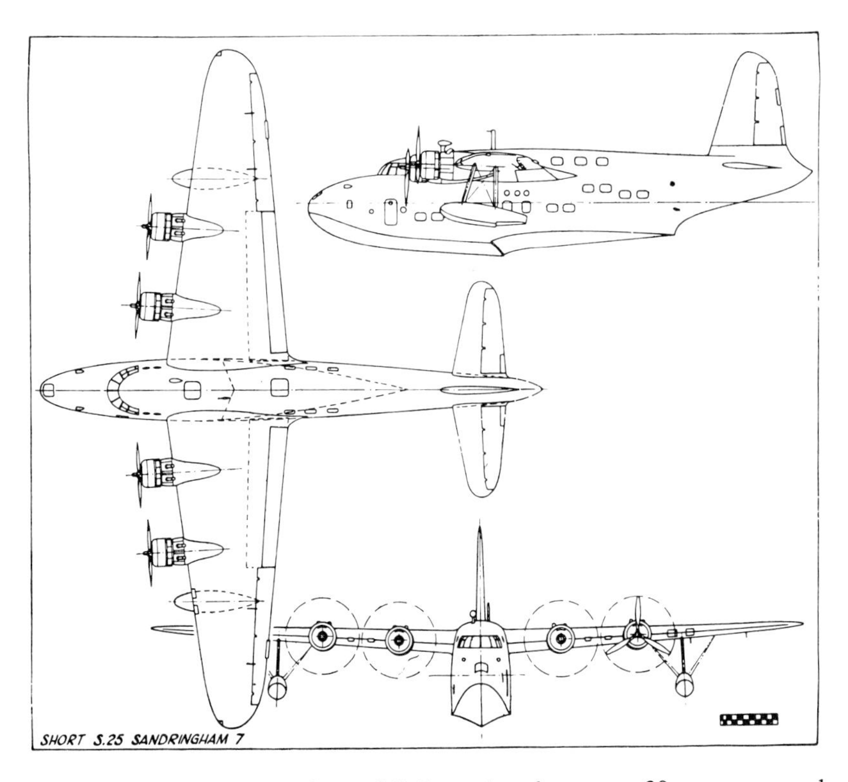

name. Three final Sandringhams, Mk.7s equipped to carry 30 passengers and known as the Bermuda Class, were then added to the B.O.A.C. fleet.

In 1949 the Sunderlands were replaced by Constellations after covering 10 million miles and carrying 31,000 passengers on the Australia route alone. In the same year Sandringhams were superseded on Far East routes by Canadair C-4s, after flying nearly six million miles in the Corporation's employ. Three Sunderlands, 'Hampshire', 'Haslemere' and 'Halstead', sold to Aquila Airways Ltd., were thereafter maintained at Hamble, but used Berth 50, Southampton, when making 6, 118 and 141 sorties respectively to the Havel Lake, during the Berlin Air Lift, 26 June 1948 to 6 October 1949. Seven more B.O.A.C. Sunderlands and the Sandringham 1 were then acquired, some for scheduled services to Madeira and the Canary Islands and others for reduction to spares. An R.A.F. Sunderland 5, PP162, ferried to Hamble in 1953, was destroyed in a storm before conversion to G-ANAK, so that, paradoxically, the last Sunderland to remain in service was 'Hadfield', the first ever civilianised. Three former B.O.A.C. Sandringham 3s went to the Pacific in Qantas service, and two Sandringham 7s joined their sister ships in Uruguay. The third, 'St. George', was overhauled at Cowes by Saunders-Roe Ltd. for Capt. Sir Gordon P. G. ('Bill') Taylor, who took delivery on 14 October 1954, afterwards flying home to Australia to inaugurate a series of South Seas flying boat cruises. It was sold later to Réseau Aérien Inter-insulaire as F-OBIP.

The T.E.A.L. Sandringhams were sold to Ansett Airways 1949–50 as VH-BRC, 'RD, VH-EBW and 'BX and later joined by former B.O.A.C. boats VH-EBV/G-AHZD and 'BY/G-AHZF. All but VH-BRC 'Beachcomber' were wrecked by tropical storms but services were maintained with this and an R.N.Z.A.F. Sunderland 5, NZ4108, which Ansett converted to near-Sandringham standard at Rose Bay, Sydney in 1963 as VH-BRF 'Islander'. This aircraft was still operational in 1973.

SPECIFICATION

Manufacturers: Short Bros. (Rochester and Bedford) Ltd., Seaplane Works, Rochester, Kent and Windermere, Cumberland; Short Bros. and Harland Ltd., Queen's Island, Belfast, N.I.; Blackburn Aircraft Ltd., Dumbarton, Dunbartonshire.

Power Plants:
(Sunderland 3) Four 1,030 h.p. Bristol Pegasus XVIII, 38 or 48.
(Sandringham 1) Four 1,030 h.p. Bristol Pegasus 38.
(Sandringham 2) Four 1,200 h.p. Pratt & Whitney Twin Wasp R-1830-92.
(Sandringham 3) Four 1,200 h.p. Pratt & Whitney Twin Wasp R-1830-92B.
(Sandringham 4) Four 1,200 h.p. Pratt & Whitney Twin Wasp R-1830-92C.
(Sandringham 5,6,7) Four 1,200 h.p. Pratt & Whitney Twin Wasp R-1830-92D.

	Sunderland 3	Sandringham 1	Sandringham 2 and 3	Sandringham 5 and 7
Span	112 ft. 9½ in.	112 ft. 9½ in.	112 ft. 9½ in.	112 ft. 9½ in.
Length	88 ft. 6¾ in.	85 ft. 4¼ in.	86 ft. 3 in.	86 ft. 3 in.
Height	22 ft. 10½ in.	22 ft. 10½ in.	22 ft. 10½ in.	22 ft. 10½ in.
Wing area	1,687 sq. ft.	1,687 sq. ft.	1,687 sq. ft.	1,687 sq. ft.
Tare weight	35,862 lb.	34,150 lb.	41,370 lb.	39,498 lb.
All-up weight	50,000 lb.	56,000 lb.	56,000 lb.	60,000 lb.
Maximum speed	178 m.p.h.	216 m.p.h.	238 m.p.h.	206 m.p.h.
Cruising speed	165 m.p.h.	184 m.p.h.	221 m.p.h.	176 m.p.h.
Initial climb	720 ft./min.	557 ft./min.	1,000 ft./min.	840 ft./min.
Ceiling	16,000 ft.	16,150 ft.	21,300 ft.	17,900 ft.
Range	2,350 miles	2,550 miles	2,410 miles	2,440 miles

Conversions by Short and Harland Ltd., Belfast:

(a) Sandringham 2: Three British registered aircraft G-AGPT, 'PZ and G-AHRE.

(b) Sandringham 3: Two British registered aircraft G-AGPY and 'TZ.

(c) Sandringham 4: Four aircraft initially for T.E.A.L.: (c/n SH.30C) ML761/ZK-AMB/VH-EBW; (SH.32C) NJ255/ZK-AMD/VH-EBX/VH-BRE; (SH.33C) NJ179/ZK-AME/VH-BRD; (SH.55C) JM715/ZK-AMH/VH-BRC.

(d) Sandringham 6: Five aircraft initially for D.N.L., Norway: (c/n SH.48C) ML809/LN-IAU; (SH.51C) ML807/LN-IAV; (SH.52C) JM720/LN-IAW; (SH.62C) W4037/LN-LAI; (SH.71C) JM714/LN-LMK/LV-PAE/LV-AHM.

(e) Sunderland 5: (c/n SH.60C) DP195/CX-AKR; (SH.69C) EJ171/LV-AHH; (SH.70C) EK579/LV-AHG.

Solent 2 'Southampton' of British Overseas Airways Corporation, showing the original type of wing-tip floats. (*Charles E. Brown*)

Short S.45 Solent

A larger and longer version of the Sunderland, 1 ft. wider in the beam, with a planing bottom of increased area to permit a greater take-off weight, was flown in 1945 as the Seaford 1, and NJ201, one of a small batch built for the R.A.F., was loaned to B.O.A.C. for civil evaluation as G-AGWU in 1946. As a result, an order was placed for 12 similar aircraft, powered by Hercules 637 engines, for operation with seven crew and up to 30 passengers on two decks, with full promenade, cocktail bar and dining saloon facilities. Construction was undertaken at Rochester, where the prototype, G-AHIL 'Salisbury', designated Solent 2, was launched on 11 November 1946. The twelfth, G-AHIY 'Southsea', launched on 8 April 1948, was the last aircraft ever built at Rochester.

During its $2\frac{1}{2}$-year accident-free B.O.A.C. service, the Solent 2 became famous for the luxury travel it introduced after replacing the Yorks on the South Africa route. 'Southampton', named by the Mayoress of that city on 14 April 1948, made a proving flight which terminated at Vaaldam, the lake near Johannesburg, on 1 May, and three days later the first Solent passenger service left Southampton. The route lay via Marseilles, Augusta in Sicily, Cairo, Port Bell on Lake Victoria, and Victoria Falls, three services a week operating to a $4\frac{1}{2}$-day schedule. Teething trouble with the wing tip floats necessitated the withdrawal of the Solent fleet on 22 July, and the boats remained out of service until 17 October, during which time the floats were strengthened and re-installed on a V strut mounting 7 ft. outboard and 18 in. forward of their original position.

The Solent fleet was on lease from the M.C.A. and not owned outright by B.O.A.C., and in 1948 arrangements were made whereby six new Seaford 1s, under construction at Belfast, should be completed as Solents for the Corporation. Equipped for 39 passengers and designated Solent 3, they were

Solent 2 'Solway' flying low at the 1949 Farnborough S.B.A.C. Show to show the revised strutting of wing-tip floats. (*A. J. Jackson*)

externally identified by two extra rectangular windows in the upper rear part of the hull. The first Solent 3, G-AKNO, landed on the Thames at Limehouse Reach, London, on 5 May 1949, to receive the name 'City of London' from the Lord Mayor at Tower Pier five days later. Together with later Solent 3s, 'NO then served to reinforce the earlier boats on the South Africa run. From 15 May they were also routed to Lake Naivasha, Kenya, replacing Yorks on the Nairobi service and cutting the journey from 48 to 27½ hours. Ten days later they also relieved Sandringhams on the Karachi service, but with the departure of 'Somerset' to South Africa from Berth 50 on 10 November 1950, all B.O.A.C. flying-boat operations ceased.

'Somerset' and 'City of Cardiff', two of four (G-AKNO, 'NP, G-AHIV and 'IO) flown to Australia for the Sydney–Hobart and Sydney–Port Moresby services of Trans-Oceanic Airways, became VH-TOA to 'OD respectively, but were sold again and arrived at Oakland, California, in June 1956 as N9945F and N9946F respectively. They acquired South Pacific Airlines livery, joining N9947F, formerly G-AKNT, which arrived from Belfast via Australia and Honolulu in November 1955.

'City of Liverpool' was loaned to the Marine Aircraft Experimental Establishment during 1951 for overload rough weather tests at weights up to 84,000 lb., take-off and landing tests being conducted at Felixstowe, Gibraltar and Tangier in temporary R.A.F. markings as WM759.

Tasman Empire Airways Ltd. already operated four heavier Solent 4s, ZK-AML to 'MO, custom-built to carry 44 passengers on the 1,350 mile ocean crossing from Auckland to Sydney, the first, 'Aotearoa II', having been named at Belfast by Princess Elizabeth on 26 May 1949 and used for certification trials before leaving for New Zealand on 26 November. In June 1950 T.E.A.L. also took over the Auckland–Suva–Labasa routes from the N.Z.N.A.C. Sunderlands and were joined in the following August by B.O.A.C.'s Solent 3 G-AKNR 'City of Belfast', ferried via Gander, San Francisco, Honolulu and Fiji to become ZK-AMQ 'Aparimu'.

When they were superseded by Douglas DC-6Bs in 1954, ZK-AML and sister ship ZK-AMN 'Awateri' were ferried back to England and joined Aquila Airways Ltd. at Hamble for routes between Southampton and Montreux,

Santa Margherita, Madeira and the Canary Islands. T.E.A.L. retained ZK-AMO 'Aranui' until it flew the last flying boat service between Fiji and Tahiti on 14 September 1960.

The last Solent 3 to be built, G-AKNU 'Sydney', served with Aquila Airways Ltd. from December 1951 until it was joined in April 1954 by the most remarkable of all Solents. Originally the turretted evaluation Seaford 1 G-AGWU, it was later fitted with Solent nose and tail as a trainer but retained its original serial NJ201, and flew from Hythe to Felixstowe on 7 November 1950, when the B.O.A.C. fleet disbanded. Aquila Airways Ltd. brought it back to Hamble in 1953 for conversion to Solent 3 standards as G-ANAJ. One other Seaford 1, NJ200, registered to R. L. Whyham as G-ALIJ in February 1949, was not collected from the R.A.F.

All British commercial flying-boat activity ceased on 30 September 1958, when Aquila Airways Ltd. withdrew its Madeira service. The three surviving Solents G-AHIN, G-ANYI and G-AOBL were then taken over by Aerovias Aquila, to resume their flights to Madeira under Portuguese registry. The scheme fell through and all three were beached in the Tagus estuary near Lisbon and eventually suffered a similar fate to those in California.

Aquila Airways' Solent 4 G-ANYI at Hamble in 1958 awaiting ferrying to Portugal. (*Aviation Photo News*)

Solent 3 N9946F 'Isle of Tahiti', formerly VH-TOB, G-AKNP and NJ203, at Oakland, California in 1958 in the second paint scheme devised for it by South Pacific Air Lines.

SPECIFICATION

Manufacturers: Short Bros. (Rochester and Bedford) Ltd., Seaplane Works, Rochester, Kent; Short Bros. and Harland Ltd., Queens Island, Belfast, N.I.

Power Plants: (Seaford 1) Four 1,800 h.p. Bristol Hercules 130.
(Solent 2 and 3) Four 1,690 h.p. Bristol Hercules 637.
(Solent 4) Four 2,040 h.p. Bristol Hercules 733.

Dimensions: Span, 112 ft. 9½ in. Length, 87 ft. 8 in. Height, 34 ft. 3¼ in. Wing area, 1,687 sq. ft.

	Seaford 1	Solent 2	Solent 3	Solent 4
Tare weight	45,000 lb.	47,760 lb.	48,210 lb.	49,145 lb.
All-up weight	75,000 lb.	78,000 lb.	78,600 lb.	81,000 lb.
Maximum speed	242 m.p.h.	273 m.p.h.	267 m.p.h.	282 m.p.h.
Cruising speed	207 m.p.h.	244 m.p.h.	236 m.p.h.	251 m.p.h.
Initial climb	875 ft./min.	925 ft./min.	830 ft./min.	925 ft./min.
Ceiling	13,000 ft.	17,000 ft.	15,500 ft.	17,100 ft.
Range	2,800 miles	1,800 miles	2,190 miles	3,000 miles.

Production: Twelve Solent 2 and six Solent 3 registered in Britain; four Solent 4 (c/n SH.1556–SH.1559) ZK-AML to 'MO; two Seaford 1s allotted British civil markings.

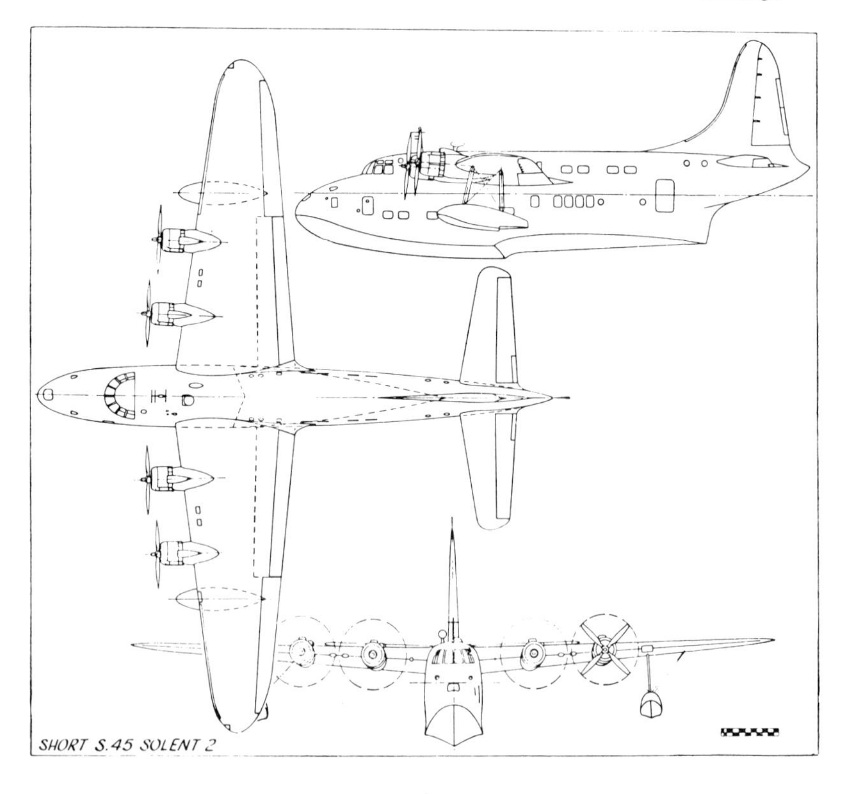
SHORT S.45 SOLENT 2

Sealand G-AKLO photographed en route to the 1950 S.B.A.C. Show.
(*Short Bros. and Harland Ltd.*)

Short S.A.6 Sealand

Allotted the S.B.A.C. designation S.A.6, the all-metal Sealand, designed in 1947 by C. T. P. Lipscomb, was Britain's first post-war civil amphibian and carried up to seven passengers with two crew on the power of two Gipsy Queen 70 motors. The hull was of the normal single step type, fitted with a pneumatically retractable undercarriage for land operations. G-AIVX, the prototype, made its maiden flight from the waters of Belfast Lough piloted by H. L. Piper on 22 January 1948 and a production batch of 14 Sealand 1s, later increased to 24, was laid down. A projected Sealand 2 with Alvis Leonides radials was not built.

The first Sealand 1, G-AKLM, averaged 169 m.p.h. in the Elmdon King's Cup Race of 1 August 1949, and later left on a sales tour of Scandinavia, but was burned out with the loss of Flt. Lt. D. G. McCall and crew when it hit a mountainside in fog at the southern tip of Norway in the following October. The fourth aircraft, G-AKLP, first of three ordered by British West Indian Airways for inter-island services, was exhibited as VP-TBA 'R.M.A. St. Vincent' at the 1949 Farnborough S.B.A.C. Show. During the completion of tropical trials in the West Indies, Short's chief test pilot, T. W. Brook-Smith, found that the Sealands were expected to operate from unsuitable areas of open sea at St. Vincent and Dominica and recommended the shelving of the scheme. 'St. Vincent' therefore reverted to the manufacturers, was renamed 'Festival of Britain' and left Trinidad on 6 January 1951, under British marks for a 50,000-mile sales tour of South and North America, which included a double crossing of the Andes. The second and third West Indian aircraft were then disposed of to Jugoslovenski Aero Transport for services along the Dalmatian coast and passed through Short's establishment at Rochester en route to Zagreb in September 1951. One at least was transferred to the Jugoslav Air Force, as in 1972 it was stored at the Air Museum at Surcin with military serial 0662.

During 1950–52 the European demonstrator, G-AKLO, ranged far and wide, from the Canary Islands in the south to Scandinavia in the north, resulting in the purchase by Vestlandske Luftfartselskap, Bergen, of 'LN and

'LU for scheduled services along the difficult coastline to Trondheim, with undercarriages removed as Sealand 3s.

G-AKLN, shown at the 1951 Farnborough S.B.A.C. Show was the first Sealand with strengthened hull, wing fences and 2 ft. 6 in. greater wing span. Shell then acquired the European and American demonstrators 'LO and 'LP, which, after long periods in storage at Rochester and Croydon respectively, departed for Balik Papaan for amphibious service over remote jungle areas in Borneo as VR-SDS and 'DV. Another, G-AKLW, was sold to Egyptian business man Ahmed Abboud Pasha and left Croydon on delivery as SU-AHY 'Nadia' piloted by D. Tanton and S. Omar on 23 February 1952.

The disposal of 'LT to the Christian and Missionary Alliance in January 1951 was a triumph of salesmanship. This, the first post-war British aeroplane sold to an American buyer, was shipped to Djakarta for operation by the veteran bush pilot evangelist Mason, from a base at Tandjoengselor, Indonesia. Like those in Borneo, it reduced a month's trek to a matter of minutes, but ended its year's career in a jungle watercourse after a forced landing with a split fuel tank and was replaced by the last production Sealand, JZ-PTA. G-AKLV 'Pegasus', which left Blackbushe on delivery on 7 May 1952, was operated in East Pakistan by Ralli Bros. Ltd. between their riverside jute stations as AP-AFM; and two others, G-AKLX and 'LY served with the local Transport Commission as AP-AGB and 'GC respectively.

G-AKLU at Bergen in 1951 as Sealand 3 LN-SUH with undercarriage removed and wheel wells blanked off. (*John Stroud*)

Only the first 12 of the total production of 24 Sealands were initially of British registry, the last two being first of 10 special aircraft built for the Indian Navy in 1952. They were equipped with dual control, tankage for 6 hours endurance and, for higher continuous cruising power, Gipsy Queen 70-4 engines driving constant speed feathering and reversing airscrews. The first, INS-101, left Rochester on 13 January 1953, piloted by R. Gough and C. C. Dash of Short's Ferry Flight, en route to Cochin. The remaining machine of the supplementary batch, YV-P-AEG, was shipped to Venezuela for use by the Shell Company on Lake Maracaibo.

SPECIFICATION

Manufacturers: Short Bros. and Harland Ltd., Queen's Island, Belfast, N.I.

Power Plants:	(Prototype)	Two 345 h.p. de Havilland Gipsy Queen 70-2.
	(Production)	Two 340 h.p. de Havilland Gipsy Queen 70-3.
	(Indian)	Two 340 h.p. de Havilland Gipsy Queen 70-4.

	Prototype and Early Production	Late Production
Span	59 ft. 0 in.	61 ft. 6 in.
Length	42 ft. 2 in.	42 ft. 2 in.
Height	15 ft. 0 in.	15 ft. 0 in.
Wing area	353 sq. ft.	358·6 sq. ft.
Tare weight	7,397 lb.	7,065 lb.
All-up weight	9,100 lb.	9,100 lb.
Maximum speed	189 m.p.h.	185 m.p.h.
Cruising speed	175 m.p.h.	169 m.p.h.
Initial climb	880 ft./min.	780 ft./min.
Ceiling	20,600 ft.	21,000 ft.
Range	660 miles	525 miles

Production: One prototype, 14 British registered aircraft and the following for export: (c/n SH.1760–SH.1764) Indian Navy INS-103 to INS-107; (SH.1765) YV-P-AEG; (SH.1766–SH.1768) INS-108 to INS-110; (SH.1769) JZ-PTA; (SH.1770–SH.1772) cancelled.

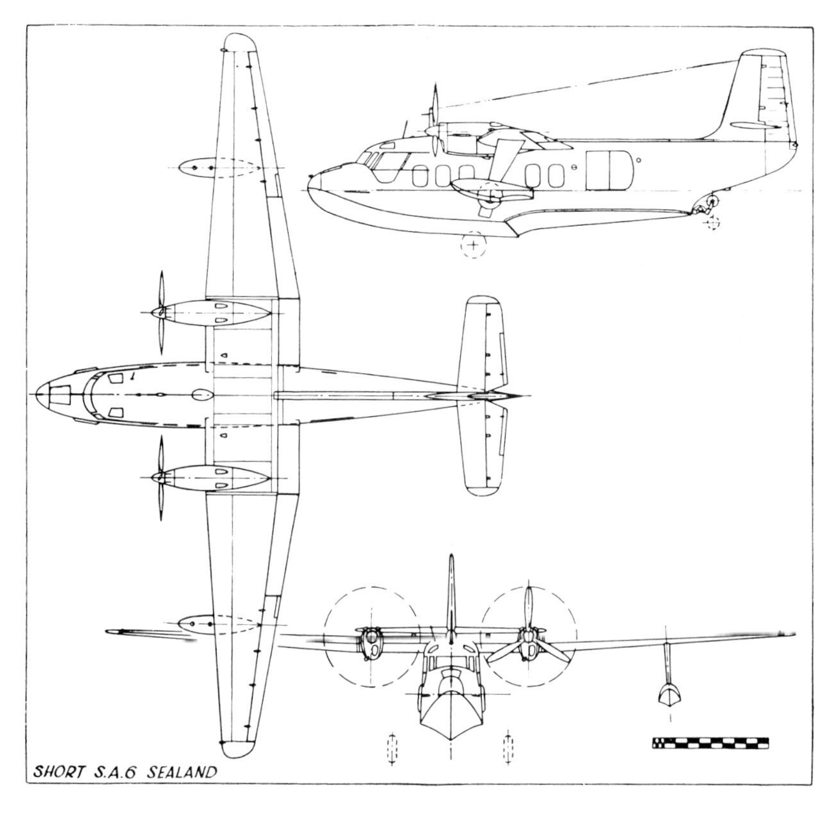

Skyvan 3 N4917 taking off at the September 1968 Farnborough S.B.A.C. Show prior to delivery to Wien Consolidated Airlines, Fairbanks, Alaska. (*Richard Riding*)

Short S.C.7 Skyvan

Design of the Skyvan freighter followed an approach made to Shorts in 1958 by F. G. Miles Ltd. who were seeking production backing for their projected H.D.M.106 Caravan with Hurel Dubois high aspect ratio wing. Shorts acquired both the design and data gathered from trials with the earlier Aerovan-based H.D.M.105 prototype G-AHDM but while approving the basic concept, rejected the Caravan in its original form because of probable manoeuvring and hangarage problems during small strip operations.

They therefore designed a strictly utility all-metal box-car version known as the Short S.C.7 Skyvan with strut braced, 64 ft. span, rectangular wing, to carry 3,000 lb. loads or 15 passengers on the power of two 390 h.p. Continental GTSIO-520 turbosupercharged piston engines. The rear hold, 6 ft. 6 in. square and 16 ft. 6 in. long, was unobstructed internally and loaded through a full width, upward opening door in the underside of the rear fuselage taper. The undercarriage was the simplest possible fixed, low drag type.

Construction of the prototype Skyvan 1, G-ASCN, commenced in 1960 but proceeded slowly due to pressure of work on the Belfast military transport, so that the first flight by chief test pilot D. Tayler did not take place at Sydenham until 17 January 1963. Market research showed a preference for propeller turbines and greater payload, with the result that G-ASCN was re-engined with 520 e.s.h.p. Turboméca Astazou IIs with which it flew again on 2 October 1963 as the Skyvan 1A with all-up weight increased from 8,600 lb. to 9,500 lb. and the payload to 4,000 lb.

In February 1964 the British Government authorised a production batch of 20 Skyvans, increased to 50 in April 1966, to be equipped with more powerful 670 e.s.h.p. Astazou Xs, and G-ASCN flew with these engines, lowered tailplane and fin and rudder assemblies raised as the Skyvan 1A Series 2 in March 1965. It was shown at the Paris Salon in Aeralpi colours, made ski undercarriage trials at Sydenham in April 1966, and flew for the last time on 15 August 1966. It was subsequently dismantled.

G-ASCO, first of three Skyvan 2 pre-production trials aircraft with revised nose shape, larger main wheels and square windows, flew on 29 October 1965 followed by G-ASZI and 'ZJ early in 1966, all three powered by the definitive 730 e.s.h.p. Astazou XII and operating at a maximum all-up weight of 12,500 lb. The first production Skyvan 2, I-TORE for operation by Aeralpi out of its mountain encircled base-strip at Cortina d'Ampezzo, Italy, flew on 13 May 1966 and was joined later by I-CESA but was lost in a training accident at Venice on 6 March 1967.

The second and fourth production Skyvans, G-ATPF and 'PG, were delivered to Emerald Airways Ltd. in August and October 1966, the second having appeared at the September S.B.A.C. show. G-ATPF flew their first Eglinton–Glasgow service on 23 September but both Skyvans returned to Shorts in January 1967 when the company ceased operations. Two others ordered by Papuan Airlines and three with 'quick change' interiors for palletised freighting by Ansett-MAL had 18 ft. 7 in. freight holds but after tropical trials with G-ASZI at Addis Ababa, Mombasa and Nairobi, the Astazou XII was found to be temperature-limited under hot and high conditions resulting in a further change of engine to the American 715 e.s.h.p. Garrett-AiResearch TPE331-201 propeller turbine with which G-ASZI and 'ZJ first flew on 15 December 1967 and 20 January 1968 respectively.

With these engines the standard model became the Skyvan 3 from the 17th production airframe. Some earlier machines were also converted or completed to this standard but in the interim period others were ferried across the Atlantic to the U.S. distributor, Remmert Werner Inc., as Skyvan 2s. These included N4906, for lease to Northern Consolidated Airlines in Alaska, which became G-AVGO for F.A.A. certification in Belgium prior to delivery in April 1967; and N732R in which Caribbean Air Services shuttled dirty linen from arid St. Croix, Virgin Islands to San Juan, Puerto Rico for laundering.

Introduction of the Skyvan 3 resulted in a steady stream of orders, mainly from the U.S.A., Canada and Australia but G-AWCS was delivered to Southwest Aviation Ltd., Exeter, on 1 July 1968 after the earlier lease of G-ATPF; and G-AWYG was delivered to Loganair Ltd., Abbotsinch on 4 March 1969 for its Scottish schedules. Gulf Aviation Ltd. received G-AYJN and 'JO in November 1970 with G-AXFI following in March 1971, for oil company charters in the Persian Gulf area. They were used also to transport 34 ft. pipe sections projecting from the open freight door. A special variant

The prototype Skyvan, G-ASCN, undergoing static testing before first flight in its original form with Continental piston engines.

Skyvan 3 N20CK, formerly G-AXAD, one of three used on Cherokee Airlines' 'Mini Jumbo' services out of Los Angeles in 1969. (*Aviation Photo News*)

Skyvan 2 G-ATPF in the livery of South West Aviation Ltd., Exeter in 1968. (*Aviation Photo News*)

The Royal Nepalese Army's Skyvan 3M RA-N14 ready to leave Heathrow on 26 August 1971 with ferry registration G-AYZD. (*Aviation Photo News*)

The third pre-production Skyvan, G-ASZJ, after conversion to all-passenger Skyliner configuration.

for Questor International Surveys in November 1970 was CF-QSL fitted with a Barringer INPUT transmitting loop encircling the aircraft from wing tip pylons to booms projecting 8 ft. 4 in. ahead of the flight deck and 11 ft. 6 in. aft of the tail. Another of note was the luxuriously furnished 9N-RAA, first flown as G-AYIX, for the Royal Flight of Nepal. N3201, delivered to Continental Air Services of Los Angeles, saw service in South Vietnam as XW-PGL.

Further development led to the 22 seat 'Skyliner', all-passenger version with airstair-equipped entry door on the port side and all-up weight increased to 13,500 lb., in which form it was shown at the 1970 S.B.A.C. Show. It was then evaluated on inter-city and Scottish routes in the livery of British Air Services Ltd. and took part in the Japan International Aerospace Show at Nagoya, 29 October–3 November 1971. Flown by Tim Woods with Fred Edwards as engineer, it made a seven-week sales tour along the route home.

The first all-passenger aircraft to be sold was Skyvan 3 9M-AQG, flown out to Malaysia Air Charter Ltd., Kuala Lumpur, as G-AYYR in August 1971. A year later the first production Skyliner, G-BAHK, joined Gulf Aviation Ltd.'s Skyvan 3s in Bahrein. In April 1973, Skyliners G-AZYW and G-BAIT were delivered to B.E.A. to replace D. H. Heron 1Bs on its Scottish routes.

Military interest led to the evolution of the Skyvan 3M for supply dropping, paratrooping, assault landing and casualty evacuation. Two supplied to the Austrian Army in February 1969 were followed by batches for the Indonesian Air Force, Argentine Naval Prefecture, Ecuador Army Air Service, the Muscat and Oman Air Force and Royal Nepalese Army.

SPECIFICATION

Manufacturers: Short Bros. and Harland Ltd., Queen's Island, Belfast, N.I.

Power Plants: (Skyvan 1) Two 390 h.p. Continental GTSIO-520
(Skyvan 2) Two 730 e.s.h.p. Turboméca Astazou XII
(Skyvan 3 and 3M) Two 715 e.s.h.p. Garrett-AiResearch TPE331-201

Dimensions: Span, 64 ft. 1 in. Length, 40 ft. 1 in. Height, 9 ft. 5 in. Wing area, 373 sq. ft.

**Weights:* Tare weight, 7,700 lb. All-up weight, 12,500 lb.

*Performance: Maximum cruising speed, 201 m.p.h. at 10,000 ft. Range, 270 miles with 4,000 lb. payload and reserves.

* Skyvan 3

Production: More than 50 registered in Britain by 1973 and the following for export:

(a) Skyvan 2

(c/n SH.1832) I-TORE; (SH.1834) I-CESA, later G-AXCS; (SH.1836) not completed; (SH.1840) VH-PNI; (SH.1841) VH-PNJ ntu, later N725R; (SH.1843) N729R; (SH.1844) G-14-1/N732R; (SH.1845) N734R/CF-GSC

(b) Skyvan 3

(c/n SH.1846) N4916; (SH.1848) 6Y-JFL ntu/N3201/XW-PGL; (SH.1849) VH-PNJ; (SH.1850) N4917; (SH.1864) G-14-36/CF-TAI, later G-AYYR; (SH.1883) G-14-55/CF-QSL

(c) Skyvan 3M

(c/n SH.1855) G-14-27/Austrian 5S-TA; (SH.1860) G-14-32/5S-TB; (SH.1875) G-14-47/Muscat and Oman '902'; (SH.1877) G-14-49/'904'; (SH.1878) G-14-50/'905'; (SH.1880) G-14-52/'906'; (SH.1881) G-14-53/Indonesian T-702; (SH.1882) G-14-54/T-703; (SH.1887–SH.1891) Argentine PA-50 to PA-54; (SH.1895) G-14-67/'907'; (SH.1896) G-14-68/'908'

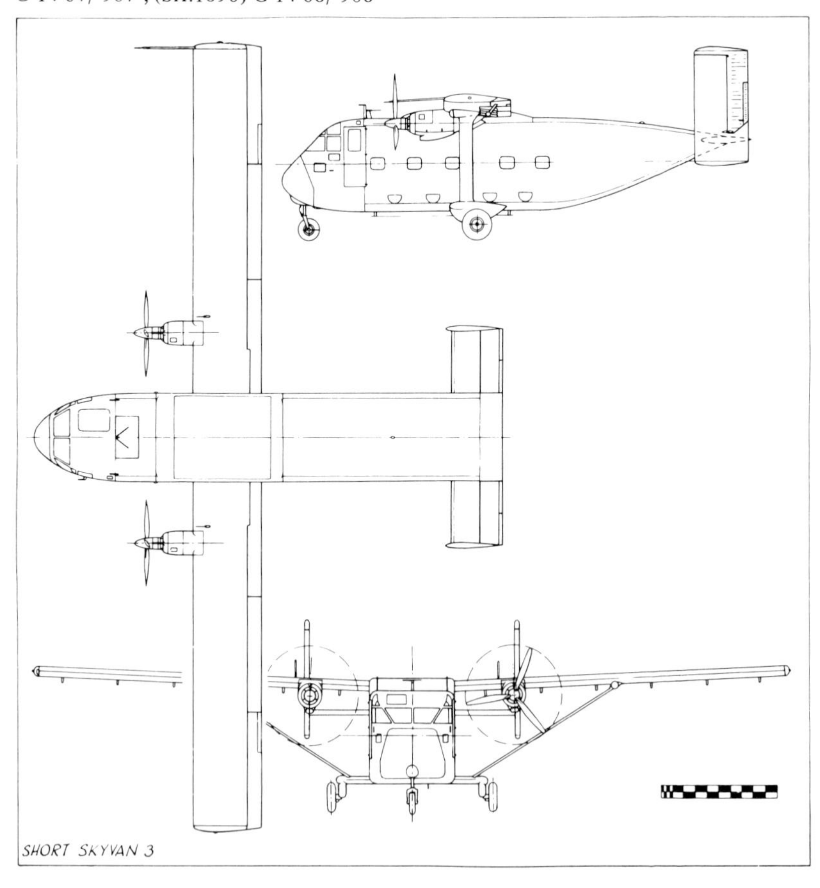
SHORT SKYVAN 3

T. Neville Stack demonstrating the prototype Simmonds Spartan G-EBYU at Croydon in 1928. (*Flight Photo 6288*)

Simmonds Spartan

Dissatisfied with the high manufacturing and maintenance costs of contemporary light aeroplanes, O. E. (later Sir Oliver) Simmonds designed and built a wooden two seat biplane in 1928 which sought economy through interchangeability. All four wings and ailerons were identical and had a symmetrical aerofoil section to enable one spare wing to fit in any of the four positions. The rudder was also interchangeable with the half elevator, the fin was identical with the outer third of the tailplane, each half of the undercarriage would fit on either the port or starboard side, and all main bracing wires were of the same length and size. Spares needed to cover even serious damage were therefore few.

Known as the Simmonds Spartan and powered by a 95 h.p. Cirrus III, the prototype, G-EBYU, was completed at Woolston, Southampton, in time for the King's Cup Race of 20–21 July 1928 in which it averaged 73·06 m.p.h. and came 18th piloted by Flt. Lt. S. N. Webster. Later in the year the Spartan was loaned to the short-lived Isle of Purbeck Flying Club whose chief instructor, Flg. Off. H. W. R. Banting, flew it from Croydon to the Berlin Aero Show on 24 October 1928 in the remarkable non-stop time of 7 hours 10 minutes. Lt. Col. L. A. Strange was carried as passenger and the return trip was made on 27 October in 5 hours 55 minutes.

Production then began at Weston, Southampton, and final erection and test flying took place at Hamble. During the next 15 months at least 49 were built, the majority for the Dominions but 24 were of British registry, including a fleet of 12, G-AAMA to G-AAML, ordered by National Flying Services Ltd. for instructional use at Hanworth and elsewhere. Unlike those of the prototype, the main undercarriage legs were not raked forward on production aircraft, four of which, G-AAFP, 'GN, 'GY and 'MC, were flown in the King's Cup Race of 5–6 July 1929.

Five sold in Australia in 1929 via the Spartan agents, Robert Bryce and Co. Pty. Ltd., included G-AUIT which flew for ten years with various owners and G-AUKQ which crashed in New Guinea in 1942.

The eighth aircraft, ZK-AAP, built for a solo flight from England to New Zealand by H. F. Mase, was a single seater with an 80 gallon fuel tank in the front fuselage and named 'The All Black' by long distance pilot Lady Bailey at Croydon on 19 April 1929. Mase left Lympne at 6.15 a.m. on 26 April but crashed on take-off from a field after a forced landing at Commelle Cernay, France, a few hours later. New Zealand was nevertheless the largest overseas buyer, commencing with the third Australian, G-AULI, re-registered in October 1929 as ZK-AAY for the Hawkes Bay Aero Club which also acquired a second machine ZK-ABC.

ZK-ABL was used by the Wellington Aero Club but the most remarkable were Air Travel's ZK-ABU and 'BZ. On 13 June 1932 the former became the first aircraft to land on the Waiho Gorge glacier and the latter, after service with the Marlborough Aero Club and New Zealand Airways (Fleet No.3), was stored until refurbished for the Marlborough Aero Club's 40th anniversary in April 1968.

One Spartan was evaluated by the South African Air Force at Roberts Heights; CF-ABC and 'BD were supplied to Dominion Aircraft Ltd., Montreal; and VT-AAT 'Frontier of Dawn' left Le Bourget on 7 June 1929 in an attempt to fly to Karachi, piloted by F. N. Kabali, but got no further than Tripoli.

Five engine variants were produced: an unidentified machine (but possibly c/n 2 certificated on 23 January 1929) flown with a prototype 85 h.p. seven cylinder Redrup Fury Mk.II air-cooled lever engine at Hamble on 17 July 1929; G-AAGO fitted temporarily with a Gipsy II as H. T. Andrew's mount in the King's Cup Race, 5 July 1930; G-AAHA supplied to C. Coombes of Shanklin with a Hermes II (also fitted to the first and last N.F.S. machines, the rest being Hermes I powered); and finally G-ABNU, built at Brooklands in 1931 as an exercise by students of the College of Aeronautical Engineering, which was fitted with a Gipsy I.

First of three airframe variants, G-AAMH was experimentally fitted with wings of 4 ft. greater span, with a consequent improvement in take-off and climb. Another, 'MG, was evaluated at the M.A.E.E. Felixstowe on twin metal

The second production Simmonds Spartan showing the revised undercarriage. *(John Hopton)*

H. M. Mackay (left), managing director of New Zealand Airways and Capt. 'Tiny' White with the coupé three seater ZK-ABN 'Southern Cross Kitten' at Timaru in 1931. (*R. M. Mackay*)

floats and fitted with an enlarged rudder of the type fitted to O. E. Simmond's later design, the Spartan Arrow.

Several aircraft were also built to seat two passengers in tandem in a double cockpit ahead of the pilot, but were otherwise similar to the two seater and used all the same interchangeable assemblies. The three sold on the home market were G-AAGV (Cirrus III) and 'HV (Hermes I), which went to Cramlington for joyriding with Pleasure Flying Services Ltd., and 'JB flown by Flg. Off. H. R. L. Wood in the 1930 King's Cup Race. 'GV crashed in September 1930, but was painstakingly rebuilt by Cramlington Aircraft Ltd. and reappeared in June 1932 as G-ABXO. Its sister machine, G-AAHV, passed through several ownerships, including that of an airminded cleric, who used it as an open air pulpit along the East Coast in 1935.

The sole three seat Spartan on floats was VQ-FAA operated in Fiji by Gordon Fenton from 18 April 1930 (when it made its first wheeled landing at Levuku) until August 1933, during which time it was also used by Fiji Airways Ltd. New Zealand Airways Ltd. acquired ZK-ABK (Fleet No.1) in 1929 for its pioneer Dunedin–Timaru airline, and also rebuilt ZK-ABN and ZK-AAY (Fleet No.2) in three seat configuration at Timaru, the former with cabin top. During the visit of Fokker monoplane VH-USU 'Southern Cross' to New Zealand in January 1933, ZK-ABN was repainted as 'Southern Cross Kitten'.

When National Flying Services Ltd. standardised the Moth at the end of 1930, its remaining Spartans were retired. G-AAMD was then modified at Hanworth and fitted with a Gipsy I and seven hour tankage for Lt. Finch White, who left Hanworth on 29 January 1931, in an abortive attempt to reach India, crashing at Tunis a few days later.

Fame rarely came to the Simmonds Spartan, but the former N.F.S. machine G-AAMI was equipped with skis and sold to Wilhelm Omsted at Oslo in April 1930. It made many Arctic flights, covering more than 45,000 miles over the mountain ranges of Northern Norway.

SPECIFICATION

Manufacturers:	Simmonds Aircraft Ltd., Weston, Southampton and Hamble Aerodrome, Hants.	
Power Plants:	One 85 h.p. Redrup Fury Mk.II One 100 h.p. de Havilland Gipsy I or 120 h.p. Gipsy II. One 100 h.p. A.D.C. Hermes I or 105 h.p. Hermes II.	
Dimensions:	Span, 28 ft. 7 in. Length, 23 ft. 11 in. Height, 9 ft. 3 in. Wing area, 240 sq. ft.	
Weights:	(Two seater)	Tare weight, 940 lb. All-up weight, 1,680 lb.
	(Three seater)	Tare weight, 1,050 lb. All-up weight, 1,750 lb.
Performance:	(Two seater)	Maximum speed, 100 m.p.h. Cruising speed, 85 m.p.h. Initial climb, 600 ft./min. Range, 320 miles.
	(Three seater)	Maximum speed, 107 m.p.h. Cruising speed, 95 m.p.h. Initial climb, 500 ft./min. Ceiling, 16,000 ft. Range, 300 miles.

Production: Forty-nine aircraft including 24 British registered, seven (c/n 2, 13, 16, 30, 40 and 41) untraced, and the following for export: (c/n 3) G-AUIT/VH-UIT; (4) G-AULI/ZK-AAY; (5) G-AUKQ/VH-UKQ; (6) CF-ABC; (7) CF-ABD; (8) ZK-AAP; (9) South African Air Force; (28) VH-UMP; (31) VT-AAT; (39) ZK-ABL; (42) ZK-ABN; (43) ZK-ABZ; (45) VH-UMQ; (46) ZK-ABK*; (47) VQ-FAA*; (48) ZK-ABC; (49) ZK-ABU

* Built as three seater.

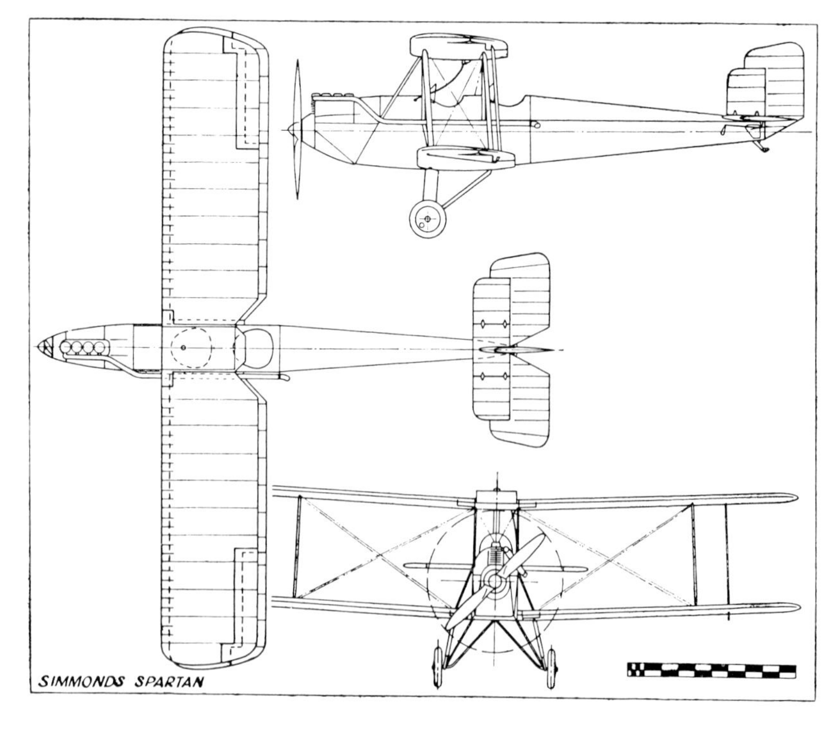

Harry Hawker flying the prototype cabin Gnu K-101, second British civil registered aeroplane, at Hendon, 29 May 1919. (*Flight Photo 330*)

Sopwith Gnu

Introduced in May 1919, the Sopwith Gnu three seat tourer or taxi machine was one of the first cabin aircraft designed for civil use and was an orthodox two bay biplane of fabric-covered wooden construction, seating the pilot in an open cockpit under the centre section, one panel of which was left open for improved vision. Two passengers sat side by side in the rear cockpit under a hinged and glazed cabin roof.

Fresh from his historic mid-Atlantic rescue, Harry Hawker flew his wife from Brooklands to Hendon in the Bentley B.R.2 powered prototype Gnu, K-101, on 29 May 1919, to attend the reception given to the crews of the successful American transatlantic flying-boats NC-1, 2 and 4. The honour of making the first passenger flight in the Gnu, piloted by the idol of the aviation world, fell to a Miss Daisy King of Leeds, who paid 60 guineas in an auction conducted by Claude Grahame-White. K-101 then went to Southport to give pleasure flights piloted by C. D. Barnard but was damaged beyond repair on 10 June after a life of but a few weeks.

Twelve Gnus were completed, the second of which, K-136, flew to Hendon in formation with the prototype. In common with several later specimens it was powered by a 110 h.p. Le Rhône but the cramped cabin was not popular and commencing with the next machine, K-140, the majority of Gnus were open models.

Although the post-war slump ended production in six months, several were sold abroad including K-169 and G-EAIL shipped to the Larkin-Sopwith Aviation Co. Ltd. in Melbourne. As G-AUBX and 'BY they gave quite outstanding service for many years, and one, piloted by W. 'Skipper' Wilson, won the speed prize in the first Australian Aerial Derby at Mascot, Sydney, in 1920. In 1924 they joined Sopwith's Wallaby and Antelope on the Adelaide–Sydney mail route of Larkin's pioneer company, Australian Aerial Services Ltd., and were thereafter based at Hay, mid-point of the route. G-AUBX was destroyed when taking off from Mildura on 23 August 1924 but 'BY was re-engined with a 110 h.p. Le Rhône and later with a Wright Whirlwind with which it came 11th in the East–West Air Race in September 1929 piloted by K. R. Farmer.

Four Gnus, G-EAME to 'MH, remained unsold in the Kingston works when Sopwiths closed down and the cabin model exhibited without registration at the Olympia Aero Show in July 1920 was probably G-EAMG (Bentley B.R.2), the only one of the four to receive a C. of A.

Only the first and fourth production Gnus had lengthy careers in the United Kingdom. These were the cabin model G-EADB and the open cockpit 'GP. The latter became the property of Lt. Col. F. K. McClean and won the Grosvenor Trophy at Lympne on 23 June 1923, piloted by Flt. Lt. W. H. Longton. The 404 mile course round Southern England was completed at an average speed of 87·6 m.p.h., the Filton–Croydon leg being covered in 62 minutes. The other Gnu, G-EADB, was owned and flown during 1923–24 by Brooklands racing driver E. A. D. Eldridge but in June 1925 was sold to J. R. King who entered it for the Lympne Races on 1–3 August 1925. The Gnu's performance was not outstanding, and 'DB came fourth at 86·95 m.p.h. in the 100 mile International Handicap, and fifth at 84·86 m.p.h. in the 50 mile Private Owners' Handicap.

W. H. Longton taxying in at Lympne after winning the 1923 Grosvenor Trophy in the open cockpit Gnu G-EAGP. (*Flight Photo*)

Both Gnus were then purchased by the Southern Counties Aviation Company of Shoreham and spent the remainder of the 1925 season giving pleasure flights from fields along the South Coast. In the following year they were taken over by G. M. Lloyd, a professional stunt man, who extended their activities to embrace the East Coast and to include exhibition flying to attract would-be passengers. It was their undoing, the first to go being 'DB, which stalled on the approach to a field at Horley, Surrey, on 2 March 1926, injuring the pilot, L. R. Goodman. Two months later 'GP spun into a cemetery at King's Lynn, the pilot, A. O. Bigg-Wither, being killed after the engine failed at the conclusion of a wing walking exhibition by G. M. Lloyd.

A small passenger, Arthur Golding-Barrett (later to be Avro test pilot and the Tiger Club's well known 'G-B'), was unscathed.

SPECIFICATION

Manufacturers:	The Sopwith Aviation Co., Canbury Park Road, Kingston-on-Thames, Surrey. Name changed to The Sopwith Aviation and Engineering Co. Ltd., June 1919.
Power Plants:	One 200 h.p. Bentley B.R.2. One 110 h.p. Le Rhône. One 300 h.p. Wright Whirlwind J-5.
Dimensions:	Span, 38 ft. 1 in. Length, 25 ft. 10 in. Height, 9 ft. 10 in.
Weights:	All-up weight, 3,350 lb.
Performance:	Maximum speed, 93 m.p.h. Initial climb, 645 ft./min. Range, 300 miles.

Production: One prototype and twelve production aircraft, all British registered: (c/n A.16) K-101/G-EAAH and two production batches to Works Orders 2976/1 to 6 and 3005/1 to 6. See Appendix E.

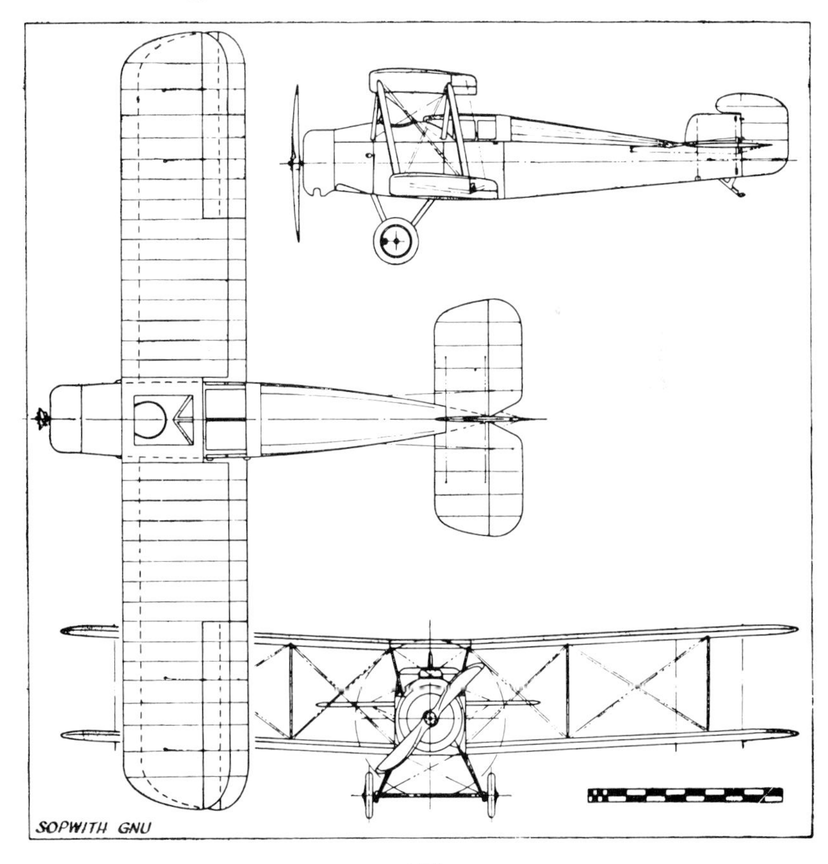

The prototype Martlet with Hornet engine. (*Flight Photo 7663*)

Southern Martlet

In 1926 F. G. Miles bought a quantity of aircraft components and complete airframes from the former Avro factory at Hamble which included the two-seat Avro Baby G-EAUM which he re-engined at Shoreham with a 60 h.p. Cirrus I engine of approximately the same weight as the original water-cooled 35 h.p. Green. Its lively performance on nearly twice the power led to an order from Shoreham private owner L. E. R. Bellairs for a single seat aerobatic biplane of the same type. Assisted by former Avro design draughtsman Horace Miles, Southern Aircraft Ltd.'s production team built him a machine based on the Avro Baby and using metal fittings purchased at Hamble, but with an entirely new tail unit and a new oleo and coil spring undercarriage designed for it by the Hendy Aircraft Co.

The prototype, G-AAII, first flown at Shoreham by F. G. Miles in August 1929 with 85 h.p. A.B.C. Hornet flat four, made its first public appearance at the opening of Hanworth on 30 August but soon afterwards was re-engined with an 80 h.p. Genet II radial and named Martlet after the heraldic emblem of Sussex.

Five dissimilar production aircraft were built at Shoreham during 1930–31, G-AAVD with Genet II for W. R. Westhead, 'YX with Genet Major and untapered ailerons for L. E. R. Bellairs, 'YZ with Gipsy II for the Rt. Hon. F. E. Guest, G-ABBN with Genet II for the Marquess of Douglas and Clydesdale and G-ABIF with Genet II and untapered ailerons for Miss Maxine Freeman-Thomas, later Mrs. F. G. Miles. Although obvious racing mounts, their King's Cup record was disappointing. Miss Winifred Spooner flew 'YZ into 14th place in the 1930 event at a round-Britain speed of 125·5 m.p.h., but F. G. Miles in 'VD retired at Hanworth. That redoubtable pair M. L. Bramson and H. H. Leech were no luckier in 1931. Flying 'BN and 'IF, they retired at Shoreham and Sherburn-in-Elmet respectively, while in the following year, Flg. Off. E. C. T. Edwards, then the owner of 'YZ, damaged it in a forced landing near Runcorn. In 1933 T. C. Sanders retired in 'IF and for the 1934 race, 'YZ was fitted with a Gipsy I, bringing Edwards into 6th place at 119·77 m.p.h., but Martlets were never again flown in the classic event.

G-ABBN was acquired by National Aviation Day Displays Ltd. in 1932, and for one season toured the country giving aerobatic and aerodrome racing performances. The prototype, veteran of six ownerships, spent 1935 at Hanworth in the possession of A. H. Tweddle and was then sold in Ireland. In common with other Martlets, 'VD had several owners, ending its flying days

G-AAYZ, the Gipsy II Martlet at Brooklands prior to the start of the King's Cup Race, 8 July 1932. (*Flight Photo 8889*)

The last production Martlet G-ABIF combined the Genet II with untapered ailerons. (*Photo: Miles Aircraft Ltd.*)

at Redhill in 1939 with H. Whittaker after a period at Walsall with H. M. Goodwin. The Gipsy model, 'YZ, spent 1935–37 in a red colour scheme with Marius Maxwell at Croydon, while 'IF toured with C. W. A. Scott's Air Display 1936–37, flown by pilots of Air Travel Ltd. When war came, its final owner, G. D. Tucker of Hatfield, gave it to the A.T.C.

Unique among Martlets by virtue of its Genet Major engine, G-AAYX was at first the all-red personal mount of F. G. Miles and went with him to Reading, passing into the ownership of Phillips and Powis Aircraft Ltd. in August 1934. Its presence among the new Reading-built Miles machines then gave rise to the oft used, but wholly inaccurate, designation Miles Martlet. After spending 1937–38 at West Malling with G. K. Lawrence and W. K. Vinson, it was taken to Witney by M. N. Mavrogordato. One of the first pre-war aircraft to reappear after VJ Day, it flew again at Woodley on 17 June 1947, after overhaul by Miles Aircraft Ltd. for Butlins Ltd., who acquired it for the aerobatic entertainment of holiday-makers at Broomhall, Pwllheli. In 1949 it was sold to the Ultra Light Association, but finally returned to its birthplace and progressive dereliction. In 1973, as the only survivor of an important breed, it was in the hands of the Shuttleworth Trust at Old Warden.

The last Martlet left the Shoreham works in 1931, but was followed by a new version, the Metal Martlet. This had a fuselage of plate-jointed steel tubing covered by detachable wood and fabric fairings and split axle undercarriage with low pressure wheels and differential brakes. Powered by a

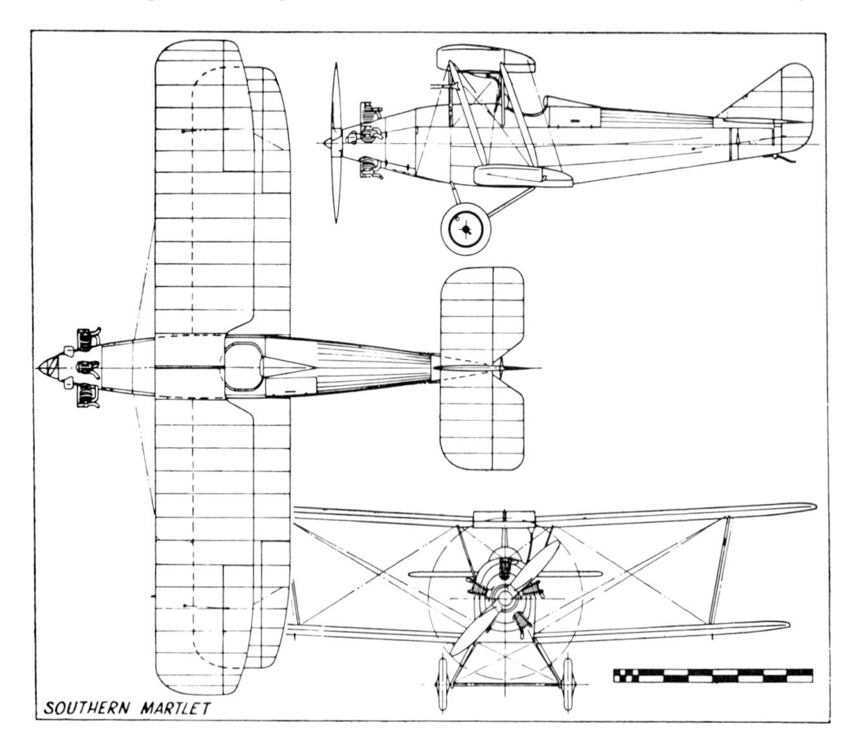

The Metal Martlet, G-ABJW, showing the incorrect lettering.

Hermes I, it had unstaggered folding wings and little in common with the true Martlet. Registered G-ABJW, it flew at Shoreham during the 1931 season, mispainted first as G-AAII and later as G-AAJW, and then went to the scrap heap. A second machine, G-ABMM, ordered by W. R. Westhead, was not completed.

SPECIFICATION

Manufacturers: Southern Aircraft Ltd., Shoreham Aerodrome, Sussex.

Power Plants: (Martlet) One 85 h.p. A.B.C. Hornet
One 80 h.p. Armstrong Siddeley Genet II.
One 100 h.p. Armstrong Siddeley Genet Major.
One 100 h.p. de Havilland Gipsy I.
One 120 h.p. de Havilland Gipsy II.
(Metal Martlet) One 105 h.p. A.D.C. Hermes I.

Dimensions: (Martlet) Span, 25 ft. 0 in. Length, 20 ft. 3 in. Height, 7 ft. 7 in. Wing area, 180 sq. ft.
(Metal Martlet) Span, 23 ft. 6 in. Length, 20 ft. 6 in. Height, 8 ft. 0 in. Wing area, 156 sq. ft.

	Martlet			Metal Martlet
	Hornet	Genet II	Gipsy II	
Tare weight	630 lb.	705 lb.	–	–
All-up weight	1,040 lb.	1,030 lb.	1,105 lb.	–
Maximum speed	112 m.p.h.	112·5 m.p.h.	130 m.p.h.	130 m.p.h.
Cruising speed	–	95·5 m.p.h.	95 m.p.h.	115 m.p.h.
Initial climb	1,100 ft./min.	1,100 ft./min.	1,700 ft./min.	1,400 ft./min.
Ceiling	–	–	–	20,000 ft.
Range	–	280 miles	–	400 miles

Production: One prototype (c/n 2SH) G-AAII; five production aircraft (c/n 201–205); and two Metal Martlets (c/n 31/1 and 31/2), the second not completed.

The Spartan Group's Hermes powered Spartan Arrow G-ABWP, last survivor of its type, at Elstree in 1960. (*Richard Riding*)

Spartan Arrow

Simmonds Aircraft Ltd. was reconstituted early in 1930 and renamed Spartan Aircraft Ltd. A new two seater, the Spartan Arrow, was then built which used a non-symmetrical wing section, but much of the original interchangeability was ingeniously retained by a system of detachable wing tips and trailing edge sections. These enabled a wing to be fitted on either side and an aileron at either end. The two halves of the undercarriage were still interchangeable but the vertical tail surfaces were of entirely new outline. The Arrow was otherwise structurally orthodox with spruce and plywood fuselage and wooden, fabric-covered, folding wings but the cockpits, entered via large doors, were more roomy than those of contemporary light aircraft.

Use of the Clark Y, high-lift aerofoil section and an increase of 2 ft. in the span, imparted a rate of climb superior to that of its predecessor. The prototype, G-AAWY, flew with a Hermes II engine in May 1930 but G-AAWZ and G-ABBE, first of the 12 production Arrows, were powered by Gipsy IIs for the King's Cup Race of 5 July 1930 piloted by W. A. Andrews and Capt. H. H. Balfour, M.P. for Thanet, at average speeds of 100·5 and 94·3 m.p.h. respectively. The Andrews/'WZ combination also put up a fine performance in the International Round Europe Touring Competition a month later.

First Spartan Arrow deliveries, made in December 1930, were G-ABGW to B. S. Thynne, Hamble, and 'HR, the only Arrow fitted with a Cirrus III, to the Household Brigade Flying Club, Heston. G-ABKL went to the Bristol and Wessex Aeroplane Club, Whitchurch, in April 1931. A single seater, 'HD, with Gipsy II, was delivered to the Australian pilot G. P. Fairbairn at Hanworth on 25 January 1931, for an attempt on the Australia record, but the flight ended at Nice on 20 February, one day after leaving Hanworth. The remaining distance was covered by sea, the Arrow subsequently seeing considerable service in Australia as VH-UQD before being destroyed in a crash at Essendon aerodrome, Melbourne, on 11 June 1935.

Capt. Balfour's G-ABBE went to the M.A.E.E., Felixstowe, at the end of 1930 for floatplane trials, which were followed by an order from the Hon. A. E. Guinness for G-ABMK, a Hermes powered Arrow on floats. This was first flown at Cowes under B conditions as S-1 in June 1931, but the owner's interest in larger marine aircraft led to its sale as a landplane to George Duller at Woodley in February 1933.

G-ABBE was later shipped to New Zealand and after erection at Wigram was delivered to new owner Frank Lysons on 31 May 1931 as ZK-ACQ. He flew it to Blenheim on the same day but on arrival, spun in off a subsequent take-off. The remains were carefully pieced together at Wellington by A. J. Dingle and its career as a politician's aeroplane was resumed in 1934 when, in a lurid checked paint scheme, it was sold to M. H. Oram (later Sir Matthew, Speaker of the House of Representatives). It was then based at Palmerston North where it was destroyed when a gale blew in the hangar roof on 2 February 1936.

Although no Arrow ever again raced for the King's Cup, Flt. Lt. G. H. Stainforth flew the 9th production aircraft, G-ABOB, in the *Morning Post* Race at Heston on 21 May 1932, but averaged a humble 79·2 m.p.h. to come 13th, an unhappy position reached in the same machine by Lt. Col. L. A. Strange in the Heston–Cramlington Race of 16 August 1933. It went on to enjoy a successful career in private and club ownership, ended with the Exeter and Thanet Aero Clubs in 1938–39, but was more noteworthy as the last Arrow fitted with ailerons on all four wings. The remaining six Arrows had them only on the lower mainplanes, and included a special aircraft, G-ABST, with non-standard rudder, built as a flying test bed for the new Napier E.97 six cylinder, air-cooled engine, later known as the Javelin. Relays

The Gipsy powered Arrow floatplane G-ABBE at Felixstowe, December 1930.
(*Crown Copyright Reserved*)

G-ABST, the Napier Javelin III flying test bed. (*Flight Photo*)

of pilots put in hundreds of hours of test flying with this Arrow at Heston in 1932–33 and during the same period the second prototype, 'WZ, was in similar employ at Croydon by Cirrus Aero Engines Ltd., fitted with their Hermes II and flown by J. V. Holman.

Production of the Arrow ended in 1933 with the delivery of G-ACHE, 'HF and 'HG, the second of which was the centre of a fatal drama at Brooklands on 13 September 1933, when its first owner, Lady Clayton East Clayton, fell out on take-off and was killed. Later it went to Lympne to be flown by the Marquess of Kildare in 1935 and by T. A. S. Webb in the following year, coming 4th in the Wakefield Trophy Race. Bought by the Romford Flying Club in March 1939, its end came in the fire at Maylands on 6 February 1940. Its career was rivalled only by the fifth production Arrow, G-ABWR, which, between 1932 and its sale in Denmark in August 1938, was owned successively by R. V. L'Estrange Malone, Heston; H. V. K. Atkinson and Flying Hire Ltd. at Chilworth; Rollason Aircraft Services Ltd., Croydon, and W. J. Gunther, Gravesend.

G-ACHG, which also went to Denmark, was further sold in Sweden in 1937 and had an even longer career, being still in service with the Östersunds Flygklubb in 1951.

At the outbreak of the 1939–45 war the first prototype, re-engined with a Gipsy II, was in use by the Isle of Wight Flying Club at Sandown, where it was eventually dismantled and the parts used to build a primary glider. The second Arrow, 'WZ, was at Ford with the Yapton Aero Club and 'KL, owned by E. D. Ward, was destroyed in the Hooton fire of 8 July 1940. One other, the Hermes II model G-ABWP, bought by R. O. Shuttleworth in December 1936, reappeared at the Fifty Years of Flying Exhibition at Hendon in July 1951 after years in storage at Old Warden. Two years later it began a post-war career with a brand new C. of A. with W. G. Lilleystone's group at Croydon, passing in April 1955 into the hands of the Spartan Group with which it flew at Denham until sold to R. E. Blain in August 1964. After 1967 it was stored at Baginton awaiting overhaul.

SPECIFICATION

Manufacturers: Spartan Aircraft Ltd., Weston, Southampton, moved to East Cowes, Isle of Wight, 20 February 1931.

Power Plants: One 100 h.p. de Havilland Gipsy I.
One 120 h.p. de Havilland Gipsy II.
One 95 h.p. A.D.C. Cirrus III.
One 105 h.p. Cirrus Hermes II.
One 160 h.p. Napier Javelin III.

Dimensions: Span, 30 ft. 7 in. Length, 25 ft. 0 in. Height, 9 ft. 6 in. Wing area, 251 sq. ft.

Weights: (Standard) Tare weight, 965 lb. All-up weight, 1,750 lb.*
(Javelin) Tare weight, 1,207 lb. All-up weight, 1,730 lb.

Performance: Maximum speed, 106 m.p.h. Cruising speed, 92 m.p.h. Initial climb, 830 ft./min. Range, 432 miles.

* Late production 1,850 lb.

Production: Fifteen British registered aircraft comprising (c/n 51 and 52) G-AAWY and 'WZ, followed by a batch of 13 running consecutively from c/n 75.

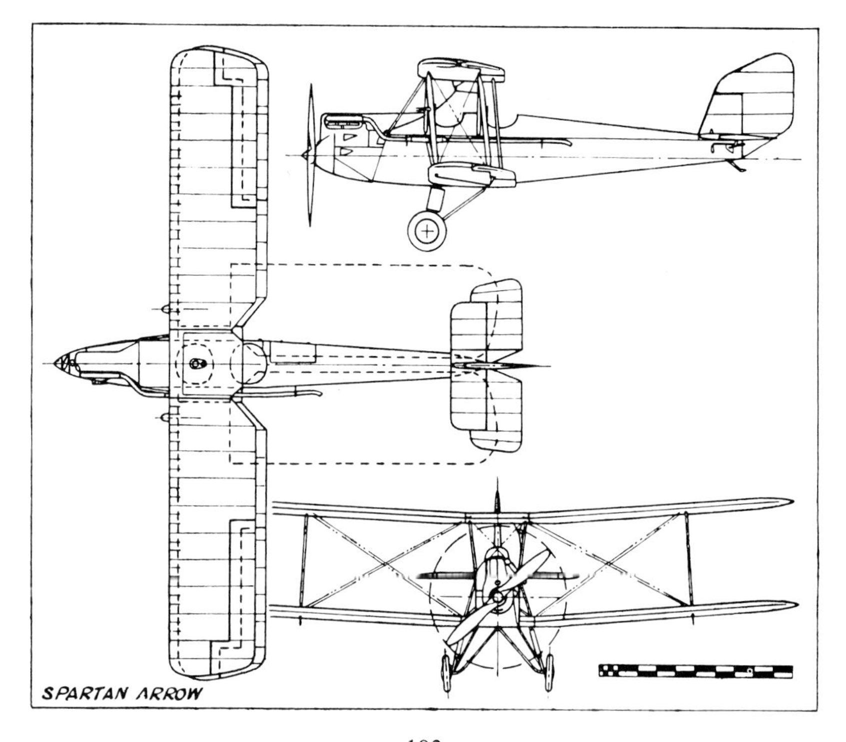

The Hermes II powered Spartan Three Seater I G-ABRA of the Spartan Air Circus 1932.

Spartan Three Seater I and II

Spartan Aircraft Ltd. produced both two and three seat successors to the original Simmonds Spartan and these were designated Spartan Arrow and Spartan Three Seater respectively. The latter was structurally similar to the Arrow, with plywood fuselage and wooden wings, but retained the characteristic rudder of the original Simmonds Spartan. Commencing with Sandown and Shanklin Flying Services' red G-ABAZ 'Island Queen', 19 Three Seaters were built at Cowes 1930–32, all of British registry except the 11th, which was sold in Australia as VH-URB and crashed at Mundaring, W.A. on 16 October 1938. Five were fitted with Gipsy IIs and the rest with Hermes IIs.

Although few in number, Spartan Three Seaters became one of the mainstays of the pleasure flight trade in the 1930s. In 1939 'AZ was still circuiting Sandown Bay, while the second and third aircraft, 'ET and 'KJ, were similarly employed along the East Coast by Lawn Parks (Skegness) Ltd. British Air Transport's black and white G-ABTU worthily upheld the Avro tradition at Croydon, Addiscombe and Redhill; 'JS toured with C. D. Barnard's Circus in 1931; 'WU spent 1933 doing 10*s*. flights round Southend Pier; Rollason's 'WV toured with National Aviation Day Displays; and 'LJ spent its life on the same errand, first with Portsmouth, Southsea and Isle of Wight Aviation Ltd. and later at Ford with the Yapton Aero Club. Hayling Island's Three Seater was 'YH, destroyed there in 1935 in a fatal crash when attempting a publicity loop at low altitude. Spartan joyriding activities also extended to Africa, where G-ABPZ, 'RA and 'RB of Skywork Ltd., piloted by Oscar Garden, E. D. Ayre and others, toured 64 towns in 1932. G-ABRA then returned home to spend a season at Allhallows, Kent, piloted by John Stark; 'PZ staying at the Cape while Oscar Garden took 'RB into the Sudan and Egypt with Tanganyikan marks during 1933.

Trading as Air Trips Ltd., those immortal ladies Pauline Gower and

Dorothy Spicer made 'KK the best remembered of the Spartan Three Seaters. Named 'Helen of Troy', it ranged between Shoreham, Blackpool and Haldon with the Crimson Fleet in 1932, visited 185 towns with British Hospital's Air Pageants in 1933 and spent 1934–35 at Hunstanton and with Jubilee Air Displays. Its career ended in 1936, with Campbell Black's Air Circus, in a take-off collision at Westwood, Coventry. Several flying clubs augmented their incomes with Spartan joyriding, including Peterborough with 'KT and Romford with 'WO in 1939, but few were privately owned. J. Miskelly kept the cabin Three Seater 'WX at Dumfries for a few months in 1933 and Neville Browning had 'YG at Abridge in 1935. G-ABLJ, kept at Tangmere by A. C. Douglas in 1939, was acquired by C. J. Rice in 1942 and conveyed on a trailer to Leicester, where it was given to the A.T.C. Only one Three Seater essayed a racing career, G-ABTT, winner of a local race at Skegness on 14 May 1932, piloted by Capt. Gordon Store of Imperial Airways. Exactly a week later it flew into a tree during the *Morning Post* Race, Flt. Lt. F. G. Gibbons being killed.

Two years at the most gruelling form of aerial work had shown the need for better pilot view and less difficult entry for passengers. In the Three Seater II, the prototype of which, G-ABTR, was introduced by Lt. Col. L. A. Strange at Henlys' Rally, Heston on 4 June 1932, both requirements were brilliantly met by cockpit reversal and the use of the Hermes IIB inverted engine. The earlier model then became known as the Three Seater I, but neither should be identified with the original three seat Simmonds Spartan, which was an entirely different aeroplane. 'TR then embarked on a racing programme for publicity purposes, winning the Skegness Race at 100·25 m.p.h. on 31 July, coming 4th in the Heston–Cramlington Race on 6 August and winning the Thanet Air Race at Ramsgate at 96·5 m.p.h. on 17 September.

Only six production models were built, all Hermes IV powered. The first, G-ABYN, privately owned by E. G. Croskin at Hedon, Hull, in 1935, eventually went to Ireland and was still flying in Tipperary in 1950. Aerofilms Ltd. used 'ZH as a photographic aircraft, but it also toured with the circuses, as did the Cornwall Aviation Company's G-ACAF, and 'AD

G-ABWX, only Three Seater I to be fitted with an enclosed passenger cockpit. (*Aerofilms Ltd.*)

Prototype Spartan Three Seater II G-ABTR (Hermes IIB) and the first production machine G-ABYN (Hermes IV) at the special Spartan demonstration, Heston, 30 August 1932. (*Flight Photo 12216*)

Sole example of a cabin Three Seater II, G-ABTR flew with Spartan Air Lines during the 1933 season. (*Flight Photo 13146*)

successor to the Gower/Spicer 'KK. The last Spartan of all, G-ACEF, privately owned at Christchurch by H. Pritchett 1935–37, ended its days with Malling Aviation Ltd. Only one, 'ZI, exchanged a hard-working for an eventful career, going to Iraq Airwork Ltd. as YI-AAB in January 1933 and returning to Hendon two years later for the use of officers of No. 601 Squadron. It was burned out on the roof of the station buildings at Farnborough in August 1936 after an haphazard take-off.

The last surviving Spartan Three Seater was G-ABTR operated by United

Airways Ltd. and British Airways Ltd. 1934–36 and later employed joyriding with F. G. Barnard at Hayling Island. It was burned as a derelict in 1947 after wartime storage at Gatwick.

SPECIFICATION

Manufacturers: Spartan Aircraft Ltd., Weston, Southampton, moved to East Cowes, Isle of Wight, 20 February 1931.

Power Plants: (Three Seater I) One 120 h.p. de Havilland Gipsy II.
One 115 h.p. Cirrus Hermes II.
(Three Seater II) One 115 h.p. Cirrus Hermes IIB.
One 120 h.p. Cirrus Hermes IV.

Dimensions: Span, 28 ft. 10 in. Length, 26 ft. 3 in. Height, 9 ft. 8 in. Wing area, 240 sq. ft.

Weights: Tare weight (Mk.I), 1,030 lb. (Mk.II), 1,150 lb. All-up weight (Mk.I), 1,680 lb. (Mk.II), 1,850 lb.

Performance: (Three Seater I) Maximum speed, 103 m.p.h. Cruising speed, 90 m.p.h. Initial climb, 600 ft./min. Ceiling, 15,000 ft. Range, 300 miles.
(Three Seater II) Maximum speed, 107 m.p.h. Cruising speed, 95 m.p.h. Initial climb, 750 ft./min. Range, 260 miles.

Production: Nineteen Three Seater Is, including (c/n 63) VH-URB; and a total of seven Three Seater IIs, all British registered.

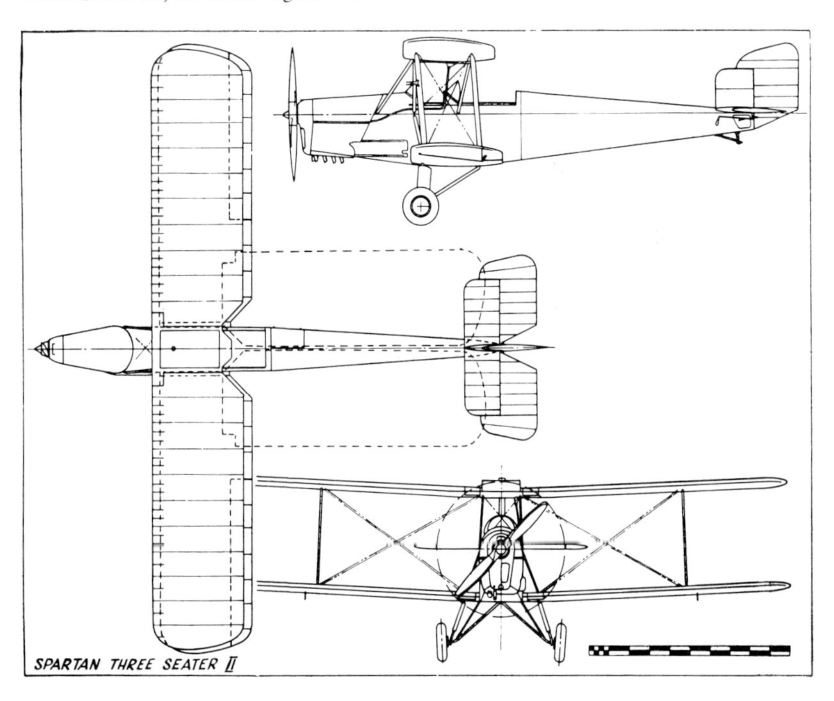

Cruiser II G-ACVT at Croydon in 1934 showing the revised windscreen and cabin windows incorporated in the four final aircraft.

Spartan Cruiser

The Cruiser stemmed from the Saro-Percival Mailplane, G-ABLI, designed by E. W. Percival and built under his supervision at Cowes in 1931 as a joint project with Saunders-Roe Ltd. It was a low-wing cantilever monoplane, with typically Percival plywood fuselage and wooden wing, powered by three 120 h.p. D.H. Gipsy III engines, and carried a single pilot ahead of the mail compartment. It was test flown and seen through the Martlesham C. of A. trials by E. W. Percival early in 1932 but soon afterwards he sold his interests in the aircraft when Saunders-Roe Ltd. was financially reorganised. The aircraft was then redesignated Saro A.24 Mailplane, but when close ties between the Saunders-Roe and Spartan companies, both of East Cowes, led to development being transferred to Spartan, the name was changed finally to Spartan Mailplane.

The single fin and rudder was then replaced by a twin unit and two cramped passenger seats, fitted in the mail compartment with windows, for a flight to India piloted by T. Neville Stack. Named 'Blackpool', it left Stanley Park Aerodrome with civic blessings on 15 June 1932, reaching Drigh Road, Karachi, in an elapsed time of 5 days 23 hours 50 minutes. After demonstration before the Director of Civil Aviation, it returned home, making a forced landing in Greece with an oil leak en route.

Although the pure mail carrier had no future, the design held promise for passenger work, team effort at East Cowes being rewarded by successful trials of the Spartan Cruiser I, G-ABTY, by Lt. Col. L. A. Strange in May 1932. As indicated by the constructor's number 24M, E. W. Percival's low-wing trimotor layout had been retained, but an all-metal fuselage had been built to accommodate six passengers and two crew. The structural features of the stressed-skin hull and plywood-covered wing of the Cutty Sark, had been adapted for the Cruiser, which also used cabin glazing reminiscent of the Saro Segrave Meteor. The new machine was demonstrated at the first Hendon S.B.A.C. Show of 27 June 1932, and alongside its predecessor, the Mailplane, at the Spartan demonstration at Heston on 30 August. Piloted by Lt. Col. L. A. Strange, it conveyed H.R.H. the Prince of Wales from Sunningdale to

Croydon on 22 September, carried the Lord Mayor of London from Heston to Maylands to open the Essex Air Display on the 24th and left on 14 October for a European sales tour. On its return to Heston on the 25th, 3,593 miles had been covered at an average speed of 113 m.p.h. Demonstrations made to the Jugoslav airline Aeroput at Belgrade on 19 October eventually led to an order for two aircraft and a licence to build further examples in Jugoslavia, although only YU-SAP, c/n 1, completed in 1935, is believed to have resulted.

The first Cruiser II, flown in February 1933, was ordered by Iraq Airwork Ltd. for an experimental air route between Baghdad and Mosul, and although initially registered G-ACBM, was flown out in Airwork white and green as YI-AAA by T. Neville Stack. It was powered by three Hermes IVs and entered by a cabin door instead of via folding side and roof panels, while the pilot's windscreen was V-shaped for improved vision. During the next two years, eleven more Cruiser IIs were built, five of which, fruits of the overseas sales tours, were sold abroad. Two were flown to Belgrade on delivery to the Jugoslav airline Aeroput and two to the Bata Shoe Company at Zlin,

The Saro-Percival Mailplane.

Cruiser I showing the early type of cabin glazing. (*Aeroplane*)

Cruiser III G-ADEM, last of all the Cruisers. (*J. G. Ellison*)

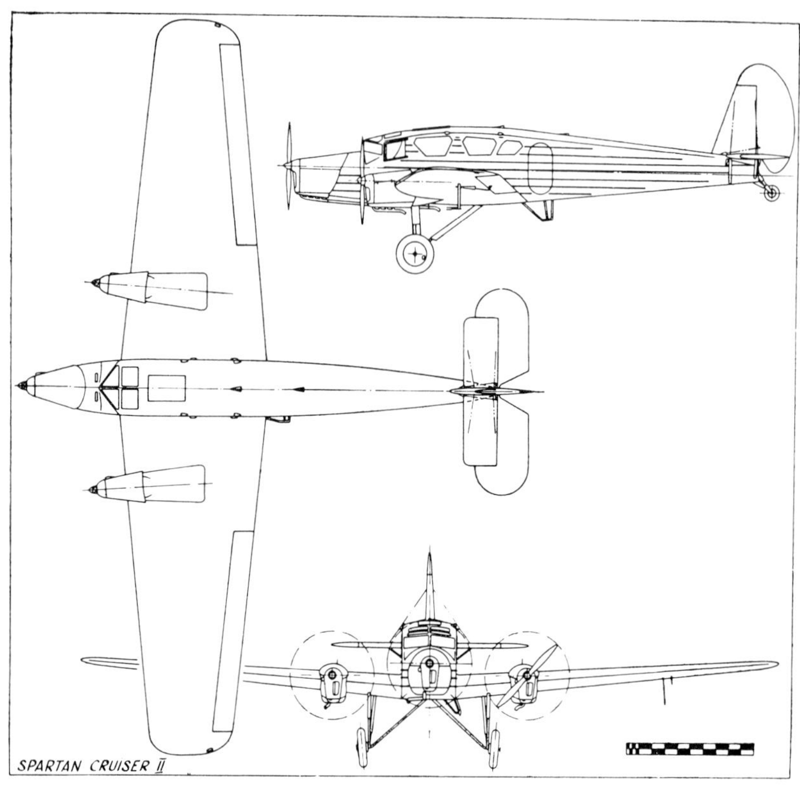

Czechoslovakia. In May–June 1934 the first of these, G-ACNO/OK-ATQ 'Cape of Good Hope', carried out a successful 21,900 mile business trip of Europe, the Near East, Egypt, Sudan and South Africa.

The majority of Cruisers were Gipsy Major powered but the 5th aircraft, G-ACKG, shipped to India as VT-AER for the Maharaja of Patiala in November 1933, had Hermes IVs while G-ACOU, second for Bata, had Czech-built Walter Major 4s.

An operating company known as Spartan Air Lines Ltd., formed to open an internal air route between Heston and Cowes, began operations on 1 April 1933, with the Cruiser I and two new Cruiser IIs, G-ACDW and 'DX. The firm's chief pilot, P. W. Lynch Blosse, flew 'DW, specially named 'Faithful City', to Australia and back at the end of the season, on charter to Capt. W. P. Crawford Green and Lord Apsley. Leaving on 9 October 1933, Sydney was reached on the 30th, and the machine eventually arrived home to make a precautionary landing on St. Osyth beach, Essex. The Southern Railway then acquired a controlling interest in Spartan Air Lines and the London terminus was transferred to Croydon on 1 May 1934. Two new Cruiser IIs, G-ACSM and 'VT, were then commissioned together with 'BM, back from Iraq to replace 'DW, which had left Heston as SU-ABL on delivery to Misr Airwork Ltd., at Almaza, Cairo, in April. They were joined in the following year by the final Cruiser II, G-ACZM, built to replace the Cruiser I G-ABTY which had been sold to the Hon. Mrs. Victor Bruce in February 1935 for Channel Air Lines' early morning newspaper runs to Le Bourget, during which it was lost in a forced landing in the Channel a few months later. The penultimate Cruiser II, 'YL, built for United Airways Ltd., operated between Heston, Stanley Park, Blackpool and Ronaldsway throughout 1935.

Cruiser production finally ended in May 1935 with the delivery to Spartan Air Lines of the third Spartan Cruiser III, of similar design to the Mk.II but with aerodynamically refined fuselage, modified windscreen, empennage and trousered undercarriage. Passenger accommodation was increased to eight and the prototype, G-ACYK, made its public debut at the Heathrow Garden Party of the Royal Aeronautical Society on 5 May 1935.

The year 1936 saw the absorption of Spartan Air Lines by British Airways Ltd., and the transference of the surviving Cruisers to a new base at Eastleigh, from which they worked over the Isle of Wight, Heston, Blackpool, Isle of Man network. The Cruiser IIIs carried Railway Air Services Ltd.'s livery during the season, but G-ADEM was burned out at Stanley Park in November of that year, Capt. O'Connell and a passenger being killed when it flew into a hangar when taking off in fog. The four surviving Cruisers were then taken over by Northern and Scottish Airways Ltd., Renfrew, continuing in service to the Highlands and Islands until the outbreak of war. From August 1937 they did so under Scottish Airways ownership, three being impressed by the R.A.F. in April 1940. G-ACYK lay in the hills near Largs after it crashed on 14 January 1938, until the cabin section was retrieved by a R.N. Sea King helicopter on 25 July 1973.

SPECIFICATION

Manufacturers: Spartan Aircraft Ltd., East Cowes, Isle of Wight, Hants.

Power Plants:
(Mailplane) Three 120 h.p. de Havilland Gipsy III.
(Cruiser I) Three 120 h.p. de Havilland Gipsy III.
(Cruiser II) Three 130 h.p. de Havilland Gipsy Major.
Three 130 h.p. Cirrus Hermes IV.
Three 130 h.p. Walter Major 4.
(Cruiser III) Three 130 h.p. de Havilland Gipsy Major.

	Mailplane	Cruiser I	Cruiser II	Cruiser III
Span	56 ft. 0 in.	54 ft. 0 in.	54 ft. 0 in.	54 ft. 0 in.
Length	41 ft. 6 in.	39 ft. 2 in.	39 ft. 2 in.	41 ft. 0 in.
Height	9 ft. 0 in.	10 ft. 0 in.	10 ft. 0 in.	9 ft. 6 in.
Wing area	470 sq. ft.	436 sq. ft.	436 sq. ft.	436 sq. ft.
Tare weight	4,425 lb.	3,400 lb.	3,650 lb.	4,010 lb.
All-up weight	5,645 lb.	5,500 lb.	6,200 lb.	6,200 lb.
Maximum speed	122 m.p.h.	135 m.p.h.	133 m.p.h.	135 m.p.h.
Cruising speed	105 m.p.h.	110 m.p.h.	115 m.p.h.	118 m.p.h.
Initial climb	500 ft./min.	600 ft./min.	630 ft./min.	600 ft./min.
Ceiling	–	13,000 ft.	15,000 ft.	15,000 ft.
Range	400 miles	660 miles	310 miles	550 miles

Production: One Cruiser I; 12 Cruiser II (c/n 13 not used); three Cruiser III. The entire production was British registered.

G-EAED/N1529, the first civil Channel, leaving Southampton on the inaugural flight to Le Havre, August 1919. (*The Supermarine Aviation Works Ltd.*)

Supermarine Channel

The A.D. two-seat patrol flying boat of 1916 was designed jointly by Lt. Linton Hope, Harold Bolas, Harold Yendall and Clifford W. Tinson and had a flexible wooden monococque hull which unconcernedly absorbed punishment from rough seas. The wings folded forward and construction took place at the Woolston, Southampton, works of Pemberton Billing Ltd. where 27 had been completed by the 1918 Armistice. A number of these were repurchased from the Air Ministry by the Supermarine Aviation Works Ltd., successors to the Pemberton Billing concern, and converted for civil use with 160 h.p. Beardmore engine driving a pusher airscrew and with the forward part of the hull seating two passengers in tandem with a third in the bows and the pilot behind.

An initial batch of ten, redesignated Supermarine Channels, were registered to Supermarine as G-EAED to 'EM on 11 June 1919, three of which, G-EAED, 'EE and 'EK, still bearing R.A.F. serials, began pleasure flights along the South Coast with the first Cs. of A. issued to British commercial flying boats. Brisk business was done at Bournemouth Pier and chief pilot Cdr. B. D. Hobbs organised the daily positioning flight from Woolston into a regular service. During Cowes Week a Channel stationed on the Medina was chartered on 7 August for a flight round H.M.S. *Renown* as it left Portsmouth with H.R.H. the Prince of Wales aboard. Later in the month 'ED received a civic send-off at the inauguration of the world's first international flying boat service to Le Havre and a local service to Cowes also began. The Channels taxied from the Woolston works to embark passengers at Royal Pier but 'EE overturned and sank during a pleasure flight at Bournemouth on 15 August and commercial operations ceased at the end of the season.

In 1920 Channels G-EAEH, 'EI and 'EL were despatched to Norway in crates for Norske Luftreideri's mail and passenger service between Stavanger and Bergen. From difficult anchorages, over difficult terrain and frequently in marginal weather, they operated with 94·4% regularity until the company was wound up in December 1920. A fourth Channel, believed to have been G-EAEM, was a dual control trainer for the Royal Norwegian Navy based at Horten.

G-EAEF, 'EG and 'EJ were shipped to Bermuda in April 1920 and spent the following winter in highly successful pleasure flying operations with the Bermuda and Western Atlantic Aviation Co. Ltd. One of several novel charters involved overtaking and landing alongside a United States bound steamship and transferring actress Pearl White. Shortage of spares ended their careers within a few months but 'EG was shipped to Trinidad in March 1921 to join two Channel Mk.IIs G-EAWC and 'WP.

Powered by the 240 h.p. Siddeley Puma, these had strutted wing tip floats and watertight camera doors let into the hull bottoms. Flown by C. E. Ward and F. Bailey of Bermuda and Western Atlantic Aviation Co. Ltd., they prospected for oil in the Orinoco Delta, Venezuela, under the direction of Major Cochran Patrick. Neither carried markings and one was detached later for the aerial survey of Georgetown, British Guiana, but sank in the River Essequibo after colliding with driftwood.

In May 1921 another unmarked Channel, actually G-NZAI, was shipped to Walsh Bros. and Dexter for the New Zealand Flying School, Auckland. It was a hybrid with 160 h.p. Beardmore and Mk.II airframe and made the first ever Auckland–Wellington flight on 4 October 1921 piloted by George Bolt. Early in July 1922 it was shipped to Fiji for a two-week, 1,000 mile, survey of the main islands of the group, flown by Capt. A. C. Upham and on its return was fitted with a 240 h.p. Puma and remained in service until 1926. Its hull was still used as a boat in 1943.

Six more Channel IIs received certificates of airworthiness in 1920–21 for export without markings, including four for the Imperial Japanese Navy taken out by the British Aviation Mission, and one each for Cuba and Chile.

Launching Channel G-EAEJ of the Bermuda and Western Atlantic Aviation Co. Ltd.

SPECIFICATION

Manufacturers:	The Supermarine Aviation Works Ltd., Woolston, Southampton, Hants.
Power Plants:	(Channel Mk.I) One 160 h.p. Beardmore.
	(Channel Mk.II) One 240 h.p. Siddeley Puma.
Dimensions:	Span, 50 ft. 4 in. Length, 30 ft. 7 in. Height, 13 ft. 1 in. Wing area, 479 sq. ft.
**Weights:*	All-up weight 3,400 lb.
**Performance:*	Maximum speed 100 m.p.h. Ceiling 10,000 ft. Duration 5 hours.

* Channel Mk.I.

Production: (a) Channel Mk.I

Ten aircraft of British registry listed in Appendix E.

(b) Channel Mk.II

Two aircraft of British registry and the following for export: (c/n 1037), unregistered, C. of A. 13.7.20, British Controlled Oil Field Co., Trinidad; (1142), G-NZAI, 17.12.20; (1148), Imperial Japanese Navy, 3.12.21; (1149), unregistered, 24.8.21, Cuba; (1150 and 1155), Imperial Japanese Navy, 17.12.21; (1156), Imperial Japanese Navy, 20.12.21.

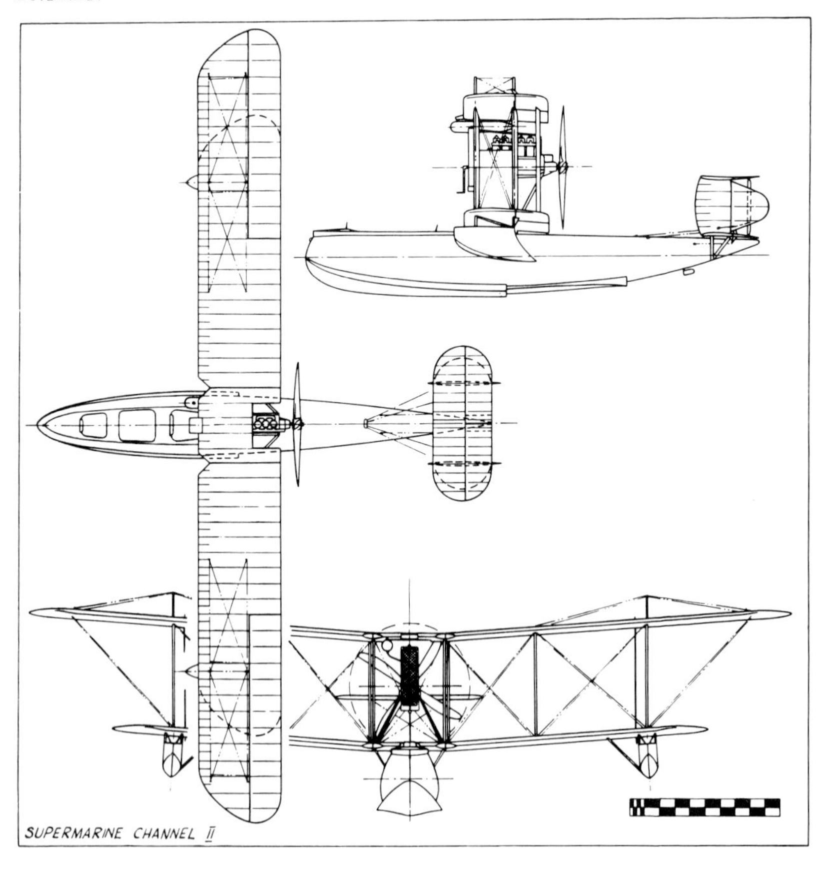

The Romford Flying Club's Taylorcraft Plus C, flying at Maylands, August 1939.

Taylorcraft Plus C and D

Taylorcraft Aeroplanes (England) Ltd. was formed in November 1938 to build the Taylorcraft side-by-side, two seat, high-wing monoplane under licence from the Taylor Young Airplane Corporation in the U.S.A. Following contemporary American practice, the Taylorcraft Model A was fabric-covered with welded steel tube fuselage and a wing of mixed construction braced by steel struts. Six examples, powered by the 40 h.p. Continental flat four engine had already been imported, the first of which, G-AFDN, was exhibited as a 'Taylor Young' at the Heathrow Garden Party of the Royal Aeronautical Society on 8 May 1938. After a season with C. N. Prentice at Ipswich, it joined a similar machine, 'KN, at the West Suffolk Aero Club, Bury St. Edmunds. The other four comprised 'HF of Cambridgeshire Flying Services Ltd., Ely; 'JO with Reid and Sigrist Ltd., Desford; 'JP at Meir with the South Staffs Aero Club, and 'JW with the County Flying Club, Rearsby, Leicester. A seventh, 'KO, a Model B with 50 h.p. Continental, was also based at Rearsby for publicity and test purposes by the new British licensee, who had opened a factory at Thurmaston, three miles away.

To differentiate them from the American machines the British versions were designated Taylorcraft C, later changed to Taylorcraft Plus C. The prototype, G-AFNW, completed at Thurmaston in April 1939, was taken to Rearsby for erection and flight, over a road traversed by all aircraft built by the firm during the next seven years. Powered by a 55 h.p. Lycoming and fitted with dual control for use by the County Flying Club, 'NW was the forerunner of 22 production aircraft delivered in the summer of 1939 to private owners, the Coventry, Derby, Grimsby, Luton, Maidstone, Romford and West Suffolk clubs and the Wiltshire School of Flying.

The 11th airframe, built with 90 h.p. Cirrus Minor 1 in June 1939, was delivered to the R.A.F. as T9120 under the designation Auster I. Two months later the 25th aircraft, G-AFWN, also flew with this type of engine to become prototype of the civil Taylorcraft Plus D. Eight production aircraft appeared too late for bona fide civil use, four being impressed in 1940 for communications work in France and A.O.P. duties with No. 651 Squadron, a fate which befell the majority of Plus C machines. They were then re-engined by the R.A.F. with Cirrus Minor 1s and redesignated Taylorcraft Plus C.2. The prototype Plus D, G-AFWN, remained stored in a crashed condition until rebuilt as the prototype Autocrat in 1945 (See Volume 1, page 63).

Air Ministry trials of the Auster I led to a contract for 100 similar aircraft in 1941, final development work being undertaken at Larkhill by No. 651 Squadron with the last two civil machines G-AGBF and 'DB in August 1940 and September 1941 respectively. After a short Service life, the Auster Is, many in new condition, were stored at M.U.s until disposed of by public tender in 1945–46, when 58 became civil as Taylorcraft Plus Ds. Seven pre-war civil machines also survived, four of which had lost their previous identities and received post-war registrations. The prototype Auster I, T9120, also reappeared to fly at Thruxton with the Wiltshire School of Flying as G-AHAF until wrecked by a sister machine G-AHUG, which landed on top of it on 29 May 1948. At Rearsby, three former R.A.F. aircraft G-AHCR, 'GX and 'HC were temporarily fitted with 55 h.p. Lycoming engines in 1947, approximating to Plus Cs until the Cirrus Minors were re-installed in 1948.

Plus C.2 G-AHLJ, flown by the Fairoaks Aero Club in 1959, was first delivered to the Suffolk Aero Club in May 1939 as G-AFTZ, suffered

Taylorcraft Plus D G-AHUG, formerly an Auster I LB282, operated by the Reading Aero Club at Woodley 1960 but previously in executive use by Feltrex Ltd. and Polythene Ltd. (*A. J. Jackson*)

impressment and later spent 12 post-war years at Chilbolton on Vickers-Armstrongs communications work. Two American-built Taylorcraft Model As, G-AFJO and 'JP, spent the war in storage, to fly again in 1946 with P. S. Clifford, Walsall, and T. C. Sparrow, Christchurch, respectively. For six years mainstay of the Rotol Flying Club at Staverton, 'JO crashed in 1952, a year before the other passed away at Woodbridge, Suffolk, under group ownership with the Flying Tiger Cubs.

In the post-war years the Taylorcraft Plus C.2 and D machines did yeoman service with private owners, they took the hard knocks of instructional flying and served with 23 flying clubs. Seldom in the sporting headlines, the type made history at Woolsington on 12 July 1952, when Cyril Gregory flew a brilliant race in G-AHGZ, cunningly tuned, to win the King's Cup at an average speed of 113·5 m.p.h.

Advancing age, accidents and sales in Finland, Southern Rhodesia, Germany, Ireland and Switzerland took their toll and in 1973 only seven remained active in Britain. The last 'new' machine, G-ARRK, built at Rearsby for the Shropshire Flying Group, Sleap, in 1961 using parts of three deceased machines G-AHUM, 'XG and G-AIIU, was sold to the Munster Aero Club at Cork in April 1962 as EI-AMF.

SPECIFICATION

Manufacturers: (Taylorcraft A) Taylor Young Airplane Corporation, Alliance, Ohio, U.S.A.
(Taylorcraft Plus C and D) Taylorcraft Aeroplanes (England) Ltd., Britannia Works, Thurmaston and Rearsby Aerodrome, Leicester.

Power Plants: (Taylorcraft A) One 40 h.p. Continental A-40-4.
One 40 h.p. Continental A-40-5.
One 50 h.p. Continental A-50.
(Taylorcraft Plus C) One 55 h.p. Lycoming O-145-A2.
(Taylorcraft Plus C.2 and D) One 90 h.p. Blackburn Cirrus Minor 1.

Dimensions: Span, 36 ft. 0 in. Length, 22 ft. 10 in. Height, 8 ft. 0 in. Wing area, 167 sq. ft.

	Model A	Model C	Model C.2	Model D
Tare weight	586 lb.	720 lb.	833 lb.	890 lb.
All-up weight	1,050 lb.	1,200 lb.	1,300 lb.	1,450 lb.
Maximum speed	91 m.p.h.	110 m.p.h.	125 m.p.h.	120 m.p.h.
Cruising speed	80 m.p.h.	90 m.p.h.	107 m.p.h.	102 m.p.h.
Initial climb	390 ft./min.	550 ft./min.	1,000 ft./min.	1,000 ft./min.
Ceiling	14,000 ft.	–	–	–
Range	230 miles	275 miles	325 miles	325 miles

Production: Twenty-three British registered Plus C and (c/n 110) T9120 for the R.A.F. (post-war G-AHAF); nine British registered Plus D; and 58 post-war Auster I conversions including six for export: (c/n 176) LB317/HB-EUL; (203) LB344/EI-ACJ; (218) LB371/OO-ABI, later F-BEXR; (226) LB379/EI-ACN; (227) LB380/OO-YES; (232) OO-JAQ.

Tipsy Belfair G-AOXO flying near Blackbushe in 1971. (*Tony Leigh*)

Tipsy Trainer 1 and Belfair

The performance and handling qualities of the S.2 single seater led E. O. Tips to produce a two seater of similar design, powered by the Czech-built 62 h.p. Walter Mikron and known as the Tipsy B. Following a demonstration of the prototype, OO-DON, at Heathrow on 14 May 1937, Brian Allen Aviation Ltd., acquired the selling rights in the United Kingdom and imported two Tipsy Bs, G-AFCM and 'EI, early in the following year. Arrangements were also made for Tipsy Aircraft Ltd. to acquire premises at Hanworth for its manufacture under licence. The Heathrow Garden Party of the Royal Aeronautical Society on 8 May 1938, thus saw a formation by Belgian Tipsy Bs 'CM and 'EI flown by Brian Allen and E. D. Ward and the first British-built model G-AFGF piloted by F. Wesson. A number of important differences were evident between the models, the Britisher having a strengthened mainplane with wash-out at the tips, camber changing flaps, mass balanced controls and a one-piece elevator with the hinge line of the latter normal to the fore-and-aft axis of the aircraft.

Before war stopped production, 15 Tipsy two seaters had been constructed but in view of the many differences from the Tipsy B, the designation was changed to Tipsy Trainer at the 6th aircraft and to Tipsy Trainer 1, with an increase in gross weight to 1,200 lb. at the 9th. Eight were used for Civil Air Guard training: G-AFJR and 'JS at Sherburn-in-Elmet by the Yorkshire Aeroplane Club; 'RU, 'RV and 'VN at Kidlington by Airtraining (Oxford) Ltd.; 'RT and 'VP at Bekesbourne by the Kent Flying Club; and 'SC by the Airwork Flying Club at Heston.

The seventh aircraft was shipped to the Indian Air Transport and Survey Co. Ltd., Calcutta, as VT-AKQ in March 1939 and the remainder were sold privately.

After the war three final Tipsy Trainer 1 machines, G-AISA–'SC, were erected by Tipsy Aircraft Ltd. in new premises on the Slough Trading Estate, two of which flew in 1947 and the other a year later. The last was used for tuition by the employees of the Fairey Aviation Co. Ltd., which on 1 July 1949, presented the other two to the Royal Naval Flying Club, Gosport. Tipsy Aircraft Ltd. finally closed down in 1952, burning Tipsy B G-AFCM and Trainers 'GF and 'RT at Slough in the process.

Ten Hanworth-built machines survived the war, most of which were still flying nearly three decades later. Three went overseas, the first of which, 'VO, was sent to Gosselies by the Fairey Company in 1946. G-AFJT, winner of the Grosvenor Trophy at Woolsington on 29 July 1950, piloted by K. C. Millican at 97·5 m.p.h., was sold to Kauhavan Ilmailukerho in Finland and the third, 'KP, which had flown throughout the war on Hordern-Richmond communications, went to Khartoum for the private use of W. C. Jelliss. It was damaged during a post-overhaul test flight in 1952 and later destroyed by local workmen who cut it up to fit the crate for shipment home.

In the post-war years Tipsy Trainer 1 G-AISC flew with the Armstrong Siddeley Flying Club at Baginton; 'VN at Heldre Hill, Welshpool, with the Montgomeryshire Ultra Light Flying Club; and 'SA with the Cardiff Ultra Light Aeroplane Club and as recently as 1973 three were still flying.

The second Tipsy B, OO-DOP, built at Gosselies in 1937, was fitted in 1939 with raised decking to the rear fuselage and perspex canopy to become

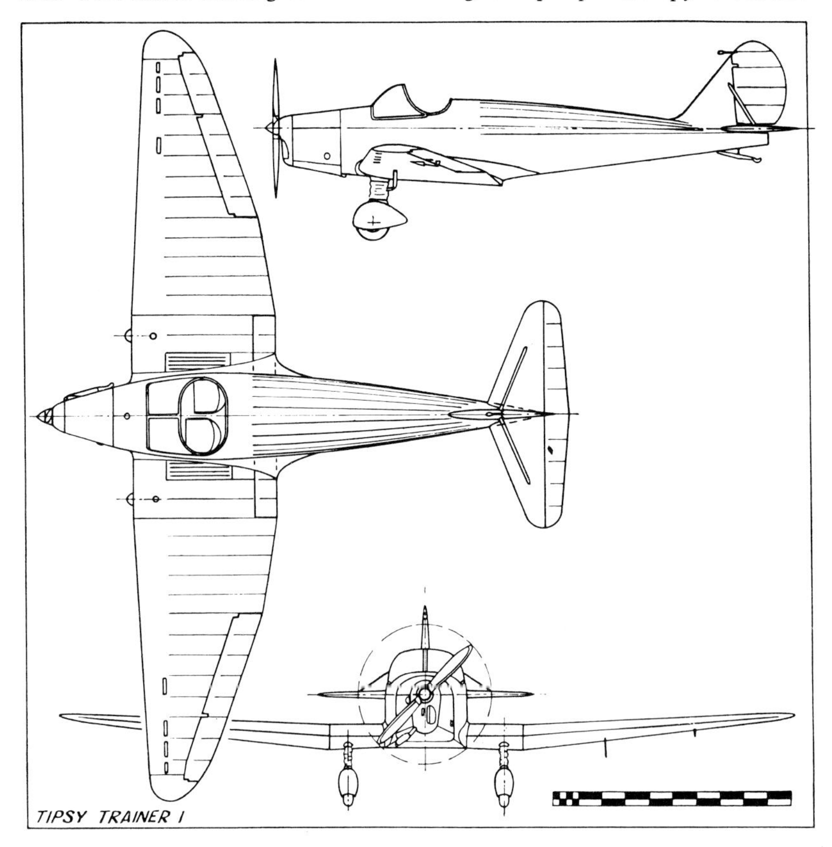
TIPSY TRAINER I

the prototype Tipsy BC cabin model. Escaping to England in 1940, it was used as a wartime communications aircraft, G-AGBM, by the Fairey Aviation Co. Ltd., but flew with Class B marking F-0222 until impressed by the R.A.F. as HM494 in June 1941. In 1946 it was demobilised and sold to E. O. Tips by J. C. Rice, returning to its native land as prototype of the post-war Tipsy Belfair. Seven of these little cabin two seaters were built at Gosselies in 1947, the last three of which were sold partially finished to D. Heaton at Speeton, Yorks. In 1957 they all went to Sherburn-in-Elmet for completion with the culinary registrations G-AOXO, G-APIE and G-APOD. The miniature production line also included the Barton Flying Group's Tipsy Trainer 1 G-AFJR, which was converted to Belfair standard so successfully that the group's pilot, J. Hill, had no difficulty in averaging 109·5 m.p.h. to win the Osram Cup at Baginton on 12 July 1958. All four were still active in 1973.

G-AFJT, fourth British built two seat Tipsy showing the one-piece elevator. *(W. K. Kilsby)*

SPECIFICATION

Manufacturers: Avions Fairey S.A., Gosselies, Belgium. Also the Tipsy Aircraft Co. Ltd., London Air Park, Hanworth, Middlesex; moved to Liverpool Road, Trading Estate, Slough, Bucks. in 1939.

Power Plants: (Tipsy B, Trainer 1 and Belfair) One 62 h.p. Walter Mikron 2.

Dimensions: Span, 31 ft. 2 in. Length, 21 ft. 8 in. Height, 5 ft. 8 in. Wing area, 129 sq. ft.

	Tipsy B	Tipsy Trainer 1	Belfair
Tare weight	496 lb.	668 lb.	624 lb.
All-up weight	992 lb.	1,073 lb.*	1,073 lb.
Maximum speed	124 m.p.h.	110 m.p.h.	110 m.p.h.
Cruising speed	106 m.p.h.	100 m.p.h.	100 m.p.h.
Initial climb	450 ft./min.	650 ft./min.	500 ft./min.
Ceiling	19,680 ft.	19,000 ft.	20,000 ft.
Range	450 miles	400 miles	300 miles

* 1,200 lb. commencing with the 9th aircraft.

Production: Nineteen aircraft, all but two of British registry: (c/n 7) VT-AKQ; (16) incomplete at the outbreak of war in 1939.

The Air Ministry Competition Vimy Commercial at Martlesham in August 1920. *(G. Clephane)*

Vickers F.B.27 Vimy and Vimy Commercial

The Vickers F.B.27 Vimy twin engined bomber of 1918 saw no war service but was the fastest weight lifter of its age. Designed by R. K. Pierson as a three bay, fabric-covered biplane of mixed construction, powered by two 360 h.p. Rolls-Royce Eagle VIIIs, it found employment in many peacetime Service roles and six became famous as civil aeroplanes. The first of these was the 13th Weybridge-built machine which was shipped to Newfoundland in April 1919 to be made ready for its historic Atlantic crossing. This was some weeks before civil flying was permitted officially and it was therefore too early to receive a registration. Piloted by Jack Alcock and Lt. Arthur Whitten Brown, it took-off from St. John's, Newfoundland on 14 June 1919 with 865 gallons of petrol and 50 gallons of oil at an all-up weight of 13,300 lb. and touched down 1,890 miles away at Clifden, Ireland, 15 hr. 57 min. later, bogged and broken at the end of the world's first transatlantic flight. After reconstruction at Weybridge it was presented to the Science Museum in London.

The first prototype Vimy, B9952, with 260 h.p. Salmson engines was allotted markings G-EAAR on 1 May 1919 but these were never carried and during its short career—a flight from Brooklands to Amsterdam in August 1919 for static display at the First Air Traffic Exhibition—wore the constructor's number C-105. Active flying by the Vickers contingent was done by K-107, the Vimy Commercial prototype which had first flown at Joyce Green on 13 April and used the standard Vimy wing structure and tail unit mated to a rotund, oval section, plywood monocoque front fuselage seating 10 passengers. Entry was via a narrow opening in the port side, closed by a roller blind, and two pilots sat in an open cockpit high in the nose.

First flown on 20 September 1919, the next civil Vimy, G-EAOL, was a three seat bomber which left Brooklands in the following month for demonstration to the Spanish Government at Madrid. Although it disappeared into obscurity, its sister ship, G-EAOU, achieved immortality as winner of the Australian Government's £10,000 prize for the first England–Australia flight. Piloted by Capts. Ross and Keith Smith and carrying Sgts. W. H. Shiers and J. M. Bennett as engineers, 'OU left Hounslow on 12 November 1919 and landed 11,340 miles away at Darwin, N.T., 27 days 21 hr. later on 10 December having averaged 75 m.p.h. for 350 flying hours, an incredible feat for those days and for which both pilots were knighted. After Sir Ross Smith's death in the Viking IV accident at Brooklands (see page 206), the Vimy was stored for 35 years but in 1957 it was taken south from Canberra on two R.A.A.F. trailer vehicles for permanent exhibition in a glass memorial hall specially erected at Adelaide airport. Mainplanes, airscrews and cowlings were damaged by fire at Keith, 160 miles east of Adelaide while in transit on 3 November 1957 necessitating lengthy repairs which delayed final display for two years.

Inspired by the Australia flight, the *Daily Mail* put up a £10,000 prize for a flight from Cairo to the Cape for which three aircraft competed including Handley Page O/400 G-EAMC (Volume 2, page 226) and Vimy G-UABA 'Silver Queen' manned by Lt. Col. P. Van Ryneveld and Flt. Lt. C. J. Quintin Brand who left Brooklands on 4 February 1920 but crashed at Korosko in Upper Egypt. They continued in a borrowed R.A.F. Vimy named 'Silver Queen II' which crashed at Bulawayo.

After Martlesham trials the Vimy Commercial K-107 was fitted with rectangular windows replacing the original portholes and an additional door with built-in 'airstairs' in the rear fuselage. Carrying the permanent registration G-EAAV, it too left Brooklands for the Cape, a week or so before G-UABA, on 24 January 1920. It was sponsored by *The Times* and flown by Capts. S. Cockerell and F. C. G. Broome but crashed at Tabora, Tanganyika, on 27 February.

Sir John Alcock of Atlantic flight fame, with Sir Ross and Keith Smith's 1919 Australia Flight Vimy IV. (*Shell Photo*)

The Vimy Commercial prototype, K-107, at Hendon in July 1919, showing the circular windows. (*Central Press*)

Large scale production of 40 Vimy Commercials for China then began at Weybridge. They inaugurated a mail service between Pekin and Tsinan and two were named 'Ta Peng' and 'Chengku' but the majority remained in their crates unused. The 39th was allotted, but never used, the registration G-EAUY and the 40th, G-EAUL, was runner-up in the Air Ministry's Heavy Commercial Aeroplane Competition at Martlesham in August 1920 flown by Capts. Cockerell and Broome.

British air transport pioneers S. Instone and Co. Ltd. took delivery of the 41st Vimy Commercial G-EASI, named 'City of London' for its inaugural flight from Croydon to Brussels with jockeys on 9 May 1920. This aeroplane, Vickers Type 66, was the best known of all pre-1939 passenger aircraft, flying continually, almost relentlessly, on the Paris, Brussels and Cologne routes piloted by F. L. Barnard, G. J. Powell and others. As early as July 1921 it had completed 360 hr. flying and had carried 10,600 passengers, many on pleasure flights, and when handed over to Imperial Airways Ltd. on 1 April 1924, had flown 107,950 miles. It was scrapped in 1926 but the inimitable K.L.M. representative at Croydon, Spry Leverton, acquired the cabin as a summer house in the garden of his house in Waterer Rise, Wallington, where it was finally burned in 1935.

The 42nd aircraft, shown at the Paris Aero Show in November 1921 in Grands Express Aériens livery as F-ADER, later returned to Brooklands to be re-engined with 400 h.p. Lorraine-Dietrich units and left again for Paris in June 1922. This and the 43rd machine, supplied to Russia in September 1922, were similar to the R.A.F. Vickers Vernon, with Napier Lions faired into the lower mainplane.

After its success with the F.B.5 Gunbus replica (see page 351), the Vintage Aircraft and Flying Association built a Vimy replica, G-AWAU, powered by two Eagle VIIIs found in Holland, to commemorate the 50th anniversary of the first Atlantic flight. It was first flown at Wisley on 3 June 1969 by B.A.C. test pilot D. G. Addicott who flew it to the Paris Air Show a few days later. Repainted in R.A.F. colours as H651 it then went to Ringway for exhibition to Alcock and Brown's fellow Mancunians but was seriously damaged by fire due to the heat of the sun on 16 July. After repair it was donated to the R.A.F. Museum, Hendon, bearing a different R.A.F. serial, F8614.

SPECIFICATION

Manufacturers:	Vickers Ltd., Vickers House, Broadway, Westminster, S.W.1; Brooklands Aerodrome, Surrey and Joyce Green Aerodrome, Kent.	
Power Plants:	Two 360 h.p. Rolls-Royce Eagle VIII.	
Dimensions:	Span, 67 ft. 2 in. Height, 15 ft. 3 in. Wing area, 1,330 sq. ft. Length (Vimy IV), 43 ft. 6½ in. (Commercial), 42 ft. 8 in.	
Weights:	(Vimy IV)	Tare weight, 7,101 lb. All-up weight, 12,500 lb.
	(Commercial)	Tare weight, 7,790 lb. All-up weight, 12,500 lb.
Performance:	(Vimy IV)	Maximum speed, 103 m.p.h. Initial climb, 300 ft./min. Ceiling, 10,500 ft.
	(Commercial)	Maximum speed, 103 m.p.h. Cruising speed, 84 m.p.h. Initial climb, 375 ft./min. Ceiling, 10,500 ft. Range, 450 miles.

Production with export C. of A. dates: Forty-three Vimy Commercials: (c/n 1–40) China, including (39) G-EAUY and (40) G-EAUL; (41) G-EASI; (42) F-ADER Lions 23.12.21, Lorraine-Dietrich 30.6.22; (43) Russia 18.9.22.

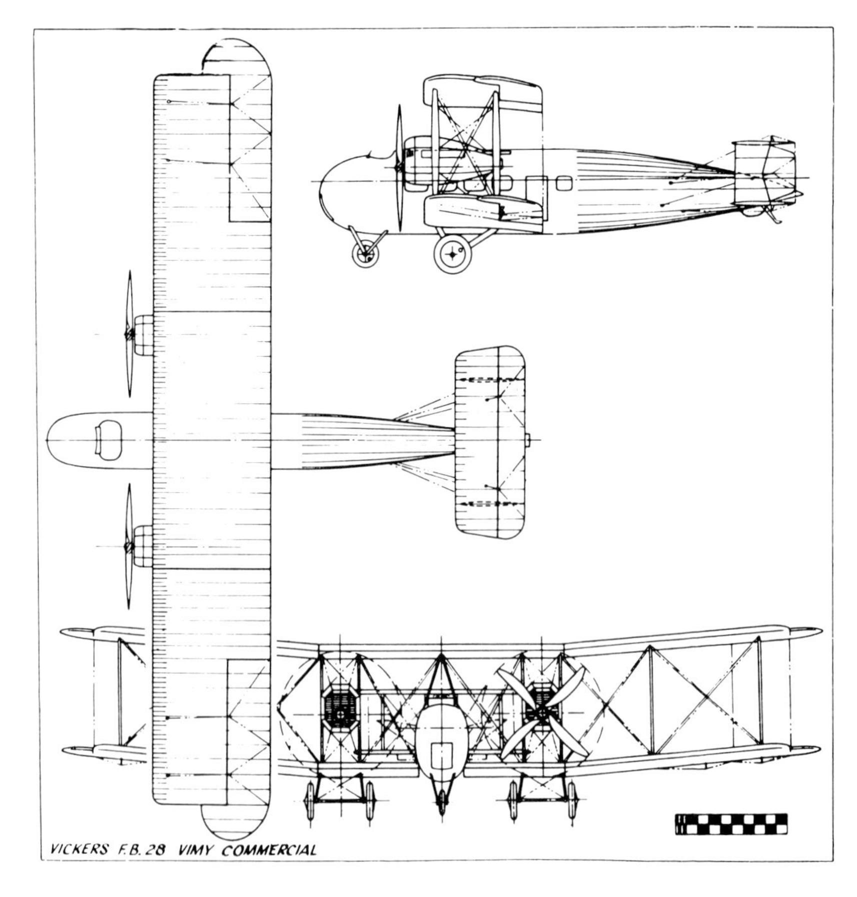

Viking Mk.III G-EAUK on the Thames at Westminster in February 1921. (*Flight Photo 1144*)

Vickers Viking Amphibian

The prototype Viking, G-EAOV, was a four seat cabin amphibian of wooden construction designed by R. K. Pierson and powered by a 275 h.p. Rolls-Royce Falcon III mounted under the top centre section driving a four bladed pusher airscrew. It was first flown at Brooklands in October 1919 but crashed while making a precautionary landing in fog near Rouen while en route to the Paris Aero Show on 18 December 1919 flown by Sir John Alcock of transatlantic fame who was killed.

The Viking Mk.II, G-EASC, with 360 h.p. Rolls-Royce Eagle VIII, increased wing span, wider undercarriage track and three rudders, was first flown at Cowes by Capt. S. Cockerell in June 1920 before exhibition at the Olympia Aero Show in July. In August it gained first prize in the Antwerp Seaplane Trials but was then withdrawn from use in favour of the Viking Mk.III, G-EAUK, with 450 h.p. Napier Lion, longer nose and wide chord wings, which won the £10,000 first prize in the Air Ministry Amphibian Competition held at Martlesham and Felixstowe in September 1920. In January 1921 it was sold to the Air Council as N147 and wearing both this and its civil marks, made trial landings on the Thames at Westminster on 7 February and 17 March, and on the Seine in Paris on 29 April, to test the feasibility of a service between city centres.

The successful performance of G-EAUK led to orders for the Viking Mk.IV production version, 28 of which were built, some with folding wings. The first, Type 54 F-ADBL, delivered to the French Navy in October 1921, was followed by eight Type 55 (and two further crash replacements) with increased span for the Dutch East Indies Air Force; two Type 58 for the

Imperial Japanese Navy and a third, serial A6073, for the U.S. Navy; two Type 59 tested by the R.A.F. in Iraq as N156 and N157; one Type 64 for Russia; two Type 73 with cabin tops for the Buenos Aires–Montevideo service of the River Plate Aviation Co. Ltd.; four Type 84 for the Argentine Navy; and two Type 85s, G-CYES and 'ET, for Royal Canadian Air Force forestry patrol work, for which six more, G-CYEU to 'EZ, were built by Canadian Vickers Ltd. at Montreal.

Type 60 G-EBBZ was a special Viking Mk.IV with long range tanks for Sir Ross Smith's round-the-world flight. After Capt. Cockerell made the first flight at Brooklands on 13 April 1922, Sir Ross took-off in it with his mechanic Sgt. Bennett but spun off a turn into the Byfleet banking and was killed. The only other British registered machine, Type 67 G-EBED, was demonstrated in Spain in 1922 and chartered to Belgian financier Alfred Lowenstein for flights between Croydon and Nice between January and March 1926. In the following July it was sold to Capt. Leslie Hamilton who ran a winter sports taxi service with it from St. Moritz.

One Type 69, G-CAEB, with 360 h.p. Eagle VIII, delivered to the Laurentide Air Service in June 1922, was based initially at Remi Lake, Moonbeam, Ontario but moved west in 1929 for survey work in the Vancouver area with Aero Mineral Locaters Ltd. and was written off there in an accident on 16 September 1932 after a long and useful life.

The first production Viking Mk.IV, F-ADBL, at Brooklands before delivery to France, October 1921. (*Flight Photo 1513*)

SPECIFICATION

Manufacturers: Vickers Ltd., Vickers House, Broadway, Westminster S.W.1; and Brooklands Aerodrome, Surrey

Power plants:	(Viking Mk.I)	One 275 h.p. Rolls-Royce Falcon III
	(Viking Mk.II and IV)	One 360 h.p. Rolls-Royce Eagle VIII
	(Viking Mk.III and IV)	One 450 h.p. Napier Lion

	Viking Mk.I	Viking Mk.III	Viking Mk.IV Type 60	Viking Mk.IV Type 69
Span	37 ft. 0 in.	46 ft. 0 in.	50 ft. 0 in.	50 ft. 0 in.
Length	30 ft. 0 in.	32 ft. 0 in.	35 ft. 0 in.	34 ft. 0 in.
Height	13 ft. 0 in.	13 ft. 0 in.	14 ft. 0 in.	14 ft. 2 in.
Wing area	368 sq. ft.	585 sq. ft.	635 sq. ft.	635 sq. ft.
Tare weight	2,030 lb.	2,740 lb.	3,728 lb.	4,020 lb.
All-up weight	3,600 lb.	4,545 lb.	5,600 lb.	5,650 lb.
Maximum speed	104 m.p.h.	110 m.p.h.	105 m.p.h.	100 m.p.h.
Initial climb	500 ft./min.	475 ft./min.	950 ft./min.	350 ft./min.
Range	340 miles	420 miles	925 miles	500 miles.

Production: Twenty-eight Viking Mk.IV (with export C. of A. dates):

Type 54 (c/n 1) F-ADBL, 10.10.21; Type 55 (2–9) Dutch East Indies, 23.12.21; Type 58 (10) U.S. Navy Bu A6073, 24.3.22; (11–12) Japan; Type 59 (13–14) N156, N157; Type 60 (15) G-EBBZ; Type 64 (16) Russia, 14.11.22; Type 67 (17) G-EBED; Type 69 (18) G-CAEB, 20.6.22; Type 73 (19-20) River Plate Aviation Co. Ltd., 6.4.23; Type 55 (21-22) Dutch East Indies, 13.4.23; Type 84 (23–26) Argentine R-3 to R-6; Type 85 (27–28) G-CYET, G-CYES, 25.5.23.

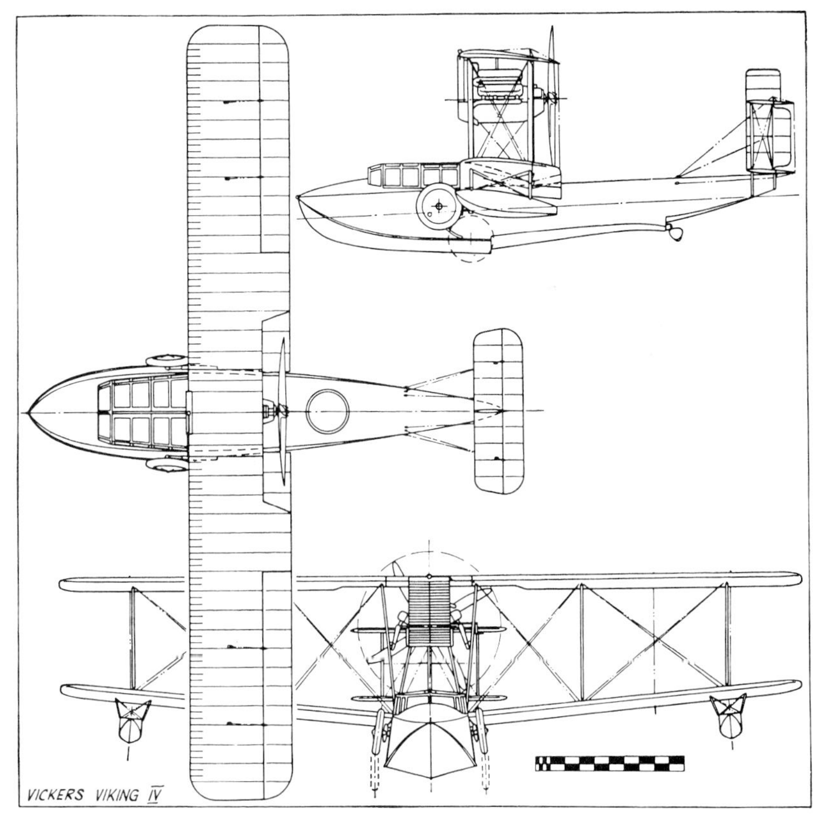

The prototype Vulcan before the addition of the small central fin. (*Vickers Ltd.*)

Vickers Vulcan

Designed by R. K. Pierson and first flown at Brooklands by chief test pilot S. Cockerell in May 1922, the Vulcan was an attempt to build a commercial aeroplane which would pay its way without Government subsidy, performance being rated second to low initial cost and cheapness of operation. It was a compact, single bay biplane of great rotundity, every inch a descendant of the Vimy Commercial. Pilot, eight passengers and baggage were carried into the air on the mere 360 h.p. of one Rolls-Royce Eagle VIII obtainable in new condition at a fraction of original cost from the Aircraft Disposal Co. Ltd. The entire mainplane gap was occupied by an oval section, plywood fuselage supporting a small biplane tail unit. The single pilot sat in front of the upper mainplane with a magnificent view, the nose falling away sharply to a car type radiator.

Early trials revealed some directional instability and the necessity for a central auxiliary fin, and also a reluctance to take-off at the designed maximum weight. Nevertheless, the construction of eight more Vulcans began at Brooklands, two of which, G-EBDH and 'EA, were sold with the prototype 'BL, to Instone Air Line Ltd. Delivery in the company's dark blue livery took place in August 1922 at Croydon, where their obese appearance, small tails, squat undercarriages and snub noses promptly earned them the permanent soubriquet of 'Flying Pigs'. The three Vulcans were chiefly employed on the Brussels route, 'BL 'City of Antwerp' alone receiving a name. A fourth Vulcan, 'EK, was completed to Air Ministry order as the Type 63 freighter without windows and subjected to exhaustive Martlesham trials. The next, 'EM, was acquired by Douglas Vickers, M.P., for entry in the first King's Cup Race. Piloted by Capt. S. Cockerell and carrying several passengers, it started from Croydon on 8 September 1922, arriving back in 7th place on the following day, having covered the 810 mile course to Renfrew and back in 9 hours 24 minutes flying time.

Later in 1922 two Vulcans, G-EBES and 'ET, were registered to Queensland and Northern Territory Aerial Services Ltd. and 'ET was shipped to Melbourne to be evaluated for the Charleville–Cloncurry service. With midsummer temperatures standing at 110 degrees in the shade, tests on 'ET at Longreach in March 1923 proved the Vulcan's performance entirely inadequate and it was shipped back to England. The aircraft's lack of power reserve was further underlined by the loss of Instone's 'DH in a crash at Oxted, Surrey, after which 'EA was relegated to the scrap heap.

These experiences led to the installation of the more powerful Napier Lion engine in the last two Vulcans, 'FC and 'LB, both of which operated at the increased maximum weight as Type 74. G-EBFC, first flown on 3 March 1923, was Douglas Vickers' entry in the 1923 King's Cup Race, but retired on the first leg. Additional power enabled these Vulcans to be employed on Imperial Airways' scheduled services, their work being publicised at the 1925 Empire Exhibition, Wembley, by the presence of the Air Council's G-EBEK.

In the following year 'FC was withdrawn from service, dismantled and

The Air Council's windowless Type 63 Vulcan freighter G-EBEK.

Lion powered Type 74 Vulcans were identified by two exhaust stacks on the starboard side. (*Vickers Ltd.*)

burned, leaving only the Eagle engined 'EM and the Lion powered 'LB, airworthy. They were thereafter relegated to charter work, the first, leased to Leslie Hamilton by the manufacturers to succeed his Viking IV G-EBED, was lost at sea off the Italian coast in May 1926. The second, 'LB, completed more flying hours than any other Vulcan, remaining in commission until July 1928, when it crashed and burned in Purley with the loss of several Imperial Airways employees, soon after taking off on a test flight.

SPECIFICATION

Manufacturers: Vickers Ltd., Vickers House, Broadway, Westminster, London, S.W.1 and Brooklands Aerodrome, Surrey.

Power Plants: One 360 h.p. Rolls-Royce Eagle VIII.
One 450 h.p. Napier Lion.

Dimensions: Span, 49 ft. 0 in. Length, 37 ft. 6 in. (Lion) 38 ft. 0 in. Height, 14 ft. 3 in. Wing area, 840 sq. ft.

Weights: (Eagle) Tare weight, 3,775 lb. All-up weight, 6,150 lb.
(Lion) Tare weight, 4,400 lb. All-up weight, 6,750 lb.

**Performance:* Maximum speed, 105 m.p.h. Cruising speed, 90 m.p.h. Initial climb, 450 ft./min. Range, 360 miles.

* With Eagle VIII engine.

Production: Nine British registered aircraft commissioned 1922–25.

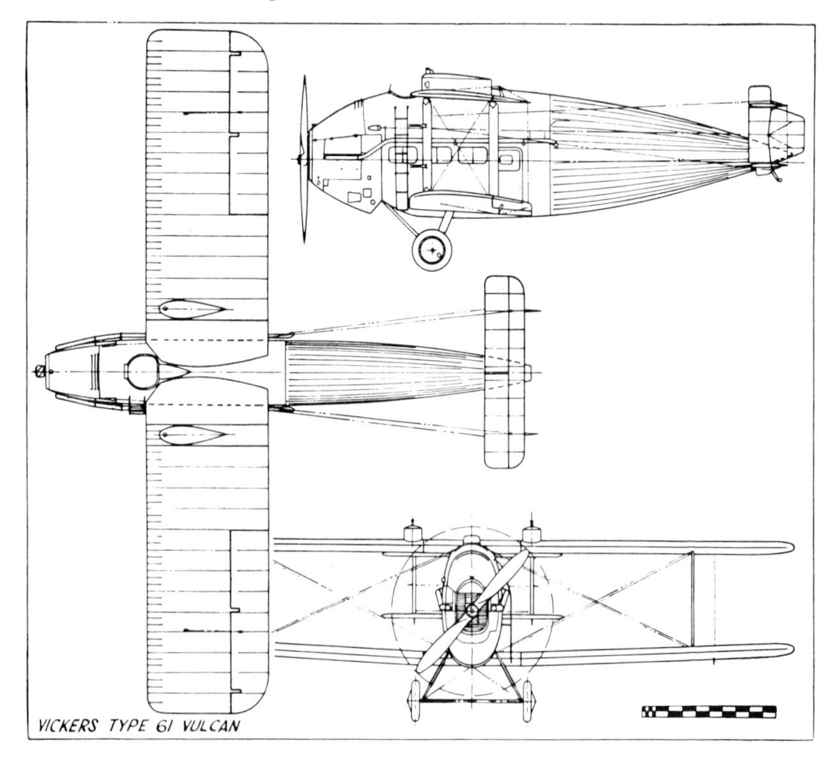

The prototype Viastra, G-AAUB, at Brooklands in 1932 in its final form as Vickers Type 220 with three 450 h.p. Bristol Jupiter VIFMs.

Vickers Viastra

Vickers Ltd., one of the first British firms to foresee that metal-clad aircraft would be able to remain in the open for long periods with minimum maintenance, flew the Vickers Type 121 Wibault Scout single seater with thin corrugated metal skin in 1926. Then followed the Type 125 Vireo naval fighter and the single and twin engined Vellore freighters G-EBYX and G-AASW described on pages 326–327.

In 1929 designs were put in hand for a large, high-wing transport using this form of construction, known as the Viastra and stressed to take one, two or three engines according to the customer's route conditions and financial position. The fuselage for the prototype, G-AAUB, was built at Vickers' Crayford works but was transferred to the Supermarine Aviation Works at Woolston, Southampton (in which Vickers had just acquired a controlling interest), for completion. It was equipped for 10 passengers and two crew (with dual control) and powered by three 230 h.p. Armstrong Siddeley Lynx V radials as the Type 160 Viastra I and like the four Supermarine-built Viastras which were to follow, was towed down the River Itchen on a lighter and taken ashore for first flight at Hamble, made by J. 'Mutt' Summers on 1 October 1930.

Well aware of the immense strength and reliability of the Junkers metal covered transports operating in remote areas of New Guinea, Maj. Norman Brearley ordered Viastras to supplement D.H.66 Hercules aircraft on the 2,000 mile West Australian Airways Perth–Adelaide service. His pilots had flown behind Bristol Jupiter engines for years and the engineers were skilled in Jupiter maintenance and well equipped with spares, so that the 525 h.p. Jupiter XIF was a natural choice of power plant for the two twin engined Type 198 Viastra II twelve passenger machines and for the single engined Type 203 Viastra VI freighter ordered by the company.

The Viastra IIs were shipped to Fremantle where the first, VH-UOO, arrived on 16 February 1931 and left Perth on its maiden flight piloted by Maj. Brearley on 2 March. When it reached Adelaide on 4 March in 11 hr. flying time, newspaper men were loud in their approval of the aircraft because they had been permitted to smoke during flight. In July 1931 VH-UOO demonstrated the ruggedness of its construction by completing schedules without difficulty in gale force winds, covering the 400 mile Kalgoorlie–Forrest leg at an average speed of 155 m.p.h. The second aircraft, VH-UOM, was eventually damaged beyond repair in a landing accident at Redcliffe, W.A., on 11 October 1933 but 'OO continued alone until withdrawn from service when the Perth–Adelaide route was sold to Australian National Airways Ltd. in 1936.

The Viastra VI freighter flown from Hamble to Brooklands with Supermarine Class B registration N-1 on 22 April 1931 and flight tested with Vickers marking O-6, was never delivered. Registration G-ABVM, allotted when the W.A.A. order was cancelled, was also not used. The aircraft made a solitary public appearance at the G.A.P.A.N. Air Display at Brooklands on 28 May 1932 and was then dismantled.

The single engined Viastra VI freighter built for West Australian Airways but not delivered. (*Vickers Ltd.*)

Ground running the Jupiter XIF engines of West Australian Airways first Type 198 Viastra II at Brooklands in 1930. (*Vickers Ltd.*)

Viastra X G-ACCC as a radio test vehicle at Croydon in 1936. (*W. K. Kilsby*)

The Lynx engined Viastra I was fitted with two 490 h.p. Armstrong Siddeley Jaguar VIC radials in 1930 as Type 199 Viastra III and was inspected by an Indian delegation at the Brooklands Air Display on 4 January 1931, but in the following year, as the result of an enquiry by Maj. Brearley, reverted to a more powerful tri-motor layout with three 450 h.p. Jupiter VIFMs as Type 220 Viastra VIII. In this form the Viastra was at last able to maintain height if an engine failed but as this was achieved purely at the expense of payload, no Australian order resulted.

The final Viastra, Type 259 Viastra X, was a special machine powered by two 650 h.p. Bristol Pegasus II.L3 radials (in nacelles attached directly to the wing), with seven seat VIP interior for the use of the Prince of Wales (later Duke of Windsor) and painted externally in the red and blue of the Brigade of Guards. It was registered to the Royal pilot, Flt. Lt. E. H. Fielden A.F.C. as G-ACCC and first flown at Hamble by chief test pilot Summers in April 1933. An inaugural Royal flight was made from Smiths Lawn, Windsor, to Hendon via Cardiff on 16 May but utilisation was low and 'CC made a final appearance as Royal Barge when it conveyed the Prince of Wales to the Hendon R.A.F. Display on 30 June 1934. It was then transferred to Air Ministry ownership as a radio test vehicle operating at Croydon with Imperial Airways crews until June 1936. Although nominally on R.A.F. charge as L6102, it remained G-ACCC until scrapped at Croydon in 1937.

SPECIFICATION

Designers:	Vickers (Aviation) Ltd., Broadway, Westminster, S.W.1.	
Manufacturers:	Supermarine Aviation Works, Woolston, Southampton.	
Power Plants:	(Viastra I)	Three 230 h.p. Armstrong Siddeley Lynx V.
	(Viastra II)	Two 525 h.p. Bristol Jupiter XIF.
	(Viastra III)	Two 490 h.p. Armstrong Siddeley Jaguar VIC.
	(Viastra VI)	One 540 h.p. Bristol Jupiter IXF.
	(Viastra VIII)	Three 450 h.p. Bristol Jupiter VIFM.
	(Viastra X)	Two 650 h.p. Bristol Pegasus II.L3.

	Viastra I	Viastra II	Viastra VI	Viastra X
Span	70 ft. 0 in.	70 ft. 0 in.	70 ft. 0 in.	70 ft. 0 in.
Length	48 ft. 6 in.	45 ft. 6 in.	48 ft. 6 in.	45 ft. 6 in.
Height	13 ft. 6 in.	13 ft. 6 in.	13 ft. 6 in.	13 ft. 6 in.
Wing area	745 sq. ft.	745 sq. ft.	745 sq. ft.	745 sq. ft.
Tare weight	–	7,880 lb.	6,440 lb.	7,850 lb.
All-up weight	11,850 lb.	10,750 lb.	9,960 lb.	12,350 lb.
Maximum speed	130 m.p.h.	145 m.p.h.	127 m.p.h.	160 m.p.h.
Cruising speed	105 m.p.h.	128 m.p.h.	103 m.p.h.	130 m.p.h.
Initial climb	–	970 ft./min.	500 ft./min.	–
Ceiling	–	17,000 ft.	11,500 ft.	–
Range	–	535 miles	900 miles	1,050 miles

Production: One Type 160 Viastra I: (c/n 1) G-AAUB, converted to Viastra III and VIII. Two Type 198 Viastra II: (c/n 1) VH-UOO, C. of A. 12.1.31; (2) VH-UOM, C. of A. 2.9.31. One Type 203 Viastra VI: (c/n 1) N-1/O-6/G-ABVM. One Type 259 Viastra X: (c/n 1) G-ACCC.

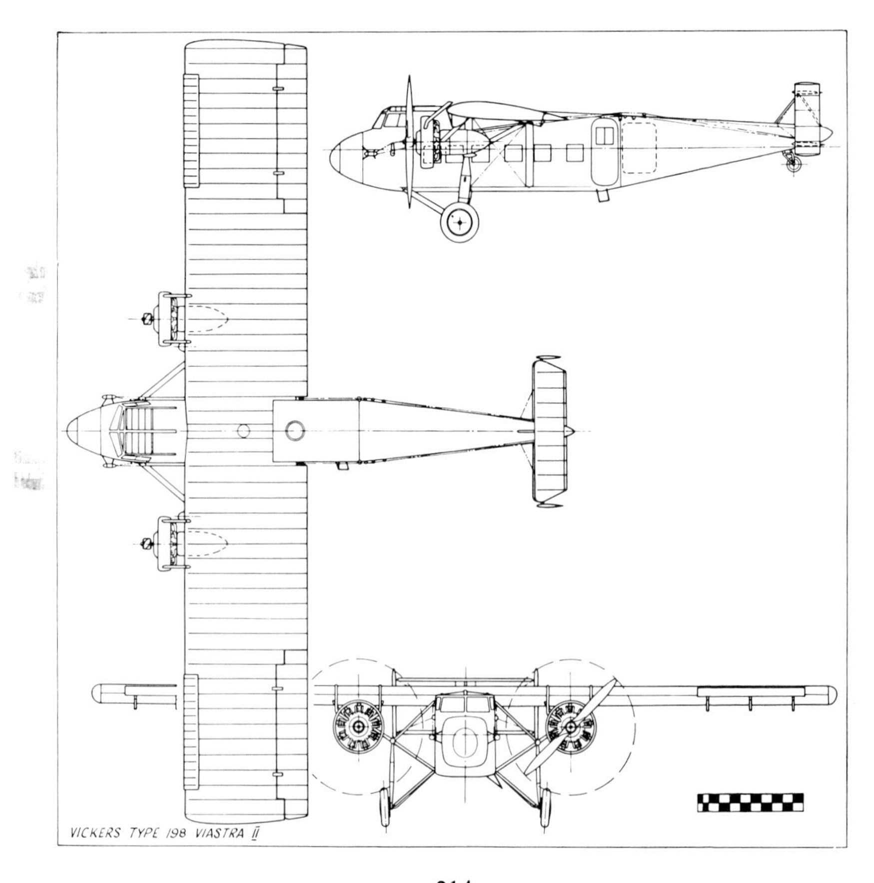

G-AHPC, in Hunting service, showing the seven cabin windows of the short nose Viking 1.

Vickers Viking

For some 18 years the Vickers Commercial 1, or V.C.1 Viking, was one of the mainstays of British aviation, first with British European Airways Corporation, and in later years with independent operators. It was the first post-war British transport aeroplane to enter airline work, the first ever to be built in quantity and the last to be designed by R. K. Pierson. Assessing in advance the possible peacetime requirement for a medium–short haul passenger aircraft, the Ministry of Supply and Aircraft Production ordered three prototype 'Wellington Transport Aircraft' in October 1944 to Spec. 17/44 for which serials TT191, TT194 and TT197 were allotted. For speed and cheapness of production the greatest possible use was made of Wellington bomber assemblies, including the fabric-covered geodetic outer wing panels and nacelle/undercarriage units. The entirely new, large-capacity, stressed skin, metal fuselage, seating 21 passengers, perpetuated the familiar rotundity of most Vickers transports since the Vimy Commercial of 1919. A crew of four was carried consisting of two pilots, radio officer and stewardess.

When the first prototype, designated Type 491, made its maiden flight in the hands of J. 'Mutt' Summers at Wisley on 22 June 1945, it did so as a civil aeroplane G-AGOK, all three R.A.F. serials having been transferred to aircraft built by other firms. Continuing existing practice, each new Viking prototype or custom-built production variant was allotted a distinguishing type number. Thus the second prototype, G-AGOL, was Type 495 by virtue of increased fin area and the third, G-AGOM, became Type 496. Development proceeded apace, and by December 1945 the three aircraft had completed 100, 50 and 10 hours respectively. Nineteen Type 498 aircraft were then ordered for the European services of B.O.A.C. (later reorganised as B.E.A.C.), the first aircraft G-AGON, flying on 23 March 1946. Together with subsequent Vikings 'RM and 'RN and the prototypes 'OL and 'OM, 'ON was later taken over by the R.A.F. for trials which led to orders for military counterparts, the Viking C.Mk.2 and Valetta C.Mk.1. Three aircraft were earmarked for crew training at Northolt, and five were modified internally as Type 657 for service in Trinidad with British West Indian Airways, leaving only 11 to earn revenue for B.E.A.C. and to receive V Class names (see Appendix E). Following a proving flight Northolt–Stavanger–Oslo by Capt. L. G. James in 'Vagrant' on 20 August 1946, 'Valerie' inaugurated the first regular Viking service over the Northolt–Copenhagen route on 1 September.

A second batch of Vikings included 13 Type 614 for B.E.A.C., commencing with 'Vanguard', delivered in October 1946. In response to the operator's wishes they were fitted with mainplanes of stressed skin, instead of geodetic construction, with the designation Viking 1, the earlier model becoming the Viking 1A. As before, certain B.E.A.C. aircraft were released to other companies, three to B.W.I.A., one to Central African Airways and one to South Africa. Twelve Type 621 Viking C.Mk.2 freighters were also built for the Ministry of Supply, two of which were used by the Civil Air Test Section, Boscombe Down, for a number of years in alternate military and civil roles as VL226/G-AIJE and VL227/G-AIKN.

The 20th airframe, completed as VT-AZA for Indian National Airways and first flown on 6 August 1946, was the first 'long nose' Viking 1B with a 28-in

'Lord Rodney', an eight windowed long nose Viking 1B in the Mayfair Class livery of Eagle Aviation Ltd. in 1953.

The Nene Viking G-AJPH (*Vickers-Armstrongs Ltd.*)

extension to the front fuselage permitting the carriage of three more passengers over stage lengths of up to 600 miles. A preliminary batch of eight Viking 1B Type 610, G-AHPK–'PS, was delivered to B.E.A.C. early in 1947, followed by G-AIHA, a Type 616 flown out to Central African Airways. Large-scale production followed for the Argentine, Southern Rhodesia, Denmark and Eire. Additionally 68 (later reduced to 39) were ordered for B.E.A.C., three of which were released to Iraqi Airways and one to Central African Airways. The manufacturers also commissioned a demonstrator, G-AJJN, Type 636, which left Hurn on 13 April 1947, piloted by Sqn. Ldr. P. Robarts, for a sales tour to New Zealand, covering 40,000 miles and returning on 15 June. It was sold to B.E.A.C. and named 'Vulcan' in 1950. By the end of 1947 Vikings had ousted the well-worn Dakota from all major European services and were working between Northolt and Paris, Amsterdam, Brussels, Geneva, Lisbon, Gibraltar, Berlin, Prague, Oslo, Glasgow and Belfast.

Viking production terminated at the end of 1947, when 113 long-nosed aircraft had been delivered in addition to the original 48 short-nosed type. Final deliveries included eight Type 635 to South African Airways.

The unobtrusively efficient Viking seldom made headline news, but did so tragically when 'Vimy' was lost with 10 passengers and crew on 5 April 1948, its starboard wing cut off in collision with a Soviet Yak fighter when approaching to land at Gatow, Berlin. Two years later, on the night of 13 April 1950, 'Vigilant', Capt. J. Harvey, suffered an internal explosion which almost severed the tail unit. The immense strength of the Viking, coupled with superb airmanship, brought the 31 occupants safely back to Northolt. The aircraft was then rebuilt by Airwork Ltd. at Gatwick, reappearing in January 1951 in a new colour scheme, which, in modified form, was adopted as the Corporation's new Admiral Class livery, prelude to a complete new naming process (see Appendix E). Operating at an increased all-up weight of 36,712 lb. and carrying 36 instead of 27 passengers, Admiral Class Vikings made possible the first cheap fare of £9 15s. return between London and Paris, the service being inaugurated on 1 October 1952 by G-AMNJ. This was one of the entire batch of eight South African Airways Viking 1Bs which were purchased to augment the already considerable B.E.A. fleet, four in time for the 1951 season as G-AMGG–'GJ and four a year later as G-AMNJ, 'NR, 'NS and 'NX. The fleet continued in service until replaced by Viscounts in 1953–4, and in eight years of service flew 65 million miles in 414,000 hours, carried 2,748,000 passengers and earned £35 million revenue.

As a charter aircraft the Viking began its career in 1948 with Hunting Air Transport Ltd., which acquired nine redundant B.E.A.C. Viking 1A and 1 aircraft G-AGRP, 'RV, 'RW, G-AHOY, 'PB–'PD, 'PI and 'PJ. Geodetic wings were eventually scrapped and all became Viking 1s, joined in 1951 by G-AMNK, a former Egyptian Airlines Viking 1B SU-AFM, reclaimed from a desert crash after an epic feat of reconstruction by an engineering team from Field Aircraft Services Ltd. The other main British users during the 1950s were Airwork Ltd. and Eagle Aviation Ltd., both of Blackbushe, the majority of B.E.A.C. Viking 1Bs being taken over by Eagle in 1953 as they were replaced by Viscounts. Both firms flew trooping services to the Canal Zone with their Vikings in temporary R.A.F. markings.

Flying in West Germany, banned since 1945, was permitted again in 1956

Airline liveries–Invicta Airways' Viking 1 G-AHOY at Manston in 1967. (*Richard Riding*); Viking 1B G-AHPL flying in Autair (Luton) Ltd. colours in 1962. (*Autair*); Maitland Drewery Viking 1B G-AHPR at Biggin Hill in 1960. (*Colin Bruce*); Continental Air Services' Viking 1B G-AJJN. (*Hugo Hooftmann*).

The Varsity 1, ultimate Viking variant, used by Kelvin and Hughes Ltd. 1959–63. *(College of Aeronautics)*

at the beginning of a boom in inclusive tour holidays and over the next few years a considerable number of Vikings were sold to West German charter operators and a few in France and elsewhere. The Viking was given a new lease of life and more than 50, mainly in 32 seat configuration, served a variety of airlines and many new names appeared such as Air Ferry Ltd., Air Safaris Ltd., Autair (Luton) Ltd., B.K.S. Air Transport Ltd., Continental Air Services Ltd., East Anglian Flying Services Ltd. (later Channel Airways Ltd.), Eros Airline (U.K.) Ltd., Falcon Airways Ltd., Independent Air Travel Ltd., Orion Airways Ltd., Overseas Aviation (C.I.) Ltd., Pegasus Airlines Ltd. and Tradair Ltd.

Non-standard aircraft also played an important part in the Viking story. The 107th airframe, completed to Ministry of Supply order with two Rolls-Royce Nene turbojets, metal-clad elevators and heavier main and tail-plane skinning, became the first British pure jet transport. First flown at Wisley by J. Summers on 6 April 1948 as the Type 618 G-AJPH/VX856, the 24 passenger Nene Viking set up a new fashion in intercapital speed by flying from London Airport to Villacoublay, Paris, in 34 minutes 7 seconds on 25 July 1948, 39th anniversary of Blériot's first cross-Channel flight. It was eventually sold to Eagle Aviation Ltd. and converted into a standard Viking 1B freighter with 5½ ft. square door and named 'Lord Dundonald' by P. G. Masefield at Northolt on 24 September 1954. It was used on trooping flights as XJ804, forced landed four miles from Nicosia, Cyprus, on 19 January 1956 and was eventually scrapped at Blackbushe in 1962. Both Ministry of Supply Type 621 Vikings C.2 G-AIJE and 'KN also returned, the former to Independent Air Travel Ltd., in whose service it crashed at Southall, Middlesex, on 2 September 1958, and the latter to fly with Continental Air Services Ltd. in the Netherlands.

Five former R.A.F. Viking C.Mk.2s also acquired civil status as Viking 2s. G-APAT was delivered to Eagle Aviation Ltd. in May 1957 and later passed to Orion Airways Ltd. and Air Safaris Ltd.. while three Queen's Flight machines were delivered to Tradair Ltd. at Southend as G-APOO to 'OR on 12 August 1958 but VL229, once the Napier Naiad test bed, delivered to the same owner from Ringway on 10 October 1959 to become G-APWS, was never converted. The first three later adopted Channel Airways livery.

Four former R.A.F. Valetta C.Mk.1s, differing from the Viking 1A externally by their lack of tail cones, also gained civil registrations. G-APII and 'IJ were delivered to Eagle Aviation Ltd. at Ringway on 3 December 1957 but were never converted, and G-APKR and 'KS went to Biggin Hill for the Decca Navigator Co. Ltd. Using 'KS as a source of spares, 'KR remained airworthy as a flying laboratory until written off after an undercarriage failure at Gatwick on 21 September 1963.

An example of the wide span, long fuselage, tricycle undercarriage R.A.F. trainer variant, the Type 668 Varsity T.Mk.1, was acquired for research purposes by Kelvin and Hughes Ltd. at Cranfield as G-APAZ. After it passed to Smith's Instruments Ltd. for similar use at Staverton, it crashed on a house in Gloucester on 27 March 1963 and was replaced by G-ARFP for autoland research. This returned to the R.A.F. in 1967.

ZS-BWT 'Rex', the last production Viking, at Nairobi in 1948 while in service with Suidair International Airways Ltd.

By the end of 1964 most Vikings had been scrapped but three British operators continued to use them and some were still flying in 1969: Autair International Airways Ltd., Luton had G-AGRW, G-AHPB and 'PJ; Air Ferry Ltd., Manston had G-AIVD and G-AJBX; and Invicta Airways Ltd., also of Manston had G-AHOW, 'OY, 'PL, G-AIVF and G-AOCH. Airwork's G-AHOP, equipped for calibration duties in the livery of the Marconi company, was active until its retirement at Hurn in August 1967. A few Vikings still remained in 1973 as monuments to a famous aeroplane: Channel's G-AGRU and Autair's G-AGRW and G-AHPB as hamburger stalls at Soesterberg in Holland, G-AHPG served a similar purpose at Blantyre, Malawi, and ZS-DKH (once G-AHOT), formerly of Protea Airways, was mounted on the roof of a garage near Johannesburg. The Argentine Air Force Type 635, T-90 formerly G-AMNS, and the Pakistan Air Force Type 649, J750, were both in military museums in their respective countries.

SPECIFICATION

Manufacturers: Vickers-Armstrongs Ltd., Broadway, Westminster, London, S.W.1; Brooklands and Wisley Aerodromes, Surrey.

Power Plants:	
(Prototypes Type 401, 495, 496)	Two 1,675 h.p. Bristol Hercules 130.
(Viking 1A Type 498)	Two 1,690 h.p. Bristol Hercules 630.
(Viking 1, 1B and C.2 Types 610, 614, 616, 621, 623)	Two 1,690 h.p. Bristol Hercules 634.
(Nene Viking Type 618)	Two 5,000 lb. s.t. Rolls-Royce Nene 1.
(Valetta C.Mk.1 Type 637)	Two 1,975 h.p. Bristol Hercules 710.
(Varsity T.Mk.1 Type 668)	Two 1,950 h.p. Bristol Hercules 764.

	Viking 1 and 1A	Viking 1B	Nene Viking	Valetta C.Mk.1	Varsity T.Mk.1
Span	89 ft. 3 in.	89 ft. 3 in.	89 ft. 3 in.	89 ft. 3 in.	95 ft. 7 in.
Length	62 ft. 11 in.	65 ft. 2 in.	65 ft. 2 in.	62 ft. 11 in.	67 ft. 6 in.
Height	19 ft. 6 in.	19 ft. 6 in.	19 ft. 6 in.	19 ft. 6 in.	23 ft. 11 in.
Wing area	882 sq. ft.	882 sq. ft.	882 sq. ft.	882 sq. ft.	974 sq. ft.
Tare weight	22,910 lb.	23,250 lb.	21,050 lb.	24,854 lb.	27,040 lb.
All-up weight	34,000 lb.	34,000 lb.	34,000 lb.	36,500 lb.	37,500 lb.
Maximum speed	252 m.p.h.	263 m.p.h.	457 m.p.h.	294 m.p.h.	288 m.p.h.
Cruising speed	210 m.p.h.	210 m.p.h.	393 m.p.h.	172 m.p.h.	239 m.p.h.
Initial climb	1,390 ft./min.	1,275 ft./min.	3,500 ft./min.	1,200 ft./min.	1,400 ft./min.
Ceiling	22,000 ft.	23,750 ft.	44,000 ft.	22,200 ft.	27,000 ft.
Maximum range	1,875 miles	1,700 miles	312 miles	1,410 miles	2,648 miles

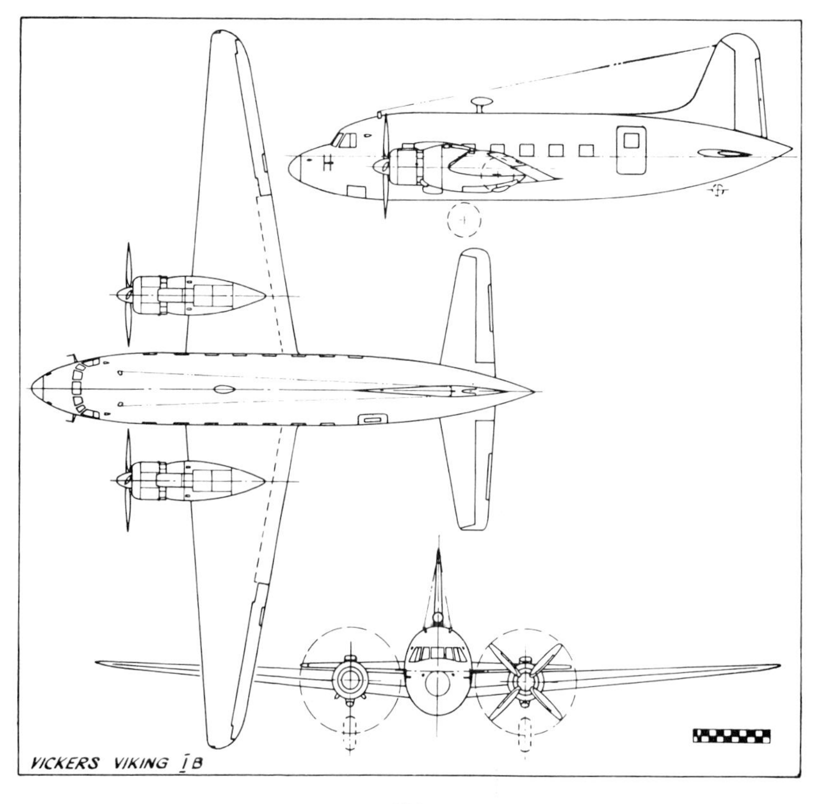

Production: One hundred and sixty-three aircraft, mainly of British civil registry plus the following for export or the R.A.F.:

Type 604 (Viking 1B for Indian National Airways, two Hercules 634): (c/n 120) VT-AZA; (126) VT-AZB; (143) VT-CEJ; (154) VT-CEK; (166) VT-CEL; (186) VT-CEM.

Type 607 (Valetta prototype for Ministry of Supply, two Hercules 230): (c/n 158) VL249, sold as spares for civil Vikings and scrapped at Blackbushe 3.59.

Type 615 (Viking 1 for Argentine Government, two Hercules 634): (c/n 135) LV-XEQ/Argentine Air Force T-2; (151) LV-XER/T-3; (161) LV-XES/T-4; (163) LV-XET/T-9; (180) LV-XEU/T-6; (181) LV-XEV/T-5; (182) LV-XEW/T-7; (183) LV-XEX/T-8; (184) LV-XEY/T-184/LV-AEW; (185) LV-XEZ/T-185/T-76/LV-AEV; (187) LV-XFD/T-10; (188) LV-XFE/T-11; (189) LV-XFF/T-13; (190) LV-XFG/T-12; (191) LV-XFH/LV-AFF; (192) LV-XFI; (193) LV-XFJ/T-80; (194) LV-XFM; (200) LV-XFL/T-88/LV-AFU.

Type 616 (Viking 1 for Central African Airways, two Hercules 634): (c/n 159) VP-YEX; (168) VP-YEY; see also G-AIHA and G-AJCF.

Type 620 (Viking 1 for Argentine Government, two Hercules 630): (c/n 113) LV-XEN/Argentine Air Force T-1.

Type 621 (Viking C.Mk.2 for King's Flight* or R.A.F., two Hercules 130): (c/n 127) VL226*, later G-AIJE; (131) VL227*, later G-AIKN; (136) VL228; (140) VL229, later G-APWS; (145) VL230, later G-ANZK; (150) VL231, later R.A.A.F. A82-1 and G-AOCH; (153) VL232, later G-APAT; (156) VL233, later G-APOO; (169–176) VL237 to VL244 order cancelled.

Type 623 (Viking C.Mk.2 for King's Flight, two Hercules 134): (c/n 177) VL246, later G-APOP; (178) VL247, later G-APOR.

Type 624 (Viking C.Mk.2 for King's Flight, two Hercules 134): (c/n 144) VL245.

Type 626 (Viking C.Mk.2 for King's Flight, two Hercules 134): (c/n 179) VL248, later G-AOBY, ferried to Mexico in 1955 as XB-FIP 'Jorge' for Pasquel Organization.

Type 628 (Viking 1B for D.D.L., two Hercules 634): (c/n 195) OY-DLA, later SU-AGO; (196) OY-DLE, later SU-AGN; (197) OY-DLI; (198) OY-DLO, later SU-AGM and ZS-DPA; (199) OY-DLU.

Type 632 (Viking 1B for Air-India, two Hercules 634): (c/n 201) VT-CIY; (202) VT-CIZ; (203) VT-CKW; (204) VT-CKX; (205) VT-CLY; (206) VT-CLZ.

Type 634 (Viking 1B for Aer Lingus, two Hercules 634): (c/n 208) EI-ADF, later G-AKTV; (209) EI-ADG, later SU-AFN; (210) EI-ADH, later SU-AFM and G-AMNK; (211) EI-ADI, later G-AKTU; (212) EI-ADJ, later SU-AFO; (213) EI-ADK, later SU-AFK; (214) EI-ADL, later SU-AFL and G-ASBE.

Type 635 (Viking 1B for South African Airways, two Hercules 634): (c/n 290) ZS-BNE, later G-AMGG; (291) ZS-BNF, later G-AMNR; (292) ZS-BNG, later G-AMNX; (293) ZS-BNH, later G-AMGH; (294) ZS-BNI, later G-AMNS; (295) ZS-BNJ, later G-AMGJ; (296) ZS-BNK, later G-AMNJ; (297) ZS-BNL, later G-AMGI.

Type 637 (Valetta C.Mk.1 for the R.A.F., two Hercules 230): (c/n 162) VL262; (165) VL263, later G-APKS; VL275, later G-APII.

Type 643 (Viking 1 for Suidair International, two Hercules 630): (c/n 298) last built, ZS-BWT, later VP-YIE, D-BLUP and F-BJEQ.

Type 649 (Viking 1B for Pakistan Air Force, two Hercules 634): (c/n 261) J750.

Type 651 (Civil conversion of production Valettas, two Hercules 230): VW802/G-APKR; WD162/G-APIJ.

Type 668 (Civil conversion of Varsity T.Mk.1, two Hercules 264): WF387/ G-ARFP; WF415/G-APAZ; SA-R-6.

Not built: c/n 265 to 288 inclusive.

B.E.A.'s Viscount 802 G-AOHS flying near Abbotsinch with Scottish Airways titles, 1972. (*B.E.A.*)

Vickers Viscount

Design projects for an unpressurised Viking development with four propeller turbine engines were commenced in April 1945 under designation Vickers Type 453 V.C.2 but when, in the following month, the Brabazon IIB specification was published calling for a similar aeroplane with pressurised fuselage seating 24 passengers, a further Type 453 variant with double-bubble fuselage was offered to this specification. Following the appointment of R. K. Pierson as chief engineer in September 1945, design responsibility fell to his successor G. R. (later Sir George) Edwards, and the finalised Type 453 emerged in December 1945 as a 55 ft. span monoplane with pressurised circular section fuselage featuring the now familiar oval windows and seating 24 passengers at an all-up weight of 35,000 lb. Rolls-Royce Dart engines were proposed but on 9 March 1946 the Ministry of Supply ordered two prototypes of an enlarged 32 seat version with Armstrong Siddeley Mambas to specification 8/46 and known as the V.609 Viceroy. A third prototype was to be financed by Vickers.

Later it was decided to complete the Ministry's prototypes G-AHRF and 'RG with four Rolls-Royce Darts as V.630 and Vickers' third aircraft G-AJZW with four Napier Naiads as V.640. Construction then went ahead at Foxwarren, but in 1947 the partition of India resulted in a change of name to Viscount. When the first aircraft, G-AHRF, assembled at Wisley, made its maiden flight on 16 July 1948, piloted by J. Summers and G. R. Bryce, it was not merely the world's first turbo-prop transport, a natural flier and an almost trouble-free prototype but also a truly sensational advance over contemporary piston engined aircraft.

The prospect of a developed Dart, the R.Da.3 (Mk.505) giving 50% more power, made it possible to design a stretched 40 seat version, more exactly fulfilling British European Airways Corporation requirements. Construction

The first prototype Viscount 630, G-AHRF, landing at Farnborough during the S.B.A.C. Show, September 1949. (*E. J. Riding*)

of a prototype, known as the V.700 with fuselage lengthened by 6 ft. 8 in. and the inner span increased by 5 ft. was then undertaken, to specification 21/49, the second V.630 being completed as the V.663 flying test bed with two Rolls-Royce Tay turbojets. This first flew in R.A.F. markings as VX217 at Wisley on 15 March 1950 and after demonstration at the Farnborough S.B.A.C. Show in the following September, was used in the development of powered controls for the Valiant bomber. It was later flown experimentally by Boulton Paul Ltd. at Seighford as test bed for their electronic control system. The first V.630 G-AHRF flew as VX211 during trials which culminated in the issue of a restricted C. of A. on 19 August 1949 and eventually to full passenger carrying clearance for a month's scheduled operations with B.E.A. commencing on 29 July 1950. This historic aircraft remained in continual use until written off at Khartoum on 27 August 1952, after completing 931 hours 50 minutes of experimental flying.

Components intended for the abandoned third prototype were used in the construction of the V.700 prototype G-AMAV, the fuselage of which was built at South Marston and the wings at Itchen. Assembly took place at Brooklands, and after the first flight on 19 April 1950, 20 (later increased to 27), slightly modified 53 seat V.701 production aircraft were ordered by B.E.A. The prototype V.700 was shown at the S.B.A.C. Show a month later, completing 250 hours of test flying before leaving on 5 October 1951, for tropical trials at Khartoum, captained by S. N. Sloan. The same pilot took it to India, Pakistan and the Near East for demonstration in the June and July, Capt. A. S. Johnson made the first B.E.A. proving flight in it to Rome, Athens and Cyprus on 21 August and George Lowdell showed its paces in West Germany a month later. Six weeks winterisation trials in Canada were completed when G. R. Bryce returned to Wisley via the northern route on 5 April 1953. Meanwhile the first V.701, G-ALWE, flown on 20 August 1952, in time for exhibition at the S.B.A.C. Show, had been named at Wisley by Lady Douglas on 11 February 1953, as flagship of the new Discovery Class. Rapid deliveries then permitted route proving trials on all the Corporation's services in Europe, Scandinavia and the United Kingdom, culminating in the introduction of the world's first propeller turbine scheduled services on 18 April 1953 when G-AMNY, Capts. A. S. Johnson and A. Wilson, flew the

London–Rome–Athens–Nicosia route.

Delivery of the first of twelve V.708s for Air France began in May and after G-AMAV, in B.E.A. styling, numbered 23, and bearing the Discovery Class name 'Endeavour' had been flown in the England–New Zealand Race by Capt. W. Baillie and a B.E.A. crew, orders materialised from all over the world, as detailed in the accompanying production list. Leaving Heathrow on 8 October 1953, 'AV covered the 11,795 miles to Harewood Airport, Christchurch, in an elapsed time of 40 hr. 45 min. at an official average speed of 290 m.p.h.

Although all the V.700 sub-series were basically the same, additional fuel capacity was provided in the seven V.720s for Trans-Australia Airlines by adding extra wing tanks and pick-up points for external slipper tanks under the wings, a configuration also specified by some other customers. More extensive reworking to incorporate American equipment and a revised fuel system was undertaken for Trans-Canada Air Lines which ordered fifteen V.724s and later 36 similar V.757s, deliveries commencing in December 1954. Improved air conditioning, weather radar, integral airstairs, strengthened wing spars and more powerful Dart R.Da.6 (Mk.510) engines were introduced for the U.S. operator Capital Airlines to whom the delivery of sixty V.745s

The Rolls-Royce Tay powered Viscount 663 VX217/G-AHRG. (*Charles W. Cain*)

began in November 1955, the F.A.A. Type Certificate having been gained on 13 June after trials with three of the V.744s delivered previously.

Later the suffix D was applied to any V.700 series ordered with Dart R.Da.6 engines and V.720, 724 and 725 standard features, while numbers above 790 were allocated to a short stage 65 seat version for local service operations. Other British V.700 customers included Hunting-Clan Air Transport Ltd. whose V.732s G-ANRR, 'RS and 'RT were delivered in 1955, followed by G-AOGG and 'GH late in 1956. B.O.A.C. Associated Companies Ltd. ordered 22 under various designations, all of which operated initially under foreign registry with British West Indian Airways, Hong Kong Airways, Middle East Airlines, and Turk Hava Yollari. Airwork Ltd. also ordered V.755s G-AOCA, 'CB and 'CC, but these went direct to Cubana de Aviacion in 1956.

An enlarged version designated V.801, with 1,690 e.h.p. Dart R.Da.5s and fuselage lengthened by 13 ft. 6 in. to accommodate 86 passengers, was proposed in 1952. B.E.A. ordered 12 of these on 11 February 1953 but decided later that the stretch was too great and further design work around the more powerful R.Da.6 eventually resulted in a reduced fuselage extension of 3 ft. 10 in. with the rear pressure bulkhead moved aft to provide 65 seats. This version, the V.802, was ordered by B.E.A. on 14 April 1954 and 24 were eventually delivered.

All V.700 series construction was then concentrated at Weybridge and a V.800 series production line set up at Hurn. In January 1956 B.E.A. placed an additional order for 59 seat mixed-class aircraft powered by the improved Dart R.Da.7 (Mk.520) and known as the V.806. The first of these, G-AOYF 'Michael Faraday', was used by the makers for certification trials but made a crash landing at Johannesburg on 20 October 1957, and never saw B.E.A. service. Designated V.806A, it first flew on 9 August 1957 with Dart R.Da.7/1 (Mk.525), an even more powerful engine destined for the V.810 series aircraft then under construction. Due to their higher design weight and speed, these were the first Viscounts to embody major structural strengthening and modification, and were externally recognisable by the simplified aerodynamic balance of the rudder. The first V.810, G-AOYV, which first flew on 23 December 1957, became the maker's test vehicle and was assisted throughout the certification trials by the V.700 prototype G-AMAV, re-engined for the purpose. F.A.A. type certification was obtained on 22 April 1958 and deliveries of fifteen V.812s to the U.S.A. for Continental Airlines began in the following month. New British V.800 aircraft were Transair Ltd.'s V.804s G-AOXU, 'XV and G-APKG; Eagle Aviation Ltd.'s V.805s G-APDW and 'DX delivered to Blackbushe in December 1957 for operation in Bermuda; Airwork Ltd.'s V.831s G-APND and 'NE, with a third (ST-AAN) for the associated Sudan Airways Ltd.; and Hunting-Clan's G-APTB, 'TC and 'TD delivered in 1959. The last were fitted with uprated Dart Mk.530s for 'hot and high' operations.

Viscount production declined from the end of 1959 and eventually terminated at the 459th aircraft. Among final deliveries, made over the next few years, were nine V.828s for All Nippon Airways, Japan and six V.843s for the People's Republic of China, all of which had temporary British civil markings for test flights and ferrying. Chinese aircraft were powered by Dart R.Da.10 (Mk.541) engines and the last of the six, serialled 84306 (ex G-ASDV), was also the last Viscount to be delivered, on 16 April 1964. Over 60 operators in some 40 countries had bought them, including 48 airlines with scheduled services, five governments and seven private owners, the total value of the 445 aircraft sold being £177 million.

In the late 1950s surviving B.E.A. V.701s were modified to 63 passenger layout with airstairs and two additional windows for the Corporation's new German internal services. A proving flight to Moscow via Copenhagen on 21 April 1959 by G-AOYI, Capt. G. G. McLannahan, heralded a permanent, twice weekly, V.806 mixed class service to the Soviet capital, inaugurated on 14 May by G-AOYS. Despite its already sizeable fleet of 77 Viscounts, the demand during this era resulted in the Corporation short-leasing a number of others: Fred Olsen's V.736s LN-FOF and 'OL operated as G-AODG and 'DH from 1955–57 before being sold to Airwork Ltd.; V.779s LN-FOH and 'OM from the same operator became G-APZP and G-ARBW during 1960; and V.776 G-APNF and V.793 G-APNG were leased from Vickers Ltd. during 1958.

Somali Airlines' Viscount 785 6OS-AAK, purchased from Alitalia, ex I-LIFE, in June 1969. (*Aviation Photo News*)

Botswana National Airways' A2-ZEL, once Trans-Australia Airlines' VH-TVN, acquired in March 1969. (*Aviation Photo News*)

In 1962, however, disposal of the V.701 fleet began with the sale of several to V.A.S.P. of Brazil and of G-AMNZ, 'OG, 'OL, 'ON and 'OP to Cambrian Airways Ltd. for its Welsh, West Country and Midlands scheduled services. A year later the last seven, G-ALWF, G-AMOA, 'OC, 'OE, 'OH, 'OJ and 'OO, were sold to Channel Airways Ltd., primarily for inclusive tour work. All but one of these were leased, for varying periods, to British Eagle International Airways Ltd. for its scheduled routes and inclusive tour network.

Later in the 1960s when major operators were re-equipping with jet aircraft, there came a considerable world-wide movement in secondhand Viscounts. Among early sales were four Air France V.708s which returned to England, one as G-ARIR for Starways Ltd., Speke and three as G-ARBY, 'ER and 'GR to Maitland Drewery Ltd., Biggin Hill. All four went back to France in 1966 to join the Air Inter fleet along with four former Trans-Canada Air Lines V.724s which became F-BMCF, 'CG, 'CH and F-BNAX.

Channel Airways' V.701s were sold to Cambrian Airways 1966–67 and replaced by eleven V.812s purchased from Continental Airlines in Denver and flown back by the North Atlantic route. On the other side of the world All

Nippon's V.828s dispersed in 1970 to Merpati Nusantara in Indonesia and to SAETA, Ecuador; former Cubana aircraft operated by Ansett-ANA were sold in Formosa; Alitalia machines went to Somalia; Americans to Italy; Austrians to India; Lebanese to Rhodesia; these and many others being outlined in the Appendix E aircraft register.

As permanent memorials to a great aeroplane, Air Canada's CF-THI was presented to the Canadian Aeronautical Collection, Museum of Science and Technology in December 1969, and in 1972 the oldest surviving Viscount, Cambrian Airways' G-ALWF, which had flown its last service on 24 December 1971, was placed on public display at Liverpool Airport, Speke.

SPECIFICATION

Manufacturers: Vickers-Armstrongs (Aircraft) Ltd., Vickers House, Westminster, S.W.1; Brooklands Aerodrome, Byfleet, Surrey; Hurn Airport, near Bournemouth, Hants.

Viscount Type	630	663	700	701
Engines	Dart R.Da.1	Tay R.Ta.1	Dart R.Da.3	Dart R.Da.3
Mark	502	–	505	506
Power	1,380 e.h.p.	6,250 lb.s.t.	1,540 e.h.p.	1,540 e.h.p.
Span	88 ft. 11 in.	88 ft. 11 in.	93 ft. $8\frac{1}{2}$ in.	93 ft. $8\frac{1}{2}$ in.
Length	74 ft. 6 in.	74 ft. 6 in.	81 ft. 2 in.	81 ft. 2 in.
Wing area	885 sq. ft.	885 sq. ft.	963 sq. ft.	963 sq. ft.
Passengers	32	–	47	47
Tare weight	29,060 lb.	–	32,000 lb.	35,522 lb.
All-up weight	40,400 lb.	–	50,000 lb.	60,000 lb.
Economical cruising	276 m.p.h.	–	316 m.p.h.	316 m.p.h.
Maximum range	1,380 miles	–	950 miles	1,450 miles

Viscount Type	802	806	810
Engines	Dart R.Da.6	Dart R.Da.7	Dart R.Da.7/1
Mark	510	520	525
Power	1,742 e.h.p.	1,890 e.h.p.	1,990 e.h.p.
Span	93 ft. $8\frac{1}{2}$	93 ft. $8\frac{1}{2}$ in.	93 ft. $8\frac{1}{2}$ in.
Length	85 ft. 8 in.	85 ft. 8 in.	85 ft. 8 in.
Wing area	963 sq. ft.	963 sq. ft.	963 sq. ft.
Passengers	53–71	59	52–75
Tare weight	40,430 lb.	40,980 lb.	41,276 lb.
All-up weight	63,000 lb.	64,500 lb.	67,500 lb.
Economical cruising	320 m.p.h.	320 m.p.h.	360 m.p.h.
Maximum range	1,490 miles	–	1,380 miles

Production: Four hundred and fifty-nine aircraft including the following for export, with initial operators and later British registrations or last foreign markings:

V.702 for British West Indian Airways Ltd.: (c/n 71) VP-TBK, later G-APTA; (72) VP-TBL, later G-APOW; (73) VP-TBM, later G-APPX; (81) VP-TBN/YV-C-AMT.

V.707 for Aer Lingus: (c/n 30) EI-AFV, later G-APZB; (31) EI-AFW, later VR-BBJ/G-ARKH; (32) EI-AFY, later VR-BBH/G-ARKI; (34) EI-AGI, later G-APZC.

Viscount 838 9G-AAW which was delivered new to Ghana Airways in July 1958. (*Aviation Photo News*)

V.708 for Air France: (c/n 8) F-BGNK; (10) F-BGNL, later G-ARBY; (12) F-BGNM, later G-ARER; (14) F-BGNN, later G-ARGR; (16) F-BGNO; (18) F-BGNP; (33) F-BGNQ; (35) F-BGNR; (36) F-BGNS, later G-ARIR; (37) F-BGNT; (38) F-BGNU; (39) F-BGNV.

V.720 for Trans-Australia Airlines: (c/n 44) VH-TVA; (45) VH-TVB/VH-RMQ; (46-49) VH-TVC to 'VF; (84) VH-TVG.

V.723 for the Indian Air Force: (c/n 79) IU-683/VT-DWI.

V.724 for Trans-Canada Air Lines: (c/n 40) CF-TGI; (41) CF-TGJ/N117H; (42) CF-TGK; (43) CF-TGL; (50) CF-TGM/F-BMCH; (51) CF-TGN/N1898M; (52) CF-TGO/F-BMCG; (53) CF-TGP; (54) CF-TGQ/F-BMCF; (55) CF-TGR/F-BNAX; (56–60) CF-TGS to 'GW.

V.730 for the Indian Air Force: (c/n 80) IU-684/VT-DWJ.

V.734 for the Pakistan Air Force: (c/n 83) J751/ to Chinese Government 1968.

V.735 for Iraqi Airways: (c/n 67–69) YI-ACK to 'CM.

V.736 for Fred Olsen Air Transport: (c/n 77) LN-FOF, later G-AODG; (78) LN-FOL, later G-AODH.

V.737 for Canadian Department of Transport: (c/n 70) CF-GXK.

V.739 for Misrair, later United Arab Airlines: (c/n 85) SU-AIC; (86) SU-AID; (87) SU-AIE, later G-ATDU; (393) SU-AKN, later G-ATDR; (394) SU-AKO, later G-ATFN; (427) SU-AKW.

V.742 for the Brazilian Air Force: (c/n 141) FAB-2100/C90-2100.

V.744 for Capital Airlines: (c/n 88) N7402, later G-APKJ; (89) N7403, later G-APKK: (90) N7404; (103) N7405; (104-111) N7406 to N7413; (112) N7414/OE-LAN; (113) N7415/OE-LAO; (114) N7416/I-LIRC; (115) N7417; (116) N7418/I-LIRE, later G-AWGV; (117) N7419; (118) N7420, later G-ARHY; (119) N7421/I-LITS; (120–123) N7422 to N7425; (124) N7426, later G-ATTA; (125–129) N7427 to N7431; (130) N7432/CX-BHA; (131) N7433/CX-BHB; (132–139) N7434 to N7441.

V.745 for Capital Airlines: (c/n 198) N7442, later G-ARUU; (199) N7443; (200) N7444; (201) N7445/N923RC; (202–210) N7446 to N7455; (211) N7456/N1898K; (212) N7457/YS-28C; (213–217) N7458 to N7462; (231) N7465; (285) N7464; (287) N7463.

V.748 for Central African Airways Corporation: (c/n 98) VP-YNA/9Q-YDK; (99–102) VP-YNB to 'NE.

V.749 for Linea Aéropostale Venezolana: (c/n 94) YV-C-AMV; (95) YV-C-AMX; (96) YV-C-AMZ.

V.754 for Middle East Airlines: (c/n 239) OD-ACT; (240) OD-ACU/VP-WAR; (241) OD-ACV/VP-YTE; (242) OD-ACW/N7410; (245) OD-ACX.

V.756 for Trans-Australia Airlines: (c/n 146–148) VH-TVH to 'VJ; (181) VH-TVK; (197) VH-TVL; (373) VH-TVM; (374) VH-TVN/A2-ZEL.

V.757 for Trans-Canada Air Lines: (c/n 142) CF-TGX; (143) CF-TGY; (218–224) CF-THA to 'HG; (269) CF-THH; (270) CF-THI; (271–279) CF-THK to 'HS; (301) CF-THJ; (302-310) CF-THT to 'IB; (383–387) CF-TIC to 'IG.

V.760 for Hong Kong Airways Ltd.; (c/n 186) VR-HFI/9M-ALY/VR-AAW, later G-AWCV; (187) VR-HFJ.

V.761 for Union of Burma Airways: (c/n 188) XY-ADF; (189) XY-ADG; (190) XY-ADH, later G-APZN.

V.763 for T.A.C.A., Salvador: (c/n 82) YS-09C.

V.764 for United States Steel Corporation: (c/n 183) N905/N905G; (184) N906/N906RB; (185) N907/N907G.

V.765 for Standard Oil Co. of America: (c/n 191) N306.

V.768 for Indian Airlines Corporation: (c/n 192) VT-DIO; (193–196) VT-DIF to 'II; (292) VT-DIX; (293–296) VT-DIZ to 'JC.

V.769 for P.L.U.N.A., Uruguay: (c/n 321–323) CX-AQN to 'QP.

V.772 for British West Indian Airways Ltd.: (c/n 235) VP-TBS/9Y-TBS; (236) VP-TBT/9Y-TBT; (237) VP-TBU/9Y-TBU; (238) VP-TBX/9Y-TBX.

V.773 for Iraqi Airways: (c/n 331) YI-ACU.

V.776 for Aer Lingus: (c/n 225) EI-AJW, later G-APNF.

V.779 for Fred Olsen Air Transport: (c/n 247) LN-FOM/OE-LAE, later G-ARBW; (250) LN-FOH/OE-LAB, later G-APZP; (251) LN-FOI/VT-DOH; (252) LN-FOK/VT-DOI.

V.781 for the South African Air Force: (c/n 280) '150'.

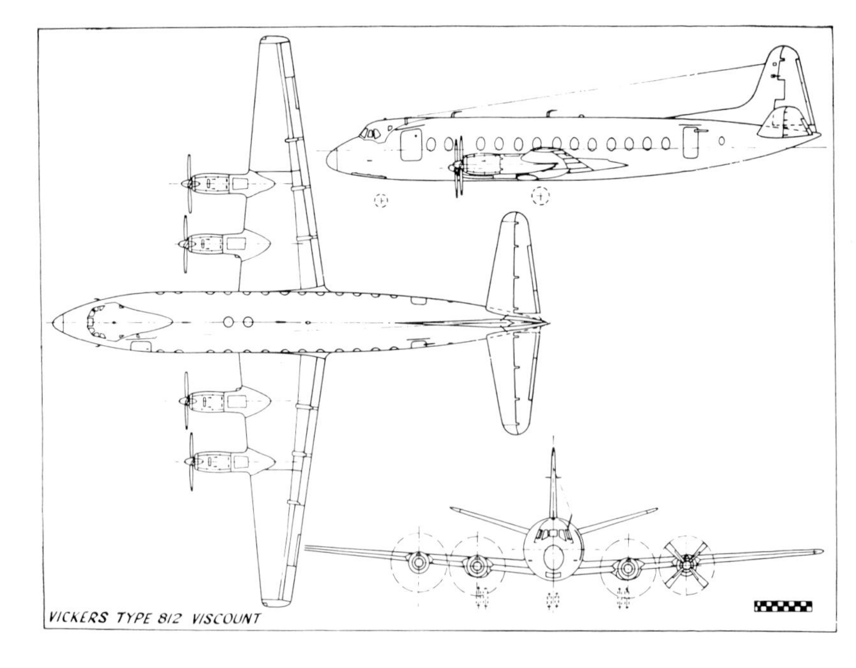
VICKERS TYPE 812 VISCOUNT

V.782 for Iran Government: (c/n 297) EP-AHA/VP-WAS; (298) EP-AHB/VP-WAT; (299) EP-AHC.

V.784 for Philippine Air Lines: (c/n 227) VH-TVO/PI-C772/SE-CNK; (300) PI-C770; (324) PI-C771.

V.785 for LAI/Alitalia; (c/n 325) I-LIFE/6OS-AAK; (326) I-LIFT; (327) I-LILI/HK-1061; (328) I-LAKE; (329) I-LARK/HC-APV; (330) I-LOTT; (377) I-LIRS/HC-ARS; (378) I-LIZT; (379) I-LIRP/6OS-AAJ; (380) I-LIZO/HK-1058.

V.786 for Lloyd Colombiano: (c/n 332) HK-943X/YS-08C; (333) HK-946X/AN-AKP/YS-011C, later G-AVIY; (334) HK-947X/AN-AKQ/N200Q.

V.789 for the Brazilian Air Force: (c/n 345) FAB-2101/C90-2101.

V.793 for Aer Lingus: (c/n 228) EI-AJV, later G-APNG.

V.794 for Turk Hava Yollari: (c/n 246) TC-SEC; (429) TC-SEV; (430) TC-SEL; (431) TC-SES; (432) TC-SET.

V.798 for Northeast Airlines: (c/n 232) N6590C/N7416; (233) N6591C/N1898T; (234) N6592C; (284) N6594C/I-LIRG; (286) N6593C/N746HA/YS-07C, later G-AVED; (288) N6596C/HC-ART; (391) N6597C/N8989V; (392) N6598C/N897C.

V.803 for K.L.M.: (c/n 172) PH-VIA/EI-AOG; (173) PH-VIB/EI-AOJ; (174) PH-VIC/EI-APD; (175) PH-VID/EI-AOL, later G-AYTW; (176) PH-VIE/EI-AOF; (177) PH-VIF/EI-AOE; (178) PH-VIG/EI-AOM; (179) PH-VIH/EI-AOI; (180) PH-VII/EI-AOH.

V.807 for New Zealand National Airways Corporation: (c/n 281–283) ZK-BRD to 'RF; (428) ZK-BWO.

V.808 for Aer Lingus: (c/n 289) EI-AJI; (290) EI-AJJ; (291) EI-AJK/HB-ILR; (421) EI-AKJ/EI-AKO/D-ADAN; (422) EI-AKK; (423) EI-AKL/D-ADAM (reallocation).

V.812 for Continental Airlines: (c/n 353) N240V/N501T; (354) N243V; (355) N241V/B-2021; (356) N242V; (357) N244V, later G-ATUE; (358) N245V, later G-AVIW; (359) N246V, later G-AVHK; (360) N248V, later G-AVJZ; (361) N249V, later G-AVNJ; (363) N251V, later G-AVHE; (364) G-APPU/N252V, later G-APPU; (365) N253V, later G-ATVR; (366) N254V, later G-ATVE; (389) N247V, later G-AVJL.

V.813 for South African Airways: (c/n 346–352) ZS-CDT to 'DZ.

V.814 for Deutsche Lufthansa/Condor: (c/n 338) D-ANUN; (339) D-ANOL, later G-AWXI; (340) D-ANAD; (341) D-ANIP; (342) D-ANUR; (343) D-ANEF; (344) D-ANIZ; (368) D-ANAM; (369) D-ANAB; (370) D-ANAC, later G-AYOX; (447) D-ANAF.

V.815 for Pakistan International Airlines: (c/n 335) AP-AJC; (336) AP-AJD, later G-AVJA; (337) AP-AJE; (375) AP-AJF, later G-AVJB; (376) AP-AJG/LX-LGC.

V.816 for Trans-Australia Airlines: (c/n 433) VH-TVP; (434) VH-TVQ.

V.818 for Cubana de Aviacion: (c/n 317) CU-T621/ZS-CVA; (318) CU-T622/VH-TVR; (319) CU-T623/B-2019; (320) CU-T624/N500T.

V.827 for V.A.S.P., Brazil: (c/n 397–401) PP–SRC to 'RG.

V.831 for Sudan Airways Ltd.: (c/n 419) ST-AAN, later G-ASED.

V.832 for Ansett-ANA: (c/n 414) VH-RMG/B-2015; (415–417) VH-RMH to 'MJ.

V.836 for Union Carbide, U.S.A.: (c/n 435) N40N/N140N/R.A.A.F.A6-435/VH-EQP/Muscat and Oman '501'.

V.837 for Austrian Airlines: (c/n 437) OE-LAF; (438) OE-LAG, later to R.R.E., Defford as XT575; (439) OE-LAH, later G-AZOV; (440) OE-LAK; (441) OE-LAL; (442) OE-LAM/OE-IAM.

V.838 for Ghana Airways: (c/n 371) 9G-AAV, later to R.R.E., Defford as XT661; (372) 9G-AAW; (446) 9G-AAU.

V.839 for Iran Government: (c/n 436) EP-MRS/R.A.A.F.A6-436/VH-EQQ/Muscat and Oman '502'.

Note: As a result of cancelled orders, c/n 313–315, 388, 390 and 420 were not used.

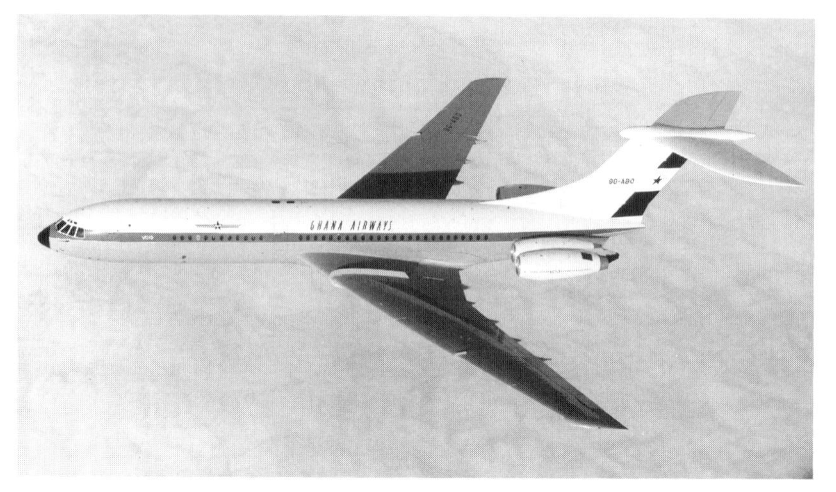

The first VC10 Type 1102 for Ghana Airways, 9G-ABO, delivered on 27 January 1965. (*B.A.C. Ltd.*)

Vickers VC10

The VC10 second generation turbojet transport with four tail-mounted 21,000 lb. s.t. Rolls-Royce Conway R Co 42s and aerodynamically clean, swept wing, was built to cover B.O.A.C.'s long distance routes at high subsonic cruising speed and yet be capable of full load operation out of hot and high airfields at Kano, Nairobi, Johannesburg and elsewhere. Short field performance and superb handling near the ground were ensured by the use of full span, leading edge slats and extensive Fowler trailing edge flaps.

A contract 'for 35 aircraft was placed on 14 January 1958 and construction commenced at Brooklands in new assembly shops built over the sewage farm that once had seen the undoing of so many pioneer (and other) aviators. The prototype VC10 Type 1100, G-ARTA, made its first flight from Brooklands to Vickers' flight test centre at Wisley on 29 June 1962, piloted by G. R. Bryce with B. Trubshaw as co-pilot and W. Cairns as flight engineer.

In 1961, when Vickers announced the enlarged Super VC10 with 13 ft. fuselage stretch to increase economy class accommodation from 135 to 163 passengers, B.O.A.C. cut its order for the standard VC10 Type 1101 to 12 aircraft and ordered 30 Super VC10 Type 1151s with 22,500 lb. s.t. Conway R Co 43s. Later this fleet was seen to exceed forecast requirements and was cut to 17 and although the first B.O.A.C. Super VC10, G-ASGA, flew on 7 May 1964, deliveries were irregular and were not completed until May 1969, G-ASGG being retained for Autoflare development until June 1967.

The standard VC10 went into regular B.O.A.C. passenger service on 29 April 1964 with the departure of G-ARVJ from London to Lagos; and the Super VC10 on the London–New York route on 1 April 1965. The travelling public was quick to appreciate the quiet cabin environment imparted by the rear-engined layout and during the next few years consistently high VC10 load factors caused real concern among B.O.A.C.'s competitors.

Two mixed traffic VC10 Type 1103s, G-ASIW and 'IX, built for British United Airways Ltd., Gatwick in 1964, were the first of a number completed with large side-loading freight doors in the front fuselage. These included 9G-ABP, second of two VC10 Type 1102s for Ghana Airways; three Super VC10 Type 1154s for East African Airways; and 14 Type 1106 VC10 C.Mk.1s for No.10 Squadron, R.A.F. Transport (later Air Support) Command. The military version was equipped with 150 rearward facing, removable seats for world wide troop transport and freighting; or up to 78 stretchers for aero medical evacuation; and for flight refuelling. One aircraft, XR809, was detached to Rolls-Royce Ltd. in 1969 for conversion to flying test bed for the enormous RB.211 engine then under development for the Lockheed TriStar. It first flew at Hucknall as G-AXLR on 6 March 1970 with this engine replacing the two port Conways.

Production of this, the last aeroplane designed and built solely by Vickers, terminated at the 37th VC10 (XV109 for the R.A.F.) in 1968 and the 27th Super VC10 (East African 5H-MOG) in 1970 but like so many other transports the aircraft became the subject of inter-airline leasing. B.O.A.C.'s G-ARVC flew for Nigeria Airways 1967–69; G-ARVG and 'VH for Air Ceylon; and Ghana Airways' 9G-ABP for Middle East Airlines 1967–68. The prototype, G-ARTA, was reworked to production standard for Laker Airways Ltd. in 1968 and then leased to M.E.A. 1968–69 as OD-AFA, mercifully escaping the fate of 9G-ABP which was destroyed by Israeli commandos at Beirut Airport on 28 December 1968. It was not the only VC10 to meet a violent end as B.O.A.C.'s G-ARVA, sold to Nigeria Airways in September 1969, crashed on approach to Lagos Airport on 20 November that year at the end of its delivery flight from Heathrow; and Super VC10 G-ASGN was wantonly destroyed with explosives by Palestinian guerillas in the Jordanian desert on 17 September 1970 after being hijacked at Beirut.

VC10 Type 1103 G-ASIX in Caledonian/B.U.A.'s interim colour scheme 1970 as 'Loch Maree'. (*British Caledonian Airways Ltd.*)

SPECIFICATION

Manufacturers: Vickers Aviation Ltd., Brooklands and Wisley Aerodromes, Surrey.

Power Plants: (Type 1101) Four 21,000 lb. s.t. Rolls-Royce R Co 42 Conway Mk.540
(Type 1106) Four 22,500 lb. s.t. Rolls-Royce R Co 43 Conway Mk.301
(Type 1151) Four 22,500 lb. s.t. Rolls-Royce R Co 43 Conway Mk.550

Dimensions: Span, 146 ft. 2 in. Length (VC10), 158 ft. 8 in. Length (Super VC10), 171 ft. 8 in. Height, 39 ft. 6 in. Wing area, 2,932 sq. ft.

	Type 1101	Type 1106	Type 1151
Tare weight	139,505 lb.	142,220 lb.	146,962 lb.
All-up weight	312,000 lb.	322,000 lb.	335,000 lb.
Maximum cruise	580 m.p.h.	580 m.p.h.	580 m.p.h.
Service ceiling	38,000 ft.	38,000 ft.	38,000 ft.
Maximum range	6,725 miles	6,860 miles	7,190 miles

Production: Prototype aircraft: (c/n 801–802) static test fuselages; (803) Type 1101 prototype G-ARTA.

VC10 Type 1101 for B.O.A.C.: (c/n 804–815) G-ARVA to G-ARVM excepting G-ARVD not used; (816–818) cancelled.

VC10 Type 1102 for Ghana Airways: (c/n 823) 9G-ABO; (824) 9G-ABP; (825) 9G-ABQ undelivered, became Type 1103 G-ATDJ; (840) 9G-ABU cancelled.

VC10 Type 1103 for British United Airways Ltd.: (c/n 819) G-ASIW; (820) G-ASIX; (821–822) cancelled; (825) G-ATDJ first built as Type 1102 9G-ABQ.

VC10 Type 1106 for the R.A.F.: (c/n 826–830) XR806 to XR810; (831–839) XV101 to XV109.

Super VC10 Type 1151 for B.O.A.C.: (c/n 851–867) G-ASGA to G-ASGR; (868–875) G-ASGS to G-ASGZ cancelled.

Super VC10 Type 1154 for East African Airways: (c/n 881) 5X-UVA; (882) 5H-MMT; (883) 5Y-ADA; (884) 5X-UVJ; (885) 5H-MOG.

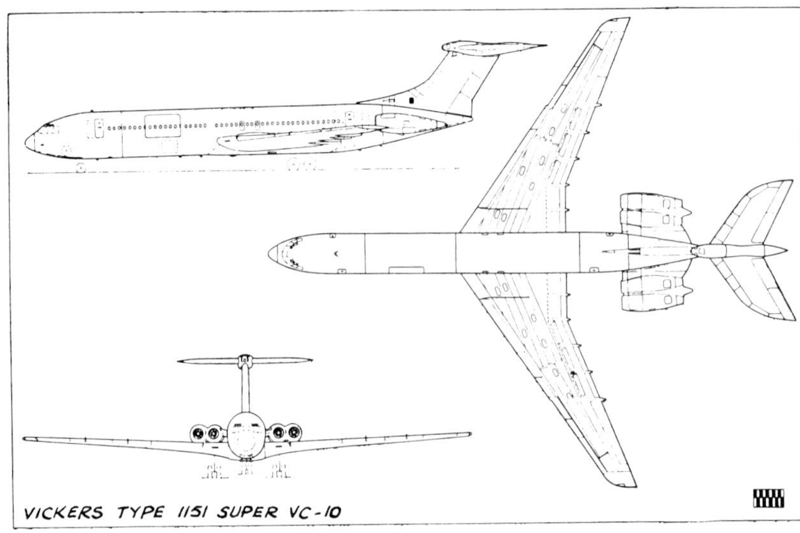
VICKERS TYPE 1151 SUPER VC-10

The prototype Rolls-Royce Falcon powered Westland Limousine I.
(*Westland Aircraft Works*)

Westland Limousine

Designed by Arthur Davenport, the Limousine I was the Westland Aircraft Works' first commercial aeroplane and one of the earliest attempts to introduce saloon car comfort into flying. It was a two bay biplane of conventional fabric-covered, wooden construction powered by one well-proven and economical 275 h.p. Rolls-Royce Falcon III, complete with Bristol Fighter type radiator. Situated amidships, the cabin was a plywood-covered structure for three passengers and pilot, the latter in the port rear seat, 30 in. higher than the passengers, with his head through a hole in the roof, open cockpit fashion. The prototype, K-126, first flown at Yeovil by chief test pilot Capt. A. S. Keep in July 1919, made a considerable number of publicity flights in 1919–20, including one during which Westland director R. J. Norton's secretary typed letters to his dictation in flight.

October 1919 saw the completion of the Limousine II, G-EAJL, also with a 275 h.p. Rolls-Royce Falcon but externally identified by the rectangular radiator and increased fin and rudder area. The prototype, now registered G-EAFO, was demonstrated at the air meeting held at Winton Racecourse by the Bournemouth Aviation Company on 1 May 1920. Later, on 13 September 1920, it was leased, together with G-EAJL, to a new company known as Air Post of Banks Ltd. for an experimental Croydon–Le Bourget express mail service during which it made fastest time of the month by crossing in a time of 1 hour 52 minutes. The firm's chief pilot was F. T. Courtney but after two months the Limousines returned to Yeovil where G-EAFO became the manufacturer's communications aircraft. It gave useful service until struck and demolished by a Fairey Fawn on the ground at Netheravon in September 1925, while on a business visit, piloted by Major L. P. Openshaw.

The Limousine II G-EAJL with modified cowlings and enlarged vertical tail surfaces. (*Westland Aircraft Works*)

The Jupiter powered Limousine II G-EAMV with the pilot's head projecting above the rear fuselage. (*Westland Aircraft Works*)

Manhandling the Limousine III G-EARV during ski operations in Newfoundland in 1921. (*via K. M. Molson*)

A third Limousine, also Mk.II, had flown in April 1920 as test bed for the new 400 h.p. Cosmos Jupiter but later reverted to standard. It was followed by a small batch of four, two of which, 'RE and 'RF, flown in October 1920, were leased to Instone Air Line, flying regularly on the Paris and Brussels routes until purchased outright in June 1922. Limousine 'RE, which was fitted with a 300 h.p. Hispano-Suiza, set up a new London–Brussels time of 2 hours 8 minutes later in the year.

Publication of the rules for the 1920 Air Ministry Commercial Aeroplane Competition resulted in the construction of the Lion powered Limousine III, a much larger, three bay biplane for pilot and five passengers. It was fitted with wheel brakes and a nose wheel to permit their maximum use in the short landing test. Fuel tanks were fitted under the lower mainplanes to reduce fire risk and to allow smoking in the cabin, a feature also incorporated in the Instone Air Line Limousine IIs. Piloted at Martlesham by A. S. Keep, it just beat the Sopwith Antelope to win £7,500, first prize in the small commercial aeroplane section. An interesting sidelight was the presence of maker's serial W.A.C.7 on the rear fuselage in contradiction of the aircraft's documents, which quoted W.A.C.8. It is therefore probable that construction of the true W.A.C.7, the final Limousine II, G-EARH, was not completed. Although inherently stable and in advance of the time–Capt. Keep was able to leave the

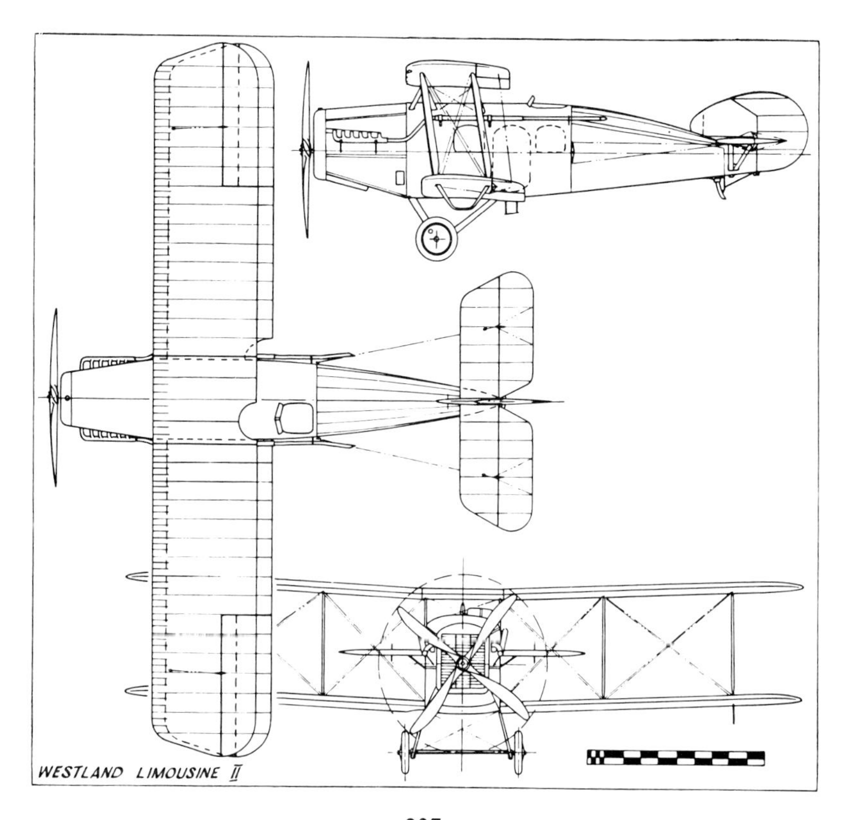

controls and join his passengers in the cabin—the market for commercial aeroplanes was non-existent due to the post-war slump, and only one other Limousine was built. This was a Mk.III supplied to the Air Council in April 1921 under a Contract placed on 11 November 1920 and was to have appeared in R.A.F. markings as J6851 but was registered G-EAWF instead and joined the small fleet of miscellaneous transports on loan to approved firms under the Government's subsidy scheme. It thus became the Instone Air Line reserve aircraft, joining its smaller brethren 'RE and 'RF at Croydon until all three were pensioned off in 1923.

Competition winner G-EARV pioneered air transport in Newfoundland with the Aerial Survey Company (Newfoundland) Ltd. formed in November 1920 by Maj. F. S. Cotton, A. S. Butler and Capt. S. Bennett. Successful, if difficult, seal and fishery spotting on wheels and skis in January 1921 was followed by a long charter flight to Cartwright, Labrador, piloted by T. K. Breakell during the gold rush. In July 1922 the Limousine IIs G-EAJL and 'MV were overhauled for C. of A. renewal and then also shipped to Newfoundland, followed in November by G-EARG.

The company operated in Newfoundland until the end of 1923, carrying mail and passengers between remote outposts. The large Limousine III G-EARV was then purchased by Laurentide Air Service Ltd. for $5,000 and registration G-CAET was reserved but on arrival at the company's maintenance base at Lac à la Tortue near Grand'Mere, Quebec, the aircraft was condemned and scrapped because of rot in the wooden structure.

SPECIFICATION

Manufacturers:	The Westland Aircraft Works, Yeovil, Somerset.	
Power Plants:	(Limousine I and II)	One 275 Rolls-Royce Falcon III.
	(Limousine II)	One 300 h.p. Hispano-Suiza.
		One 410 h.p. Cosmos Jupiter III.
	(Limousine III)	One 450 h.p. Napier Lion.

	Limousine I	Limousine II	Limousine III
Span	38 ft. 2 in.	37 ft. 9 in.	54 ft. 0 in.
Length	27 ft. 9 in.	27 ft. 9 in.	33 ft. 6 in.
Height	10 ft. 9 in.	10 ft. 9 in.	12 ft. 6 in.
Wing area	440 sq. ft.	440 sq. ft.	726 sq. ft.
Tare weight	2,183 lb.	2,010 lb.	3,823 lb.
All-up weight	3,383 lb.	3,800 lb.	5,850 lb.
Maximum speed	100 m.p.h.	100 m.p.h.	118 m.p.h.
Cruising speed	85 m.p.h.	90 m.p.h.	90 m.p.h.
Initial climb	600 ft./min.	650 ft./min.	–
Ceiling	17,000 ft.	17,000 ft.	12,300 ft.
Range	290 miles	400 miles	520 miles

Production: One Limousine I: (W.A.C.1) K-126/G-EAFO. Five Limousine II: (W.A.C.2) G-EAJL; (W.A.C.3) G-EAMV; (W.A.C.4) G-EARE; (W.A.C.5) G-EARF; (W.A.C.6) G-EARG. Two Limousine III: (W.A.C.8) G-EARV; (W.A.C.9) J6851/G-EAWF.

Note: (W.A.C.7) Limousine II G-EARH not completed.

Carill S. Napier landing in his Gipsy I powered Widgeon III. (*Aeroplane*)

Westland Widgeon

Built for the 1924 Lympne Trials, the two seat Widgeon was a parasol monoplane with fabric-covered, spruce girder fuselage and powered by a 35 h.p. Blackburne Thrush. The unusual folding wing tapered sharply in chord and thickness to give the pilot an exceptional range of vision. The maiden flight took place at Yeovil on 22 September 1924 but during a qualifying circuit of the Lympne course on the 27th, the Widgeon encountered a down current and sideslipped into the ground. Capt. Winstanley was uninjured, and the damaged aircraft, obviously underpowered, was rebuilt as the Widgeon II with 60 h.p. Armstrong Siddeley Genet I and less rudder area. Competitive trials against the Woodpigeon led to the eclipse of the biplane and to the introduction of the Widgeon III production version with plywood fuselage and constant chord mainplane. It was not only robust and free from rigging problems but also faster than contemporary light biplanes, and the Cirrus II powered prototype, G-EBPW, first flown by chief test pilot L. P. Openshaw in April 1927, was piloted by Sqn. Ldr. T. H. England in the Bournemouth Easter Races in competition with the Widgeon II. During Whitsun racing over the same course, 'PW collided in the air with Blackburn Bluebird G-EBKD, both aircraft being burned out with the loss of pilots L. P. Openshaw and W. H. Longton. Dr. E. D. Whitehead Reid bought Widgeon II G-EBJT in January 1928 and flew it from Bekesbourne until he was killed through striking trees in a dusk forced landing at East Sutton Park, near Detling, Kent, in October 1930.

Pressure of work on the Wapiti contract brought production to an end in 1929 after nearly 30 Widgeons had been constructed, 17 of which were of British registry, sold in two well-defined batches in 1927 and 1929. Westland managing director R. A. Bruce's G-EBRL, second in the 1927 King's Cup Race at 102·8 m.p.h. piloted by W. J. McDonough, was experimentally fitted, but not flown, with an 80 h.p. A.B.C. Hornet in 1928. It was also flown at Cowes on Saunders-Roe floats with 95 h.p. Cirrus III in 1929.

The Widgeon I with three cylinder Thrush radial before the Lympne Trials, September 1924. (*Westland Aircraft Works*)

The Widgeon II, showing Genet engine and revised rudder. (*Flight Photo 7166*)

G-EBRN, Cirrus II engined single seater with 50 gallon fuel tank in the front cockpit, left Lympne for Australia on 23 April 1928, piloted by Wing Cdr. E. R. Manning. After considerable bad luck the flight was abandoned at Baghdad and 'RN was shipped home and sold to H. R. Law for a similar attempt. Again damaged, this time at Athens on 18 January 1930, it returned to become the longest-lived British owned Widgeon, flown privately by Flt. Lt. (later Air Commodore) A. H. Wheeler from November 1933 until the outbreak of war in 1939. After C. of A. renewal at Balado in February 1948, however, it was burned at Stranraer because the owner could no longer house it.

Sqn. Ldr. H. M. Probyn's G-EBRQ, winner of the 1928 Grosvenor Trophy, was unique in having an alternative centre section giving 11 in. instead of 4 in. of sweepback to compensate for the lower installed weight of a 75 h.p. Genet II. During the winter of 1928–29, owner and wife made a 4,200 mile tour to Naples, Catania, Tunis, Algiers, Seville, Madrid and Biarritz in a flying time of 60 hours 50 minutes. Cirrus Widgeon G-EBRO, Gipsy Widgeon G-AADE flown respectively by J. G. Ormston and C. S. Napier, and 'RQ, all competed without success in the King's Cup Race of July 1930, averaging 98 m.p.h. G-EBRQ ended its days at R.A.F. Hinaidi, Iraq, flown by Wing Cdr. E. L. Howard Williams.

Those sold overseas comprised G-AUGI used initially by Airgold Ltd. in New Guinea; an unregistered machine for T. K. Breakall in Newfoundland; G-UAAH for the Port Elizabeth Light Aero Club, South Africa; G-IAAW for the French Motor Car. Co. Ltd., Delhi; and at least five for Australia. One of these, G-AUKP/VH-UKP, was flown by owner J. A. Marsh in the gruelling 1,410 mile Brisbane–Adelaide Race in 1936, and G-AUKA 'Kookaburra' was the Widgeon III under which Keith Anderson and Bobby Hitchcock died of thirst after forced landing in the bush between Alice Springs and Wyndham on 10 April 1929 while searching for Kingsford Smith's Fokker monoplane VH-USU 'Southern Cross'. In 1973 the world's only airworthy Widgeon was VH-UHU flown from a strip at Boort, Victoria, by owner A. L. Whittaker but VH-UGI was dismantled and stored by Marshall Airways at Bankstown.

The remaining aircraft of the first batch, G-EBRM, built for R. G. Cazalet, was the first of several Widgeon IIIA aircraft with metal fuselage and divided undercarriage. With the original Cirrus III replaced by a 105 h.p. Hermes I, 'RM made fastest time in the Grosvenor Trophy Race at Cramlington on 5 October 1929. The divided undercarriage, fitted retrospectively to some wooden Widgeons such as G-EBRO and 'RP, was not therefore a recognition

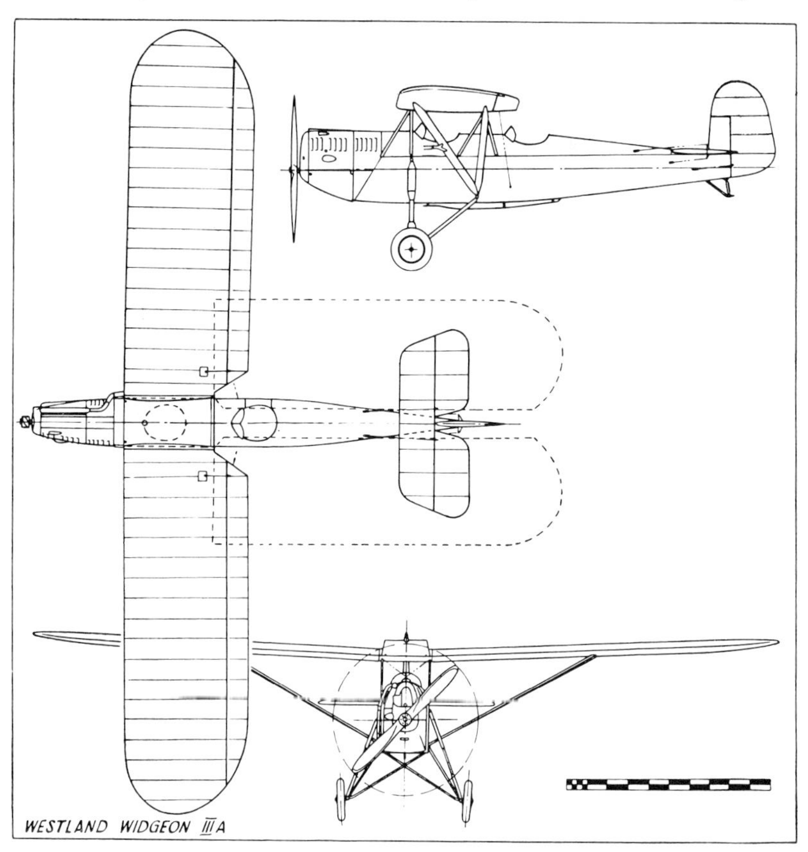
WESTLAND WIDGEON IIIA

Widgeon III G-EBRL moored off Cowes during trials on Saunders-Roe floats in 1929.

Widgeon III G-EBRO with the temporary cabin fitted in 1928.

Sqn. Ldr. Probyn's Widgeon III G-EBRQ, Genet II radial, at the opening of the Bristol and Wessex Aeroplane Club at Filton on 8 October 1927. (*Flight Photo 5118*)

feature of the Widgeon IIIA.

The second, or 1929 batch, comprised C. S. Napier's Gipsy I powered Widgeon III G-AADE and seven Widgeon IIIAs. These were Miss C. R.

Leathart's Cramlington based G-AAJF; Westland's Cirrus III powered demonstrator G-AAFN; the Anglo-American Oil Co. Ltd.'s Gipsy I engined G-AAFD 'Miss Ethyl'; G-AALB taken to Canada by W. J. McDonough and fitted with a front seat coupé top in 1939; G-AUKS sold to Milton Kent in Australia, stored during the 1939–45 war as VH–UKS and written off in a forced landing at Sugarloaf Point, N.S.W. on 6 October 1947; and one, believed c/n 1781, flown in South America.

Last of all the Widgeons, G-AAGH, fitted with a Hermes I, was the manufacturer's communications aircraft for over 19 years, flown throughout the war in military colours with civil marks. In the hands of H. J. Penrose it gave memorable postwar displays until burned out at Merryfield, Somerset, in July 1948 after striking a hangar during an attempted pilotless take-off.

SPECIFICATION

Manufacturers:	The Westland Aircraft Works, Yeovil, Somerset.	
Power Plants:	(Widgeon I)	One 35 h.p. Blackburne Thrush.
	(Widgeon II)	One 60 h.p. Armstrong Siddeley Genet I.
	(Widgeon III)	One 85 h.p. A.D.C. Cirrus II.
		One 90 h.p. A.D.C. Cirrus III.
		One 75 h.p. Armstrong Siddeley Genet II.
		One 85 h.p. A.B.C. Hornet.
		One 100 h.p. de Havilland Gipsy I.
	(Widgeon IIIA)	One 90 h.p. A.D.C. Cirrus III.
		One 100 h.p. de Havilland Gipsy I.
		One 105 h.p. Cirrus Hermes I.
		One 120 h.p. Cirrus Hermes II.

	Widgeon I	Widgeon II	Widgeon III	Widgeon IIIA
Span	30 ft. 8 in.	30 ft. 8 in.	36 ft. 4½ in.	36 ft. 4½ in.
Length	21 ft. 0 in.	21 ft. 0 in.	23 ft. 5¼ in.	23 ft. 5¼ in.
Height	7 ft. 3 in.	7 ft. 3 in.	8 ft. 5 in.	8 ft. 5 in.
Wing area	145 sq. ft.	145 sq. ft.	200 sq. ft.	200 sq. ft.
Tare weight	475 lb.	–	852 lb.*	935 lb.
All-up weight	815 lb.	1,150 lb.	1,400 lb.*	1,650 lb.
Maximum speed	72 m.p.h.	110 m.p.h.	100 m.p.h.	104 m.p.h.
Cruising speed	–	–	85 m.p.h.	86 m.p.h.
Initial climb	300 ft./min.	–	560 ft./min.	640 ft./min.
Ceiling	–	–	14,000 ft.	15,000 ft.
Range	–	–	–	315 miles

* 775 lb. and 1,323 lb. respectively with Genet II.

Production: Prototype Widgeon I/II (c/n W.1/WA.1671) G-EBJT; prototype Widgeon III (WA.1677) G-EBPW; and production batches WA.1679–WA.1684, WA.1693–WA 1698, WA.1724, WA.1773–WA.1783, and WA.1866. These included 11 British registered Widgeon IIIs and six for export: (c/n WA.1681) G-AUGI/VH-UGI; (WA.1683) Newfoundland; (WA.1693) G-UAAH; (WA1773) G-AUIY/VH-UIY; (WA.1774) G-AUKA; (WA.1777) G-AUKE/VH-UKE. Also five British Widgeon IIIAs and two for export: (WA.1780) G-AUKS/VH-UKS; (WA.1781) South America unconfirmed.

The Imperial Airways Westland Wessex G-ACHI landing at Yeovil in June 1935. (*Flight Photo*)

Westland IV and Wessex

The Westland IV, designed in 1928, was a small, high wing, taxi or feeder line aircraft built of wood, fabric covered and fitted with standard Wapiti rudder. Risk of forced landings was lessened by fitting three 95 h.p. Cirrus III engines, the outboard units mounted on the undercarriage outriggers. Pilot, mechanic and four passengers were carried, with a generous baggage compartment behind the cabin. The prototype, G-EBXK, was first flown at Yeovil by chief test pilot L. C. Paget on 22 February 1929 and a second, G-AAGW, with rear fuselage of metal construction and three closely cowled 105 h.p. Hermes I engines, was completed in time for exhibition at the Olympia Aero Show, London, in the following July. After the Show it went into service with the private hire department of Imperial Airways Ltd. at Croydon and work started on two others, G-AULF for the Shell Co. of Australia Ltd. and G-AAJI ordered by Wilson Airways Ltd., Nairobi.

After extensive trials the use of in-line engines was discontinued and when the two overseas orders fell through, G-AAJI was completed as the prototype Wessex with three 105 h.p. Armstrong Siddeley Genet Major radials in streamlined nacelles strutted to the mainplane. First flights with Class B marking P-1 were made in May 1930 after which this and the frustrated Australian machine became two of the four Wessex aircraft supplied to the Belgian airline SABENA for its shorter Continental services. The original Westland IV, similarly re-engined, was used as the manufacturer's demonstration and communications aircraft until 1935.

Early in 1931 the Armstrong Siddeley company introduced the Genet Major IA, a 140 h.p. engine with seven instead of five cylinders. When fitted to the Wessex, it imparted a considerable improvement in performance and the demonstrator, G-ABEG, was chartered for a survey of the South Yorkshire canals in 1931. It was also used by H.R.H. the Prince of Wales for the opening of Roborough Aerodrome on 15 July 1931, and for a trip to the French Riviera. On 24 September 1932 it also carried the Lord Mayor's guests to the Essex Air Display at Maylands. Both 'EG and another 'high performance' Wessex G-ACHI were acquired by Imperial Airways Ltd. in 1933, joining their original Westland IV G-AAGW, which had been modified to the same standard. Chartered by the Great Western Railway, 'GW operated a pioneer internal air route from Cardiff to Plymouth via Haldon from 12 April–20 May 1933, then extended to Castle Bromwich until the service ceased on 30 September. In the following year 'EG went to Baghdad on charter to the Iraq Petroleum Transport Co. Ltd., and spent 1935 in service with Rhodesia and Nyasaland Airways, finally coming to grief in a forced landing at Chirindu, Northern Rhodesia. Its sister aircraft was then relegated to radio and navigation training with Air Pilots Training Ltd., Hamble, until 1940.

Only two more Wessex aircraft were built, the first of which, G-ABVB, was a special machine with square dural tubes replacing wood in the wings, for use on the Portsmouth–Ryde and Shoreham–Portsmouth high density ferry services of Portsmouth, Southsea and Isle of Wight Aviation Ltd. Eight passengers were accommodated by a reduction in baggage space, while the cockpit was raised, undercarriage strengthened and rudder area increased. G-ACIJ, the final Wessex, a standard aircraft, left Heston in March 1934 on delivery to the Egyptian Air Force.

On 8 December 1934 Wessex OO-AGD was destroyed by fire when Belgian Air Force Fairey Fox O-47 crashed into SABENA's hangar at Evere

The Cirrus III powered Westland IV prototype landing at Croydon. (*Flight Photo 6976*)

G-AAGW in its original form with Hermes engines. (*Westland Aircraft Works*)

Aerodrome, Brussels and in the following March the other three returned to England for use as G-ABAJ, G-ADEW and 'FZ by Cobham Air Routes Ltd. on a Portsmouth–Christchurch–Guernsey service which opened on 6 May 1935. Two months later the starboard engine of G-ADEW failed half an hour out from Guernsey and the machine sank after a forced landing at sea off the Needles. The route then closed and 'AJ became a Ryde ferry, while 'FZ and the veteran 'XK joined National Aviation Day Displays Ltd. for pleasure flying. Early in 1936 'AJ and 'FZ were taken over by the Trafalgar Advertising Co. Ltd. and were based at Croydon, carrying out nightly publicity sorties with battery-operated neon advertising under the wings.

The special Wessex built for Portsmouth, Southsea and Isle of Wight Aviation Ltd. in 1932.

G-ACIJ, the V.I.P. Wessex supplied to the Egyptian Air Force in 1934. Late production machines had metal clad front fuselages. (*Westland Aircraft Works*)

SPECIFICATION

Manufacturers: The Westland Aircraft Works, Yeovil, Somerset.

Power Plants: (Westland IV) Three 95 h.p. A.D.C. Cirrus III.
Three 105 h.p. Cirrus Hermes I.
(Wessex) Three 105 h.p. Armstrong Siddeley Genet Major.
Three 140 h.p. Armstrong Siddeley Genet Major 1A.

Dimensions: Span, 57 ft. 6 in. Length, 38 ft. 0 in. Height, 9 ft. 6 in. Wing area, 490 sq. ft.

	Westland IV	Wessex		
		Genet Major	Genet Major IA	G-ABVB
Tare weight	3,150 lb.	3,810 lb.	3,891 lb.	3,930 lb.
All-up weight	5,500 lb.*	5,750 lb.	6,300 lb.	6,300 lb.
Maximum speed	108 m.p.h.	118 m.p.h.	122 m.p.h.	122 m.p.h.
Cruising speed	100 m.p.h.	100 m.p.h.	100 m.p.h.	108 m.p.h.
Initial climb	520 ft./min.	600 ft./min.	680 ft./min.	610 ft./min.
Ceiling	14,000 ft.	12,300 ft.	14,900 ft.	13,700 ft.
Range	525 miles	520 miles	420 miles	340 miles

* Prototype 4,900 lb.

Production: (a) Westland IV

Two aircraft only: (c/n WA.1771) G-EBXK; (WA.1867) G-AAGW.

(b) Wessex

Eight aircraft only: (c/n WA.1897) G-AAJI/VP-KAD ntu/G-ABAJ/OO-AGC, later G-ABAJ; (WA.1898) G-AULF/OO-AGD; (WA.1899) OO-AGE, later G-ADEW; (WA.1900) OO-AGF, later G-ADFZ; (WA.1901) G-ABEG; (WA.2152) G-ACIJ; (WA.2156) G-ABVB.

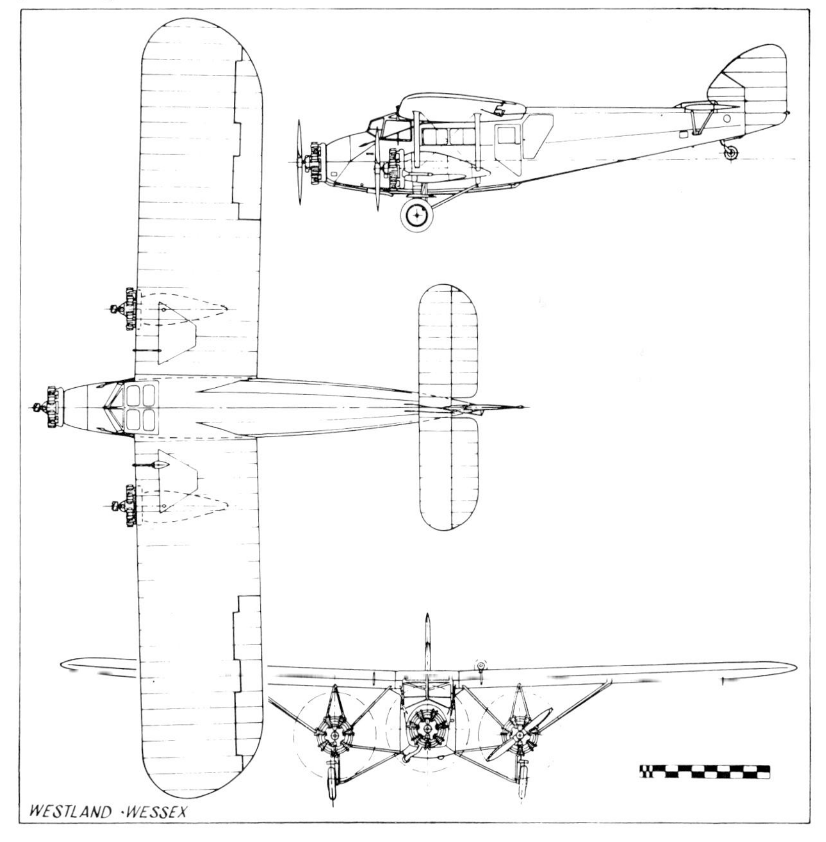

APPENDIX A

Other British-built Civil Aircraft

This section of the book describes civil aircraft of British design which existed only in prototype form or in small numbers and includes designs intended for amateur construction which, although of foreign origin, were built in Britain from British materials to British standards of airworthiness. Exceptions are the Jodel D.9 Bébé and Jodel D.11 Club which are included in Appendix C for continuity with other Jodel designs. Replicas of vintage foreign types built for film purposes will also be found in Appendix C with the exception of the Slingsby-built Rumpler C IV which, having a British designation, logically finds a place here.

Whenever possible registration details are included in the text but when this is not possible through lack of space, they are listed in Appendix E. Omission of the date of issue of C. of A. indicates that none was issued. Dates are given in the British way, viz. day, month, year.

Abbreviations are limited to those used in Volumes 1 and 2 and to the following:

A/L	Airlines or Air Lines
A.T.C.	Air Training Corps
C.A.A.	Central African Airways
c.s.	constant speed
H.A.P.S.	Historic Aircraft Preservation Society
I.A.L.	Imperial Airways Ltd.
LIAT	Leeward Islands Air Transport
P.A.A.	Pan American World Airways
P. and P.	Phillips and Powis
SATA	Sociedade Acoriana de Transportes Aereos
STOL	Short Take-Off and Landing
T.A.I.P.	Transportes Aereos da Indias Portugesas
U.A.S.	University Air Squadron

(*E. J. Riding*)

Heath Parasol (Tomtit)

Single seat ultra light of American design powered by one 696 cc. Blackburne Tomtit. One British aircraft only, G-AFZE, c/n P.A.1, built by R. H. Parker 1939, first flown at Elstree by C. H. Debenham 9.1.49, A. to F. 1.49. Sold to F. G. Lowe, Redhill 7.51 and fitted with 32 h.p. Bristol Cherub III at Croydon; L. G. Foley, Prestwick 9.60; last owner F. R. Brimecombe, Luton. Crashed at Luton 1.4.66. Span, 23 ft. 0 in. Length, 17 ft. 3 in. Tare wt., (Tomtit), 448 lb. A.U.W., 560 lb. Max. speed, 71 m.p.h. Cruise, 62 m.p.h.

(*A. J. Jackson*)

Heath Parasol (J.A.P.)

Similar airframe initially powered by one 30 h.p. A.B.C. Scorpion. One British aircraft only, G-AJCK, c/n S.H.1, built by South Hants Ultra Light Air Club, Christchurch, 1948, A. to F. 15.1.49, trial hops by G. B. S. Errington only. Sold to the Airways Aero Association, fitted at Hurn with 40 h.p. Aeronca J.A.P. J-99, A. to F. reissued 12.5.50, sold to R. A. Mann, Redhill 5.51, flown till 1954. Tare wt. (J.A.P.), 464 lb. A.U.W., 700 lb. Max. speed, 82 m.p.h. Cruise, 73 m.p.h.

(*Flight 16951S*)

Helmy Aerogypt I

Four seater powered by three 22 h.p. Douglas Sprites, designed and built at Heston by S. Helmy, an Egyptian, 1938. One aircraft only. G-AFFG, c/n 3, incorporating a hinged roof which acted as a landing flap, first flown at Heston 2.39. Later flown as Aerogypt II with hinged roof removed. Last flown 26.9.40 as Aerogypt III with end plate fins. Span, 26 ft. 4 in. Length, 19 ft. 0 in.

Helmy Aerogypt IV

G-AFFG modified to Aerogypt IV at White Waltham 1943 with two 65 h.p. Continental A65 and tricycle undercarriage by the newly formed Aerogypt High Speed Development Co. Ltd., C. of A. 29.10.46. Dropped by salvage crane and damaged beyond repair following a landing accident at Northolt 26.11.46 when outward bound for Egypt. Fuselage used as a hen house near White Waltham Aerodrome until the late 1960s. Tare wt., 1,150 lb. A.U.W., 2,400 lb. Max. speed, 160 m.p.h. Cruise, 145 m.p.h.

(*Flight 7315*)

Henderson–Glenny H.S.F.II Gadfly I and II

Single seater, 35 h.p. A.B.C. Scorpion II, designed by K. N. Pearson, built by Glenny and Henderson Ltd. at York Road, Byfleet, Surrey 1929. Two only: Gadfly I G-AAEY, c/n 1, f/f at Brooklands 4.29; fitted with Pearson rotary ailerons as Gadfly II, World's altitude record of 3,021 m. in 200 kg. class 16.5.29 piloted by G. L. P. Henderson, C. of A. 16.9.29; to O. Greig, Brooklands 9.29; C. F. Parker, Wolverhampton 5.31; E. Bradley, Wolverhampton 2.33, scrapped 6.34. G-AARJ, c/n 2, Gadfly II, f/f 8.29, C. of A. 31.10.29, to R. Foley, Hamilton, Ontario 4.30 as CF-AMG, d.b.f. at Kitchener, Ontario 25.8.31. Span, 25 ft. 10 in. Length, 17 ft. 10 in. Tare wt., 455 lb. A.U.W., 750 lb. Cruise, 72 m.p.h. Range, 350 miles.

(*Aeroplane*)

Henderson–Glenny H.S.F.II Gadfly III

Gadfly II fitted with 40 h.p. Salmson A.D.9 radial. One aircraft only, G-AARK, c/n 1, built 7.29, owner G. L. P. Henderson, demonstrated at Heston 20.7.29. Withdrawn from use 1930, in storage at Brooklands until 6.33. Dimensions as for Gadfly I.

Henderson H.S.F.I

Six seat, twin boom pusher monoplane powered by one 240 h.p. Siddeley Puma, designed by J. Bewsher, built in a shed near Byfleet station and assembled at Brooklands 1928 by the Henderson School of Flying Ltd. One aircraft only: G-EBVF, c/n H.S.F.I, initially with cabin top which was removed before the first flight by G. L. P. Henderson who carried 30 passengers on the first day. Tested at Martlesham 4.30, scrapped after Henderson's death in the crash of Junkers F.13 G-AAZK at Meopham 21.7.30. Span, 51 ft. 0 in. Length, 38 ft. 0 in. Tare wt., 3,300 lb. A.U.W., 4,112 lb. Max. speed, 105 m.p.h.

(*Aeroplane*)

Hendy 281 Hobo

Single seater powered by one 35 h.p. A.B.C. Scorpion II, designed by Basil B. Henderson and built by the Hendy Aircraft Company at Shoreham in 1929. One aircraft only: G-AAIG, c/n 1, first flown 10.29 by E. W. Percival. Rebuilt at Shoreham 1934 with 90 h.p. Pobjoy Cataract, mass balanced ailerons and modified undercarriage for Lord Patrick Crichton-Stuart, C. of A. 9.7.34, based at Hanworth. Owner won the Hatfield–Cardiff Race 6.10.34 at 125·4 m.p.h. Raced with varying success until 1939, destroyed by German bombing at Lympne 30.8.40. Span, 32 ft. 0 in. Length, 19 ft. 6 in. A.U.W., 650 lb. Max. speed, 130 m.p.h.

(*Aeroplane*)

Hendy 302A

Two seater with 105 h.p. Cirrus Hermes I, designed by Basil B. Henderson and built as the Hendy 302 by Geo. Parnall & Co. Ltd. at Yate 1929. One aircraft only: G-AAVT, c/n 1, C. of A. 27.6.30, E. W. Percival averaged 121.5 m.p.h. in 1930 King's Cup Race. To the Cirrus Hermes Engineering Co. Ltd. 7.31, rebuilt for C.S. Napier at Croydon 1934 as 302A with inverted 130 h.p. Cirrus Hermes IV and revised cabin. Averaged 133·5 m.p.h. in 1934 King's Cup Race. Test bed for 150 h.p. Cirrus Major II in 1936, w.f.u. at Gravesend 1938. Span, 35 ft. 0 in. Length 22 ft. 10 in. Tare wt., 1,045 lb. A.U.W., 1,900 lb.

Heston Type 5 Racer

Wooden single seater designed by A. E. Hagg and G. Cornwall for an attempt on the world's air speed record, powered by one 2,300 h.p. derated Napier Sabre. Two aircraft only, financed by Lord Nuffield, built by the Heston Aircraft Co. Ltd. 1939–40 and registered to D. Napier and Son Ltd. G-AFOK, c/n 1, made one flight at Heston 12.6.40 piloted by Sqn. Ldr. G. L. G. Richmond. Damaged beyond repair in forced landing with overheated engine and inadequate elevator control after five minutes flight. G-AFOL, c/n 2, construction not completed. Span, 32 ft. 0½ in. Length, 24 ft. 7¼ in. A.U.W., 7,200 lb. Duration, 18 minutes. Estimated max. speed, 480 m.p.h.

Hillson Pennine

Side-by-side, two seat cabin monoplane of wooden construction powered by one 36 h.p. Praga B, designed by Norman Sykes and built by F. Hills and Sons Ltd. at Trafford Park, Manchester in 1937. Fitted with an unorthodox control system consisting solely of a normal elevator and spoilers on the leading edge of the mainplane. One aircraft only: G-AFBX, c/n H.A.100, registered 27.10.37 in the name of the manufacturers. Registration cancelled 19.11.45.

Hillson Helvellyn

Two seat, mid-wing training monoplane powered by one 90 h.p. Blackburn Cirrus Minor 1, designed by Norman Sykes and built by F. Hills and Sons Ltd. at Trafford Park, Manchester in 1939. One aircraft only: G-AFKT, c/n H.A.200, A. to F. 30.4.40, flown early in the 1939–45 war on the firm's communications duties, mainly between Barton and Ipswich. Dismantled 11.42. Span, 33 ft. 0 in. Length, 22 ft. 0 in. Tare wt., 900 lb. A.U.W., 1,500 lb. Cruise, 110 m.p.h.

(*Flight 9218*)

Hinkler Ibis

Two seat, wooden monoplane powered by two 40 h.p. Salmson A.D.9, designed and built at Hamble 1929–30 by H. J. Hinkler with the assistance of R. H. Bound. The wing was designed by Basil B. Henderson and built at Shoreham by Hendy Aircraft Ltd. One aircraft only, G-AAIS, c/n 1, first flown at Hamble without markings 5.30 and thereafter stored in Hinkler's garden at Sholing, Southampton. Rediscovered semi-derelict 2.53, acquired by H. C. G. Stisted and exhibited at the Hatfield Garden Party of the R.Ae.S. 14.6.53, scrapped at Lee-on-Solent 1959.

(*Flight 13657S*)

Hordern–Richmond Autoplane

Three seat, low-wing monoplane of wooden construction, powered by two 40 h.p. Continental A40. Built at Heston 1936 by the Heston Aircraft Co. Ltd. to the joint specification of their test pilot E. G. Hordern and the Duke of Richmond and Gordon. Rudder control from wheel on control column. One aircraft only, G-AEOG, c/n 1, A. to F. 16.10.36, owned by the Duke of Richmond and Gordon and after 14.4.38 by Hordern-Richmond Aircraft Ltd. at Denham. Scrapped during the 1939–45 war. Span, 43 ft. 4 in. Length, 24 ft. 6 in. Tare wt., 1,125 lb. A.U.W., 1,750 lb. Max. speed, 100 m.p.h. Cruise, 85 m.p.h.

(*via R. P. Smith*)

Howitt Monoplane

Single seater with plywood covered fuselage and fabric covered mainplane, powered by one 600 cc. Douglas, designed by R. C. Howitt and built at Garsington, near Cowley, Oxford in 1937. One aircraft only: G-AEXS, c/n H.32D, first flown at R.A.F. Abingdon by a Mr. Hutchinson of the Oxford U.A.S. and later by Flt. Lt. H. R. A. Edwards. Re-engined with a four cylinder air-cooled type in 1939 but not flown again. Stored in U.A.S. hangar at Abingdon but disappeared during the 1939–45 war. Span, 31 ft. 3 in. Length, 21 ft. 0 in. A.U.W., 510 lb.

(*J. O. Isaacs*)

Isaacs Fury Mk.1

Single-seat, wood and fabric sporting biplane using Currie Wot constructional methods but redesigned as a seven-tenths scale replica of the 1935 Hawker Fury fighter. One aircraft only: G-ASCM, c/n 1, one 65 h.p. Walter Mikron III, designed and built at Southampton 1961–63 by owner/pilot J. O. Isaacs and first flown at Thruxton 30.8.63 by John Heaton. A. to F. 14.4.64. Span, 21 ft. 0 in. Length, 18 ft. 9 in. Tare wt., 540 lb. A.U.W., 800 lb. Max. speed, 87 m.p.h. Cruise, 75 m.p.h.

(*Air Portraits*)

Isaacs Fury Mk.2

The original Fury, G-ASCM, re-engined by J. O. Isaacs at Kings Somborne airstrip, Hants. 1966–67 with one 125 h.p. Lycoming O-290-D. First flown by V. H. Bellamy 5.67, repainted in black and white insignia of No.43 Sqn., R.A.F.; A. to F. 9.5.68; sold 8.68 to M. Raper, Biggin Hill; flown to Wildenrath, Germany 6.69. A second Fury Mk.2, G-AYJY (PFA.1373), under construction by A. V. Francis at Dunstable 1973 and others abroad. Span, 21 ft. 0 in. Length, 19 ft. 3 in. Tare wt., 720 lb. A.U.W., 1,000 lb.

(*Air Portraits*)

Jurca MJ.2 Tempête

All-wood, single seat sportplane for amateur construction designed in France by Marcel Jurca 1955–56. Two British-built aircraft by 1973: G-ASUS, c/n PFA.2001, 90 h.p. Continental C90, built at Coventry by D. G. Jones, A. to F. 31.1.66, based at Baginton, re-engined 1970 as MJ.2B with 125 h.p. Lycoming O-290-3. G-AYTV, PFA.2002, MJ.2A with 65 h.p. Continental C65-8F, built by A. Baggallay and first flown at Blackbushe 4.3.72 by C. Rogers, C. of A. 21.7.72, based at Shoreham. Data for MJ.2A: Span, 19 ft. 8 in. Length, 19 ft. $2\frac{1}{2}$ in. Tare wt., 640 lb. A.U.W., 950 lb. (MJ.2B) 1,430 lb. Cruise, 100 m.p.h. Range, 330 miles.

(*A. J. Jackson*)

Kay Gyroplane Type 33/1

Single seat autogiro, powered by one 75 h.p. Pobjoy R, designed by David Kay and built by Oddie, Bradbury and Cull Ltd. at Eastleigh 1934–35. One aircraft only, G-ACVA, c/n 1002, Kay Gyroplanes Ltd., first flown 18.2.35, last flown at Perth 16.8.47, presented to Museum of Transport, Glasgow in 1969. A second aircraft, G-ACVB, c/n 1003, was not completed. The earlier model, Type 32/1, flown at Leuchars in 1932, was unregistered. Rotor diameter, 22 ft. 0 in. Length, 17 ft. 11 in. Tare wt., 664 lb. A.U.W., 920 lb.

(*Aeroplane*)

Kronfeld Monoplane

Single seat parasol monoplane powered by one 30 h.p. Carden-Ford driving a pusher airscrew, designed as a Drone replacement by Robert Kronfeld and built at Hanworth 1937. One aircraft only, G-AESG, c/n 33, A. to F. 7.5.37, first public appearance at the Heathrow Garden Party of the Royal Aeronautical Society 9.5.37. Scrapped during the 1939–45 war. Registration G-AESH reserved for unfinished second aircraft. Span, 39 ft. 8 in. Length, 21 ft. 2 in. Tare wt., 390 lb. A.U.W., 640 lb. Max. speed, 73 m.p.h.

(*Flight*)

L. and P. Biplane

Two seater powered by one 50 h.p. Gnôme, designed by A. A. Fletcher, built at Hendon 1916 by the London and Provincial Aviation Company as Type No.4 for their own flying school. After the 1914–18 war, five were registered for use at Stag Lane, Edgware: K-117/G-EABQ, c/n E121; K-118/G-EABR, c/n E120; K-119/G-EABS, c/n D147, all registered 20.5.19, broken up 8.19 when A.I.D. approval was refused. K-138/G-EADT, c/n E122, registered 11.6.19, wrecked by gale 10.20. Improved version G-EAQW, 100 h.p. Anzani (illustrated), no c/n, used during the 1914–18 war for parachuting experiments, registered to R. A. Whitehead 6.2.20, later sold to J. Coe and scrapped. Span, 37 ft. 0 in. Length, 25 ft. 0 in. Duration 3 hours.

Lockspeiser Land Development Aircraft

Seven-tenths scale research and demonstration model of a projected low cost utility transport. Designed by D. Lockspeiser as a single seat canard monoplane of fabric covered metal construction having a foreplane identical to each half of the mainplane, rugged box fuselage, four wheeled under-carriage and 85 h.p. Continental C85-12 rear mounted pusher engine. One aircraft only: G-AVOR, c/n LDA.01/PFA.1346, registered 8.6.67, built at Shalford, Surrey, and first flown by the designer at Wisley 24.8.71. Span, 29 ft. 0 in. Length, 22 ft. 6 in. A.U.W., 1,400 lb.

(*via G. A. Jenks*)

Lowe H.L.(M).9 Marlburian

Side-by-side, two seat braced monoplane powered by one 60 h.p. Gnome rotary, designed and built at Heaton, Newcastle-upon-Tyne, 1921 by F. Harold Lowe, trading as the Northern Aerial Transport Company. One aircraft only, G-EBEX, c/n H.L.(M).9, registered to the designer 7.10.22, crashed 25.11.22. Span, 28 ft. 6 in. Length, 17 ft. 0 in. Tare wt. 450 lb. Max. speed, 100 m.p.h. Cruise, 85 m.p.h.

(*Flight 12952S*)

Luton Buzzard I

Open cockpit, single seat ultra light of wooden construction, powered by one 35 h.p. Anzani inverted twin, designed by C. H. Latimer-Needham and built by Luton Aircraft Ltd. at Barton-in-the-Clay, Beds. One aircraft only, G-ADYX, c/n L.A.B./1, first flown 1936, fitted with split flaps and all-flying tailplane. Serious damage to rear fuselage landing at Christchurch 16.11.36. Span, 40 ft. 0 in. Length, 20 ft. 0 in. Tare wt., 600 lb. A.U.W., 800 lb. Max. speed, 85 m.p.h. Cruise, 75 m.p.h.

(*Aeroplane*)

Luton Buzzard II

The original Buzzard G-ADYX, rebuilt in 1937 with short-span wings, enclosed cockpit, orthodox tailplane, revised cowlings and undercarriage, A. to F. 8.8.36. Damaged beyond repair in baulked landing during demonstration by Robert Kronfeld at the Heathrow Garden Party of the Royal Aeronautical Society 8.5.38. Destroyed in hangar fire Gerrards Cross 1943. Span, 35 ft. 6 in. Length, 21 ft. 6 in. Tare wt., 400 lb. A.U.W., 600 lb. Max. speed, 95 m.p.h. Cruise, 81 m.p.h.

(*Richard Riding*)

Luton L.A.5 Major

Two seat cabin type, one 62 h.p. Walter Mikron II, designed by C. H. Latimer-Needham, built by Luton Aircraft Ltd., Gerrards Cross 1939. One aircraft initially: G-AFMU, c/n L.A.5/1, A. to F. 4.3.39, f/f by Sqn. Ldr. E. L. Mole 12.3.39, exhibited at the Heathrow Garden Party of the R. Ae. S. 14.5.39, destroyed in hangar fire at Gerrards Cross 1943. Design rights acquired 1958 by Phoenix Aircraft Ltd. who up-dated the drawings for amateur constructors as the L.A.5A. Construction of 17 had begun in Britain by 1973, of which 12 were registered, including G-AVXG with 100 h.p. Continental O-200-A. Span, 35 ft. 2 in. Length, 23 ft. 9 in. Tare wt., 600 lb. A.U.W., 1,100 lb. Max. speed, 105 m.p.h. Cruise, 95 m.p.h.

(*A. J. Jackson*)

Marendaz Mk.III

Four seater with retractable undercarriage, powered by one 200 h.p. de Havilland Gipsy VI, designed by D. M. K. Marendaz and built by International Aircraft and Engineering Ltd. Two aircraft only: an unregistered prototype, c/n 1, built at Cordwallis Works, Maidenhead, was lost when the factory was destroyed by fire 6.37; G-AFGG, c/n 2, built at Barton-in-the-Clay, Beds, was exhibited in unfinished state at the Heathrow Garden Party of the Royal Aeronautical Society 8.5.38. The machine remained uncompleted and was destroyed in 1940.

(*Aeroplane*)

Marendaz Trainer

Two seat instructional aircraft powered by one 90 h.p. Blackburn Cirrus Minor I, designed by D. M. K. Marendaz and built by Marendaz Aircraft Ltd. at Barton-in-the-Clay, Beds, 1939. One aircraft only: G-AFZX, c/n A.B.T.1, first flown 12.39, given to the Halton Squadron of the Air Training Corps, 1940. Span, 34 ft. 0 in. Length, 22 ft. 4 in. Tare wt., 960 lb. A.U.W., 1,500 lb. Max. speed, 124 m.p.h. Cruise, 95 m.p.h.

(R. P. Howard)

Martin Monoplane

Single seater designed and built at Denham 1937 by C. H. Latimer-Needham and H. Best-Devereux of Luton Aircraft Ltd. using the 32 h.p. Bristol Cherub III, mainplanes and other D.H.53 components taken from the Clarke Cheetah q.v. One aircraft only: G-AEYY, c/n 1, built for Flg. Off. Martin Hopkinson, first flown at Denham 10.37. A. to F. 4.11.37, crashed on second flight and rebuilt with new plywood fuselage. Used by owner to commute Denham–Ringway. Damaged in forced landing near Meir circa 1938, acquired by a Mr. Ford of Stoke-on-Trent and still in store 1973. Span, 30 ft. 0 in. Max. speed, 80 m.p.h.

(Aeroplane)

Martin–Baker M.B.1

Two seat, all-metal, experimental aircraft powered by one 160 h.p. Napier Javelin IIIA, designed by James Martin and built by the Martin-Baker Aircraft Co. Ltd. at Denham, Bucks, 1934, to demonstrate the Martin system of lattice girder construction. One aircraft only, G-ADCS, c/n M.B.1, first flown by V. H. Baker 3.35, destroyed by fire 3.38. Span, 37 ft. 0 in. Length, 28 ft. $10\frac{1}{2}$ in. Wing area, 206 sq. ft.

(G. J. R. Skillen)

McCandless M–4 Gyroplane

Single-seat gyroplane powered by one 1,500 cc. Volkswagen, designed and first built in 1962 as the M-2 with 650 cc. Triumph engine, by R. McCandless of McCandless Aviation Ltd., Newtownards. Six aircraft completed (including one two seat M-4/T1 trainer, G-ATXY, with 1,600 cc. Volkswagen) before production was taken over by W. H. Ekin (Engineering) Ltd., Crumlin, Co. Down. A further six aircraft registered by 1971. Rotor diameter, 22 ft. 0 in. Length, 10 ft. 11 in. Tare wt., 310 lb. A.U.W., 520 lb. Cruise, 100 m.p.h. Range, 120 miles.

Miles M.1 Satyr

Single seat wooden aerobatic biplane powered by one 75 h.p. Pobjoy R, designed by F. G. Miles and built by George Parnall and Company at Yate, Glos., 1932. One aircraft only, G-ABVG, c/n 1 (later J.7), first flown 8.32, C. of A. 1.2.33. Sold to the Hon. Mrs. Victor Bruce's firm Luxury Air Tours Ltd. 5.33, painted in red and white squares and flown by J. B. Pugh at the displays of British Hospitals Air Pageants Ltd. until crashed 8.36. Span, 21 ft. 0 in. Length, 17 ft. 8 in. Tare wt., 594 lb. A.U.W., 900 lb. Max. speed, 122 m.p.h.

Miles M.7 Nighthawk

Four seat instrument trainer powered by one 200 h.p. de Havilland Gipsy Six, built at Woodley from 1935. Five production aircraft only: G-ADXA, c/n 263, prototype, first flown as U-5, C. of A. 7.12.35, crashed during spinning trials at Woodley 22.1.36, Wing Cdr. F. W. Stent escaped by parachute; G-AEBP, c/n 282, C. of A. 19.3.36, withdrawn 5.37; G-AEHN and 'HO, c/n 283–4, Cs. of A. 14.8.36, left on delivery to the Rumanian Air Force 15.8.36; L6846 to No.24 Sqn., Hendon. Span, 35 ft. 0 in. Length, 25 ft. 0 in. Tare wt., 1,650 lb. A.U.W., 2,400 lb. Max. speed, 175 m.p.h. Cruise, 155 m.p.h.

(E. J. Riding)

Miles M.7A Nighthawk

Four seater erected in 1944 using a Nighthawk fuselage, the wings of the second Mohawk, revised glazing, rudder trim tab and one 205 h.p. de Havilland Gipsy Six Series II driving a variable-pitch airscrew. One aircraft only, c/n 286, flown by Miles Aircraft Ltd. as U-0225 and later as G-AGWT, C. of A. 15.3.46. Taxi work by Raceways Ltd., Woodley 1946–47; raced by Tommy Rose and other owners 1947–54; to Kenya 6.54 as VP-KMM; returned 8.61 as VR-TCM; left for Singapore 1.3.63 but abandoned at Lignane near Aix-en-Provence. Dimensions as M.7, A.U.W., 2,650 lb. Max. speed, 170 m.p.h. Cruise, 150 m.p.h.

(*Flight 13599*)

Miles M.8 Peregrine

The first Miles twin engined aircraft. Transport with retractable undercarriage to carry two crew and six passengers, built at Woodley 1936. Two aircraft only: G-AEDE, c/n 300, two 205 h.p. Gipsy Six II, f/f as U-9 by C. O. Powis 12.9.36, entered for the Schlesinger Race to Johannesburg by Flt. Lt. H. R. A. Edwards but was not ready in time, dismantled 12.37; L6346, c/n 485, two 250 h.p. Menasco Buccaneer B6S, to R.A.E., Farnborough 1938 for boundary layer trials. Span, 46 ft. 0 in. Length, 32 ft. 0 in. Tare wt., 3,000 lb. A.U.W., 5,200 lb. Max. speed, 188 m.p.h. Cruise, 164 m.p.h.

(*A. J. Jackson*)

Miles M.12 Mohawk

Two seater powered by one 250 h.p. Menasco Buccaneer B6S, built at Woodley 1936 to the specification of Col. Charles Lindbergh. Two aircraft only, G-AEKW, c/n 298, C. of A. 28.1.37, used by Lindbergh and wife for European inter-Capital travel 1937. Impressed 11.41 as HM503, restored 5.46 by Southern Aircraft (Gatwick) Ltd., flown in 1947 Folkestone Trophy Race by Wg. Cdr. Earle. Sold to E. G. F. Lyder 1947; to B. P. Pini, Broxbourne 7.48 and converted to open cockpits. Sold in Spain 2.50; G-AEKX, c/n 301, built but not erected. Span, 35 ft. 0 in. Length, 25 ft. 6 in. Tare wt., 1,605 lb. A.U.W., 2,620 lb. Max. speed, 190 m.p.h. Cruise, 170 m.p.h.

(*A. J. Jackson*)

Miles M.13 Hobby

Single seat research monoplane with retractable undercarriage, powered by one 145 h.p. de Havilland Gipsy Major 2 driving a variable-pitch airscrew. One aircraft only, G-AFAW, c/n 1.Y, completed at Woodley and f/f by F. G. Miles 4.9.37 as U-2. Retraction difficulties prevented it from competing in the King's Cup Race 11.9.37 although a public appearance was made at Hatfield on that day. Transferred to the R.A.E. for full scale wind tunnel research 5.38 as L9706, scrapped 1945. Span, 21 ft. 5 in. Length, 22 ft. 8 in. Tare wt., 1,140 lb. A.U.W., 1,527 lb. Max. speed estimated in excess of 200 m.p.h.

Miles M.18 Mk.1

Two seat trainer powered by one 130 h.p. de Havilland Gipsy Major 1, designed by W. Capley. One aircraft only, G-AFRO, c/n 1075, first flown at Woodley by F. G. Miles 4.12.38 as U-2. Converted to single seater in 1941 with tricycle undercarriage and fin and rudder moved forward 22 in. Flown as U-0222. Reverted to tail wheel undercarriage, flew with span reduced to 22 ft. and in 1946–47 with 110 h.p. Jameson FF engine. Scrapped 12.47. Span, 31 ft. 0 in. Length, 24 ft. 10 in. Tare wt., 1,180 lb. A.U.W., 1,800 lb. Max. speed, 140 m.p.h.

(*E. J. Riding*)

Miles M.18 Mk.2

Second prototype M.18 with fin and rudder moved forward 22 in., powered by one 150 h.p. Blackburn Cirrus Major III. One aircraft only: c/n 4426, first flown at Woodley 11.39 as U-8 and on Air Ministry acceptance trials as U-0224. Miles communications aircraft as HM545 until civilianised post-war as G-AHKY, C. of A. issued 29.8.46. Sold to Flt. Lt. H. B. Iles 3.48, won 1956 Goodyear Trophy at 130 m.p.h., 1957 Osram Cup at 136 m.p.h. and 1961 King's Cup at 142 m.p.h. To R. E. Coates, Blackbushe 1.70. Span, 31 ft. 0 in. Length, 24 ft. 10 in. Tare wt., 1,306 lb. A.U.W., 1,925 lb. Max. speed, 130 m.p.h. Cruise, 120 m.p.h.

(*G. A. Cull*)

Miles M.18 Mk.3

Third prototype M.18, fitted with enclosed cockpits and powered by one 150 h.p. Blackburn Cirrus Major III. One aircraft only: c/n 4432, first flown at Woodley 10.42 as U-3. Used for communications, becoming U-0238 in 1945 and civil as G-AHOA in 1946, C. of A. 3.4.48. Owned by Mrs. E. M. Porteous, Burnaston 1948, sold to T. W. Hayhow, crashed at Littondale, Yorks, 25.5.50. Specification as for M.18 Mk.2.

(*C. A. Nepean Bishop*)

Miles M.28 Mercury 2

Three seater with knuckled retractable undercarriage, designed by G. H. Miles, built at Woodley 1942. One aircraft only: U-0237 later HM583, initially powered by one 145 h.p. de Havilland Gipsy Major IIA and later one 140 h.p. Blackburn Cirrus Major II. Civilianised 1947 as G-AJVX and fitted with 150 h.p. Blackburn Cirrus Major III for the Hulland Gravel Co. Ltd., Burnaston, C. of A. 11.12.47. Sold to J. E. Nicholson, Croft, flown to Australia in 64 days as VH-BBK by F. Burt, arrived Perth, W.A., 17.1.51. Span, 30 ft. 8 in. Length, 24 ft. 0 in. Tare wt., 1,400 lb. A.U.W., 2,500 lb. Max. speed, 155 m.p.h. Cruise, 135 m.p.h.

(*Miles Aircraft Ltd.*)

Miles M.28 Mercury 3

Three seat, triple control trainer with thinner centre section allowing retracted wheels to protrude, powered by one 150 h.p. Blackburn Cirrus Major III. One aircraft only: c/n 4684, built 1943, initially flown as U-0242 and later PW937. Registration G-AISH reserved 12.46, scrapped 2.48. Span, 30 ft. 8 in. Length, 24 ft. 0 in. Tare wt., 1,480 lb. A.U.W., 2,500 lb. Max. speed, 155 m.p.h. Cruise, 135 m.p.h.

(*E. J. Riding*)

Miles M.28 Mercury 4

Four seat tourer powered by one 145 h.p. de Havilland Gipsy Major IIA driving a constant speed airscrew. One aircraft only: c/n 4685, built at Woodley 1944, first flown as U-0243, registered to Miles Aircraft Ltd. 11.45 as G-AGVX, C. of A. 26.4.46. Sold to Aerotaxi A.G. Zürich 4.47 as HB-EED, restored to H. W. H. Moore 3.48, five subsequent owners. Sold in Australia 1.53 as VH-AKH, later VH-AKC. Span, 30 ft. 8 in. Length, 24 ft. 0 in. Tare wt., 1,425 lb. A.U.W., 2,400 lb. Max. speed, 157 m.p.h. Cruise, 139 m.p.h.

(*A. J. Jackson*)

Miles M.28 Mercury 5

Four seater powered by one 150 h.p. Blackburn Cirrus Major III, fitted with revised undercarriage and the square rear window. One aircraft only: G-AJFE, c/n 6697, built at Woodley 1947, C. of A. 28.10.47, sold to K. Hole, White Waltham, and later J. F. Schumaker, Geneva. Re-registered in Switzerland 6.51 as HB-EEF. Restored to A. T. C. Carey, Denham, 12.54, damaged beyond repair in forced landing at West Hyde, Bucks, 13.3.55. Span, 30 ft. 8 in. Length, 24 ft. 0 in. Tare wt., 1,460 lb. A.U.W., 2,500 lb. Max. speed, 157 m.p.h. Cruise, 139 m.p.h.

(*E. J. Riding*)

Miles M.28 Mercury 6

Four seater powered by one 150 h.p. Blackburn Cirrus Major III, fitted with the oval rear window of the Messenger 2A. One aircraft only: G-AHAA, c/n 6268, built at Woodley 1946, C. of A. 3.5.46, personal aircraft of chairman of B.E.A.C., used by the Airways Aero Association 1947, sold 3.48 to K. E. Millard & Co. Ltd., Wolverhampton. Sold in Germany 9.56 by Adie Aviation Ltd. as D-EHAB. Specification as for Mercury 5.

(*E. J. Riding*)

Miles M.68

Aerovan derivative carrying one crew, unofficially known as the Boxcar, carrying 1,600 lb. of freight in a detachable and roadable central container and powered by four 90 h.p. Blackburn Cirrus Minor IIs. One aircraft only; G-AJJM, c/n 6696, first flown at Woodley by G. H. Miles 22.8.47 and demonstrated with and without freight hold at the Radlett S.B.A.C. Show 9.47. Scrapped 1948. Span, 50 ft. 0 in. Length, 36 ft. 0 in. Tare wt., 3,618 lb. A.U.W., 6,000 lb. Max. speed, 140 m.p.h. Cruise, 130 m.p.h. Range, 610 miles.

(*Aeroplane*)

Miles M.71 Merchantman

The largest Aerovan development, of all-metal construction, powered by four 250 h.p. de Havilland Gipsy Queen 30 and carrying two crew and 20 passengers or 5,000 lb. of freight. One aircraft only: G-AILJ, c/n 6695, first flown at Woodley by K. H. F. Waller 7.8.47 as U-21 and demonstrated at the Radlett S.B.A.C. Show 9.47. Scrapped 1948. Span, 66 ft. 6 in. Length, 42 ft. 9 in. Tare wt., 6,810 lb. A.U.W., 13,000 lb. Max. speed, 163 m.p.h. Cruise, 157 m.p.h. Range, 850 miles.

(*Lorna Minton*)

Mitchell–Procter Kittiwake I

All-metal, single seat sport or glider tug aircraft, one 100 h.p. Rolls-Royce Continental O-200-A, designed by Dr. C. G. B. Mitchell for amateur construction. Two completed by 1973: G-ATXN (c/n 001/PFA.1306) at Camberley, Surrey 1965–67, C. of A. 2.5.67 to Mitchell-Procter Aircraft Ltd. (restyled Procter Aircraft Associates Ltd. when the Mitchell-Procter partnership dissolved 10.68), f/f by R. G. Procter at Lasham 23.5.67, sold to T. A. McMullin, Dunstable 6.70; XW784 (PFA.1352), begun by R.N. apprentices at Arbroath 1969, f/f at Lee-on-Solent 21.10.71 by Lt. Cdr. C. Allen R.N. Span, 24 ft. 0 in. Length, 19 ft. 8 in. Tare wt., 925 lb. A.U.W., 1,350 lb. Cruise, 122 m.p.h. Range, 490 miles.

(*Aviation Photo News*)

Mitchell Kittiwake II

Side-by-side, two seat development of the all-metal Kittiwake I, one 130 h.p. Rolls-Royce Continental O-240, designed by Dr. C. G. B. Mitchell who was formerly associated with R. G. Procter in Mitchell-Procter Aircraft Ltd. Prototype, G-AWGM (c/n 002/PFA.1329), built by Robinson Aircraft Ltd. and first flown at Blackbushe 19.3.72 by Sqn. Ldr. B. Hopkins. Span, 25 ft. 6 in. Length, 20 ft. 5 in. (estimated data); Tare wt., 1,070 lb. A.U.W., 1,600 lb. Cruise, 130 m.p.h. Range, 500 miles.

(*Flight 16355S*)

Moss M.A.1

Two seat cabin monoplane of wooden construction powered by one 95 h.p. Pobjoy Niagara III, designed and built by Moss Bros. Aircraft Ltd. at Chorley, Lancs. 1937. One aircraft only: G-AEST, c/n 1, C. of A. 6.9.37, converted to open cockpits 1938, stored during 1939–45 war, flown with rear cockpit faired over in the 1949 and 1950 King's Cup Races by W. H. Moss who was killed when it crashed at the Newport turn, near Wolverhampton 17.6.50. Span, 34 ft. 0 in. Length, 23 ft. 3 in. Tare wt., 950 lb. A.U.W., 1,400 lb. Cruise, 120 m.p.h.

(A. J. Jackson)

Moss M.A.2

Open two seater, 90 h.p. Blackburn Cirrus Minor I, built at Chorley 1939. One aircraft completed only: G-AFMS, c/n 2, first shown at Heathrow 14.5.39, converted to cabin, C. of A. 18.10.40, shipped to Canada as CF-BUB, crossed the Rockies 1941, returned 1947. Flown in 1949 King's Cup Race by W. H. Moss and in 1950 by G. F. Bullen. To the Fairwood Flying Group 9.53, crashed 10 miles south of Builth Wells 7.7.58. Reservations G-AFHA and 'JV not used but an unfinished M.A.2 found at Chorley 1964 was acquired by Carl Schofield for completion at Coventry as M.A.1 G-AFHA. Span, 34 ft. 0 in. Length, 23 ft. 3 in. Tare wt., 950 lb. A.U.W., 1,400 lb. Cruise, 110 m.p.h.

(E. J. Riding)

Newbury A.P.4 Eon

Four seater powered by one 100 h.p. Blackburn Cirrus Minor II, designed by Aviation and Engineering Projects Ltd. and built 1947 by Elliotts of Newbury Ltd. One aircraft only: G-AKBC, c/n Eon/1, first flown at Welford, Berks. by P. Stanbury 8.8.47, C. of A. 8.9.47. Fitted 7.48 with 145 h.p. de Havilland Gipsy Major 10 and lengthened nose-wheel leg, and redesignated Eon 2. Destroyed in pilotless take-off at Lympne 14.4.50. Span, 37 ft. 0 in. Length, 25 ft. 0 in. (Eon 1) A.U.W., 1,950 lb. Max. speed, 112 m.p.h. Cruise, 100 m.p.h. (Eon 2) A.U.W., 2,340 lb. Max. speed, 136 m.p.h. Cruise, 115 m.p.h.

Nieuport Nighthawk

Two seater designed by H. P. Folland, powered by one 320 h.p. A.B.C. Dragonfly I and built from Nighthawk single seat fighter components by the Nieuport and General Aircraft Co. Ltd. at Cricklewood 1919. One British civil aircraft only: K-151, c/n L.C.1 No.1, flown in the Aerial Derby, Hendon, 21.6.19 by L. R. Tait-Cox, forced landed at West Thurrock, Essex. Became G-EAEQ, C. of A. 7.7.19, made first newspaper flight in India, from Bombay to Poona 2.20. Sold in India 9.20. Span, 28 ft. 0 in. Length, 18 ft. 0 in. Tare wt., 1,500 lb. A.U.W., 2,180 lb. Max. speed, 138 m.p.h.

(Flight 286)

Nieuport Nieuhawk

Single seat wooden racing and demonstration aircraft powered by one 320 h.p. A.B.C. Dragonfly I, designed by H. P. Folland and built at Cricklewood 1919 by the Nieuport and General Aircraft Co. Ltd. One aircraft only: G-EAJY, c/n L.C.1 No.2, first flown 3.9.19, fourth at 132·67 m.p.h. in the Aerial Derby, Hendon, 24.7.20 piloted by J. H. James. Forced landed after completing one lap of the Aerial Derby 16.7.21 at 142·6 m.p.h. piloted by Flt. Lt. J. Noakes. Sold 1921 to C. P. B. Ogilvie, Willesden. Span, 26 ft. 0 in. Length, 18 ft. 6 in. A.U.W., 2,120 lb. Max. speed, 151 m.p.h.

(*Flight 571*)

Nieuport Goshawk

Single seat racing biplane powered by one 320 h.p. A.B.C. Dragonfly I, designed by H. P. Folland and built at Cricklewood 1920. One aircraft only: G-EASK, c/n L.S.3 No.1, set up British speed record of 166·5 m.p.h. in Class C4B piloted by L. R. Tait-Cox at Martlesham 17.6.20. Forced down at Brooklands in the Aerial Derby 24.7.20, same pilot. Flown to Etampes by J. H. James for the Gordon Bennett Race 26–27.9.20. H. G. Hawker suffered haemorrhage in the air and was killed when the machine crashed at Hendon 12.7.21. Span, 20 ft. 6 in. Max. speed, 167 m.p.h.

(*Flight F68 15/10*)

Nipper Mk. III

Single seat sporting monoplane of fabric covered steel tube construction similar to 14 Belgian-built Tipsy Nipper Mk.IIs imported 1960–67. Design rights then acquired by Nipper Aircraft Ltd., Castle Donington for whom 32

continued on page 278

(Air Portraits)

Owl OR65-2 Racer

Single seat Formula 1 racer with wooden wing and fabric covered steel tube fuselage, designed by George Owl who built the first aircraft, N8787 'Pogo', in California, U.S.A., in 1969. The second machine, G-AYMS 'Richochet', c/n OR65-2-1/PFA.1519, one 90 h.p. Continental C90-12F, was built by Farm Aviation Ltd. at Rush Green, Herts. 1970–71 and sold to Chequair Ltd. First flown by Sqn. Ldr. M. A. Kelly at Panshanger 13.4.71; raced at North Weald 31.5.71, crashed into the River Thames at Greenwich later that day through propeller failure. Span, 16 ft. 0 in. Length, 17 ft. 5 in. Tare wt., 600 lb. A.U.W., 840 lb. Max. speed over 200 m.p.h.

(via John Pothecary)

Parmentier Wee Mite

Two seater powered by one 35 h.p. A.B.C. Scorpion, designed and built in Guernsey 1932 by Messrs. Noel and Parmentier. One aircraft only, c/n 1, first flown off the sands of Vazon Bay 10.4.33, metal airscrew burst, damaging the
continued on page 281

(P. T. Capon)

Parnall Pixie I and II

Wooden single seat ultra light designed by Harold Bolas for the 1923 Lympne Trials and built by Geo. Parnall and Co. at their Coliseum Works, Bristol. One unregistered aircraft initially, first flown at Filton 13.9.23 and entered for the Consumption Test as Pixie I (No.9) with 29 ft. wings and 500 cc. Douglas. The same aircraft, first flown at Lympne 4.10.23 as Pixie II (No.24) with 18 ft. wings and 736 cc. Douglas, averaged 76·1 m.p.h. to win the £500 speed prize 11.10.23 and won the Wakefield Prize at 81 m.p.h., Hendon 27.10.23, piloted throughout by Capt. Norman Macmillan. Two military examples, J7323 and J7324 with 696 cc. Blackburne Tomtits and larger rudders, were ordered by the Air Ministry 9.3.24 for comparative trials with the ANEC I, Avro 560 and D.H.53. J7323, shown at Hendon R.A.F. Display 28.6.24, later flown at Wittering and owned in succession by the Linnell brothers and the Bedford Flying Club, was last heard of with C. P. B. Ogilvie at Watford in 1935; J7324, now known to have been registered to Parnalls 2.12.24 as G-EBKM, flew in the Lympne Races 8.25 piloted by F. T. Courtney. It was flown at Wittering and elsewhere until sold to F. J. Cleare at Maylands, Romford 4.36, A. to F. 7.8.37. Sold to Ray Bullock, Fraddon, Cornwall 1.39, crashed at nearby Colan 19.4.39. Data for Pixie II; Span, 18 ft. 0 in. Length, 18 ft. 0 in. Tare wt., 280 lb. A.U.W., 450 lb.

---

continued from page 276

Nipper Mk.IIIs, mainly with Rollason Ardem Mk.X engines, were built by Slingsby Sailplanes Ltd., Kirkbymoorside, Yorks. After production was halted by a factory fire 18.11.68, plans were available to amateur constructors. Span, 19 ft. 8 in. Length, 14 ft. 9 in. Tare wt., 458 lb. A.U.W., 725 lb. Cruise, 90 m.p.h. Range, 200 miles.

Parnall Pixie IIIA

Two seater with detachable upper mainplane built for the 1924 Lympne Trials. Two aircraft only: G-EBJG, 32 h.p. Bristol Cherub III, first flown at Yate 5.9.24, flown as No.17 (biplane) and No.18 (monoplane) by Flt. Lt. R. A. de Haga Haig; G-EBKK, 35 h.p. Blackburne Thrush, flown as No.19 by Wing Cdr. W. F. Sholto Douglas, both retired with engine trouble. G-EBKK fitted with 1,100 cc. Anzani (illustrated) in 1925. Span, 32 ft. 5 in. Length, 21 ft. 2 in. Tare wt., 540 lb. A.U.W., 891 lb.

(W. K. Kilsby)

Parnall Pixie III

The two Pixie IIIA biplanes permanently converted to monoplanes with 32 h.p. Bristol Cherub III engines 1926. G-EBJG, C. of A. 4.9.26, flown as No.14 into 4th place in the 1926 Lympne Trials by F. T. Courtney, sold to C. B. Thompson, Rugby 3.33, to S. L. Dodwell, Hinckley 4.35, stored at Hanworth 1936. To R. G. Carr, Kirklinton during 1939–45 war, later to D. I. Taylor and to K. C. D. St. Cyrien, Reigate 1957. Some components held by the Midland Aircraft Preservation Society at Coventry in 1973. Span, 32 ft. 5 in. Length, 21 ft. 2 in. Tare wt., 522 lb. A.U.W., 925 lb.

Note: Constructor's numbers were not allotted to Pixie airframes.

(*P. T. Capon*)

Parnall Imp

Two seat cantilever biplane with fuselage of plywood-covered, stressed-skin construction, powered by one 80 h.p. Armstrong Siddeley Genet II, designed by Harold Bolas, first flown at Yate 1927. One aircraft only: G-EBTE, C. of A. 4.5.28, 8th in the 1928 King's Cup Race at 109·93 m.p.h. piloted by Flt. Lt. D. W. Bonham Carter. Later used for flight trials of the 65 h.p. Pobjoy P prototype radial. Sold to Flg. Off. A. T. Orchard, Worthy Down, 8.33, scrapped 12.33. Span, 25 ft. 6 in. Length, 21 ft. 2 in. Tare wt., 850 lb. A.U.W., 1,320 lb.

Parnall Elf

Two seat biplane with plywood-covered fuselage and Warren girder-braced, fabric-covered, folding wings, designed by Harold Bolas and built at Yate 1928–32. Three aircraft only: G-AAFH (c/n 1), Mk.I with 105 h.p. A.D.C. Hermes I, first shown without markings at the Olympia Aero Show, London 7.29; G-AAIN (2, later J.6), Mk.II with horn balanced rudder and 120 h.p. A.D.C. Hermes II, preserved by the Shuttleworth Trust in 1973; G-AAIO (3, later J.5), Mk.II. See Appendix E. Span, 31 ft. $3\frac{1}{2}$ in. Length, 22 ft. $10\frac{1}{2}$ in. Tare wt., 1,020 lb. A.U.W., 1,700 lb. Cruise, 103 m.p.h. Range, 400 miles.

(D. J. Penn-Smith)

Penn–Smith Gyroplane

Single seater, similar to Bensen, designed and built by D. J. Penn-Smith at Markfield, Leicester 1969–70, powered by one Volkswagen rebuilt from 1,200 cc. to 1,584 cc. by the designer who also finished and balanced the two bladed rotor supplied by Campbell Aircraft Ltd. One aircraft only: G-AXOM, c/n DJPS.1, first flown at Wymeswold 5.4.70, first public appearance (non-flying) at Sywell 11.7.70, P. to F. 25.8.70. Rotor diameter, 20 ft. 0 in. Length, 9 ft. 8 in. Tare wt., 302 lb. A.U.W., 512 lb. Cruise, 55 m.p.h. Minimum level speed, 40 m.p.h. Endurance, 1 hr. 40 min.

---

continued from page 277

front fuselage. Rebuilt with lengthened fuselage, 18 in. of wing sweep back and 40 h.p. Salmson A.D.9 radial. Successfully flown round the island by C. W. Noel for 50 minutes 15.9.33. Registered G-ACRL 24.4.34, dismantled 3.36. (With Salmson engine.) Span, 31 ft. 0 in. Length, 20 ft. 0 in. Tare wt., 650 lb. A.U.W., 970 lb. Max. speed, 92 m.p.h. Cruise, 75 m.p.h.

Perman Parasol

Single seat ultra light powered by one 30 h.p. Perman-Ford, designed and built by E. G. Perman and Co. Ltd. at Brownlow Mews, Guildford St., Grays Inn Road, W.C.1, and first flown at Gravesend 5.36. One aircraft only: G-ADZX, c/n E.G.P.56, using marks originally reserved for one of the company's Poux du Ciel. Sold to Airworthiness Ltd., Gravesend, 13.10.36, and believed burned at fire fighting display 7.37. Span, 25 ft. 6 in. Length, 15 ft. 6 in. A.U.W., 600 lb. Max. speed, 80 m.p.h.

Peterborough Guardian

Side-by-side, two seat, cabin monoplane with tricycle undercarriage, powered by one 90 h.p. Blackburn Cirrus Minor I, designed by J. H. Payne for the Peterborough Aero Club, 1939. One aircraft only: G-AFZT, c/n G.1, (illustrated) completion abandoned due to the outbreak of 1939–45 war, unfinished airframe transferred to Slingsby Sailplanes Ltd., Kirkbymoorside. Span, 33 ft. 4 in. Length, 23 ft. 4 in. Tare wt., 840 lb. A.U.W., 1,350 lb. Max. speed, 120 m.p.h. Cruise, 100 m.p.h. Range, 500 miles.

(Aeroplane)

Pickering–Pearson KP.2

Single seat, experimental pusher of wooden construction powered by one 40 h.p. Aeronca E.117 designed by K. N. Pearson and built at Hanworth 1933 by G. L. Pickering. No rudder was fitted, directional and lateral control being effected by the Pearson rotary ailerons. One aircraft only: G-ACMR, c/n 2, completed 10.33, scrapped 1935.

(R. H. Nicholls)

Planet Satellite

Four seater of magnesium alloy construction, with retractable undercarriage, ventral fin and rudder and one 250 h.p. de Havilland Gipsy Queen 32 amidships driving a pusher airscrew in the tail. Designed by J. N. D. Heenan, built in the Redwing factory, Croydon, erected at Redhill 1948. One aircraft only: c/n 1, shown at the Farnborough S.B.A.C. Show 9.48, registered G-ALOI 4.49. Initial take-off attempts at Blackbushe abandoned and the aircraft never flew. Dismantled at Redhill and melted down 1958. Span, 33 ft. 6 in. Length, 26 ft. 3 in. Tare wt., 1,600 lb. A.U.W., 2,905 lb. Max. speed, 208 m.p.h. Cruise, 191 m.p.h.

Pobjoy Pirate

Three seat, plywood-covered monoplane with 90 h.p. Pobjoy Niagara III and folding wings, designed by H. D. Boultbee and built at Rochester by Pobjoy Airmotors and Aircraft Ltd. One aircraft only: G-ADEY, c/n 101, first flown, without markings, by J. Lankester Parker 25.6.35 and again on 29.6.35 and 10.7.35. Performance was disappointing and when the firm began Short Scion production, the Pirate was pushed into a corner of the flight shed until scrapped in 1936, having flown only 1 hr. 10 min. Span, 34 ft. 0 in. A.U.W., 1,600 lb. Designed max. speed, 125 m.p.h.

Portsmouth Aerocar Major

Twin-boom, high-wing monoplane with retractable undercarriage, powered by two 155 h.p. Blackburn Cirrus Major III, seating pilot and five passengers in a pod type fuselage. One aircraft only: G-AGTG, c/n 2, built by Portsmouth Aviation Ltd. at Portsmouth City Airport 1947, first flown by F. L. Luxmoore 18.6.47, exhibited at 1948 and 1949 S.B.A.C. Shows, C. of A. 3.9.48. Production abandoned, scrapped 1950. Span, 42 ft. 0 in. Length, 26 ft. 3 in. Tare wt., 2,600 lb. A.U.W., 3,950 lb. Max. speed, 167 m.p.h.

R.A.E. Zephyr

Single seat, twin-boom ultra light powered by one 500 cc. Douglas driving a pusher airscrew, designed and built at Farnborough 1922–23 by the Royal Aircraft Establishment Aero Club. One aircraft only: G-EBGW, c/n 1, first flight (illustrated) at Farnborough by Flt. Lt. P. W. S. Bulman 6.9.23, scrapped 1925. Span, 29 ft. 0 in. A.U.W., 635 lb. Cruise, 45 m.p.h.

(*Leonard Bridgman*)

R.A.E. Hurricane

Single seat ultra light powered by one 600 cc. Douglas, designed by S. Childs and built at Farnborough by the R.A.E. Aero Club 1922–23. One aircraft only: G-EBHS, c/n 2, flown in Lympne Trials 10.23 by Flt. Lt. P. W. S. Bulman but was underpowered. Rebuilt with strutted undercarriage and 32 h.p. Bristol Cherub III (illustrated) for Lympne Races 1–3.8.25, C. of A. 2.8.25. Won the Grosvenor Trophy at 81·19 m.p.h. and £300 in prize money, piloted by Flt. Lt. J. S. Chick. Span, 23 ft. 0 in. Length, 17 ft. 3¾ in. Tare wt. (Douglas), 375 lb. A.U.W. (Douglas), 565 lb. Max. speed (Douglas), 58 m.p.h. (Cherub), 85 m.p.h.

R.A.E. Scarab

Single seater powered by one 32 h.p. Bristol Cherub III, designed by P. G. N. Peters and C. R. Brewer (whose initials gave its alternative designation P.B. Scarab) and built by the Royal Aircraft Establishment Aero Club, Farnborough 1930–31. An entirely new fuselage was fitted with de Havilland D.H.53 tail unit and mainplanes, the latter shortened and rigged with five degrees of sweepback. One aircraft only: G-ABOH, c/n 5, first flown by Flg. Off. H. H. Leech 2.32, stored from 1938 until scrapped at Farnborough in 1945. Span, 30 ft. 0 in. Length, 21 ft. 0 in. A.U.W., 650 lb. Max. speed, 78 m.p.h.

(*Flight 17085S*)

Reid and Sigrist R.S.1 Snargasher

Three seat, twin engined trainer of plywood-covered, wooden construction, powered by two 205 h.p. de Havilland Gipsy Six Series II. Built by Reid and Sigrist Ltd. at Desford 1938–39. One aircraft only: G-AEOD, c/n 1, first flown by G. E. Lowdell 1939, first public appearance at the Heathrow Garden Party of the Royal Aeronautical Society 14.5.39, C. of A. 3.6.39. Used for manufacturer's communications during the 1939–45 war. Scrapped 1944. Span, 36 ft. 4 in. Length, 25 ft. 4 in. Tare wt., 3,000 lb. A.U.W., 4,900 lb. Max. speed, 205 m.p.h. Cruise, 190 m.p.h.

(Aeroplane)

Reid and Sigrist R.S.3 Desford

Two seat, twin engined cantilever monoplane with wooden monocoque fuselage powered by two 130 h.p. de Havilland Gipsy Major I, built by Reid and Sigrist Ltd., Desford, 1945. One aircraft only: G-AGOS, c/n 3, first flown 9.7.45, C. of A. 30.5.46, sold to the Air Council 5.49 and modified for prone-pilot experiments as the R.S.4 Bobsleigh VZ728, first flown 13.6.51. Span, 34 ft. 0 in. Length, 25 ft. 6 in. Tare wt., 2,413 lb. A.U.W., 3,300 lb. Max. speed, 162 m.p.h. Cruise, 148 m.p.h.

(John Goring)

Reid and Sigrist R.S.4 Desford Trainer

At the end of Service experiments the R.S.4 Bobsleigh was disposed of to Air Courier (Transport) Ltd. and restored 1.56 as G-AGOS. Overhauled at Croydon, fitted with two 145 h.p. de Havilland Gipsy Major 10 Mk.2, redesignated Desford Trainer and C. of A. renewed 10.1.58. In use by Film Aviation Services Ltd. as a photographic aircraft 3.58 to 9.58 and by Kemp's Aerial Surveys Ltd., Thruxton 1963–72. Specification as for Desford except: Length, 26 ft. 6 in.

(*A. J. Jackson*)

Rollason D.62 Condor

Side-by-side two seater by French designer Roger Druine, built at Croydon by Rollason Aircraft and Engines Ltd. commencing 1961 with D.62 prototype G-ARHZ (75 h.p. Continental A75). Two D.62As (100 h.p. Continental O-200-A), G-ARVZ and G-ASEU, followed by over 50 production D.62Bs (4 in. shorter in length, some with clipped wings and end plates, all but the first four with flaps) and a number of D.62C glider tugs (130 h.p. Rolls-Royce Continental O-240-A). The D.62B G-AVCZ won the Manx Air Derby 28.4.68 at 126·25 m.p.h. flown by Norman Jones. In use by clubs at 20 British aerodromes in 1973. Span, 27 ft. 6 in. Length, 22 ft. 10 in. Tare wt., 900 lb. A.U.W., 1,475 lb. Cruise, 100 m.p.h. Range, 385 miles.

(*Tony Leigh*)

Rollason Beta

Wooden single seat racer based on the Luton Group's winning design in a competition promoted by Mr. Norman Jones in 1965. Luton's G-ATEE not completed; Rollason-built Beta B.1 G-ATLY (65 h.p. Continental A65) f/f at Redhill 21.4.67, later converted to Beta B.2 (90 h.p. Continental C90-8F and airframe refinements) similar to G-AWHV (f/f 15.2.69) and 'HX; and Beta B.4 (100 h.p. Rolls-Royce Continental O-200-A) G-AWHW, built Redhill 1968–72. Home-built G-AXYV and G-BADC under construction 1973, see Appendix E. Data for B.4: Span, 20 ft. 5 in. Length, 16 ft. 8 in. Tare wt., 575 lb. A.U.W., 850 lb. Max. speed, 185 m.p.h.

Rotorcraft Grasshopper Series 1

Two seat private or business helicopter powered by two 100 h.p. Walter Minor engines driving contra-rotating, co-axial rotors, designed by J. S. Shapiro and developed for Rotorcraft Ltd. by Servotec Ltd. One research prototype only: G-ARVN, c/n 1, registered to Rotorcraft Ltd. and built at the Feltham Trading Estate, Middlesex. A. to F. 1.3.62, withdrawn from use 5.63, conveyed to Redhill and dismantled circa 1967. Rotor diameter, 25 ft. 0 in. Length, 17 ft. 10 in. Tare wt., 1,240 lb. A.U.W., 2,880 lb. Cruise, 105 m.p.h. Range, 265 miles.

(*G. Wansborough White*)

Salmon Tandem Monoplane

Single seat, ultra light monoplane, powered by one $3\frac{1}{2}$ h.p. Bradshaw motorcycle engine, designed by Percy Salmon, chief draughtsman at the R.A.E. drawing office. One aircraft only: G-EBHQ, registered to the designer 11.8.23, completed at Farnborough 9.23, entered for the Lympne Trials and allotted competition number 27. During one of several take-off attempts on Farnborough Common, piloted by Flg. Off. C. A. Bouchier, the airscrew disintegrated and the aircraft is believed never to have flown, or to have carried registration markings. Stored and later burned. A.U.W., 445 lb.

(*Saunders-Roe Ltd.*)

Saunders Kittiwake

Wooden amphibian for two crew and seven passengers, powered by two 200 h.p. A.B.C. Wasp II radials, designed by F. P. H. Beadle and completed at East Cowes by S. E. Saunders Ltd. just too late for the 1920 Air Ministry Commercial Amphibian Competition. Full span leading and trailing edge camber-changing gear necessitated interplane ailerons. One aircraft only: G-EAUD, c/n 101, first flown 19.9.20 by Capt. Norman Macmillan, immediately landed through loss of leading edge camber gear. Made several experimental flights 3.21 piloted by F. Warren Merriam. Scrapped 7.21. Span, 68 ft. 3 in. Length, 43 ft. 8 in. Tare wt., 3,840 lb. A.U.W., 6,000 lb.

(*Imperial War Museum MH.2794*)

Saunders A.4 Medina

Plywood-covered wooden flying-boat for two crew and 10 passengers, powered by two 450 h.p. Bristol Jupiter VI, built for the Air Council by S. E. Saunders Ltd. at East Cowes 1925–26. One aircraft only: G-EBMG, c/n A.4/1, withdrawn from use 1929. Span, 58 ft. 0 in. Length, 49 ft. 0 in. Tare wt., 8,060 lb. A.U.W., 11,560 lb. Max. speed, 115 m.p.h.

Saro A.19 Cloud (Whirlwinds)

Amphibian with metal hull and wooden wing, for two crew and eight passengers, powered by two 300 h.p. Wright Whirlwind J-6, built by Saunders-Roe Ltd., East Cowes, 1930–33. Two aircraft only: G-ABCJ, prototype, c/n A.19/1, first flown as L-4, C. of A. 1.8.30, owner Capt. R. Holt, to Canada 12.31 as CF-ARB, returned to makers for trial engine installations 1.34; G-ABXW 'Cloud of Iona', c/n A.19/4, C. of A. 15.7.32, used on the Glasgow–Belfast service of British Flying Boats Ltd., to Guernsey Airways Ltd. 9.34, lost off Jersey with 10 occupants 31.7.36. Span, 64 ft. 0 in. Length, 47 ft. 9 in. Tare wt., 5,500 lb. A.U.W., 8,100 lb. Max. speed, 120 m.p.h. Cruise, 95 m.p.h.

Saro A.19 Cloud (Lynx)

Special Cloud amphibian built for the Hon. A. E. Guinness 1930, powered by three 215 h.p. Armstrong Siddeley Lynx IVC. One aircraft only: G-ABHG, c/n A.19/2, nominally registered to the owner's pilot O. S. Baker, test flown 12.30 by Sqn. Ldr. L. S. Ash. Re-engined with Wasps before delivery. Specification as for Whirlwind model except: Tare wt., 6,075 lb.

Saro A.19 Cloud (Wasps)

The Hon. A. E. Guinness' Cloud G-ABHG, named 'Flying Amo' and re-engined 1931 with two 425 h.p. Pratt & Whitney Wasp C radials (of the type fitted to the owner's Ford 5AT-D), driving three bladed airscrews. Lower landing speed and improved directional control achieved by fitting auxiliary aerofoil and twin fins and rudders. C. of A. 31.7.31. Based at Eastleigh until sold to Imperial Airways Ltd. for crew training 1.40, damaged beyond repair at Ibsley 6.41. Sold as scrap, fuselage used as caravan at St. Leonards, Ringwood, Hants. 1952. Specification as Whirlwind model except: Tare wt., 5,687 lb. A.U.W., 10,000 lb.

(D. Napier and Son Ltd.)

Saro A.19 Cloud (Rapiers)

The prototype Cloud G-ABCJ re-engined 1934 with two 340 h.p. Napier Rapier IV and fitted with small auxiliary aerofoil behind and below the engine nacelles to smooth out the airflow and improve control. Allotted revised c/n A.19/1A. Demonstrated at Hendon S.B.A.C. Shows of 1.7.34 and 1.7.35, loaned to Jersey Airways Ltd. 8.35, withdrawn from use 12.36. Span, 64 ft. 0 in. Length, 49 ft. 9 in. Tare wt., 6,450 lb. A.U.W., 9,700 lb. Max. speed, 121 m.p.h. Cruise, 102 m.p.h.

Saro A.19 Cloud (Servals)

Main Cloud production comprised 18 aircraft powered by two 340 h.p. Armstrong Siddeley Serval III radials. Prototype K2681, c/n A.19/3, numbered '12' for the Hendon R.A.F. Display 6.31 followed by K2894–K2898, K3722–K3729 and K4300–K4302 delivered for navigation training by 6.35. One civil aircraft only: G-ACGO, A.19/5, first flown 15.7.33, C. of A. 23.7.33, returned to Cowes 10.8.33 after long sales tour of Europe by Saro test pilot S. D. Scott. To Czechoslovak State Airline 7.34 as OK-BAK and re-engined with Walter Pollux radials. Span, 64 ft. 0 in. Length, 49 ft. 9 in. Tare wt., 6,500 lb. A.U.W., 9,500 lb. Cruise, 95 m.p.h. Range, 380 miles.

(*Imperial War Museum MH.2816*)

Saro A.21 Windhover

Metal-hulled amphibian for two crew and six passengers powered by three 120 h.p. D.H. Gipsy II. Two aircraft only: ZK-ABW, c/n A.21/1, C. of A. 10.10.30, built for Dominion Airways, N.Z., delivered instead to Matthews Aviation Co., Hobart 12.31 as VH-UPB, wrecked off King Island, Bass Strait 14.5.36. G-ABJP, A.21/2, 8.7.31, F. Francis, Heston; Gibraltar Airways Ltd. 9.31; Mrs. Victor Bruce 'City of Portsmouth' 7.32 (with undercarriage removed temporarily for flight-refuelled endurance record of 54 hr. 13 min., 9–11.8.32); Jersey Airways Ltd. 5.35, withdrawn from use 1938. Span, 54 ft. 4 in. Length, 41 ft. 4 in. Tare wt., 4,200 lb. A.U.W., 5,700 lb. Cruise, 90 m.p.h.

Saro A.37 Shrimp

Two seat, flying scale research aircraft of metal construction, powered by four 95 h.p. Pobjoy Niagara III, designed by H. Knowler and built as part of a development programme on large flying-boat design by Saunders-Roe Ltd. at Cowes 1939. One aircraft only: G-AFZS, c/n A.37/1, first flown at Cowes late in 1939 before transfer to Beaumaris, Anglesey, in 1940 where a slipway was built for it at Fryars, a local waterside residence. Taken over by the Ministry of Aircraft Production 1944 as TK580 for flight testing a scaled-down model of the Short Shetland 1 tail unit. Scrapped at Felixstowe in 1949. Span, 50 ft. 0 in. Length, 42 ft. 8¾ in.

(*Saunders-Roe Ltd.*)

Saro S.R.45 Princess

All-metal, 200-passenger flying-boat powered by ten 3,780 e.h.p. Bristol Proteus 600, designed by H. Knowler and built by Saunders-Roe Ltd. 1947–52. Three aircraft only, ordered for B.O.A.C. 1946, registered to the Ministry of Supply 13.10.49: G-ALUN, c/n SR.901, launched 20.8.52, first flown by Geoffrey Tyson 22.8.52, flown at 1952 and 1953 S.B.A.C. Shows, cocooned at Cowes 1954; G-ALUO, c/n SR.902, launched in cocooned state 13.2.53, beached at Calshot next day; G-ALUP, c/n SR.903, cocooned and beached at Calshot 1953. All scrapped in 1967. Span, 219 ft. 6 in. Length, 148 ft. 0 in. Tare wt., 191,000 lb. A.U.W., 330,000 lb. Cruise, 360 m.p.h. Max. range, 5,270 miles.

Saro Skeeter

Two seat development of the Cierva W.14 helicopter built by Saunders-Roe Ltd. Five prototypes variously engined (see Appendix E), flown at Eastleigh: G-AMTZ, Mk.5 laid down 1952 as Cierva Skeeter 5 G-AMDC, to Boscombe Down 1954 as XG303, re-engined 1957 as Skeeter Mk.6, flown briefly with Napier NRE.19 rotor tip rockets; three Mk.6s G-ANMG to 'MI flown in military marks 1956; G-APOI, Mk.8, flown 9.58, reservations G-APOJ and 'OK ntu. A production Skeeter 12, XM553, released by the Army 1969, became G-AWSV. Data for Skeeter 5: Rotor diameter, 32 ft. 0 in. Length, 28 ft. 5 in. Tare wt., 1,500 lb. A.U.W., 2,100 lb. Cruise, 97 m.p.h. Range, 220 miles.

Saro P.531

All-metal five seat helicopter built by Saunders-Roe Ltd. 1958–59. Four civil prototypes only: Two Mk.1s with 325 s.h.p. Blackburn Turboméca Turmo 600, viz. G-APNU, c/n S2/5267, first flown at Eastleigh by K. M. Reed 20.7.58; G-APNV, S2/5268, to the Royal Navy 1959 as XN332; and two

continued on page 329

(*Flight 13017*)

Shackleton–Murray S.M.1

Two seat, wooden parasol monoplane powered by one 70 h.p. Hirth H.M.60 driving a pusher airscrew, designed by W. S. Shackleton and L. C. Murray and built by Airspeed Ltd. at York 1933. One aircraft only: G-ACBP, Airspeed c/n 8, first flown at Sherburn-in-Elmet 1933, C. of A. 28.9.33, based at Hanworth until sold to Lord Apsley, Whitchurch, 1.35. Dismantled 1937. Span, 40 ft. 0 in. Length, 25 ft. 7 in. Tare wt., 840 lb. A.U.W., 1,450 lb. Max. speed, 90·5 m.p.h. Cruise, 75 m.p.h.

(*Aeroplane*)

Shapley Kittiwake

Side-by-side two seater with gull wing, designed and built at Torquay by E. S. Shapley 1937–38. Two aircraft only: G-AEZN, c/n E.S.S.1, Mk.1 open model, 50 h.p. Continental A50, first flown at Roborough, A. to F. 29.6.37, dismantled pre-1939; G-AFRP, c/n E.S.S.2, Mk.2 cabin model, 90 h.p. Pobjoy Niagara III, flown at Roborough 1938, stored, flown at Rochester 4.46, crashed near Exeter during C. of A. spinning trials 10.5.46. Mk.2 data in parentheses. Span, 20 ft. 3 in. (32 ft. 0 in.). Length, 20 ft. 3 in. (20 ft. 10 in.). Tare wt., 630 lb. (901 lb.). A.U.W., 1,000 lb. (1,600 lb.). Max. speed, 116 m.p.h. (120 m.p.h.). Cruise, 99 m.p.h. (110 m.p.h.).

(*P. H. T. Green*)

Shield Xyla

As the name Xyla (a contraction of xylon, Greek for wood) implies, this was a wooden, single seat, aerobatic ultra light, powered by one 65 h.p. Continental GPU conversion, designed and built at the Mexborough Grammar School, Yorks. by the headmaster, Mr. G. W. Shield, builder of Luton Minor G-ATFW. One aircraft only: G-AWPN, c/n 2 (PFA.1320), first flown at Hemswell, Lincs. 30.10.71, C. of A. 11.7.72, ferried to Doncaster 15.7.72, based there in 1973. Span, 27 ft. 3 in. Length, 19 ft. 3 in. A.U.W., 995 lb. Cruise, 110 m.p.h. Range, 500 miles.

Short Silver Streak

The first British all-metal aeroplane. A single seater powered by one 240 h.p. Siddeley Puma, with semi-monocoque duralumin fuselage and duralumin-covered wings with steel tubular spars, built by Short Bros. Ltd. at Rochester 1920. One aircraft only: G-EARQ, c/n S.543, exhibited without markings at Olympia 7.20, first flown at Grain by J. Lankester Parker 20.8.20, converted to two seater and delivered to the Air Ministry at Farnborough 1.2.21. On charge as J6854 for flight tests 5.21, static tests 6.21, 100 hours of vibration testing 9–11.21. Span, 37 ft. 6 in. Length, 26 ft. 6 in. Tare wt., 1,865 lb. A.U.W., 2,870 lb. Max. speed, 120 m.p.h. Cruise, 90 m.p.h.

Short Shrimp

Commercial seaplane sometimes known as the Short Sporting Type, powered by one 240 h.p. Siddeley Puma, built at Rochester 1919–20. Two front seats in tandem with dual control, two rear seats side by side. Three aircraft only: G-EAPZ, c/n S.540, initially with 160 h.p. Beardmore, sold in Australia 3.21 as G-AUPZ; G-EAUA, c/n S.541, exhibited at Olympia 7.20, damaged in heavy landing, Rochester 24.9.20, rebuilt with 300 h.p. Hispano-Suiza and camber-changing flaps; G-EAUB, c/n S.542, first flown 21.1.21, dismantled 1924. Span, 44 ft. 6 in. Length, 36 ft. 9 in. A.U.W., 3,554 lb. Max. speed, 85 m.p.h.

(Short Bros. Ltd.)

Short S.1 Cockle

Single seat, all-metal flying-boat powered by two 696 cc. Blackburne Tomtit driving tractor airscrews through extension shafts, built by Short Bros. Ltd. at Rochester 1924 for, but not delivered to, Lebbaeus Hordern. One aircraft only: G-EBKA, c/n S.638, first flown by J. Lankester Parker 7.11.24, evaluated at Felixstowe 7.25 as N193. Returned to Rochester, first flown 14.6.27 with two 32 h.p. Bristol Cherub IIs, returned to Felixstowe 10.27 for exposure tests. Span, 36 ft. 0 in. Length, 24 ft. $8\frac{1}{2}$ in. Tare wt., 814 lb. A.U.W., 880 lb. Max. speed, 68 m.p.h.

(*Flight*)

Short S.4 Satellite

Two seater with metal monocoque fuselage, powered by one 32 h.p. Bristol Cherub III, built at Rochester for the 1924 Lympne Trials. One aircraft only: G-EBJU, c/n S.644, first flown 16.9.24, competed as No. 8 piloted by J. Lankester Parker, who raced it as a single seater, Lympne 1–3.8.25. Fitted with 40 h.p. A.B.C. Scorpion II by the Seven Aero Club, C. of A. 8.9.26, flown in the 1926 Lympne Trials and Grosvenor Trophy Race by Flg. Off. G. E. F. Boyes. Dismantled 1.28. Span, 34 ft. 0 in. Length, 23 ft. 9 in. (Cherub III) Tare wt., 640 lb. A.U.W., 1,014 lb. (Scorpion II) Tare wt., 610 lb. A.U.W., 1,010 lb.

(*Flight*)

Short S.7 Mussel I

Two seat seaplane with metal fuselage powered by one 60 h.p. A.D.C. Cirrus I, built at Rochester 1925. One aircraft only: G-EBMJ, c/n S.678, first flown 6.4.26, converted to landplane 9.26, C. of A. 16.9.26, flown by J. Lankester Parker in the 1926 Grosvenor Trophy Race and at the 1927 Bournemouth Easter Meeting. Fitted with new floats and enclosed 85 h.p. Cirrus II, raised the world's altitude class record to 13,400 ft. piloted by Lady Heath 10.7.28. Sank in the Medway 24.8.28. To R.A.F. Halton as instructional airframe 1929. Span, 36 ft. 0 in. Length, 25 ft. 0 in. Tare wt., 907 lb. A.U.W., 1,400 lb. (Cirrus II 1,135 lb. and 1,636 lb.). Max. speed, 82 m.p.h. Cruise, 65 m.p.h.

Short S.7 Mussel II

Similar floatplane with revised undercarriage strutting, powered by one 90 h.p. A.D.C. Cirrus III, built at Rochester 1929. One aircraft only: G-AAFZ, c/n S.750, first flown by J. Lankester Parker 17.5.29, exhibited at the Olympia Aero Show, London, 7.29. Fitted with Short amphibian undercarriage and flown 8.3.30 under B conditions as M-1, last flown 15.9.33, scrapped 1.34. Span, 37 ft. 3½ in. Length, 24 ft. 11½ in. Tare wt., 1,061 lb. (Amphibian 1,300 lb.) A.U.W., 1,640 lb. Max. speed, 102 m.p.h.

Short L.17

Transport for 39 passengers, powered by four 595 h.p. Bristol Jupiter XFBM, using the superstructure and tail unit of the S.17 Kent, built at Rochester for the European services of Imperial Airways Ltd. 1933–34. Two aircraft only: G-ACJJ 'Scylla', c/n S.768, first flown by J. Lankester Parker 26.3.34, C. of A. 1.5.34, wrecked by gale at Drem, Scotland 14.9.40; G-ACJK 'Syrinx', c/n S.769, C. of A. 8.6.34, re-engined 1935 with four 660 h.p. Bristol Pegasus XC, scrapped at Exeter in 1940. Span, 113 ft. 0 in. Length, 83 ft. 10 in. Tare wt., 22,650 lb. A.U.W., 33,500 lb. Cruise, 105 m.p.h.

Short S.11 Valetta

Transport for 16 passengers and two crew built to Air Ministry order for comparison with the pure flying-boat, and in its day was the world's largest floatplane. One aircraft only: G-AAJY, c/n S.747, powered by three 525 h.p. Bristol Jupiter XIF, built at Rochester 1929–30, first flown 21.5.30, C. of A. 17.7.31. Left Rochester 22.7.31 piloted by Sir Alan Cobham on an African survey flight to Lakes Albert, Victoria, Edward and Kivu, covering 12,300 miles before returning to Rochester 1.9.31. Span, 107 ft. 0 in. Length, 70 ft. 5 in. Tare wt., 14,535 lb. A.U.W., 23,000 lb. Max. speed, 135 m.p.h.

(*Flight 11564*)

Short S.11 Valetta (Landplane)

The Valetta G-AAJY was last flown as a seaplane by J. Lankester Parker at Rochester 16.11.31 before conversion to landplane for comparative trials. Transported by road to Croydon and first flown there by Parker 13.5.32; shown at the Hendon R.A.F. Display 25.6.32; flown by Imperial Airways Ltd. on test 6–7.32; delivered to Martlesham 26.7.32 and withdrawn from use there 12.33; then used as an instructional airframe in the Radio School at R.A.F. Halton. Span, 107 ft. 0 in. Length, 69 ft. 8 in. Tare wt., 16,070 lb.

(*Flight 15005S*)

Short–Mayo S.20/S.21 Composite

Built to test Maj. R. H. Mayo's theory for extending the range of one aircraft by assisting it into the air on the back of a larger, lightly loaded type.

Upper Component: Short S.20 G-ADHJ 'Mercury', c/n S.796, four 340 h.p. Napier Rapier Vs, launched at Rochester 25.8.37, first flown by J. Lankester Parker 5.9.37, C. of A. 2.7.38, later fitted with four 370 h.p. Rapier VIs, flown Hythe–Felixstowe 18.6.40 by Capt. D. C. T. Bennett and handed over to No.320 (Netherlands) Squadron, a Dutch seaplane reconnaissance unit, with whom it served at Pembroke Dock. Returned to Felixstowe 1941, flown back to Rochester by an R.A.F. pilot 9.8.41 and scrapped. Span, 73 ft. 0 in. Length, 51 ft. 0 in. Tare wt., 10,000 lb. A.U.W. (individual flying), 15,500 lb. (air launched), 20,500 lb. Max. speed, 207 m.p.h. Cruise, 180 m.p.h.

Lower Component: Short S.21 G-ADHK 'Maia', c/n S.797, four 920 h.p. Bristol Pegasus XC, first flown by Parker 27.7.37, C. of A. 1.6.38, navigation trainer when not used in its composite role, destroyed by enemy action in Poole harbour 11.5.41. Span, 114 ft. 0 in. Length, 84 ft. 10¾ in. Tare wt., 24,000 lb. A.U.W. (individual flying), 38,000 lb. Max. speed, 200 m.p.h. Cruise, 165 m.p.h.

Composite: First flown at Rochester 21.1.38 with J. Lankester Parker in 'Maia' and H. L. Piper in 'Mercury'. First air separation 6.2.38, first commercial separation at Foynes 21.7.38 when 'Mercury', flown by Capt. D. C. T. Bennett with radio operator A. J. Coster, flew non-stop to Montreal in 20 hours 20 minutes. Flew New York–Azores in 7 hours 33 minutes on the return journey. Separated at Dundee 6.10.38 when the same crew flew 'Mercury' 6,045 miles non-stop to the mouth of the Orange River, South Africa, and established a world's long distance record for seaplanes. Last commercial separations 29.11.38 and 12.1.39 when the same crew flew Christmas mail 2,200 miles non-stop Southampton–Alexandria. Tare wt., 34,000 lb. A.U.W., 47,500 lb. Cruise, 167 m.p.h.

(Flight)

Short S.22 Scion Senior

Floatplane for nine passengers and pilot, powered by four 90 h.p. Pobjoy Niagara III. A total of five built at Rochester 1935–36: VT-AGU, 'HI and 'IJ (c/n S.837) for the Irrawaddy Flotilla Co. Ltd., Rangoon; G-AENX used by Elders Colonial Airways Ltd., Sierra Leone, and G-AETH equipped for the Air Ministry with a half scale model of the Sunderland planing bottom for test purposes as L9786. Span, 55 ft. 0 in. Length, 42 ft. 0 in. Tare wt., 3,886 lb. A.U.W., 5,750 lb. Cruise, 115 m.p.h.

(Short Bros. Ltd.)

Short S.22 Scion Senior (Landplane)

Landplane version. One civil aircraft only, G-AECU, c/n S.834, C. of A. 28.7.36, demonstrator, flown by H. L. Piper in the King's Cup Race 11.9.37, loaned to Jersey Airways Ltd. 1938, sold to the Iraq Petroleum Transport Co. Ltd., Haifa, 12.38, impressed in the Middle East 2.42 as HK868. Lost in action 22.9.43. Dimensions as floatplane. Tare wt., 3,546 lb. A.U.W., 5,750 lb. Max. speed, 140 m.p.h. Cruise, 122 m.p.h.

(*Associated Press*)

Short S.40 Shetland 2

A second generation, very-long-range reconnaissance flying-boat built to Specification R.14/40 and embodying all the experience gained from large scale production of the Sunderland. Two prototypes, DX166 and DX171, were laid down, the mainplanes and nacelles by Saunders-Roe Ltd. who conveyed these massive components by road to Rochester for mating to the Short-built hulls and tail units.

Fitted with four 2,500 h.p. Bristol Centaurus VII radials and designated S.35 Shetland 1, DX166 was first flown by J. Lankester Parker and Geoffrey Tyson 14.12.44, but with gun turrets removed, the aircraft having been relegated to the role of unarmed transport. It was delivered to the M.A.E.E., Felixstowe 10.45 but was burned out at moorings 28.1.46 as a result of a galley fire.

The second aircraft, designated S.40 Shetland 2 and powered by four 2,500 h.p. Centaurus 660, was completed as a civil transport very reminiscent of the earlier S.26 boats at nose and tail. There was sufficient space on two decks for 70 passengers but seats were installed for only 40 and a crew of 11. The allotted serial DX171 was never used and during erection the Shetland 2 was given c/n S.1313 and registered G-AGVD to the Ministry of Supply and Aircraft Production. Launched 15.9.47, it was first flown 17.9.47 by H. L. Piper and T. Brooke-Smith but after preliminary trials was ferried to Short's works, Belfast where it was scrapped in 1951 without ever having carried a fare paying passenger. Span, 150 ft. 4 in. Length, 105 ft. 0 in. Tare wt., 80,140 lb. A.U.W., 125,000 lb. Cruise, 240 m.p.h. Range, 2,750 miles.

(*P. R. March*)

Slingsby Type 29B Motor Tutor

Single seater made by fitting a Slingsby Tutor glider airframe with an undercarriage and one 40 h.p. Aeronca-J.A.P. J-99. Three aircraft only: G-AKEY, c/n W.N.544, built by Slingsby Sailplanes Ltd. at Kirkbymoorside 1948, first flown 6.48 as AB-1, later G-26-1, sold in the Bahamas 1963; G-AKJD, c/n W.N.599, Slingsby-built, A. to F. 3.11.50, evaluated at the Southend Municipal Flying School 1951, last owner J. E. G. Harwood, crashed at Dunstable Downs 21.6.64; G-AZSD, registered 7.4.72 with c/n RGB.01/PFA.1574, and completed by R. G. Boyton at Epsom. Span, 43 ft. 3¾ in. Length, 20 ft. 0 in. Tare wt., 555 lb. A.U.W., 798 lb. Cruise, 65 m.p.h.

(*Air Portraits*)

Slingsby/Osbourn Twin Cadet Mk. 1

Slingsby Type 8 Tutor primary glider fitted with two 197 cc. Villiers 9E single cylinder, two stroke engines by E. W. Osbourn at Cranfield in 1969. One conversion only: G-AXMB, formerly VM590 and BGA.805, first flown with power 20.9.69, A. to F. 2.7.70, public debut (illustrated) at the Air League's Flying for Fun Rally at Sywell 11.7.70. Re-engined and first flown at Cranfield 22.1.72 with one 500 cc. Triumph T.100 motor-cycle engine as Cadet Mk.2, A. to F. 6.6.72. Span, 38 ft. 6 in. Length, 20 ft. 10½ in. Tare wt., 455 lb. A.U.W., 657 lb. Max. speed, 60 m.p.h. Cruise, 40 m.p.h. Range, 100 miles.

(*Bernard Martin*)

Slingsby/Martin Motor Cadet Mk.3

Two seat Slingsby Type 31 Tandem Tutor acquired from the Dorset Gliding Club in 1970 and converted to single seat ultra light with 1,600 cc. Volkswagen and Luton Minor undercarriage by P. J. Martin and D. R. Wilkinson at Twinwood Farm aerodrome, Beds., a 6½ gallon fuel tank replacing the front seat. One conversion only: G-AYAN 'Thermal Hopper', c/n 003/PFA.1385, A. to F. 15.1.71, to D. R. Wilkinson, Twinwood Farm 8.72. Span, 43 ft. 4¾ in. Length, 22 ft. 0 in. Tare wt., 470 lb. A.U.W., 830 lb. Cruise, 57 m.p.h. Endurance, 2¾ hours.

(*Yorkshire Evening Press*)

Slingsby Type 49C Powered Capstan

Slingsby Type 49 Capstan two seat sailplane powered by one 45 h.p. Nelson H-63CP air-cooled engine driving a pusher airscrew. One aircraft only: G-AWDV, c/n 1599, registered 26.2.68 to Slingsby Aircraft Ltd. and first flown at Kirkbymoorside by Derek Piggott 15.2.68. Registration cancelled 8.68 as sold in the U.S.A. Not delivered, destroyed in works fire at Kirkbymoorside 17.11.68. Span, 55 ft. 0 in. Length, 26 ft. 6 in. Tare wt., 761 lb. A.U.W., 1,250 lb. Max. speed, 85 m.p.h.

(*G. Bailey-Woods*)

Slingsby Type 58 Rumpler C IV replica

Replica of the 1916 German two-seater entirely designed by Slingsby Aircraft Ltd., using the steel fuselage frame of the Tiger Moth and the 130 h.p. de Havilland Gipsy Major 1 modified to run upright. Two aircraft only built for film use by Universal Pictures Ltd.: G-AXAL (illustrated) and G-AXAM, c/n 1705 and 1704, first flown at Rufforth, Yorks. 24 and 25.3.69, A. to Fs. 26.3.69, shipped to Tunisia 4.69, thence to Flying Circus Aerodrome, Bealeton, Virginia, U.S.A. 1970 as N1915E and N1916E respectively. Span, 39 ft. 4¾ in. Length, 23 ft. 11 in. Tare wt., 1,381 lb. A.U.W., 1,800 lb. Max. speed, 120 m.p.h.

Slingsby Type 61 Falke

Side-by-side, two seat, dual trainer version of the Scheibe SF-24A Motorspatz, in production in Germany from 1968. Two SF-25A aircraft G-AVBK and 'IZ (26 h.p. Hirth F10A) imported into Britain 1967; five SF-25B (45 h.p. Starck Stamo MS1500) with larger tail surfaces, improved fuselage lines and cabin glazing were imported 1969–70. Licence production from 1970 by Vickers-owned Slingsby Sailplanes Ltd. at Kirkbymoorside, Yorks. as the Slingsby Type 61A Falke, commencing G-AYPY (illustrated), or Type 61C (Stamo MS1500/2). See Appendix E. Span, 50 ft. 2½ in. Length, 24 ft. 10½ in. Tare wt., 739 lb. A.U.W., 1,220 lb. Cruise, 80 m.p.h. Range, 240 miles.

(*R. A. Cole*)

Somers–Kendall SK-1

Two seat wooden jet racer with retractable bicycle undercarriage, powered by one 330 lb. s.t. Turboméca Palas 1 turbojet, designed by Hugh Kendall and built for J. N. Somers by Somers-Kendall Aircraft Ltd. at Woodley 1954–55. One aircraft only: G-AOBG, c/n 1, first flown 14.10.55, C. of A. 27.3.56. Minor defects prevented participation in 1956 racing events, and the aircraft was stored at Cranfield following turbine failure in the air 11.7.57. Span, 22 ft. 9½ in. Length, 20 ft. 10½ in. Tare wt., 685 lb. A.U.W. 1,500 lb. Max. speed, 332 m.p.h. Cruise, 285 m.p.h.

(*P. T. Capon*)

Sopwith Scooter

Single seat monoplane comprising a Sopwith Camel fuselage fitted with a wire-braced wing and powered by one 130 h.p. Clerget. One aircraft only, somewhat resembling the Sopwith Swallow, first flown at Brooklands 6.18, registered 29.5.19 as K-135/G-EACZ as an aerobatic mount for H. G. Hawker, to whom it was sold 4.21. Overhauled for C. Clayton, Hendon, 5.25, C. of A. 1.8.25, exhibition flying by J. Phillips, sold 8.26 to Dudley Watt, by whom it was extensively raced. Sold as scrap 1927. Wing area, 162 sq. ft. Length, 18 ft. 9 in. Tare wt., 890 lb. A.U.W., 1,420 lb. Max. speed, 115 m.p.h.

(*L. T. Mason*)

Sopwith Grasshopper

Two seat tourer of wooden construction powered by one 100 h.p. Anzani, built at Kingston-on-Thames by the Sopwith Aviation and Engineering Co. Ltd. 1919. One aircraft only: G-EAIN, c/n W/O 2698/1, C. of A. 22.3.20. Sold 12.22 to L. C. G. M. Le Champion, 5.23 to E. A. D. Eldridge, 2.25 to John R. Cobb, 8.25 to Dudley Watt, all of Brooklands; 2.28 to Miss C. R. Leathart, Cramlington. C. of A. not renewed on expiry 30.5.29. Span, 33 ft. 1 in. Length, 23 ft. 1 in. A.U.W., 1,670 lb. Max. speed, 90 m.p.h.

Sopwith Dove

Two seat version of the Pup, with swept-back wings and 80 h.p. Le Rhône, built at Kingston-on-Thames by the Sopwith Aviation and Engineering Co. Ltd. 1919–20. Ten British civil aircraft shown in Appendix E. Last machine modernised 1925 with horn balanced rudder as G-EBKY, C. of A. 12.4.27. Sold to C. H. Lowe-Wylde 9.30, abandoned at West Malling after owner's
continued on page 329

Sopwith Schneider

Single seat racer of fabric-covered wooden construction with $2\frac{1}{2}$ in. backward stagger, powered by one 450 h.p. Cosmos Jupiter, built at Kingston-on-Thames for the 1919 Schneider Trophy contest. One aircraft only: G-EAKI, c/n W/O 3067, flown in the race by H. G. Hawker over a course between Bournemouth and Swanage 10.9.19. Retired through fog, contest abandoned. Span, 24 ft. 0 in. Length, 21 ft. 6 in. A.U.W., 2,200 lb. Speed, 170 m.p.h.

(*Flight 846*)

Sopwith Rainbow

Sopwith Schneider with wheeled undercarriage and 320 h.p. A.B.C. Dragonfly as a mount for H. G. Hawker in the Hendon Aerial Derby 24.7.20. Disqualified for incorrect finish. Rebuilt 1922 with 500 h.p. Bristol Jupiter II by the H. G. Hawker Engineering Co. Ltd., and is the only aircraft to which the transitional nomenclature Sopwith/Hawker may strictly be applied. Second in the 1923 Aerial Derby at Croydon piloted by Flt. Lt. W. H. Longton at 165 m.p.h. Re-registered to the Hawker Company 18.7.23, crashed at Burgh Hill Golf Course, Surrey 1.9.23. Span, 24 ft. 0 in. Length, 18 ft. 0 in. Max. speed (Dragonfly), 165 m.p.h.; (Jupiter), 175 m.p.h.

Sopwith Wallaby

Long range open biplane with two seats retracting into the cabin, powered by one 375 h.p. Rolls-Royce Eagle VIII, built at Kingston-on-Thames 1919 to compete for the Australian Government's £10,000 England–Australia Flight prize. One aircraft only: G-EAKS, c/n W/O 3109, left Hounslow 21.10.19 piloted by Capt. G. C. Matthews and Sgt. T. Kay, C. of A. 22.10.19, crashed when landing on the Island of Bali, Dutch East Indies, 17.4.20. Shipped to Australia, rebuilt as an 8 seater, G-AUDU, for Australian Aerial Services Ltd. Span, 46 ft. 6 in. Length, 31 ft. 6 in. Tare wt., 2,780 lb. A.U.W., 5,200 lb. Max. speed, 115 m.p.h. Cruise, 107 m.p.h.

Sopwith Antelope

Transport seating two passengers in a cabin behind the pilot's open cockpit, powered by one 200 h.p. Wolseley Viper, built at Kingston-on-Thames 1919. One aircraft only: G-EASS, c/n W/O 3398, modified with four wheel braked undercarriage, C. of A. 10.8.20, awarded the second prize of £3,000 in the Air Ministry Small Commercial Aeroplane Competition Martlesham 8.20, piloted by H. G. Hawker. Won the Surrey Open Handicap Race, Croydon 5.6.22, piloted by F. P. Raynham. To the Larkin Sopwith Aviation Company with Puma engine 4.23 as G-AUSS. Span, 46 ft. 6 in. Length, 31 ft. 0 in. Tare wt., 2,387 lb. A.U.W., 3,450 lb. Max. speed, 110·5 m.p.h. Cruise, 84 m.p.h.

Spartan Clipper

Two seater using outer wings of the Monospar ST-4, powered by one 75 h.p. Pobjoy R, designed by H. E. Broadsmith and built at East Cowes by Spartan Aircraft Ltd. 1932. One aircraft only: c/n 201, first flown 14.12.32 as S-3. After undercarriage, cabin glazing and cowling modifications, registered as G-ACEG, C. of A. 29.6.33, averaged 93·39 m.p.h. in the 1933 King's Cup Race piloted by L. A. Strange. Fitted with 90 h.p. Pobjoy Niagara III in 1938, used on the firm's communications, destroyed in an air raid, Cowes, 4.5.42. Span, 34 ft. 0 in. Length, 28 ft. 2 in. Tare wt., 770 lb. A.U.W., 1,300 lb.

Supermarine Amphibian Mk. I

Unnamed wooden amphibian seating two passengers in a glazed cabin ahead of the pilot's open cockpit, powered by one 360 h.p. Rolls-Royce Eagle VIII and built by the Supermarine Aviation Works Ltd. at Woolston, Southampton, for the 1920 Air Ministry Commercial Amphibian Competition. One aircraft only: G-EAVE, c/n 1152, registered to Hubert Scott-Paine. Land and sea trials at Martlesham and Felixstowe 9.20, won the Second Prize of £8,000, crashed at Great Bookham, Surrey 13.10.20. Span, 50 ft. 0 in. Length, 33 ft. 0 in. Tare wt., 3,996 lb. A.U.W., 5,700 lb. Max. speed, 94 m.p.h. Cruise, 77 m.p.h.

(*A. J. Jackson*)

Storey T.S.R.3

Single seat racing monoplane (Tom Storey Racer) of wood and fabric construction, powered by one 90 h.p. Continental C90-8F flat four, designed by T. M. Storey and built at Redhill 1967–68. One aircraft only: G-AWIV, c/n PFA.1325, first flown by the designer at Redhill 25.7.68 and shown in public during the National Air Race meeting at Tollerton 24.8.68. Dorsal fin added later. Span, 18 ft. 6 in. Length, 17 ft. 10 in. Tare wt., 590 lb. A.U.W., 925 lb. Max. speed, 138 m.p.h. Cruise, 108 m.p.h. Range, 345 miles.

(*Central Press*)

Supermarine Sea Lion I

Single seat, wooden racing flying-boat, powered by one 450 h.p. Napier Lion driving a pusher airscrew, built at Woolston for the 1919 Schneider Trophy Race. One aircraft only: G-EALP, no c/n, piloted in the race, which was declared void through fog, 10.9.19 by Cdr. B. D. Hobbs. Struck flotsam and holed the hull when taking off from Swanage Bay after a precautionary landing and sank on alighting off Bournemouth Pier. Hull loaned to the Science Museum, South Kensington, 1921. Span, 35 ft. 0 in. Length, 24 ft. 0 in. A.U.W., 2,900 lb. Max. speed, 147 m.p.h.

Supermarine Sea Lion II

Originally the single seat Sea King II amphibian scout powered by one 300 h.p. Hispano-Suiza, built at Woolston 1921. One aircraft only: G-EBAH, c/n 1154, registered to the manufacturers 16.12.21, first flown by H. C. Biard 3.22. Rebuilt as flying-boat with 450 h.p. Napier Lion, wings of reduced area and renamed Sea Lion II. Winner of the Schneider Trophy contest at Naples 10–12.8.22 piloted by H. C. Biard, who averaged 145·7 m.p.h. over the course of 200·2 nautical miles. Span, 32 ft. 0 in. Length, 24 ft. 9 in. Tare wt., 2,115 lb. A.U.W., 2,850 lb.

(*Leonard Bridgman*)

Supermarine Sea Lion III

The Sea Lion II G-EBAH, rebuilt with two bay wings and increased rudder area for the 1923 Schneider Trophy Race at Cowes. Piloted by H. C. Biard, it averaged 151·16 m.p.h. to come third. Transferred to the R.A.F. 4.12.23 as N170. Span, 32 ft. 0 in. Length, 27 ft. 6 in. Tare wt., 2,400 lb. A.U.W., 3,275 lb. Max. speed, 155 m.p.h. Cruise, 125 m.p.h.

Supermarine Sea Eagle

Cabin amphibian for six passengers, designed by R. J. Mitchell and powered by one 350 h.p. Rolls-Royce Eagle IX. Three aircraft only, built for the Woolston–Cherbourg and Channel Islands services of the British Marine Air Navigation Co. Ltd. 1923: G-EBFK, c/n 1163, C. of A. 11.7.23, flew in the 1923 King's Cup Race, crashed 21.5.24; G-EBGR and 'GS, c/n 1164–5, Cs. of A. 2.10.23, handed over to Imperial Airways Ltd. 10.6.24, 'GR withdrawn from use 1929, 'GS sunk by a ship, Guernsey, 10.1.27, hull salvaged, stored at Hythe, burned at Heston 1953. Span, 46 ft. 0 in. Length, 37 ft. 4 in. Tare wt., 3,950 lb. A.U.W., 6,050 lb. Max. speed, 93 m.p.h. Cruise, 84 m.p.h.

Supermarine Swan

Experimental wooden amphibian powered by two 350 h.p. Rolls-Royce Eagle IX, designed by R. J. Mitchell, built at Woolston 1924. One completed aircraft only: N175, c/n 1173, first flown by H. C. Biard 25.3.24. Re-engined with two 450 h.p. Napier Lions and the undercarriage removed for evaluation by the M.A.E.E. 8.24 as a 12 seater G-EBJY. Twenty hours of test flying by 4.12.24, C. of A. 30.6.26, loaned to Imperial Airways Ltd., scrapped 1927. Span, 69 ft. 0 in. Length, 37 ft. 4 in. Tare wt., 10,114 lb. A.U.W., 12,832 lb. Max. speed, 105 m.p.h. Cruise, 92 m.p.h.

(*Flight*)

Supermarine Sparrow I

Two seat ultra light with plywood fuselage, powered by one 35 h.p. Blackburne Thrush, designed by R. J. Mitchell and built at Woolston for the 1924 Lympne Trials. One aircraft only: G-EBJP, c/n 1211, first flown by H. C. Biard 11.9.24, competed as No. 9, but was eliminated by engine failure. Fourth at 62·08 m.p.h. in the Grosvenor Trophy Race, Lympne 4.10.24, 10 hours total flying by 12.24. Span, 33 ft. 4 in. Length, 22 ft. 8 in. Tare wt., 475 lb. A.U.W., 860 lb.

(*Flight*)

Supermarine Sparrow II

The original Sparrow G-EBJP, rebuilt as a parasol monoplane with 32 h.p. Bristol Cherub III for the 1926 Lympne Trials, C. of A. 9.9.26. Flown by H. C. Biard as No. 7, but forced landed near Beachy Head 12.9.26. Sold to the Halton Aero Club 5.29, and although later sold, was still in existence at Wilstead 8.33. Span, 34 ft. 0 in. Length, 22 ft. 8 in. Tare wt., 605 lb. A.U.W., 1,000 lb. Max. speed, 65 m.p.h.

(*Vickers Ltd.*)

Supermarine S.4

Single seat, wooden racer, powered by one 680 h.p. Napier Lion VII, designed by R. J. Mitchell and built at Woolston for the 1925 Schneider Trophy Race. One aircraft only: G-EBLP, c/n 1215, first flown by H. C. Biard 9.25, raised the world's seaplane speed record to 226·752 m.p.h., Southampton Water 13.9.25, C. of A. 4.10.25. Shipped to the U.S.A., but during Schneider trials, piloted by H. C. Biard, at Bay Shore Park, Baltimore, 24.10.25, sideslipped into the water from 200 ft. and was wrecked. Span, 30 ft. 6 in. Length, 26 ft. 3 in. A.U.W., 3,150 lb. Max. speed, 239 m.p.h.

Supermarine Air Yacht

All-metal flying-boat for six passengers and two crew, powered by three 490 h.p. Armstrong Siddeley Jaguar VI, designed by R. J. Mitchell and built at Woolston 1929 for Hon. A. E. Guinness. One aircraft only: G-AASE, c/n 1285, C. of A. 22.12.31, used for cruises to the Irish lakes. Sold 10.32 to Mrs. J. J. James, re-engined with three 525 h.p. Armstrong Siddeley Panther IIA to carry 20 passengers and two crew. Named 'Windward III' and left Woolston for Egypt piloted by Tommy Rose 11.10.32; forced down in the Gulf of Salerno 25.1.33; dismantled, returned to Woolston and scrapped. Span, 92 ft. 0 in. Length, 67 ft. 6 in. (Panthers) Tare wt., 15,050 lb. A.U.W., 25,000 lb. Max. speed, 117·5 m.p.h.

(*J. G. Ellison*)

Surrey Flying Services A.L.1

Side-by-side two seat trainer of fabric-covered, wooden construction, powered by one 95 h.p. Salmson A.C.7, designed by J. Bewsher and built by Surrey Flying Services Ltd. at Croydon 1929. One aircraft only: G-AALP, no c/n, registered to F. J. Grant 29.8.29, transferred to Surrey Flying Services Ltd. 7.31. Stored at Croydon until sold to Bertram Arden 5.38 and taken by road to Exeter, where it flew a good deal until 1939. In store at Heavitree, Exeter in 1973. Span, 28 ft. 9 in. Length, 20 ft. 0 in. Tare wt., 680 lb. A.U.W., 1,200 lb. Max. speed, 110 m.p.h. Cruise, 100 m.p.h.

(*Flight 13897S*)

Taylor Experimental

Two seater of fabric-covered metal construction, powered by one 90 h.p. Cirrus Minor I, incorporating many untried features such as lattice girder wing spars and a system of diagonal surface bracing. One aircraft only: G-AEPX, c/n T.E.2, designed and built at Hamsey Green Aerodrome, Surrey, 1936 by Richard Taylor, who was killed when the wings failed on its first flight (illustrated) 7.1.37. Two similar aircraft: G-AEPY, c/n T.E.3, a single seater and G-AEPZ, c/n T.E.4, two seater, were registered 7.12.36 but not built. Registration G-AERA was reserved for a fourth Taylor Experimental.

(*via J. W. R. Taylor*)

Tawney Owl

All-metal, two-seat light pusher monoplane, with twin booms and dual controls, designed by A. M. Creedon and developed and built by Tawney Aircraft Ltd., a subsidiary of Thurston Engineering Ltd., Stapleford. One aircraft only: G-APWU, c/n TA.1, powered by one 75 h.p. Porsche 678/4 air-cooled flat four. Overturned during its first take-off at Stapleford 22.4.60, dismantled and stored. Span, 24 ft. 0 in. Length, 19 ft. 6 in. Tare wt., 800 lb. A.U.W., 1,200 lb. Max. cruise, 110 m.p.h. Range, 500 miles.

(*Air Portraits*)

Taylor J.T.1 Monoplane

Single seater designed by John Taylor for home construction in wood. Prototype, G-APRT with 36 h.p. Aeronca J.A.P. J-99, built by the designer at Ilford, Essex 1958–59 and first flown by Wg. Cdr. O. V. Holmes at White Waltham 4.7.59. Rebuilt 1966 with 40 h.p. Ardem 4CO2 Mk.4, bubble canopy and mass balanced ailerons (illustrated). Many built and flown overseas and three, G-AVPX, G-AWGZ and G-AXYK had flown in Britain by 1973 with six others registered and more than 30 under construction. Span, 21 ft. 0 in. Length, 15 ft. 0 in. Tare wt., 450 lb. A.U.W., 660 lb. Cruise, 90 m.p.h. Range, 300 miles.

(*B. C. Hockley*)

Taylor J.T.2 Titch

High performance single seater designed by John Taylor who built the prototype, G-ATYO, c/n JFT.1, with one 85 h.p. Continental C85, at Leigh-on-Sea, Essex 1965–66, A. to F. 12.10.66. First flown at Southend 4.1.67 by the designer who was killed when it crashed there 16.5.67. Others built and flown in Canada, New Zealand, Rhodesia and U.S.A., with six, registered G-AXWY, 'ZR, G-AYZH, G-AZLA, G-BABE and 'BY, and some 20 others under construction in Britain by 1973. See Appendix E. Span, 18 ft. 9 in. Length, 16 ft. 1½ in. Tare wt., 500 lb. A.U.W., 750 lb. Max. speed, 180 m.p.h.

(*Miss D. E. Wright*)

Thruxton Jackaroo

Four seat cabin adaptation of the de Havilland D.H.82A Tiger Moth, powered by one 130 h.p. de Havilland Gipsy Major 1 or 145 h.p. Gipsy Major 1C. Eighteen listed in Appendix E were produced by Jackaroo Aircraft Ltd., Thruxton 1957–59 and one, G-APOV, by Rollason Aircraft and Engines Ltd., Croydon. G-AOEY, G-APAP and 'HZ were equipped initially with Britten-Norman crop spraying gear, and a large number served with the Wiltshire School of Flying, Thruxton. Span, 30 ft. 4¼ in. Length, 25 ft. 0 in. Tare wt., 1,360 lb. A.U.W., 2,180 lb. Cruise, 90 m.p.h.

(*R. P. Howard*)

T.K.1

Wooden two seater, designed and built at Stag Lane 1934 by the students of the de Havilland Technical School under the direction of Marcus Langley, the initials T.K. arising from the title 'Tekniese Kollege No.1' given by the Dutch student responsible for the drawings. One aircraft only: G-ACTK, c/n 1, powered by one 120 h.p. de Havilland Gipsy III, first flown 6.34 under B conditions as E-3, C. of A. 6.7.34, 5th in the King's Cup Race 13–14.7.34 at 124·24 m.p.h. piloted by Geoffrey de Havilland. Sold to Flt. Lt. E. H. Fielden, Hendon, 2.36 and flown as a single seater. Scrapped 1936. Span, 27 ft. 0 in. Length, 24 ft. 0 in. Tare wt., 950 lb. A.U.W., 1,450 lb. Max. speed, 118 m.p.h. Cruise 100 m.p.h.

(*Flight 11795S*)

T.K.2

Wooden two seater powered by one 140 h.p. de Havilland Gipsy Major IC, designed by de Havilland Technical School students and built at Hatfield 1935. One aircraft only: G-ADNO, c/n 1998, completed as a single seater with long range tank in place of passenger, first flown 16.8.35 as E-3, C. of A. 29.8.35, 4th in the King's Cup Race 6–7.9.35 at 165·88 m.p.h. piloted by Hubert Broad. Span, 32 ft. 0 in. Length, 22 ft. 2½ in. Tare wt., 1,078 lb. A.U.W., 1,600 lb. Max. speed, 174 m.p.h.

(*W. K. Kilsby*)

T.K.2 (First Modification)

The original T.K.2 with aerodynamically refined cockpit canopy and lengthened spats. Sixth in the King's Cup Race 11.7.36 at 172·05 m.p.h. piloted by R. J. Waight, won the Heston–Cardiff race at 190 m.p.h. Second in the Heston–Newcastle race 3.7.37, piloted by Geoffrey de Havilland, who won the Heston–Cardiff race 10.7.37 at 161·4 m.p.h. but retired in the King's Cup Race 11.9.37 after averaging 165 m.p.h. Specification as before except: A.U.W., 1,630 lb.

(*A. J. Jackson*)

T.K.2 (Second Modification)

G-ADNO modified for the 1938 season with reduced span, improved cabin glazing and 140 h.p. de Havilland Gipsy Major II, test flown as E-5. Piloted by Geoffrey de Havilland, won the 1938 Heston–Cardiff race at 187·5 m.p.h. and the 1939 Heston–Isle of Man at 168·4 m.p.h. Flew on de Havilland's communications as E-0235 during the war, 2nd in 1947 Manx Air Derby at 179 m.p.h. piloted by Bruce Campbell. Final appearance in Folkestone Trophy Race 31.8.47 when W. I. P. Fillingham broke the 100 km closed circuit class record at 178·33 m.p.h. Scrapped 12.47. Span, 28 ft. 0 in. Length, 22 ft. 5 in. Tare wt., 1,135 lb. A.U.W., 1,650 lb. Max. speed, 182 m.p.h.

(*Flight 15992*)

T.K.4

Built at Hatfield by de Havilland Technical School students in 1937 as the smallest single seat racer that could be designed around a 140 h.p. de Havilland Gipsy Major II. It was equipped with retractable undercarriage, variable-pitch airscrew, slots and flaps. One aircraft only: G-AETK, c/n 2265, first flown 30.7.37 as E-4, C. of A. 1.9.37. Ninth in King's Cup Race 11.9.37 at 230·5 m.p.h. piloted by R. J. Waight, who was killed when the aircraft crashed near Hatfield 1.10.37 while practising for an attempt on the 100 km class record. Span, 19 ft. 8 in. Length, 15 ft. 6 in. Tare wt., 928 lb. A.U.W., 1,357 lb.

(*Aeroplane*)

T.K.5

Last of the T.K. series, designed and built at Hatfield 1938–39. Single seat canard research aircraft powered by one 140 h.p. de Havilland Gipsy Major IC driving a pusher airscrew. One aircraft only: G-AFTK, c/n 2266, completed late 1939, tested by Geoffrey de Havilland, but refused to leave the ground and was scrapped. Span, 25 ft. 8 in. Length, 18 ft. 3 in. A.U.W., 1,366 lb.

Tipsy S.2

Single seater powered by one 28 h.p. Douglas Sprite, developed by E. O. Tips of Avions Fairey, Gosselies, Belgium from his S.1 prototype OO-TIP which had flown to England 5.36. Three Belgian-built S.2s and six of the nine built under licence by Aero Engines Ltd., Kingsdown, Bristol flew in Britain 1936–39. Two Belgian-built, G-AFFN (32 h.p. Sarolea Epervier) and G-AFVH, survived the war, the latter returning to Brussels for preservation in 1947. Span, 24 ft. 7 in. Length, 18 ft. 8½ in. Tare wt., 287 lb. A.U.W., 532 lb. Cruise, 80 m.p.h. Range, 470 miles.

Vickers Type 78 Vulture Mk.I

Three seat amphibian powered by one 450 h.p. Napier Lion, built for a round the world flight. Two aircraft only: G-EBHO, c/n 2, C. of A. 18.2.24, left Calshot 25.3.24 in command of Sqn. Ldr. A. C. S. MacLaren and piloted by Flg. Off. J. Plenderleith, crashed on take-off at Akyab 24.5.24; G-EBGO, c/n 1, C. of A. 11.11.23, spare aircraft positioned at Tokyo, shipped back to Akyab, left 25.6.24, wrecked in forced landing in heavy seas near the Aleutian Islands 2.8.24. Span, 49 ft. 0 in. Length, 38 ft. 2 in. A.U.W., 6,000 lb. Max. speed, 104 m.p.h. Cruise, 82 m.p.h.

Vickers Type 89 Viget

Single seat wooden ultra light powered by one 750 cc. Douglas, designed by R. K. Pierson and built at Weybridge for the 1923 Lympne Trials. One aircraft only: G-EBHN, c/n 1, flown in the trials by chief test pilot S. Cockerell. Performed well but earned no prize money. Fitted with 35 h.p. Blackburne Thrush in 1924. Withdrawn from use 1928. Span, 25 ft. 0 in. Length, 17 ft. 3 in. Tare wt., 395 lb. A.U.W. (Douglas), 575 lb.; (Thrush), 625 lb. Max. speed, 58·1 m.p.h.

Vickers Type 98 Vagabond

Two seat wooden ultra light powered by one 32 h.p. Bristol Cherub III, designed for the 1924 Lympne Trials and built for Vickers Ltd. by A. V. Roe and Co. Ltd. at Hamble. One aircraft only: G-EBJF, c/n 1, not flown until fitted with one 35 h.p. Blackburne Thrush (illustrated) in 1925. Scrapped 1927. Span, 28 ft. 0 in. Length, 21 ft. 0 in. Tare wt., 527 lb. A.U.W., 887 lb. Max. speed, 77 m.p.h.

(*Vickers Ltd.*)

Vickers Type 133 Vendace II

Two seat, general purpose aircraft of mixed construction powered by one 300 h.p. A.D.C. Nimbus, built by Vickers Ltd. at Weybridge 1926. One British civil aircraft only: G-EBPX, c/n 1, C. of A. 10.1.28, sold to the Aircraft Operating Co. Ltd. 6.28, equipped with cameras and twin float undercarriage for the aerial survey of Rio de Janeiro, shipped on S.S. *Andorra* 6.6.28, withdrawn from use 9.30. Span, 45 ft. 0 in. Length, 31 ft. 4 in. Tare wt., 2,604 lb. A.U.W., 3,270 lb. Max. speed, 119 m.p.h.

(*Flight 6859*)

Vickers Type 134 Vellore I

All-metal, two seat freighter for the Air Ministry, powered by one 525 h.p. Bristol Jupiter IX, first flown 17.5.28. One aircraft only: G-EBYX, allocated R.A.F. serial J8906 during construction, shown at Hendon R.A.F. Display 30.6.28. Fitted with one 490 h.p. Armstrong Siddeley Jaguar IV for Australia flight by Flt. Lt. S. J. Moir and P/O H. C. Owen, C. of A. 14.3.29, left Brooklands 18.3.29, crashed at Cape Don, Northern Territory, 26.5.29. Span, 76 ft. 0 in. Length, 51 ft. 6 in. Tare wt., 4,771 lb. A.U.W., 9,500 lb. Max. speed, 110 m.p.h.

Vickers Type 170 Vanguard

Transport for 22 passengers and two crew developed from the Vickers Victoria. One aircraft only: G-EBCP/J6924, built for the Air Ministry and first flown with 450 h.p. Napier Lions 18.7.23 as Type 62. Re-engined 1925 with 650 h.p. Rolls-Royce Condor IIIs as Type 103, C. of A. 11.3.26. Reconditioned as Type 170 for Imperial Airways route proving trials to Paris and Cologne 5.28. World's load carrying record 6.7.28. Crashed at Shepperton, Middlesex, E. R. C. Scholefield killed 16.5.29. Span, 87 ft. 9 in. Length, 53 ft. 10 in. Tare wt., 12,040 lb. A.U.W., 18,500 lb. Max. speed, 112 m.p.h.

Vickers Type 172 Vellore III

Metal transport for two crew and eight passengers developed from Vellore I. Two aircraft only: G-AASW, c/n 1, powered by two 550 h.p. Bristol Jupiter IXF, last aircraft built at Joyce Green. First flown at Brooklands 24.6.30, C. of A. 27.6.30, averaged 126·8 m.p.h. in the King's Cup Race 5.7.30, flown by Flg. Off. J. 'Mutt' Summers. Tested on floats as O-4, scrapped 1934; G-ABKC, c/n 1, completed as mailplane Type 173 with two 525 h.p. Bristol Jupiter XIF, transferred to the R.A.F. 8.31 as K2133. Span, 76 ft. 0 in. Length, 48 ft. 0 in. Tare wt., 7,435 lb. A.U.W., 12,000 lb. Max. speed, 138 m.p.h. Cruise, 120 m.p.h.

Vickers Type 212 Vellox

Heavy freighter of fabric-covered metal construction, powered by two 580 h.p. Bristol Pegasus IM3. One aircraft only: G-ABKY, c/n 1, first flown 23.1.34, C. of A. 30.1.34, exhibited at the Hendon S.B.A.C. Show 2.7.34, sold to Imperial Airways Ltd. for night freighting 5.36. Fitted with two 600 h.p. Bristol Perseus III radial engines, burned out in night take-off crash at Croydon 10.8.36. Span, 76 ft. 0 in. Length, 50 ft. 6 in. Tare wt., 8,150 lb. A.U.W., 13,500 lb. Cruise, 130 m.p.h. Range, 690 miles.

Vickers Type 950–953 Vanguard

Second generation propeller-turbine aircraft in production at Weybridge 1958–64. Prototype Type 950, G-AOYW, first flown by G. R. Bryce 20.1.59, was followed by six Type 951 (5 crew, 126 passengers) and 14 Type 953 (135 passengers) for B.E.A. with four 4,985 e.s.h.p. Rolls-Royce Tyne Mk.506; and 23 Type 952 (5 crew and 139 passengers) for Trans-Canada Air Lines (later Air Canada) with four 5,545 e.s.h.p. Tyne Mk.512. Freight conversions later in Canada and by Aviation Traders Ltd., Southend as Type 953C Merchantman for B.E.A. (illustrated), and as Type 952F for Air Holdings Ltd. The disposal of the Air Canada fleet is recorded in Appendix E. Data for Type 953: Span, 118 ft. 0 in. Length, 122 ft. 10½ in. Tare wt., 85,000 lb. A.U.W., 141,000 lb. Max. range, 2,070 miles at 412 m.p.h.

(*Wallis Autogyros Ltd.*)

Wallis WA-116 Agile

Single seater, 72 h.p. Wallis-McCulloch 4318A, designed and built by Wg. Cdr. K. H. Wallis. Prototype, G-ARRT, first flown 2.8.61, was followed by five Beagle-built WA-116s for Army evaluation 1962, and five WA-116 Agile aircraft built by Wallis Autogyros Ltd. Variants were one WA-116-T pillion two seater; three WA-117s with 100 h.p. Rolls-Royce Continental O-200-B; two WA-118 Meteorites with 120 h.p. Meteor Alfa; one WA-119 with 990 cc. Hillman Imp; and the small, streamlined WA-121 with 90 h.p. Wallis-McCulloch, for high speed, high altitude research 1972. Data for WA-116: Rotor diameter, 20 ft. 4 in. Length, 11 ft. 1 in. Tare wt., 255 lb. A.U.W., 550 lb. Cruise, 60–80 m.p.h. Range, 130 miles.

---

continued from page 295

Mk.2s G-APVL, S2/5311, 650 s.h.p. Blackburn A.129 Nimbus, first flown at Eastleigh 9.8.59; G-APVM, S2/5312, derated 1,000 s.h.p. de Havilland Gnome, H.1000. The last were trials aircraft for the Navy's Westland Wasps, evaluated 1960 as XP166 and XR493. Rotor diameter, 32 ft. 6 in. Length, 29 ft. 0 in. Tare wt., 2,092 lb. A.U.W., 3,800 lb. Cruise, 115 m.p.h.

---

continued from page 309

death 1933, rebuilt as Sopwith Pup by R. O. Shuttleworth 1937–38. Span 24 ft. 9½ in. Length, 19 ft. 4 in. Tare wt., 1,065 lb. A.U.W., 1,430 lb. Max. speed, 95 m.p.h.

(*Wallis Autogyros Ltd.*)

Wallis WA-120

High performance, long range, single seat autogyro with fully enclosed cockpit and bubble canopy, powered by one 130 h.p. Rolls-Royce Continental O-240-A driving a four bladed wooden airscrew, and carrying internal fuel for more than four hours. One experimental aircraft only: G-AYVO, c/n K/602/X, first flown by Wg. Cdr. K. H. Wallis 13.6.71. Rotor diameter, 20 ft. 4 in. Length, 12 ft. 0 in. Tare wt., 460 lb. A.U.W., 750 lb. Cruise, 103 m.p.h. Range, 360 miles.

(*K. Lumb*)

Ward Gnome

Minimum size, low-wing, single seat monoplane of wooden construction, designed and built by Mr. M. Ward at North Scarle, Lincs. in 1966. One aircraft only, c/n 45, powered by a 1925 two cylinder, horizontally opposed Douglas motor-cycle engine tuned to give 14 h.p. First flown by the designer at Wigsley, Lincs. 4.10.67. Sold to R. A. Fixter, to whom it was registered 25.4.69 as G-AXEI. Loaned to the Lincolnshire Aircraft Museum, Tattershall in 1971. Span, 15 ft. 9 in. Length, 11 ft. 6 in. Tare wt., 210 lb. A.U.W., 380 lb. Cruise, 50 m.p.h. Range, 50 miles.

(*Flight 16389S*)

Watkinson Dingbat

Single seat ultra light of wooden construction powered by one 30 h.p. Carden Ford, designed by E. T. Watkinson and C. W. Taylor and built at Teddington, Middlesex, 1938. One aircraft only: G-AFJA, c/n DB.100, first flown at Heston 6.38 by R. L. Porteous, P. to F. 29.7.38. Restored post-war to J. A. Allen but not re-erected, dismantled at Croydon 4.53. Rebuilt by J. H. Pickrell and D. O. Wallis, North Weald, 1959, A. to F. reissued 10.12.59, owned by A. J. Christian, Overton strip, Wilts., 1972. Span, 28 ft. 0 in. Length, 16 ft. 0 in. Tare wt., 460 lb. A.U.W., 700 lb. Max. speed, 90 m.p.h.

Westland Woodpigeon I

Wooden two seater built for the 1924 Lympne Trials, powered by one 32 h.p. Bristol Cherub III. Two aircraft only: G-EBIY, c/n W.P.1, and G-EBJV, c/n W.P.2. The latter first flown by L. P. Openshaw 17.9.24, piloted in the Trials as No. 5 without success by Flg. Off. Gaskell. Second in the Grosvenor Trophy Race 4.10.24. Re-engined with 30 h.p. A.B.C. Scorpion (illustrated) for the Seven Aero Club, C. of A. 8.9.26, unsuccessful in the 1926 Lympne Trials. Span, 22 ft. 9 in. Length, 19 ft. 6 in. Tare wt., 439 lb. A.U.W., 779 lb. Max. speed, 72 m.p.h.

Westland Woodpigeon II

The original Woodpigeon fitted with 60 h.p. Anzani radials and mainplanes of greater span in 1927. G-EBIY sold to Flg. Off. A. F. Scroggs, Henlow, C. of A. 12.5.27, last owner Miss Cicele O'Brien 8.30, in Bowers' scrap yard, Ferrybridge, Yorks in 1949: G-EBJV, sold to L. Taylor 6.27; to L. J. C. Mitchell, Chard 10.27, to J. E. Crossland McClure, No.41 (Fighter) Sqn., Netheravon, 2.30. Last C. of A. renewal at Northolt 6.5.32. Span, 27 ft. 0 in. Length, 20 ft. 9 in. Tare wt., 515 lb. A.U.W., 890 lb.

(Westland Aircraft Ltd.)

Westland S-51

Following the import in 1947 of six American-built Sikorsky S-51 four seat helicopters, 139 were produced by Westland Aircraft Ltd. at Yeovil as the S-51 Mk.1A with 540 h.p. Alvis Leonides 521/1 and S-51 Mk.1B with 450 h.p. Pratt & Whitney Wasp Junior R-985-B4, mainly for the R.A.F. and foreign air forces but including 22 British civil Mk.1A and five Mk.1B. Rotor diameter, 49 ft. 0 in. Length, 57 ft. 6½ in. Tare wt., 4,397 lb. A.U.W., 5,700 lb. Cruise, 80 m.p.h. Range, 300 miles.

(*Westland Aircraft Ltd.*)

Westland S-51 Series 2 Widgeon

Yeovil-built S-51A with one 520 h.p. Alvis Leonides 521/2, the improved rotor head of the larger S-55 and a new Westland-designed light-weight front fuselage to seat five. Prototype G-ALIK first flown 23.8.55 was followed by 14 production aircraft, some being conversions of existing S-51 Mk.1As. Two were for the Brazilian Navy, one each for the Royal Arab Air Force and Japan, and 11 British civil registered. Rotor diameter, 49 ft. 2 in. Length, 57 ft. 8 in. Tare wt., 4,322 lb. A.U.W., 5,900 lb. Cruise, 88 m.p.h. Range, 310 miles.

Westland S-55

Developed version of the American Sikorsky S-55 seven seat helicopter, over 500 built under licence from 1952 by Westland Aircraft Ltd. at Yeovil as the Series 1 with one 600 h.p. Pratt & Whitney Wasp R-1340-40, Series 2 with one 750 h.p. Alvis Leonides Major 755 and Series 3 (illustrated) with 720 s.h.p. Bristol Siddeley Gnome 101. R.A.F. and Royal Navy versions were known as Whirlwinds. Data for Series 3: Rotor diameter, 53 ft. 0 in. Length, 44 ft. 2 in. Tare wt., 4,760 lb. A.U.W., 8,000 lb. Cruise, 100 m.p.h. Range, 260 miles.

(*P. R. March*)

Westland Westminster

Aerodynamic test rig for a 6 ton crane or 40 seat transport helicopter powered by two 2,400 s.h.p. Napier Eland 229 turboshaft engines and using the five bladed rotor of the Sikorsky S-56. Two aircraft only: G-APLE, c/n WA.1, first flown at Yeovil in skeleton form 15.6.58 by W. H. Sear, shown at Farnborough 9.58, C. of A 26.1.59; G-APTX, c/n WA.2, first flown 4.9.59. Development abandoned in 1960 and both dumped at Yeovilton in 1963. Rotor diameter, 72 ft. 0 in. Length, 86 ft. 9 in. Tare wt., 21,245 lb. A.U.W., 33,000 lb. Cruise, 115 m.p.h. Range, 210 miles.

Westland Wessex 60 Series 1

Westland version of the two crew/12 passenger Sikorsky S-58, first flown at Yeovil 6.58, built in quantity for the world's navies and air forces. Registration G-APLF reserved but not used 1958 for the Wessex 1 (one 1,450 s.h.p. Napier Gazelle N.Ga.13 turbine). Main civil production as Wessex 60 Series 1 (two 1,350 s.h.p. Bristol Siddeley Gnome 660), 13 delivered to Bristow Helicopters Ltd., Redhill 1965–72 for oil rig support. Data for Wessex 60 Series 1; Rotor diameter, 56 ft. 0 in. Length, 48 ft. 5 in. Tare wt., 8,657 lb. A.U.W., 13,500 lb. Cruise, 121 m.p.h. Max. range, 335 miles.

(*A. H. Wheeler*)

Wheeler Slymph

Single seater powered by one 696 cc. Blackburne Tomtit designed and built by Flt. Lt. (later Air Commodore) A. H. Wheeler at the Aircraft Depot, Hinaidi, Iraq, 1931. One aircraft only: G-ABOI, c/n A.H.W.1, modified and re-engined with one 35 h.p. A.B.C. Scorpion at R.A.F. Henlow 1932. Never flown. Stored at Old Warden with the Shuttleworth Collection until loaned to the Midlands Aircraft Preservation Society, Coventry for restoration in 1969. Span, 22 ft. 0 in. Length, 14 ft. 9 in. A.U.W., 530 lb.

Willoughby Delta F

Wooden experimental two seater with triangular aerofoil section tail booms, powered by two 125 h.p. Menasco Pirate C-4, designed by P. N. Willoughby and built by the Willoughby Delta Company at Witney 1938–39. One aircraft only: G-AFPX 'St. Francis', c/n 1, demonstrated by A. N. Kingwill at the Heathrow Garden Party of the R.Ae.S. 14.5.39, destroyed in crash at Caulcott, near Bicester 10.7.39, pilot H. N. Olley and designer killed. Span, 34 ft. 6 in. Length, 26 ft. 1 in. Tare wt., 1,585 lb. A.U.W., 2,350 lb. Max. speed, 183 m.p.h. Cruise, 165 m.p.h.

(*M. D. N. Fisher*)

Wittman W-8 Tailwind

Side-by-side two seater of fabric-covered composite construction, designed by S. J. Wittman and first flown in the U.S.A. 1953, plans and components later being available to amateur builders. The first British example, G-AYDU, c/n PFA.1363, 90 h.p. Continental TC60, built by A. J. E. Perkins at Maiden Hill Farm, near Hertford as the AJEP Developments Tailwind, was first flown at Panshanger 24.3.72 by W. S. Bowker, C. of A. 15.5.72. G-BALR, c/n TW4/381, under construction at Preston by R. L. Hughes 1973. Span, 22 ft. 6 in. Length, 20 ft. 7 in. Tare wt., 743 lb. A.U.W., 1,300 lb. Max. cruise, 142 m.p.h. Range, 550 miles.

Wren Goldcrest

Single seat, ultra light, low-wing monoplane, powered by one 25 h.p. Scott Squirrel, designed by R. G. Carr and built by the Wren Aircraft Co. Ltd. at Kirklinton, Carlisle, 1946. One aircraft only: G-AICX, c/n 1, registered 13.8.46 to the designer, scrapped in 1947. Production plans abandoned due to difficulty in obtaining approved materials. Span, 23 ft. 0 in. Length, 16 ft. 8 in. Tare wt., 370 lb. A.U.W., 580 lb. Max. speed, 98 m.p.h. Cruise, 75 m.p.h.

(A. J. Jackson)

Youngman–Baynes High Lift

Experimental two seater using some Proctor components, designed by L. E. Baynes and built by Heston Aircraft Ltd. 1947 to test a system of full span, slotted flaps invented by R. T. Youngman. One aircraft only: c/n 1, powered by one 250 h.p. Gipsy Queen 32, first flown at Heston 5.2.48 as VT789 by R. Munday. Registered 10.5.50 to R. T. Youngman as G-AMBL, shown at the White Waltham Garden Party of the R.Ae.S. 6.5.51, presented to the College of Aeronautics, Cranfield, 1954. Span, 33 ft. 0 in. Length, 29 ft. 0 in. Tare wt., 2,380 lb. A.U.W., 3,500 lb. Max. speed, 180 m.p.h.

APPENDIX B

Military Types Used for Civil Purposes

Aircraft listed in this section were either demilitarised in small numbers for normal commercial or private usage or were military aircraft flown under civil markings for demonstration, test or overseas delivery. As it constitutes a breach of international law to fly an aircraft in military marks over foreign soil without special permission, British military aircraft being delivered by air usually receive temporary civil status.

The introductory notes to Appendix A apply equally to this section. British military types civilianised overseas are outside the scope of this book.

(*Air Portraits*)

Hunting Percival P.56 Provost T. Mk.1

Side-by-side two-seat trainer, one 550 h.p. Alvis Leonides 503/6A, produced by Hunting Percival Aircraft Ltd., Luton from 1953. One civil demonstrator G-AMZM initially, for tour of Turkey 7.53, S.B.A.C. Show 9.54; Lockheed Aerobatic Contest, Baginton 20.7.56 piloted by R. G. Wheldon. One R.A.F. aircraft civilianised 1963 as G-ASMC for the Rapid F/G, Baginton; nine more released by the R.A.F. 1968 became G-AWPH, 'PI, 'TB to 'TG and 'VF, the first and last converted by Alvis Ltd., Baginton. Span, 35 ft. 2 in. Length, 28 ft. 8 in. Tare wt., 3,350 lb. A.U.W., 4,700 lb. Max. speed, 200 m.p.h. Cruise, 162 m.p.h.

Hunting Percival P.84 Jet Provost Mk.1

Two seat, side-by-side, all-metal, basic trainer using Provost mainplane and empennage, powered by one 1,640 lb. s.t. Armstrong Siddeley Viper 5 Mk.101 turbojet, built by Hunting Percival Aircraft Ltd. at Luton 1954. One civil aircraft only: G-AOBU, c/n 6, C. of A. 25.5.55; demonstrated at Blackbushe 9.55; flight trials of Viper 8 at Bitteswell 1956 as G-42-1, presented to the Shuttleworth Trust 4.61 and loaned to Loughborough College as an instructional airframe. Span, 35 ft. 5 in. Length, 31 ft. 11 in. A.U.W., 6,038 lb. Max. speed, 330 m.p.h. Cruise, 303 m.p.h.

Hunting Percival P.84 Jet Provost (Other Marks)

Developed versions with shortened undercarriage legs, improved fuselage lines and dorsal fin. Five aircraft allotted civil registrations 1956–65 for demonstration, test or ferrying: G-AOHD, Mk.2 (1,750 lb. s.t. Bristol Siddeley Viper 8); G-AOUS, Mk.2B (2,500 lb. s.t. Viper 11); G-APVF, reservation dated 7.59; G-ASEZ, T.Mk.52 and G-ATAJ, T.Mk.4 (2,500 lb. s.t. Viper 201). Span, 35 ft. 5 in. Length, 32 ft. 5 in. A.U.W., (G-AOHD) 6,200 lb. (G-AOUS) 7,150 lb. (G-ASEZ) 6,650 lb. Max. speed, 411 m.p.h. at 20,000 ft.

Martin–Baker M.B.2

Private venture, single seat, eight gun fighter to Specification F.5/34, powered by one 1,000 h.p. Napier Dagger III, designed by James Martin and built at Heston by the Martin-Baker Aircraft Co. Ltd. 1937. One aircraft only: G-AEZD, c/n M.B.2, first flown at Harwell under B conditions as M-B-1 by V. H. Baker 3.8.38. Transferred to the R.A.F. 3.39 as P9594. Span, 34 ft. 0 in. Length, 34 ft. 6 in. A.U.W., 5,400 lb. Max. speed, 300+ m.p.h.

(*Miles Aircraft Ltd.*)

Miles M.9 Kestrel Trainer

Private venture, two seat advanced trainer of wooden construction, fitted with retractable undercarriage, powered by one 745 h.p. Rolls-Royce Kestrel XVI, designed by F. G. Miles and built by Phillips and Powis Aircraft Ltd. at Woodley 1937. One aircraft only: G-AEOC, c/n 330, first flown by F. G. Miles 3.6.37, demonstrated at the Hendon R.A.F. Display 26.6.37, flown under B conditions as U-5 until transferred to R.A.F. marks 5.38 as N3300. Dismantled at Woodley 1943. Span, 39 ft. 0 in. Length, 29 ft. 6 in. Tare wt., 4,159 lb. A.U.W., 5,337 lb. Max. speed, 296 m.p.h. Cruise, 254 m.p.h.

(E. J. Riding)

Miles M.16 Mentor

Three seat training and communications aircraft developed from the Miles Nighthawk and powered by one 200 h.p. de Havilland Gipsy Six Series 1. One aircraft only: L4420, c/n 462, sole survivor of 45 Mentors supplied to the R.A.F. 1938–39, civilianised at White Waltham as G-AHKM 1947. Based at Wolverhampton by P. W. Bayliss, sold to J. C. Turnhill 12.48. Competed for 1948 Siddeley Trophy and 1949 King's Cup. Crashed in bad visibility at Clayhidon, Devon, 1.4.50, en route Wolverhampton–Exeter, J. C. Turnhill killed. Span, 34 ft. $9\frac{1}{2}$ in. Length, 26 ft. $1\frac{3}{4}$ in. Tare wt., 1,978 lb. A.U.W., 2,710 lb. Max. speed, 156 m.p.h.

(A. J. Jackson)

Miles M.19 Master 2

Two seat advanced trainer of all-wood construction powered by one 870 h.p. Bristol Mercury 20, 1,799 built by Phillips and Powis Aircraft Ltd. at Woodley from 1940. Three British civil aircraft only. G-AHOB, c/n 6434, converted at Woodley 5.46 for demonstration flying, scrapped 1950; G-AIZM and 'ZN, formerly EM300 and DM442 respectively, registered to Southern Aircraft (Gatwick) Ltd. 30.12.46, not converted, broken up for spares 1948. Span, 35 ft. 9 in. Length, 29 ft. 6 in. Tare wt., 4,053 lb. A.U.W., 5,673 lb. Max. speed, 243 m.p.h.

(*Miles Aircraft Ltd.*)

Miles M.25 Martinet

Two seat target tug using many Master 2 components, powered by one 870 h.p. Bristol Mercury 20 engine, 1,724 built by Phillips and Powis Aircraft Ltd. at Woodley from 1942. Six Swedish registered aircraft, SE-AZC to 'ZG and SE-BCI shipped to Svensk Flygtjänst for target towing 3.47, were followed by three British registered, G-AJJK, 'JL and 'JO, crated at Hanworth and shipped 23.5.47. Two others, G-AJZB and 'ZC, registered to W. S. Shackleton Ltd. 18.6.47, remained unconverted and were scrapped at Bovingdon 3.48. Span, 39 ft. 0 in. Length, 30 ft. 11 in. Tare wt., 4,600 lb. A.U.W., 6,600 lb. Max. speed, 232 m.p.h. Cruise, 225 m.p.h.

(*J. J. Masterson*)

Miles M.27 Master 3

As Master 2 but powered by one 825 h.p. Pratt & Whitney Twin Wasp Junior R-1535-SB4G, 602 built by Phillips and Powis Aircraft Ltd. at Woodley from 1940. One British civil aircraft only: G-AGEK, R.A.F. serial DL670, registered to the Secretary of State for Air 3.7.42 and ferried to Ireland in civil markings for demonstration to the Irish Air Corps. Span, 35 ft. 9 in. Length, 30 ft. 2 in. Tare wt., 4,204 lb. A.U.W., 5,570 lb. Max. speed, 232 m.p.h.

Miles M.37 Martinet Trainer

Two seat trainer conversion of the Miles M.25 Martinet powered by one 870 h.p. Bristol Mercury 20. One British civil aircraft only: G-AKOS, second prototype, formerly JN668, registered 22.12.47 to L. A. Andrews, trading as the Gloucester Flying Club, Staverton. Not converted for civil use, becoming derelict in an orchard adjacent to Staverton aerodrome in 1949. Specification as standard Martinet.

(*Aeroplane*)

Miles M.100 Student

Two seat, side-by-side, private venture trainer powered by one 880 lb. s.t. Blackburn Turboméca Marboré 2A turbojet, designed by G. H. Miles and built at Shoreham 1956–57. One aircraft only: G-APLK, c/n 100/1008, first flown by the designer 14.5.57; exhibited at the Farnborough S.B.A.C. Show 9.57 as G-35-4, C. of A. 20.6.58 for Continental tour, London–Paris Race and Paris Air Show 7.59. First flown as XS941 by G. H. Miles 22.4.64 as Mk.2 with 1,050 lb. s.t. Marboré 6F and underwing pods; stored at Ford and Shoreham from 10.65. Span, 29 ft. 2 in. Length, 31 ft. 6 in. (Mk.1) Tare wt., 2,400 lb. A.U.W., 3,900 lb. Max. speed, 298 m.p.h. Cruise 262 m.p.h. Range, 440 miles.

(*via K. M. Molsen*)

Norman Thompson N.T.2B

Two seat wooden flying-boat powered by one 160 h.p. Beardmore pusher. Admiralty trainer N2290, built 1918 by the Norman Thompson Flight Co. Ltd., registered to Handley Page Ltd. 9.1.20 as G-EAQO, was shipped to Canada as G-CACG for forestry patrols from Lake St. John, Quebec. Believed scrapped at Hamilton 1929. Span, 48 ft. 4¾ in. Length, 27 ft. 4½ in. Tare wt., 2,320 lb. A.U.W., 3,170 lb. Max. speed, 85 m.p.h.

Parnall Panther

Two seat Fleet reconnaissance biplane of wooden monocoque construction, powered by one 200 h.p. Bentley B.R.2 rotary, designed 1917 by Harold Bolas for Parnall and Sons, 150 built by the British and Colonial Aeroplane Co. Ltd. at Filton 1919–21. One civil aircraft only: G-EBCM, formerly N7530, completed at Filton 23.6.20. First flown at Croydon 13.4.22, after conversion by the Aircraft Disposal Co. Ltd., solely for the Royal Aero Club race meeting at Croydon 17.4.22, at which it was flown by A. F. Muir. Span, 29 ft. 6 in. Length, 24 ft. 11 in. Tare wt., 1,328 lb. A.U.W., 2,369 lb. Max. speed, 108·5 m.p.h.

Parnall Plover

Single seat Fleet fighter powered by one 420 h.p. Bristol Jupiter III, designed by Harold Bolas and built at Coliseum Works, Bristol, by George Parnall and Company 1923–24. One civil aircraft only: G-EBON, formerly N9705, C. of A. 7.7.26, flown in the King's Cup Race of 9–10.7.26 by Sqn. Ldr. Sir C. J. Quintin Brand, retired with petrol feed trouble. Crashed 1.29. Span, 29 ft. 0 in. Length, 23 ft. 0 in. Tare wt., 2,035 lb. A.U.W., 3,020 lb.

(*Aeroplane*)

Percival P.40 Prentice 1

Two/three seat basic trainer, powered by one 250 h.p. de Havilland Gipsy Queen 30-2, delivered to the R.A.F. in quantity 1948. Overseas tours by demonstrators G-AKLF and 'LG in 1947 led to orders from Argentina, Lebanon and India. Aviation Traders Ltd. bought 252 obsolete R.A.F. Prentices for civil conversion 1955–58 and two others, VS652 and VR211, acquired by Vendair Ltd. Croydon and H. H. Bushell, were registered G-APIF and G-ARGA respectively. Only 28 eventually found civil employment including the 'one-off' seven seat G-APJE. Span, 46 ft. 0 in. Length, 31 ft. 6½ in. Tare wt., 3,232 lb. A.U.W., 4,350 lb. Cruise, 126 m.p.h. Range, 350 miles.

(Sqn. Ldr. C. A. Rea)

Short 184

Two seater designed by Short Bros. Ltd. in 1915 and widely sub-contracted. Five British civil aircraft only, all with 260 h.p. Sunbeam Maori III, converted to five seaters for one season's seaside pleasure flying: G-EAJT, N2986, C. of A. 8.8.19 and G-EALC, N2998, C. of A. 17.6.19, the Eastbourne Aviation Co. Ltd., scrapped 8.20; G-EBBM, N9096, C. of A. 24.8.22 and G-EBBN, N9118, C. of A. 1.6.22, Seaplane and Pleasure Trip Co. Ltd.; G-EBGP, N2996, Manchester Airways, not converted. Span, 63 ft. 6¼ in. Length, 40 ft. 7½ in. Tare wt., 3,638 lb. A.U.W., 5,287 lb. Max. speed, 82 m.p.h.

(Flight 5212)

Short S.5 Singapore I

The first large all-metal flying-boat. One aircraft only: N179, c/n S.677, two 650 h.p. Rolls-Royce Condor IIIA, first flown by J. Lankester Parker at Rochester 17.8.26. Loaned to Sir Alan Cobham by the Air Council 1927 as G-EBUP for a 20,000 mile African Survey Flight, C. of A. 7.11.27. Left Rochester 17.11.27, held up at Malta until 21.1.28, first flying-boat to visit the Cape 30.3.28, returned to Rochester 4.6.28. Returned to the R.A.F. 10.28 as N179, exhibited at Olympia 7.29. Later fitted with Rolls-Royce Buzzard engines. Span, 93 ft. 0 in. Length, 65 ft. 6 in. Tare wt., 12,955 lb. A.U.W., 21,000 lb. Max. speed, 128 m.p.h.

(*E. J. Riding*)

Short S.29 Stirling 5

All-metal transport powered by four 1,600 h.p. Bristol Hercules XVI, 160 built at Belfast 1945 by Short and Harland Ltd. One British civil aircraft only: G-AKPC, formerly PK148 (illustrated), registered 6.1.48 for ferrying from R.A.F. Polebrook to Airtech Ltd., Thame, for overhaul and delivery to the Belgian operator Trans-Air as OO-XAM. The Belgian marks were not taken up, and the aircraft is believed to have been scrapped at Thame late in 1948. Span, 99 ft. 1 in. Length, 90 ft. $6\frac{3}{4}$ in. Tare wt., 43,500 lb. A.U.W., 70,000 lb. Max. speed, 280 m.p.h. Cruise, 233 m.p.h.

(*Short Bros. and Harland Ltd.*)

Short S.C.5 Belfast

Long range freighter for outsize loads, powered by four 5,730 e.s.h.p. Rolls-Royce Tyne 12 propeller-turbines. Ten aircraft XR362-XR371 (c/n SH.1816–SH.1825) built at Belfast for the R.A.F. The first, rolled out 8.10.63 as G-ASKE, was first flown 5.1.64 from Sydenham to Aldergrove as XR362 by D. Tayler and P. Lowe. Used civil marks for high level take-off tests at Torrejon, Madrid 10.64 and tropical trials at Nairobi 12.65; issued to No.53 Sqn., Brize Norton 2.68 as XR362 'Samson'. Span, 158 ft. 10 in. Length, 136 ft. 5 in. Tare wt., 125,000 lb. A.U.W., 225,000 lb. Max. cruise, 358 m.p.h. Max. range, 5,200 miles.

(*P. T. Capon*)

Sopwith Pup

Single seat fighter, one 80 h.p. Le Rhône, designed 1916. Eight civilianised: G-EAVF, and 'VV to 'VZ, by Handley Page Ltd. 1920; G-EBAZ based at Erith, Kent, by P. T. Capon 1922; G-EBFJ converted by J. T. Norquay 1923. One rebuild, G-APUP, completed by K. St. Cyrien in 1973; replica G-AVPA being built by C. Warrilow, High Wycombe 1974. The Shuttleworth Trust's airworthy N5180 was a conversion of Sopwith Dove G-EBKY. See Appendix E. Span, 26 ft. 6 in. Length, 19 ft. 3¾ in. Tare wt., 787 lb. A.U.W., 1,330 lb. Max. speed, 111 m.p.h.

(*Flight 296*)

Sopwith R.M.1 Snapper

Fabric-covered, wooden, single seat fighter powered by one 360 h.p. A.B.C. Dragonfly IA, built by the Sopwith Aviation Co. Ltd. at Kingston-on-Thames 1919. One civil aircraft only: K-149/G-EAFJ, c/n P.W.14, demilitarised and registered to the manufacturers 19.6.19. Flown to Hendon by H. G. Hawker for the Aerial Derby 21.6.19, but participation was forbidden as the Dragonfly engine was still on the Secret List. Scrapped 8.20. Span, 28 ft. 0 in. Length, 20 ft. 7 in. Tare wt., 1,244 lb. A.U.W., 2,190 lb. Max. speed, 140 m.p.h.

Sopwith F.1 Camel

1916 single seat fighter with 130 h.p. Clerget. Two, H2700 and F6302, built by Boulton and Paul Ltd., civilianised respectively as: G-EAWN, f/f 12.12.19, H.S. Broad sixth in Aerial Derby 16.7.21 at 95.61 m.p.h., aerobatics for the Welsh Aviation Co. 8.21, dismantled at Stag Lane 1922; G-EBER registered 9.8.22 to W. J. McDonough, crashed 4.11.22. One Slingsby Type 57 replica, G-AWYY, c/n 1701, 145 h.p. Warner Super Scarab, built for Universal Pictures Ltd., f/f at White Waltham 4.3.69, A. to F. 12.5.69, sold to Flying Circus, Bealeton, Virginia, U.S.A. 1970. Span, 28 ft. 0 in. Length, 18 ft. 9 in. A.U.W., 1,474 lb. Max. speed, 115 m.p.h.

(*Flight 389*)

Sopwith 7F.1 Snipe

Single seat fighter powered by one 230 h.p. Bentley B.R.2, widely sub-contracted from 1918. Four unused R.A.F. aircraft registered 1920 by the

continued on page 356

Supermarine Seagull III

Fleet Air Arm amphibian powered by one 450 h.p. Napier Lion V, built by the Supermarine Aviation Works, Woolston, 1923. Three aircraft converted to six seaters 1928–29: G-EBXH, N9653, C. of A. 16.7.28, F. Tyllyer and F. H. Winn, t/a Coastal Flying Boat Services, Shoreham for South Coast joyrides and abortive Dieppe service with G-EBXI, N9654, both scrapped 1930; G-AAIZ, N9605, Lion IIB, C. of A. 10.7.29, Travel and Tour Association Ltd., Brooklands, flown to Jersey 10.29, sold to G. W. Higgs 2.30, burned at Brooklands 12.33. Span, 46 ft. 0 in. Length, 37 ft. 0 in. Tare wt., 3,897 lb. A.U.W., 5,668 lb. Max. speed, 108 m.p.h.

Supermarine Solent

Torpedo-carrying derivative of the Southampton powered by three 420 h.p. Armstrong Siddeley Jaguar IVA built for the Danish Navy as the Nanok (Ice Bear) in 1928. One undelivered aircraft only: Danish serial 99, c/n 1244, civilianised as G-AAAB for the Hon. A. E. Guinness and redesignated Solent, C. of A. 5.9.28. Numerous flights between Woolston and the Irish ports. Scrapped 1934. Span, 75 ft. 0 in. Length, 50 ft. 2 in. Tare wt., 9,849 lb. A.U.W., 16,300 lb. Max. speed, 111 m.p.h. Cruise, 90 m.p.h.

(Aviation Photo News)

Vickers F.B.5 Gunbus replica

Two seat fighter first flown in 1914 and used by the R.F.C. in France until 1916. One replica aircraft, G-ATVP, c/n VAFA.01, built at Weybridge 1966 by the Vintage Aircraft and Flying Association to honour the centenary of the R.Ae.S. Its 100 h.p. Gnome Monosoupape was built from two stored engines. First flown by D. G. Addicott at Wisley 14.6.66 with serial 2345 and took part in the R.Ae.S. centenary display at Cranfield 19.6.66. Presented to the R.A.F. Museum, Hendon in 1969. Span, 36 ft. 6 in. Length, 27 ft. 2 in. Tare wt., 1,220 lb. A.U.W., 2,050 lb. Max. speed, 70 m.p.h. Range, 250 miles.

(Vickers Ltd.)

Vickers F.B.14A

Two seat scout first flown 8.16. Total of 150 built, two of which were registered 5.19 to Vickers Ltd. as G-EAAS and G-EAAT, c/n C-103 and C-104 respectively. Civil conversion, begun at Bexleyheath, Kent and shown in the illustration, was abandoned 7.19 even though a 150 h.p. Lorraine-Dietrich water-cooled engine had been installed in one of them. Span, 39 ft. 6 in. Length, 28 ft. 5 in. Tare wt., 1,662 lb. A.U.W., 2,603 lb. Max. speed, 99 m.p.h.

Vickers Type 71 Vixen I

Two seat general-purpose biplane powered by one 450 h.p. Napier Lion, first flown at Brooklands by Capt. F. C. G. Broome 2.23. First flown 13.8.23 as Type 87 Vixen II with longer fuselage, C. of A. 10.9.23. Cleaned up aerodynamically and fitted with 650 h.p. Rolls-Royce Condor III in 1924 as the Type 105 Vixen IV night interceptor. (Vixen I) Span, 40 ft. 0 in. Length, 29 ft. 0 in. Tare wt., 3,098 lb. A.U.W., 4,720 lb. Max. speed, 137 m.p.h.

(*Imperial War Museum MH.2948*)

Vickers Type 91 Vixen III

Two seat marine reconnaissance biplane similar to Vixen II with modified cowlings, decking and rudder horn balance, powered by one 450 h.p. Napier Lion. One aircraft only: G-EBIP, c/n 1, first flown at Brooklands 4.24, registered to Douglas Vickers 8.24, flown by Sqn. Ldr. H. J. Payn in 1924 King's Cup Race. Fitted with floats at Hamble 12.24, to M.A.E.E., Felixstowe 1925. Demilitarised as landplane for 1925 King's Cup Race as Vickers Type 106 q.v. Span, 45 ft. 1 in. Length, 36 ft. 6 in. Tare wt., 3,900 lb. A.U.W., 5,500 lb. Max. speed, 125 m.p.h.

(Flight)

Vickers Type 106 Vixen III

The original Vixen III G-EBIP demilitarised as a high performance two seater for the 1925 King's Cup Race and fitted with ailerons on the lower wing only. Modified to single seater Type 148 with 500 h.p. Napier Lion V, C. of A. 1.2.26, 2nd and 3rd respectively in the 1926 and 1927 King's Cup Races, averaging 141·6 m.p.h., piloted by E. R. C. Scholefield, scrapped 1929. Span, 45 ft. 1 in. Length, 36 ft. 6 in. Tare wt., 3,900 lb. A.U.W., 5,500 lb. Max. speed, 125 m.p.h.

Vickers Type 113 Vespa I

High altitude Army Co-operation biplane of wooden construction, one 425 h.p. Bristol Jupiter IV, first flown at Brooklands 9.25. One demonstrator only: G-EBLD, c/n 1, C. of A. 28.1.26, re-engined 4.26 with 455 h.p. Jupiter VI. Rebuilt 1927 with metal wings as Type 119 Vespa II. Averaged 115·5 m.p.h. in the King's Cup Race 30.7.27, flown by Sqn. Ldr. H. J. Payn. Rebuilt 1930 as Type 210 Vespa VI q.v. Span, 50 ft. 0 in. Length, 31 ft. 3 in. Tare wt., 2,468 lb. A.U.W., 3,925 lb. Max. speed, 129 m.p.h.

(Vickers Ltd.)

Vickers Type 123

Private venture single seat fighter of fabric-covered metal construction, powered by one 400 h.p. twelve cylinder Hispano-Suiza T52, built at Weybridge 1926. One aircraft only: G-EBNQ, c/n 1, first flown at Brooklands 11.9.26, modified to Type 141 Scout with 480 h.p. Rolls-Royce F.XI in 1927. Span, 34 ft. 0 in. Length, 28 ft. 6 in. Tare wt., 2,278 lb. A.U.W., 3,300 lb. Max. speed, 149 m.p.h.

(Vickers Ltd.)

Vickers Type 124 Vixen VI

The Type 105 Vixen IV, G-EBEC, modified later in 1924 with improved fuselage lines and controls as well as increased wing, rudder and elevator area, and powered by one 650 h.p. Rolls-Royce Condor IIIA geared engine. Flown by Capt. Charles Russell and Flg. Off. J. 'Mutt' Summers on experimental mail flights to connect with transatlantic liners, the first Croydon-Baldonnel service being flown 26.8.29. Scrapped in 1930. Span, 45 ft. 1 in. Length, 34 ft. 6 in. A.U.W., 5,550 lb. Max. speed, 151 m.p.h.

Vickers Type 131 Valiant

Two seat, general purpose biplane of fabric-covered metal construction powered by one 455 h.p. Bristol Jupiter VI, built at Weybridge 1927. One aircraft only, c/n 1, shown as No.11 in the New Types Park at the Hendon R.A.F. Display 2.7.27. Registered 15.12.27 as G-EBVM, C. of A. 3.1.28, shipped to Valparaiso and demonstrated by Flt. Lt. E. R. C. Scholefield to the Chilean Air Force which afterwards purchased the machine. Span, 45 ft. 7 in. Length, 34 ft. 0 in. Tare wt., 2,973 lb. A.U.W., 5,550 lb. Max. speed, 125 m.p.h.

Vickers Type 141

Vickers Type 123 G-EBNQ modified in 1927 and fitted with one 480 h.p. Rolls-Royce F.XI for the Air Ministry fighter competition 1.28. Further modified as fleet fighter to Spec.21/26 for trials on H.M.S. *Furious* 6.29. Scratch machine in the King's Cup Race, 5–6.7.29 piloted by Flg. Off. J. Summers but retired at Castle Bromwich. Scrapped in 1930. Max. speed, 174 m.p.h.

(*Flight 10242*)

Vickers Type 142 Vivid

Two seat, general purpose biplane powered by one 590 h.p. Napier Lion XIA, first flown 27.6.27. One aircraft only: G-EBPY, c/n 1, C. of A. 29.8.28, flown at Woolston on twin floats; and to Bucharest as a landplane by Flt. Lt. E. R. C. Scholefield 6.9.28. Sold to J. R. Chaplin 3.31, set up one-day out-and-home records from Heston piloted by T. Neville Stack and owner: Berlin 12.4.31, Copenhagen 23.5.31, Warsaw 24.6.31. Burned in hangar fire at Broomfield Aerodrome, Chelmsford, Essex 18.9.32. Span, 45 ft. 1 in. Length, 34 ft. 5 in. Tare wt., 3,560 lb. A.U.W., 5,550 lb. Max. speed, 153 m.p.h. Cruise, 130 m.p.h.

---

continued from page 349

Aircraft Disposal Co. Ltd.: G-EATF, J365, built at Lincoln by Ruston and Hornsby Ltd., demonstrator; G-EAUU/J459, G-EAUV/J453, G-EAUW (illustrated)/J455, built at Norwich by Boulton and Paul Ltd. and flown in the Hendon Aerial Derby 24.7.20 by J. S. T. Fall, W. H. Longton (both forced landed) and W. L. Jordan (5th) respectively. A fifth Snipe G-EBBE, J461, Norwich-built, flown Croydon–Brussels for Belgian Air Force 28.1.22. Span, 31 ft. 1 in. Length, 19 ft. 10 in. Tare wt., 1,127 lb. A.U.W., 2,075 lb. Max. speed, 121 m.p.h.

Vickers Type 209 Vildebeest III

Two seat torpedoplane of fabric-covered, metal construction powered by one 550 h.p. Bristol Jupiter XIF. One aircraft only: G-ABGE, c/n 1, formerly the prototype N230, modified for the Paris Aero Show 12.30, C. of A. 1.12.30. Modified to Spanish requirements 9.31 as Type 216 Vildebeest VII and flown as O-3. Span, 49 ft. 0 in. Length, 36 ft. 8 in. Tare wt., 3,571 lb. A.U.W., 7,529 lb. Max. speed, 123 m.p.h.

Vickers Type 210 Vespa VI

Vespa I G-EBLD converted to two seat fighter prototype with modified undercarriage but retaining the Jupiter VI engine. Re-registered G-ABIL 1.31, C. of A. 12.3.31 for sales tour of China by H. W. R. Banting. Loaned to the Bristol Aeroplane Co. Ltd., converted to single seat Type 250 Vespa VII with one 550 h.p. Bristol Pegasus IS.3 under the direction of F. S. Barnwell. Pegasus development flights at Filton under B conditions as O-5, culminating in a new world's altitude record of 43,976 ft. piloted by C. F. Uwins 16.9.32. To the R.A.F. 6.33 as K3588. Span, 50 ft. 0 in. Length, 32 ft. 6 in. Tare wt., 2,917 lb. A.U.W., 4,370 lb. Max. speed, 148 m.p.h.

Vickers Type 216 Vildebeest VII

Similar to Type 209 Vildebeest III but fitted with one 595 h.p. Hispano-Suiza 12Lbr. Two British civil aircraft only: demonstrator G-ABGE flown at Woolston 10.31 with twin float undercarriage, and later with wheeled undercarriage as O-3, C. of A. reissued 22.3.32, sold to Spanish Ministry of Marine, ferried to Seville as EC-W11 by H. W. R. Banting 24–27.3.32; markings G-ABJK reserved 10.3.31, but not used, for the second prototype (flown as O-1 with 525 h.p. Panther IIA) in revised form as Type 217. Span, 49 ft. 0 in. Length, 40 ft. 0 in. Tare wt., 4,702 lb. A.U.W., 8,500 lb. Max. speed, 155 m.p.h. Cruise, 106 m.p.h.

Vickers Type 440 Wellington T.Mk.10

Navigation trainer of fabric-covered, geodetic construction designed by B. N. Wallis, and powered by two 1,650 h.p. Bristol Hercules 16. One British civil aircraft only: G-ALUH, an R.A.F. aircraft RP468, fitted at Langley 1949 with a tail boom radar device and allotted civil status for test flights to the Norwegian coast. C. of A. 22.7.49, called at Ringway 8.9.49, returned to the R.A.F. 10.49 as RP468. Span, 86 ft. 2 in. Length, 60 ft. 10 in.

Vickers Type 252 Vildebeest XI

Modified Vildebeest II aircraft with one 660 h.p. Bristol Pegasus IIIM3 to Specifications S9/30 and M1/30 for entry in the Air Ministry TSR competition. First flown at Brooklands 1933 as O-7, registered 5.10.34 to Vickers Ltd. as G-ACYV, c/n 1, for demonstration purposes. Scrapped in 1938. Span, 49 ft. 0 in. Length, 38 ft. 6 in. Tare wt., 4,229 lb. A.U.W., 8,100 lb. Max. speed, 143 m.p.h.

Vickers Type 456 Warwick I

Long range transport of fabric-covered, geodetic construction, powered by two 1,850 h.p. Pratt & Whitney Double Wasp R-2800-S1A4-G, designed by B. N. Wallis and built at Weybridge 1942. Fourteen British civil aircraft only: G-AGEX–'FK, R.A.F. aircraft BV243–BV256, diverted 11.42 for wartime use by British Overseas Airways Corporation on routes to North Africa and the Mediterranean. All transferred to No. 167 Sqn., Holmesley South 8.43. Span, 96 ft. 8½ in. Length, 70 ft. 9 in. A.U.W., 45,000 lb. Max. speed, 260 m.p.h. Cruise, 180 m.p.h.

(*W. K. Kilsby*)

Vickers-Supermarine Type 236 Walrus

Three seat amphibian with fabric-covered mainplanes and metal hull (Supermarine-built Mk.I) or wooden hull (Saunders-Roe built Mk.II), designed by R. J. Mitchell and powered by one 775 h.p. Bristol Pegasus VI. Seventeen war surplus aircraft converted, or earmarked for conversion for civil use (see Appendix E). None saw real service except G-AHFL-'FO, three of which spotted for whales aboard the S.S. *Balaena* in the Antarctic 1947. G-AHFN, piloted by John Grierson, won the Folkestone Trophy at 121 m.p.h. at Lympne 31.8.46. Span, 45 ft. 10 in. Length, 37 ft. 7 in. Tare wt., 4,900 lb. A.U.W., 7,200 lb. Max. speed, 135 m.p.h. Cruise, 95 m.p.h.

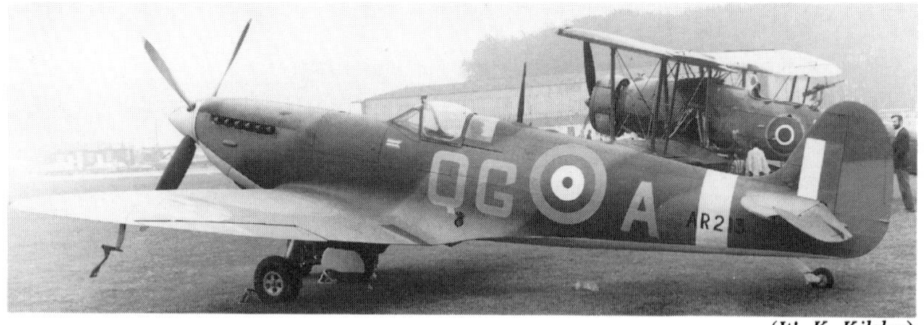

(*W. K. Kilsby*)

Vickers-Supermarine Type 300 Spitfire IB

Single seat fighter of all-metal, monocoque construction, designed by R. J. Mitchell, armed with four machine guns and two cannon, powered by one 1,030 h.p. Rolls-Royce Merlin II, 1,566 built for the R.A.F. 1937–39. Civil marks G-AIST reserved 25.10.46 for one aircraft, AR213, by Grp. Capt. (later Air Commodore) A. H. Wheeler. Stored at Old Warden until made airworthy as AR213 in 1968 for the film 'Battle of Britain'. Based at Booker in 1972. Span, 36 ft. 10 in. Length, 29 ft. 11 in. A.U.W., 5,820 lb. Max. speed, 355 m.p.h.

(*E. J. Riding*)

Vickers-Supermarine Type 309 Sea Otter

Four seat amphibian with metal hull, powered by one 855 h.p. Bristol Mercury 30, built at Cowes by Saunders-Roe Ltd. 1943–46. Twenty-four surplus aircraft converted, or earmarked for conversion, for civil use (see Appendix E). One aircraft only: G-AIDM illustrated, converted by Vickers-Armstrongs Ltd. at Eastleigh 1947, to special civil standard as Type 503. Span, 46 ft. 0 in. Length, 39 ft. 5 in. Tare wt., 6,805 lb. A.U.W., 10,000 lb. Max. speed, 150 m.p.h. Cruise, 100 m.p.h.

(*E. J. Riding*)

Vickers-Supermarine Type 329 Spitfire II

Modified Spitfire I with 1,175 h.p. Rolls-Royce Merlin XII built at the Castle Bromwich Aeroplane Factory from 6.40. Two British civil examples only: Mk.IIB G-AHZI 'Josephine', c/n CBAF.960, P8727, fitted with 1,440 h.p. Merlin 45 at Cambridge for M. L. Bramson, C. of A. 22.10.46, crashed on take-off from Kastrup, Copenhagen 15.4.47; Mk.IIA G-AWIJ, CBAF.14, P7350, registered 25.4.68 to Spitfire Productions Ltd. for flying in the film 'Battle of Britain', returned to the Coltishall Historic Aircraft Flight 1969 as P7350. Span, 36 ft. 10 in. Length, 29 ft. 11 in. A.U.W., 6,527 lb. Max. speed, 357 m.p.h.

(*A. J. Jackson*)

Vickers-Supermarine Type 349 Spitfire VB

Modified Spitfire IIB with one 1,440 h.p. Rolls-Royce Merlin 45M. Two British civil aircraft only: G-AISU, c/n CBAF.1061, formerly AB910, built 1942, C. of A. at White Waltham 17.10.47 for A. H. Wheeler, fitted Merlin 55M at Eastleigh 5.50, flown by Geoffrey Quill as AB910/QJ:J until presented to Coltishall Historic Aircraft Flight 15.9.65; G-AWII, formerly AR501, registered 25.4.68 to Spitfire Productions Ltd. for flying in film 'Battle of Britain', based at Thurleigh for Shuttleworth Trust 1972. Span, 36 ft. 10 in. Length, 29 ft. 11 in. A.U.W., 6,785 lb. Max. speed, 374 m.p.h.

(*Tony Leigh*)

Vickers-Supermarine Type 361 Spitfire IX

Development of the Spitfire V with progressively more powerful Merlin engines in production from 1944. Three aircraft powered by 1,720 h.p. Merlin 76 engines repurchased from COGEA, Brussels, received British civil status 1963–66 as G-ASJV, 'SD and G-AVDJ, the first flown extensively as a private aircraft by T. A. Davies, Elstree, and all three flew in the film 'Battle of Britain' in 1968. See Appendix E. Span, 36 ft. 10 in. Length, 31 ft. 1 in. A.U.W., 9,500 lb. Max. speed, 408 m.p.h.

(*W. L. Lewis*)

Vickers-Supermarine Type 379 Spitfire 14

High-altitude fighter developed from the Spitfire F.Mk.VIII, powered by one 2,050 h.p. Rolls-Royce Griffon 65. One civil aircraft only: G-ALGT, c/n 6S/432263, formerly RM689, built by the Supermarine Division of Vickers-Armstrongs Ltd. at Eastleigh 1944. Civilianised by Rolls-Royce Ltd. for use at Hucknall as an engine test vehicle, C. of A. 8.6.50. Flown in film 'Battle of Britain' in 1968. Based at Castle Donington in 1973. Span, 36 ft. 10 in. Length, 32 ft. 8 in. A.U.W., 8,500 lb. Max. speed, 448 m.p.h.

(*Richard Riding*)

Vickers-Supermarine Spitfire Trainers

Two seat trainer conversions of the Spitfire VIII and IX, powered by the 1,720 h.p. Rolls-Royce Merlin 66. Prototype Type 502 Trainer 8 first flown as N 32, later became G-AIDN; and one other, G-AKBD, was contemplated in 1947. One Type 509 Trainer 9 ferried to Egyptian Air Force 3.50 as G-ALJM, and six serialled 158–163 to the Irish Air Corps, three of which, 158, 159 and 163, returned to England for film purposes 1963–68 as G-ASOZ, G-AVAV and G-AWGB respectively. See Appendix E. Span, 36 ft. 10 in. Length, 31 ft. $4\frac{1}{2}$ in. A.U.W., 7,300 lb. Max. speed, 386 m.p.h.

Westland Wapiti V

Two seat Army Co-operation aircraft of fabric-covered, metal construction powered by one 550 h.p. Armstrong Siddeley Panther II, built at Yeovil 1929. Two civil aircraft only: G-AAWA, c/n WA.1822, C. of A. 30.10.30, demonstrated in Argentina and Uruguay by H. J. Penrose 1931, also on floats; modified to Westland PV-6 prototype P-6 and ultimately to Wallace; VR-HAC, c/n WA.2150, C. of A. 30.10.30, to Far East Aviation Co. Ltd. for sale in China. Span, 46 ft. 5 in. Length, 34 ft. 2 in. Tare wt., 3,200 lb. A.U.W., 4,950 lb. Max. speed, 139 m.p.h.

Westland Wallace

The prototype Wapiti V G-AAWA further modified in 1932 with rear cabin and 525 h.p. Bristol Pegasus I.S3, re-registered G-ACBR, c/n WA.1822, C. of A. 10.2.33, taken to India by the Houston Everest Flight, flown over Mt. Everest by Flt. Lt. D. F. McIntyre, 3.4.33. Reconverted to standard Wallace and returned to the R.A.F. 12.33 as K3488. One other civil Wallace only: G-ACJU, c/n WA.2302E, C. of A. 21.11.33, to the R.A.F. 6.35 as K5116. Span, 46 ft. 5 in. Length, 34 ft. 2 in. Tare wt., 3,840 lb. A.U.W., 5,750 lb. Max. speed, 158 m.p.h. Cruise, 135 m.p.h.

(*Flight 12603*)

Westland PV-3

Carrier-borne torpedoplane powered by one 575 h.p. Bristol Jupiter XFA first flown as P-3 by L. C. Paget in 1931. One aircraft only: c/n WA.2419, remodelled with rear cabin and 525 h.p. Bristol Pegasus I.S3 as G-ACAZ for the Houston Everest Flight. Test flown at Yeovil to 35,000 ft. by H. J. Penrose 25.1.33, C. of A. 31.1.33, flew over Everest piloted by Lord Clydesdale 3.4.33, exhibited at Selfridges, London 7.33, transferred to Bristols 12.33 as engine test bed K4048. Span, 46 ft. 6 in. Length, 34 ft. 2 in. Tare wt., 3,580 lb. A.U.W., 4,870 lb.

(*Westland Aircraft Works*)

Westland Whirlwind

All-metal, single seat fighter powered by two 885 h.p. Rolls-Royce Peregrine I, 112 built at Yeovil for the R.A.F. 1940–42. One civil aircraft only: G-AGOI, formerly P7048, civilianised at Yeovil by Westland Aircraft Ltd. 1945–46, C. of A. 23.10.46, dismantled at Yeovil 5.47. Span, 45 ft. 0 in. Length, 32 ft. 9 in. Tare wt., 7,840 lb. A.U.W., 10,270 lb. Max. speed, 360 m.p.h.

APPENDIX C

Foreign and Commonwealth Types

This section of the book describes all aircraft of foreign or Commonwealth design and construction flown in British civil markings since the inception of the registration system in 1919 and should be read in conjunction with Appendix E.

The introductory notes to Appendix A apply equally to this section.

(*Flight 13024*)

Heinkel He 64C

Two seater powered by one 120 h.p. de Havilland Gipsy III built by Ernst Heinkel Flugzeugwerke at Warnemünde, Germany in 1932. One British registered aircraft only: G-ACBS, c/n 47, formerly D-2305, imported by the Air Council 12.32 for slot and flap research by Handley Page Ltd. Transferred to the R.A.E., Farnborough 7.33 as K3596; restored 9.35 to Flt. Lt. B. Paddon, Brooklands; C. of A. 6.1.36. Flown to Southern Rhodesia by A. H. Elton 1.37 on delivery to H. Perrem and re-registered VP-YBI. Scrapped 1952. Span, 32 ft. 2 in. Length, 27 ft. 4 in. Tare wt., 1,120 lb. A.U.W., 1,783 lb. Max. speed, 146 m.p.h. Min. speed, 39 m.p.h.

(*Rolls-Royce Ltd.*)

Heinkel He 70G

Transport for two crew and four passengers, fitted with retractable undercarriage, built at Warnemünde 1935. One British aircraft only: G-ADZF, c/n 1692, formerly D-UBOF, built to the order of Rolls-Royce Ltd. for Kestrel engine development. Delivered Rostock–Hucknall 27.3.36 with Kestrel V installed, C. of A. 6.4.36. Flown at R.Ae.S. Garden Party, Heathrow 10.5.36. Later fitted with 745 h.p. Kestrel XVI; flown 10.38 with 885 h.p. Peregrine engine which gave a top speed of 300 m.p.h. Scrapped in 1944. Span, 48 ft. 6½ in. Length, 37 ft. 9 in. Tare wt., 5,291 lb. A.U.W., 7,700 lb.

(*John Goring*)

Heinkel He 111H (C.A.S.A. 2-111)

German bomber of the 1939–45 war licence-built in Spain by Construcciones Aeronauticas S.A. for the Spanish Air Force, many of the 200 produced having two 1,600 h.p. Rolls-Royce Merlin 500s. Two aircraft with these engines, B2-177 (c/n 025) and B2-157 (c/n 049) registered to Spitfire Production Ltd. as G-AWHA and 'HB (illustrated) for delivery Madrid–Duxford via Jersey 21.5.68. After extensive flying in the film 'Battle of Britain', both stored at West Malling until 'HA sold in the U.S.A. 8.70 and 'HB to the Southend Historic Aircraft Museum 3.72. Span, 74 ft. 3 in. Length, 54 ft. 6 in. A.U.W., 30,865 lb. Max. speed, 260 m.p.h.

(*Richard Riding*)

Helio H-395 Super Courier

Four/five seat STOL monoplane with full-span leading edge slots and extensive trailing edge flaps powered by (H-391 Courier) one 260 h.p. Lycoming GO-435-C2B2 or (H-395 Super Courier) one 295 h.p. Lycoming GO-480-G1D6. Built by the Helio Aircraft Corporation at Norwood, Mass., U.S.A. from 1958. One Courier G-APXH and four Super Couriers G-ARLD, 'MU, G-ATGM and G-BAGT imported 1959–72. Span, 39 ft. 0 in. Length, 30 ft. 0 in. Tare wt., 2,037 lb. A.U.W., 3,000 lb. Max. speed, 162 m.p.h. Cruise, 145 m.p.h. Range, 842 miles.

(*Richard Riding*)

Hiller 360 Series UH-12A and Variants

Three seater designed by Stanley Hiller Jnr. and built by United Helicopters Inc. at Palo Alto, California from 1958. Three variants British registered in some numbers for crop spraying in the U.K., the Near East, Central America and the West Indies; also for pilot training by Air Service Training Ltd., Hamble and by Bristow Helicopters Ltd. at Middle Wallop. (Ser. UH-12A) 178 h.p. Franklin 6V4-178-B33; (Ser. UH-12B and UH-12C) 200 h.p. Franklin 6V4-200-C33; (Ser. UH-12E) 305 h.p. Lycoming VO-540-C2A. Rotor diameter, 35 ft. 0 in. Length, 26 ft. 6 in. Tare wt., 1,628 lb. A.U.W., (UH-12A) 2,400 lb. (UH-12B and C) 2,500 lb. Max. speed, 84 m.p.h. Cruise, 76 m.p.h.

(*Aviation Photo News*)

Hiller 360 Series UH-12E-4

Stretched version of the Hiller 360 Series UH-12E with cabin lengthened by 25 in. to accommodate a fourth occupant and powered by one 305 h.p. Lycoming VO-540-B2D. Two British registered examples only: G-ASAZ, c/n 2070, formerly N5372V, C. of A. 30.7.62, operated by Bouley Investments Ltd., Guernsey in 1972; G-ATDW, c/n 2030, formerly N5350V and VP-YXR, C. of A. 7.8.65, to New Zealand 8.68 as ZK-HCQ. Rotor diameter, 35 ft. $4\frac{3}{4}$ in. Length, 29 ft. 10 in. Tare wt., 1,813 lb. A.U.W., 2,800 lb. Max. speed, 96 m.p.h. Cruise, 90 m.p.h. Range, 225 miles.

(*A. J. Jackson*)

Hirtenberg H.S.9A

Two seater powered by one 120 h.p. de Havilland Gipsy Major, built by the Hirtenberger Patronen Zündhutchen und Metallwarenfabrik A.G. at Hirtenberg, Austria. One British aircraft only, c/n 001, built for J. H. Davies 7.37 as OE-DJH. Flew to England as D-EDJH 7.39, registered G-AGAK, C. of A. 22.11.39. Stored at Filton until overhauled at Gatwick 10.46. Flown privately by J. H. Davis, sold to D. D. Budworth at Boxted and named 'Zamiel' 9.50, to A. J. Stocks 8.54, J. E. Coxon 11.55 and C. H. Cosmelli, Denham, 4.56. Crashed at Butser Hill, Petersfield, Hants, 15.2.58. Span, 36 ft. 0 in. Length, 26 ft. 5 in. Tare wt., 1,254 lb. A.U.W., 2,090 lb. Max. speed, 118 m.p.h. Cruise, 102 m.p.h.

(*A. J. Jackson*)

Hughes 269A and Variants

Two seat light helicopter (also known as Model 200), one 180 h.p. Lycoming HO-360-A1A, built by the Hughes Tool Co., at Culver City, California from 1961. Externally similar three seat 269B (Model 300), 180 h.p. Lycoming HIO-360-A1A, introduced 1965 and 269C (Model 300C), 190 h.p. Lycoming HIO-360-D1A, in 1970. Twenty British registered by 1973. Rotor diameter, 25 ft. 3½ in. Length, 21 ft. 10¾ in. A.U.W. (269A), 1,600 lb. (269B), 1,670 lb. (269C), 1,900 lb. Max. speed, 86 m.p.h. Cruise, 66 m.p.h. Range, 200 miles.

(*Tony Leigh*)

Hughes 369HE and 369HS

Five seat transport helicopter (also known as Model 500), powered by one 250 h.p. Allison 250-C18A turbine engine, in production by Hughes at Culver City from 1966. Hughes 369HE with executive interior and operating at 2,400 lb. A.U.W., identical externally with Hughes 369HS convertible passenger/freight version, A.U.W. of 2,550 lb. One 369HE and four 369HS registered in Britain by 1972. Rotor diameter, 26 ft. 4 in. Length, 30 ft. 2½ in. Max. speed, 150 m.p.h. Cruise, 125 m.p.h. Range, 485 miles.

(*Air Pictorial*)

Jodel D.9 Bébé

Single seat ultra light of wooden construction designed by MM. Joly and Delemontez, who formed the Société des Avions Jodel at Dijon, France, in 1948 to supply kits, materials and plans to amateur constructors. Eight British-built 1966–72 are listed in Appendix E. One French-built example, D.92 F-PHFC, c/n 59, was registered 13.11.72 as G-BAGF. Power plants were either the 1,200 cc. or 1,500 cc. converted Volkswagen engines. Span, 22 ft. 11 in. Length, 17 ft. 10½ in. Tare wt., 396 lb. A.U.W., 705 lb. Cruise, 85 m.p.h. Range, 250 miles.

(*Tony Leigh*)

Jodel D.11 Club and D.112

Two seat version of the D.9 introduced in 1950. Four aircraft with 90 h.p. Continental C90 engines built in Britain 1969–72. The D.112 version, 65 h.p. Continental A65-8F, was factory-built by Wassmer Aviation at Issoire, France, and imported in small numbers from 1961. Two, G-ATJN and G-AXFN, with 90 h.p. Continental C90-12F and imported 1965 and 1970, were factory-built by M. Dumois at Chateau Thierry, France, and known as D.119s. Span, 26 ft. 10 in. Length, 20 ft. 10 in. Tare wt., 635 lb. A.U.W., (D.11) 1,375 lb. (D.112) 1,166 lb. (D.119) 1,360 lb. Cruise, 105 m.p.h. Range, 370 miles.

(*Tony Leigh*)

Jodel D.117 Grand Tourisme

Two seat cabin monoplane of wooden construction, developed from the D.112 and powered by one 90 h.p. Continental C90-14F. Built in quantity by the Société Aéronautique Normande (S.A.N.) at Bernay, France, the first exported to Britain, G-APOZ, c/n 846, C. of A. 1.10.58, being ferried to Croydon by Norman Jones 4.10.58. More than 30 secondhand examples imported 1961–72 are listed in Appendix E. Span, 26 ft. 10 in. Length, 20 ft. 10 in. Tare wt., 808 lb. A.U.W., 1,360 lb. Max. speed, 130 m.p.h. Cruise, 120 m.p.h. Range, 600 miles.

(*Richard Riding*)

Jodel D.120 Paris-Nice

De luxe version of the Jodel D.112 trainer/tourer fitted with the more powerful 95 h.p. Continental C90-12F, developed, built and marketed by Wassmer Aviation, Issoire, France. Used specimens, including three improved D.120As with air brakes, imported in small numbers 1964–71 as well as one new D.120A aircraft, G-AVLY, by Altair Aviation & General Trading Co. Ltd., Cambridge, 1968. Span, 27 ft. 0 in. Length, 20 ft. 10 in. Tare wt., 825 lb. A.U.W., 1,430 lb. Cruise, 118 m.p.h. Range, 620 miles.

(*A. J. Jackson*)

Jodel D.140 Mousquetaire

Four/five seat tourer, with 180 h.p. Lycoming O-360-A2A and sharp pointed rudder, built by the Société Aéronautique Normande (S.A.N.) at Bernay, France from 1958. Imported in small numbers, including improved D.140A and D.140B versions, initially by Rollason Aircraft and Engines Ltd. The D.140C Mousquetaire III of 1966 with swept fin and rudder, was followed by the D.140E Mousquetaire IV featuring an all-moving tailplane and increased wing, flap and rudder areas. One D.140C imported 1966 and one D.140E in 1968. See Appendix E. (D.140) Span, 33 ft. 6 in. Length, 25 ft. 11 in. Tare wt., 1,320 lb. A.U.W., 2,645 lb. Cruise, 140 m.p.h. Range, 800 miles.

(*Richard Riding*)

Jodel DR.1050 Ambassadeur

Wooden three seater first built as the DR.100 (90 h.p. Continental C90-14F) and the DR.105 (100 h.p. Continental O-200-A) bearing the initials of MM. Pierre Robin and Delemontez who formed the Centre Est Aéronautique (C.E.A.), Dijon in 1957. The DR.1050 production version was also built by S.A.N. In 1964 C.E.A. introduced the DR.1051 Sicile with improved canopy, cowlings and spats and 105 h.p. Potez 4E-20 or 100 h.p. Continental O-200-A. Two DR.100A, four DR-105A and nearly 50 DR.1050/1051s imported by 1972. (DR.1050) Span, 28 ft. 7½ in. Length, 21 ft. 4 in. Tare wt., 882 lb. A.U.W., 1,650 lb. Cruise, 120 m.p.h. Range 650 miles.

(*A. J. Jackson*)

Jodel DR.1050-M Excellence and DR.1051-M Sicile Record

High performance variants of the Jodel DR.1050 and DR.1051 introduced in 1965 with one-piece all-moving tailplane and swept vertical tail surfaces with orthodox fin and rudder in place of the previous horn balanced fin-less unit, were designated DR.1050-M Excellence (100 h.p. Continental O-200-A) and DR.1051-M Sicile Record (105 h.p. Potez 4E-20-B1) respectively. Six Excellence and three Sicile Record registered in Britain 1966–72. Span, 28 ft. 7½ in. Length, 21 ft. 4 in. Tare wt., 903 lb. A.U.W., 1,720 lb. Max. speed, 155 m.p.h. Cruise, 146 m.p.h. Range, 650 miles.

(*Air Portraits*)

Jodel D.150 Mascaret

Two seater with fuselage similar to the Jodel D.117, mainplane of the DR.1050 Ambassadeur, all-moving tailplane and swept fin and rudder. In production by S.A.N. at Bernay and Alpavia S.A. at Gap, France from 1963 with 100 h.p. Continental (later Rolls-Royce) O-200-A, or as the D.150A with 105 h.p. Potez 4E-20. Four aircraft, G-ASKL, 'PG, 'RT and G-AVEF, imported by Rollason Aircraft and Engines Ltd. 1963–68, as well as G-AZBI by J. M. Bisco, Staverton 1971 and G-BACL by G. R. French 1972. Span, 26 ft. 9 in. Length, 20 ft. 8 in. Tare wt., 912 lb. A.U.W., 1,588 lb. Cruise, 135 m.p.h. Range, 1050 miles.

(*P. R. March*)

Jodel DR.221 Dauphin and DR.250 Capitaine

The three seat DR.221 with 108 h.p. Lycoming O-235-C2A was introduced in 1967 and built by C. E. A., Dijon, in parallel with the high performance, four seat, DR.250 based on the DR.1051-M Sicile Record and powered by one 160 h.p. Lycoming O-320-D2A. Two DR.221s, one DR.200 pre-production aircraft, G-AYDZ, with 105 h.p. Potez 4E-20-B2, and five DR.250s were imported 1967–72. Span, 28 ft. 7½ in. Length, 22 ft. 11 in. Tare wt., 1,047 lb. A.U.W., 1,850 lb. (DR.250) 2,116 lb. Cruise, 135 m.p.h. (DR.250) 150 m.p.h. Range, 565 miles (DR.250) 680 miles.

Junkers F.13

All-metal, low wing transport for four cabin passengers and two crew in an open cockpit, powered by one 385 h.p. Junkers L.5 and built by Junkers Flugzeug und Motorenwerke A.G. at Dessau, Germany from 1919. One model F.13fe aircraft, G-EBZV, imported 1928 for Rt. Hon. F. E. Guest, Hanworth, was re-engined in 1930 with one 450 h.p. Bristol Jupiter VI. Four 1929 model F.13ge aircraft with enclosed cockpits were imported by Trost Bros. Ltd., Croydon for air taxi work 1929–30. Span, 58 ft. 3 in. Length, 31 ft. 6 in. Tare wt., 3,330 lb. A.U.W., 5,960 lb. Max. speed, 123 m.p.h. Cruise, 106 m.p.h.

(Flight 8305)

Junkers A.50 Junior

Two seat monoplane of all metal construction powered by one 80 h.p. Armstrong Siddeley Genet II, in production at Dessau, Germany from 1929. Two British aircraft only: G-AATH, c/n 3512, formerly D-2155, delivered Amsterdam–Croydon 21.3.30, C. of A. 26.3.30, H. R. Trost, sold in Germany via Croydon–Amsterdam 20.2.31; G-AAXB, c/n 3523, delivered Amsterdam–Heston 12.5.30, C. of A. 22.5.30, J. Parkes, crashed 6.31. Span, 32 ft. 10 in. Length, 23 ft. 6 in. Tare wt., 770 lb. A.U.W., 1,330 lb. Max. speed, 109 m.p.h. Cruise, 87 m.p.h.

(R. P. Howard)

Junkers Ju 52/3m

All-metal transport with corrugated duralumin skin, powered by three 770 h.p. B.M.W. licence-built Pratt & Whitney Hornets, in production by Junkers Flugzeug und Motorenwerke A.G., Dessau, Germany from 1932. G-AERU, 'RX and G-AFAP bought 1937–38 for British Airways Ltd. freight services; G-AGAE, war-refugee Polish aircraft abandoned at Bucharest 1939; twelve captured Ju 52/3m.g8e aircraft, G-AHBP and G-AHOC to 'OL, converted by Short Bros. & Harland Ltd. at Belfast for use on B.E.A. internal services as 'Jupiter' Class 1946–48. Span, 95 ft. 10 in. Length, 62 ft. 0 in. Tare wt., 14,326 lb. A.U.W., 23,150 lb. Cruise, 160 m.p.h. Range, 546 miles.

(John Blake)

Kensinger KF

All-metal, single seat racing monoplane similar to the Midget Mustang, powered by one 90 h.p. Continental C85-12F, completed by Ned Kensinger at Fort Worth, Texas, U.S.A. in 1962. One aircraft only: N23S, c/n 2, imported as G-ASSV, A. to F. 9.6.65, P. G. Bannister, Halfpenny Green. Flown in the National Air Races at Shoreham 11.6.65. Re-engined with 100 h.p. Continental C90 and flown in the National Air Races 2.9.68 at Halfpenny Green where it was destroyed in a crash 2.7.69 after a flying life of some 50 hours. Span, 18 ft. 6 in. Length, 16 ft. 5 in. A.U.W., 997 lb. Max. speed, 184 m.p.h.

(R. Nerou)

Klemm L25

Two seater of plywood-covered wooden construction in production by Leichtflugzeugbau Klemm GmbH at Böblingen, Germany from 1927. One L25, G-AAFV (30 h.p. Daimler), seven L25-Is (40 h.p. Salmson A.D.9) and four L25a-Is (horn balanced rudders), imported by S. T. Lea Ltd., Croydon 1929–31. Three later models, G-ABRG and 'TE (70 h.p. Hirth HM60) and G-ABZO (75 h.p. Pobjoy R) imported by A. B. Gibbons, Heston 1931–32. Span, 42 ft. 7½ in. Length, 24 ft. 7 in. Tare wt., 627 lb. A.U.W., 1,364 lb. Cruise, 87 m.p.h. Range, 600 miles.

(R. P. Howard)

Klemm L26

Larger and heavier version of the Klemm L25, in production at Böblingen from 1930. Six aircraft imported for private owners 1930–31 comprised two L26a-II, G-AAVS and G-ABFS (80 h.p. Siemens & Halske Sh13), three L26a-III, G-ABBU, 'CI and 'OJ (95 h.p. A.D.C. Cirrus III); and one L26a-X, G-ABRP (120 h.p. de Havilland Gipsy III). Span, 42 ft. 7½ in. Length, 24 ft. 7½ in. Tare wt., 924 lb. A.U.W., 1,544 lb. Max. speed, 109 m.p.h.

(Aeroplane)

Klemm L27

Three seat version of the Klemm L26 with enlarged front cockpit for two passengers. Four aircraft only imported 1930–31: Two L27a-III, G-AAWW and G-ABJX (95 h.p. A.D.C. Cirrus III); one L27a-VIII, G-ABOP (105 h.p. Cirrus Hermes IIB) and one L27a-IX G-ABOR (120 h.p. de Havilland Gipsy III). Data similar to L26 except A.U.W. 1,584 lb.

(*R. P. Howard*)

Klemm L32

Three seat cabin monoplane of wooden construction built at Böblingen 1932–34. Two British examples only: G-ACLH (c/n 401), L32-X, C. of A. 17.11.33, A. B. Gibbons, Heston (120 h.p. D.H. Gipsy III, formerly the 135 h.p. Argus As 8 powered 1932 Rundflug machine CH-360), to Ireland 11.36 as EI-ABF; G-ACYU (402), L32-V, (the Argus engined Klemm demonstrator D-2299 delivered Berck–Heston 21.7.32 by Lord Carberry), C. of A. 19.11.34, Aircraft Exchange & Mart Ltd., Hanworth, N. B. Littlejohn, Eastleigh 3.35, to Australia 12.35 as VH-UVE, burned out at Archerfield, Brisbane 28.6.39. Span, 39 ft. 4 in. Length, 23 ft. 7 in. Tare wt., 1,320 lb. A.U.W., 2,090 lb. Cruise, 111 m.p.h. Range, 465 miles.

(*A. J. Jackson*)

KZ-VII Lark

Four seat, high-wing monoplane powered by one 125 h.p. Continental C-125-2, in production at Copenhagen by Skandinavisk Aero Industri A.S. from 1946. Two British aircraft only, imported by R. K. Dundas Ltd.: G-AJHM, c/n 148, formerly OY-AAN, C. of A. 21.7.47, sold to G. J. Dawson and later to the Guernsey Salvage Co. Ltd., to France 7.49 as F-BFXA: G-AJZV, c/n 151, C. of A. 10.9.47, crashed 4 miles N.W. of Manston, Kent 20.12.47. Span, 31 ft. 6 in. Length, 21 ft. 6 in. Tare wt., 1,022 lb. A.U.W., 1,911 lb. Max. speed, 125 m.p.h. Cruise, 115 m.p.h.

(*Air Portraits*)

KZ-VIII

Single seat aerobatic aircraft of wooden construction powered by one 145 h.p. de Havilland Gipsy Major 8, designed by Björn Andreasson and built by S.A.I. at Copenhagen. First flown at Kastrup 14.11.49 and delivered to the Sylvest Jensen Air Circus as OY-ACB, c/n 202, in 1950; sold as HB-EPB 1957 to Swiss aerobatic champion Arnold Wagner who delivered it Zürich–Elmdon 23.12.69 for British owner R. Mitchell. Appropriately re-registered 13.10.70 as G-AYKZ. The only other KZ-VIII built was sold in Germany 1949 as D-EBIZ. Span, 23 ft. 7 in. Length, 18 ft. $7\frac{1}{2}$ in. Tare wt., 897 lb. A.U.W., 1,268 lb. Max. speed, 171 m.p.h. Range, 360 miles.

(*Richard Riding*)

Le Vier Cosmic Wind

All-metal, single seat racer built 1947–48 by Lockheed engineers led by test pilot Tony Le Vier. Two of the three built initially were registered later in Britain: G-ARUL, c/n 103, N22C 'Ballerina', 85 h.p. Continental C85, A. to F. 18.4.62, N. H. Jones (Tiger Club), Redhill, crashed at Halfpenny Green 29.8.66, rebuilt by P. G. Bannister 1969–72 as PFA.1311; G-AYRJ, c/n 101, NX67888 later N20C 'Little Toni', 100 h.p. Continental O-200-A and modified controls, f/f at Blackbushe 28.1.71, C. of A. 20.5.71, R. McCowen, Redhill. A fourth, built in the 1960s, was completed as G-BAER, c/n PFA.1571, by R. Voice at Redhill 1973. Span, 18 ft. $11\frac{1}{4}$ in. Length, 16 ft. $8\frac{1}{2}$ in. Tare wt., 540 lb. A.U.W., 850 lb. Max. speed, 185 m.p.h.

(*John Strangward*)

Leopoldoff L.7 Colibri

Two seat touring biplane designed by MM. Leopoldoff and Levavasseur and first flown with 35 h.p. Anzani in 1933. Built in small numbers pre-1939 and post-1945 with various engines, the last to be constructed, F-PCZX (c/n 125), with 65 h.p. Continental A65-8S and designated L.7, ferried Le Touquet–Southend–Purleigh strip, Hazeleigh Grange, Essex 8.7.70 for W. H. Cole and G. A. Mason, was re-registered G-AYKS. Expected to fly in British marks in 1974. Span, 29 ft. 4 in. Length, 19 ft. 5 in. Tare wt., 660 lb. A.U.W., 1,145 lb. Cruise, 96 m.p.h. Range, 280 miles.

(*John Goring*)

LET Z-37 Čmelák (Bumble Bee)

Single seat agricultural aircraft of fabric-covered metal construction powered by one 310 h.p. M462-RF Russian-designed, licence-built radial, in production by LET Národní Podnik (LET National Corporation) at Kunovice, Czechoslovakia, from 1965. Fitted with 25 cu. ft. chemical hopper and spray gear. One British registered aircraft only: G-AVZB, c/n 0408, C. of A. 4.2.68, A.D.S. (Aerial) Ltd., Southend. Span, 40 ft. $1\frac{1}{4}$ in. Length, 28 ft. $0\frac{1}{2}$ in. Tare wt., 2,140 lb. A.U.W., 4,080 lb. Cruise, 115 m.p.h.

(*Flight 9774*)

Lockheed Model DL-1A Vega

Transport for six passengers, powered by one Pratt & Whitney Wasp SC1, built at Los Angeles by Lockheed Aircraft Inc. 1929. One British aircraft only: G-ABFE, c/n 155, formerly NC372E, re-registered G-ABGK using initials of owner Glen Kidston, C. of A. 3.1.31. Left Netheravon 31.3.31 and lowered the Cape record to 6 days 9 hours, piloted by O. Cathcart Jones and owner. Sold to H. C. Miller 8.34, named 'Puck', flown in MacRobertson Race by D. C. T. Bennett, crash landed at Aleppo 21.10.34. Shipped to Australia, rebuilt 1936 as VH-UVK. Span, 41 ft. 0 in. Length, 27 ft. 6 in. Tare wt., 2,595 lb. A.U.W., 4,500 lb. Max. speed, 178 m.p.h. Cruise, 153 m.p.h.

Lockheed Model 8D Altair

Two seat, long distance monoplane fitted with retractable undercarriage and one 550 h.p. Pratt & Whitney Wasp S1D1. One British aircraft only: c/n 152, built 1934 for Sir Charles Kingsford Smith, test flown as X118W 'Anzac' and shipped to Australia 27.6.34. Became VH-USB 'Lady Southern Cross', made first eastbound trans-Pacific flight, Brisbane–San Francisco 20.10.34–4.11.34. Shipped to U.K., taken ashore by barge at Allhallows, Kent, and flown to Croydon 8.10.35, registered G-ADUS, C. of A. 18.10.35, for attempt on England–Australia record. Left Croydon 6.11.35, with J. T. Pethyridge navigating, lost in Bay of Bengal 8.11.35, wreckage found 20 years later. Span, 42 ft. 9½ in. Length, 27 ft. 10 in. Tare wt., 3,297 lb. A.U.W., 5,800 lb. Max. speed, 230 m.p.h. Cruise, 205 m.p.h.

(*Flight 14018S*)

Lockheed Model 10A Electra

All-metal transport for 10 passengers and 2 crew, with two 450 h.p. Pratt & Whitney Wasp Junior R-985-SB2 radials, produced by Lockheed at Burbank, California from 1934. Five aircraft, G-AEPN to 'PR and 'SY, imported by British Airways Ltd., Croydon 1937 followed by G-AFCS and 'EB in 1938. Five belonging to the Polish airline LOT, which escaped to Bucharest when the Germans invaded 1.9.39, were registered G-AGAF to 'AJ but the Germans seized them before they could be flown to the Imperial Airways base, Cairo. Span, 55 ft. 0 in. Length, 38 ft. 7 in. Tare wt., 6,325 lb. A.U.W., 10,500 lb. Cruise, 185 m.p.h. Range, 810 miles.

(*A. J. Jackson*)

Lockheed Model 12A

All-metal executive transport for 6 passengers and 2 crew, powered by two 450 h.p. Pratt & Whitney Wasp Junior R-985-SB2 radials, in production at Burbank from 1936. Eight aircraft (including G-AFTL used by F. S. Cotton to photograph Wilhelmshaven 16.9.39) imported by the Aeronautical Research & Sales Corporation of Heston, and others 1938–39; three R.A.F. and two American examples (including G-AGTL used for 11 years by F. S. Cotton for radio aid development) registered in Britain 1946–47. Span, 49 ft. 6 in. Length, 36 ft. 4 in. Tare wt., 6,040 lb. A.U.W., 9,200 lb. Max. speed, 225 m.p.h. Cruise, 212 m.p.h.

Lockheed Model 14 and Model 414 Hudson

Fourteen passenger transport introduced 1937. Nine Model 14-WF62 (two 760 h.p. Wright Cyclone GR-1820-F62) operated by British Airways Ltd. 1938–39; four Polish registered Model 14-H (two 750 h.p. Pratt & Whitney Hornet R-1690-S1E2-G) which escaped to Bucharest 9.39, re-registered to Imperial Airways Ltd. as G-AFZZ to G-AGAC; two others which escaped to Perth were registered G-AGAV and 'BG. One R.A.F. Model 414 Hudson 1 (two 1,200 h.p. Cyclone GR-1820-G205A) allocated to F. S. Cotton 5.40 as G-AGAR; five others released to B.O.A.C. 1941–42; one Model 14-08 (two 1,200 h.p. Twin Wasp R-1830-S1C3-G) registered to R. A. Brand and Co. Ltd., Croydon 1948 as G-AKPD. Span, 65 ft. 6 in. Length, 44 ft. 4 in. Tare wt., 10,300 lb. A.U.W., 17,500 lb. Cruise, 230 m.p.h. Range, 2,100 miles.

Lockheed Model 18 Lodestar

Stretched version of the Lockheed 14 for 14 passengers and 3 crew, in production at Burbank from 1939. Nine Model 18-07 (two 875 h.p. Pratt & Whitney Hornet R-1690-S1E3-G), and 14 Lend-Lease Model 18-08 (two Twin Wasp R-1830-S1C3-G), used on B.O.A.C. trans-Africa routes from 1941; two Norwegian-owned aircraft were based at Leuchars as G-AGDD and 'DE. Fourteen Lend-Lease Model 18-56 (two 1,200 h.p. Wright Cyclone GR-1820-G202A) operated by B.O.A.C. 1944–48. Span, 65 ft. 6 in. Length, 49 ft. 10 in. Tare wt., 11,790 lb. A.U.W., 17,500 lb. Max. speed, 272 m.p.h. Cruise, 248 m.p.h. Range, 1,890 miles.

(*Flight F65 43/7*)

Lockheed 049E and 749A Constellation

Long range transport for 43 passengers and 7 crew, powered by four 2,200 h.p. Wright Duplex Cyclone R-3350-C18-BA1 radials, produced at Burbank from 1943. Eight used on B.O.A.C. transatlantic services from 1948, four by Euravia Ltd. from 1962. Seventeen 749A developed versions acquired by B.O.A.C. 1948–55, five later operated by Skyways Ltd. (three with double freight door modifications). Three, including G-ALAL (illustrated), and four former South African Airways aircraft, were acquired by Ace Freighters Ltd., Gatwick 1964. (749A): Span, 123 ft. 0 in. Length, 95 ft. 1 in. Tare wt., 60,140 lb. A.U.W., 107,000 lb. Cruise, 298 m.p.h. Range, 3,000 miles.

Lockheed L.1011 Tristar

Large capacity, wide bodied, medium range transport for a maximum of 400 passengers in 10 abreast seating, powered by three 42,000 lb. s.t. Rolls-Royce RB.211 22B three spool turbofans, built by the Lockheed Aircraft Corporation at Palmdale, California, U.S.A. from 1972. Two examples imported by Court Line Aviation Ltd. 1973: G-BAAA, c/n 1024, 'Halcyon Days', C. of A. 27.2.73; G-BAAB, c/n 1032, 'Halcyon Breeze', C. of A. 30.4.73. Span, 155 ft. 4 in. Length, 177 ft. 8 in. A.U.W., 430,000 lb. Cruise 405 m.p.h. Normal range, 2,970 miles.

(*John Goring*)

Maule M-4 Bee Dee

Four seat touring aircraft of fabric-covered tubular steel construction powered by one 145 h.p. Continental O-300-A in production by the Maule Aircraft Corporation at Jackson, Michigan, U.S.A., from 1963. One British registered aircraft only: G-ASPH, c/n 45, N4702T, C. of A. 3.4.64, R.W.S. and Co. (Aircraft) Ltd., Stapleford (British agents); to E. Andersen and partner, Skanderborg, Denmark 8.64 as OY-BAD. Span, 29 ft. 8 in. Length, 22 ft. 0 in. Tare wt., 1,100 lb. A.U.W., 2,100 lb. Max. speed, 157 m.p.h. Cruise, 130 m.p.h. Range, 750 miles.

(*D. A. Conway*)

McCulloch J-2

Two seat cabin gyrocopter powered by one 180 h.p. Lycoming O-360-A2D driving a pusher airscrew, designed by D. K. Jovanovich, in production by the McCulloch Aircraft Corporation at Lake Havasu, Arizona, U.S.A. from 1970. One British registered aircraft only: G-AZWZ, c/n 066, C. of A. 23.6.72, imported by C.S.E. Aviation Ltd. as N4356G, uncrated at Kidlington 5.6.72, demonstrated at the P.F.A. Flying for Fun Rally at Sywell 14–16.7.72 by M. Hudson. Rotor diameter, 26 ft. 0 in. Length, 16 ft. 0 in. Tare wt., 1,000 lb. A.U.W., 1,550 lb. Cruise, 105 m.p.h. Range, 200 miles.

McDonnell Douglas DC-10 Series 10

Large capacity, wide bodied, medium range transport for a maximum of 300 passengers in 9 abreast seating, powered by three 40,000 lb. s.t. General Electric CF6-6D two-spool turbofans, built by McDonnell Douglas Aircraft Corporation at Long Beach, California, U.S.A. First deliveries were made to U.S. airlines in 1971 and two British registered examples were imported 1972: G-AZZC, c/n 46905, 'Eastern Belle', delivered to Laker Airways (International) Ltd. at Gatwick 12.11.72; G-AZZD, c/n 46906, 'Western Belle', delivered to Laker at Gatwick 23.11.72. Span, 155 ft. 4 in. Length, 181 ft. 5 in. A.U.W., 430,000 lb. Cruise, 430 m.p.h. Normal range, 3,325 m.p.h.

(E. J. Riding)

Messerschmitt Bf 108B-1 Taifun

Four seat luxury tourer of all-metal, stressed-skin construction, fitted with retractable undercarriage and powered by one 270 h.p. Argus As 10E or As 10C3 inverted 8 cylinder engine. Four British registered aircraft only: G-AFRN and 'ZO imported 1939 (post-impressment identities entangled with the German D-IJHW seized at Croydon 3.9.39); French-built, ex Luftwaffe Nord 1000, G-AGUZ, unconverted at Gatwick 1946; G-AKZY sold abroad unconverted 1.50. Span, 34 ft. 5 in. Length, 27 ft. 2 in. Tare wt., 1,887 lb. A.U.W., 3,087 lb. Max. speed, 196 m.p.h. Cruise, 187 m.p.h.

(*P. J. Howard*)

Messerschmitt Bf 109 (Hispano HA-1112-M1L)

Modernised version of the all-metal wartime single-seat fighter, licence-built in Spain by Hispano-Aviacion S.A. from 1951, powered by one 1,400 h.p. Rolls-Royce Merlin 500 engine. Sixteen former Spanish Air Force aircraft registered 14.5.68 to Spitfire Productions Ltd. as G-AWHD to 'HP and G-AWHR to 'HT for ferrying to Duxford via Jersey and Manston to be used in the film 'Battle of Britain', after which 12 were sold to the 'Confederate Air Force', Harlingen, Texas, U.S.A. Span, 32 ft. 6½ in. Length, 29 ft. 10 in. Tare wt., 5,855 lb. A.U.W., 7,011 lb. Max. speed, 420 m.p.h

(*Air Pictorial*)

Messerschmitt Bf 109-C4 (Hispano HA-1112-M4L)

Two seat trainer version of the Messerschmitt Bf 109 with 1,400 h.p. Rolls-Royce Merlin 500, built in small numbers by Hispano-Aviacion in Spain from 1951. One British aircraft only: G-AWHC (illustrated), c/n 40/2, formerly Spanish Air Force C4X-112, registered 14.5.68 to Spitfire Productions Ltd. and flown to England for the film 'Battle of Britain'. To the 'Confederate Air Force', Harlingen, Texas, U.S.A., 2.69 as N4110G. Data similar to single seater.

(*W. K. Kilsby*)

Monocoupe 70

Tandem, two seat, cabin monoplane powered by one 55 h.p. Velie radial, built 1928 by Mono Aircraft Inc. at Moline, Illinois, U.S.A. One British aircraft only: G-AADG, c/n 194, imported 12.28 by H. G. Hamer, sold to R. W. H. Knight, Hereford 2.31, re-engined with 80 h.p. Armstrong Siddeley Genet II, C. of A. 14.7.31, flown to Guernsey and back 25–27.3.32. Last owner A. O. Humble-Smith, Maylands, 1939. Stored during 1939–45 war, broken up at Gatwick 1947. Span, 30 ft. 0 in. Length, 19 ft. 9 in. Tare wt., 700 lb. A.U.W., 1,175 lb. Max. speed, 92 m.p.h.

Monocoupe 110

Side-by-side, two seat, cabin monoplane powered by one 110 h.p. Warner Scarab, built 1930 by Mono Aircraft Inc. at Moline, Illinois, U.S.A. One British aircraft only: G-ABBR, prototype, mispainted as G-ABAR, c/n 5W40,
continued on page 402

(*N. B. Rivett*)

Mooney M.20E Mk.21 and M.20F Mk.21

Wooden four seater with one 180 h.p. Lycoming O-360, built as the M.20A Mk.21 by the Mooney Aircraft Corp. at Kerville, Texas, U.S.A. from 1957. All-metal M.20B Mk.21 with 180 h.p. Lycoming O-360-A1A introduced 1960, improved as the M.20C Mk.21 with O-360-A1A in 1961, with square windows 1967 as the M.20C Ranger, and with 200 h.p. IO-360-A1A as the M.20E Super 21 (illustrated) 1964. Executive M.20E Mk.21 with lengthened fuselage, three side windows and 200 h.p. IO-360-A1A introduced 1967. Over 20 of all marks British registered 1959–72. (M.20E): Span, 35 ft. 0 in. Length, 24 ft. 0 in. Tare wt., 1,600 lb. A.U.W., 2,575 lb. Cruise, 140 m.p.h. Range, 900 miles.

(*Tony Leigh*)

Morane-Saulnier Type N replica

Replica of the wire-braced, mid-wing Bullet fighter designed and built in France for the Royal Flying Corps and the French Army in 1913. One aircraft only: G-AWBU, c/n PPS/REP/7, built from modern materials by D. E. Bianchi of Personal Plane Services Ltd., powered by one 145 h.p. Warner Super Scarab radial and first flown at Booker in 1969. Data for original 80 h.p. Le Rhône model: Span, 27 ft. 5 in. Length, 22 ft. 7 in. A.U.W., 1,122 lb. Max. speed, 102 m.p.h. Range, 150 miles.

(Air Portraits)

Morane-Saulnier M.S.230

Tandem two-seat parasol monoplane powered by one 230 h.p. Salmson 9AB radial built in France in large numbers for military training before 1939. A few were also constructed 1948–49, one subsequently being registered in Britain: G-AVEB, c/n 1076, formerly F-BGJT, C. of A. 21.5.69, owned by Hon. P. Lindsay, Booker in 1973. Span, 35 ft. 2 in. Length, 22 ft. 9 in. Tare wt., 1,944 lb. A.U.W., 2,535 lb. Cruise, 111 m.p.h. Range, 370 miles.

(C. Wood)

Morane-Saulnier M.S.500 Criquet

German four seat Fieseler Fi 156 Storch with one 240 h.p. Argus As 10C, built by Morane-Saulnier at Puteaux, France, during and after the 1939–45 war. Two British registered aircraft only: G-AYKI, c/n 43, formerly F-BJQB, registered 2.10.70 to D. E. Bianchi but forced landed at Briare, near Paris, during delivery Nevers–Booker and was sold on the spot to an American; G-AZMH, c/n 637, formerly F-BJQG and EI-AUU, registered 20.1.72 to Hon. P. Lindsay, Booker public debut at Vintage Flying Display, Booker 24.9.72. Span, 46 ft. 9 in. Length, 31 ft. 8 in. Tare wt., 2,100 lb. A.U.W., 3,140 lb. Cruise, 85 m.p.h. Range, 435 miles.

(*Aeroplane*)

Morane-Saulnier M.S.760 Paris

All-metal four seater powered by two 880 lb. s.t. Turboméca Marboré IIC, built by Aéroplanes Morane-Saulnier at Puteaux, Seine, France 1958. One British aircraft: G-APRU, c/n 8, delivered to the College of Aeronautics at Cranfield 10.12.58 as F-WJAC. Later flown as G-36-2 and equipped as a high performance flying classroom. Flown in the London–Paris Race 7.59. Span, 33 ft. 3 in. Length, 33 ft. 0 in. Tare wt., 4,280 lb. A.U.W., 7,725 lb. Max. speed, 405 m.p.h. Cruise, 350 m.p.h.

(*Richard Riding*)

Morane-Saulnier M.S.880B and M.S.885 Rallye

The M.S.880B Rallye Club all-metal, three seat tourer (100 h.p. Continental O-200-A) and M.S.885 Super Rallye (145 h.p. Lycoming O-300-A), both with extensive high-lift devices and slow flying characteristics, were in large scale production in France by the Société d'Exploitation des Etablissements Morane-Saulnier (and later by the Sud-Aviation-controlled Gerance des Etablissements Morane-Saulnier) from 1960. Imported into Britain in considerable numbers, mainly by Air Touring Services Ltd., Biggin Hill. Data for M.S.885: Span, 31 ft. 5 in. Length, 22 ft. 9 in. Tare wt., 1,100 lb. A.U.W., 1,880 lb. Cruise, 124 m.p.h. Range, 680 miles.

(*John Goring*)

Morane-Saulnier M.S.890A Rallye Commodore Variants

The enlarged and strengthened four seat M.S.890A Rallye Commodore 145 (145 h.p. Lycoming O-300-A), M.S.892A Rallye Commodore 150 (150 h.p. Lycoming O-320-E) M.S.893A Rallye Commodore 160 (160 h p. Lycoming GO-360-A2A) and M.S.894A Rallye Minerva (220 h.p. Franklin 6A-350-C1), all externally similar, were introduced progressively from 1965. By 1972 more than 40 of all variants were in use under British registry, imported mainly by Air Touring Services Ltd., Biggin Hill. Data for M.S.894A: Span, 31 ft. 5 in. Length, 23 ft. 5¾ in. Tare wt., 1,355 lb. A.U.W., 2,425 lb. Cruise, 155 m.p.h. Range, 620 miles.

(*J. M. G. Gradidge*)

N.H.I. H-3 Kolibrie Series I

Two seat, two bladed helicopter powered by two 49·5 lb. s.t. TJ-5 tip mounted ramjets, built by N. V. Nederlandse Helicopter Industrie at Rotterdam 1958. Two British aircraft only: G-APRZ, c/n 3009, formerly PH-ACD, delivered to European Helicopters Ltd. at Ipswich for agricultural use 11.58, C. of A. 6.4.59, sold in Ecuador in 1960; PH-NIW, c/n 3011, was to have been G-APVB, same owners, but crashed at St. Andrews, Fife 4.6.59. Rotor diameter, 33 ft. 0 in. Length, 13 ft. 10½ in. Tare wt., 530 lb. A.U.W., 1,430 lb.

(*Tony Leigh*)

Nord 1002 Pingouin II

Four seat version of the retractable undercarriage Messerschmitt Bf 108 Taifun, powered by one 233 h.p. Renault 6Q 10, built by S.N.C.A. du Nord at Les Mureaux, France, for French Air Force communications from 1945. Many later released to civil operators and four were imported into Britain 1965–67 as G-ASTG, 'UA, G-ATBG and G-AVJS as listed in Appendix E. Span, 34 ft. 5 in. Length, 28 ft. 1 in. Tare wt., 1,980 lb. A.U.W., 3,270 lb. Cruise, 165 m.p.h. Range, 530 miles.

(*W. L. Lewis*)

Nord 1101 Noralpha

Production version of the four seat retractable tricycle undercarriage Messerschmitt Me 208, powered by one 233 h.p. Renault 6Q 10, built by S.N.C.A. du Nord at Les Mureaux, France, for French Air Force and civil use from 1945. Six imported into Britain 1965–67 as G-ASTN, G-ATDB, 'HH. 'HN, 'IX and 'JW as listed in Appendix E. Span, 37 ft. 8 in. Length, 28 ft. 10 in. Tare wt., 2,090 lb. A.U.W., 3,630 lb. Cruise, 172 m.p.h. Range, 745 miles.

(*N. D. Pratt*)

Nord 262A

All-metal, 26 passenger, pressurised transport powered by two 1,080 e.s.h.p. Turboméca Bastan VI B2 propeller-turbines, in production by Nord Aviation Bourges, France, from 1964. The 29th. aircraft, formerly F-BNKX, delivered to Air Ceylon 24.3.67 as 4R-ACL, was re-worked by Nord for Dan-Air Services Ltd. as G-AYFR, c/n 029, C. of A. 17.6.70, and delivered to Gatwick 1.7.70 for the company's inter-city services. Sold to Rousseau Aviation and delivered Gatwick–Dinard 22.2.72 as F-BTDQ. Span, 71 ft. 10 in. Length, 63 ft. 6 in. Tare wt. 14,390 lb. A.U.W., 23,370 lb. Cruise, 224 m.p.h. Range, 1,080 miles.

(*D. J. Calvert*)

North American AT-16 Harvard IIB

Two seat advanced trainer designed by North American Aviation Inc. in 1937 as the BC-1. Built in quantity 1939–45 including 1,500 by Noorduyn Aircraft Ltd. at Montreal, Canada, as AT-16s with 600 h.p. Pratt & Whitney R-1340-49 radials for the R.C.A.F. and R.A.F. Surplus aircraft sold to European air forces from 1946, five of which, plus one similar North American-built AT-6D, returned to Britain 1969–72 for display use. See Appendix E. Span, 42 ft. 0¼ in. Length, 29 ft. 6 in. Tare wt., 4,270 lb. A.U.W., 5,620 lb. Cruise, 170 m.p.h. Range, 870 miles.

(R. W. Cranham)

North American Mustang

A late production version of this famous 1939–45 war P-51 fighter, powered by one 1,450 h.p. Packard Merlin V-1650-7, was erected by the Commonwealth Aircraft Corporation at Melbourne for the R.A.A.F. as the CA-17 Mk.20, and later as the wholly Australian-built CA-18 Mk.21. One CA-17 Mk.20, G-ARKD, and one CA-18 Mk.21, G-ARUK, registered to racing driver Ron Flockhart 1961–62 for attempts to lower the Sydney–London record as detailed in Appendix E. Span, 37 ft. 0 in. Length, 32 ft. 3 in. Tare wt., 7,125 lb. A.U.W., 11,600 lb. Max. speed, 395 m.p.h. Max. range, 2,080 miles.

North American F-86E Sabre F.Mk.1

All-metal, single seat fighter, one 5,200 lb. s.t. General Electric J-47 GE-13 turbojet, built by Canadair Ltd., Montreal, for R.C.A.F. and R.A.F. 1952–53. One example, R.C.A.F.19477/R.A.F. XB546, c/n 19607 (illustrated), ferried Lyneham–Stansted 25.8.55 for overhaul by Aviation Traders Ltd., delivered to Italian Air Force, Naples 11.7.57, became MM.19477. Dismantled at Novara, Italy 1965, presented to H.A.P.S., Biggin Hill; registered 24.3.66 to M. D. N. Fisher and B. R. Clarkson as G-ATBF. Due to transport problems a substitute aircraft arrived. Painted in U.S.A.F. colours as FU-617, this was widely mistaken for G-ATBF. Span, 37 ft. 1 in. Length, 37 ft. 6 in. Tare wt., 10,000 lb. A.U.W., 16,500 lb. Max. speed, 670 m.p.h.

Northrop 1C Delta

Transport for eight passengers, powered by one 700 h.p. Pratt & Whitney Hornet SD, built at Los Angeles by the Northrop Corporation 1934. Third production aircraft, N13755, c/n 7, sold to A. B. Aerotransport, Stockholm 4.34 as SE-ADI. Non-starter in the Australia Race 10.34. Registered 5.37 by Mrs. Beryl Markham as G-AEXR for long distance flight. Not delivered. Went to Iraq as YI-OSF. Span, 47 ft. 9 in. Length, 33 ft. 1 in. Tare wt., 4,200 lb. A.U.W., 7,350 lb. Max. speed, 221 m.p.h. Cruise, 201 m.p.h.

Northrop 2L Gamma Commercial

Two seater of all metal, monocoque construction, built at Santa Monica, California, 1937. One British aircraft only: G-AFBT, c/n 347, imported by the Bristol Aeroplane Co. Ltd. 9.37 and flown at Filton as test bed during the early flight trials of the 1,400 h.p. Bristol Hercules, 14-cylinder, two row radial. Dismantled at Filton during the 1939–45 war. Span, 47 ft. 8 in. Length, 31 ft. $8\frac{5}{8}$ in. A.U.W., 8,315 lb. Max. speed, 270 m.p.h.

(*A. J. Jackson*)

Orlikan Meta-Sokol L-40

All-metal, four seat tourer with reversed tricycle undercarriage, powered by one 110 h.p. Letadlovy M-332SC, in production at Chocen, Czechoslovakia from 1954. Eight imported into Britain via the Omnipol sales organisation 1959–63, the first two, G-APUE and G-APVU, arriving in Czech lettering as OK-NMB and OK-NMI. See Appendix E. Span, 33 ft. 9½ in. Length, 24 ft. 9½ in. Tare wt., 1,177 lb. A.U.W., 2,095 lb. Cruise, 127 m.p.h. Range, 680 miles.

(*John Goring*)

Orlikan Aero 145

All-metal, four/five seat tourer designed by Ladislav Smrcek and built at Kunovice, Czechoslovakia from 1957 as the Super Aero 45 with two 105 h.p. Walter Minor 4-III (G-APRR, G-ASYY and G-AYLZ imported 1959–70), and later as the Aero 145 Series 20 with improved glazing and 110 h.p. Letadlovy M-332 engines. Seven aircraft imported, including G-ASWT (illustrated), 1961–65. Data for Aero 145: Span, 40 ft. 2½ in. Length, 25 ft. 6 in. Tare wt., 2,116 lb. A.U.W., 3,530 lb. Cruise, 155 m.p.h. Range, 1,055 miles.

(W. K. Kilsby)

Orlikan Morava L-200A

Twin-finned development of the Aero 145 with two 210 h.p. Letadlovy M-337 engines built at Chocen from 1960 and as the strengthened L-200D with three bladed airscrews from 1961. Two L-200A, G-ARYJ and G-ASFD, imported by Peter S. Clifford 1960–63 and one L-200D, G-ASHM, in 1963. Span, 40 ft. 4½ in. Length, 28 ft. 3 in. Tare wt., 2,810 lb. A.U.W., 4,300 lb. Cruise, 183 m.p.h. Range, 1,180 miles.

(B. Richards)

Partenavia P.64 Oscar

Four seat tourer powered by one 180 h.p. Lycoming O-360-A1A and built at Arzano near Naples, Italy, by Partenavia S.p.A. from 1965. One British registered example only: G-AVND, c/n 16, registered 18.5.67 to J. Hess (London) Ltd., delivered Naples–Toussus–Rochester 2.6.67, crated for shipment to South Africa next day. Registered ZS-FCH as an R.S.A.200 on arrival. Span, 32 ft. 9 in. Length, 23 ft. 3½ in. Tare wt., 1,499 lb. A.U.W., 2,535 lb. Cruise, 145 m.p.h. Range, 800 miles.

(J. O. Isaacs)

Pfalz D.III replica

Two replicas of the 1917 German single seat fighter, with de-inverted 145 h.p. Gipsy Major 10 Mk.2 engines, built for 20th Century Fox productions Ltd. 1965 for the film 'Blue Max': G-ATIF, c/n PPS/PFLZ/1, by D. E. Bianchi at Booker, airfreighted to Dublin by Aer Lingus Carvair 7.65, P. to F. 4.12.65; G-ATIJ, c/n PT.16, (illustrated), built at Eastleigh to the designs of Ray Hilborne, first flown by V. H. Bellamy 8.65, ferried to Dublin via Valley by Peter Bernest 11–12.8.65, P. to F. 29.8.65. Re-registered 6.67 as EI-ARC and 'RD respectively. Span, 30 ft. 11 in. Length, 23 ft. 2 in. A.U.W. (G-ATIF) 1,600 lb. (G-ATIJ) 1,400 lb.

Piaggio P.136-L

Five seat amphibian built by Societa per Azioni Piaggio at Finale Ligure, Italy. Two British aircraft only, both imported by Lamberts Trust Ltd.: G-AOFN, c/n 195, model P.136-L1, two 260 h.p. Lycoming GO-435-C2B, C. of A. 4.8.55, formerly I-RAIA, based Monte Carlo by Onassis, sold in Italy 9.58; G-APNY 'Christine', c/n 242, model P.136-L2, two 320 h.p. Lycoming

continued on page 402

(*John Goring*)

Piaggio P.166

All metal six/eight seat executive transport powered by two 340 h.p. Lycoming GSO-480-B1C6 driving pusher airscrews, built by Societa per Azioni Piaggio at Finale Ligure, Italy from 1959. Eight British registered by 1970 including the Marconi company's Luton-based flying laboratory G-APWY; Charrington United Breweries' Yeadon-based G-ARUJ; and G-AVSM (P.166B Portofino with two 380 h.p. Lycoming IGSO-540-A1C) operated on executive charter by McAlpine Aviation Ltd., Luton. Span, 46 ft. 9 in. Length, 38 ft. 0¼ in. Tare wt., 5,004 lb. A.U.W., 8,115 lb. Max. speed, 226 m.p.h. Cruise, 208 m.p.h. Range, 1,200 miles.

(*Richard Riding*)

Piel CP.301 Emeraude

Wood and fabric two seat tourer with 90 h.p. Continental C90-14F, designed by Claude Piel, in production by Scintex and other French manufacturers from 1953. Numerous British registered examples listed in Appendix E include several CP.301As with hinged entry doors as well as CP.301Bs and -Cs with one-piece sliding canopies. G-ARUV was homebuilt in 1964. Two aircraft, G-ASMV and 'NI, imported in 1964, were CP.1310-C3 Super Emeraudes with 100 h.p. Continental O-200-A engines. Span, 27 ft. 3 in. Length, 19 ft. 9 in. (CP.1310) 21 ft. 6 in. Tare wt., 583 lb. A.U.W., 1,345 lb. (CP.1310), 1,540 lb. Cruise, 100 m.p.h. Range, 500 miles.

(*Flight L70-180-30*)

Pierre Robin DR.253 Regent and Variants

Four/five seat tourer with 180 h.p. Lycoming O-360-A2A and tricycle undercarriage, built at Dijon, France, by Avions Pierre Robin (formerly C.E.A., established 10.57 by Jodel engineer Delemontez and designer Pierre Robin). Variants flying in Britain 1973 included the three/four seat DR.300 and DR.315 Petit Prince (illustrated) with 125 h.p. Lycoming O-235-F2B and 115 h.p. Lycoming O-235-C2A respectively; the DR.340 Major with 140 h.p. Lycoming O-320-E2A; and the DR.360 Chevalier with 160 h.p. Lycoming O-320-D, improved controls and canopy. See Appendix E. Data for DR.253: Span, 28 ft. 7½ in. Length, 22 ft. 11½ in. Tare wt., 1,323 lb. A.U.W., 2,425 lb. Cruise, 165 m.p.h. Range, 750 miles.

---

continued from page 389

imported by J. E. Carberry for the International Light Plane Tour of Europe 20.7.30–7.8.30, C. of A. 8.7.30. Fitted with Townend ring, averaged 141·8 m.p.h. in 1931 Heston–Cramlington Race, sold to Air Taxis Ltd. 3.32, sold in Germany to Leo Lammertz 7.33. Span, 32 ft. 0 in. Length, 20 ft. 5 in. Tare wt., 991 lb. A.U.W., 1,620 lb. Max. speed, 133 m.p.h. Cruise, 112 m.p.h. Range, 460 miles.

---

continued from page 400

GSO-480-B1C6, C. of A. 14.8.58, sold in Switzerland 8.59 as HB-LAV. Span, 44 ft. 4⅝ in. Length, 35 ft. 5¼ in. Tare wt., 4,460 lb. (L1) A.U.W., 6,000 lb. Cruise, 153 m.p.h. (L2) A.U.W., 6,615 lb. Cruise, 167 m.p.h.

(*M. D. N. Fisher*)

Pierre Robin DR.400 Variants

The 1972 and later models of the DR.253 Regent and its variants were slightly modified versions equipped with the forward-sliding canopy of the new HR.100/200 Royale. First examples imported were DR.400/2 + 2 Dauphin G-BAGS; DR.400/125 Petit Prince G-BAEM; DR.400/140 Earl G-BAFX; DR.400/160 Knight G-BAFP; DR.400/180 Regent G-BAEN. With span 28 ft. 1 in. and length 22 ft. 1 in., airframes were almost identical but engine type and power varied as shown in Appendix E. Data for DR.400/160: Tare wt., 1,240 lb. A.U.W., 2,330 lb. Max. cruise, 158 m.p.h. Range, 885 miles.

(*Aspenair Ltd.*)

Pierre Robin HR.100/200 Royale

Fast, four seat, luxury tourer, powered by one 200 h.p. Lycoming IO-360-A1D6 (HR.100/200), or 210 h.p. IO-360-D (HR.100/210), manufactured by Avions Pierre Robin at Dijon, France. Introduced in 1971 it was the company's first all metal design and broke from Jodel tradition by dispensing with the cranked wing in favour of dihedral from the wing roots. Imports into Britain commenced 1972 through Avions Robin (U.K.) Ltd., Sywell and their U.K. dealers, Aspenair Services Ltd., Biggin Hill. See Appendix E. Span, 29 ft. 1 in. Length, 24 ft. 0 in. Tare wt., 1,532 lb. A.U.W., 2,650 lb. Cruise, 142 m.p.h. Range, 790 miles.

(John Goring)

Pilatus P-6 Porter

Utility aircraft for STOL operations from short strips, in production by Pilatus Flugzeugwerke A.G. at Stans, Switzerland, from 1961. Two British registered aircraft only: G-ASTO, c/n 541, formerly HB-FAM, C. of A. 9.10.64, PC-6/H2, one 350 h.p. Lycoming IGO-540-A1A, sold in Algeria 4.70 as 7T-VSV; G-AWDS, c/n 616, formerly ST-ADF and HB-FCK, PC-6/B1-H2 Turbo Porter, one 525 s.h.p. Pratt & Whitney PT6A-20, C. of A. 15.9.68. Both used by A.D.S. (Aerial) Ltd., Southend, for crop spraying in the Sudan and Indonesia. Data for Turbo Porter: Span, 49 ft. 10½ in. Length, 36 ft. 1 in. Tare wt., 2,270 lb. A.U.W., 4,850 lb. Cruise, 155 m.p.h. Range, 620 miles.

(Richard Riding)

Piper J3C-65 Cub

Cub J-2 two seater (50 h.p. Continental A50-5) built by the Taylor Aircraft Co. at Lockhaven, Penn., U.S.A. 1935–37. The firm was re-organised 1937 by W. T. Piper as the Piper Aircraft Corp. which mass produced it as the Piper J-3 Cub with horn balanced rudder. Five J-2 and four J-3 flown in Britain 1936–39; five J3C-65 (65 h.p. Continental A65-1) and 26 similar, surplus U.S.A.F., L-4 Grasshopper variants with extra rear glazing (some from France) registered 1946–72. Span, 35 ft. 2½ in. Length, 22 ft. 4½ in. Tare wt., 730 lb. A.U.W., 1,220 lb. Cruise, 87 m.p.h. Range, 300 miles.

(A. J. Jackson)

Piper J-4A Cub Coupé

Side-by-side version of the tubular steel, fabric-covered Cub J-3 (65 h.p. Continental A65-1) introduced in 1938. Twenty-four registered to British flying clubs 1939 including one J-4 demonstrator (50 h.p. Continental A50-3) G-AFPP; and one J-4B (60 h.p. Franklin 4AC-171), G-AFTC, flown by the Ipswich Aero Club. The J-4A reduced the cost of flying instruction quite considerably but the majority were impressed for R.A.F. communications 1940–42. Five were restored briefly to civil owners in 1946. Span, 36 ft. 2 in. Length, 22 ft. 6 in. Tare wt., 710 lb. A.U.W., 1,200 lb. Cruise, 83 m.p.h.

(A. J. Jackson)

Piper PA-12 Supercruiser

Three seater powered by one 104 h.p. Lycoming O-235-C, in production by the Piper Aircraft Corp. at Lockhaven from 1945. Six British registered aircraft only, commencing with G-AJGY erected at Hanworth 10.47 in which C. G. Reid-Walker won the Goodyear Trophy Race at Wolverhampton 28.5.49; and including G-AWPW reconditioned by the Mex Flying Group at Kidlington in 1968 and operated by the Kidlington Flying Group in 1973. Span, 35 ft. $5\frac{1}{2}$ in. Length, 22 ft. 10 in. Tare wt., 960 lb. A.U.W., 1,750 lb. Cruise, 105 m.p.h. Range, 600 miles.

Piper PA-15 and PA-17 Vagabond

The side-by-side two seat PA-15, powered by one 65 h.p. Lycoming O-145-B, was in limited production at Lockhaven from 1948. It was succeeded in 1949 by the PA-17 dual trainer version with 65 h.p. Continental A65-8, also built only in small numbers. One PA-15, N4164H, imported 5.63 and certificated at Thruxton as G-ASHU; and three PA-17, G-AWKD, 'OF and 'OH imported from France by Personal Plane Services Ltd., Booker in 1968 (G-AWOF being a PA-15 modified to PA-17 standard). Span, 29 ft. $3\frac{1}{4}$ in. Length, 18 ft. 8 in. Tare wt., 620 lb. A.U.W., 1,100 lb. Cruise, 90 m.p.h. Range, 250 miles.

(A. J. Jackson)

Piper PA-18 Super Cub

Strengthened version of the J3C-65 Cub with 150 h.p. Lycoming O-320 mass produced at Lockhaven from 1949. Suitable for use from short strips and used extensively for crop spraying and glider towing. More than 40 registered in Britain 1957–73, including one Super Cub 135 G-AWDN (135 h.p. Lycoming O-290-D2), five Super Cub 90s (90 h.p. Continental C90-8F or -12F), and ten 90 h.p. former military PA-19s (L-18C), some for the Three Counties Aero Club, Blackbushe in 1971. Span, 35 ft. $2\frac{1}{2}$ in. Length, 22 ft. 6 in. Tare wt., 1,126 lb. A.U.W., 2,070 lb. Cruise, 113 m.p.h. Range, 460 miles.

(P. R. March)

Piper PA-16 Clipper and PA-20 Pacer

The PA-16 Clipper, a four seat development of the PA-15 Vagabond, was produced in 1949 but because 'Clipper' was a name registered by P.A.A., the improved 1950 model was known as the PA-20 Pacer. Two British examples only, both with 135 h.p. Lycoming O-290-D2 engines: G-BAMR, PA-16, c/n 16-392, formerly F-BFMS, registered 1.73 to C. C. Lovell, Worthy Down; G-ATBX, PA-20, c/n 20-904, formerly VR-TCH and VP-KKE, flown Nairobi–Andover 11.53 as VP-KRX, C. of A. 19.5.65, based at Old Sarum 1973 by J. W. Felton. Span, 29 ft. 4 in. Length, 20 ft. 5 in. Tare wt., 900 lb. A.U.W., 1,650 lb. Cruise, 112 m.p.h. Range (Pacer), 580 miles.

Piper PA-22 Tri-Pacer

Nose wheel version of the PA-20 Pacer 135 introduced in 1951 as the PA-22-135, followed in 1955 by the PA-22-150 with 150 h.p. Lycoming O-320 and in 1957 by the PA-22-160 with 160 h.p. Lycoming O-320-B. Low-cost Caribbean version with 150 h.p. Lycoming O-320 marketed in 1958 and the final variant was the two seat Colt club trainer with 108 h.p. Lycoming O-235-C1B. A considerable number of all variants were registered in Britain 1957–68. Data for PA-22-160: Span, 29 ft. $3\frac{1}{2}$ in. Length, 20 ft. $7\frac{1}{4}$ in. Tare wt., 1,110 lb. A.U.W., 2,000 lb. Cruise, 130 m.p.h. Range, 530 miles.

(Richard Riding)

Piper PA-23 Apache

All-metal four seat private, executive or taxi aircraft in continuous production at Lockhaven from 1952 and first imported into Britain in 1957. By 1971 seven early Apache 150 aircraft (two 150 h.p. Lycoming O-320) and 30 Apache 160s (two 160 h.p. Lycoming O-320-B1A) had been registered. Fleet of 12 used by the College of Air Training (Pty.) Ltd. at Hamble was equipped to airline standards of instrumentation and radio. Span, 37 ft. 0 in. Length, 27 ft. 1¼ in. Tare wt., 2,280 lb. A.U.W., 3,800 lb. Cruise, 170 m.p.h. Range, 840 miles.

(Aviation Photo News)

Piper PA-24 Comanche

All-metal four seater built at Lockhaven from 1957 as the Comanche 180 (one 180 h.p. Lycoming O-360-A1A) and Comanche 250 (one 250 h.p. Lycoming O-540-A1D5). Later models introduced in 1964 were the Comanche 260 (260 h.p. Lycoming IO-540-N1A5) and Comanche 400 (or PA-26) with enlarged tail surfaces, 400 h.p. Lycoming IO-720-A1A and three bladed airscrew. All four types were among nearly fifty British registered Comanches. Miss Sheila Scott's record breaking Comanche 260 illustrated. Data for PA-24-250: Span, 36 ft. 0 in. Length, 24 ft. 11 in. Tare wt., 1,690 lb. A.U.W., 2,900 lb. Cruise, 180 m.p.h. Range, 1,650 miles.

(*John Goring*)

Piper PA-25 Pawnee

Single seat agricultural aircraft with 1,200 lb./150 gallon load capacity, mass produced at Lockhaven from 1959. More than forty registered in Britain in two variants commencing with a Pawnee 150, G-APVY, (150 h.p. Lycoming O-320-B) in 1960 but the majority were Pawnee 235s (260 h.p. Lycoming O-540-B2B5). Used by specialist crop spraying and dusting firms at home and abroad. At least one, the Lasham-based G-ATFR, used for glider towing. Data for Pawnee 235: Span, 36 ft. 2 in. Length, 24 ft. 7 in. Tare wt., 1,472 lb. A.U.W., 2,900 lb. Cruise, 115 m.p.h. Range, 285 miles.

(*Tony Leigh*)

Piper PA-27 Aztec

All-metal, six seat development of the PA-23 Apache, introduced 1959 as the PA-23-235 Aztec (two 235 h.p. Lycoming O-540-B1A5). The 1962 model PA-23-250 Aztec with elongated nose (two 250 h.p. Lycoming O-540-A1D5), was developed via C and D variants to the Europeanised PA-E23-250 Aztec (two 250 h.p. Lycoming IO-540-C4B5) of 1970. In view of their PA-27 style constructor's numbers, over 100 Aztecs used privately or for third-level operations in Britain 1960–73 are referred to in this book as PA-27s. Data for E23-250: Span, 37 ft. 2 in. Length, 31 ft. 2 in. Tare wt., 3,042 lb. A.U.W., 5,200 lb. Cruise, 200 m.p.h. Range, 1,320 miles.

(*Flight 71-5657*)

Piper PA-28 Cherokee

All-metal, four seat tourer in large scale production at Lockhaven from 1961 when the first British-registered Cherokee 160, G-ARRP, (160 h.p. Lycoming O-230-B2B) arrived as forerunner of several hundred Cherokees imported by C.S.E. Aviation Ltd., Kidlington. These included the higher powered Cherokee 180; the model 180D with extra windows; and model 235 as well as large numbers of side-by-side two seat Cherokee 140 trainers (140 h.p. Lycoming O-320-E2A). Data for 140: Span, 30 ft. 0 in. Length, 23 ft. 3 in. Tare wt., 1,213 lb. A.U.W., 2,150 lb. Cruise, 130 m.p.h. Range, 525 miles.

(*Flight 71-5648*)

Piper PA-28R Cherokee Arrow

Twenty-five examples of a Cherokee 180D development with automatic retractable undercarriage, introduced 1967 as the Cherokee Arrow 180 (180 h.p. Lycoming IO-360-B1E), registered in Britain by late 1969 were followed by the 1970 model Cherokee Arrow 200 (200 h.p. Lycoming IO-360-C1C) and the 1972 model Cherokee Arrow 200-2, commencing G-AZSE, with 26 in. greater span, 5 in. longer fuselage and 200 h.p. Lycoming IO-360-CK. Data for Cherokee Arrow 200: Span, 30 ft. 0 in. Length, 24 ft. 2 in. Tare wt., 1,459 lb. A.U.W., 2,600 lb. Cruise, 166 m.p.h. Range, 810 miles.

(*A. J. Jackson*)

Piper PA-30 and PA-39 Twin Comanche

Four seat, twin engined development of the Piper PA-24 Comanche, strengthened for operation at higher speeds and greater all-up weight. More than 80 Twin Comanche 160s (two 160 h.p. Lycoming IO-320-B1A) imported by C.S.E. Aviation Ltd. for private owners and air taxi operators 1963–71. An improved model with opposite-handed IO-320-B1A engines and designated PA-39 Twin Comanche then appeared, imports commencing with G-AYFI certificated 7.70 for the Anglo African Machinery Co. Ltd., Halfpenny Green. Data for PA-39: Span, 36 ft. 8 in. Length, 25 ft. 2 in. Tare wt., 2,416 lb. A.U.W., 3,725 lb. Cruise, 198 m.p.h. Range, 830 miles.

(*John Goring*)

Piper PA-31 Navajo

The six/eight seat Navajo (two turbo supercharged 310 h.p. Lycoming TIO-540-A2B), largest of the Piper range when introduced in 1968, featured a walk-around cabin with rear entrance door and separate flight deck for a crew of two. More than 20 imported by C.S.E. Aviation Ltd. 1968–73 for executive use by firms such as Plessey, Whitbread, Vickers, Lotus, Court Line and Unigate as well as for advanced instrument training at the Oxford Air Training School, Kidlington. Span, 40 ft. 7½ in. Length, 32 ft. 7½ in. Tare wt., 3,842 lb. A.U.W., 6,500 lb. Cruise, 247 m.p.h. Range, 1,150 miles.

Piper PA-32 Cherokee Six

Although sharing the name and general lines of the PA-28 Cherokee, the Cherokee Six 260 (one 260 h.p. Lycoming O-540-E4B5) was a larger and entirely new aircraft with six seat cabin, 12 ft. 9 in. in length, entered by a door at the rear. A large baggage hold was sited between the pilot and the engine. A small number were used privately and commercially in Britain from 1965 including a few Cherokee Six 300s (300 h.p. Lycoming IO-540-K1A5), illustrated, which first appeared in 1967. Data for Cherokee Six 300: Span, 32 ft. 8 in. Length, 27 ft. 7 in. Tare wt., 1,784 lb. A.U.W., 3,400 lb. Cruise, 168 m.p.h. Range, 1,060 miles.

Piper PA-34 Seneca 200

Twin engined development of the Cherokee Six for pilot, six passengers and 200 lb. of luggage, powered by two 200 h.p. Lycoming IO-360-C1E6 with counter rotating airscrews. Introduced in September 1971, the Seneca was also suitable for twin conversion training, for light freight work, or ambulance duties. G-AZIK, demonstrator for the U.K. distributors, C.S.E. Aviation Ltd., was the first of many imported for executive use. See Appendix E. Span, 38 ft. 11 in. Length, 28 ft. 6 in. Tare wt., 2,479 lb. A.U.W., 4,000 lb. Cruise, 185 m.p.h. Max. range, 1,070 miles.

(*Flight 13433S*)

Pitcairn PA-19

Four seat autogiro powered by one 420 h.p. Wright Whirlwind R-975-E, built by the Pitcairn Autogiro Company Inc., at Willow Grove, Pennsylvania, U.S.A., 1934–35. Two British aircraft only, both imported by the Hon. A. E. Guinness: G-ADAM, c/n H.89, C. of A. 27.12.34, believed crashed at Newtownards 1935; replaced by G-ADBE, c/n H.87, C. of A. 11.1.36, based at Eastleigh until 1939, stored during the war, scrapped at Kenley 1950. Rotor diameter, 50 ft. 7½ in. Length, 25 ft. 9 in. Tare wt., 2,690 lb. A.U.W., 4,250 lb. Max. speed, 120 m.p.h. Cruise, 100 m.p.h.

(*Aviation Photo News*)

Pitts S-1S Special

Single seat, aerobatic biplane of fabric-covered wood and metal construction, designed by Curtis Pitts 1943–44 for U.S. amateur builders. An early example, NX86401 'Little Stinker', was flown by Betty Skelton at Gatwick 7.49. One Pitts S-1S aircraft, 180 h.p. Lycoming O-360-A4A, G-AZPH, imported by Aerobatics International Ltd., Farnborough 4.72 and three, G-AXNZ, G-AYLU and G-AZCE, registered to British amateur constructors 1969–71. See Appendix E. Span, 17 ft. 4 in. Length, 15 ft. 6 in. Tare wt., 720 lb. A.U.W., 1,050 lb. Max. cruise, 140 m.p.h. Range, 350 miles.

(*R. Wood*)

Pitts S-2A Special

Open cockpit, tandem two seat version of the S-1, powered by one 180 h.p. Lycoming IO-360-B4A, first flown in 1967 and featuring improved handling and aerobatic qualities. Five aircraft, built by Aerotek in the U.S.A., were imported, and the front seats faired over, for the Rothmans Aerobatic Team: G-BADW to G-BAEA, c/n 2035–2039, registered 21.9.72 to Rothmans International Ltd., the first being delivered to Booker 12.72. Span, 20 ft. 0 in. Length, 18 ft. 3 in. Tare wt., 898 lb. A.U.W., 1,500 lb. Max. cruise, 140 m.p.h. Range, 450 miles.

(*Flight 10765*)

Potez 36

Cabin two seater powered by one 95 h.p. Renault 4Pb, in production by the Société des Avions Henri Potez at Méaulte, Somme, France, from 1929. One British aircraft only: G-ABNB, c/n 2359, imported 6.31 for joyriding with C. D. Barnard's Air Display. Retained French markings F-ALJC (illustrated) until returned to the manufacturers at the end of the season. Span, 33 ft. 3 in. Length, 25 ft. 2 in. Tare wt., 994 lb. A.U.W., 1,676 lb. Max. speed, 93 m.p.h.

(*Flight 15679*)

Porterfield 35-70

Tandem two seater with steel tube fuselage and wooden wing, powered by one 70 h.p. Le Blond radial, built 1936 by the Porterfield Aircraft Corporation as Kansas City, U.S.A. One British aircraft only: G-AEOK, c/n 246, C. of A. 11.12.36, imported by U.K. agents, Surrey Flying Services Ltd. Used for tuition at Croydon 1937–39, stored during the 1939–45 war, scrapped at Gatwick 1947. Span, 32 ft. 0 in. Length, 20 ft. 0 in. Tare wt., 813 lb. A.U.W., 1,310 lb. Max. speed, 115 m.p.h. Cruise, 100 m.p.h.

(*Richard Riding*)

Procaer F.15B Picchio 3

Aluminium covered, all-wood four seater built by Progetti Construzioni Aeronautische at Milan 1960–61, total production of this mark with 180 h.p. Lycoming O-360-A1A being 35 aircraft. Three British registered only: G-ARNV, c/n 18, C. of A. 6.9.61, owner W. H. Spence killed when it crashed near Ramsey, I.O.M., while en route Speke–Newtownards 9.9.69; G-ARNW, c/n 19, not imported, registered in Italy as I-PROE; G-ARUE not imported but I-PROE/G-ARNW inexplicably carried a data plate with this registration at the Hanover Air Show 5.62. Span, 32 ft. 6 in. Length, 24 ft. 7 in. Tare wt., 1,532 lb. A.U.W., 2,470 lb. Cruise, 170 m.p.h. Range, 990 miles.

(*W. L. Lewis*)

PZL-104 Wilga 35

The Wilga (Thrush) all-metal, four seat aerial work, club or glider towing aircraft, powered by one 260 h.p. Ivchenko AI-14RA radial, was built by the Transport Equipment Manufacturing Centre at Okecie, Poland, from 1967. One British registered aircraft only: G-AZYJ, c/n 62153, delivered via Brussels–Gatwick 20.7.72 for Worcestershire Gliding Ltd., Bickmarsh, C. of A. 6.10.72. Span, 36 ft. 4⅞ in. Length, 26 ft. 6¾ in. Tare wt., 1,830 lb. A.U.W., 2,712 lb. Economical cruise, 79 m.p.h. Range, 410 miles.

Republic RC-3 Seabee

Four seat amphibian, powered by one 215 h.p. Franklin 6A8-215-B9F, in production by the Republic Aviation Corporation at Farmingdale, New York, 1944–47. Three British aircraft only: G-AJNM, c/n 200, C. of A. 28.5.47, Short Bros. Ltd., sold in Denmark 12.48 as OY-ABZ; G-AJVO, c/n 645, C. of A. 15.4.47, Air Transport Association Ltd., Guernsey, sold 1948 to G. C. Pearson, Redhill, to Norway 5.49 as LN-TSN; G-AJVP, c/n 644, C. of A. 15.4.47, Air Transport Association Ltd., to Norway 5.48 as LN-PAM. Span, 37 ft. 8 in. Length, 27 ft. 11 in. Tare wt., 1,950 lb. A.U.W., 3,000 lb. Max. speed, 120 m.p.h. Cruise, 103 m.p.h. Range, 560 miles.

(*A. J. Jackson*)

Romeo Ro.5

Two seater with fabric-covered, welded steel tube fuselage and wooden wing, powered by one 85 h.p. Fiat A-50 seven cylinder radial, built by S.A. Industrie Aeronautiche Romeo at Naples, Italy, from 1929. One British aircraft only: G-ABVD, c/n 145, formerly I-AAVT, registered to S. H. R. Higgs 19.3.32, hangared at Woodley. Italian C. of A. was not validated, and the aircraft was withdrawn from use in 1933. Span, 36 ft. 11 in. Length, 23 ft. 3 in. Tare wt., 882 lb. A.U.W., 1,499 lb. Max. speed, 105 m.p.h. Cruise, 93 m.p.h.

(*Aeroplane*)

Ryan B-1 Brougham

Five seater with fabric-covered, welded steel tube fuselage and wooden wing, powered by one 200 h.p. Wright Whirlwind, built by the B. F. Mahoney Aircraft Corporation at San Diego, California, 1927. One British aircraft only: G-AAEK, c/n 167, imported by H. G. Hamer and W. Adamson of the Irvin Air Chute Co. Ltd., Letchworth, 6.29. The American C. of A. was not validated, and the aircraft was withdrawn from use in 1933. Span, 42 ft. 0 in. Length, 27 ft. 9 in. Tare wt., 1,800 lb. A.U.W., 3,300 lb. Max. speed, 140 m.p.h. Cruise, 120 m.p.h.

(*Air Portraits*)

Saab 91 Safir

All-metal trainer produced by Svenska Aeroplan A.B. at Linköping, Sweden, from 1945, initially as the three seat 91A Safir with 145 h.p. D.H. Gipsy Major 10 Mk.2, and via the 91B of 1951 to the four seat 91C with 190 h.p. Lycoming O-435-A and 91D with redesigned cabin and 180 h.p. Lycoming O-360-A1A. Three British only: G-ANOK, c/n 91-311, 91C, C. of A. 29.7.54, based at Turnhouse in 1973; G-ARFX, 91-136, 91A, formerly PH-UEC, C. of A. 11.11.60, crashed at Elstree 15.7.62; G-AVGS, 91-308, 91D, formerly SE-CFZ, C. of A. 2.3.67, based at Booker in 1973. Span, 34 ft. 9 in. Length, 26 ft. 4 in. Tare wt., 1,870 lb. A.U.W., 2,660 lb. Cruise, 145 m.p.h. Range, 660 miles.

(*R. P. Howard*)

S.C.A.L. F.B.30 Avion Bassou

Two seater of wooden construction powered by one 40 h.p. Menguin driving a pusher airscrew, built by Société de Constructions et d'Aviation Légère, Paris, 1935. One British aircraft only: G-AFCD, c/n 2, formerly F-APDT, imported 6.37 by H. McClelland, A. to F. 18.10.37, sold to W. L. Lewis, Hanworth, 5.38. Destroyed in fatal crash, Hanworth, 12.6.38. Span, 30 ft. 4 in. Length, 19 ft. 8 in. Tare wt., 572 lb. A.U.W., 1,100 lb. Max. speed, 106·8 m.p.h. Cruise, 93 m.p.h.

S.C.A.N. 30/1

This designation applied to 40 examples of the American-designed, five seat Grumman G-44A Widgeon amphibian built under licence at La Rochelle, France, by the Société de Construction Aéro-Navale. One British registered example only: G-ARIX, c/n 19, built 1949 as F-BGTD, frequently at Croydon and Biggin Hill 1955–61 as VP-KNV (later EI-ALE), C. of A. 11.5.61 with two 200 h.p. D.H. Gipsy Queen 2, Bruce Campbell Ltd., Hamble. Crashed and broke up when alighting off Calshot 19.5.61. Span, 40 ft. 0 in. Length, 31 ft. 1 in. Tare wt., 3,240 lb. A.U.W., 5,200 lb. Cruise, 130 m.p.h. Range, 550 miles.

(Nicholas J. Denbow)

Scheibe SF-24A Motorspatz

Single seat motorised sailplane, of fabric-covered wood and metal construction, designed by Dipl. Ing. Egon Scheibe and powered by one 25 h.p. Hirth 560A. In production by Scheibe-Flugzeugbau GmbH at Dachau, Germany, from 1959. One British registered aircraft only: G-ASPY, c/n 4010, air-freighted to Ringway 27.9.62 as D-KEBU, A. to F. 7.7.64, L. R. Swinn, Leeming (later Carlton Moors, Yorks.). No longer active in 1970. Span, 46 ft. 1 in. Length, 20 ft. 0 in. Tare wt., 485 lb. A.U.W., 760 lb. Max. speed, 93 m.p.h.

(*R. Wood*)

Scheibe SF-27M

Single seat high performance powered sailplane with one 26 h.p. Hirth F10-1A engine driving a tractor airscrew mounted behind the wing trailing edge and manually retractable into the fuselage decking after take-off. Two British registered examples only: G-AWSX, c/n 6306, formerly D-KIMK, A. to F. 2.1.69, G. and T. Mackie, Long Kesh, Co. Antrim; G-AYOT, 6310, D-KOBG, 21.1.71, P. G. Jeffers, Booker. Span, 49 ft. $2\frac{1}{2}$ in. Length, 23 ft. 6 in. Tare wt., 595 lb. A.U.W., 848 lb. Glide, 34 to 1 at 55 m.p.h. Max. speed, 95 m.p.h. Range, 160 miles.

(*R. C. B. Ashworth*)

Schleicher AS-K14

Single seat powered sailplane of semi-monocoque wooden construction with manually retractable mono wheel undercarriage, designed by Ing. Rudolf Kaiser and built by Alexander Schleicher Segelflugzeugbau at Poppenhausen, Wasserkuppe, Germany from 1967. Powered by one nose-mounted 26 h.p. Hirth F10K-1A. Two British registered aircraft only: G-AWVV, c/n 14008, A. to F. 6.3.69, to Ireland 12.69 as EI-APS; G-AYRN, 14050, 17.3.71, D. E. Cadisch and partners, Dunstable. Span, 46 ft. 11 in. Length, 21 ft. 8 in. Tare wt., 540 lb. A.U.W., 793 lb. Glide, 28 to 1 at 52 m.p.h. Max. speed, 124 m.p.h.

(*John Goring*)

SIAI-Marchetti S.205

All-metal four seat trainer/tourer in production by SIAI-Marchetti at Sesto Calende, Italy, from 1965. Two British registered examples initially: G-AVEG, S.205-18F, c/n 225, C. of A. 11.3.68, 180 h.p. Lycoming O-360-A1A and fixed undercarriage; G-AVEH, S.205-20R, c/n 346, C. of A. 11.4.68, 200 h.p. Lycoming IO-360-A1A and retractable gear, both imported as demonstrators by Channel Airways Ltd., Southend. OY-DNG, S.205-18R, c/n 4-165, 180 h.p. Lycoming and retractable gear, registered 28.4.71 as G-AYXS, C. of A. 19.8.71, J. K. Underhill, Baginton. Data for 18F: Span, 34 ft. 10½ in. Length, 26 ft. 2¾ in. Tare wt., 1,490 lb. A.U.W., 2,645 lb. Cruise, 144 m.p.h. Range, 845 miles.

(*Air Portraits*)

SIAI-Marchetti SF.260

Four seat tourer/trainer, with aerobatic capability and superior performance, designed by Ing. Stelio Frati, powered by one 260 h.p. Lycoming O-540-E4A5 and produced by SIAI-Marchetti from 1969. Six imported by the U.K. agents, Lambair Ltd., 1969–70 are detailed in Appendix E, commencing G-AXAH and including G-AXKA flown in the London–Sydney Race 12.69 by Flt. Lts. Kingsley and Evans of the R.A.F. 'Red Arrows' aerobatic team. A seventh, LN-BIV, imported 1972 as G-BAGB, see Appendix E. Span, 27 ft. 0 in. Length, 23 ft. 0 in. Tare wt., 1,488 lb. A.U.W., 2,430 lb. Cruise, 212 m.p.h. Max. range, 1,275 miles.

(*Flight 12238*)

Sikorsky S-38B

Five seat amphibian powered by two 420 h.p. Pratt & Whitney Wasp, built at Bridgeport, Connecticut, U.S.A., 1930, by the Sikorsky Aircraft Division of the United Aircraft Manufacturing Corporation. One British aircraft only: G-ABYS 'Blue Falcon', c/n 314-19, formerly NC15V, shipped to Southampton for Francis Francis, ferried to Heston 5.6.32, C. of A. 4.8.32, flown to Geneva 3.9.32 on delivery to R. H. Parrott, sold in France 2.36 as F-AOUC, crashed at Calabar, Niger Colony 12.8.39. Span, 71 ft. 8 in. Length, 40 ft. 3 in. Tare wt., 6,500 lb. A.U.W., 10,480 lb. Max. speed, 125 m.p.h. Cruise, 110 m.p.h.

(*Flight 10581*)

Sikorsky S-39A

Four seat amphibian powered by one 300 h.p. Pratt & Whitney Wasp Junior, built at Bridgeport, Connecticut, U.S.A., 1930 by the Sikorsky Aircraft Division of the United Aircraft Manufacturing Corporation. One British aircraft only: G-ABFN, c/n 908, previously NC806W, C. of A. 22.10.30. Imported by W. S. Cottingham for use by Personal Flying Services Ltd. Returned to U.S.A. 7.35, converted to five seat S-39B and later to S-39C. Span, 52 ft. 0 in. Length, 31 ft. 11 in. Tare wt., 2,678 lb. A.U.W., 4,000 lb. Max. speed, 120 m.p.h. Cruise, 100 m.p.h.

Sikorsky S-61N

Amphibious airline helicopter with retractable undercarriage and accommodating 28 passengers and two crew. Powered by two 1,250 s.h.p. General Electric CT58-110-1 turboshaft engines driving a single, five bladed, rotor. Eight imported by B.E.A. Helicopters Ltd. 1964–71 for Lands End–Scilly scheduled services and North Sea oil rig support from Dyce or North Denes. Also six by Bristow Helicopters Ltd. 1971–73 and one S-61D-2, G-ATYU, by Westland Aircraft Ltd. 8.66 for evaluation prior to Sea King production. See Appendix E. Rotor diameter, 62 ft. 0 in. Length, 59 ft. 4 in. Tare wt., 11,333 lb. A.U.W., 19,000 lb. Cruise, 140 m.p.h. Max. range, 250 miles.

Sipa S.903

Two seater of fabric-covered wooden construction designed by Yves Gardan and built in quantity with various power plants for the French aero clubs from 1946. One S.901, G-ASXC, with 75 h.p. Minié 4DC-32-B1 imported by H. Durrant, Elmdon in 1964 was followed by four S.903s, 90 h.p. Continental C90-12F, listed in Appendix E. Span, 28 ft. 8 in. Length, 18 ft. $10\frac{1}{2}$ in. Tare wt., 895 lb. A.U.W., 1,390 lb. Cruise, 96 m.p.h. Range, 280 miles.

(*Richard Riding*)

S.N.I.A. SA-313 Alouette II

Five seater first flown 1955, in production by Sud-Aviation at Marignane, France, for over ten years. Two SE-3130s, G-AVEE and G-BANR, 360 s.h.p. Turboméca Artouste IIC-6 turboshaft engines, imported 1967 and 1973; and two examples of the SE-318B variant (360 s.h.p. Turboméca Astazou II) plus four similar SE-318Cs in 1968. When Sud-Aviation became part of Société Nationale Industrielle Aérospatiale in 1970, designations became SA-313, SA-318B and SA-318C. One SA-315B Llama, G-AZNI, with engine and rotor of the SA-316 Alouette III, imported 1972. Rotor diameter, 33 ft. 6 in. Length, 31 ft. 10 in. Tare wt., 1,973 lb. A.U.W., 3,300 lb. Max. cruise, 106 m.p.h. Range, 370 miles.

S.N.I.A. SA-316 Alouette III

Derivative of the Alouette II with seven seat cabin and Turboméca Artouste IIIB turboshaft engine, in production as the SE-3160 at Marignane from 1965. Designation changed to SA-316 in 1970. Three only registered in Britain: G-ATFC, c/n 1278, C. of A. 21.7.65, Bristow Helicopters Ltd., to Iran 8.65 as EP-HAD; G-AWXG, c/n 1517, C. of A. 12.3.69. Lusair Ltd., to Irish Helicopters Ltd. 7.70 as EI-ATO; G-AXLK, c/n 1061, ex South Vietnamese Air Force, to South Africa 10.69 as ZS-HDA, later to Bermuda as VR-BEC. Rotor diameter, 36 ft. 1 in. Length, 32 ft. 8¾ in. Tare wt., 2,436 lb. A.U.W., 4,630 lb. Cruise, 120 m.p.h. Range, 345 miles.

(*H. C. Wilden*)

Snow 600D Series 2D

Single seat agricultural aircraft first produced by the Snow Aeronautical Corporation at Olney, Texas, U.S.A., and later by Aero Commander Inc. One example of the 1967 Snow 600D Series 2D with 600 h.p. Pratt & Whitney Wasp R-1340-AN1 radial, registered 15.5.70 to Agricultural Aviation and Engineering Co. Ltd., Harleston, Suffolk: G-AYDS, c/n 1370D, formerly VH-SNC, first flown in U.K. at Norwich 28.6.70, C. of A. 1.7.70, left Gatwick on delivery flight to Israel 12.6.71, became 4X-ASK. Span, 44 ft. $7\frac{1}{4}$ in. Length, 29 ft. $2\frac{1}{2}$ in. Tare wt., 3,150 lb. A.U.W., 6,000 lb. Max. cruise, 110 m.p.h. Range, 500 miles.

(*Air Portraits*)

Socata ST-10 Diplomate

All-metal, four seat tourer with retractable undercarriage, developed from the Gardan GY-80 Horizon, powered by one 200 h.p. Lycoming IO-360-C1B, and built by Société de Construction d'Avions de Tourisme et d'Affaires at Tarbes, France, from 1969. Four aircraft imported into Britain 1970–72: G-AYKG, c/n 117, C. of A. 31.12.70, Cousenon Ltd., Biggin Hill: G-AYVV, c/n 126, C. of A. 4.6.71, M. J. L. Batt, Booker; G-AZIB, c/n 141, C. of A. 13.12.71 and G-AZMM, c/n 144, C. of A. 2.6.72, Air Touring Services Ltd., Biggin Hill. Span, 31 ft. 10 in. Length, 23 ft. 3 in. Tare wt., 1,860 A.U.W., 2,690 lb. Cruise, 157 m.p.h. Range, 840 miles.

Sperry Messenger

Single seater powered by one 60 h.p. Wright L-4 radial, designed by the Eng. Div., U.S. Air Service, McCook Field, Dayton, Ohio, and built by the Lawrence Sperry Aircraft Co. Inc. at Long Island, N.Y. 1923. One British aircraft only: G-EBIJ, c/n 12, brought to England by Lawrence Sperry, registered to the Sperry Gyroscope Co. Ltd. 9.11.23. Forced landed in the English Channel off Rye, Sussex. 13.12.23. Recovered intact by lifeboat, but Sperrys' body was not found until 11.1.24. Span, 20 ft. 0 in. Length, 18 ft. 9 in. Tare wt., 581 lb. A.U.W., 820 lb. Max. speed, 95 m.p.h.

(*Flight 12084*)

Stinson Junior R

Four seater powered by one 215 h.p. Lycoming R-680, built by the Stinson Aircraft Corporation at Wayne, Michigan, U.S.A. 1932. One British aircraft only: G-AFUW, c/n 8510, imported 5.39 by Southern Aircraft (Gatwick) Ltd., C. of A. 4.8.39, impressed into the R.A.F. 2.40 as X8522. This machine was originally NC12157 (illustrated), delivered to J. H. White of the Vacuum Oil Company at Heston 7.32, used by the Club d'Aviateurs de Bruxelles as OO-HVS 1933–39. Span, 41 ft. 8 in. Length, 29 ft. 0 in. Max. speed, 125 m.p.h. Cruise, 103 m.p.h.

(Tiger Club)

Stampe et Vertongen SV-4B and SV-4C

Two seat trainer first built by Stampe et Vertongen at Antwerp in 1933. Production of the SV-4A (120 h.p. Renault 4PO5) and SV-4B (130 h.p. D.H. Gipsy Major 1) was resumed in Belgium 1947 by Stampe et Renard, and under licence by S.N.C.A. du Nord at Sartrouville, France. Also in Algeria as the SV-4C with 140 h.p. Renault 4 Pei or 4PO3. Over 50 imported into Britain 1961–73 for the Tiger Club, the Rothmans Aerobatic team and sporting pilots. Span, 27 ft. 6 in. Length, 22 ft. 10 in. Tare wt., 1,104 lb. A.U.W., 1,698 lb. Max. cruise, 109 m.p.h.

Stinson Junior S

Four seater powered by one 215 h.p. Lycoming R-680, built at Wayne 1931. Three British aircraft only: G-ABSU, c/n 8066, formerly NC10897, C. of A. 23.11.31, Lt.-Col. E. P. Johnston, Heston, sold abroad 7.36 by R. P. G. Denman; G-ABTZ, c/n 8050, formerly NC10879, C. of A. 26.2.32, E. James, Hanworth, to Lady A. C. E. Nelson, Hanworth 8.33, last owner C. Permetta, Broxbourne, scrapped 1940; G-ABZY, c/n 8093, C. of A. 21.10.32, the Nairn Motor Transport Co. Ltd., Baghdad, sold abroad 1.34. Span, 42 ft. 1 in. Length, 28 ft. 11 in. Tare wt., 2,152 lb. A.U.W., 3,265 lb. Max. speed, 125 m.p.h. Cruise, 105 m.p.h.

Stinson SR-5 Reliant

Four seater of mixed construction powered by one 215 h.p. Lycoming R-680, built at Wayne, 1934–35. Two British aircraft only: G-ACSV, c/n 8779, formerly NC13824, C. of A. 22.5.34, imported for W. Adamson, Sherburn, last owner E. G. Hayes, Heston, impressed 2.40 as X8518; G-ADDG, c/n 9326, C. of A. 30.5.35, imported for W. Caldwell, last owner C. E. Horne, Hatfield, impressed 2.40 as X8519. Span, 43 ft. 3 in. Length, 27 ft. 0 in. Tare wt., 2,250 lb. A.U.W., 3,325 lb. Max. speed, 138 m.p.h.

Stinson SR-6A Reliant

Enlarged four seater of mixed construction powered by one 225 h.p. Lycoming R-680-4, built at Wayne, Michigan, 1935. Two British aircraft only: G-ADJK, c/n 9613, C. of A. 30.9.35, imported for Halford Constant, Croydon, sold abroad 7.37; G-AEJT, c/n 9646, formerly NC15169, C. of A. 5.6.36, imported for Aeropolis Ltd., Heston, delivered to C. W. F. Wood, Dar-es-Salaam, Tanganyika, 1.37, sold abroad 5.37. Span, 43 ft. 3 in. Length, 27 ft. 0 in. Tare wt., 2,270 lb. A.U.W., 3,325 lb. Max. speed, 138 m.p.h.

Stinson SR-7B Reliant

Four seater with compound tapered wing and single bracing struts, powered by one 245 h.p. Lycoming R-680-B6, built at Wayne 1936. One British aircraft only: G-AEFY, c/n 9691, C. of A. 20.6.36, imported for L. C. Desoutter, Hanworth, with whom it was in constant use until impressed into the R.A.F. 2.40 as W7979. Span, 41 ft. 10 in. Length, 28 ft. 0 in.

(*W. T. Larkins*)

Stinson SR-8 Reliant

Five seat version of the SR-7 Reliant, built at Wayne 1936. Four British aircraft only. Two SR-8B, 245 h.p. Lycoming R-680-B6; G-AEMC, c/n 9758, formerly NC16175, C. of A. 11.11.36, personal aircraft of Richard Fairey, Heathrow, crashed 9.39; G-AEOR, c/n 9820, C. of. 22.1.37, Fairey Aviation Co. Ltd. communications, scrapped at Ringway 12.42. Two SR-8D, 320 h.p. Wright Whirlwind R-760-E1: G-AEJI, c/n 9728, C. of A. 18.9.36, imported for J. C. Knowles, Hatfield, last owner Brian Allen Aviation Ltd., Croydon, impressed 3.40 as X8520; G-AELU, c/n 9759, C. of A. 4.11.36, imported by Brian Allen Aviation Ltd., sold to Aeropolis Ltd., Heston, 5.38, impressed 5.40 as X9596. Span, 41 ft. $10\frac{1}{4}$ in. Length, 27 ft. $5\frac{3}{8}$ in. Cruise, 140 m.p.h.

(*Aeroplane*)

Stinson SR-9 Reliant

Improved five seater with rounded front windscreen, powered by one 245 h.p. Lycoming R-680-B6 or R-680-D6 (SR-9B), one 245 h.p. Lycoming R-680-D5 (SR-9C) or one 320 h.p. Wright Whirlwind R-760-E1 (SR-9D), built at Wayne 1937. Six British registered aircraft only, as detailed in Appendix E. Span, 41 ft. 10 in. Length, 27 ft. 11 in. Tare wt., 2,530 lb. A.U.W., 3,700 lb. Cruise, 143 m.p.h.

Stinson SR-10 Reliant

Five seater with panelled windscreen and modified rudder horn balance, powered by one 245 h.p. Lycoming R-680-D6 or R-680-E3 in helmeted cowling (SR-10B and SR-10J), or R-680-D5 in smooth cowling (SR-10C), built at Wayne 1938. Four British aircraft only, see Appendix E: G-AFHB (SR-10B, later SR-10J); G-AFRS, 'VT and G-AGZV (SR-10C). G-AFVT, later SR-10J, saw 20 years service with the Fairey Aviation Co. Ltd. Span, 41 ft. 10½ in. Length, 27 ft. 7½ in. Tare wt. (SR-10C), 2,525 lb; (SR-10J), 2,610 lb. A.U.W. (SR-10C), 3,900 lb.; (SR-10J), 4,500 lb. Cruise (SR-10C), 147 m.p.h.; (SR-10J), 151 m.p.h.

Stinson V-77 Reliant

Navigational trainer powered by one 290 h.p. Lycoming R-680-E3B, built in quantity for the Royal Navy by the Stinson Aircraft Division of Vultee Aircraft Inc., at Wayne, Michigan, U.S.A., 1942. Two British civil aircraft only: G-AIYW, c/n 1410, formerly U.S.A.A.F. 43-44123 and Royal Navy FB682, civilianised by Scottish Aviation Ltd., C. of A. 28.4.47, delivered to Noon and Pearce Air Charters Ltd., Nairobi, 10.47 as VP-KEH; G-AJKZ, c/n 1404, reserved for Noon and Pearce 22.3.47, not proceeded with. Span, 41 ft. 10½ in. Length, 29 ft. 4¼ in. Tare wt., 2,810 lb. A.U.W., 4,000 lb. Max. speed, 141 m.p.h. Cruise, 130 m.p.h.

Stinson 105 Voyager

Two seater of mixed construction, powered by one 80 h.p. Continental A80-9, in production pre-war by the Stinson Division of the Aviation Manufacturing Corporation at Wayne, Michigan, U.S.A. One British aircraft only, c/n 7504, built 1940, purchased by the Air Council for experimental use at Farnborough as X1050. Sold to the Clifford Cab Co. Ltd. 1.46, civilianised by Southampton Air Services Ltd. at Eastleigh as G-AGZW 9.46, sold to R. R. Harrington, White Waltham 9.51 and to A. S. Dubey, Croydon 4.53. Sold in Sweden 5.53 as SE-BYI. Span, 34 ft. 0 in. Length, 22 ft. 0 in. Tare wt., 923 lb. A.U.W., 1,580 lb. Max. speed, 115 m.p.h. Cruise, 109 m.p.h.

(*E. J. Riding*)

Stinson L-5 Sentinel

Two seat, fabric-covered communications aircraft powered by one 185 h.p. Lycoming O-435-1, built by Vultee Aircraft Inc., Wayne, Michigan, 1942. One British civil aircraft only: G-AKYF, formerly U.S.A.A.F. 42-98552, first flown at Fairoaks 4.48 with R.A.F. colours and unofficial serial LG552, C. of A. 29.7.48, owned successively by R. C. Cox, H. C. V. Hext and Southern Aircraft (Gatwick) Ltd. Sold in Kenya 9.49 as VP-KHM. Registration G-AGUY, reserved 11.45 for T. N. L. B. Guinness, was not used. Span, 34 ft. 0 in. Length, 24 ft. 1¾ in. Tare wt., 1,472 lb. A.U.W., 2,045 lb. Max. speed, 120 m.p.h.

(*Robin G. Ridley*)

Sud-Aviation SO-1221 Djinn

Two seat general purpose tip-jet helicopter in production by Sud-Aviation at Marignane, near Marseilles, France, from 1954. Powered by one 260 e.h.p. Turboméca Palouste 4B-1 turbo generator supplying compressed air to the rotor tips. Details of seven, G-AXBX and G-AXFO to 'FU, used for crop spraying in Britain by Agricultural Air Services Ltd., Kidlington during one year, 1969–70, are given in Appendix E. Rotor diameter, 36 ft. 0 in. Length, 17 ft. 5 in. Tare wt., 794 lb. A.U.W., 1,675 lb. Cruise, 62 m.p.h. Range, 120 miles.

Temco D.16 Twin Navion

Twin engined conversion of Ryan Navion four seater, in production by the Temco Aircraft Corporation at Greenville, Texas, U.S.A. from 1953. One British registered aircraft only: G-ARIT, c/n NAV-4-1832, two 150 h.p. Lycoming O-320, formerly N4832K, C. of A. 3.10.61, Whiteley (Rishworth) Ltd., Crosland Moor airfield, Yorks; to Mrs. A. Driessen, Boxted 10.63. Sold in Iceland 5.65 as TF-AIP. Span, 33 ft. 10½ in. Length, 27 ft. 2 in. Tare wt., 2,150 lb. A.U.W., 3,350 lb. Cruise, 160 m.p.h. Range, 900 miles.

(Air Portraits)

Thurston TSC-1A Teal

Two/three seat sport or training amphibian with aluminium main structure and fibreglass bow deck and cabin top, built by the Thurston Aircraft Corporation at Sanford, Maine, U.S.A., and powered by one 150 h.p. pylon-mounted Lycoming O-320-A3B. One registered in Britain by 1972: G-AXZN, c/n 8, formerly N2008T, C. of A. 1.8.70, imported by Marinair (Transport) Ltd. and based initially at Goodwood. Forced landed near Addington, Surrey about 13.1.73 and burned out by vandals on the night of 27–28.1.73. Span, 31 ft. 11 in. Length, 23 ft. 7 in. Tare wt., 1,300 lb. A.U.W., 2,200 lb. Cruise, 105 m.p.h. Range, 400 miles.

Tipsy M

Ab initio and aerobatic trainer powered by one 145 h.p. de Havilland Gipsy Major 10, designed by E. O. Tips and built by Avions Fairey S.A. at Gosselies, Belgium, 1947. One aircraft only: G-AKSX, c/n 1, formerly OO-POM, registered to the Fairey Aviation Co. Ltd. 24.2.48, flown under B conditions as G-6-1, dismantled at the company's Hayes, Middlesex, works 3.48 to enable jigs to be made for production of the Fairey Primer (see Volume 2 page 308). Span, 32 ft. 10 in. Length, 27 ft. 6 in. Tare wt., 1,572 lb. A.U.W., 1,960 lb. Max. speed, 134 m.p.h. Cruise, 122 m.p.h.

(P. A. Mann)

Valton Lentokonetehdas Viima II

Two seat primary trainer of fabric-covered wood and metal construction, powered by one 150 h.p. Siemens Sh 14A radial. Two prototypes and 23 production machines built by the Finnish State Aircraft Factory 1935–36 for the Finnish Air Force. Survivors were sold to flying clubs in Finland post-1945. One aircraft, originally Finnish Air Force VI-3 (illustrated), later OH-VIG, was registered in Britain 12.8.72 as G-BAAY and delivered to P. A. Mann and overhauled by Personal Plane Services Ltd. at Booker. Span, 34 ft. 5 in. Length, 25 ft. 10 in. Tare wt., 1,300 lb. A.U.W., 2,050 lb. Cruise, 87 m.p.h. Range, 465 miles.

(Air Portraits)

Tipsy Junior

Single seat ultra light of wooden construction designed by E. O. Tips and built by Avions Fairey S.A. at Gosselies, Belgium, 1948. One British aircraft only, c/n J.111, imported 1948 as OO-ULA powered by one 36 h.p. Aeronca J.A.P. J-99, re-engined 1952 with 62 h.p. Walter Mikron 2 and registered to the Fairey Aviation Co. Ltd. as G-AMVP, C. of A. 5.3.53. Owned by A. R. Wershat, Fairoaks and flying with bubble canopy in 1973. Span, 22 ft. 7½ in. Length, 18 ft. 6½ in. Tare wt., 486 lb. A.U.W., 770 lb. Max. speed, 108 m.p.h. Cruise, 98 m.p.h.

(Flight)

Waco UIC

Fabric-covered, metal four seater powered by one 210 h.p. Continental R-670, built by The Waco Aircraft Company at Troy, Ohio, U.S.A., 1933. One British aircraft only: G-ACGJ, c/n 3749, shipped to Hamble, flown to Heston by H. F. Jenkins 2.6.33 on delivery to Lady Hay Drummond Hay, C. of A. 19.6.33. Sold in Australia 8.35 as VH-UAX, crashed at Brisbane 22.5.41. Span, 33 ft. 3 in. Length, 25 ft. 2½ in. Tare wt., 1,755 lb. A.U.W., 2,800 lb. Max. speed, 143·5 m.p.h. Cruise, 120 m.p.h.

(*W. L. Lewis*)

Wassmer WA.41 Super IV Baladou

High performance, four seat, cabin tourer of fabric-covered steel tube construction, with moulded plywood wing covering, all-moving tailplane, swept fin and rudder and fixed tricycle undercarriage. Powered by one 180 h.p. Lycoming O-360-A2A, the WA.41 went into production by Wassmer Aviation at Issoire, France, in 1965. Five imported by Altair Aviation and General Trading Co. Ltd., Haverhill, Suffolk, commencing with demonstrator G-ATSY in 1966; and one other, G-BAGM, was registered 10.72 to Alderney Flying Services Ltd. See Appendix E. Span, 32 ft. 9½ in. Length, 26 ft. 6½ in. Tare wt., 1,540 lb. A.U.W., 2,646 lb. Cruise, 155 m.p.h. Range, 1,055 miles.

(*D. A. Conway*)

Wassmer WA.51A Pacific and WA.52 Europa

Four seat tourers of polyester resins and woven fibreglass construction powered by one 150 h.p. Lycoming O-320-E2A, built by Wassmer Aviation at Issoire, France, and distributed in the U.K. by Rollason-Wassmer of Fairoaks. First WA.51A to be imported, F-OCSE, c/n 30, ferried Issoire–Fairoaks 12.2.72 by N. H. Jones, was re-registered 14.7.72 as G-AZYZ, C. of A. 25.8.72. It was followed by WA.52 Europa G-BADN, c/n 54. with 160 h.p. Lycoming and c.s. airscrew, registered 11.9.72 to N. H. Jones. Data for WA.51A: Span, 31 ft. 0 in. Length, 24 ft. 7 in. Tare wt., 1,300 lb. A.U.W., 2,295 lb. Cruise, 134 m.p.h. Range, 565 miles.

(*W. L. Lewis*)

Yakovlev YAK-11

Two seat military trainer with retractable undercarriage, powered by one 730 h.p. Shvetsov ASh-21 radial, designed by A. S. Yakovlev and first produced in Russia 1946. Also built in Czechoslovakia by Strojviny Privni Petiletsky as the C-11, one of which, OK-WIE, c/n 172701, forced landed at Philia, Cyprus 27.3.64 and lay damaged until shipped to Booker in 1970 to be rebuilt by Personal Plane Services Ltd. as G-AYAK for Mann and Son (London) Ltd. First flown by Neil Williams 6.72, C. of A. 27.6.72. Span, 30 ft. 10 in. Length, 27 ft. 10¾ in. Tare wt., 4,410 lb. A.U.W., 5,500 lb. Max. speed, 263 m.p.h. Max. range, 795 miles.

(*A. J. Jackson*)

Zlin 12

Open two seater of wooden construction powered by one 45 h.p. Persy II, designed and built by Zlinska Letecka A.S. at Zlin, Czechoslovakia, 1938. Two British aircraft only, imported by Essex Aero Ltd. 1938 and employed on Civil Air Guard training by Southend Flying Services Ltd. until September 1939: G-AFMW, c/n 1001, formerly OK-LZX; G-AFMX, c/n 153, formerly a cabin model, OK-TBK; Cs. of A. 18.1.39, scrapped at Gravesend during the war. Span, 32 ft. 9½ in. Length, 25 ft. 7 in. Tare wt., 650 lb. A.U.W., 1,102 lb. Cruise, 77 m.p.h.

(*John Blake*)

Zlin 226/326/526

Two seat aerobatic trainers powered by the 160 h.p. Walter Minor 6-III in-line engine, built in quantity at the Morava works, Otrokovice, Czechoslovakia from 1947. Flown by the world's leading aerobatic pilots at major championships from 1960, nine imported into Britain comprising: One 226 Trener G-ATMZ (illustrated); two 326 Trener Masters with retractable undercarriage; five 526 Trener Masters with constant speed airscrews and flown from the rear seat; and one 526A Akrobat single seat variant. Data for 526: Span, 34 ft. 9 in. Length, 25 ft. 7 in. Tare wt., 1,499 lb. A.U.W., 2,150 lb. Cruise, 129 m.p.h. Range, 360 miles.

Amendments to Volume 1

Page 16 Airspeed Courier, paragraph 3, line 1, for A.S.5 read A.S.5A.
29 Airspeed Ambassador. Production (b), for (5223–5226) read (5223–5225). Add (5226) G-ALZO.
369 Bücker Jungmann, G-ASLI, for 397 read 20.
370 Bücker Jungmeister, for four read five, add G-AYSJ.
530 Bristol Type 175 Britannia Series 312, G-AOVF, delete last flight etc., add International Aviation Services (U.K.) Ltd., Gatwick 11.72.

Amendments to Volume 2

Page 37 Currie Wot, line 12, Dr. Urmston did not sell the design rights.
213 Monospar ST-11, Pobjoy Niagara I engines, not Gipsy Majors.

APPENDIX D

This section of the book gives details of British registered civil aircraft for which illustrations have not been found despite many years of intensive search. It also describes those which were not completed, and therefore not photographed in complete form, and also those under construction at the time of going to press.

The introductory notes to Appendix A apply equally to this section.

Houston Gyroplane

Projected single seat gyroplane designed by P. J. Houston as an advance on similar contemporary types. It was to have been constructed at South Nutfield, Surrey, and registration G-ARSZ was allotted to the designer in September 1961 but the scheme was eventually shelved.

Jurca MJ.5 Sirocco

Tandem two seat development of the Jurca MJ.2 Tempête, designed by Marcel Jurca in France 1961–62 for the benefit of amateur constructors. Nine aircraft begun in Britain, two of which were registered by 1973: G-AWKB, c/n PFA.2204, registered 24.5.68 and partly constructed at Luton by K. Bywater, was sold incomplete to G. D. Claxton; G-AZOS, c/n 001/PFA.2206, registered 1.3.72, was under construction by O. Smith at Durham in 1973. Span, 23 ft. 0 in. Length, 19 ft. 8 in. Tare wt., 727 lb. A.U.W., 1,390 lb. Max. speed. 146 m.p.h. Cruise, 124 m.p.h.

Jurca MJ.10 Spitfire XIV

Two-thirds scale Vickers-Supermarine Spitfire XIV designed by Marcel Jurca for amateur builders in 1969. At least two under construction in Britain 1973, but only one registered: G-AXWD, c/n PFA.1345, registered 13.1.70 to G. R. Ferriman, M. E. Pendlebury and D. Adlington (the F.P.A. Group), and under construction at Nottingham in 1973.

Knight Twister

Single seat sport biplane with 90 h.p. Continental C90, designed in the U.S.A. by Vernon W. Payne, plans and kits for home builders being marketed by the Knight Aircraft Corporation. Steel tube fuselages for two British-built aircraft, G-APXZ, c/n BKT-001/PFA.1307, and G-ARGJ, c/n BKT-002/PFA.1308, registered to C. J. de Vere in 1960, were built at Bristol by Coventry and Jeffs Ltd. These were delivered to Eastleigh in January 1962 but other components did not arrive and the Knight Twisters were not completed. Span, 15 ft. 0 in. Length, 14 ft. 0 in. Tare wt., 535 lb. A.U.W., 960 lb. Max. speed, 160 m.p.h. Cruise, 125 m.p.h. Range, 390 miles.

Landon and Chacksfield L.C.1 Tean

Single seat, low-wing racing monoplane powered by one 85 h.p. Continental C85-5, designed by A. J. Landon and J. E. Chacksfield, to whom it was registered in September 1964 as G-ASWZ, the unusual constructors number L.C.1-190-01, referring to the 190 cu. in. racing formula. The aircraft was not completed. Span, 17 ft. 0 in. Length, 17 ft. 3 in. A.U.W., 840 lb.

Lederlin 380-L Ladybug

Side-by-side, two seat, tandem wing biplane with welded steel tube fuselage, variable incidence front wing, and long-span trailing edge flap on the rear wing. This was a redesign of the Mignet H.M.380 by Francois Lederlin of Grenoble, France, and intended for amateur construction. One British aircraft only: G-AYMR, c/n EAA.55189/PFA.1513, 90 h.p. Continental C90-14F, registered 19.11.70 to J. S. Brayshaw, Harrogate, Yorks. Span, 26 ft. 0 in. Length, 15 ft. 7¾ in. Tare wt., 794 lb. A.U.W., 1,323 lb. Cruise, 100 m.p.h. Range, 550 miles.

Manning-Flanders M.F.1

Single seat, wire braced mid-wing monoplane with steel tube fuselage and fabric-covered wooden wing, similar to the Vickers Type 22 flown in the film 'Magnificent Men in their Flying Machines' of 1964. Although designed by W. O. Manning and L. Howard Flanders before the 1914–18 war, the prototype was not constructed until 1972–73 when a slightly modernised version was built to the original drawings by D. E. Bianchi of Personal Plane Services Ltd., Booker, builder of the Vickers Type 22. One aircraft only: G-BAAF, c/n PPS/REP/8, 75 h.p. Continental A75, registered 27.7.72 to D. E. Bianchi and expected to fly in the spring of 1974.

McClure Aircraft

Registration G-AFJY was reserved 1.9.38 for a machine described on the Certificate of Registration as the 'McClure Aircraft'. This machine did not materialise and the markings were not used.

Norman Thompson N.T.4A

Three seat coastal patrol and training biplane flying boat of wooden construction, powered by two 200 h.p. Hispano-Suiza engines driving pusher airscrews. One civil aircraft only: G-EAOY, formerly N2155, built 1917 by the Norman Thompson Flight Co. Ltd. at Bognor, Sussex. Registered 29.10.19 to Handley Page Ltd. but believed not civilianised. Span, 78 ft. 7 in. Length, 41 ft. 6 in. Tare wt., 4,572 lb. A.U.W., 6,469 lb. Max. speed, 95 m.p.h.

Parnall Peto

Two seat reconnaissance biplane of fabric-covered stainless steel construction, powered by one 135 h.p. Armstrong Siddeley Mongoose or one 115 h.p. Bristol Lucifer IV, fitted with twin metal floats for operation from the submarine *M.2.* Two prototypes, N181 and N182, and one production aircraft, N255 (a rebuild of N181), were constructed by George Parnall and Co. at Yate, Glos. 1929–30. Peto N182 was acquired by F. C. H. Allen for civil use as G-ACOJ and prepared for C. of A. at Ford Aerodrome, Sussex 1934–35 but the project was eventually abandoned. Span, 28 ft. 5 in. Length, 22 ft. 6½ in. Tare wt., 1,300 lb. A.U.W., 1,950 lb. Max. speed, 113 m.p.h.

Pilot Sprite

All-metal, side-by-side two seat trainer/tourer with one 130 h.p. Rolls-Royce Continental O-240-A and tricycle undercarriage, designed for amateur construction by L. Jenkinson and P. Sharman of Loughborough University to a specification prepared by *Pilot Magazine* in 1968, plans and kits being marketed by Practavia Ltd., Booker. At least 20 under construction by 1973, of which four were registered: G-AXRK, c/n PFA.1381, E. G. Thale, Ickenham, Middlesex; G-AXUZ, PFA.1337, C. B. Healey, under construction at Heathrow by B.E.A. apprentices 1971–73; G-AZZH, PFA.1532, K. G. Stewart, Dagenham, Essex; G-BALY, c/n OS-130009, A. L. Young. Span, 24 ft. 0 in. Length, 20 ft. 0 in. Tare wt., 850 lb. A.U.W., 1,400 lb. Max. cruise, 128 m.p.h.

Pixie Monoplane

Single seat monoplane with converted Volkswagen engine and tricycle undercarriage, registered 16.9.69 to J. van Geest as G-AXNY, c/n S.B.S.1, and tested at Postland, Lincs. in the same month but is believed never to have flown. According to *Air-Britain Digest* for January 1970, the constructor's number 'is alleged to mean Safety Before Sophistication' and 'construction work is apparently by building contractors Parkers of Spalding Ltd. and is based on designs by Ray Fixter, with financial backing by J. van Geest, banana importer'.

Portsmouth Aerocar Minor

Twin boom, high-wing monoplane powered by two 90 h.p. Blackburn Cirrus Minor 2 engines, fitted with retractable undercarriage and seating pilot and four passengers in a pod-type fuselage. Prototype G-AGNJ, c/n 1, partially constructed by Portsmouth Aviation Ltd. at Portsmouth City Airport 1946. Completion abandoned 1947. Span, 42 ft. 0 in. Length, 25 ft. 7 in. Max. speed, 131 m.p.h. Cruise, 120 m.p.h.

Procter Petrel

Side-by-side, two seat aerobatic or glider tug aircraft for amateur construction, powered by one 130 h.p. Rolls-Royce Continental O-240-A, similar to the Mitchell-Procter Kittiwake I but an entirely different design from the two seat Kittiwake II (see page 273). Prototype, G-AXSF, c/n P.003/PFA.1516, under construction 1972–73 by Southborough Engineering Ltd. at West Byfleet, Surrey; and one other, G-BACA, PFA.1516, registered 21.8.72, by British Aircraft Corporation apprentices at Weybridge 1973. Span, 30 ft. 0 in. Length, 20 ft. 8 in. Tare wt., 1,137 lb. A.U.W., 1,680 lb. Max. speed, 130 m.p.h. Cruise, 120 m.p.h.

R.A.E. Sirocco

Single seat ultra light monoplane powered by one 32 h.p. Bristol Cherub III, designed by the Royal Aircraft Establishment Aero Club at Farnborough, Hants. in 1926. One aircraft only: G-EBNL, c/n 3, registered 26.1.26 as a projected entry for the Grosvenor Trophy Race at Lympne 18.9.26. Non-starter, completion abandoned.

Short S.32

Projected long range transport monoplane for 16 day or 12 night passengers, with alternative high density layout for 24, powered by four 1,250 h.p. Bristol Hercules radials, designed by Arthur Gouge for construction at Rochester by Short Bros. (Rochester and Bedford) Ltd. Three prototypes, G-AFMK, 'ML and 'MM, c/n S.1022–1024, one of which was to have been pressurised for high altitude operation, were registered 19.12.38 to the Secretary of State for Air. Construction abandoned due to the manufacturer's switch to urgent Stirling production. Standard model: Span, 127 ft. 0 in. Length, 89 ft. 0 in. Tare wt., 39,050 lb. A.U.W., 71,000 lb. Cruise, 246 m.p.h. Range, 3,420 miles.

Slingsby Type 10 Kirby Kitten

Low-wing, single seat monoplane similar to the Tipsy S.2 (see page 324), designed by F. N. Slingsby and built by Slingsby Sailplanes Ltd. at Kirkbymoorside, Yorks. in 1938. The 25 h.p. Scott Squirrel and 62 h.p. Walter Mikron engines were considered but the aircraft was overweight and no engine was ever fitted. The airframe, c/n 1, hung in the roof of the Slingsby factory until registered 11.1.49 to the Speedbird Flying Club Ltd. as G-ALGA and taken to Denham to be completed and flown. The scheme fell through but the machine was still extant near Luton in the 1960s. Span about 24 ft. 0 in.

Sopwith 1½ Strutter

Two seat day bomber of fabric-covered wooden construction, in large scale production by The Sopwith Aviation Co. Ltd., Canbury Park Road, Kingston-on-Thames, and numerous sub-contractors from 1915. One civil aircraft only: G-EAVB, c/n 3541, registered 7.8.20 to C. H. Oliver and converted to three seater with 130 h.p. Clerget rotary. History obscure. Span, 33 ft. 6 in. Length, 25 ft. 3 in. Tare wt., 1,305 lb. A.U.W., 2,200 lb. Max. speed, 100 m.p.h.

Sopwith 5F.1 Dolphin

Single seat fighter biplane with backward stagger, powered by one 200 h.p. Hispano-Suiza, in large scale production 1917–18. One civil aircraft only: G-EATC, formerly R.A.F. D5369, built by Hooper and Co. Ltd. at Chelsea, London, registered 7.5.20 to Handley Page Ltd. for demonstration and overseas ferrying by the Aircraft Disposal Co. Ltd. Span, 32 ft. 6 in. Length, 22 ft. 3 in. Tare wt., 1,406 lb. A.U.W., 1,911 lb. Max. speed, 131·5 m.p.h.

Squaircraft SA.102-5 Cavalier

Redesign of the Gardan GY-20 Minicab by S. McLeod of K. & S. Aircraft Supply, Alberta, Canada, strengthened to take engines up to 135 h.p., simplified for amateur construction, and featuring a tricycle undercarriage and swept tail surfaces. Prototype, CF-YIK, built by the designer. At least six under construction in Britain in 1973, three of which were registered: G-AZHH, c/n 69194/PFA.1393, D. W. Buckle, Nunthorpe, Yorks: G-BAJV, c/n PFA.01-10002, A. J. Starkey, Lightwater, Surrey; G-BALS, c/n PFA.1598, L. W. Shaw, Ascot, Berks. Data with 85 h.p. Continental C85: Span, 27 ft. 8 in. Length, 18 ft. 4 in. Tare wt., 800 lb. A.U.W., 1,500 lb. Cruise, 140 m.p.h.

Stinton-Warren S.31-2

Single seat prototype aircraft G-AYJC, c/n S.31-2/001, with Hall Warren wings of rhomboidal shape, powered by one 55 h.p. Ardem 4CO2 flat four and using detail designs completed by Sqn. Ldr. D. Stinton in collaboration with the College of Aeronautics, Cranfield. Full-scale mock-up was begun by Phoenix Aircraft Ltd. at Cranleigh, Surrey, in 1971 but construction of the prototype was abandoned as a result of wind tunnel tests.

Stolp SA-300 Starduster Too

Two seat aerobatic biplane developed from the single seat Starduster designed and built by Louis A. Stolp and G. M. Adams at Riverside, California, U.S.A., in 1957. Four ailerons were fitted for high rate of roll and the prototype was powered by one 180 h.p. Lycoming O-360-A1A. Two British examples only: G-AYMA, c/n EAA.50553, registered 2.11.70 to P. J. Leggo of Tallahassee, Florida, U.S.A.; one other, unregistered, c/n PFA.1349, under construction at Yateley, Surrey, by R. E. Coates 1972. Span, 24 ft. 0 in. Length, 20 ft. 0 in. A.U.W., 1,950 lb. Max. cruise, 210 m.p.h. Max. range, 830 miles.

Stolp SA-500 Starlet

Single seat parasol monoplane with fabric-covered wooden wing (incorporating nine degrees of sweep-back), welded steel tube fuselage and cantilever undercarriage. The prototype, designed and built by Louis A. Stolp, powered by one 1,500 cc. Volkswagen conversion, first flew in California in 1969. One British registered example under construction in 1973: G-AZTV, c/n SSM.2/PFA.1584, by S. S. Miles at Haynes, Bedford, fitted with one 90 h.p. Continental C90-8F. Data for G-AZTV: Span, 25 ft. 0 in. Length, 17 ft. 0 in. Tare wt., 720 lb. A.U.W.. 1,058 lb. Cruise, 90 m.p.h.

Supermarine Southampton II

Five seat reconnaissance flying-boat with metal hull and fabric-covered wooden wings, powered by two 500 h.p. Napier Lion Vs, in production at the Supermarine Aviation Works, Woolston, Southampton, 1925–28. One British civil aircraft only: G-AASH, c/n 1235, C. of A. 12.11.29, an R.A.F. aircraft loaned to Imperial Airways Ltd. for the carriage of the Indian airmail between Genoa and Alexandria during the three month gap between the loss of Short Calcutta G-AADN and the delivery of its replacement, G-AASJ. Left Calshot on delivery about 1.12.29, forced down by fog 10 miles south of Naples 5.12.29, arrived at Athens 6.12.29 to pick up its first airmail load. Handed back to the R.A.F. at Calshot 3.30. Span, 75 ft. 0 in. Length, 51 ft. 1½ in. Tare wt., 9,000 lb. A.U.W., 15,200 lb. Max. speed, 108 m.p.h. Cruise, 83 m.p.h.

Vickers F.B.19 Bullet

Single seat, single bay, fighter biplane powered variously by the 100 h.p. Gnome, 110 h.p. Le Rhône or 110 h.p. Clerget rotary engines, built for the R.F.C. by Vickers Ltd. and first flown 8.16. One civil aircraft only: G-EAAU, c/n C-104, registered 13.5.19 to Vickers Ltd., registration cancelled 7.19, believed not civilianised. Span, 24 ft. 0 in. Length, 18 ft. 2 in. The precise mark of this aircraft was not stated and no other details are known.

Vickers Type 196 Jockey III

Single seat fighter of all-metal construction powered by one 530 h.p. Bristol Jupiter VIIF. Registration G-AAWG was reserved 5.4.33 in the name of Vickers Ltd. for a projected aircraft, c/n 1, which was never built.

Vickers Type 474 Warwick V

Coastal reconnaissance version of the Warwick, powered by two 2,520 h.p. Bristol Centaurus radials, in production from 1944. One civil aircraft only: G-AGLD, formerly R.A.F. PN703, first flown at Brooklands 24.8.44, C. of A. 17.10.44 for loan to the B.O.A.C. Development Flight at Hurn as a Centaurus VII testbed. Flown to South Africa 10.45, scrapped at Wisley 10.46. Span, 96 ft. 8½ in. Length, 70 ft. 6 in. A.U.W., 50,000 lb. Max. speed, 290 m.p.h.

Vickers-Supermarine Type 179

All-metal, monoplane transport flying-boat for seven crew and 40 day passengers, powered by six 850 h.p. Rolls-Royce Buzzard water-cooled engines mounted above the wing. One aircraft only: G-ABLE, c/n 1316, design commenced 8.29, keel laid 1931, registered 7.4.31 to the Air Council, construction abandoned 1932. Span, 165 ft. 0 in.

Registration re-allotted to a Cessna 170A in 1961 (see Volume 1, page 375).

Volmer VJ-22 Sportsman

Side-by-side, two seat light amphibian with wooden hull mated to Aeronca Champion wing assemblies and powered by one 85 h.p. Continental C85 driving a pusher airscrew. Designed for amateur construction by Volmer Jensen of Burbank, California, U.S.A., who first flew the prototype in 1958. Two British-built examples by 1973: G-BAHP, c/n PFA.1313, registered 9.11.72 to J. P. Crawford and completed by Rollason Aircraft and Engines Ltd., at Croydon 1973, using the wing panels of Aeronca Champion G-ATXC; G-BAME, c/n VHB.1/PFA.1309, completed by V. H. Bellamy at St. Just 1972. Span, 36 ft. 6 in. Length, 24 ft. 0 in. Tare wt., 1,000 lb. A.U.W., 1,500 lb. Cruise, 85 m.p.h. Range, 300 miles.

Westland Wapiti I

Two seat, general purpose biplane of fabric-covered metal construction, powered by one 525 h.p. Armstrong Siddeley Panther IIA radial, built by the Westland Aircraft Works Ltd. at Yeovil for the Central Chinese Government in 1932. Four aircraft were ordered, c/n WA.2295C–WA.2298C, the first three exported with Cs. of A. dated 22.2.32, 25.2.32 and 4.3.32 respectively. The fourth was registered to the manufacturers 9.3.32 as G-ABUY and never delivered. Later in 1932 it was fitted with the standard 550 h.p. Bristol Jupiter XFA and transferred to the R.A.F. along with the large batches then being supplied. Span, 46 ft. 5 in. Length, 32 ft. 6 in. Tare wt., 3,180 lb. A.U.W., 5,400 lb. Cruise, 110 m.p.h.

Westland Lysander Mk.III

High-wing, two seat Army Co-operation monoplane of fabric-covered metal construction, powered by one 890 h.p. Bristol Mercury XII radial and built in quantity for the R.A.F. by Westland Aircraft Ltd., Yeovil 1937–42. An additional 225 aircraft, including 150 Mk.III, were built by the National Steel Car Corporation at Hamilton, Ontario, Canada for the R.C.A.F., one of which, 2355, was shipped to Britain 6.72, registered G-AZWT and stored at Strathallan airfield, Perthshire pending restoration to flying condition for W. J. D. Roberts. Span, 50 ft. 0 in. Length, 30 ft. 6 in. Tare wt., 4,065 lb. A.U.W., 5,920 lb. Max. speed, 229 m.p.h. Range, 600 miles.

Westland/S.N.I.A. SA-341G Gazelle 1

Civil version of the five seat, all-metal, general purpose helicopter developed and produced jointly by Westland Helicopters Ltd., Yeovil, and the French Société Nationale Industrielle Aérospatiale, using rotor blades designed and developed in co-operation with the German firm of Bölkow. These were driven by one 590 s.h.p. Turboméca Astazou IIIA turboshaft engine, through the transmission system of the SA-318 Alouette Astazou. The first three British examples, G-BAGJ, G-BAGK and G-BAGL (c/n 1039, 1058, 1075), were registered 26.10.72 to Westland Helicopters Ltd., one for its own use and one each for Point to Point Helicopters Ltd. and Christian Salvesen (Managers) Ltd. respectively. Rotor diameter, 34 ft. 5½ in. Length, 39 ft. 2 in. Tare wt., 1,947 lb. A.U.W., 3,747 lb. Economical cruise, 147 m.p.h. Max. range, 416 miles.

Woodsbird Woody Pusher Mk.1

Two seat parasol monoplane powered by one 75 h.p. Continental A75 arranged as a pusher, designed in the U.S.A. and first flown 1.71 by H. L. Woods, former chief engineer of the Bensen Aircraft Corporation, who formed Aerosport Inc. to market plans for amateur constructors. Five under construction in Britain in 1973: G-AWWP, c/n PFA.1323, registered 7.1.69 to M. S. Bird, construction begun at St. Albans continued at Brighstone, I.O.W. in 1971 as Mk.3 with cockpit canopy and 90 h.p. Continental C90-12F; G-AYVP, c/n 181, registered 6.4.71 to J. R. Wraight, Chatham; and PFA.1330, 1515 and 1550 unregistered. Span, 29 ft. 0 in. Length, 20 ft. 5 in. Tare wt., 630 lb. A.U.W., 1,150 lb. Cruise, 87 m.p.h. Max. endurance, 2 hr. 30 min.

APPENDIX E

Register of British Civil Aircraft

A survey of the rate at which civil aircraft were commissioned in Britain in the 54 years, from April 1919 to March 1973, shows remarkable similarities in fluctuations in growth pattern between the post-1919 and post-1945 eras. Each period commenced with a large influx of converted war surplus machines, continued through an interim period when there were few new designs, and ended with an almost explosive increase in the number of new aircraft registered.

Before 1939 this was mainly the result of an enormous demand for thoroughbred light aeroplanes of British design and manufacture but the next 30 years saw the end of this once great industry. The upsurge in the registration rate during the 1960s and 1970s was, alas, almost entirely due to the large scale importation of mass-produced foreign types. These trends are shown clearly by the following chronology, which lists the date on which each registration sequence of approximately 625 aircraft began.

G-EAAA	April 1919	G-AMAA	April 1950
G-EBAA	December 1921	G-ANAA	June 1953
G-AAAA	July 1928	G-AOAA	February 1955
G-ABAA	May 1930	G-APAA	March 1957
G-ACAA	October 1932	G-ARAA	April 1960
G-ADAA	December 1934	G-ASAA	May 1962
G-AEAA	January 1936	G-ATAA	January 1965
G-AFAA	July 1937	G-AVAA	October 1966
G-AGAA	November 1939	G-AWAA	December 1967
G-AHAA	January 1946	G-AXAA	February 1969
G-AIAA	August 1946	G-AYAA	March 1970
G-AJAA	January 1947	G-AZAA	June 1971
G-AKAA	June 1947	G-BAAA	July 1972
G-ALAA	May 1948		

In more detail this Appendix continues and concludes the complete listing of British civil aircraft since registrations were first used in 1919. As in Volumes 1 and 2, details for each aircraft are given in the following order: constructor's number in parentheses; variant number (where necessary); previous identities; date of issue of Certificate of Airworthiness, Authorisation or Permit to Fly; representative ownership changes; fate or disposal. If no C. of A. was issued or the date of issue of an export C. of A. was not available for publication, the date of registration is substituted.

Where first flight dates are included, or where certification came late in the life of an aircraft, this is made clear. Airworthy aircraft and those on overhaul in April 1973 have no disposal details.

Space considerations compel a condensed form for all foreign types as well as for British machines built in very large numbers and if, in these cases, the last recorded fact is the date of issue of C. of A., the aircraft was still active in April 1973.

Abbreviations are limited to those included in the introductory notes to Appendix A.

Hawker Siddeley H.S.748 Series 1

G-APZV (1534), first flown 24.6.60, C. of A. 6.9.60, A. V. Roe and Co. Ltd., Woodford; last flight 11.7.62 before conversion to Avro 748MF (later H.S. 748MF) prototype as G-ARRV q.v.

G-ARAY (1535), first flown 10.4.61, C. of A. 29.5.61, A. V. Roe and Co. Ltd., Woodford; converted to Series 2, first flown 6.11.61, temporarily 'Pride of Perth'; leased LAV 1965 as YV-C-AMC; leased VARIG 12.65 as PP-VDQ, leased LIAT 4.66 as VP-LIO; leased PAL 2.67 as PI-C784; sold to Falcks Flyvetjeneste, Kastrup 8.67 as OY-DFV; rest. 5.71 to Dan-Air Services Ltd.

G-ARMV (1536), first flown 31.8.61, C. of A. 30.3.62, Skyways Coach Air Ltd., Lympne; crashed at Lympne 11.7.65

G-ARMW (1537), first flown 8.5.62, C. of A. 28.5.62, Skyways Coach Air Ltd.; leased to LIAT 8.65 as VP-LII; leased to B.K.S. 1967–68; International Skyways Ltd., Lympne 2.71; Dan-Air Services Ltd. 4.72

G-ARMX (1538), first flown 19.10.62, C. of A. 15.3.63, Skyways Coach Air Ltd., Lympne; leased to B.K.S. 1967–68; International Skyways Ltd., Lympne 2.71; Dan-Air Services Ltd. 4.72

G-ARRW (1549), first flown 9.4.63, C. of A. 18.4.63, B.K.S. Air Transport Ltd., Yeadon; Skyways Coach Air Ltd., Lympne 3.67; leased B.K.S. 1967; International Skyways Ltd. 2.71; Dan-Air Services Ltd. 4.72

G-ASJT (1559), first flown 24.10.63, C. of A. 15.11.63, S. Smith and Sons (England) Ltd., Staverton; to R.A.E. Farnborough 1.70 as XW750

G-ASPL (1560), first flown 31.3.64, C. of A. 13.4.64, B.K.S. Air Transport Ltd., Yeadon; Skyways Coach Air Ltd., Lympne 4.67; International Skyways Ltd. 2.71; Dan-Air Services Ltd. 4.71; Dan-Air Skyways Ltd., Lympne 5.72

H.S.748 Series 1, G-ASJT, used by Smith's Aviation Division, Staverton, for autopilot development from 1963, after it was transferred to the R.A.E. in January 1970 as XW750. (*Aviation Photo News*)

Hawker Siddeley H.S.780 (Avro 748MF)

G-ARRV (1548), G-APZV, first flown 21.12.63, A. V. Roe and Co. Ltd., Woodford; grounded 1965; to Apprentices Training School as instructional airframe 1.68

Hawker Siddeley H.S.748 Series 2

G-ATAM (1576), first flown 9.2.65, C. of A. 16.2.65, B.K.S. Air Transport Ltd., Yeadon; Hawker Siddeley Aviation Ltd., Woodford 7.67; leased Aerotaxis 6.66 as XA-SEI; leased PAL 8.67 as PI-C1020; leased Ghana Airways 3.69 as 9G-ABV but not used; leased Falck Air 1.70 as OY-DFS; leased Zambia Airways 3.70 as 9J-ABL; leased South African Airways 7.70 as ZS-HSA; sold to Transgabon 8.72 as TR-LQY 'Libreville'

G-ATEH (1585), first flown 24.8.65, C. of A. 24.9.65, Channel Airways Ltd., Southend; leased COPA, Panama 10.65 to 5.66 as HP-416; to LIAT 4.68 as VP-LIW

G-ATEI (1586), first flown 1.11.65, C. of A. 18.11.65, Channel Airways Ltd., Southend; leased LIAT 12.65 to 5.66 as VP-LIN; leased Transair, Canada 5.69 to 11.69 as CF-TAX; leased Rousseau Aviation 5.70 to 8.70 as G-ATEI; sold to Philippine Air Lines 9.70 as PI-C1029

G-ATEJ (1587), first flown 27.1.66, C. of A. 2.2.66, Channel Airways Ltd., Southend; sold to Midwest Airlines Ltd., Winnipeg 12.67 as CF-MAL

G-ATEK (1588), first flown 11.2.66, C. of A. 3.3.66, Channel Airways Ltd., Southend; sold to LIAT 5.68 as VP-LIV

G-ATMI (1592), first flown 16.3.66, C. of A. 29.3.66, Autair International Airways Ltd., Luton; leased LIAT 11.67 as VP-LIU; leased Skyways Ltd. 5.68 to 10.68 and 3.69 to 11.69; leased LIAT 11.69 to 4.70 as VP-LIU; leased SATA 5.70 to 10.70; leased LIAT 11.70–3.71 as VP-LIU; leased British Air Ferries Ltd., Southend 4.71 to 12.71; to LIAT 12.71 as VP-LIU 'Halcyon Breeze'

G-ATMJ (1593), first flown 6.4.66, C. of A. 19.4.66, Autair International Airways Ltd., Luton; leased Jamaica Air Services Ltd. 1.68 to 4.69 as 6Y-JFJ; leased SATA 4.69 to 5.70 as G-ATMJ; leased Rousseau Aviation 8.70 to 10.70; leased British Air Ferries Ltd., Southend 10.70 to 11.71; leased LIAT 12.71 as VP-LAJ; leased Rousseau Aviation 3.72 as VP-LAJ; rest. 10.72 to C.A.A. Flying Unit, Stansted

G-AVXI (1623), first flown 13.2.69, C. of A. 4.7.70, Board of Trade Flying Unit, Stansted (style changed to C.A.A. Flying Unit 4.72)

G-AVXJ (1624), first flown 4.6.69, C. of A. 27.8.70, Board of Trade Flying Unit, Stansted (style changed to C.A.A. Flying Unit 4.72)

G-AXVG (1589), OE-LHS, first flown 22.4.66, C. of A. renewal 17.1.70, Skyways Coach Air Ltd., Lympne; International Skyways Ltd. 2.71; Dan-Air Services Ltd. 4.72

G-AZSU (1612), VP-BCM, first flown 5.4.67, C. of A. renewal 20.5.72, B.O.A.C. Associated Companies Ltd.; delivered to Dan-Air Services Ltd. 6.72

Hawker Siddeley H.S.748 Series 2A

G-AVRR (1635), first flown 5.9.67, C. of A. 15.9.67, Hawker Siddeley Aviation Ltd., leased SATA 2.69; leased Transair, Canada 4.69 to 5.69 as CF-YQD; leased Olympic Airways 6.69 to 10.69; leased Air Cape, N.A.C. and Suidwes Lugdiens 12.69 as ZS-IGI; leased Zambia Airways 3.70 to 4.70 as

9J-ABM; leased South African Airways 4.70 to 9.70 as ZS-HSI; leased Merpati Nusantara Airlines, Indonesia 1.71; leased Transgabon 10.71 as TR-LQJ and sold to them 8.72

G-AVZD (1601), A10-601, first flown 21.2.68, C. of A. 5.4.68, Hawker Siddeley Aviation Ltd., Woodford; handed over to R.A.A.F. at Woodford 30.8.68 as A10-601 at conclusion of Dart R.Da.8 flight trials

G-AXVZ (1671), first flown 15.12.69 as 9N-AAU; first flown 15.1.70 as G-AXVZ, C. of A. 31.12.69, Hawker Siddeley Aviation Ltd., Woodford; to Royal Nepal Airlines 21.1.70 as 9N-AAU at conclusion of maker's trials

Royal Nepal Airlines' H.S.748 Series 2A 9N-AAU on a pre-delivery flight near Woodford, January 1970, after a brief period as G-AXVZ.

G-AYDH (1678), first flown 7.5.70 as G-11-2, C. of A. 13.5.70, Hawker Siddeley Aviation Ltd., Woodford; to Rousseau Aviation, Dinard 5.70 as F-BSRA

G-AYFL (1679), first flown 24.4.70 as G-11-1, C. of A. 14.7.70, Hawker Siddeley Aviation Ltd., Woodford; to Chevron Standard Oil, Canada 10.70 as CF-CSE

G-AYIM (1687), first flown 17.7.70 as G-11-5, Hawker Siddeley Aviation Ltd., Woodford; to SATA, Azores 10.70 as CS-TAG

G-AYIR (1681), first flown 21.5.70 as G-11-3, C. of A. 27.8.70, Hawker Siddeley Aviation Ltd., Woodford; leased to SATA, Azores 10.70 as CS-TAF; to Rousseau Aviation, Dinard 11.70 as F-BSRU

G-AYVR (1700), G-11-7, first flown 17.3.71, C. of A. 21.4.71, Hawker Siddeley Aviation Ltd.; to Bouraq Airlines, Indonesia 10.72 as PK-IHD; temporarily restored 12.72 and left Woodford on delivery 3.1.73 as G-AYVR

G-AYYG (1697), first flown 7.5.71, C. of A. 24.5.71, Hawker Siddeley Aviation Ltd., Woodford

G-AYYH (1701), G-11-8, first flown 15.4.71, C. of A. 28.5.71, Hawker Siddeley Aviation Ltd., Woodford; to Polynesian Airlines, Samoa 1.72 as 5W-FAN

G-AZAE (1695), G-11-10, first flown 16.6.71, C. of A. 16.6.71, Hawker Siddeley Aviation Ltd.; to Merpati Nusantara Airlines, Indonesia 12.71 as PK-MHD; re-registered PK-MHM on arrival

G-AZJH (1698), freighter prototype, first flown 31.12.71, C. of A. 25.8.72, Hawker Siddeley Aviation Ltd., Woodford

G-BABJ (1718), first flown 10.7.72, Hawker Siddeley Aviation Ltd., Woodford

G-BAFY (1716), first flown 23.10.72, Hawker Siddeley Aviation Ltd.; for Air Illinois, U.S.A.; to Atlantic Aviation, Canada 1.73 for fitting out as N666

Helio H-391B Courier

G-APXH (061), N7805B, 22.12.59, to Southern Rhodesia 9.61 as VP-YTD; rest. 8.62 to Strathallan Air Services Ltd., Strathallan, Perthshire; damaged beyond repair landing at Athens 8.11.64

Helio H-395 Super Courier

G-ARLD (522), N13B, N1890B, 25.4.61, Sir N. K. L. Nuttall, Leicester East; G-ARMU (523), N13B, N4172D, 14.6.61, Strathallan Air Services Ltd. 11.63 to 5.66, to Ireland 10.68 as EI-ATG, rest. 7.70, crashed at Ormesby Hall, near Caister, Norfolk 30.8.70; G-ATGM (593), N4199D, 8.11.65, J. Carter Jones & Sons Service Co., Cambridge; G-BAGT (1288), CR-LJG, registered 31.10.72 to Tanganyika Holdings Ltd., Elstree

Heston Type 1 Phoenix I

G-ADAD (1/1), first flown 18.8.35, C. of A. 1.10.35, Heston Aircraft Co. Ltd., Heston; to E. Xidis, Athens 9.36 as SX-AAH

G-AEHJ (1/3), 7.5.36, Heston Aircraft Co. Ltd., Heston; British American Air Services Ltd., Heston 6.39; crashed into Mersey at Liverpool 13.2.40

Heston Type 1 Phoenix II

G-AEMT (1/4), 22.5.37, Heston Aircraft Co. Ltd., Heston; loaned to No.4 Sqn., Farnborough until sold to Luton Flying Club 7.39; impressed 3.40 as X9393, reduced to spares 1943

G-AESV (1/5), 23.3.37, Standard Telephones and Cables Ltd., Hatfield; impressed 3.40 as X2891; rest. 2.46 to Heston Aircraft Co. Ltd.; A. R. Pilgrim, Elstree 3.50; crashed in the French Alps 4.52

G-AEYX (1/6), 25.6.37, C. Randrup and S. T. Worth, Heston, Allflight Ltd., Heston 4.39, impressed 3.40 as X9338, scrapped 6.44.

Hiller 360 Series UH-12A

G-AMDN (166), 3.10.50; G-AMDO (172), 3.10.50, crashed in Panama 3.3.58; G-AMGY (165), 18.1.51, dismantled at Redhill 6.63; G-AMMY (148), N8148H, OO-MAT, 3.11.51, crashed at Grantchester, Cambs. 20.11.56; G-ANOA (170), F-BEEG, 22.2.54; G-ANOB (120), N8120H, HB-XAI, I-ELAM, F-BGGZ, 20.4.54, d.b.r. at Barton, Cambs. 30.5.61; G-ANOC (115), F-BFGY, 25.3.54, crashed at Gleatham, Lincs. 23.8.55; G-ANZM (106), N8106H, OO-APR, rebuilt 1.56 with fuselage of LN-FOH (c/n 122), 1.2.56, dismantled at Redhill 11.62; G-APKX (337), CF-HAP, N24C, 30.6.58, crashed near Chilbolton, Hants. 4.7.66; G-APLA (137), F-BFLX, 24.4.58, crashed at High Roding, Essex 28.5.58; G-APZO (167), N8167H, to Egypt 2.61 as SU-ALK

Hiller 360 Series UH-12B

G-AOFK (745), 28.6.55, crashed at Hamble 4.10.55; G-AOFL (746), 28.6.55, crashed at Bourn 13.12.65; G-AOFV (748), 14.11.55, crashed at Ludham, Norfolk 6.4.65; G-APJN (686), HB-XAH, 7.2.58; G-APKY (673), PH-NFL, 4.6.58; G-APSH (747), N5313V, 4.3.59; G-APSL (555), N5300V, 25.4.59, d.b.f in Dominica 19.4.60; G-APTM (674), PI-C364, 10.5.69; G-APTN (680), PI-C365, 10.6.59, to the U.S.A. 8.62 as N9742F; G-APUH (744), D-HABA, 29.5.59, d.b.f. in the Sahara 19.12.59

G-ASTM (538), Royal Navy XB478, 26.8.64; G-ASTR (542), XB513, 26.8.64; G-ASVH (510), XB474, 1.10.64; G-ASVI (536), XB476, 10.11.64; G-ASVJ (537), XB477, 6.12.64, crashed at Middle Wallop 4.8.66; G-ASVK (539), XB522, 2.9.64; G-ASVL (541), XB481, 15.1.65; G-ATKG (496), Thai Air Force 496, 29.11.65; G-ATLG (505), Thai 105, 18.3.66; G-ATZB (497), Thai 102, 6.10.66

G-AVAJ (726), Thai 116, 29.11.66; G-AWKG (669), 2.7.69; G-AYCH (687), 54-872, Dutch O-26, registered 27.4.70; G-AYCI (736), 54-2942, Dutch O-8

Hiller 360 Series UH-12C *(improved control system)*

G-AOFA (785), 18.9.56, d.b.r. 1961; G-AOZR (847), 5.4.57, sold in the U.S.A. 5.62; G-AOZS (848), 5.4.57, d.b.r. 1965; G-APDU (849), 31.7.57, sold in the U.S.A. 1.62; G-APDV (856), 31.7.57, to Trinidad 4.61 as VP-TCE/9Y-TCE, rest. 10.68; G-APMP (1041), 21.7.58; G-APMR (1037), 6.6.58; G-APMS (1038), N9778C, 6.6.58; G-APNI (1039), 14.7.58, crashed in Panama 4.59; G-APNR (784), F-BHTG, 3.7.58; G-APOF (776), PH-NGP, F-BBDZ, 31.7.58, crashed at Redhill 25.5.68; G-APOT (1040), 2.9.58 to the U.S.A. 2.62 as N9755C; G-APRD (777), N5319V, 31.12.58, to the U.S.A. 5.62 as N9738C, rest. 1.64, to Norway 9.69 as LN-ORX; G-ARTG (936), HP-262, 14.6.63; G-ARUF (903), HP-263, 18.1.63, ditched in Loch Awe, Argyllshire 6.7.63; G-ASOE (778), N5818V, 26.8.64, w.f.u. 11.68; G-ASTP (1045), N9750C, 19.6.64

Hiller 360 Series UH-12E

G-ARXV (2193), 24.5.62, to Bermuda 6.63 as VR-BCA, to Nigeria 12.64 as 5N-AGG, rest. 4.67, to Iran 9.67 as EP-HAJ, rest. 4.68, to South Africa 2.69 as ZS-HCT; G-ASIG (2190), 24.5.63, to New Zealand 8.68 as ZK-HCN; G-ASIH (2192), 24.5.63, crashed at Tynron, Dumfries 11.3.71; G-ASUJ (2317), 7.9.64, crashed at Platy, Thessalonika, Greece 15.5.65; G-ASUK (2339), 7.9.64, crashed at Spilsby, Lincs. 15.3.66; G-ATDM (2288), 28.6.65

G-ATED (2342), 14.6.65; G-ATFJ (2349), 5.7.65, crashed at Thorney, Peterborough 1.3.66; G-ATVG (2191), 5N-ABX, 8.6.66, to Iran 1.67 as EP-HAL, rest. 5.67; G-ATVM (2123), 5N-AGH, to Iran 7.66 as EP-HAH, rest. 5.68, crashed near Agadir, Morocco 16.7.68; G-ATVN (2133), 5N-AGC, 21.6.66, crashed at Balderton, Notts. 28.2.72; G-AVKX (2103), CN-MAO, 8.1.68; G-AVKY (2104), CN-MAP, 24.1.68; G-AWME (2130), 5N-AGB, 10.8.68, to Bermuda 10.69 as VR-BBU, rest. 8.70, to Nigeria 8.70 as 5N-AIP; G-AZSV (2114), ZS-HAV, 5N-AGJ, EP-HAH, 27.4.72; G-BAIU (2138), D-HAFA, registered 29.11.72

Hillson Praga *(including Czech-built Praga E.114 demonstrator G-ADXL)*

Note: Praga monoplanes with constructor's numbers up to and including H.A.16 were issued with Authorisations to Fly in lieu of C. of A.

G-ADXL (107), OK-PGC, 27.2.36, F. Hills and Sons Ltd., Barton; flown to South Africa by H. L. Brook 5.36; re-registered ZS-AHL, converted to glider 9.53

G-AEEU (H.A.2), 13.4.36, F. Hills and Sons Ltd., Barton; J. S. Boumphrey, Hunts Cross, Liverpool (dismantled) 2.43; F. Bosworth, Hooton 1.46; stored there until sent by road to Gosport 1.51 as spares for G-AEUT

G-AEEV (H.A.3), 13.4.36, F. Hills and Sons Ltd., Barton; R. J. Pattinson, Sherburn 8.36; H. Poskett, Whitley Bridge, Yorks. 12.39; to Hatfield Motor Wreckers, Doncaster, Yorks 12.45; remains burned at Yeadon 1955

G-AELK (H.A.13), 11.9.36, F. Hills and Sons Ltd., Barton; flown by R. Jagger and partners, Barton; crashed at Abbey Village, near Chorley, Lancs. 7.6.37

Newly completed Hillson Praga monoplanes G-AEUO (without airscrew and not yet flown) and G-AEOL, lined up at Barton Aerodrome, Manchester, in May 1937. (*E. J. Riding*)

G-AELL (H.A.14), 25.10.36, F. Hills and Sons Ltd., Barton; remained unsold; dismantled at Barton during 1939–45 war

G-AEOL (H.A.15), 8.12.36, R. Jagger and partners, Barton; dismantled at Barton during 1939–45 war

G-AEOM (H.A.16), 18.1.37, F. Hills and Sons Ltd., Barton; remained unsold; dismantled during 1939–45 war

G-AEON (H.A.20), 4.12.36, F. Hills and Sons Ltd., Barton; sold abroad 12.36

G-AEPI (H.A.12), 21.12.36, F. Hills and Sons Ltd., Barton, Northern Aviation School and Club Ltd., Barton 7.39; scrapped during 1939–45 war

G-AEPJ (H.A.25), 11.2.37, F. Hills and Sons Ltd., Barton; Northern Aviation School and Club Ltd., Barton 4.39; scrapped during 1939–45 war

G-AEPK (H.A.26), 16.3.37, F. Hills and Sons Ltd., Barton; Midland Aircraft Repair Ltd., (North Staffs. Aero Club) Meir 3.39; scrapped during 1939–45 war

G-AEPL (H.A.23), 4.2.37, F. Hills and Sons Ltd., Barton; Malayan Motors Ltd., Singapore 3.37; sold abroad 1937

G-AEPM (H.A.24), 1.2.37. F. Hills and Sons Ltd., Barton; Malayan Motors Ltd., Singapore 3.37; re-registered in Singapore as VR-SAU

G-AEUK (H.A.27), 23.3.37
G-AEUL (H.A.28), 8.4.37
G-AEUM (H.A.29), 28.4.37
G-AEUN (H.A.30), 18.5.37
} Northern School of Aviation Ltd., Barton; stored during part of 1939–45 war; registrations cancelled 12.46

G-AEUO (H.A.31), 3.6.37, F. Hills and Sons Ltd., Barton; Northern Aviation School and Club Ltd., Barton 11.38; scrapped during 1939–45 war

G-AEUP (H.A.32), 31.7.37, F. Hills and Sons Ltd., Barton; Ipswich Aero Club Ltd., 12.38; I. H. Cameron, Perth 8.39; crashed in Turkey 23.7.47

G-AEUR (H.A.33), 12.8.37, Northern Aviation School and Club Ltd., Barton; crashed 1.4.39

G-AEUS (H.A.34), 21.9.37, Northern Aviation School and Club Ltd., Barton; crashed at Barton 4.6.39

G-AEUT (H.A.35), 5.1.38, F. Hills and Sons Ltd., Barton; Ipswich Aero Club Ltd., 11.38; A. Harcus, Kirkwall 10.44; F. Bosworth, Hooton 12.46; Lt. Cdr. G. A. J. Goodhart, Gosport 4.51; V. H. Hallam, Abingdon 5.52; C. M. Roberts, Panshanger 7.56; crashed at Sinalunga, Siena, Italy 19.6.57

G-AEUU (H.A.36), 30.12.37, F. Hills and Sons Ltd., Barton; Ipswich Aero Club Ltd., 11.38; scrapped during 1939–45 war

G-AEYK (H.A.37), 15.12.37, F. Hills and Sons Ltd., Barton; Northern Aviation School and Club Ltd. 1.39; not repaired after accident at Barton 8.8.39

G-AEYL (H.A.38), 19.1.38, F. Hills and Sons Ltd., Barton; Ipswich Aero Club Ltd. 10.38; Thanet Aero Club Ltd., Ramsgate 2.39; scrapped during 1939–45 war

G-AEYM (H.A.39), 19.1.38, F. Hills and Sons Ltd., Barton; Ipswich Aero Club Ltd., 11.38; crashed at Weston-super-Mare 1.9.39

Note: Registrations G-AEYN to G-AEYU (H.A.40–H.A.46) not used, aircraft not completed. A further reservation, G-AFBE, was not taken up.

Hughes 269A *(also known as Model 200)*

G-ASBD (42-0081), G-17-2, 8.8.62, temporarily to Boscombe Down 1962 as XS684; G-AVSU (62-0102), N8778F, 23.8.67; G-AWVL (63-0234), VP-YWB, ZS-HCN, 1.1.69

Hughes 269B *(also known as Model 300)*

G-ASBL (42-0066), G-17-1, 18.9.62, temporarily to Boscombe Down 1962 as XS349, crashed at Fairlop, Essex 27.10.64; G-ASTZ (54-0085), N8761F, 31.7.64; G-AVUM (0317), 8.11.67; G-AVVS (16-0284), EI-APN, 9.11.67; G-AVZC (45-0189), EI-AOU, 15.12.67, G-AWKC (16-0234), EI-APH, 6.6.68; G-AXXD (16-0228), N9451F, 25.2.70

Hughes 269C *(also known as Model 300C)*

G-AYLX (90-0041), 27.11.70; G-AYNO (100-0054), 18.1.71; G-AZEJ (100-0059), 14.9.71; G-AZXI (41-0110), 3.7.72; G-BAAN (41-0136), 16.8.72; G-BABI (41-0149), 11.9.72; G-BABN (41-0140), 1.9.72; G-BAEH (41-0150), 28.2.73; G-BAFC (41-0148), 20.10.72; G-BAKG (41-0155), 5.1.73

Hughes 369HE* and 369HS *(also known as Model 500)*

,G-AXEJ (69-0101S), 23.7.69; G-AXPL (89-0112S), 3.12.69; G-AYIA (99-0120S), 5.8.70; G-AYNK* (59-0102E), N9012F, EI-AUA, 3.2.71; G-AZVM (61-0326S), N9091F, 2.6.72

Hunting Percival P.56 Provost T.Mk.1

G-AMZM (20), 29.6.53, Hunting Percival Aircraft Ltd., Luton; stored at C. of A. expiry 3.10.57; to the Malayan Air Force 5.61 as FM1036

G-ASMC (417), XF908, 13.3.64, Rapid Flying Group Ltd., Baginton; W. Walker, Baginton 5.65

G-AWPH (3), WV420, first flown after conversion at Baginton 28.3.69, C. of A. 15.5.69, J. A. D. Bradshaw, Thruxton

G-AWPI (330), XF685, registered 6.9.68 to J. A. D. Bradshaw and used as spares

G-AWTB (342), XF838
G-AWTC (338), XF693
G-AWTD (285), XF554
G-AWTE (336), XF691
G-AWTF (4), WV421
G-AWTG (86), WV540
} Registered 31.10.68 to Target Towing Aircraft Ltd., Blackbushe; cancelled 3.69 as sold in West Germany; still at Fairoaks 7.69 with R.A.F. Air Traffic Control School codings H, V, Z, K, B and C respectively

G-AWVF (375), XF877, 8.5.69, J. R. Walgate, Hemswell

The Rapid Flying Group's Provost T.Mk.1 G-ASMC. (*Richard Riding*)

Hunting Percival P.84 Jet Provost

G-AOHD (12), Mk.2, 30.5.56, Hunting Percival Aircraft Ltd., Luton; fitted with new wing and Mk.3 undercarriage 9.58; shipped to No.1 F.T.S., R.A.A.F., Point Cook 5.59; evaluated as A99-001; sold to the R.A.A.F. 8.61

G-AOUS (14), Mk.2B, 25.9.56, Hunting Percival Aircraft Ltd., Luton; crashed at Langford Common, near Biggleswade, Beds. 16.11.60

G-APVF Reserved 7.59 for Hunting Aircraft Ltd., not taken up

G-ASEZ (1093), T.Mk.52, 28.2.63, Hunting Aircraft Ltd., Luton; allotted Sudanese Air Force serial 181 but flown out as G-ASEZ, damaged en route in forced landing at Idjilidje, near Fort Lamy, Chad 7.4.63. Brought back to Luton, stored until rebuilt 3.65

G-ATAJ (BAC/166), T.Mk.4, XS231, registered 1.65 to B.A.C. (Operating) Ltd., Hunting Division, Luton. Last T.Mk.4 for R.A.F. released to makers for T.Mk.5 development. Civil marks not used, fitted with Viper 20 engine and first flown as T.Mk.5 interim type 16.3.65.

Jodel D.9 Bébé *(British-built)*

G-AVPD (PFA.927), 1,500 cc. Volkswagen, erected at Heathrow 1968–69, first flown 14.6.69, A. to F. 1.8.69, S.W. McKay, Booker 'Louis Lady'; redesignated D.92 with c/n MAC.1 in 1971

G-AWFT (PFA.932), 1,200 cc. Volkswagen, A. to F. 23.7.68, W. H. Cole, Willingale; dismantled at Purleigh strip, Essex in 1972

G-AXKI (SAS/001), 1,500 cc. Volkswagen, A. to F. 26.2.70, Southdown Aero Services Ltd., Lasham; P. L. Cyster, Rye, Sussex 6.71

G-AXKJ (SAS/002), 1,500 cc. Volkswagen, A. to F. 29.12.69, Southdown Aero Services Ltd., Lasham

G-AXOI (PFA.930), 1,400 cc. Volkswagen, C. of A. 2.9.71, G. K. Penson and P. M. Bowden, Barton

G-AXYU (537), 1,300 cc. Volkswagen, A. to F. 15.1.71, J. A. Littlechild, St. Albans

G-AZBL (PFA.938), 1,500 cc. Volkswagen, C. of A. 17.10.72, D. S. Morgan, Shoreham

G-AZSS (PFA.939), registered 20.4.72 to M. W. Rice, Rickmansworth

Jodel D.11 Club *(British-built)*

G-AVOP (PFA.900), Continental C90-8F, registered 8.6.67 to A. V. J. Lester, West Malling; completed by R. Emerson at Rudgwick, Sussex, C. of A. 27.11.70, to Horsham Self-Build F/G, d.b.r. at Slinfold 8.8.71

G-AWMD (PFA.904), Continental C90-14F, C. of A. 12.6.70, F. H. French, Swansea
G-AXWT (PFA.911), Continental C90-14F, built at Sharpthorn, Sussex by C. King and R. Owens, first flown at Redhill 11.71, C. of A. 6.1.72
G-AYVZ (PFA.907), built by the Fledgling Flying Group using parts of PFA.902, fuselage destroyed in fire at Rochester 6.71

Jodel D.112 (*with date of issue of Authorisation to Fly*)

G-ARDO (146), F-WBTE, F-BBTE, 6.10.61; G-AWIG (1067), F-BKAA, 10.10.68; G-AWVZ (898), F-PKVL, 30.5.69; G-AXTX (1077), F-BKCA, 27.2.70; G-AYBP (1131), F-BMEK, HB-SOV, 18.5.69; G-AYBR (1259), F-BMIG, 29.5.69, d.b.r. in pilotless take-off at Ipswich 17.3.71; G-AYCP (67), F-BGKO, 23.6.72; G-AYEB (586), F-BIQR, 5.6.70; G-AYEO (684), F-BIGG, 22.6.70; G-AYMU (1015), F-BJPB, 1.7.71, wrecked in ground collision with parked Beagle 206s G-ATYD and G-ASMK at Shoreham 8.9.71; G-AZHC (585), F-BIQQ, 11.4.72; G-AZVL (794), F-BILB, 10.7.72; G-BAAW (366), F-BHMY, 6.9.72

Jodel D.117

G-APOZ (846), 1.10.58, crashed at Wembury, Devon 13.8.65; G-ARNX (296), F-BHGE, 24.8.61; G-ARNY (595), F-BHXQ, 30.6.61; G-ARYW (639), F-BIBS, 21.5.62, crashed at Rhoose 16.8.62; G-ASJZ (826), F-BITD, 20.9.63; G-ASPB (596), F-BHXR, 27.2.64, crashed at Eton-on-Tern, Salop 26.10.66; G-ASXY (914), F-BIVA, 3.12.66; G-ASZH (705), F-BIDP, 9.7.68; G-ATIN (437), F-BHNV 8.10.66; G-ATIZ (636), F-BIBR, 5.10.66; G-ATWB (423), F-BHNH, 11.7.67, w.f.u. 12.72; G-AVEI (294), F-BHGI, 20.4.67; G-AVPM (593), F-BHXO, 4.8.67; G-AVVM (624), F-BIBF, 27.5.68

G-AWFW (599), PH-VRE, 2.5.68; G-AWVB (604), F-BIBA, 4.7.69; G-AWWI (728), F-BIDU, 2.4.69; G-AXAT (836), F-BITJ, 23.5.69; G-AXCG (510), PH-VRA, 24.10.69; G-AXCY (499), F-BHXB, 6.8.69; G-AXHV (695), F-BIDF, 10.7.69; G-AXXW (632), F-BIBN, 11.12.70; G-AXZT (607), F-BIBD, 24.2.71; G-AYGA (436), F-BHNU, registered 30.6.70; G-AYHX (903), F-BIVE, 25.9.70; G-AYKJ (730), F-BIDX, 19.4.71; G-AYKK (378), F-BHGM, 2.9.71; G-AYKT (507), F-BGYY, 21.10.70; G-AYWH (844), F-BIVO, 23.7.71; G-AYXP (693), F-BIDD, 28.7.71; G-AZFF (1175), F-BLFI, 14.10.71; G-AZFK (602), F-BHXY, 1.6.72; G-AZII (848), F-BNDO, 15.12.71; G-AZKP (419), F-BHND, 10.3.72; G-BAKR (814), F-BIOV, registered 27.12.72

Jodel D.119 (from a batch of eleven built in the furniture factory of M. Dumois at Chateau Thierry, France in 1950)

G-ATJN (863), F-PINZ, A. to F. issued 25.10.65; G-AXFN (980), F-PHBU, registered 19.5.69

Jodel D.120 Paris-Nice

G-ASPF (02), F-BFNP, 17.4.64; G-ATGX (134), F-BIXQ, 30.8.65, crashed at Wombleton 3.1.66; G-ATLV (224), F-BKNQ, 1.2.66; G-ATWL (209), F-OBUF, 14.12.66; G-AXDX (328), F-BOBL, 10.5.69; G-AXNJ (52), F-BHYO, registered 29.8.69; G-AYGG (184), F-BJPH, 5.8.70; G-AYLV (300), F-BNCG, 3.3.71; G-AZEF (321), F-BNZS, 31.12.71; G-AZGA (144), F-BIXV, 23.5.72; G-AZLF (230), F-BLFL, 10.5.72; G-BACJ (315), F-BNZC, 20.9.72; G-BAFR (72), F-BIKV, 31.3.73

Jodel D.120A Paris-Nice

G-ASXU (196), F-BKAG, 17.12.66; G-AVLY (331), 19.6.68; G-AVLZ (333), not imported; G-AVYV (252), F-BMAM, 2.1.69; G-AYRS (255), F-BMAV, 19.4.71; G-AZXE (296), F-BNCL, 6.9.72

Jodel D.140 Mousquetaire

G-AOVZ (42), D.140, 6.5.60; G-ARDZ (49), D.140A, 23.12.60; G-ARLX (66), D.140B, 26.5.61; G-AROW (71), D.140B, 21.10.61; G-ARRY (72), D.140B, 13.9.61; G-ATKX (163), D.140C, 4.5.66; G-ATSU (80), D.140B, F-BKSA, 25.7.66; G-AWFE (166), D.140E, 9.4.68; G-AYFP (18), D.140, F-OBLH, F-BMSI, 7.8.70; G-AZMA (65), D.140B, PH-SBB, 2.6.72

Jodel D.150 Mascaret

G-ASKL (27), D.150A, 24.10.63, converted to D.150 in 1970; G-ASPG (41), 27.4.64, crashed at Ingleby Greenhow, Yorks. 10.6.66; G-ASRT (45), 8.5.66; G-AVEF (16), F-BLDK, 10.3.68; G-AZBI (43), F-BMFB, 31.8.71; G-BACL (31), CN-TYY, F-BSTY, 25.6.73

Jodel DR.100A Ambassadeur

G-ATHX (74), F-OBMM, 28.10.65; G-AXUY (51), F-BIZI, 10.3.70

Jodel DR.105A Ambassadeur

G-ASAB (87), F-BIVS, 13.2.63, crashed at Fairoaks 14.6.67; G-AVHL (90), F-BIVY, 25.6.69; G-AXLS (86), F-BIVR, 22.9.69; G-AXUE (59), F-BKFX, 12.3.70

Jodel DR.1050 Ambassadeur

G-ARFT (170), 27.10.60; G-ARRD (274), 20.7.61; G-ARRE (275), 23.8.61; G-ARUH (284), 29.12.61; G-ARXT (355), 10.5.62; G-ASMB (127), F-OBMN, F-BKMN, 22.11.63, crashed at Dinard, France 18.7.67; G-ASRP (64), F-BITI, 13.4.64; G-ASXS (133), F-BJNG, 3.9.65; G-ATAG (226), F-BKGG, 3.5.65; G-ATEV (18), F-BHJL, 23.6.65; G-ATGE (114), F-BJJF, 30.7.65, G-ATGP (122), F-BJNB, 30.7.65; G-ATIC (06), F-BJCJ, 21.9.65; G-ATJA (378), F-BKHL, 16.11.65; G-ATWA (296), F-BKHA, 10.8.66

G-AVGJ (265), F-BJYJ, 22.6.67; G-AVIU (134), F-BJJN, 24.8.67; G-AVOA (195), F-BJYY, 7.7.67; G-AWEN (67), F-BIVD, 28.3.68; G-AWUE (299), F-BKHE, 25.3.69; G-AWWO (552), F-BLOI, 5.2.69; G-AXUK (292), F-BJYU, 9.1.70; G-AXVS (155), F-BJNL, 6.2.70; G-AYEA (369), F-BKHG, 5.6.70, crashed in the Bristol Channel 26.3.72; G-AYEH (455), F-BLJB, 4.12.70; G-AYEJ (253), F-BJYG, 10.7.70; G-AYEK (282), F-BJYL, 25.11.70; G-AYEV (179), F-BERH, F-OBTH, 12.8.70; G-AYJA (150), F-BJJJ, 5.10.70; G-AYKD (351), F-BKHR, 21.4.71; G-AYLL (11), F-BJHK, 3.2.72; G-AYMT (454), F-BKHY, 18.5.72; G-AYUT (479), F-BLTZ, 7.5.71; G-AZHO (157), F-BJNK, 31.10.72, G-AZWF (130), F-BJJT, 26.7.72; G-BAMW (278), F-BJYI, 8.5.73

Jodel DR.1051 Sicile

G-ATFD (311), F-BKIM, 11.7.67; G-AVCB (411), F-BLAK, 22.12.66; G-AVGZ (341), F-BKPR, 24.2.67, redesignated DR.1050 in June 1967; G-AVTH (243), F-BKGT, 12.9.67; G-AWWN (398), F-BLJA, 5.2.69; G-AXSM (512), F-BLRH, 10.4.70; G-AYEW (443), F-BLMJ, 31.7.70; G-AYGD (515), F-BLRE, 31.7.70; G-AYLC (536), F-BLZG, 9.11.70; G-AYLF (547), F-BLZQ, 30.11.70; G-AZAD (501), F-BLMX, 3.3.72; G-AZOU (354), F-BJYX, 19.5.72

Jodel DR.1050-M Excellence and DR.1051-M Sicile Record

G-ATBR (625), Sicile Record, 8.4.65, to Libya 5.68 as 5A-CAA; G-ATLB (78), Excellence, F-BIVG, 7.1.66; G-AVJK (453), F-BLJH, Excellence, 15.6.68; G-AWVE

G-ATHX, first of two early production Jodel DR.100A Ambassadeurs to be registered in Britain.

(612), F-BMPQ, Sicile Record, 7.1.69; G-AYYO (622), F-BMPZ, Excellence, 1.7.71; G-AYYT (587), F-BMGU, Excellence, 6.7.71; G-AYZK (590), F-BMGY, Excellence, 17.8.71; G-AZAH (580), OY-DFM, Excellence, 20.4.72; G-BAEE (579), F-BMGN, Sicile Record, 20.10.72

Jodel DR.200 and DR.221 Dauphin

G-AVOC (67), DR.221, 28.6.67, crashed at Framfield, Sussex 7.3.71; G-AVOM (65), DR.221, 3.10.67; G-AYDZ (1), DR.200, F-BLKV, 16.7.70

Jodel DR.250 Capitaine

G-ATTM (65), 11.5.66; G-ATZL (87), 18.5.67; G-AVIV (92), 13.4.67, crashed near Bethesda, Caernarvonshire, North Wales 22.8.69; G-AVOB (52), F-OCIB, 7.6.67, crashed in the English Channel 6.7.69; G-AZSB (18), F-OCGL, 6.10.72

Junkers F.13fe* and F.13ge

G-EBZV* (2024), 13.7.28, Rt. Hon. F. E. Guest, Hanworth, Sempill, Hanworth 5.30, re-engined with 450 h.p. Bristol Jupiter VI, Lord Lissant Beardmore, Hanworth 5.32, to Sweden 4.37 as SE-AFW; G-AAGU (2047), delivered Berlin–Croydon 26.5.29, C. of A. 30.5.29, Trost Bros. Ltd., Croydon, Walcot Airlines Ltd., Croydon 5.30, to Union Airways Ltd. 12.32 as ZS-AEN; G-AAZK (2052), 4.6.30, Walcot Airlines Ltd., Croydon, structural failure in the air, Meopham, Kent 21.7.30, G. L. P. Henderson and 5 passengers killed; G-ABDC (2074), delivered Rotterdam–Croydon 22.8.30, C. of A. 23.8.30, Personal Flying Services Ltd., Heston, Brooklands Airways Ltd. 4.33, to Sweden 12.34 as SE-AEC; G-ABDD (2005), delivered via Lympne–Croydon 22.7.30, Trost Bros. Ltd., flew to Berck, France 1.8.30 and did not return, sold abroad 8.30

Junkers Ju 52/3m

G-AERU (5440), SE-AER, 19.2.37, British Airways Ltd. 'Juno'*, to B.O.A.C., Takoradi 11.40, to SABENA as spares 4.41; G-AERX (5518), SE-AES, 7.4.37, British Airways Ltd. 'Jupiter'*, to B.O.A.C., Takoradi 11.40, to SABENA, Leopoldville 9.41 as OO-CAP; G-AFAP (5881), 28.1.38, British Airways Ltd. 'Jason', captured by the

Germans at Oslo 9.4.40; G-AGAE (5588), SP-AKX, three Bristol Pegasus VI, 7.11.39, Imperial Airways Ltd., interned at Bucharest 1939

* Re-engined at Gatwick 1940 with three 600 h.p. Pratt & Whitney Wasp R-1340-S3H1-G radial engines

LOT's famous Junkers Ju 52/3m SP-AKX (Bristol Pegasus VI engines) which escaped the 1939 German invasion, fled to Bucharest and just failed to become G-AGAE. *(Bristol Photo)*

Junkers Ju 52/3m.g8e *(British European Airways 'Jupiter' Class)*

Note: These aircraft were all scrapped at Warrington 2.48 unless otherwise stated. The Short & Harland conversion numbers are given before the C. of A. date.

G-AHBP (6750), D-APZX, VM908, (SH.7C), 7.10.46, scrapped at Castle Bromwich 2.48; G-AHOC (501441), VM923, (SH.16C), 5.11.46; G-AHOD (131150), VN740, (SH.10C), 12.12.46; G-AHOE, VN723, (SH.8C), 11.11.46; G-AHOF, VN729, (SH.9C), 29.11.46; G-AHOG (3317), VM979, (SH.17C), 5.11.46; G-AHOH (641364), VN746, (SH.14C), 14.3.47; G-AHOI (641227), VN744, (SH.13C), 8.2.47; G-AHOJ (500138), VN756, (SH.15C), 28.2.47; G-AHOK (2998), VN742, (SH.12C), 8.1.47, beyond repair in accident at Renfrew 26.1.47; G-AHOL (614213), VN741, (SH.11C), 19.12.46

Klemm L25

G-AAFU (129), L25-I, D-1565, 20.6.29, scrapped in 1939; G-AAFV (136), L25, 8.5.29, scrapped in 1931; G-AAHL (144), L25-I, 26.8.29, crashed at Whitchurch, Bristol 27.2.32; G-AAHW (152), L25-I, 26.8.29, w.f.u. 7.57, reconstructed by R. Nerou at Coventry, f/f by K. Sedgwick at Halfpenny Green 23.4.72, C. of A. renewal 6.6.72; G-AARO allotted to Klemm 9.29, n.t.u.; G-AATD (163), L25-I, 4.1.30, sold abroad pre-1939; G-AAUP (145), L25-I, 5.3.30, w.f.u. 12.39, reconstructed by R. S. Russell at Prestwick, f/f at Prestwick 31.5.72; G-AAWE (181), L25-I, 7.4.30, w.f.u. at Broxbourne 12.33; G-AAXK (182), L25-I, 16.6.30, stored at Sevenoaks in 1972; G-AAZH (180), L25a-I, D-1776, 14.7.30, impressed 4.40 as X5009

G-ABBT (216), L25a-I, 27.11.30, registration cancelled 5.36; G-ABCY (215), L25a-I, 16.7.30, in storage 1939; G-ABOS (214), L25a-I, 3.10.31, w.f.u. at Gravesend 3.37; G-ABRG (358), L25b-VII, D-2393, 12.10.31, sold abroad 1.33; G-ABTE (360), L25b-XI, 25.1.32, sold abroad 1.38; G-ABZO (413), L25c-XI, D-7, 30.9.32, to Ireland 10.36 as EI-ABJ

Klemm L26

G-AAVS (197), L26a-II, 26.3.30, sold abroad 12.34; G-ABBU (225), L26a-III, 2.7.30, almost certainly the machine refurbished at Brooklands 1939 as VR-HCY but never delivered due to the 1939–45 war (registration VR-HCY re-allotted to Porterfield 70, c/n 245, in 1941); G-ABCI (226), L26a-III, D-3, 7.7.30, to Holland 9.37 as PH-APA; G-ABFS (208), L26a-II, D-1833, sold abroad 9.33; G-ABOJ (325), L26a-III, 21.7.31, scrapped at Knowle, Birmingham 1945; G-ABRP (350), L26a-X, 7.11.31, w.f.u. at Heston 1937

Klemm L27

G-AAWW (196), L27a-III, 17.4.30, crashed at Croydon 2.33; G-ABJX (247), L27a-III, 27.3.31, scrapped at Burton, Wilts. 1946; G-ABOP (307), L27a-VIII, 21.8.31, scrapped at Whitchurch, Bristol 1939; G-ABOR (330), L27a-IX, 25.8.31, to Australia 6.36 as VH-USZ, crashed at Salisbury, S.A. 13.3.38

Klemm L26a-III VR-HCY outside the College of Aeronautical Engineering's hangar at Brooklands in 1939. It was never delivered and is believed to have been the former G-ABBU. (*C. A. Nepean Bishop*)

Lockheed Model 10 Electra

G-AEPN (1080), 12.3.37, impressed 4.40 for No.24 Sqn. as W9105, destroyed in German night raid on Hendon 6–7.11.40; G-AEPO (1081), 17.3.37, impressed 4.40 for No.24 Sqn. as W9106, dismantled at Hendon 6.42; G-AEPP (1082), 17.3.37, crashed in night landing at Croydon in blizzard 13.12.37; G-AEPR (1083), 17.3.37, to B.O.A.C., Cairo 4.40 as 'Leith', destroyed in accident 1944; G-AESY (1102), 15.6.37, crashed in sea off Copenhagen 15.8.39; G-AFCS (1025), NC14936, 16.2.38, to B.O.A.C., Cairo 4.40 as 'Lea', crashed at Almaza 19.11.43; G-AFEB (1122), 14.3.38, impressed 4.40 for No. 24 Sqn. as W9104, damaged beyond repair landing at Clifton 12.10.41

Five Lockheed 10A Electras belonging to Polske Linje Lotnicze (LOT), which escaped to Bucharest, Rumania, when the Germans invaded Poland 1.9.39, were registered to Imperial Airways Ltd. and their Cs. of A. validated 7.11.39 in readiness for ferry flights to Cairo. When it proved impossible to repaint them in British marks, they were interned by the Rumanian Government and later seized by the Germans. The allocated markings were: G-AGAF (1087), formerly SP-BGG; G-AGAG (1047), SP-AYC; G-AGAH (1086), SP-BGF; G-AGAI (1085), SP-BGE; G-AGAJ (1088), SP-BGH

The Earl of Granard's Lockheed 12A, G-AHLH, outside the terminal building at Croydon Airport in 1948. (*A. J. Jackson*)

Lockheed Model 12A

G-AEMZ (1206), 3.4.37, impressed 9.39 as R8987, d.b.r. at Farnborough 15.4.42; G-AEOI (1212), 10.3.37, impressed 12.39 as X9316, rest. 2.46, to Shell Co. of Venezuela 1947 as YV-P-AEJ, later YV-C-TAD; G-AFCO (1238), 18.11.37, to Maharajah of Jammu and Kashmir 3.38 as VT-AJS, impressed in India 1941 as AX803; G-AFKR (1267), 15.2.39, to France 5.39 as F-ARQA; G-AFPF (1270), to France 5.39 as F-ARPP; G-AFTL (1203), NC16077, 11.6.39, to British West Indian Airways 11.42 as VP-TAI; G-AFXP (1274), 12.1.40, to Maharajah of Jaipur 3.40 as VT-AMB, impressed in India 1942 as HX798

G-AGDT (1285), Y-0233 (Cunliffe-Owen Aircraft Ltd., Eastleigh, Class B marking), 13.9.40, to Sweden 1.51 as SE-BTO; G-AGTL (1287), NC33615, U.S. Navy 02947, F. S. Cotton 'Caprice', to France 12.60 as F-BJJY; G-AGVZ (1277), R.A.F. LA621, to U.S.A. 2.47 as NC79820; G-AGWM (1211), LA620, Short and Harland Ltd. civil conversion SH.49C, to Belgium 3.47 as OO-AFA; G-AGWN (1275), LA623, Short and Harland Ltd. civil conversion SH.50C, 21.5.47, to Australia 2.53 as VH-BHH; G-AHLH (1226), NC18130, 28.5.47, re-registered in Ireland 3.61 as EI-ALV but based at Le Bourget

Lockheed Model 14-WF62

G-AFGN (1467), 15.9.38, burned out after forced landing at Luxeuil, France 11.8.39; G-AFGO (1468), 15.9.38, crashed at Walton, Somerset 22.11.38; G-AFGP (1469), 15.9.38, to B.O.A.C. 4.40 as 'Livingstone', crashed at Khartoum 4.8.41; G-AFGR (1470), 15.9.38, to B.O.A.C. 4.40 as 'Lafayette', crashed at El Fasher, Sudan 19.1.41; G-AFKD (1484), 22.11.38, to B.O.A.C. 4.40 as 'Loch Invar', crashed near Loch Lomond 23.4.40; G-AFKE (1485), 30.11.38, to B.O.A.C. 4.40 as 'Lothair', to the R.A.F. 10.43 as HK982; G-AFMO (1490), 18.3.39, crash landed at Heston 15.1.40; G-AFMR (1491), 21.3.39, to B.O.A.C. 4.40 as 'Leander', to the R.A.F. 10.43 as HK984, serial not used, scrapped at Kabrit 11.43; G-AFYU (1444), PH-ASL, 19.8.39, lost at sea off Malta 21.12.39

Lockheed Model 14-H

G-AFZZ (1493), SP-BPL, 7.11.39, crashed at Bucharest 24.7.40; G-AGAA (1492), SP-BPK, 7.11.39, interned in Rumania 12.39; G-AGAB (1420), SP-BNE, interned in

Rumania 12.39; G-AGAC (1423), 7.11.39, SP-BNH, interned in Rumania 12.39; G-AGAV (1425), SP-LMK, 15.3.38, scrapped at Croydon 2.46; G-AGBG (1421), SP-BNF, 13.10.38, to Sweden 3.51 as SE-BTN; G-AKPD (1429), CF-TCD, converted to Model 14-08, 27.7.48, lost at sea off Elba 29.10.48

Lockheed Model 414 Hudson 1

G-AGAR (1761), N7364, 3.5.40, destroyed by enemy action, Le Luc, France 29.5.41; G-AGCE (2789), AM707, 6.6.41, returned to the R.A.F. 8.41; G-AGDC (2585), V9061, 8.7.41, B.O.A.C. 'Loch Lomond', to R.A.F. 8.45 as VJ416; G-AGDF (3772), 29.9.41, B.O.A.C. 'Loch Leven', crashed off Swedish coast near Skredewick 23.6.42; G-AGDK (3757), 28.1.42, B.O.A.C. 'Loch Lyon', to R.A.F. 8.45 as VJ421; G-AGDO (c/n not given), AE581, B.O.A.C. 'Loch Loyal'; returned to the R.A.F. 4.42

Lockheed Model 18-07 Lodestar *(all B.O.A.C. aircraft except G-AJAW)*

G-AGBO (2018), 3.1.41, 'Lanark', to R.A.F. 10.43 as HK973; G-AGBP (2024), 3.1.41, 'Leicester', to R.A.F. 10.43 as HK980; G-AGBR (2070), 3.2.41, converted to Model 18-56, 'Lewes' (later 'Lake George'), to East African Airways 4.48 as VP-KFE (later SE-BUF); G-AGBS (2071), 10.2.41, conv. 18-56, 'Lichfield' (later 'Lake Nyasa'), to East African Airways 2.48 as VP-KFB; G-AGBT (2076), 18.2.41, conv. 18-56, 'Lincoln' (later 'Lake Victoria'), to East African Airways 2.48 as VP-KFA (later SE-BUU); G-AGBU (2090), 21.3.41, conv. 18-56, 'Lowestoft', to Australia 6.49 as VH-FAD (later ZK-BJM); G-AGBV (2091), 24.3.41, conv. 18-56, 'Ludlow' (later 'Lake Albert'), to East African Airways 2.48 as VP-KFC; G-AGBW (2094), 31.3.41, conv. 18-56, 'Lyndhurst', crashed on Kinangop Peak, Kenya 29.11.44; G-AGBX (2095), 7.4.41, conv. 18-56, 'Llandaff' (later 'Lake Edward'), to East African Airways 4.48 as VP-KFF

G-AGEH (2147), 41-29635, HK851, 2.6.42, conv. 18-56, 'Lake Baringo', to R.A.F. 11.47, to U.S.A. 11.55 as N9927F, later EC-ADT; G-AGIG (2148), EW980, 26.7.43, conv. 18-56, 'Lake Karoun', to R.A.F. 11.47, to U.S.A. 5.55 as N9928F, later N1251W; G-AGIL (2143), HK855, conv. 18-56, 22.10.43, 'Lake Nyasa', scrapped at R.A.F. Kasfareet 11.47; G-AGIM (2144), EW977, 23.11.43, conv. 18-56, 'Lake Tanganyika', to R.A.F. 11.47, to U.S.A. 9.55 as N9926F; G-AGIN (2146), EW976, conv. 18-56, 'Lake Timsah', scrapped at R.A.F. Kasfareet 11.47; G-AGJH (2153), EW982, 28.1.44, conv. 18-56, 'Lake Tana' (2), scrapped at R.A.F. Kasfareet 11.47; G-AJAW (1954), NX17835, VP-TAE, 17.2.47, to Sweden 10.51 as SE-BTL

Lockheed Model 18-08 Lodestar *(Impressed American aircraft)*

G-AGCL (c/n and previous identity unrecorded), transferred direct to the Free French Air Force; G-AGCM (2093), NC33617, 20.10.41, conv. 18-56, 'Lake Mariut', to the R.A.F. 10.46 as VR955; G-AGCN (2020), NC25630, AX756, 20.10.41, conv. 18-56, 'Lake Victoria', to R.A.F. 11.47, later N9933F and ZK-BVE; G-AGCO (2021), NC25631, AX758, 25.11.41, conv. 18-56, 'Lake Albert', scrapped at R.A.F. Kasfareet 11.47; G-AGCP (2022), NC25632, AX721, 9.8.41, conv. 18-56, 'Lake Edward', scrapped at R.A.F. Kasfareet 11.47; G-AGCR (2072), NC3138, AX718, 'Lake Rudolf', beyond repair in take-off accident at Malta 13.5.42; G-AGCS (2031), NC25640, not delivered to B.O.A.C., direct to R.A.F. as AX723

G-AGCT (2001), NC25604, AX722, 'Lake Timsah', to R.A.F. 10.43; G-AGCU (2068), NC34900, AX720, conv. 18-56, 'Lake Kivu', to R.A.F. 11.47, to U.S.A. 6.56 as N9932F; G-AGCV (2042), NC6175, AX717, conv. 18-56, 23.7.41, 'Lake Chad', scrapped at R.A.F. Kasfareet 11.47; G-AGCW (1956), NC18993, AX719, 30.8.41, 'Lake

Tana' (1), to R.A.F. 9.43 as HK975; G-AGCX (2012), NC3030, 31.1.42, 'Lake Mweru', to R.A.F. 9.43 as HK981; G-AGCY (2077), NC1611, AX765, 25.11.41, 'Lake Rukwa', scrapped at R.A.F. Kasfareet 11.47; G-AGCZ (2023), NC25633, 28.11.41, 'Lake Stephanie', crashed in the Western Desert, North Africa 22.12.41

G-AGDD (2087), NX34901, 30.7.41, 'Loch Losna', to Norwegian Air Force 7.45 as '2087'; G-AGDE (2086), 11.8.41, 'Loch Lesja', crashed at sea 15 miles off Leuchars, Fife 17.12.43

Lockheed Model 18-56 Lodestar *(Lend-Lease aircraft)*

G-AGEI (2084), 20.8.42, 'Loch Leon', to Norwegian Air Force 7.45 as '2084', later OH-VKO and SE-BZK; G-AGEJ (2085), 12.9.42, 'Loch Lange', ditched in North Sea 4.4.43; G-AGIH (2491), 42-56018, 26.5.44, crashed at Kinnekulle 29.8.44; G-AGII (2492), 42-56019, 30.6.44, to Norwegian Air Force 7.45 as '2492', later SE-BTI; G-AGIJ (2593), 43-16433, 28.3.44, to Norwegian Air Force 7.45 as '2593', later OH-VKP and SE-BZE; G-AGIK (2594), 43-16434, 28.3.44, to Norwegian Air Force 7.45 as '2594', later SE-BTG

G-AGLG (2615), 43-16455, 15.11.44, to Norwegian Air Force 7.45 as '2615', later SE-BTH; G-AGLH (2616), 43-16456, 4.12.44, to Norwegian Air Force 7.45 as '2616', later SE-BTK; G-AGLI (2620), 43-16460, 30.10.44, lost in Gulf of Bothnia 2.5.45

Lockheed Model 049 Constellation

G-ARHK (2036), N88836, CU-T547, seized at Charlotte, North Carolina during delivery flight 27.1.61, registration ntu; G-ARVP (1967), 43-10315, N90828, 4X-AKB, 6.4.62, scrapped at Luton 5.65; G-ARXE (1965), 43-10313, N90827, 4X-AKA, scrapped at Luton 5.65

Lockheed Model 049E Constellation *(with B.O.A.C. names)*

G-AHEJ (1975), 21.5.46, 'Bristol', to Capital Airlines 6.55 as N2740A, rest. 1.61, scrapped at Biggin Hill 2.63; G-AHEK (1976), 21.5.46, 'Berwick', to Capital Airlines 6.55 as N2737A; G-AHEL (1977), 24.6.46, 'Bangor', to Capital Airlines 6.55 as N2736A, rest. 3.61, to Britair East Africa 1.66 as 5Y-ABF; G-AHEM (1978), 24.6.46, 'Balmoral', to Capital Airlines 6.55 as N2735A; G-AHEN (1980), 1.7.46, 'Baltimore', crash landed at Filton 8.1.51, rebuilt as N74192, to El Al as 4X-AKD, rest. 2.62, scrapped at Luton 1965

G-AKCE (1971), NX54212, 31.3.48, 'Bedford', to Capital Airlines 6.55 as N2741A; G-AMUP (2051), N90921, 9.3.53, 'Boston', to Capital Airlines 4.55 as N2738A, rest. 12.60, scrapped at Luton 1965; G-AMUR (2065), N90927, 26.3.53, 'Barnstaple', to Capital Airlines 5.55 as N2739A

Lockheed 749A Constellation *(with B.O.A.C. names)*

G-ALAK (2548), EI-ACR, 30.6.48, 'Brentford', to Trans Bolivian Airways 1.68 as CP-797, later OB-R-899; G-ALAL (2549), EI-ACS, 30.6.48, 'Banbury', sold in Puerto Rico 4.67; G-ALAM (2554), EI-ADA, 30.6.48, 'Belfast', crashed at Kallang, Singapore 13.3.54; G-ALAN (2555), EI-ADD, 30.6.48, 'Beaufort', to Pacific Northern Airlines 3.59 as N1554V; G-ALAO (2566), EI-ADE, 21.7.48, 'Braemar', to Capitol Airways 9.58 as N4902C

G-ANNT (2671), N6025C, 25.9.54, 'Buckingham', to Capitol Airways 4.58 as N4901C; G-ANTF (2504), VT-CQS, VH-EAF, 15.9.54, 'Berkeley', to Transocean Airlines 3.58 as N9816F; G-ANTG (2505), VT-CQR, VH-EAE, 15.10.54, 'Bournemouth', to Pacific Northern Airlines 11.58 as N1552V; G-ANUP (2562), VH-EAA, 9.2.55, 'Branksome', to Aero Transport 5.63 as OE-IFO; G-ANUR (2565), VH-EAB, 18.2.55, 'Basildon', sold in Puerto Rico 3.67, later to U.S.A. as N1949; G-ANUV (2551), PH-TDC, N90607, 1.7.55, 'Blantyre', to Transocean Airlines 2.58 as N9830F; G-ANUX (2556), PH-TDD, N90623, 8.12.54, 'Bala', to Pacific Northern Airlines 4.57 as N1593V; G-ANUY (2557), PH-TDE, N90625, to Avianca, Colombia 5.59 as HK-651; G-ANUZ (2559), PH-TDG, N90621, 30.5.55, 'Belvedere', to Transocean Airlines 4.58 as N9812F; G-ANVA (2564), PH-TDH, N90608, 17.5.55, 'Blakeney', to Avianca, Colombia 4.59 as HK-652; G-ANVB (2589), PH-TDI, N90624, 31.3.55, 'Blackrod'; to Transocean Airlines 4.58 as N9813F; G-ANVD (2544), PH-TDB, N90622, 30.4.55, 'Beverley', to Avianca, Colombia 5.59 as HK-650

G-ASYF (2630), ZS-DBS, 13.5.66, to U.S.A. ex Baginton 23.6.67; G-ASYS (2623), ZS-DBR, to spares at Baginton 4.67; G-ASYT (2631), ZS-DBT, to spares at Baginton 6.67; G-ASYU (2632), ZS-DBU, to spares at Baginton 4.67

Luton L.A.3 Minor

G-AEPD (L.A.3), 35 h.p. Anzani, A. to F. 3.3.37, Luton Aircraft Ltd., Barton-in-the-Clay, Beds.; A. J. Cook, Anstruther, Fife 5.39; wrecked circa 1947

Luton L.A.4 Minor *(with date of issue of Authorisation to Fly)*

G-AFBP (L.A.4), 40 h.p. A.B.C. Scorpion, Luton Aircraft Ltd., Gerrards Cross; destroyed when the Phoenix Works was burned down in 1943

G-AFIR (J.S.S.2), 35 h.p. Anzani, 14.8.38, J. S. Squires, Rearsby; rebuilt with 40 h.p. Aeronca J.A.P. J-99 at Pinner 1950 by A. W. J. G. Ord-Hume; damaged in forced landing at Oxhey, Herts. 1.5.51; rebuilt and flown again 1956; owned by A. J. Phillips, Fairoaks in 1971; crashed at Fairoaks 14.3.71

G-AFIU (C.A.4), also known as the Parker C.A.4 Parasol, partially constructed by C. F. Parker at Pembroke in 1938; fuselage in store at Cheadle, Cheshire 1972

G-AFRC (J.E.C.1), 35 h.p. Anzani, 8.3.39, J. E. Carine, Hall Caine airfield, Isle of Man; beyond repair landing at Jurby 2.9.39

G-AFUG (W.S.H.1), 40 h.p. A.B.C. Scorpion, partially constructed by W. S. Henry at Newtownards, Co. Down in 1939

G-AGEP (L.R.M.1), 40 h.p. Aeronca J.A.P. J-99, built by L. R. Miller at Seaton, Devon; registered 9.42; J. A. Bagley, Farnborough 1952; C. M. Roberts, Luton 4.59 for rebuild as PFA.538B; not proceeded with; wings to Jenny Wren G-ASRF

G-AHMO (PFA.815/R.S.F.1), 40 h.p. Aeronca J.A.P. J-99, partially constructed by R. S. Finch at Darwen, Lancs. 1946–49, reg'n. cancelled 2.49; rest. 1.66 to T. G. Thompson, Cottesmore and completed as PFA.815; A. to F. 11.5.66; crashed at Sandown, Isle of Wight 22.10.66; wreck to spares for G-ATWS

G-ALUZ (D.E.F.1), 25 h.p. Scott Squirrel, registration reserved in 1949 for D. E. Felce who completed 11 hours taxying before storing it at Hinckley, Leics.

G-AMAW (J.R.C.1), 32 h.p. Bristol Cherub III, 3.10.50, J. R. Coates, Hitchin 'Sunbury'; airworthy with same owner in 1973 with amended c/n SA.1

G-AMUW (W.P.1), registered 9.52 to W. Petrie, St. Margaret's Hope, Orkney; still incomplete in 1958; construction abandoned

G-ASAA (O-H/4), 40 h.p. Aeronca J.A.P. J-99, 19.8.63, built at Sandown by A. W. J. G. Ord-Hume and first flown 2.8.63; Four Counties Flying Syndicate, Ancaster strip, Lincs. 5.64

Luton L.A.4A Minor *(with date of issue of Authorisation to Fly)*

G-APVI (PAL.1101), construction begun by J. T. Hayes at Branston, Lincs. in 1959; nearly complete at Hemswell in 1973

G-APYV (PFA.820/PAL.1117), registration reserved 5.60 for F. W. Tilley, Maidstone, Kent

G-ARIF (PAL.1401), registered 6.60 as L.A.4C to A. W. J. G. Ord-Hume; constructed at Sandown 1965–73 as Ord-Hume OH-7 Coupé

G-ARXP (PFA.816/PAL.1119), 40 h.p. Aeronca J.A.P. J-99, 26.8.66, W. C. Hymas, Rochester; re-engined with 62 h.p. Walter Mikron III in 1967

G-ASCY (PAL.1124), 40 h.p. Aeronca J.A.P. J-99, 27.10.63, C. Bos, Norwich; P. C. Mumby, Grimsby 12.66; D. Boden, Lincoln 1.68; to Ireland 2.70 as EI-ATP

G-ASEA (PAL.1154), 40 h.p. Aeronca J.A.P. J-99, 27.9.67, built at Elmdon by G. P. Smith and M. Fawkes, first flown at Wellesbourne Mountford

G-ASEB (PAL.1149), 55 h.p. Lycoming O-145-B2, 26.6.63, built at Leeds and erected at Yeadon by J. A. Anning, first flown by J. E. G. Appleyard 4.5.63; A. Alderdice, Newtownards 9.65; Phoenix Aircraft Ltd., Cranleigh, Surrey 5.69; F. McVeigh, Cranfield, Co. Down 8.72

G-ASML (PFA.802/PAL.1148), 34 h.p. Ardem 4CO2-1, built 1963–66 by R. M. Kirby, Stapleford, Cambs.; T. A. Hampton, Roborough 10.66; A. to F. issued 23.11.66; R. C. Wingfield, St. Austell 7.68; R. Radmore, Bolt Head, Devon 3.70; R. Cole, Roborough 9.72

Luton L.A.4A Minor G-ATCN (with fin and balanced rudder) showing the 55 h.p. Lycoming installation. (*Richard Riding*)

G-ASXJ (PFA.801), 34 h.p. Ardem 4CO2-1, registered 10.64 to P. D. Lea and A. E. Lingard, Ancaster, Lincs.; to Blackbushe 5.70

G-ATCJ (PFA.812/PAL.1163/R.M.S.1), registered 3.65 to R. Sharphouse, built at Thirsk, Yorks., first flown at Dishforth 1.9.72

G-ATCN (PAL.1118), 55 h.p. Lycoming O-145-A2, 6.10.65, D. G. Peacock, Ipswich; A. C. Chapman, Hethel, Norfolk 6.72

G-ATFW (PFA.811), 55 h.p. Lycoming O-145-A2, 22.2.67, built by G. W. Shield at Mexborough Grammar School, Yorks., based at Doncaster; based Hemswell from 1971

G-ATKH (PFA.809), 40 h.p. Aeronca J.A.P. J-99, 7.6.68, 'Mayfly', built at Stourbridge by E. B. W. Woodall; L. Hepper, Rochester 8.69

G-ATWS (PFA.818/PAL.1195), 36 h.p. Aeronca E.113C, built by D. Handley at Spondon, Derby, first flown 17.2.68, A. to F. 27.3.68; K. J. Hazelwood, Tollerton 9.69

G-AVDY (PFA.808/PAL.1183), 55 h.p. Lycoming O-145-A2, 5.5.67, built at Sheffield by D. McNeill and partners; M. F. Pendlebury and partners, Tollerton 1.69

G-AVLX (PFA.814), 34 h.p. Ardem 4CO2-1, built at Belfast by N. F. O'Neill and R. S. Parke; crashed at Newtownards during preliminary trial 27.10.68

G-AVUO (PAL.1313), registered 9.67 to C. P. Butterfield, Walney Island; sold before completion to M. Vaisey, Hemel Hempstead to provide parts for G-AXKH

G-AWIP (PFA.830/PAL.1308), 65 h.p. Continental C65-8F, 17.3.70, 'Sarah', built at Crawley by T. Reagan and based at Redhill 1970–72; to N. Cranfield, Redhill 11.72

G-AWMN (PFA.827), registered 7.68 to R. E. R. Wilks, under construction at Tiptree, Essex in 1971

G-AXGR (PAL.1125), 40 h.p. Aeronca J.A.P. J-99, 8.1.70, built by R. and W. Spall at Longniddry, East Lothian 1968–70

G-AXKH (PFA.823/PAL.1316), registered 7.69 to M. E. Vaisey, completed at Hemel Hempstead in 1973

G-AYDY (PFA.817/PAL.1302), registered 5.70 to L. J. E. Goldfinch, airframe completed at Old Sarum in 1973

G-AYSK (PFA.832), 65 h.p. Continental A65-8, 7.10.71, L. Plant, Stoke-on-Trent/Meir

G-AYTT (PFA.841), two seater, 90 h.p. Continental C90, Grp. Capt. A. S. Knowles; first flown at Fairoaks 6.73; redesignated Phoenix Duet

G-AZHU (PFA.839), registered 1.11.71 to A. E. Morris, Nazeing, Essex

G-AZPV (PFA.833), registered 14.3.72 to J. Scott, Dorking

G-BAPC (MAPS.2), registered 1.73 to Midland Aircraft Preservation Society; to use wings built in Scotland pre-1939 and possibly an Anzani engine

Luton L.A.5 Major

G-AFMU (L.A.5/1), 62 h.p. Walter Mikron II, A. to F. issued 4.3.39, Luton Aircraft Ltd., Gerrards Cross; burned in factory fire 1943

Luton L.A.5A Major

G-AOVX (PAL.1207), construction commenced at Barton 1959 by J. A. Cowap; sold incomplete to V. C. Hester, Waddington 11.60

G-APUG (PFA.1205/PAL.1203), construction commenced at Sawbridgeworth, Herts. 1.59 by L. D. Blyth; sold incomplete to L. D. Firmin and transferred to Blackbushe 10.63

G-APUN (PAL.1201), registered 6.59 to W. G. Cooper, Weybridge; believed not completed

G-ARAD (PAL.1204), registered 4.60 to W. T. Sproat, Borgue, Kirkudbright, Scotland; completed with 90 h.p. Continental C90 as PFA.836 in 1973

The prototype Luton L.A.5 Major, G-AFMU, built and flown in 1939. (*W. K. Kilsby*)

G-ARAF (PAL.1209), registered 4.60 to C. E. Stones and partners (R.A.F. Waddington P.F.A. Group); constructed with components from G-AOVX

G-ARWX (PAL.1208), registered 2.62 to A. G. Cameron, Forres, Kingswells, Scotland; sold to A. Milne partly complete, and scrapped

G-ASWH (PAL.1225), 62 h.p. Walter Mikron II, built at Wincanton, Somerset 1964–65 by S. G. and T. G. Stott, first flown at Compton Abbas 2.65; A. to F. issued 24.2.65; W. H. Mansfield, Shoreham 8.72

G-AVON (PAL.1234), built by G. R. Mee at Loughborough; completed 9.69 and picketted at Rearsby; based at Hemswell 1971

G-AVXG (001), 100 h.p. Continental O-200-A, erected at Blackbushe 1968 by Robinson Aircraft Ltd.; A. to F. issued 7.5.68; R. G. Kellett, Benenden, Kent

G-AYVN (PFA.1204), registered 6.4.71 to C. T. Gough, built at Upleaden Farm, Newent, Glos.; based at Staverton

G-AYXO (PFA.1211), registered 27.4.71 to C. Drinkwater, Stapleford; completed 1972

G-BAGU (PFA.1216), registered 6.11.72 to J. Gawley, Reading

Martinsyde F.4 *(Hispano-Suiza engines)*

G-EAES K-152, registered 13.6.19 to Martinsyde Ltd., Brooklands; registration cancelled 8.20

G-EANM (E4-500), 22.10.19, Martinsyde Ltd., Brooklands; demonstrated in Spain 10.19; named 'Vasco da Gama' at Lisbon 11.11.19; to Portuguese A/F 12.19

G-EATD D4267, registered 7.5.20 to Handley Page Ltd., Cricklewood; Aircraft Disposal Co. Ltd., Croydon 5.22; grounded after Aerial Derby 29.7.22

G-EAUR D4352, registered 15.7.20 to Handley Page Ltd., Cricklewood; registration cancelled at census 10.1.23

G-EAUX H7786, first flown after conversion at Brooklands 20.5.20, C. of A. 6.9.20; overseas demonstrator; not flown after C. of A. expiry 26.11.23

G-EAWE H7780, registered 14.1.21 to Handley Page Ltd., Cricklewood; left Croydon for Warsaw 29.1.21; sold to the Polish Government

G-EAXB D4279, registered 1.6.21 to Aircraft Disposal Co. Ltd., Croydon; crashed at Croydon 5.5.22

G-EAYK R.A.F. serial not recorded, 6.10.21, Martinsyde Ltd., Brooklands; overseas demonstrator; not flown after C. of A. expiry 26.11.23

G-EAYP D4275, first flown after conversion at Brooklands 4.10.21; C. of A. 14.10.21, Martinsyde Ltd., Brooklands; overseas demonstrator; not flown after C. of A. expiry 26.11.23

G-EBDM H7692, registered 19.6.22 to Aircraft Disposal Co. Ltd., Croydon; believed sold abroad; registration cancelled 8.6.23

G-EBFA H7688, 16.4.25, Aircraft Disposal Co. Ltd., Croydon; believed sold abroad; registration cancelled 5.1.27

G-EBMI D4295, 15.4.26, Aircraft Disposal Co. Ltd., Croydon; C. of A. expired 6.5.28; stored at Croydon; flown again by Southern Aircraft Ltd., Shoreham in 1930; sold to E. D. A. Bigg, Woodley 3.30; crashed at Woodley 24.8.30

Martinsyde F.4A

G-EAPP (E4-500), registered 21.11.19 to Martinsyde Ltd., Brooklands; not flown after the Aerial Derby 24.7.20

G-EAQH (F.4A), 3.5.20, Martinsyde Ltd., Brooklands; crashed in 1920

G-EATX (310), 3.11.20, Martinsyde Ltd., Brooklands; believed sold abroad; registration cancelled 4.8.22

G-ABKH (A.V.1), 16.3.31, erected at Croydon by A.D.C. Aircraft Ltd. for C. Amherst Villiers; C. B. Field, Kingswood Knoll aerodrome, Surrey 10.32; hit telegraph pole and crashed at Bekesbourne, Kent 5.2.33

Martinsyde F.6

G-EAPI (E4-500), 25.8.20, Martinsyde Ltd., Brooklands; to the Canadian Government 10.22 as G-CYEQ, struck off charge 4.11.25

G-EATQ (61/3), registered 8.6.20 to Martinsyde Ltd., Brooklands; believed sold abroad; registration cancelled at census 10.1.23

G-EBDK (No recorded c/n), first flown at Brooklands 29.9.21; registered 16.6.22 to Martinsyde Ltd.; F. P. Raynham, Brooklands 3.23; C. of A. 11.7.23; L. C. G. M. Le Champion, Brooklands 1.25; Leslie Hamilton, Brooklands 7.25; Maj. J. C. Savage, Hendon 11.27; dismantled at Brooklands 4.30

Martinsyde Type A Mk.I

G-EAMR (E4-500), registered 10.9.19 to Martinsyde Ltd., Brooklands; left Hounslow for Australia 12.12.19; lost at sea off Corfu 17.12.19

G-EAPN (E4-500), registered 20.11.19 to Martinsyde Ltd., Brooklands; almost certainly reworked as Type A Mk.II c/n 617 for Irish Air Corps

Note: E4-500 was entered in 1919 as the constructor's number on the Certificates of Registration of several civil Martinsydes. They were not, of course, all one and the same aircraft!

Martinsyde Type A Mk.II

G-EATY (218), 6.10.20, Martinsyde Ltd., Brooklands, shipped to the Aerial Survey Co., Newfoundland in 1921; registration cancelled at census 10.1.23

Martinsyde A.D.C.I and A.D.C. Nimbus*

G-EBKL (K.501), first flown at Croydon 11.10.24, C. of A. 1.1.25, Aircraft Disposal Co. Ltd., Croydon; scrapped at Croydon and burned in 1930

G-EBMH (K.502), 11.6.26, Aircraft Disposal Co. Ltd., Croydon; sold to the Latvian Air Force with seven unregistered machines (c/n K.503–K.509)

G-EBOJ* (K.1001), 2.7.26, Aircraft Disposal Co. Ltd., Croydon; scrapped at Croydon and burned in 1930

G-EBOL* (K.1002), 2.7.26, Aircraft Disposal Co. Ltd., Croydon; Air Taxis Ltd., Stag Lane 'Gugnunc I' 3.27; d.b.r. in forced landing in fog on Epsom Downs, inbound from France 7.10.27; stored at Croydon until burned 1930

G-EATY, sole example of a Martinsyde Type A Mk.II in British civil markings. (*Martinsyde Ltd.*)

McCandless M-4 Gyroplane *(with dates of Permit to Fly)*

G-ARTZ (M-4/1), 650 cc. Triumph, 26.10.65, R. and W. A. C. McCandless, Newtownards; J. L. McGladery, Newtownards 4.69; fitted with 1,500 cc. Volkswagen in 1970

G-ATXW (M-4/2), 1,600 cc. Volkswagen, 5.6.68, W. H. Ekin, Newtownards

G-ATXX (M-4/3), registered 27.7.66 to R. McCandless, Newtownards

G-ATXY (M-4/4), McCandless M-4/T1 two seat trainer, 1,600 cc. Volkswagen, 26.12.68, R. McCandless, Newtownards

G-AXHZ (M-4/5), 28.7.69, R. McCandless, Newtownards; to G. J. Fasenfeld, Roscrea, Co. Tipperary 7.69 as EI-ASR

G-AXVN (M-4/6), registered 5.1.70 to R. McCandless, Newtownards

McCandless M-4 Gyroplane *(built by W. H. Ekin (Engineering) Ltd.)*

G-AXXN (1002), registered 13.2.70 to W. H. Ekin, Newtownards; redesignated 2.73 as W.H.E. Airbuggy

Note: G-AXYX to G-AXZB, c/n 1003–1007, registered 10.3.70 to W. H. Ekin for completion as W.H.E. Airbuggy aircraft

Messerschmitt Bf 108B-1 Taifun

G-AFRN (2039), 26.6.39, impressed 4.41 as DK280, crashed near Rugeley, Staffs. 20.7.44; G-AFZO (1660), D-IDBT, impressed 9.41 as ES955 (mis-painted as ES995), rest. 9.46 but flew as G-AFRN, to Switzerland 4.50 as HB-ESL; G-AGUZ (15), French-built Nord 1000, unconverted at Gatwick 1946; G-AKZY (3059), Bf 108D-1, not converted at Gatwick 1949, sold abroad 1.50

Note: D-IJHW, seized at Croydon 3.9.39, impressed 6.40 as AW167, demobilised 9.46 as 'G-AFZO', to Switzerland 4.50 as HB-ESM

Messerschmitt Bf 109 *(Spanish-built Hispano HA-1112-MIL)*

G-AWHD (190), Spanish Air Force C4K-126, sold in the U.S.A. 2.69; G-AWHE (67), C4K-31, to the U.S.A. 2.69 as N109ME; G-AWHF (129), C4K-61, d.b.r. landing at Duxford 21.5.68; G-AWHG (139), C4K-75, later modified to resemble P-51 Mustang with serial 123577, Fairoaks Av. Serv. Ltd., Blackbushe 2.73, G-AWHH (145), C4K-105, to the U.S.A. 10.68 as N6036; G-AWHI (166), C4K-106, sold in the U.S.A. 2.69; G-AWHJ (171), C4K-100, sold in the U.S.A. 2.69; G-AWHK (172), C4K-102, to the U.S.A. 10.68 as N9938; G-AWHL (186), C4K-122, remodelled to resemble P-51 Mustang, sold in Spain 1.69; G-AWHM (187), C4K-99, sold in the U.S.A. 2.69; G-AWHN (193), C4K-130, sold in the U.S.A. 2.69; G-AWHO (199), C4K-127, sold in the U.S.A. 2.69; G-AWHP (208), C4K-144, to the U.S.A. 2.69 as N8575; G-AWHR (220), C4K-152, to the U.S.A. 10.68 as N4109G; G-AWHS (228), C4K-170, later modified to resemble P-51 Mustang, sold in Spain 1.69; G-AWHT (234), C4K-169, to the U.S.A. 10.68 as N9939

Note: All 16 aircraft registered 14.5.68 to Spitfire Productions Ltd. and flown on location in Spain, at Duxford, North Weald, Bovingdon and elsewhere.

Mignet H.M.14 Pou du Ciel *(with date of Authorisation to Fly where issued)*

G-ADDW (T.P.1), 35 h.p. Anzani, 31.3.36, 'Blue Atom', built by T. Proctor and J. Analey at Blackburn, Lancs. and based at Barton

G-ADME (S.V.A.1), 22 h.p. Aubier et Dunne, 6.9.35, built by S. V. Appleby at Heston for Air Comm. J. A. Chamier, Hendon; shown at Selfridges 8.35

G-ADMH (S.V.A.2), 30 h.p. Carden-Ford, 24.7.35, built by S. V. Appleby at Heston; remodelled by L. E. Baynes; registration cancelled 7.38

G-ADOU (F.H.1), 9.10.35, built by F. Hills & Sons Ltd. at Manchester; crashed near Cheadle, Staffs. 5.4.36

G-ADOV (GAP/SS/50), 25 h.p. Scott Squirrel, 2.10.35, built by E. G. Perman Ltd. at Grays Inn Road, W.C.1 for J. E. W. Wheatley, Heston (later Lympne)

G-ADPP (C.B./H.S.4), 25 h.p. Scott Squirrel, 25.9.35, built by C. F. Brook at Huddersfield and flown briefly at Sherburn-in-Elmet

G-ADPU (CAR/SS/51), registration reserved for E. G. Perman Ltd., London

G-ADPV (CAR/SS/52), 25 h.p. Scott Squirrel, 24.1.36, built by E. G. Perman Ltd. at Grays Inn Road, W.C.1 for E. W. Cavendish, based at Heston

G-ADPW (CAR/SS/53), 35 h.p. Anzani, 18.10.35, built by E. G. Perman Ltd. for R. G. Doig, Lympne; performed with Campbell Black's Circus

G-ADPX (CAR/SS/54), 30 h.p. Perman-Ford, 2.2.36, built by E. G. Perman Ltd. for F. W. Broughton, Romford; registration cancelled 7.36

G-ADPY (CAR/SS/55), 25 h.p. Scott Squirrel, 14.2.36, built by E. G. Perman Ltd. for E. H. Chambers, based at Heston; based at Haddenham 1937

G-ADPZ (P.P./M/300), 11.9.35, built by P. Priest at Huddersfield and flown briefly at Sherburn-in-Elmet; registration cancelled 3.36

G-ADSC (H.M.14 No.6), 25 h.p. Poinsard, 11.9.35, built by Mignet in France for National Aviation Day Displays Ltd., Ford (also given c/n N.A.D.1), to Scott Motor Cycle Co. Ltd. and based at Yeadon 11.35; reg'n. cancelled 12.36

G-ADSD (H.M.14 No.4), 25 h.p. Poinsard, 11.9.35, built by Mignet in France for N.A.D. Displays Ltd., Ford (N.A.D.2); to W. G. Bennett, Aldenham 12.35; crashed 3.36

G-ADSE (C.F.R.G.2), 32 h.p. Bristol Cherub III, 19.10.35, built by Zander & Weyl at Dunstable for C. F. R. Griffin, Gerrards Cross, named 'Winnie the Pou'; registration cancelled as 'lapsed' 1.12.46

G-ADUB (M.L.1), 23.10.35, built by M. G. Lazaro and A. L. Bieber at Liverpool; registration cancelled as 'sold' 9.36

G-ADVI (W.B.H.1), 3.12.35, built by W. B. Haddon at Glasgow and based at Renfrew; registration cancelled 1.38

G-ADVL (R.H.P.1), built at Glasgow by R. H. Paterson; pilot A. H. Anderson killed when it became uncontrollable and crashed at Renfrew 20.4.36

G-ADVM (B.9), 25 h.p. Scott Squirrel, 25.10.35, built by H. Bowen at Chelmsford, Essex; registration cancelled as 'lapsed' 9.45

G-ADVS (C.C.L.G.1), 9.3.36, built by C. C. L. Gregory at Friern Park, London, N.12 and based at Broxbourne; registration cancelled 12.38

G-ADVU Reservation for unspecified Pou du Ciel

G-ADVW (R.L.B.1), built by R. L. Baker at Forest Hill, London S.E.23 and tested at Westerham, Kent 1936

G-ADWR (J. A. 1), 25 h.p. Scott Squirrel, 13.11.35, built at Weybridge by A. U. Tomkins and based at Brooklands; registration cancelled 1.37

G-ADWS (W.M.1), 35 h.p. Anzani, built by Whyteleafe Motors Ltd., Whyteleafe, Surrey; registration reserved 11.35 for Rollason Aircraft Services Ltd.; on show in R. G. Doig's premises at New Eltham, Kent 3.36

G-ADWX (F.B.1), built by E. M. Lamb at Canonbridge, Ross-shire 1935; registration cancelled as 'lapsed' 11.45

G-ADXF (E.H.C.1), 25 h.p. Scott Squirrel, 20.11.35, built by E. H. Chambers at Princes Risborough and based at Ramsgate; registration cancelled 12.37

G-ADXS (C.L.S.1), 25 h.p. Scott Squirrel, 9.12.35, built at Southend by C. L. Storey and flown briefly at Southend Airport 20.1.36; named 'Fleeing Fly'; re-erected for exhibition in Alexandra St., Southend postwar; exhibited at the Southend Historic Aircraft Museum from 1972

G-AEDF, built at Willesden by Arthur Rose, was a non-standard Pou with a wide-track undercarriage and Anzani engine. (*A. J. Jackson*)

The Austin Seven engine in Pou G-AEEI, built by Coopers Garages (Surbiton) Ltd., drove the airscrew through a chain reduction gear. (*A. J. Jackson*)

G-ADXY	(J.G.1), 24.12.35, built by J. Goodall at Keith, Banffshire who was killed when it became uncontrollable and crashed at Dyce 20.9.36
G-ADYO	(B.H.P.1), 24.12.35, built at Southport, Lancs. by B. H. Park; registration cancelled as 'sold' 1.37
G-ADYV	(J.S.B.1), reservation for unspecified Pou du Ciel; cancelled 11.35
G-ADZG	(GAP/SS/56), reserved for E. G. Perman Ltd.; marks not used; aircraft completed as Perman Parasol G-ADZX
G-ADZP	(J.B.P.1), 7.1.36, built by J. B. Plant at Manchester; tested at Barton; given to A.T.C. at Audenshawe Grammar School during 1939–45 war
G-ADZS	(E.1101 No.684), 35 h.p. A.B.C. Scorpion, built by R. R. Little at Herne Bay, Kent, tested at Bekesbourne; exhibited in Canterbury 8.37
G-ADZT	(S.S.M.1), 1,300 cc. Henderson motor cycle engine, built by S. S. Miles at Bedford 1936; see also Stolp Starlet G-AZTV, Appendix D.
G-ADZV	(T.M.E.1), 1.1.36, built by H. Dodson and R. C. Caunse at Wirral, Cheshire; registration cancelled 12.37
G-ADZW	(EGP/55), reserved for E. G. Perman Ltd. but not used
G-ADZY	(L.R.D.B.1), built by L. R. D. Beck at Hansworth, Birmingham 1936; registration cancelled 3.37
G-AEAD	(E.W.K.1), 36 h.p. Praga B, 4.2.36, built by E. W. Kendrew at Seamer, Yorks.; first flown at Leeming Bar 12.1.36; still in store 4.47
G-AEBA	(A.O.1), built by A. Oliver at St. Teath, Bodmin, Cornwall 1936; flown and damaged at Kennford, Devon
G-AEBB	(K.W.O.1), 2.3.36, 1,300 cc. Henderson motor cycle engine, built by K. W. Owen at Southampton; given to No.424 Sqn., A.T.C. 1941; restored with 25 h.p. Scott Squirrel by Shuttleworth Trust, Old Warden 1968
G-AEBR	(A.1), 22.9.36, built by A. S. Bacon and H. Sower-Butts at Canterbury; tested at Bekesbourne; registration cancelled 7.38

G-AEBS (C.R.D.1), 25 h.p. Scott Squirrel, 22.1.36, built by Sqn. Ldr. C. R. Davidson at R.A.F. Digby, Lincs. who was killed when it became uncontrollable and crashed at Digby 21.5.36

G-AEBT (W. and V.1), 10 h.p. Ford modified, built by J. H. V. Wood and C. Smith-Vaughan at Solihull and tested at Walsall; to J. G. Wood, Birmingham 1937; to J. A. Fortey 1944; destroyed by the weather 1951

G-AECD (W.V.S.1), 21.2.36, built by W. V. Smedley and C. Bell at Wisbech, Cambs. and tested at Cambridge; registration cancelled 12.36

G-AECE (J.S.1), 27.2.36, built by J. Stubbs at York; registration cancelled 12.37

G-AECK (EGP/58), reserved for E. G. Perman Ltd. but not used

G-AECL (EGP/59), reserved for E. G. Perman Ltd. but not used

G-AECM (EGP/60), 30 h.p. Perman-Ford, 8.4.36, built by E. G. Perman Ltd. at Grays Inn Road, W.C.1 for J. E. A. Foster, Heston; flown at Canewdon, Essex

G-AECN (D.C.B.1), built by D. C. Burgoyne at Knowle, Birmingham; registration cancelled 11.45 but used unofficially on Burgoyne-Stirling Dicer 1948

G-AECV (C.V.1), 25.2.36, built by the Clyde Battery Co. Ltd. at Glasgow for the Flying Flea Club (Glasgow), Renfrew; registration cancelled 12.37

G-AEDF (A.R.1), 35 h.p. Anzani, 11.3.36, built by A. Rose at Willesden, N.W.10 and flown at Heston and East Horndon, Essex; written off 11.36

G-AEDM (R.B.1), 11.3.36, built by R. Bullock at Fraddon, Cornwall; registration cancelled as 'sold' 4.37

G-AEDN (P.H.S.1), 35 h.p. A.B.C. Scorpion, 10.3.36, built at Southend by W. A. Pearce, H. Sawyer and L. Hendry and flown at Southend Airport; to H. C. Ferguson, London, E.5 in 1937; scrapped at Sudbury, Suffolk during the 1939–45 war.

G-AEDO (C.S.1), built by C. Watson at Portsmouth 1936; cancelled 8.45

G-AEDP (W.H.W.1), 24.2.36, built by W. H. Wardley at York; cancelled 12.38

G-AEDR (E.D.1), built by E. Dutton at York 1936; cancelled 12.36

G-AEDS (F.G.W.1), built by F. G. Wright at Louth, Lincs. 1936; cancelled 12.38

G-AEEC (PAC/5), 30 h.p. Carden-Ford, 21.3.36, built by Puttnam Aircraft Co. Ltd. at Hornsey Road, London, N.19, based at Heston; sold 12.36

G-AEED (PAC/6), reservation for Puttnam, not taken up

G-AEEE (PAC/7), reservation for Puttnam, not taken up

G-AEEF (H.J.D.1), 1.3.36, built by H. J. Dunning and G. E. Ferguson at Worthing; tested at Shoreham; registration cancelled 9.39

G-AEEH (E.G.D.1), 25 h.p. Scott Squirrel, 16.5.36, built by E. G. Davis at Bath; preserved at R.A.F. Colerne in 1973

G-AEEI (C.G.1), 847 cc. Austin, 1.4.36, built by Coopers Garage (Surbiton) Ltd. at Surbiton, exhibited at Ashingdon, Essex 10.4.36

G-AEEJ (I.D.P.C.1), 30 h.p. Carden-Ford, 9.4.36, built by the Ipswich & District Pou Club at Felixstowe; tested, damaged and repaired at Ipswich; scrapped 11.36

G-AEEW (RGD/A/22), 1.4.36, built by R. G. Doig of Aircraft Constructions Ltd., Sidcup, Kent; Flt. Lt. A. M. Cowell killed when it became uncontrollable and crashed at Penshurst, Kent 4.5.36

G-AEEX (H.32C), built by C. Howitt at Garsington, near Cowley, Oxford 1936; flown at R.A.F. Abingdon by Flt. Lt. H. R. A. Edwards

G-AEEY (R.B.1), 35 h.p. Anzani, 1.4.36, built by R. Butler at Hastings, Sussex and based at Lympne; registration cancelled 3.37

The first Cantilever Pou, G-AEGD, showing the revised bracing and control system. (*Aeroplane*)

G-AEFC (R.L.T.1), built by R. L. Thorn at Hull 1936 and tested at Hedon; registration cancelled 3.37

G-AEFD (G.F.B.1), 8.4.36, built by G. F. Briggs at Preston, Lancs.; registration cancelled as 'lapsed' 11.45

G-AEFE (L.V.G.B.1), 25 h.p. Scott Squirrel, 3.4.36, built by L. V. G. Barrow at Southwell, Notts.; tested at Ipswich on one day only 5.6.36; registration cancelled 1.39

G-AEFF (E.C.1), built by E. Crossley at Banbury, Oxon. 1936; cancelled 12.36

G-AEFG (J.N.1), 1.4.36, built by J. Nolan at Accrington, Lancs.; registration cancelled 12.38

G-AEFI (L.E.M.1), built by L. E. Mottram at Northfield, Birmingham 1936 and tested at Walsall; registration cancelled 12.36

G-AEFJ (M.L.C.1), built by M. L. Curtiss at Winchmore Hill, London, N.21 and tested at Enfield 1936; registration cancelled 9.38

G-AEFK (S.F.D.1), 30 h.p. Carden-Ford, 3.4.36, built by C. W. A. Scott's Flying Displays Ltd. at Hanworth; registration cancelled 3.37

G-AEFL (C.R.S.1), built by C. R. Shoults at Nazeing, Essex 1936 and tested at Broxbourne; registration cancelled as 'lapsed' 12.46

G-AEFO (W.T.1), 15.5.36, built by W. Turner at Helensburgh, Scotland; registration cancelled as 'lapsed' 1.46

G-AEFP (G.C.T.1), 16.4.36, built by Glasgow Corporation Tramways Flying Club at Airdrie; registration cancelled 12.36

G-AEFV (A2.S1), 25 h.p. Scott Squirrel, 26.3.36, built by Malling Aviation Ltd. at West Malling for C. E. Mercer; to R.A.E., Farnborough for wind tunnel tests 1937; registration cancelled 2.38

G-AEFW (A8/C.B.1), 23 h.p. Douglas Sprite, 16.5.36, built by the Aero 8 Flying Club at Ashingdon, Essex and initially painted incorrectly as G-AERF; crashed south of Gravesend, Kent in 1936

G-AEGD (C.P.1), 30 h.p. Carden-Ford, 25.4.36, cantilever Pou built by E. D. Abbott Ltd. at Farnham, Surrey and based at Heston; to India 1.37 as VT-AID

G-AEGT (R.P.H.1), 35 h.p. Anzani, built by R. P. Hartley at Winster, Windermere 1936; registration cancelled as 'lapsed' 12.46

G-AEGU (G.A.E.1), 15.5.36, built by G. A. Essex at Penrhyn Bay, Llandudno, North Wales; registration cancelled as 'lapsed' 12.46

G-AEGV (E.M.A.C.1), 25 h.p. Scott Squirrel, 27.5.36, built by the East Midlands Aviation Co. at Northampton and test flown at Sywell; given to the A.T.C. in 1943; restored 1969 by Midland Aircraft Preservation Society, Coventry

G-AEHD (L.P.M.1), 30.6.36, built by G. A. Litchfield, G. Price and J. Marshall at Nottingham and tested at Tollerton; sold 1.37

G-AEHG (L.F.P.C.1), 1.5.36, built by Leicestershire Flying Pou Clubs Ltd. at Leicester and tested at Melton Mowbray; registration cancelled 5.37

G-AEHH (C.H.C.1), built by C. H. Cooper at Chaddesden, Derby 1936; registration cancelled as 'lapsed' 12.46

G-AEHM (H.J.D.1), 35 h.p. A.B.C. Scorpion, built by H. J. Dolman at Staplehill, Bristol 1936; exhibited at 50 Years of Flying Exhibition, Hendon 7.51; stored at Hayes 1972

G-AEIA (H.F.B.1), 24.4.36, built by H. F. Bouskill at Adel, Leeds and tested at Yeadon; registration cancelled 12.37

G-AEIE (W.B.1), built by E. D. Abbott Ltd. at Farnham, Surrey 1936 and based at Heston; exhibited at Simpson's, Piccadilly 5.36; cancelled 12.37

G-AEII (1A), 35 h.p. A.B.C. Scorpion, 11.5.36, built by H. D. Killick at Bowdon, Cheshire and based at Barton; registration cancelled 6.36

The 35 h.p. A.B.C. Scorpion engined Pou du Ciel G-AEII at Barton during its brief month of existence in 1936. (*E. J. Riding*)

G-AEIO (J.S.S.1), 25 h.p. Scott Squirrel, 11.5.36, built by J. S. Squires at Barrow-on-Soar, Leicestershire and tested at Melton Mowbray; canc. 12.37

G-AEIP (P.A.C.C.O.1), 30 h.p. Carden-Ford, 9.4.36, built by the Phoenix Aircraft Construction Co. at Ashingdon, Essex and based at Heston; registration cancelled 12.38

G-AEIX (J.C.C.G.1), built by J. C. C. Green at Stroud, Glos. 1936; canc. 12.38

G-AEIZ (B.F.C.1), 25 h.p. Scott Squirrel, built by the Birkenhead Flying Club at Oxton, Birkenhead 1936; registration cancelled 12.37

G-AEJA (O.W.C.M.1), built by the Oldham Welding & Central Motors Ltd. at Oldham, Lancs. and tested at Barton 1936; registration cancelled 12.38

G-AEJC (C.P.3), 30 h.p. Carden-Ford, 28.7.36, cantilever Pou built by E. D. Abbott Ltd. at Farnham, Surrey and based at Heston; canc. 12.37

G-AEJD (C.P.4), 30 h.p. Carden-Ford, 28.7.36, cantilever Pou built by E. D. Abbott Ltd., Farnham, Surrey; registration cancelled 12.37

G-AEJE to G-AEJG (C.P.5 to C.P.7), reserved for E. D. Abbott Ltd. but not used

G-AEJO (H.J.T.1), 20.5.36, built by H. J. Tuckett at Chelmsford, Essex and based at Hawkinge R.A.F. Station, Kent; registration cancelled 8.39

G-AEJU (C.E.B.1), 27.5.36, built by C. E. Baker at Wimborne, Dorset; registration cancelled 12.38

G-AEJX (S.H.1), 12.6.36, built by Small & Hardie at Brechin, Angus, named 'The Angus Flea', in store near Perth in the 1960s

G-AEJZ (T.L.C.1), 29.5.36, built by T. L. Crosland at Hull and tested at Hedon; registration cancelled 12.38

G-AEKA (E.H.G.1) built by E. H. Gray at Swindon, Wilts. and tested at Highworth, Wilts., registration cancelled 7.37

G-AEKH (C.L.B.1), 35 h.p. Anzani, 18.7.36, built by C. L. Berrington at Burnham, Bucks. and based at Heston; registration cancelled as 'lapsed' 11.45

G-AEKR (C.A.C.1), 35 h.p. Anzani, 23.6.36, built by E. Claybourn & Co. Ltd. at Doncaster; first flown at Doncaster by R. Parker 28.5.36; made four flights, the last on 23.6.37; loaned to the Finningley Vintage Aircraft Club; destroyed by fire in hangar at Finningley 5.9.70

G-AELM (N.L.L.P.C.1), 1.8.36, built by the North Liverpool Light Plane Club at Maghull, Lancs.; registration cancelled as 'lapsed' 12.46

G-AELN (C.L.A.C.1), 30.7.36, built by the Cheltenham Light Aeroplane Club; registration cancelled 12.37

G-AEME (W.B.1), 26.8.36, built by R. and D. Weaver at Wolverhampton; registration cancelled 12.37

G-AEMY (N.M.B.1), built by N. M. Bird at Wetherden, Stowmarket, Suffolk 1936; registration cancelled 7.37

G-AEND (T.R.1), 17.9.36, built by H. R. Toy and D. P. Riley at Ormskirk, Lancs.; registration cancelled 9.38

G-AENI (F.W.B.1), built by F. W. Brown at Peterborough 1936; registration cancelled as 'lapsed' 9.42

G-AENJ (J.P.1), built by J. Patston at Eyebury Eye, Peterborough 1936; registration cancelled 10.37

G-AEOH (R.C.S.1), 5.10.36, built by R. C. Streather at Sutton Coldfield and tested at Walsall; restored by the Midland Aircraft Preservation Society, Solihull 1969

G-AEOJ (M.D.S.A.1), 7.2.37, built by Dr. M. D. S. Armour at Anstruther, Fife; registration cancelled as 'lapsed' 11.45

G-AERJ (W.B.M.1), 847 cc. Austin, 1.12.36, built by W. B. Millichamp at Belton, Suffolk, named 'Madam Butterfly' and flown at Ely, Cambs.; later sold to V. M. Stoudley, Sheerness, Kent; cancelled 12.46

G-AFBU (N.H.S.1), 23.8.37, built by N. H. Shaw at Stafford; cancelled 10.38

G-AFUL (T.H.F.1), 1.5.39, built by T. H. Fouldes at Derby; registration cancelled as 'lapsed' 12.46

Mignet H.M.18 Cabin Pou du Ciel

G-AENV (H.M.18), 38 h.p. Menguin, P. to F. 18.9.36, S. V. Appleby, Heston; flown back to France for Paris Aero Show 9.36; sold in France 12.37

Mignet H.M.293 Pou du Ciel

G-AXPG (PFA.1333), built by W. D. Cole at Hazeleigh Grange, Purleigh, Essex 1969–71, first flown 6.71; to Southend Historic Aircraft Museum 1972

Miles M.2 Hawk

G-ACGH (1), first flown at Woodley 29.3.33, registered 19.4.33 to F. G. Miles, Woodley; registration cancelled 12.33

G-ACHJ (3), 4.7.33, Wg. Cdr. H. M. Probyn, Farnborough; F. J. C. Bloomfield, Newtownards 6.38; crashed at Clyst St. George, Devon 20.7.38

G-ACHK (4), 22.7.33, J. C. V. K. Watson; Germ Lubricants Ltd., Heston 11.33; crashed at Cherangani, Kenya 16.12.33

G-ACHL (5), 25.8.33, F. D. Bradbrooke, Hanworth; Southern Aircraft & Motors Ltd., Warlingham 4.38; G. W. Alexander, Gatwick 1.39; sold in Palestine 1940

G-ACHZ (6), 9.9.33, Lt. Col. W. E. Duncan; Kent Flying Club, Bekesbourne 8.34; Airsales & Service Ltd., Bekesbourne 1.36; crashed at Bekesbourne 25.6.39

G-ACIZ (7), 19.10.33, Dr. U. Whitby, Woodley; Mrs. Gabrielle Patterson, Woodley 11.33; W. J. Martin, Tollerton 5.36; crashed at Tollerton 30.6.36

G-ACJC (8), 30.9.33, Mrs. B. Macdonald, Baghdad; delivered by Flt. Lt. H. R. A. Edwards 10.33; to Lt. Lønborg 3.35 as OY-DAK, crashed 20.4.35

G-ACJD (9), 14.10.33, Sir Alfred Beit; crashed nr Wimbourne, Dorset, 9.8.34

G-ACJY (10), 5.9.33, F. G. Miles, Woodley; returned from Paris via Lympne 24.9.33; struck telegraph pole landing at Woodley and crashed 25.9.33

G-ACKI (11), 20.1.34, first Hawk with brakes, G. T. Armstrong-Evans, Woodley; crashed at Morston, Norfolk, 25.8.34

G-ACKX (13), 27.10.33, H. L. Krayenhoff, Woodley; to Sourabaya Aero Club 10.33 as PK-SAL; used by local auxiliary squadron 1940, believed as 'M.1'

G-ACLA (15), registered 24.10.33 to Phillips & Powis Aircraft Ltd., Woodley; not certificated; sold abroad 12.33

G-ACLB (16), 8.11.33, E. D. Spratt, Heston; sold abroad 12.35

G-ACMH (17), 24.11.33, Phillips & Powis Aircraft Ltd., Woodley; V. N. Buchan 2.34; sold in Denmark 9.34

G-ACMM (18), 23.12.33, G. L. Harrison; E. E. Marsh, Croydon 5.35; R. A. Walley, Wolverhampton 5.38; E. Brockhouse, Meir 3.39; scrapped during 1939–45 war

G-ACMX (23), 25.1.34, F. R. Hill, Dublin; registered in Ireland 6.38 as EI-ABQ

G-ACNW (26), 17.3.34, Phillips & Powis Aircraft Ltd., Woodley; crashed at Woodley 21.9.35

G-ACNX (24), 20.2.34, Lady Cathleen Nelson, Drogheda; to Everson Flying Services, Dublin 3.34 as EI-AAX; rest. 1.35 to Henlys Ltd., Heston; C. R. Pitt, Warlingham 11.35; Staffordshire Airplanes Ltd., Meir 3.36; impressed 1.41 as DG578; to No.1211 A.T.C. Sqn., Swadlincote 4.42 as 2617M

G-ACOC (25), 10.3.34, Cdr. C. Croxford, Catterick; P. R. Bradley, Tollerton 6.37; registration cancelled 3.44

G-ACOP (41), 4.6.34, Phillips & Powis Aircraft Ltd., Woodley (bearing initials of C. O. Powis); used by P. & P. School of Flying; crashed at Woodley 4.8.35

G-ACRB (27), 21.4.34, E. A. Bailey and C. B. Wilson, Hanworth; P. B. King, Woodley 4.35; A. G. Ortega, Woodley 1.37; to W. Fairweather, Renfrew 1939; last heard of in Calcutta; registration cancelled 2.43

G-ACRT (31), 12.5.34, Viscount Clive, Hanworth; derelict at Kidlington 1946

Miles M.2 Hawk G-ACNX at Dublin's airfield in 1934 while in use by Everson Flying Services as EI-AAX. (*via J. J. Masterson*)

G-ACSD (28), 13.5.34, Marshalls Flying School Ltd., Cambridge; crashed in severe snow storm at Kelshall, near Royston, Herts. 4.4.35

G-ACSL (29), 12.5.34, H. S. Uberoi, Woodley; Phillips & Powis Aircraft Ltd., Woodley 1.36; registration cancelled 12.36

G-ACTI (37), 9.6.34, P. T. Petley, Woodley; C. G. Alington, Hatfield 12.36; registration cancelled 2.43

G-ACTN (103), 4.6.34, North Staffordshire Aero Club, Meir; crashed while attempting to land at Meir, Stoke-on-Trent in severe snowstorm 15.12.35

G-ACTO (34), 24.4.34, Herts & Essex Aero Club, Broxbourne; sold abroad; rest. 7.37 to Ely Aero Club; Airsales & Service Ltd., Bekesbourne 2.39; impressed 6.40 as AW152

G-ACUD (38), 17.8.34, Phillips & Powis Aircraft Ltd., Woodley; crashed at West Woodhay, Berks, 5.6.36

G-ACVN (39), 19.7.34, W. L. Foster, Woodley; destroyed 7.35

G-ACVO (106), 20.12.34, Phillips & Powis Aircraft Ltd., Woodley; K. W. Hole, Hatfield 10.34; crashed at Flamsread nr. Harpenden 15.11.34

G-ACVP (107), 28.11.34, Phillips & Powis Aircraft Ltd., Woodley; to Denmark 11.34 as OY-DEI; crashed 10.10.36

G-ACXZ (104), 12.9.34, Capt. N. A. Blandford-Newson, Macmerry, Edinburgh; sold abroad 3.37

G-ACYA (105), 1.10.34, H. J. Hardy, Barton; S. B. Wilmot, Steventon strip, Ludlow 4.38; burned out in hangar fire at Hooton 8.7.40

G-ACZD (130), 13.12.34, Eastern Counties Aeroplane Club, Ipswich; to Sweden 5.37 as SE-AFS; crashed at Styrsö 1937

G-ACZW (136), 16.1.35, P. C. Kendall, Woodley; sold abroad 12.34

G-ADBK (146), 26.1.35, Kent Flying Club, Bekesbourne; crashed at Bekesbourne 9.8.37

G-ADDM (142), 4.3.35, S. Hawley, Meir; crashed at Melton Mowbray 2.5.36

G-ADGI (175), 11.5.35, Kent Flying Club, Bekesbourne; Airsales & Service Ltd., Bekesbourne 8.39; impressed 6.40 as AW150 and flown to Lossiemouth

G-ADGR (192), 29.5.35, C. A. Nepean Bishop, Woodley; Insurance Flying Club, Hanworth 12.36; J. Rowntree 5.37; crashed at Évère Airport, Brussels, 18.7.37

G-ADVR (171), 9.5.35 (certificated as YR-ITR for Interprinderila Technica Romana but not delivered), Phillips & Powis Aircraft Ltd., Woodley; Airsales & Service Ltd., Bekesbourne 5.38; crashed at Broadoak, Kent, 29.8.39

Miles M2A Hawk *(cabin version)*

G-ACLI (14), 1.12.33, S. B. Cliff, Woodley; burned out in hangar fire at Brooklands 24.10.36

Miles M.2B Hawk *(long range)*

G-ACKW (12), 21.12.33, Man Mohan Singh, Woodley; re-registered in India 1.34 as VT-AES; crashed near Paris at beginning of flight to India 20.1.34

Miles M.2C Hawk *(Gipsy III version)*

G-ACOB (19), 29.3.34, Phillips & Powis Aircraft Ltd., Woodley; to France 5.34 as F-AMZW

Miles M.2D Hawk *(three seaters)*

G-ACPC (20), 3.4.34, Air Pageants Ltd., Woodley; scrapped 5.37

G-ACPD (30), 7.4.34, T. C. Place, Woodley; destroyed in ground collision with Avro 504N G-ACLV at Claybury, Woodford, Essex, during air pageant 30.9.34

G-ACPW (33), 11.5.34, Phillips & Powis Aircraft Ltd., Woodley; sold abroad 5.35

G-ACSC (35), 18.5.34, H. R. Dimock, Peterborough; Aircraft Distributors Ltd., Skegness 4.35; registration cancelled as 'lapsed' 12.46

G-ACSX (42), 18.5.34, Harlow Mill Flying Fields Ltd., Hatfield; destroyed when it struck high ground in mist at Bilsdale, Yorks. 5.6.34

G-ACVR (108), 18.7.34, Harlow Mill Flying Fields Ltd., Hatfield; Aircraft Distributors Ltd., Skegness 8.35; registration cancelled as 'lapsed' 11.45

Miles M.2F Hawk Major

G-ACTD (36), 5.7.34, G. R. D. Shaw, Woodley; K. Crawford, Macmerry 7.35; crashed at Doncaster Airport 31.8.36

G-ACVM (109), 28.7.34, Sir John Carden, Heston; Executors to Sir John Carden's estate, Woodley 3.36; crashed at Hurst nr Woodley 2.6.36

G-ACWV (110), 28.8.34, Phillips & Powis Aircraft Ltd., Woodley; The British Instrument Co. Ltd., Hendon 7.35; scrapped during the 1939–45 war

G-ACWW (111), 6.10.34, Phillips & Powis Aircraft Ltd., Woodley; G. A. M. Vandeleur, Heston 9.38; L. R. Hiscock, Brooklands 2.39; shipped to the Kuala Lumpur Flying Club 4.40

G-ACWX (112), 5.10.34, Phillips & Powis Aircraft Ltd., Woodley; G. Lissant Beardmore, Woodley 8.34; registration cancelled as 'crashed' 6.36

G-ACWY (113), 30.8.34, Phillips & Powis Aircraft Ltd., Woodley; Lady Blanche Douglas, Whitchurch 9.34; F. W. Griffith, Croydon 2.39; impressed 2.43 as NF748, by road to No.50 M.U. Oxford, struck off charge 3.43

G-ACXL (114), 17.9.34, Phillips & Powis Aircraft Ltd., Woodley; Aircraft Distributors Ltd., Skegness 10.35; scrapped during the 1939–45 war

G-ACXM (115), 2.10.34, Phillips & Powis Aircraft Ltd., Woodley; to India 11.35 as VT-AGX

G-ACXN (116), 19.10.34, Phillips & Powis Aircraft Ltd., Woodley; to Kenya 10.34 as VP-KBL

G-ACXT (118), 8.11.34, Miss Ruth Fontes, Woodley; Mrs. N. H. Jones, Hanworth 3.38; Staffordshire Airplanes Ltd., Meir 6.39; impressed 1.41 as DG577

G-ACXU (119), 12.10.34, Phillips & Powis Aircraft Ltd., Woodley; to the Manawatu Aero Club 9.34 as ZK-ADJ for the Australian Race

G-ACYO (121), 9.11.34, J. M. Bickerton, Denham; impressed 9.43 as NF752; rest. 9.46 to Miles Aircraft Ltd.; B. C. Barton & Son Ltd., Elmdon 2.48; Miss F. M. Leaf, White Waltham 8.53; F. H. Stirling, Elstree 8.54; crashed at Elstree 28.11.54

G-ACYW (117), 10.11.34, M. A. Lacayo, Woodley; to Spain 5.35 as EC-ZZA

G-ADAC (134), 2.1.35, R. K. Dundas Ltd., Heston; to India 9.35 as VT-AGT

G-ADCI (147), 9.2.35, T. A. K. Aga, Brooklands; to the Western Federated Flying Club, New Zealand 9.37 as ZK-AFM

G-ADGA (169), 3.5.35, The British Instrument Co. Ltd., Hendon; shipped to India 5.41 and based at Juhu, Bombay

G-ADGL (166), 24.5.35, J. P. W. Topham, Lympne; destroyed by enemy action at Lympne 6.40

Miles M.2G Hawk Major

G-ACYB (120), 12.10.34, Phillips & Powis Aircraft Ltd., Woodley; to the Club George Chazez, Switzerland 10.34 as HB-OAS

Miles M.2H Hawk Major

G-ACYX (129), 18.12.34, J. A. Parker, Woodley; Old Etonian Flying Club Ltd., Brooklands 11.37; Mrs. M. Colledge, Brooklands 2.39; stored during 1939–45 war by owner; sold in France and left Heston 9.46 as F-BCEX

Hawk Major F-BCEX, formerly G-ACYX, at Broxbourne on the eve of its departure for France in September 1946. (*E. J. Riding*)

G-ACYZ (123), 20.12.34, Sir Alfred Beit, Heston; to Australia 12.38 as VH-ACC; to R. Diemert, Carman, Manitoba, Canada in 1970 as CF-AUV

G-ACZI (132), 21.12.34, E. H. F. Fuller, Heston; G. A. McPhee, Woolsington 3.36; to South Africa 11.36 as ZS-AFM; impressed 1940 as S.A.A.F. 1576

G-ACZJ (122), 18.11.34, Aircraft Distributors Ltd., Skegness; to India 6.37 as VT-AIR; impressed 1942 for Communications Flt., Peshawar as LV768

G-ADAB (137), 14.1.35, Mrs. B. Macdonald, Witney; J. M. Houlder, Brooklands 5.39; A. J. Cripps, Brooklands 8.42; C. N. Cooper, Surbiton 12.46; scrapped at Walsall 12.47

G-ADAS (138), 29.1.35, E. L. Maddox, Brooklands; Malcolm & Farquharson Ltd., Heston 11.35; registration cancelled as 'sold' 1.37

G-ADAW (139), 5.3.35, Phillips & Powis Aircraft Ltd., Woodley; crashed at Sandford Mill, near Woodley 3.5.36

G-ADBG (143), 21.1.35, British & Overseas Aircraft Ltd., Woodley; registration cancelled 12.36

G-ADBT (145), 5.2.35, Miss Rosemary Rees, Heston; S. J. Hawley, Meir 5.38; registration cancelled as 'lapsed' 1.12.46

G-ADCF (153), 2.4.35, Shell Mex & B.P. Ltd., Heston; registration cancelled as 'dismantled' 11.45

G-ADCJ (154), 16.2.35, E. G. H. Forsyth, Heston; Austin Hopkinson, Barton 2.36; registration cancelled as 'destroyed' 11.45

G-ADCU (162), 9.3.35, E. G. H. Forsyth, Heston; Maj. H. L. Higman, Woodley 8.36; registration cancelled as 'lapsed' 1.12.46

G-ADCW (152), 28.2.35, A. Sebag-Montefiore, Heston; crashed near Manston 28.4.35

G-ADCY (158), 13.3.35, R. C. Ramsey, Bekesbourne; impressed 6.40 as BD141

G-ADDC (164), 16.4.35, Capt. J. C. Hargreaves, Heston; L. C. Lewis, Brooklands 10.36; sold abroad 9.37

G-ADDU (180), 15.11.35, E. J. Lambert, Brooklands; L. C. Lewis, Brooklands 1.37; sold abroad 9.37

G-ADEN (161), 26.3.35, Phillips & Powis Aircraft Ltd., Woodley; sold to Señor Jose Mariano Rabello, Lisbon 5.35; diverted to Spanish war en route

G-ADFC (167), 16.4.35, R. K. S. Mainwaring, Woodley; to W. Fairweather, Muzzaffarpur, Behar, India 6.38 as VT-AKG

G-ADGD (165), 23.4.35, W. R. Norman, Heston; crashed at Ponders End, Middlesex 22.6.35

G-ADGE (135), 24.6.35, A. H. Cook, Woodley; E. F. Walter, Brooklands 6.36; sold abroad 12.37

G-ADHF (173), 11.5.35, Capt. H. Shaw, Heston; sold abroad as PK-SAR 9.35

G-ADIG (204), 28.6.35, Maj. R. H. Thornton, Speke; crashed between Budapest and Hamburg 8.6.36

G-ADIT (168), 28.6.35, V. A. P. Budge, Heston; Cotswold Aero Club, Gloucester 6.39; impressed 12.39 as X5125; to No.1851 Sqn., A.T.C., Norton, Suffolk 4.42 as 3017M

G-ADLA (176), 31.7.35, Mrs. E. Battye, Woodley; J. K. Matthew, Heston 6.36; J. M. Prout, Brooklands 10.38; to South Africa 2.39 as ZS-APX; impressed 1940 as S.A.A.F. 2008

G-ADLB (210), 20.8.35, Maj. G. W. G. Allen, Woodley; sold abroad 7.36

G-ADMW (177), 1.8.35, W. R. Norman, Heston; Portsmouth Aero Club 4.39; impressed 2.41 as DG590; rest. 9.46 to Miles Aircraft Ltd., Woodley (used by Reading Aero Club); J. P. Gunner, Sleap 10.52; w.f.u. 7.65; preserved as DG590

G-ADZU (184), 11.3.36, R. H. M. Grahame, Woodley; Phillips & Powis Aircraft Ltd., Woodley 3.36; crashed at Linz, Austria 15.5.37

G-AEEZ (179), 14.4.36, Phillips & Powis Aircraft Ltd.; Staffordshire Airplanes Ltd., Meir 5.38; registration cancelled as 'lapsed' 12.46

G-AEFA (183), 28.4.36, Phillips & Powis Aircraft Ltd., Woodley; to South African Air Transport Ltd. 4.36 as ZS-AHH

G-AEFS (124), 6.11.35, G. V. Carey, Northolt; to India 12.36 as VT-AFT; to Australia 3.37 as VH-AAH; crashed at Leura Station, Q. 8.6.38

G-AEGE (267), 27.4.36, O. F. H. Atkey, Woodley; impressed 9.41 as HL538; sold to the College of Aeronautical Engineering, Wimbledon 4.48; transferred to the College hangar at Redhill in 1949 as instructional airframe

G-AEGP (186), 28.5.36, Phillips & Powis Aircraft Ltd., Woodley; used by the Reading Aero Club from 1938; impressed 3.41 as DP851; to No.1889 Sqn., A.T.C., Faringdon, Berks. 4.42 as 3016M for instructional purposes

G-AEGR (188), 17.6.36, Phillips & Powis Aircraft Ltd., Woodley; crashed near Bucklebury, Newbury, Berks. 27.4.37

G-AEKJ (185), 7.7.36, W. Foster, Ligacao, Brazil; registration cancelled 11.45 as damaged beyond repair

G-AENS (198), 28.9.36, Phillips & Powis Aircraft Ltd., Woodley; used by the Reading Aero Club from 1938; impressed 3.41 as DP848; crashed and burned near Priddy, Somerset 20.11.41

G-AENT (328), 5.10.36, Phillips & Powis Aircraft Ltd., Woodley; crashed at Woodbridge, Suffolk 19.12.36

G-AEOX (205), 7.11.36, W. L. Gordon, Eastleigh; to France 1.37 as F-APOY

G-AFKL (221), 12.11.38, Reading Aero Club, Woodley; crashed 29.3.39

Miles Hawk Major *(other variants)*

G-ADCV (156), M.2M, 6.4.35, J. E. D. Houlder, Heston; R. R. Paine, Wolverhampton 4.46; Lt. Col. G. H. Wotton, Eastleigh 2.48; B. S. St. A. H. Hurle-Hobbs, Croydon 12.48; destroyed when wall collapsed in gale at Croydon 4.2.50

G-ADDK (190), M.2P, 13.6.35, S. K. Davies, Splott, Cardiff; Cardiff Aeroplane Club 10.36; impressed 8.40 as BD180; struck off charge 2.45

G-ADLH (194), M.2S, 21.8.35, J. H. Van, Broxbourne; G. P. Nair, Woodley 8.37; crashed near Rouen, France 28.10.37

G-ADLN (211), M.2R, 16.8.35, R. Cornwall & W. Verrells, Woodley; Reading Aero Club, Woodley 11.38; impressed 2.41 as DG664; struck off charge 7.41

G-ADLO (220), M.2P, 23.7.35, Airwork Ltd., Heston; to Marlborough Aero Club, New Zealand 5.37 as ZK-AFL

G-ADNJ (203), M.2T, 30.8.35, A. Henshaw, Mablethorpe, Lincs.; crashed in the Irish Sea 6.9.35

G-ADNK (222), M.2T, 30.8.35, F. D. Bradbrooke, Woodley; sold abroad 10.35

R. R. Paine's post-war modifications to the Hawk Speed Six M.2L included a large bubble canopy. (*A. J. Jackson*)

Miles M.3A Falcon Major G-ADER of Maddox Airways Ltd. flying near Brooklands in April 1935, showing the production-type cabin roof. (*Flight Photo 14745*)

Miles Hawk Speed Six

G-ACTE (43), M.2E, 5.7.34, Sir Charles Rose, Portsmouth; W. Humble, Sherburn-in-Elmet 9.35; sold abroad 9.37

G-ADGP (160), M.2L, 13.6.35, Luis Fontes, Woodley; Miles Aircraft Ltd., Woodley 8.46; R. R. Paine, Wolverhampton 2.48; W. H. Todd, Wolverhampton 10.65; Mrs. L. A. Osborne, Stapleford 7.67; D. A. Hood, Booker 2.71

G-ADOD (195), M.2U, 27.8.35, Miss Ruth Fontes, Woodley; A. E. Clouston, Woodley 8.36; crashed at Gwelo, Southern Rhodesia 1.10.36

Miles M.2W Hawk Trainer

G-ADVF (217), 10.10.35, Phillips & Powis Aircraft Ltd., used by No.8 E.R.F.T.S., Woodley; scrapped at C. of A. expiry 10.39

G-ADWT (215), 23.11.35, Phillips & Powis Aircraft Ltd., used by No.8 E.R.F.T.S., Woodley; impressed 1.43 as NF750; rest. 9.46 to Miles Aircraft Ltd.; No.47 Sqn. Flying Club, Abingdon 2.55; Panda Flying Group, Panshanger 11.58; J. MacGillivray, Soellingen, Germany 11.61; to Canada 1964 as CF-NXT

G-ADWU (224), 23.11.35, Phillips & Powis Aircraft Ltd., used by No.8 E.R.F.T.S., Woodley; scrapped at C. of A. expiry 8.40

G-ADWV (228), 23.11.35, Phillips & Powis Aircraft Ltd., used by No.8 E.R.F.T.S., Woodley; scrapped at C. of A. expiry 1.40

Miles M.2X Hawk Trainer

G-ADYZ (235), 2.7.36, Phillips & Powis Aircraft Ltd., used by No.8 E.R.F.T.S., Woodley; scrapped at C. of A. expiry 8.40

G-ADZA (241), 31.12.35, Phillips & Powis Aircraft Ltd., used by No. 8 E.R.F.T.S., Woodley; impressed 2.41 as DG665; to No.1887 Sqn., A.T.C., Lewisham 4.42 as instructional airframe 3015M

G-ADZB (242), 22.1.36, Phillips & Powis Aircraft Ltd., used by No. 8 E.R.F.T.S., Woodley; rebuilt 2.37 with new fuselage, c/n 481; scrapped 7.40

G-ADZC (249), 13.1.36, Phillips & Powis Aircraft Ltd., used by the Reading Aero Club and No.8 E.R.F.T.S., Woodley; scrapped in 1940

G-ADZE (254), 4.2.36, Phillips & Powis Aircraft Ltd., used by No.8 E.R.F.T.S., Woodley; withdrawn from use after colliding with G-AEAW 26.8.36

G-AEAW (246), 14.4.36, Phillips & Powis Aircraft Ltd., used by No.8 E.R.F.T.S., Woodley; withdrawn from use after colliding with G-ADZE 26.8.36

G-AEAX (260), 25.3.36, Phillips & Powis Aircraft Ltd., used by the Reading Aero Club, Woodley; impressed 2.41 as DG666; beyond repair at Harwarden 7.43

G-AEAZ (270), 13.3.36, Phillips & Powis Aircraft Ltd., used by No.8 E.R.F.T.S., Woodley; withdrawn from use after accident in 1937

G-AEEL (271), 26.3.36, Phillips & Powis Aircraft Ltd., used by No.8 E.R.F.T.S., Woodley; scrapped at C. of A. expiry 5.40

Miles M.2Y Hawk Trainer

G-ADZD (253), 4.2.36, Phillips & Powis Aircraft Ltd., used by No.8 E.R.F.T.S., Woodley; scrapped at C. of A. expiry 8.40

G-AEAY (261), 18.2.36, Phillips & Powis Aircraft Ltd., used by No.8 E.R.F.T.S., Woodley; scrapped at C. of A. expiry 9.39

G-AEHP (258), 12.6.36
G-AEHR (237), 12.6.36
G-AEHS (245), 12.6.36
G-AEHT (265), 12.6.36
G-AEHU (292), 10.7.36
G-AEHV (293), 15.6.36
G-AEHW (294), 2.7.36
G-AEHX (295), 26.6.36
G-AEHY (296), 10.7.36
G-AEHZ (297), 10.7.36
} delivered by air to the Rumanian Air Force, registrations cancelled 12.36

Miles M.3 Falcon prototype

G-ACTM (102), U-3, 9.10.34, H. L. Brook, Sherburn-in-Elmet, crashed 11.36

Miles M.3A Falcon Major

G-ADBF (131), 26.2.35, Maj. N. A. Blandford-Newson, Macmerry; temporarily to Italy as I-ZENA in 1935; to Switzerland 12.38 as HB-USU

G-ADBI (140), 29.4.35, Phillips & Powis Aircraft Ltd., Woodley; Air Hire Ltd., Heston 4.35; to Southern Rhodesia 3.37 as VP-YBN; crashed Bulawayo 1938

G-ADER (157), 18.4.35, Maddox A/W Ltd., Brooklands; Staffordshire Airplanes Ltd., Meir 6.36; Miss B. Wenman, Gravesend 11.36; to France 2.37 as F-AQER

G-ADFH (196), 28.6.35, E. D. Spratt, Hamble; impressed 12.41 as HM496; rest. 8.46 to T. C. Sparrow, Christchurch; D. E. Bianchi, White Waltham 4.50; R. A. Drean, Blackbushe 1.51; withdrawn from use at Redhill 8.54

G-ADHC (163), 21.2.35, Galbraith Pembroke & Co. Ltd., Woodley; to Italy 3.36 as I-ZENA (reallocation of marks first used on G-ADBF above)

G-ADHG (193), 13.6.35, Aircraft Distributors Ltd., Skegness; to Australia 5.37 as VH-AAT; impressed by R.A.A.F. 1940 as A37-3; active as VH-AAT in 1971

G-ADHH (181), 28.5.35, D. W. Gumbley, Heston; to Palestine Aviation Co. 'Aviron', Lydda 3.40 as VQ-PAO

G-ADHI (189), 29.5.35, Continental Carrosseries Ltd., Woodley; R. C. Ramsey, Bekesbourne 6.36; Airsales & Service Ltd., Bekesbourne 8.36; Portsmouth, Southsea and I.O.W. Aviation Ltd. 10.39; impressed 3.40 as X9300

G-ADIU (202), 11.7.35, Leicestershire Aero Club, Braunstone; to Australia 1.37 as VH-ACE; impressed by R.A.A.F. 5.42 as A37-6

G-ADLI (206), 12.7.35, Kennings Ltd., Skegness; K. J. Dear, Redhill 7.38; C. B. Field, Woodley 1.41; Marshall's Flying School Ltd., Cambridge 5.46; C. P. Godsall, Cambridge 7.46; Falcon Airways Ltd., Elmdon 5.48; J. W. Haggas, Hatfield 7.50; crashed at Elstree 10.9.52

G-ADZR (209), 7.10.35, Miss H. M. Harrison, Woodley; to Australia 6.36 as VH-AAS; crashed at Hatches Creek, Northern Territory 23.7.40

G-AEEG (216), U-20, 25.3.36, Phillips & Powis Aircraft Ltd., Woodley; to Bengt Eriksson, Stockholm 10.36 as SE-AFN, sometime Fv.7001; rest. 1.63 to Personal Plane Services Ltd., White Waltham; E. Eves, Baginton 4.64; P. A. Mann, Booker 12.72

G-AEFB (229), 8.6.36, Phillips & Powis Aircraft Ltd., Woodley; D. F. Peel, Heston 8.37; Portsmouth, Southsea & I.O.W. Aviation Ltd. 10.39; impressed 3.40 as X9301; struck off charge 2.41

G-AENG (234), 28.9.36, Phillips & Powis Aircraft Ltd., Woodley; crashed at foot of Scarborough cliffs during King's Cup Race 10.9.37

G-AETN (226), 22.4.37, Phillips & Powis Aircraft Ltd., Woodley; used on the company's Hire Service; crashed at Starcross, Devon 17.5.37

Miles M.3B Falcon Six

G-ADLC (213), 27.7.35, C. O. Powis, Woodley; C. Branson, Woodley 11.36; E. D. Spratt, Hamble 7.38; withdrawn from use at Gatwick in 1940

G-ADTD (255), 4.2.36, Maddox Airways Ltd., Brooklands; Vickers Aviation Ltd., Brooklands 2.36; Miles Aircraft Ltd. Woodley 2.46; R. S. Turner, Woodley 5.48; Wiltshire School of Flying Ltd., Thruxton 2.51; G. C. Marler, Thruxton 5.59; crashed in the sea off Angmering, Sussex 21.9.62

G-ADZL (262), 8.5.36, Fairey Aviation Co. Ltd., Harmondsworth (later White Waltham); withdrawn from use 12.44

G-AEAO (269), 18.1.36, T. Rose, Woodley; to Holland 3.36 as PH-EAO; rest. 6.39 to Miles Aircraft Ltd.; to R.A.E., Farnborough as R4071; rest. 1.46 to Southern Aircraft (Gatwick) Ltd. as G-AGZX; to Belgium 12.46 as OO-FLY; later to France as F-BBCN; still extant at Lognes in 1971

G-AEDL (259), 26.5.36, E. G. H. Forsyth, Heston; withdrawn from use in 1939

G-AEKK (248), 27.7.36, Dunlop Rubber Co. Ltd., Castle Bromwich; impressed 1.40 as W9373; used by the Royal Navy at Lee-on-Solent

G-AFAY (233), OE-DBB, 26.10.35, Airwork Ltd., Heston; Brian Allen Aviation Ltd., Heston 2.38; E. D. Spratt, Hamble 8.38; C. G. M. Alington, Elmdon 11.38; Hawker Aircraft Ltd., Brooklands 8.41; scrapped at Heston in 1946

G-AFBF (256), D-EGYV, 19.12.35, Airwork Ltd., Heston; Birkett Air Services Ltd., Heston 11.39; impressed 4.40 as AV973; rest. 5.46 to J. D. Habin (Southampton Air Services); Cunliffe-Owen Aircraft Ltd., Eastleigh 6.47; British Aviation Insurance Co. Ltd. 12.50; sold as spares in France 1954

Miles M.3C to M.3F Falcon Six

G-ADLS (231), M.3C, 28.8.35, S. Harris, Croydon; A. D. Farquhar, Abbotsinch 6.36; sold 1.37, almost certainly to F. T. Stanley, Singapore as VR-RAP

G-AEAG (266), M.3D, 21.3.36, H. Deterding, Sywell; A. W. A. Whitehead, Woodley 7.37; to Australia 9.40 as VH-ABT; impressed by R.A.A.F. 11.40 as A37-1

G-AECC (280), M.3D, 27.4.36, A. N. T. Rankin, Heston; impressed 1.41 as DG576; rest. 4.46 to Miles Aircraft Ltd., Newtownards; Ulster Aviation Ltd. 2.48; J. Rush, Woolsington 6.49; Crop Culture (Aerial) Ltd., Bembridge 1.58; lost at sea between Bembridge and Exeter 8.5.59

G-AFCP (289), M.3E, not certificated, registered 17.11.37 to Phillips & Powis Aircraft Ltd., Woodley; dismantled 4.38

G-AGZX (269), M.3F, see Miles M.3B Falcon Six G-AEAO

Miles M.4A Merlin

G-ADFE (151), U-8, 15.5.35, Birkett Air Service Ltd., Heston; registration cancelled 12.46 as 'lapsed'

Miles M.5 Sparrowhawk

G-ADNL (239), 21.8.35, F. G. Miles, Woodley; Phillips & Powis Aircraft Ltd., Woodley 1.36; Miss J. M. Parsons, Woodley 2.38; C. G. M. Alington, Elmdon 6.45; Oldham Tyre Cord Co. Ltd., Barton 12.50; first flown at Shoreham 14.12.53 as Miles M.77 Sparrowjet, c/n 77/1006; burned in hangar fire at Upavon 7.64

G-ADWW (264), 24.6.36, J. H. G. McArthur, Woodley; to Perry Boswell, Hyattsville, Maryland, U.S.A. 11.36 as NC191M; crashed at Palm Beach, Florida 1959

G-AELT (275), 16.9.36, Victor Smith, Cape Town; sold to B. du Preez 10.37 as ZS-ANO and fitted with cabin top; to S.A.A.F. 1940 as '1427'

G-AFGA (273), built for L. E. R. Bellairs, Shoreham; sold to W. Humble, Doncaster 4.38; C. of A. 20.5.38; withdrawn from use in 1939

G-AGDL (276), U-3, 3.12.41, Phillips & Powis Aircraft Ltd., Woodley; Miles Aircraft Ltd. 10.43; T. Shipside Ltd., Tollerton 2.48 (used by the Nottingham Flying Club); crashed on take-off at Tollerton 19.6.48

Miles M.11 Whitney Straight prototype

G-AECT (290), 9.5.36, Phillips & Powis Aircraft Ltd., Woodley; L. E. R. Bellairs, Shoreham 8.38; impressed 10.40 as BS755 as instructional airframe.

Miles M.11A Whitney Straight

G-AENH (303), 16.1.37, Whitney Straight Ltd., Heston; to F. W. Hewson, Queensland 11.37 as VH-ABN; to Auckland Aero Club, New Zealand 2.51 as ZK-AXN

G-AERS (304), 20.1.37, Airwork Ltd., Heston; R. K. Clarke, York 2.37; Miss E. Townsend, Woodley 4.40; impressed 5.41 as ES922 for Stn. Flt., Northolt

G-AERV (307), 30.1.37, H. W. H Moore, Heston; impressed 6.41 as EM999 and used by R.A.F. Abingdon; rest. to owner 6.47; R. T. Boyes, Newtownards 3.62; withdrawn from use 4.66 and loaned to the Belfast Transport Museum

G-AERY (309), 13.2.37, British Air Transport Ltd., Redhill; H. B. Legge & Sons Ltd., Redhill 2.37, to India 4.38 as VT-AKF

G-AETB (310), 12.2.37, Hon. T. S. Fermor-Hesketh, Brooklands; crashed near Beauvais while en route Le Bourget to Lympne, owner killed, 21.6.37

G-AETS (312), 25.3.37, E. G. H. Forsyth, Heston; impressed 5.41 as DR611 but mis-painted DR617; rest. 11.46 to the Straight Corporation as G-AITM; not proceeded with, scrapped at Weston-super-Mare 3.48

G-AEUJ (313), 24.2.37, Maj. C. L. Y. Parker, Gatwick; Hawker Aircraft Ltd., Langley 1.41; Mill Hill F/G, Elstree 8.57; Edward Eves, Baginton 5.61; J. Tullett, Seething 10.62; P. Hillwood and C. H. Parker, Hurn 11.66

G-AEUX (314), 2.3.37, J. Bayley, Roborough; impressed 1.41 as DJ713; used by Andover Stn. Flt.; rest. 5.46 to Wg. Cdr. H. M. Probyn and flown to Kenya, re-registered to owner 12.49 as VP-KHO; beyond repair 2.3.52

G-AEUY (315), 3.3.37, R. E. Gardner, Hamsey Green; Sir A. Beit, Heston 10.37; impressed 3.40 as W7422 for Air Attaché; Paris; abandoned at Le Bourget 5.40

G-AEUZ (316), 24.3.37, Rolls-Royce Ltd., Hucknall; A. F. Eayrs, Tollerton 2.48; H. Tempest Ltd., Tollerton 8.49; to Kenya 10.52 as VP-KKF

G-AEVA (318), 9.3.37, G. Cohen, Heston; D. de C. Smiley, Heston 8.37; E. A. Stroutts, Bekesbourne 12.38; impressed 5.41 as DR612; rest. 1.46 to J. C. Rice, Leicester East; crashed in the Swiss Alps 2.7.54

G-AEVF (317), 10.3.37, L. T. Lillington, Ratcliffe; impressed 9.40 as BS814

G-AEVG (319), 15.3.37, W. and A. Norman, Heston; impressed 3.41 as DP854; rest. 3.37 to Air Service Training Ltd., Hamble; W. A. Strauss 3.54; flown to Australia arriving Moorabbin 16.10.54; re-registered 5.55 as VH-EVG

G-AEVH (321), 24.3.37, Capt. A. V. Harvey, Heston; Reading Aero Club, Woodley 5.38; crashed 28.1.39

G-AEVL (322), 7.4.37, Maj. R. H. Thornton, Speke; Maj. H. Musker, Hanworth 3.39; impressed 3.41 as DP855; reserialled 3.43 as NF751; rest. 1.46 to G. W. Harben, Burnaston; to New Zealand 10.51 as ZK-AZX as deck cargo, fuselage rendered useless by water soakage en route

G-AEVM (324), 14.4.37, J. A. H. Parker, Hambledon, Surrey; impressed 9.41 as BS815; used by Station Flight, Northolt until scrapped 4.45

G-AEWA (320), 19.3.37, Earl of Ronaldshay, Portsmouth; T. B. Birkett 2.39; impressed 1.41 as DJ714; rest. 5.47 to H. R. Minchin, Woodley; S. J. Burt, Fairoaks 4.49; crashed on take-off from field, Neufchâtel, France 3.3.61

G-AEWK (325), 22.4.37, E. Jobling-Purser, Woolsington; impressed 4.40 as AV970; written off in accident 24.11.44 while in use at Northolt

G-AEWT (326), 5.5.37, Whitney Straight, Heston; to P. Genin, St. Didier 8.37 as F-APPZ; flown to Indo China and back 1937 by Mme. Genin; hidden during 1939–45 war; to Aéro Club du Rhône 3.54; crashed at St. Didier 7.7.54

G-AEXJ (501), 20.4.37, Air Service Training Ltd., Hamble; impressed 10.40 as BS818; crashed at Lowfield Heath Road, Gatwick, Surrey 12.5.44

G-AEYA (342), 13.7.37, W. Headlam, York; impressed 4.41 as DP237; to No.24 Sqn., Hendon for Prince Bernhardt of the Netherlands; to Northolt Stn. Flt. 4.42; crashed on take-off at Biggin Hill 10.2.45

G-AEYB (500), 2.7.37, Whitney Straight Ltd., Heston; to Gaspare Bona in Italy 12.37 as I-BONA; sold to a Frederica Cassinas 9.41

G-AEYJ (343), 14.4.37, J. B. Turnbull, Heston; Airwork Ltd., Heston 9.38; to Belgium 12.38 as OO-ZUT; destroyed during German invasion 5.40

G-AEZO (347), 21.8.37, Brig. Gen. A. C. Lewin, Nairobi, Kenya; crashed near Malakal, Sudan, while owner was ferrying it to Nairobi 9.10.37

G-AFAB (346), 18.8.37, P. P. S. Pratt, Brooklands; Venner Time Switches Ltd. 3.39; impressed 7.40 as BD145; spun in near Radlett 10.12.41

G-AFBV (497), 4.10.37, A. Batchelor, Ramsgate; Ipswich Aero Club 2.39; Thanet Aero Club, Ramsgate 3.39; crashed while landing at Ipswich 15.6.39

G-AFCC (499), 26.10.37, T. Saunders, Magellanes, Chile; based at Magellanes; registration lapsed during 1939–45 war

G-AFCN (502), 20.11.37, Whitney W. Straight, Heston; H. M. Mitchell, Castle Bromwich 10.38; Yacht Cruises Ltd., Gatwick 4.39; impressed 10.39 as V4739

G-AFGK (509), 11.4.38, Miss Rosemary Rees, Heston; Airwork Ltd., Heston or Perth 1942; F. H. Wilson, Speke 4.51; Aldenham Flying Group, Elstree 3.56; E. Wilkinson, Panshanger 1.64; W. Scott-Hill, Fairoaks 2.72

G-AFJJ (306), OO-UMK, 3.2.37, registered 27.7.38 to Airwork Ltd., Heston; impressed 8.40 as BD168; beyond repair in forced landing near Andover 1.8.44

G-AFJX (507), 14.9.38, Brig. Gen. A. C. Lewin, Njoro, Kenya; J. Tweedale, Woodford 8.39; impressed 8.40 as BD183; rest. 3.47 to Warden Aviation & Eng. Ltd.; to Mt. Cook & Southern Lakes Tourist Co., N.Z. 3.50 as ZK-AUK

G-AFZY (506), U-0227, 20.11.39, Phillips & Powis Aircraft Ltd., Woodley; impressed 11.42 as NF747; rest. 10.46 to Southern Aircraft (Gatwick) Ltd.; Lord Calthorpe, Fairoaks 1.50; to New Zealand 10.50 as ZK-AXD

G-AITM (312) – see Whitney Straight G-AETS

Whitney Straight G-AFGK, used by Airwork Ltd. for communications, in camouflage throughout the 1939–45 war, restored to peacetime colours at Farnborough, June 1946. (*E. J. Riding*)

Amherst Villiers with G-AERC, the Miles M.11B flying test bed for the 135 h.p. Villiers Maya I engine. (*Aeroplane*)

Miles M.11B Whitney Straight

G-AERC (305), 5.2.37, C. A. and Mrs. M. Villiers, Heston; conv. to M.11A when sold to Thanet Aero Club, Ramsgate 1.38; Ipswich Aero Club 5.38; impressed 4.40 as AV971; used by R.A.F., Northolt; struck off charge 6.43

Miles M.11C Whitney Straight

G-AEYI (341), 8.9.37, Phillips & Powis Aircraft Ltd., Woodley; crashed at Harefield, Berks. 28.6.38, test pilot Wg. Cdr. F. W. Stent killed

Miles M.14 and M.14A Hawk Trainer Mk.III

G-AETJ (331), 23.7.37, Phillips & Powis Aircraft Ltd., Woodley; to Auckland A/C, New Zealand 4.37 as ZK-AEX; crashed at Great Barrier Island 17.3.39

G-AETL (332), 23.7.37, Phillips & Powis Aircraft Ltd., Woodley; to the Otago Aero Club, New Zealand 4.37 as ZK-AEY; impressed as NZ586, later ZK-ALO

G-AEZR (495), 31.7.37, J. M. Barwick, Leeming; withdrawn from use 7.39

G-AEZS (538), 21.7.37, Phillips & Powis Aircraft Ltd., used by No.8 E.R.F.T.S., Woodley; flown with Miles M.18 wing as U-6 during 1939–45 war; canc. 12.46

G-AFBS (539), 6.10.37, Phillips & Powis Aircraft Ltd., used by No.8 E.R.F.T.S.; impressed 9.40 as BB661; rest. 6.48 to Airways Aero Association, Croydon; Denham Aero Club 10.52; preserved at Skyfame Museum, Staverton in 1973

G-AFDB (542), 1.12.37, Phillips & Powis Aircraft Ltd., used by No.8 E.R.F.T.S., Woodley; impressed 9.40 as BB662; to No.3 S. of TT., Blackpool as 4557M

G-AFET (556), 4.2.38, Ipswich Aero Club; Weston Aero Club 11.38; Thanet Aero Club 12.38; impressed 5.40 as AV978; beyond repair at Salcombe 18.11.44

G-AFEU (557), 17.2.38, Thanet Aero Club; crashed in the sea off Cliftonville, Kent 17.7.38

G-AFEV (558), 23.2.38, Exeter Aero Club; Weston Aero Club 11.38; Thanet Aero Club 2.39; crashed at Uplyme, Devon, 30.8.39

G-AFEW (559), 23.2.38, Plymouth Aero Club, Roborough; crashed in 1938

G-AFWY (1080), 3.8.39, Phillips & Powis Aircraft Ltd., used by No.8 E.R.F.T.S., Woodley; impressed 9.40 as BB665; struck off charge 11.44

G-AFXA (1081), 10.8.39, Phillips & Powis Aircraft Ltd., used by No. 8 E.R.F.T.S., Woodley; impressed 9.40 as BB666; rest. incorrectly 4.49 as G-ALOG to R. A. Short, Croydon; corrected to G-AFXA later; not converted; scrapped

G-AFXB (1082), 17.8.39, Phillips & Powis Aircraft Ltd., used by No.8 E.R.F.T.S., Woodley; impressed 9.40 as BB667; struck off charge 12.47

G-AFYV to G-AFYY (1083–1086), applications for registration cancelled

Miles M.14B Hawk Trainer Mk.II

G-AEZP (494), 6.9.37, Blackburn Aircraft Ltd., Brough; scrapped about 1943

G-AFTR (1078), 10.5.39, Phillips & Powis Aircraft Ltd., used by No.8 E.R.F.T.S., Woodley; impressed 9.40 as BB663; crashed at Tongham, Surrey 25.4.42

G-AFTS (1079), 18.5.39, Phillips & Powis Aircraft Ltd., used by No.8 E.R.F.T.S., Woodley; impressed 9.40 as BB664; crashed at Farley Hill, Berks. 15.8.41

G-AKNA (534), L6913, registered 29.11.47 to Herts & Essex Aero Club, Broxbourne; converted but not certificated; to Wright Aviation Ltd., Speke 1948 as spares

Miles M.14 Hawk Trainer Mk.III G-AEZS at the Royal Aeronautical Society Garden Party, Heathrow, 8 May 1938, with the prototype Monarch G-AFCR and prototype Percival Q.6 G-AEYE behind. (*A. J. Jackson*)

Miles M.14A Hawk Trainer Mk.3

G-AGEO (2022), T9755, not converted, scrapped at Thruxton 1.49; G-AGVW (1748), P6380, 19.11.45, destroyed in air collision with Auster J-1 OY-DGA near Copenhagen 21.4.46; G-AGZR (902), N3856, U-0252, 12.4.46, to Thai Navy 11.47

G-AHKP (1832), R1831, 25.9.46, crashed at Greenock 4.8.54; G-AHNE (2170), T9977, 19.3.47, to New Zealand 11.52 as ZK-BBA; G-AHNU (2033), T9766, 8.5.47, crashed near Sandbach, Cheshire 7.2.51; G-AHNV (1949), R1978, 26.8.46, beyond repair in heavy landing at Wolverhampton 25.7.52; G-AHNW (1921), R1950, 29.6.46, crashed at Elstree 2.6.57; G-AHUJ (1900), R1914, 17.9.46, stored at Strathallan Castle Perthshire; G-AHUK (1959), T9672, 16.8.46, sold abroad 8.49; G-AHUL (677), L8210, not converted, scrapped at Weston 2.47; G-AHYK (870), N3822, 26.3.47, crashed in Sussex 7.9.47; G-AHYL (2071), T9834, 14.4.47, scrapped at Denham in 1954; G-AHYM (2085), T9848, 18.3.47, crashed at Lee-on-Solent 6.10.51

G-AIAI (documented with fuselage part number PP38384 only), 13.11.46, scrapped at Northolt 6.49; G-AICD (1734), P6366, not converted, destroyed by heavy lorry at Christchurch 22.6.52; G-AICE (2049), T9812, Colomb Béchar 4.54 as F-OAPJ; G-AIDF (1766), P6411, 28.11.46, wrecked by gale at Southend 5.9.67; G-AIOJ (2105), T9888, 7.6.47, to New Zealand 6.49 as ZK-ATE; G-AIOK (2148), T9955, 20.12.46, crashed at Burnaston 23.8.50; G-AITN (1826), R1825, 10.1.49, withdrawn from use at Fairoaks 11.62; G-AITO (1842), R1841, 14.11.47, crashed at Shoreham 3.11.51; G-AITR (1845), R1844, 19.3.49, to the Egyptian Air Force 6.49; G-AITS (1997), T9730, 9.8.48, crashed at Hurstpierpoint, Sussex 16.8.55; G-AITT (1658), P2436, 22.12.48, to the Egyptian Air Force 2.49; G-AITU (423), L5991, 3.5.49, to the Egyptian Air Force 6.49; G-AITV (595), L8086, 6.9.48, to the Egyptian Air Force 9.48; G-AITW (1884), R1898, 15.2.49, to the Egyptian Air Force 2.49; G-AITX (1843), R1842, 4.1.49, to the Egyptian Air Force 2.49; G-AITY (616), L8138, 24.8.48, to Italy 6.49 as I-AITY; G-AITZ (1074), N5438, 5.9.47, scrapped at Thruxton 9.49

G-AIUA (2035), T9768, 27.3.47, under restoration at Felthorpe in 1971; G-AIUB (613), L8135, 27.3.47, crashed at Cowes 18.7.50; G-AIUC (843), N3795, 24.9.47, to Tangier 6.50 as F-OAGQ, to Morocco 2.64 as CN-TZE; G-AIUD (606), L1828, 3.10.47, to the Egyptian Air Force 1.49; G-AIUE (995), N3962, 14.7.47, crashed at Seething,

C. A. Nepean Bishop, leading post-war exponent of Magister aerobatics, climbing away from Elstree in G-AIUA in 1949. (*E. J. Riding*)

Norfolk 26.8.62; G-AIUF (1782), P6438, 21.4.53, withdrawn from use in Germany 11.59; G-AIUG (988), N3955, 10.6.47, scrapped at Croydon 9.51; G-AIYB (1840), R1839, 3.5.47, crashed at Redhill 16.1.52; G-AIYC (2087), T9870, 14.6.47, crashed at Horne, Surrey 4.8.50; G-AIYD (2132), T9915, 3.5.47, crashed at Redhill 29.11.53; G-AIYL (517), L6896, 2.4.47, to French Morocco 7.53 as F-DADV; G-AIZJ (1645), P2408, not converted, scrapped at Gatwick 1949; G-AIZK (1706), P2506, 14.5.48, scrapped at Little Snoring, Norfolk 1963; G-AIZL (592), L8083, 7.7.48, scrapped at Speke 1955

G-AJCM (1934), R1963, 15.11.50, crashed near Chesterfield 11.5.53; G-AJDR (2169), T9976, 22.5.47, preserved by the Shuttleworth Trust, Old Warden as T9976; G-AJGK (1941), R1970, 3.2.49, to the Egyptian Air Force 9.49; G-AJGL (1933), R1962, 23.2.49, to the Egyptian Air Force 9.49; G-AJGM (589), L8080, 3.7.47, beyond repair landing at Denham 21.9.48; G-AJGN (896), N3850, 16.2.49, to the Egyptian Air Force 9.49; G-AJGP (753), L8327, not converted, scrapped at White Waltham 1947; G-AJHA (1972), T9685, 2.5.47, withdrawn from use at Elmdon 4.56; G-AJHB (628), N2259, 10.6.47, withdrawn from use at Croft, Darlington 6.48, scrapped at Sherburn-in-Elmet 1957; G-AJHC (876), N3830, 14.8.47, withdrawn from use at Croft, Darlington 8.48, scrapped 1952; G-AJHD (650), 14.8.47, to spares at Woolsington 11.60; G-AJHE (825), N3777, 14.4.47, to French Morocco 12.49 as F-OAFU; G-AJHF (2081), T9844, 25.4.47, crashed at Croft, Darlington 15.2.48; G-AJHG (1984), T9697, 13.5.47, crashed in Glasgow 22.6.54; G-AJHH (1000), N3967, 8.5.47, to French Morocco 5.49 as F-OAFV; G-AJJI (1985), T9698, 21.10.47, crashed at Elstree 19.8.56; G-AJRS (1750), P6382, not converted, scrapped at Redhill 1954; G-AJRT (744), L8288, 3.1.52, cabin model, crashed at Waltham, Grimsby 15.8.59; G-AJRU (352), L5921, not converted, burned at Redhill 21.5.54; G-AJRV (1774), P6419, 3.4.48, crashed at Alexandria, Dunbartonshire 29.9.55; G-AJSF (1932), R1961, 14.4.49, crashed at Kinder Law, Derbyshire 28.7.57; G-AJZH (1641), P2404, 8.7.47, crashed at Nuthampstead 22.8.57

G-AKAS (1971), T9684, 29.6.56, crashed at Croydon 7.5.57, scrapped at Biggin Hill 10.61; G-AKAT (2005), T9738, 13.6.56, withdrawn from use 11.65, preserved by

Newark Air Museum; G-AKAU (1947), R1976, 13.7.57, withdrawn from use 10.63; G-AKGR (1982), T9695, 4.2.55, crashed at Lympne 1.4.56; G-AKGS (1765), P6410, 13.5.48, crashed near Granada, Spain 1.4.54; G-AKJV (1762), P6407, 6.4.48, cabin model, burned at Redhill 5.54; G-AKJW (528), L6907, 24.6.48, crashed at East Grinstead 19.7.48; G-AKJX (560), L8051, 6.5.48, scrapped at Lympne 7.54; G-AKKR (1995), T9708, 22.3.51, preserved by the R.A.F. Museum, Hendon, as T9967; G-AKKS (1790), P6446, 23.3.49, withdrawn from use at Renfrew 10.54; G-AKKT (405), L5973, not converted, scrapped at Denham 1951; G-AKKV (987), N3954, 15.2.49, crashed at Hemswell 13.6.60; G-AKKW (1776), P6421, 23.3.49, withdrawn from use at Denham 3.50; G-AKKX (2039), T9802, 28.1.49, crashed at Denham 28.3.51; G-AKKY (2078), T9841, 27.10.48, withdrawn from use at Renfrew 11.64; G-AKKZ (2227), V1074, 1.4.49, burned at Northolt 7.52

G-AKMJ (777), L8351, 22.1.48, to South Africa 12.48 as ZS-DBF, to Kenya 1.51 as VP-KIK; G-AKMK (897), N3851, 26.5.49, to New Zealand 7.49 as ZK-ATD; G-AKML (334), L5914, 18.3.49, to the Egyptian Air Force 9.49; G-AKMM (1712), P6344, 24.6.49, to the Egyptian Air Force 9.49; G-AKMN (424), L5992, 6.4.49, crashed at Wheaton Aston 26.2.53; G-AKMO (395), L5963, 6.4.49, to the Egyptian Air Force 9.49; G-AKMP (601), L8092, 4.2.49, to the Egyptian Air Force 9.49; G-AKMR (1820), R1819, not converted, scrapped at Lympne 1954; G-AKMS (1650), P2428, 21.1.49, to the Egyptian Air Force 9.49; G-AKMT (730), L8274, 26.3.49, to the Egyptian Air Force 9.49; G-AKMU (775), L8349, 2.7.49, beyond repair landing at Weston-super-mare 4.11.49, scrapped at Redhill 2.52; G-AKMY (2191), V1018, not converted, scrapped at Southport 1956; G-AKMZ (1775), P6420, not converted, burned at Squires Gate 1956

G-AKOL (923), N3882, 27.5.48, burned out at Dyce 12.5.49; G-AKPE (823), N3775, 26.2.48, withdrawn from use 5.54, wrecked by gale at Carlisle 1956; G-AKPF (2228), V1075, 23.4.48, withdrawn from use 4.63, in store at Ipswich 1967; G-AKPG (356), L5925, 28.6.57, crashed at Cranfield 12.11.64; G-AKPL (871), N3825, 11.9.48, crashed at Strabane, Co. Tyrone 26.1.64; G-AKPM (591), L8082, 4.4.49, struck car when landing at Lympne 22.10.50; G-AKRH (785), L8359, 27.5.48, withdrawn from use 11.56, scrapped at Squires Gate 1963; G-AKRI (623), L8145, 28.4.48, to Ireland 6.48 as EI-ADU; G-AKRJ (1862), R1876, 8.4.48, crashed in the sea off Shoreham 29.1.49; G-AKRK (1860), R1859, not converted, scrapped at Croydon 1948; G-AKRL (2042), T9805, 17.2.49, to Belgium 3.49 as OO-PAB; G-AKRM (2104), T9887, 25.3.48, crashed near Chester 8.4.53; G-AKRT (2100), T9883, 21.4.48, crashed at Elstree 8.11.53; G-AKRU (1874), R1888, 20.5.48, withdrawn from use 5.53, burned at Rochester 9.54; G-AKRV (2113), T9896, 9.3.49, cabin model, to Kenya 9.56 as VP-KNW; G-AKRW (931), N3890, 6.5.48, cabin model, beyond repair in forced landing at Hawkhurst, Kent 11.7.53; G-AKUA (1021), N3988, 6.5.48, crashed at Burnaston 21.7.57; G-AKXM (864), N3816, 17.1.49, to the Egyptian Air Force 9.49; G-AKXN (364), L5932, 21.1.49, to the Egyptian Air Force 9.49

G-ALFE (2239), V1086, 5.1.49, crashed at Ford 2.56, scrapped at Portsmouth 1957; G-ALFH (2063), T9826, not converted, scrapped at Northolt 1951; G-ALFI (2110), T9893, not converted, scrapped at Northolt 1951; G-ALGJ (2106), T9889, 25.5.49, crashed near Egremont, Cumberland 22.7.52; G-ALGK (1742), P6374, 16.3.49, single seat cabin model, ditched in the River Crouch off Burnham 21.1.51; G-ALGZ (2150), T9957, not converted, scrapped at Croydon 1950; G-ALHA (1879), R1893, not converted, scrapped at Croydon 1950; G-ALHB (971), N3933, not converted, scrapped at Croydon 1950; G-ALIM (640), N4557, 30.5.49, crashed at Kirriemuir, near Perth 14.9.56; G-ALIN (2027), T9760, not converted, burned at Rochester 3.54; G-ALIO (1700), P2500, 1.6.49, crashed near Sevenoaks 6.7.58; G-ALIP (1825), R1824, not converted, burned at Rochester 3.54; G-ALNX (678), L8211, not converted, scrapped at Elstree 10.52; G-ALNY (584), L8075, not converted, burned at Elstree 5.11.53; G-ALNZ (425), c/n checked visually as 426, not converted, scrapped at Elstree 10.52

G-ALOA (567), L8058, 27.10.49, scrapped at Elstree 10.52; G-ALOB (1044), N5408, not certificated after conversion, scrapped at Croydon 6.52; G-ALOC (1054), N5418, 27.10.49, sold abroad 2.50; G-ALOE (964), N3926, 7.12.49, to Belgium 1952 as OO-ACH; G-ALOF (1066), N5430, not converted, burned at Elstree 5.11.53; G-ALOG (732), L8276, 9.6.50, crashed at Speke 29.7.55; G-ALOH (2025), T9758, not converted, scrapped at Croydon 1949; G-ALUW (1693), P2493, 5.10.49, to Belgium 1951 as OO-AJT; G-ALUX (1649), P2427, 5.10.49, withdrawn from use at Fairoaks 4.63

G-AMBM (1625), P2388, 27.3.51, crashed at Deols, France 14.9.54; G-AMBN (752), L8326, 26.7.50, crashed at Wightwick, Staffs. 25.4.54; G-AMBO (1956), T9669, not converted, scrapped at Fairoaks 6.51; G-AMBP (1757), P6402, 13.7.50, crashed at Fairoaks 2.6.51; G-AMMC (779), L8353, to New Zealand 11.53 as ZK-AYW, preserved at Auckland as L8353; G-AMMD (741), L8285, to New Zealand 12.52 as ZK-AWX; G-ANLT (836), N3788, not converted, burned at Burnaston 1957; G-ANWO (718), L8262, 19.4.61, damaged at Kirton-in-Lindsey 21.4.62, preserved by the Newark Air Museum

The prototype Monarch flying near Woodley in 1937 piloted by H. W. C. Skinner. (*Aeroplane*)

Miles M.17 Monarch

G-AFCR (638), 1.6.38, Phillips & Powis Aircraft Ltd., Woodley; impressed 11.39 as W6461; rest. 1.46 to N. R. Harben, Burnaston; Air Schools Ltd., Burnaston 9.46; H. H. Mould, Wolverhampton 4.52; beyond repair Este, Venice 2.5.57

G-AFGL (786), 30.6.38, Airwork Ltd., Heston; sold in France 3.39 as F-ARPE

G-AFJU (789), 2.9.38, Sir V. A. G. Warrender, Heston; impressed 4.40 as X9306; rest. 3.46 to Lt. Cdr. R. H. A. Kidston, Heston; A. R. Pilgrim, Elstree 6.48; last owner K. A. Hudson, Staverton 8.64; dismantled at Staverton

G-AFJZ (790), 15.9.38, E. O. Liebert, Squires Gate; G. E. Wallace, Manston 7.39; delivered to R.A.F. Abingdon 1.11.39 as W6462; scrapped 12.48

G-AFLW (792), 18.11.38, Phillips & Powis Aircraft Ltd., Woodley; Rolls-Royce Ltd., Hucknall 3.39; Derby Aviation Ltd., Burnaston 5.58; M. F. Kirk, Leicester East 4.63; R. E. Coates, Blackbushe 7.68; J. E. Randall, White Waltham 1.72

G-AFRZ (793), 22.4.39, Lord Malcolm Douglas-Hamilton, Heston; impressed 11.39 as W6463; rest. 8.46 to B. G. Heron, Christchurch as G-AIDE q.v.

G-AFTX (795), 31.5.39, W. H. Whitbread, Heston; sold abroad 7.39

G-AGFW (787), OO-UMK, U-0226, 18.8.38, Phillips and Powis Aircraft Ltd., Woodley; re-serialled 5.44 as TP819; rest. 2.47 to J. Mahieu, Brussels; crashed near Ghent 22.11.60

G-AIDE (793), G-AFRZ, W6463, 4.1.47, B. G. Heron, Christchurch; W. P. Bowles, Elstree 5.56; based at strip at Northiam, Rye, Sussex by C. D. Cyster from 1971

Miles M.25 Martinet

G-AJJK HP145, registered 27.2.47 to D. E. Masters; shipped from Hanworth to Svensk Flygtjänst 23.5.47 as SE-BCP; scrapped 5.51

G-AJJL EM646, registered 27.2.47 to D. E. Masters; shipped from Hanworth to Svensk Flygtjänst 23.5.47 as SE-BCO; Swedish registration not taken up

G-AJJO HN913, registered 27.2.47 to D. E. Masters; shipped from Hanworth to Svensk Flygtjänst 23.5.47 as SE-BCN; scrapped 5.51

G-AJZB MS836, registered 18.6.47 to W. S. Shackleton Ltd.; not converted; dismantled for spares and derelict at Bovingdon 5.48

G-AJZC MS871, registered 18.6.47 to W. S. Shackleton Ltd.; not converted; dismantled for spares and derelict at Bovingdon 5.48

Note: Six aircraft exported by Miles Aircraft Ltd. 3.47 were: (c/n 5503) EM546/SE-AZC; (5770) SE-AZD; (5768) NR469/SE-AZE; (5567) EM629/SE-AZF; (5549) EM592/SE-AZG; (5568) EM640/SE-BCI

Miles M.38 Messenger 2A

G-AHUI (6335), 10.12.46, Derek Crouch (Contractors) Ltd., Peterborough; E. C. Francis, Hooton 2.54; withdrawn from use at Wolverhampton 9.60

G-AHZS (6331), 1.8.46, H. C. Kennard, Lympne trading as Air Kruise (Kent) Ltd.; withdrawn from use at Elstree 8.62

G-AHZT (6334), 19.2.47, H. Deterding, Sywell; Zeta Flying Group, Elstree 10.67; E. Pratt, Biggin Hill 11.70

G-AHZU (6337), 17.1.47, Tractor Spares Ltd., Wolverhampton; Strathtay Aero Club 2.54; Scottish Aero Club, Perth 9.56; crashed in Firth of Tay 10.6.57

G-AIAJ (6338),23.1.47, Maj. H. Blount, Tollerton; J. P. Sudborough, Sywell 2.54; J. A. Overton, Stapleford 10.54; temporarily to Ireland 4.55–2.56 as EI-AHL; D. P. White, Stapleford 9.63; scrapped at Stapleford in 1965

G-AIBD (6336), 23.12.46, T. Carlyle, Elmdon, later Shoreham; withdrawn from use at Portsmouth 7.63

G-AIDH (6340), 10.1.47, David Brown & Sons (Huddersfield) Ltd.; Whitehouse Industries Ltd., Yeadon 6.48; Mrs. L. K. King, Yeadon 11.49; W. S. Shackleton Ltd. 11.51; to Australia 11.51 as VH-ALN; beyond repair 1959

G-AIDK (6355), 13.9.46, G. H. Linnell, Sywell; D. C. Johnson, March, Cambs. 9.63; Wasp Flying Group, Panshanger 2.69

G-AIEK (6339), 17.1.47, A. J. Linnell, Sywell; Thames Valley Flying Group, White Waltham 9.66; R. M. Barnes, Penzance 9.68; E. C. King and J. Buckingham, Lulsgate 6.72; camouflaged and flown 1973 as 'RG333'

G-AILI (6362), 8.11.46, Miles Aircraft Ltd., Woodley; G. A. Barrow, Elmdon 3.53; H. C. Mackinnon, Lasham 8.58; Thurston Engineering Ltd., Stapleford 1.61; M. Darlington, Stapleford 6.63; crashed at Beauvais 23.5.64

Messenger 2A G-AILI with Praga E engine in 1947. (*A. J. Jackson*)

G-AILL (6341), 30.1.47, Air Schools Ltd., Wolverhampton; E. St. V. Troubridge, Eastleigh 11.53; Waveney Flying Group, Seething 7.60; G. Barker, Mablethorpe 8.70; H. Best-Devereux, Dinard 7.72

G-AISL (6346), 16.5.47, Hon. M. A. R. Cayzer, Thruxton; L. Walters, Stapleford 7.51; Smith's (Harlow) Ltd., Willingale 9.63; G. W. White, Fyfield 4.65; Allied Roofing & Insulations Ltd. 6.66; scrapped at Panshanger 7.67

G-AJDM (6347), 9.6.47, Miss E. A. Simms, Rearsby; Boston Air Transport Ltd., Wyberton 8.49; Miss D. I. Seen, Eastleigh 5.56; R. S. Bell, Portsmouth 11.59; H. G. Coward, Stapleford 5.61; reduced to spares at Stapleford 2.62

G-AJEY (6359), 23.5.47, T. Carlyle, Elmdon; beyond repair in forced landing at Bait, France 28.6.47 after the engine separated from the airframe

G-AJEZ (6360), 28.4.47, Miles Aircraft Ltd., Woodley; to Spain 11.47 as EC-ACU

G-AJFC (6349), 14.3.47, T. Shipside Ltd., Tollerton; Derek Crouch Ltd., Peterborough 11.52; G. F. Gibson, Booker 10.60; crashed at Bognor 7.7.63

G-AJFF (6363), 13.5.47, Patrick-Duval Aviation Ltd., Elmdon; Samuel Hodge & Sons Ltd., Broxbourne 11.47; G. Clifton, Spalding 7.49; Bartella Ltd., Elstree 6.59; Airscooters Ltd., Elstree 4.64; w.f.u. 3.68

G-AJFG (6364), 8.5.47, Patrick-Duval Aviation Ltd., Elmdon; to Ireland 8.48 as EI-ADT; rest. 12.66 to G. S. Medlock; later scrapped at Swanton Morley

G-AJFH (6365), 8.5.47, The Marquess of Londonderry, Newtownards; Ulster Aviation Ltd. 7.47; C. H. Bennion, Cambridge 9.52; sold in Liberia 12.60

G-AJKG (6373), 8.7.47, Ductile Steels Ltd., Wolverhampton; W. F. Stephenson, Blandford 6.50; R. C. Cox, Fairoaks 7.52; to Australia 8.53 as VH-AVQ

G-AJKK (6366), 22.5.47, W. Hopcroft & Sons Ltd., Tollerton; H. Tempest Ltd., Tollerton 4.50; A. M. Lambourne, St. Just 9.69

G-AJKL (6358), 25.7.47, Ulster Aviation Ltd., Newtownards; J. Fusco, Newtownards 2.50; M. J. Conry, Croydon 6.52; F. K. Bromley, Thruxton 6.57; Thurston Engineering Ltd., Stapleford 11.61; A.R.I. Propaflor Ltd., Panshanger 6.67

G-AJKT (6379), 3.6.47, G. O. Lawton, Burnaston; R. W. Kenny, Burnaston 9.48; Roy Wilshere Ltd., Elmdon 11.59; w.f.u. 10.62; scrapped at Sywell 1965

G-AJOC (6370), 3.6.47, C. E. Hickman, Wolverhampton; A. G. Belcher, Staverton 8.53; R. J. Sanders (Farms) Ltd., Sywell 12.62; S. B. Jolley, Dyce 5.69

G-AJOD (6698), 5.6.47, J. M. Houlder, Elstree; L. H. Wood, Carlisle 6.50; crashed into mountainside in bad weather near Dumfries 26.9.52, no casualties

G-AJOE (6367), 24.6.47, Reproducers & Amplifiers Ltd., Wolverhampton; F. Kenning, Burnaston 8.56; A. Townend, Yeadon 6.60

G-AJVC (6371), 30.6.47, Lionel Sage & Co. Ltd., Redhill; Longford Engineering Co. Ltd., Bognor 2.51; Southern Flying Schools Ltd., Portsmouth 2.55; Tyrolean Travel Ltd. 10.56; crashed at Munchen-Gladbach, Germany 19.11.56

G-AJVL (6372), 2.7.47, Tyne Taxis Ltd., Woolsington; to Australia 11.49 as VH-BJM

G-AJWB (6699), 31.7.47, Wiltshire School of Flying Ltd., Thruxton; P. Wannopp, Shoreham 6.53; W. H. Friend, Stapleford 3.60; J. L. Povey, Tees-side 7.66

G-AJYZ (H.P.R.146), 24.5.51, W. P. Bowles, Elstree; to Ireland 5.54 as EI-AGU; rest. 5.57 to W. S. Shackleton Ltd.; Middlesex Flying Group, Elstree 11.59; Wasp Flying Group, Panshanger 6.66; withdrawn from use 10.68

G-AKAH (6375), 7.8.47, Harben Aviation Ltd., Burnaston; to A.L.O.C., Ypenburg, Holland 9.48 as PH-NDR for N.L.v.S.; beyond repair at Schiedam 20.12.56

G-AKAI (6376), 16.9.47, W. G. Pearson, Thornaby; to Australia 3.52 as VH-AVD

G-AKAN (6702), 11.7.47, G. McLean, Perth; B. H. Gutteridge, White Waltham 8.51; to France 3.52 as F-BGPU

G-AKAO (6703), 26.8.47, J. C. Elwes, White Waltham; to Sweden 9.53 as SE-BYY

G-AKAV (6374), 4.9.47, W. H. Byars, Balado; W. C. Kemp, Dyce 10.52; Airscooter Flying Group, Elstree 7.57; withdrawn from use at Elstree 2.64

G-AKBL (6701), 20.8.47, Smithfield Refrigerator Co. Ltd., Elstree; to Ireland 3.50 as EI-AFH; rest. 2.53 to R. Matthews-Naper, Elstree who was lost when it was missing in the Irish Sea en route Northolt-Dublin 1.4.53

G-AKBM (6704), 12.8.47, Plymouth & District Aero Club, Roborough; withdrawn from use 5.61 and dismantled at Weston-super-Mare

G-AKBN (6377), 26.8.47, W. P. Bowles, Elstree; to Ireland 8.50 as EI-AFM; rest. 10.54 to H. Sutcliffe, Old Warden; P. F. Feeley, Elstree 12.60; Middlesex Flying Group, Elstree 8.66

G-AKBO (6378), 4.9.47, Yorkshire Aeroplane Club, Sherburn-in-Elmet; Scottish Aero Club, Perth 8.57; White Rose Flying Group, Sherburn 1.67; J. R. Ramshaw, Fairoaks 4.70

Messenger 2A G-AKBL at Elstree in March 1950, re-registered EI-AFH for its ferry flight to Dublin. (*E. J. Riding*)

G-AKCN (6705), 2.10.47, S. Bourne & Co. Ltd., Tollerton; T. Shipside Ltd., Tollerton 9.49; to New Zealand 7,50 as ZK-AUM; withdrawn from use 4.67

G-AKDF (6706), 1.10.47, Longford Engineering Co. Ltd., Bognor; L. W. Farrer, Wolverhampton 6.54; Portsmouth Aero Club 7.62; T. Carlyle, Shoreham 8.64

G-AKEZ (6707), 17.9.47, M. & H. Mining Contractors Ltd., Tollerton; Netherthorpe Aero Club 10.51; W. Nutt & Son Ltd., Yeadon 6.62; East Midlands Air Hire Ltd. 2.68; withdrawn from use 11.68; to Torbay Aircraft Museum 1971

G-AKIM (6724), 10.10.47, G. White & Co. Ltd., Denham; C. Screen, Elmdon 4.48; Wolverhampton Aero Club 10.51; Innes Ireland Ltd., Presteign 5.61; B. J. Clack, Stapleford 9.63; withdrawn from use at Stapleford 1.66

G-AKIN (6728), 7.11.47, P. A. Everard, Ratcliffe; A. J. Spiller, Sywell 7.49

G-AKIO (6729), 14.11.47, J. C. Bidgood, Yeadon; A. G. Wilson, Sherburn 6.58; to Holland 6.58 as PH-NIR; rest. 6.60; Lotus Cars Ltd., Panshanger 11.60; Elstree Caribbean F/C 5.65; Holland & Threlfall Ltd., Ringway 6.69

G-AKIP (6727), 3.11.47, Miles Aircraft Ltd., Woodley; to Switzerland 1.49 as HB-EEC, replacing c/n 6700 which had returned to U.K. to become G-AKKG

G-AKIR (6726), 17.10.47, P. Blamire, Baginton; J. W. Tomkins, Apethorpe, 4.50; J. W. Banks & Sons Ltd., Peterborough 10.68; w.f.u. at Postland 11.71

G-AKIS (6725), 15.10.47, Porter Spiers (Leicester) Ltd.; J. G. Hogg, Elstree 8.55; R. Jaffe, Elstree 6.69; withdrawn from use 2.70

G-AKKC (6369), 12.2.48, J. M. Wilkinson, Sywell; A. F. Johnson, Wyberton 4.52; D. R. Carnegie, Panshanger 11.55; E. Lloyd-Jones, White Waltham 8.59; C. Moore, Elstree 6.65; d.b.r. at St. Crowland strip, Lincs. 25.7.67

G-AKKI (6713), 8.11.48, J. Patston, Sywell; J. W. Tomkins, Apethorpe 2.55; Precision Products Ltd., Southend 8.65; destroyed in air collision with Auster Alpha 5 G-APAH over Danbury, Essex 16.3.58

G-AKKK (6712), 1.4.49, Boston Air Transport Ltd., Wyberton; to French Morocco 8.54 as F-DADU

G-AKKL (6717), 14.4.49, Godfrey Holmes Ltd., Lincoln; to New Zealand 10.50 as ZK-AWE; airworthy in 1968

G-AKKM (6714), 1.9.49, Newcastle Breweries Ltd., Woolsington; J. C. Elwes, Croydon 9.53; G. V. Barnett, Wolverhampton 8.57; damaged beyond repair 5.2.58

G-AKKN (6709), 26.9.49, P. S. Murphy, Newtownards; S. K. Davis, Cardiff 5.53; D. K. Foster, Wolverhampton 8.61; R. T. Knowles, Baginton 6.68; w.f.u. 4.69

G-AKKO (6716), 17.8.50, D. Godfrey Ltd., Rearsby; T. W. Shipside Ltd., Tollerton 1.62; J. Marriott, Tollerton 6.66; Mrs. P. M. Hugh, Ipswich 5.69; derelict at Shipdham 4.73

Miles M.38 Messenger 4A

G-AJDF RH370, 5.5.49, N. B. Williams, Wolverhampton; Scottish Flying Club, Perth 5.53; A. W. Ogsten, Perth 8.59; W. Holmes, Yeadon 6.65; w.f.u. 6.68

G-AKVZ (6352), RH427, 8.2.49, Thos. Ratcliffe & Co. Ltd., Yeadon; H. Laing, Denham 10.57; to Mk.4B 4.58 with Gipsy Major 10 Mk.2; R. W. Diggens, Denham 4.59; R. W. Spears, Jersey 11.63; P. H. Louks, Biggin Hill 5.70

G-AKZC RH372, 25.4.49, C. V. Bilbrough, Eastleigh; C. F. Westley, Old Warden 6.50; Nat. Assoc. of Training Corps for Girls, W. Waltham 12.56; w.f.u. 5.59

G-AKZU RH369, 12.11.48, Morgan Aviation Ltd., Cowes; R. H. Crofts, Rochester 2.51; F. G. Miles Ltd., Redhill 5.52; to France 8.52 as F-BGOM

G-AKZX RH424, 31.12.48, N. M. Browning, Broxbourne, later Stanford Rivers strip, Essex; crashed on take-off at Rochester 24.7.65

G-ALAE RH421, 10.2.49, E. V. Wagner, Elstree; A. R. Adair, Broxbourne 11.50; N. Middlesex F/G, Elstree 7.58; d.b.r. at Epping Upland, Essex 2.8.58

G-ALAF (6350), RH425, 26.11.48, E. J. Morton, Baginton; R. P. Sayer, Norwich 11.51; W. S. Shackleton Ltd. 11.53; to New Zealand 2.54 as ZK-BED

G-ALAG RH422, 1.5.50, J. C. Rice, Leicester; to France 3.53 as F-BGQZ; rest. 3.56 to Rosenthal China Ltd.; d.b.r. at Gittelde Harz, Germany 30.12.57

G-ALAH RH377, 6.9.48, E. P. Jenks Ltd., Wolverhampton; D. C. Jemmett, Wolverhampton 7.55; G. J. O'Neill, Baginton 10.63; w.f.u. 4.65; to R.A.F. Museum

G-ALAI RH423, 18.2.49, L. W. Hamp, Wolverhampton; Sky Flying Group, Fairoaks 1.58; Cleveland Flying Group, Tees-side 6.66; withdrawn from use 6.70

G-ALAJ (6354), RH429, 15.10.48, L. W. Farrer, Wolverhampton; Royal Artillery Aero Club, Middle Wallop 6.54; d.b.r. in gale, Christchurch 29.7.56

G-ALAP RH368, 25.5.50, Porter Spiers (Leicester) Ltd., Rearsby; L. W. Hudson, Staverton 7.53; Finch & Knight Ltd., Stapleford 2.59; crashed on take-off from Bark Island gliding site, Halifax 24.5.61

G-ALAR RH371, 30.6.49, T. W. Leadbetter, Elmdon; to H. P. Jennings, Mombasa, Kenya 2.52 as VP-KJL; returned to U.K.; dismantled at Old Warden 1959

G-ALAV (6353), RH428, 26.10.48, M. B. Neaum, Burnaston; R. Myers, Christchurch 4.55; Mell Air Ltd., Skegness 7.61; withdrawn from use at Skegness

G-ALAW (6351), RH426, 20.8.48, Skegness Steam Laundry Co. Ltd., Ingoldmells; C. A. Taylor, Tollerton 2.60; L. Booth, Sheffield 6.66; w.f.u. 4.67

G-ALBE (4691), RG327, 6.8.48, E. W. Westbrook, Redhill; Electrical Concessionaires Ltd., Ringway 12.54; withdrawn from use at Ringway 9.59

G-ALBP RH376, 13.4.51, J. P. Gunner, Redhill; D. B. Munro, Shoreham 8.52; to Wynne Bros., Adelaide, South Australia 4.55 as VH-WYN

G-ALBR RH378, 17.9.48, J. E. Nicholson, York; T. W. Hayhow, York 1.49; crashed on take-off from Elstree 2.7.49

Miles M.38 Messenger *(other variants)*

G-AGOY (4690), Mk.3, U-0247, 24.10.45, Miles Aircraft Ltd.; to Switzerland 8.46 as HB-EIP; rest. 8.48 to W. P. Bowles, Elstree; to Ireland 6.53 as EI-AGE

G-AGPX (6266), Mk.2B, 6.11.45, Blackburn Aircraft Ltd., Brough; P. J. Butterfield, Panshanger 4.58; withdrawn from use at Panshanger 3.62

G-AGUW (6267), Mk.2C, 28.2.46, Miles Aircraft of South Africa (Pty.) Ltd.; to the Belgian Congo 8.46 as OO-CCM; crashed 10.10.48

G-AHFP (6332), Mk.4, 25.11.46, Airwork Ltd., Heston; Mansfield Autos Ltd., Tollerton 3.51; to Ireland 10.52 as EI-AGB; crashed Co. Sligo 1.5.53

G-AHGE (6330), Mk.4, 13.5.46, Miles Aircraft Ltd., Woodley, on behalf of Prince Regent of Iraq; crashed at Tugela, South Africa 25.10.46

G-AHXR (6333), Mk.2B, 12.8.46, Miles Aircraft Ltd.; to Prince Regent of Iraq 2.47 as YI-HRH; rest. 5.48 to Airwork Ltd., Heston; Hon. J. B. Fermor-Hesketh 9.48; Mrs. B. Weininger, Sywell 6.53; withdrawn from use 1.62

G-AIRY (6343), Mk.4, 28.5.47, British Aviation Insurance Co. Ltd., Woodley; to Canterbury Aero Club, New Zealand 4.50 as ZK-ATT

G-AKKG (6700), Mk.4, HB-EEC, 12.9.47, Shell Mex & B.P. Ltd., Elstree; B. G. Heron, Christchurch 9.58; Dacier Ltd., Christchurch 9.63; R. E. Gold, Elstree 6.67; crashed at Partridge Green, Sussex 1.6.68

G-ALAC RH420, Mk.5, G-2-1, 20.9.51, Blackburn Aircraft Ltd., Brough; written off in forced landing at Faversham, Kent 22.9.51

Miles M.57 Aerovan Mk.1

G-AGOZ (4700), U-0248, 1.2.46, Miles Aircraft Ltd., Woodley; Western Mfg. Estates Ltd., Woodley 12.48; scrapped at Woodley in 1949

Miles M.57 Aerovan Mk.2

G-AGWO (6432), U-8, 27.6.46, Miles Aircraft Ltd., Woodley; Marquess of Londonderry, Newtownards 11.46; crashed 2.7.47

Miles M.57 Aerovan Mk.3

G-AHTX (6380), 28.6.46, Air Contractors Ltd., Woodley; S. G. Newport (Arab Contracting & Trading Co. Ltd.), Beirut 5.49; damaged beyond repair landing at Baalbeck, Lebanon 9.11.51

G-AHXH (6382), 10.9.46, Island Air Charters Ltd., Jersey; Air Contractors Ltd., Woodley 2.47; converted to Mk.4; S. G. Newport, Beirut 6.48; F. G. Miles Ltd., Shoreham 5.55; to N. V. Nastra, Rotterdam 2.59 as PH-EAB

G-AIDI (6383), 13.9.46, Air Contractors Ltd., Woodley; S. G. Newport, Beirut 2.49; broken up at Beirut, Lebanon after C. of A. expiry 1.2.51

G-AIHK (6384), 31.10.46, Air Contractors Ltd., Woodley; S. G. Newport, Beirut 2.49; beyond repair at landing ground K.1, Iraq 2.10.49 after airscrew flew off port engine in flight and severed port tailplane, fin and rudder.

G-AIHL (6385), 28.10.46, Air Contractors Ltd., Woodley; destroyed in forced landing at Dragor, south of Kastrup while en route Croydon–Kastrup 29.10.46

G-AIIG (6386), 23.1.47, Skytravel Ltd., Speke; Lancashire Aircraft Corp., Bovingdon 6.51; to Societa Transporti Aerei Mediterranei, Rome 10.53 as I-VALF

Miles M.57 Aerovan Mk.4

G-AIDJ (6387), 17.9.46, D. B. Bruce, Croydon; S. G. Newport, Beirut 5.48; crashed on take-off at Rutbah Wells, Iraq 22.11.48; wreck taken to Baghdad

G-AIHJ (6388), 10.1.47, Miles Aircraft Ltd., Woodley; to Compagnie Générale de T.S.F., Le Bourget 3.48 as F-BENO

G-AIKV (6389), 3.12.46, Air Contractors Ltd. Woodley; forced down on beach at Fremandville, east of Cherbourg by storm and washed out to sea 12.1.47

G-AILB (6391), 7.2.47, Miles Aircraft Ltd., Woodley; to Compania Auxilar de Navegacion Aerea S.A., Madrid 11.47 as EC-EAK, later EC-ACP

G-AILC (6392), 3.1.47, Miles Aircraft Ltd., Woodley; to Spain 11.47 with G-AILB above and re-registered EC-ABA; to Aerotéchnica S.A., Madrid 10.52

G-AILD (6393), 13.1.47, Miles Aircraft Ltd., Woodley; to Spain as above, became EC-ABB; to Aero Club Lérida 1950; to Aerotéchnica S.A. 10.52

G-AILE (6394), 7.2.47, Miles Aircraft Ltd., Woodley; to Spain as above 11.47 as EC-ACQ; to Aerotéchnica S.A. 7.52; crashed at Santander 4.9.52

Aerovan 4 G-AILF operating on skis early in 1947. (*Fox*)

G-AILF (6400), 14.1.47, Miles Aircraft Ltd., Woodley; flown on skis 1947; leased to Pickfords Ltd., Guernsey; beyond repair landing at Guernsey 20.8.50

G-AILM (6398), 21.2.47, Lockwoods Flying Services Ltd., Speeton nr. Filey; Silver City Airways Ltd., Blackbushe 10.51; Aero Publicity Ltd., Elstree 12.54; Sky Neon Ltd., Croydon 12.54; to Greece 5.55 as SX-DBA

G-AISE (6395), 14.3.47, Air Transport (Charter) (C.I.) Ltd., Jersey; British Nederland Airservices Ltd., Tollerton 6.47; scrapped at Tollerton 11.47

G-AISF (6396), 14.3.47, Universal Flying Services Ltd., Fairoaks; Channel Islands Air Freight Ltd., Eastleigh 12.50; Meridian Air Maps Ltd., Shoreham 10.55; fatal take-off crash at Ringway 29.4.57

G-AISG (6405), 19.5.47, North Sea Air Transport Ltd., Brough; crashed on take-off from Croydon 14.6.47 while flying racing pigeons from Ringway to Guernsey

G-AISI (6397), 31.3.47, Air Contractors Ltd., Woodley; British Nederland Airservices Ltd. 5.48; to Belgian Air Service, Grimbergen 8.50 as OO-MAR

G-AJKJ (6406), 17.4.47, Ulster Aviation Ltd., Newtownards; ditched off Southport, Lancs. 25.3.48, en route Eastleigh–Belfast with cargo of refrigerators

G-AJKM (6402), 16.5.47, East Anglian Flying Services Ltd., Southend; damaged beyond repair when blown over by gale while refuelling at Lympne 3.5.49

G-AJKO (6408), 23.4.47, Airwork Ltd., Heston; to Airwork (East Africa) Ltd., Nairobi 9.47 as VP-KEN; crashed at Rift Valley 31.12.49

G-AJKP (6401), 23.4.47, Patrick-Duval Aviation Ltd., Elmdon 'County of Stafford'; Chanair Ltd., Jersey 6.52; F. G. Miles Ltd., Shoreham 9.54 (leased to Meridian Air Maps Ltd.); fatal crash at Oldbury, Warwicks. 17.12.57

G-AJKU (6407), 6.6.47, Ulster Aviation Ltd., Newtownards; w.f.u. 7.50; taken to Squires Gate by North West Airlines Ltd. and burned there 11.57

G-AJOB (6409), 9.5.47, Ulster Aviation Ltd., Newtownards; ditched in Irish Sea off South Rock lighthouse while en route Woodley–Newtownards 27.6.47

G-AJOF (6403), 6.6.47, Patrick-Duval Aviation Ltd., Elmdon 'County of Derby'; Chanair Ltd., Jersey 6.52; to F. G. Miles Ltd., Shoreham 1.55 for conversion into the experimental H.D.M.105 with Hurel-Dubois mainplane

East Anglian Flying Services' Aerovan 4 G-AJKM joy flying at Southend in 1948. (*A. J. Jackson*)

G-AJOG (6410), 10.6.47, Universal Flying Services Ltd., Fairoaks; North Sea Air Transport Ltd., Brough 10.49; to Belgium 11.51 as OO-ERY; resold in U.K. 9.55 and lay at Chivenor for a number of years but did not fly again.

G-AJOI (6411), 27.6.47, Sivewright Airways Ltd., Ringway 'Oldhamia'; Patrick Motors Ltd., Elmdon 10.50; destroyed by gale on ground at Elmdon 7.12.50

G-AJTC (6414), 4.6.47, Miles Aircraft Ltd., Woodley; grounded 7.49 until sold to Air Ads Ltd., Southend and fitted with neon signs 9.52; crashed at Dachau near Munich, Germany 23.9.55

G-AJTD (6415), 3.7.47, Ulster Aviation Ltd., Newtownards; blown over and wrecked while taxying to take-off point, Newtownards 3.11.48

G-AJTK (6416), 27.6.47, British Nederland Airservices Ltd., Tollerton; withdrawn from use at Tollerton 11.47 and scrapped

G-AJWD (6412), 7.7.47, Skytravel Ltd., Squires Gate; grounded 7.48 until sold to Air Ads Ltd., Southend 3.55; crashed near Dunkirk 26.8.56

Aerovan 4 OO-MAR at Southend in August 1950 awaiting delivery to Grimbergen after overhaul by Aviation Traders Ltd. (*A. J. Jackson*)

G-AJWI (6418), 20.6.47, Lees-Hill Aviation Ltd., Elmdon; Mayfair Air Services Ltd., Croydon 6.48; damaged beyond repair abroad in 1950

G-AJWK (6417), 11.7.47, Airwork Ltd., Heston; to Iraq Aeroplane Society 3.48 as YI-ABV; scrapped in 1952

G-AJXK (H.P.R.144), completed by Handley Page (Reading) Ltd., Woodley; crashed on landing from C. of A. test flight at Woodley 3.12.50; parts to G-AILM

G-AJZG (6413), 8.8.47, Automobile & Aircraft Services Ltd., Croydon 'Comotas'; Culliford Airlines Ltd., Squires Gate 9.47; M. J. Conry, Croydon 10.50; G. H. Miles, Shoreham 4.53; to Soc. Transp. Aer. Med. 1.54 as I-VALT

G-AJZN (6420), 15.9.47, Kenning Aviation Ltd., Burnaston; Air Schools Ltd., Burnaston 6.48; D. Ross, Tollerton 6.51; withdrawn from use 2.52

G-AJZP (6421), 3.10.47, Kenning Aviation Ltd., Burnaston; leased Air Cargo Distributors Ltd., Woodley 2.48; to SITA, Saigon, Indochina 6.49 as F-OACN

G-AJZR (6422), 22.8.47, Skyfreight Ltd., Speke; Miles Aircraft Ltd., Woodley 10.47; to Devlet Hava Yollari, Turkey 1.49 as TC-VAN; Turkish Air Force 9.54

G-AKHD (6425), 9.4.48, Ulster Aviation Ltd., Newtownards; to France 9.49 as F-BFPF

G-AKHG (6424), 17.10.47, J. P. Cunningham, Beirut; S. G. Newport, Beirut (Arab Contracting & Trading Co. Ltd.); crashed at Hama, Syria 21.2.52

G-AKKJ (6423), 31.1.51, Western Manufacturing Estates Ltd., Woodley; to Angola 3.51 as CR-LCL

G-AMYA (H.P.R. 29), not completed by Handley Page (Reading) Ltd.; components sold to Air Ads Ltd. and stored at Elstree; to Croydon 3.55 and scrapped

G-AMYC (H.P.R. 47), as G-AMYA above but components were finally taken to Stapleford for possible preservation

Miles M.57 Aerovan Mk.5

G-AISJ (6404), registered 8.1.47 to Miles Aircraft Ltd., Woodley; damaged beyond repair during full speed braking trials at Woodley 15.7.47

Miles M.57 Aerovan Mk.6

G-AKHF (6399), 24.1.48, Miles Aircraft Ltd., Woodley; Avia Britannica Corp. 'Northern Exporter' 2.49 (t/a Air Cargo Distributors Ltd); F. G. Miles Ltd., Redhill 10.50; to Soc. Transporti Aerei Med., Rome 4.54 as I-VALK

Miles H.D.M.105

G-AHDM (105/1009), first flown 31.3.57 as G-35-3, C. of A. 20.5.57, F. G. Miles Ltd., Shoreham; H. D. et M. (Aviation) Ltd., Shoreham 12.57; dismantled at Shoreham in 1958; parts used for mock-up of H.D.M.106 Caravan

Miles M.65 Gemini 1A

G-AFLT (6520), EI-ADM, 14.11.47, crashed at Burpham, Surrey 10.1.54; G-AGUS (4701), 15.3.46, to Sweden 7.52 as SE-BUY; G-AHKL (6305), 4.11.46, w.f.u. at Lympne 2.66; G-AIDG (6308), 30.10.46, to Ethiopia 12.49, re-registered 6.51 as ET-P-14; G-AIDO (6306), 30.8.46, to Sweden 5.52 as SE-BUG; G-AIHI (6283), 6.11.46, to France 2.48 as F-BENP; G-AIHM (6307), 27.9.46, crashed at Le Touquet 18.11.62; G-AIIE (6310), 10.12.46, to France 2.50 as F-BFPP; G-AIIF (6312), 2.4.47, w.f.u. at

Lulsgate 5.71; G-AIKW (6309), 4.11.46, ditched off Island of Rum, near Skye 7.9.47; G-AILG (6311), 30.1.47, to France 6.52 as F-BGPR; G-AILK (6453), 28.11.46, to Australia 12.47 as VH-BJZ; G-AIRS (6315), 7.2.47, crashed at Oxhey, Herts. 11.3.56; G-AISD (6285), 3.4.47, to Kenya 6.47 as VP-KDH; G-AISK (6319), 3.4.47, to France 12.50 as F-BFXH, later F-BFVH; G-AISM (6454), 23.4.47, crashed near St. Ives, Cornwall 7.7.60; G-AISN (6323), 18.4.47, to France 2.53 as F-BDJD; G-AISO (6326), 18.4.47, to Australia 4.50 as VH-AAS; G-AIWS (6327), 3.5.47, w.f.u. at Woodley 5.49, scrapped at Shoreham in 1959

G-AJEX (6324), 11.4.47, crashed and burned at Panshanger 4.3.59; G-AJFA (6287), 2.4.47, to Spain 11.47 as EC-ACT; G-AJFB (6288), 9.5.47, to Spain 11.47 as EC-ACS; G-AJFD (6325), 14.4.47, w.f.u. at Exeter 10.64; G-AJKN (6286), 9.5.47, to Spain 11.47 as EC-ACR; G-AJKR (6455), 23.4.47, to Italy 10.54 as I-AJKR; G-AJKS (6289), CF-EMW, 18.7.47, scrapped at White Waltham 4.65; G-AJKV (6328), 20.5.47, w.f.u. 10.65; G-AJOH (6456), 12.6.47, to Canada 4.55 as CF-HVK; G-AJOJ (6280), 20.6.47, stored at Ford in 1971; G-AJOK (6281), 20.6.47, to Switzerland 7.51 as HB-EEE; G-AJOL (6321), 31.7.47, crashed at Cowfold, Sussex 29.8.49; G-AJOM (6282), 8.8.47, to Brazil 1.51 as PT-AHT

G-AJTA (6329), 27.6.47, to Switzerland 6.47 as HB-EEA; G-AJTB (6457), 11.8.47, damaged beyond repair at Berck, France 30.1.51; G-AJTE (6302), 3.7.47, to Kenya 11.47 as VP-KEG; G-AJTF (6303), 3.7.47, to South Africa 1.48 as ZS-BSP; G-AJTG (6459), Mk.1B, 8.5.50, converted to Mk.3B in 1951, w.f.u. at Exeter 11.60; G-AJTH (6304), 7.7.47, to Uganda 9.47 as VP-UAY, to Kenya 2.48 as VP-KFL, rest. 12.53; G-AJTI (6444), 7.7.47, to Belgian Congo 10.47 as OO-CDO; G-AJTJ (6445) 8.8.47, to Belgian Congo 5.48 as OO-CDW; G-AJTL (6461), 3.7.47, w.f.u. at Jersey 3.63; G-AJWA (6290), 20.8.47, sold in Denmark 10.65 for museum purposes; G-AJWC (6295), 22.8.47, to Cranfield 9.63 for glued joint tests; G-AJWE (6452), 11.6.47, crashed at Biggin Hill 11.4.64; G-AJWF (6291), 7.7.47, to Ireland 7.53 as EI-AGF, rest. 12.53, w.f.u. at Elstree 9.63; G-AJWG (6292), 20.8.47, w.f.u. at Sleap 3.65; G-AJWH (6293), 31.7.47, to France 8.59 as F-BJEP; G-AJWL (6460), 22.8.47, to Belgium 6.50 as OO-ODR

G-AJZI (6462), 29.8.47, crashed at Croydon 27.2.48; G-AJZJ (6465), 2.9.47, w.f.u. at Biggin Hill 1.65; G-AJZK (6466), 20.8.47, crashed near Usumbura, Urandi, Belgian Congo 10.7.48, G-AJZL (6467), 3.10.47, to Australia 10.51 as VH-ALJ; G-AJZM (6468), 1.10.47, to Australia 8.48 as VH-BLN; G-AJZO (6466), 2.9.47; G-AJZS (6297), 20.8.47, w.f.u. at White Waltham 3.64

G-AKDA (6296), 22.8.47, to Sweden 11.50 as SE-AYM; G-AKDB (6294), 2.9.47, used as spares 11.70; G-AKDC (6496), Gemini 3, U-23, G-23-2, 24.5.49, converted 7.56 to Mk.3A, converted 7.57 to Mk.3C, to Tanganyika 12.57 as VR-TBP; G-AKDD (6284), 3.10.47, ditched off Isle of Sheppey 5.3.61, wreck brought ashore at Leigh-on-Sea, Essex; G-AKDE (6298), 22.8.47, to Trinidad 3.53 as VP-TBI; G-AKDG (6450), 22.8.47, to France 6.50 as F-BBSL; G-AKDH (6449), 22.8.47, to Australia 11.50 as VH-AJW; G-AKDI (6451), 22.8.47, to France 8.53 as F-BGTM; G-AKDJ (6448), 22.8.47, crashed on beach at Bispham, Lancs. 5.1.61; G-AKDK (6469), 4.9.47; G-AKDL (6300), 22.8.47, to New Zealand 3.50 as ZK-AUA

G-AKEG (6299), 5.9.47, converted to Mk.3C in 1958, w.f.u. at Baginton 6.63; G-AKEH (6473), 4.9.47, to Singapore 8.51 as VR-SDC; G-AKEI (6470), 9.9.47, to Ireland 2.56 as EI-AHN, rest. 12.57, w.f.u. at Renfrew 11.63; G-AKEJ (6482), 9.10.47, w.f.u. at Baginton 9.65; G-AKEK (6483), 24.9.47, converted 6.52 to Mk.3A; G-AKEL (6484), 1.10.47; G-AKEM (6485), 25.9.47, w.f.u. at Lympne 4.65; G-AKEN (6486), 25.9.47, to Australia 12.53 as VH-BTP, later VH-GBB; G-AKEO (6487), 25.9.47, to Kenya 11.47 as VP-KET; G-AKEP (6493), 19.9.47, to Israel 5.50 as 4X-ACK; G-AKER (6491), 19.9.47, preserved at Lincolnshire Aircraft Museum, Tattershall 1972; G-AKES

(6447), 19.9.47, to Venezuela 3.53 as YV-P-AED

G-AKFU (6494), 25.9.47, beyond repair in forced landing 60 miles from Goose Bay, Labrador 14.8.65 while en route U.K. to Canada; G-AKFV (6495), 25.9.47, to Kenya 1.48 as VP-KEX; G-AKFW (6501), 10.10.47, to Northern Rhodesia 9.48 as VP-RBK; G-AKFX (6502), 1.10.47, converted 7.56 to Mk.8, crashed on take-off at Shoreham 26.10.60; G-AKFY (6503), 10.10.47, to Switzerland 12.47 as HB-EEF, rest. 10.48, w.f.u. at Biggin Hill 11.63; G-AKFZ (6476), 3.10.47, to the Belgian Congo 2.48 as OO-CDX; G-AKGA (6474), 23.9.47, to the Belgian Congo 6.50 as OO-CMA; G-AKGB (6504), 6.10.47, to Australia 2.49 as VH-BMW; G-AKGC (6489), 1.10.47, crashed at Anjou near Grenoble, France 3.7.61; G-AKGD (6492), 6.10.47, preserved at Southend Historic Aircraft Museum 1972; G-AKGE (6488), 7.11.47, converted 7.57 to Mk.3C, to Ireland 10.59 as EI-ALM, rest. 12.61

G-AKHA (6507), 10.10.47, crashed at Haditha, near Baghdad 25.1.49; G-AKHB (6508), 1.10.47, w.f.u. at White Waltham 4.65; G-AKHC (6490), 24.10.47, converted 5.54 to Mk.3A, w.f.u. at White Waltham 9.65; G-AKHE (6509), 1.10.47, crashed at Hilsea, Portsmouth 22.7.53; G-AKHH (6511), 24.10.47, to France 1.50 as F-BFPG; G-AKHI (6512), 24.10.47, to Egypt 12.49 as SU-AGG; G-AKHJ (6513), 24.10.47, w.f.u. at Shobdon 12.63; G-AKHK (6514), 24.10.47, crashed at Montpellier, France 30.8.59; G-AKHL (6515), 24.10.47, to Madagascar 2.48 as F-BDAF; G-AKHM (6516), 24.10.47, to Madagascar 2.48 as F-BDAG; G-AKHN (6517), 24.10.47, to Madagascar 2.48 as F-BDAH; G-AKHO (6518), 31.10.47, to Madagascar 2.48 as F-BDAI; G-AKHP (6519), 11.12.47; G-AKHR (6477), 15.10.47, to India 12.47 as VT-CQZ; G-AKHS (6510), 3.11.47, to Belgium 1.54 as OO-GAR; G-AKHT (6521), 7.11.47, to Australia 3.49 as VH-BMT; G-AKHU (6522), 7.11.47, to Australia 10.50 as VH-BMV, re-registered with Lycomings 11.56 as VH-WEJ; G-AKHV (6523), 9.12.47, w.f.u. at Biggin Hill 6.66; G-AKHW (6524), 18.11.47; G-AKHX (6525), 7.11.47, to Belgium 3.55 as OO-RVE, crashed at Grimbergen 9.71; G-AKHY (6526), 7.11.47, beyond repair in forced landing at Shebbear, Devon 4.4.65; G-AKHZ (6527), 7.11.47, converted 4.57 to Mk.7, w.f.u. at Sywell 1.64

G-AKKA (6528), 7.11.47, to Norway 4.48 as LN-TAH; G-AKKB (6537), 26.2.48; G-AKKD (6531), 27.2.48, to India 4.48 as VT-CTQ; G-AKKE (6317), Gemini Mk.4 ambulance, 14.1.48, to Angola 5.49 as CR-LCD; G-AKKF (6532), 11.5.48, to Kenya 11.51 as VP-KJC; G-AKKH (6479), OO-CDO, 5.12.47, w.f.u. at Tollerton 12.68

Gemini G-AKFX, with 155 h.p. Cirrus Major 3 engines and enlarged vertical tail surfaces, after conversion to Mk.8 by F. G. Miles Ltd. in 1956. (*A. J. Jackson*)

G-ALCS (6534), Gemini 3A, 5.4.50, converted 7.57 to Mk.3C; G-ALUG (6320), EI-ACW, 10.6.47, w.f.u. at Sywell 6.64; G-AMRG (6313), VR-GGG, VR-RGG, VR-SDJ, 17.9.54, to Switzerland 8.58 as HB-EEH; G-AOXW (6478), VP-UAZ, VP-KFJ, 4.1.59, w.f.u. at Foulsham, Norfolk 1.60

Miles M.65 Gemini 1A *(completed by Handley Page (Reading) Ltd.)*

G-ALZG (H.P.R.141), 3.6.50, P. Blamire, Baginton; converted 5.58 to Mk.3C; R. E. Winn, Cork 5.73

G-AMEJ (H.P.R.145), 21.12.50, Balfour Marine Engineering Co. Ltd., Mitchell's Farm, near Stapleford; temporarily to Miles Car Hire Ltd., Southend 4.52 to 7.52; w.f.u. at Southend 6.55; scrapped in 1957

Miles M.65 Gemini 1A *(completed by F. G. Miles Ltd., Redhill)*

G-AMBH (65/1001), 30.5.50, E. G. Hayes, Scilly Isles; East Riding Flying Club, Speeton 5.53; Wescol Construction Co. Ltd., Yeadon 6.57; converted to Mk.3A; to the Belgian Congo 8.58 as OO-COA

Miles M.65 Gemini 3A *(completed by Wolverhampton Aviation Ltd.)*

G-ALMU (WAL/C.1004), 6.10.51, Fairway Engineering Co. Ltd., Barton; L. R. Snook, Portsmouth 5.54; LEC Refrigeration Ltd., Bognor 3.55; J. G. Ratcliff, Elmdon 10.57; J. P. Snelling, Biggin Hill 7.66; w.f.u. 5.67

G-AMDE (WAL/C.1002), 30.3.51, L. S. Dawson, Yeadon; Yorkshire Flying Club, Yeadon 6.59; J. F. McClory, Woolsington 9.61; crashed at Sibson 24.9.67

G-AMGF (WAL/C.1003), 27.3.51, Shell Refining & Marketing Co. Ltd., Croydon; converted 6.55 to Mk.7; dismantled and scrapped at Heathrow 11.63

G-AMKZ (WAL/C.1005), 22.12.52, J. Brockhouse & Co. Ltd., Wolverhampton; S. M. Henry, Newtownards 11.58; to Sweden 8.61 as SE-CMX

G-AMME (WAL/C.1006), 1.7.52, Ind, Coope & Allsopp Ltd., Wolverhampton; Whiteley (Rishworth) Ltd., Yeadon 7.56; P. Jackson, Elmdon 4.64; w.f.u. at Baginton 4.71

Miles M.75 Aries

G-AMDJ (75/1002), G-35-1, 13.6.52, F. G. Miles Ltd., Redhill; Hon. M. A. R. Cayzer, Redhill 4.53; A. Vigano, Melbourne 5.54; to Australia 5.54 as VH-FAV

G-AOGA (75/1007), 9.3.56, Pasolds Ltd., White Waltham; to Ireland 6.63 as EI-ANB; rest. 9.63 to J. H. Kenny, Dublin; Aries Flying Group, Baginton 9.65; Telearchics Ltd., Staverton 6.68; R. F. Winn, Cork 6.69

Mooney M.20 Mk.21 and M.20A Mk.21

G-APVV (1474), M.20A, N8164E, 30.7.59; G-ARWY (1305), M.20A, N1079B, 26.4.62; G-BAFB (1161), M.20, D-ELER, OE-DOZ, OY-DII registered 26.9.72

Mooney M.20B Mk.21

G-ARNA (1806), 26.6.61; G-ARTB (1866), 3.10.61

Mooney M.20C Mk.21

G-ASBN (2183), 6.7.62; G-ASLZ (2596), N6892U, 20.12.64; G-ASNP (2689), 18.4.64; G-ASTH (2701), N6906U, 2.6.64, d.b.r. in forced landing at La Bouexiere, near Dinard, France 16.11.66; G-ASUC (2768), 3.11.64, to Australia 4.67 as VH-CYG;

G-ARNA, first of two Mooney M.20B Mk.21 four seat touring aircraft imported from America in 1961.

G-ATAD (2863), N79394, 22.4.65; G-AWIH (680107), 2.7.68; G-AYYS (2002), YV-T-RTG, 23.9.71

Mooney M.20E Super 21

G-ASNR (278), 7.4.64, lost in the English Channel 10.10.71; G-ASUB (397), N7158U, 23.9.64; G-ATHW (805), N5881Q, 6.1.66; G-ATOU (961), N5946Q, 24.3.66; G-AZOP (0023), N9617V, 24.3.72

Mooney M.20F Mk.21

G-AVHD (670260), N9700M, to France 4.67 as F-BOSJ; G-AVWW (670501), N6422Q, 6.11.67; G-AWLP (680200), 10.7.69; G-AXZV (680129), N3848N, 21.5.70; G-AYBF (670383), N3290F, 24.4.70

Morane-Saulnier M.S.880B Rallye Club

G-ARTT (008), 24.12.61; G-ARXX (106), 28.5.62; G-ARXY (108), 28.5.62; G-ASAR (177), 3.8.62; G-ASAT (178), 12.3.63; G-ASAU (179), 21.4.63; G-ASAV (180), 21.4.63; G-ATYZ (848), 28.2.67; G-AVIM (880), 8.5.67; G-AVIN (884), 13.6.67; G-AVIO (901), 3.7.67; G-AVVK (1143), 2.12.67, to Ireland 10.70 as EI-AUP; G-AVZX (1165), 26.1.68; G-AVZY (1166), 26.1.68; G-AWAA (1174), 26.1.68; G-AWJI (1217), 24.6.68; G-AWJK (1218), 15.7.68; G-AWKS (1225), 12.7.68; G-AWKT (1235), 15.7.68; G-AWOA (1258), 7.8.69; G-AWOB (1270), 3.2.69; G-AWXT (835), F-BNXU, 26.2.69; G-AWYX (1311), 24.4.69

G-AXAK (1304), 2.4.69; G-AXCL (1321), 14.5.69; G-AXCM (1322), 29.5.69; G-AXCN (1328), 29.5.69; G-AXGC (1349), 3.7.69; G-AXGD (1352), 3.7.69; G-AXGE (1353), 3.7.69; G-AXHF (1370), 17.3.70, to Ireland 5.70 as EI-AUJ; G-AXHG (1371), 12.6.70; G-AXHH (1616), 10.6.70, to Ireland 6.70 as EI-AUN; G-AXHI (1617), 17.7.70; G-AXHS (1357), 22.8.70; G-AXHT (1358), 10.6.70; G-AXHU (1359), 1.4.70, to Ireland 4.70 as EI-AUE

G-AYCR (70), F-BKDX, 29.7.70, crashed at Southleigh, Devon 9.10.70; G-AYFJ (333), F-BKZR, 16.11.70; G-AYKE (1783), 18.1.71; G-AYKF (1784), 5.2.71; G-AYKH (1785), 8.2.71; G-AYLE (1123), F-BPBJ, 19.6.71; G-AYMD (1734), 27.11.71; G-AYTA

(1789), 2.4.71; G-AYTB (1790), 8.4.71; G-AYYX (1812), 30.7.71; G-AYYY (1849), 30.7.71; G-AYYZ (1850), 14.10.71; G-AZEE (74), F-BKKA, registered 1.9.71; G-AZGH (1895), 5.11.71; G-AZGI (1896), 24.3.72; G-AZGJ (1897), 12.11.71; G-AZGK (1901), 13.3.72; G-AZKA (1911), 25.5.72; G-AZKB (1913), 7.6.72; G-AZKC (1914), 7.6.72; G-AZKD (1949), 30.6.72; G-AZKE (1950), 24.8.72; G-AZKF (1951), 24.8.72; G-AZNJ (5375), F-BKZS, registered 14.2.72; G-AZZF (174), F-BKKO, registered 18.7.72

Morane-Saulnier M.S.885 Super Rallye

G-ARXW (100), 6.4.62; G-ASAO (139), 27.6.62, ditched in the English Channel 20.1.67; G-ASAP (140), 27.6.62; G-ATGG (144), F-BKLR, 6.8.65; G-AWXY (5097), EI-AMG, 29.7.70; G-AXCH (265), F-BKUT, 11.7.69

Morane-Saulnier M.S.890B Rallye Commodore 145

G-AZSL (10324), F-BLBB, 19.4.72

Morane-Saulnier M.S.892A Rallye Commodore 150

G-ATGF (10547), 29.7.65; G-ATIW (10561), 6.5.66; G-ATWE (10364), 29.6.66; G-ATWZ (10636), 14.7.66; G-ATYT (10637), 21.9.66, ditched between Dinard and Jersey 21.5.70; G-AVPK (10736), 5.7.67; G-AVPL (10737), 11.7.67; G-AWOC (10926), 22.8.68; G-AXHX (11424), 27.8.69; G-AYES (10513), F-BMVJ, 10.7.70; G-AYET (10565), F-BNBR, 17.7.70; G-AYRH (10558), F-BNBX, 30.4.71; G-AZVI (12039), 12.7.72

Morane-Saulnier M.S.893A Rallye Commodore 180

G-ATMG (10567), 16.3.66; G-ATST (10618), 2.6.66; G-ATYY (10674), not imported; G-AVAK (10664), 17.2.67, sold in Ireland 11.72; G-AVTV (10725), 6.9.67; G-AVVJ (10752), 4.1.68; G-AWAB (10786), 20.12.68, crashed at Lansdown, Bath 2.8.69; G-AWJJ (10918), 15.7.68; G-AWMM (10924), 22.5.68; G-AXIT (11430), 7.11.69; G-AXOT (11433), 8.12.69; G-AYVX (11637), 17.5.71; G-AZMZ (11927), 14.2.72; G-AZUT (10963), VH-TCH, 5.6.72; G-AZYD (10645), F-BNSE, 10.10.72; G-AZYX (10640), F-BNXJ, 4.8.72; G-BAAI (10705), F-BOVG, 11.8.72

Morane-Salnier M.S.894A Rallye Minerva

G-AWSZ (11005), F-BPSO, 1.2.69; G-AXIU (11065), 19.9.69; G-AXOH (11062), D-EAGU, 7.11.69; G-AXOS (11082), 28.5.70; G-AYDG (11620), 10.7.70; G-AYVW (11836), not imported, became D-EAHL; G-AYYD (11826), 30.6.71; G-AZGL (11929), 28.4.72; G-AZIC (11888), not imported, became F-BTHZ; G-AZIZ (11883), 26.1.72; G-AZVF (11999), 9.6.72; G-AZVH (12017), 21.3.73

Nipper Mk.III *(see also Tipsy Nipper II)*

G-AVKH (Nipper S.101/Slingsby 1585), 30.6.67, Air Touring Shops Ltd., Elstree; F. R. Brimecombe, Wilstead strip, Beds. 1.70

G-AVKI (S.102/1586), 30.6.67, Nipper Aircraft Ltd., Castle Donington; P. F. Eycken, Elstree 6.68; K. D. Courtney, Fairwood Common 10.69

G-AVKJ (S.103/1587), 11.7.67, A. O. Boyle, Shoreham; Glen Flying Group, Aylestone 5.69; M. P. Boulton, Lympne 1.70; I. M. Kirkwood, Elstree 3.72

G-AVKK (S.104/1588), 6.12.67, 1,600 cc. Ardem 4CO2 Mk.6, Nipper Aircraft Ltd., Castle Donington; demonstrator with tip tanks; S. R. Young, Lulsgate 1.71

G-AVTB (S.105/1565), 12.1.68, Nipper Aircraft Ltd.; struck tree at West Tanfield, Yorks. 8.6.68; rebuilt as c/n S.129/1676, first flown thus 18.10.68; J. G. Faber, Sutton Bank; T. R. Wardle, Speke 5.72

G-AVTC (S.106/1583), 20.10.67, Altair Aviation & General Trading Co. Ltd.; leased to County Flying Club, Biggin Hill

G-AVTD (S.107/1604), left Kirkbymoorside crated for South Africa 30.11.67; registered on arrival to Grand Central Aviation (Pty.) Ltd. as ZS-UDT

G-AVXC (S.108/1605), first flown 8.2.68, C. of A. 13.2.68, 1,600 cc. Ardem 4CO2 Mk.6, G. J. C. Paul, Fairoaks; W. G. Wells and partner, Clacton 6.73

G-AVXD (S.109/1606), first flown 22.2.68, C. of A. 22.2.68, Aerosport Ltd., Dundee (later Leuchars); S. Russell, Cupar strip, Fife 1.72

G-AVXE (S.110/1607), left Kirkbymoorside 1.2.68 crated for shipment to Marina 2-15 Ltd., Zambia; re-registered on arrival as 9J-RID

G-AWCE (S.111/1617), first flown 12.3.68, C. of A. 19.3.68, M. Z. de Ferranti, Gorddinjog, Carmarthenshire; P. G. Bassford, Castle Donington 1.69; to Norway by air via Southend 24.6.70; crashed at Groenoera, Norway 28.6.70

G-AWCF (S.112/1618), left Kirkbymoorside 21.3.68 crated for shipment to Marina 2-15 Ltd., Zambia

G-AWCG (S.113/1619), left Kirkbymoorside 8.4.68 crated for shipment to Marina 2-15 Ltd., Zambia; registered 9J-AAJ on arrival

G-AWDA (S.117/1624), 9.5.68, East Midlands Air Hire Ltd., Castle Donington

G-AWDB (S.118/1625), 7.1.70, Nipper Aircraft Ltd., Elstree; H. Swift and D. A. Taylor, Paull, Hull 7.71; E. Gardiner, Blyborough 10.72

G-AWDC (S.119/1626), 6.6.68, T. Iskrzak, Castle Donington

G-AWDD (S.120/1627), 2.5.68, T. R. Whitham, Lulsgate

G-AWIZ (S.100), Belgian-built Mk.II (c/n 9), OO-NIK, G-AVDK, withdrawn from use 4.68 for conversion to Mk.III but was abandoned when found to be non-standard; destroyed in factory fire at Kirkbymoorside 18.11.68

G-AWJE (S.121/1628), 13.6.68, N. H. Jones, Rochester; to Fairoaks in 1972

G-AWJF (S.122/1629), 8.7.68, East Midlands Air Hire Ltd., Weston-super-Mare; to Roborough 1969

G-AWJG (S.123/1630), left Kirkbymoorside 11.8.68 crated for shipment to Australia; registered 3.69 to A. W. Upton, Corowa, N.S.W. as VH-EOK

G-AWJH (S.124/1633), 9.8.68, East Midlands Air Hire Ltd., Staverton

G-AWLR (S.125/1662), 6.8.68, East Midlands Air Hire Ltd., Newtownards

G-AWLS (S.126/1663), 12.9.68, East Midlands Air Hire Ltd., Castle Donington; leased briefly to Southend Light Aviation Centre 9.68

G-AWLT (S.127/1674), for export to Kenya; destroyed in factory fire at Kirkbymoorside 18.11.68

G-AWLU (S.128/1675), first flown 5.11.68, Nipper Aircraft Ltd.; destroyed in factory fire at Kirkbymoorside 18.11.68

G-AXLH (S.130/1706), registered 29.7.69 to Nipper Aircraft Ltd.; crated at Castle Donington 1.70 and shipped to K. Brooksbank, Kuala Lumpur as 9M-APH

G-AXLI (S.131/1707), 5.1.70, Nipper Aircraft Ltd., Castle Donington; D. P. L. Antill, Castle Donington 6.71

G-AXLJ (S.132/1708), registered 29.7.69 to Nipper Aircraft Ltd.; to Switzerland 4.70 as HB-SPN

G-AXZM (PFA.1378), built from kit using main parts of S.133/1709, registered 16.3.70 to Miss W. Mills, Doncaster

G-AZBA (PFA.1390/ESJT.1), built from kit, registered 30.6.71 to E. Shouler, Lincoln

Note: G-AVKH to G-AVKK used Belgian-built fuselages, Fairey c/n 27, 31, 32 and 74. The following were exported: (c/n S.114), CS-AJN; (S.115/1622 and S.116/1623) were kits for Zambia which returned to be factory-built as Slingsby c/n 1680 and 1681, burned in the works fire 18.11.68; one kit sent to South Africa was completed as ZS-UEO

Nipper Mk.III CS-AJN (c/n S.114) at Southend on 12 May 1968 prior to delivery to the Aero Club of Portugal at Cascais. (*John Goring*)

Nord 1002 Pinguoin II

G-ASTG (183), F-BGKI, 9.11.64, scrapped at Gatwick 10.70; G-ASUA (248), F-BFDY, 29.7.64, d.b.r. landing at Elstree 30.7.64; G-ATBG (121), F-OTAN-5, F-BGVX, 30.7.65; G-AVJS (196), F-BFKA, registered 12.4.67, not proceeded with, to private museum near Bath 1973

Nord 1101 Noralpha

G-ASTN (54), F-BLTR, 31.7.64, crashed at Oldenburg, Germany 5.8.64; G-ATDB (186), F-OTAN-6, 12.5.65; G-ATHH (162), F-BLQS, 6.8.65; G-ATHN (84), F-BFUZ, 12.8.66; G-ATIX (154), F-BLYO, 9.2.66; G-ATJW (167), F-BLQP, 23.11.65

North American AT-6D* and AT-16 Harvard IIB

G-AXCR (14-324), 42-787, FE590, Swiss Air Force U-322, registered 27.3.69, delivered Gatwick 13.4.69, to Germany 10.69 as D-FHGK; G-AZBN (14A-1431), 43-13132, FT391, Dutch Air Force B-97, PH-HON, C. of A. 18.1.72; G-AZJD*, 41-33931, EX958, Belgian Air Force H-9, F-BJBF, 17.8.72; G-AZKI (14A-1269), 43-12970, FT229, Dutch Air Force B-45, PH-SKM, 24.2.72; G-AZSC (14A-1363), 43-13064, FT323, Dutch Air Force B-19, PH-SKK, 23.6.72; G-BAFM (14A-868), 43-12569, FS728, Dutch B-104, PH-SKL, 4.5.73

North American Mustang

G-ARKD (1330), CA-17 Mk.20, A68-5, VH-BVM, 25.8.60, abandoned at Athens following engine trouble and cockpit fire 7.9.61, still there in 1969; G-ARUK (1438), CA-18 Mk.21, A68-113, VH-UWB, repainted 4.4.62 as G-ARUK, crashed at Kalista, Vic. in the Dandenong Ranges and Ron Flockhart killed 12.4.62

Orlikan Meta-Sokol L.40

G-APUE (150708), OK-NMB, 23.6.59; G-APVU (150706), OK-NMI, 1.9.59; G-APWV (150707), 14.4.60, d.b.r. landing at Stapleford 14.7.65; G-ARJO (150704), 7.4.61, crashed at Biggin Hill 4.6.65; G-AROF (150905), 5.4.62; G-ARSO (150906), 15.6.63, d.b.r. landing at Dinard 29.9.71; G-ARSP (150907), 7.5.62; G-ASTT (150908), 12.6.64, d.b.r. landing at Bembridge, I.O.W. 6.6.71

Orlikan Super Aero 45

G-APRR (04-014), OK-KFQ, 16.1.59; G-ASYY (51186), F-BKGY, 3.6.65; G-AYLZ (06-014), F-BILP, 9M-AOF, 12.5.72

Orlikan Aero 145

G-AROE (19-014), OK-NHF, 4.7.61; G-ARYL (20-003), 5.4.62, resold in Czechoslovakia 9.62; G-ASTU (172012), 30.6.64, d.b.r. landing at Sherburn 16.8.71; G-ASWK (172003), 3.10.64, d.b.r. at Thruxton 24.4.68; G-ASWS (172004), 18.11.64; G-ASWT (172005), 6.3.65; G-ATBH (172015), 14.4.65

Orlikan Morava L-200A and L-200D

G-ARYJ (170804), L-200A, 6.10.61, resold in Czechoslovakia 1.63; G-ASFD (170808), L-200A, 19.4.63; G-ASHM (171207), L-200D, 14.4.63, crashed 7 miles N.E. of Norwich 21.12.69

Parnall Elf

G-AAFH (1), Mk.I, Geo. Parnall and Co., Yate; shown at Olympia 7.29, C. of A. 25.6.30; Lord Apsley, Badminton, Glos. 12.32, d.b.r. in forced landing at Herongate, near Rickmansworth, Herts. 20.3.34

G-AAIN (2, later J.6), Mk.II, 15.6.32, Geo. Parnall and Co., Yate; Lord Apsley, Badminton 11.34; stored 1939–45; W. J. Nobbs, Fairoaks 6.50; Shuttleworth Trust 7.51; short loan to Southend Historic Aircraft Museum 1972

G-AAIO (3, later J.5), 2.9.31, Geo Parnall and Co., Yate; R. Hall, c/o Cotswold Aero Club 11.33; crashed and burned at Sapperton, Glos. 13.1.34

Mustang Mk.21 VH-UWB bearing Brookes Aviation (Pty.) Ltd. titling at Moorabbin before sale to Ron Flockhart in April 1962 as G-ARUK. (*P. R. Keating*)

Parnall Heck

G-ACTC (341), prototype, 18.3.35, Mrs. L. Elmhurst, Yeovil; Aircraft Exchange & Mart Ltd., Hanworth 12.35; scrapped after C. of A. expiry 29.4.37

G-AEGH (J.10), 23.12.36, Parnall Aircraft Ltd., Yate; impressed 3.43 as NF749; to Turnhouse 12.3.43, for No.17 Group Comm. Flt.; scrapped at Kemble 5.44

G-AEGI (J.11), 30.11.37, Parnall Aircraft Ltd., Yate; J. G. Crammond, Rochester 11.46; wrecked on the ground at Wolverhampton 17.6.50; scrapped in 1953

G-AEGJ (J.12), 6.9.38, Parnall Aircraft Ltd., Yate; used as spares after C. of A. expiry 5.9.39

G-AEGK (J.13), ntu. Its C. of R., No. 6925, was re-allotted 25.8.36 to the change of ownership of D. H. Dragon 1 G-ACHV to Jack Morris, Hanworth

G-AEGL (J.14), registration not used. Almost certainly flown in R.A.F. markings for experimental purposes as K8853 to Contract 486334/36; later 3125M

G-AEMR (J.13), G-AEGK ntu, 23.8.39, Parnall Aircraft Ltd., Yate; British Parachute Co. Ltd., Cardiff 9.44; scrapped at Cardiff in 1948

G-AFKF (T.20), Heck III, J-1, 29.9.39, Parnall Aircraft Ltd., Yate; scrapped during 1939-45 war

Percival Gull Four

G-ABUR (D.20), Hermes IV, 3.7.32, E. W. Percival; temporarily fitted with Javelin III in 1933 before being re-engined with Gipsy Major; Man Mohan Singh, Brooklands 6.35; d.b.r. at Luwinga, Northern Rhodesia 26.8.35

G-ABUV (D.22), Hermes IV, 24.3.33, C. S. Napier, Croydon; Surrey Flying Services Ltd., Croydon 8.33; M. Maxwell, Croydon 10.35; crashed at Nice, France 2.11.36

G-ACAL (D.21), Javelin III, 10.11.32, W. Lindsay Everard, Ratcliffe; sold to British Air Navigation Co. Ltd., Heston in 1933; crashed at Sandhurst, Kent 1.10.33

G-ACAT (D.24), Hermes IV, 20.3.33, E. W. Percival; to Australia 4.33 as VH-UQW

G-ACFJ (D.23), Gipsy Major, 8.4.33, E. W. Percival; to Guy de Chateaubrun 1.36 as F-AOZS

G-ACFY (D.26), Hermes IV, 8.4.33, E. W. Percival; A. V. Roe and Co. Ltd., Woodford 1.35; A. Collinge, Woodford 6.36; sold abroad 6.37

G-ACGC (D.25), Gipsy Major, 8.4.33, British Air Navigation Co. Ltd., Heston; Flt. Lt. N. C. Forbes, Netheravon 1.35; to Brazil 1.37 as PP-BAA

G-ACGP (D.28), Javelin III, 11.5.33, A.V.M. A. E. Borton, Hamble; C.T.F. Aviation Ltd., Thame 6.40; F. C. Bettison 1.46; scrapped at Thame 1946

G-ACGR (D.29), Javelin III, 12.5.33, Sir Philip Sassoon, Lympne; Sir John Kirwan, Heston 6.34; crashed 12.34

G-ACHA (D.30), Javelin III, 17.6.33, E. W. Percival; Airwork Ltd., Barton 8.33; fitted with Gipsy Six engine and sold in Australia 12.35 as VH-UTF

G-ACHM (D.31), Gipsy Major, 24.5.33, I. C. MacGilchrist, Heston; Brian Allen Aviation Ltd., Croydon 5.35; to France 5.36 as F-AQLZ

G-ACHT (D.32), Gipsy Major, 14.6.33, E. W. Percival, Gravesend; Percival Aircraft Co. Ltd., Luton 7.36; sold abroad 12.36

G-ACIP (D.33), Javelin III, 20.7.33, Mrs. A. Cleaver, Heston; to H. M. Schmit Crans, Holland 12.35 as PH-HCA

G-ACIR (D.34), Javelin III, 26.10.33, W. G. Robson, Heston; to Henlys Ltd., Heston in 1934; crashed and burned on take-off from Heston 20.2.35

G-ACIS (D.35), Gipsy Major, 25.7.33, Air Service Training Ltd., Hamble; to Indian National Airways Ltd., Delhi 11.34 as VT-AFU

G-ACJP (D.36), Gipsy Major, 1.11.33, Percival Aircraft Co. Ltd., Gravesend; to Japan 3.34 as J-BASC

G-ACJR (D.37), Gipsy Major, 7.11.33, N. M. Gazdar, Hamble; crashed in the English Channel 1.5.34; parts washed ashore at Berck 15.5.34

G-ACJV (D.39), Gipsy Major, 2.10.33, Sir Charles Kingsford Smith 'Miss Southern Cross'; record flight to Australia 12.33; re-registered later as VH-CKS

G-ACJW (D.38), Gipsy Major, 18.9.33, Lt. P. Randolph, Sherbourne, Dorset; to Australia 11.34 as VH-UTC; withdrawn from use 1.46

G-ACLG (D.27), Gipsy Major, 8.5.33, Loel Guinness, Heston; to Indian National Airways Ltd., Delhi 11.34 as VT-AFV

G-ACLJ (D.40), Javelin III, 18.11.33, Percival Aircraft Ltd., Gravesend; Henlys Ltd., Heston 3.34; to Indian National Airways Ltd., Delhi 6.35 as VT-AGO

G-ACPA (D.44), Javelin III, 16.4.34, Lt. Cdr. E. W. B. Leake, Gravesend; S. L. Turner, Gravesend 2.35; Brian Allen Aviation Ltd., Croydon 8.35; fitted with Gipsy Six engine; crashed at Avignon, France 2.10.35

G-ACUL (D.45), Gipsy Major, 18.8.34, Lt. P. Randolph, Sherbourne, Dorset; fitted with Gipsy Six engine; flown to New Zealand 10–11.36, became ZK-AES

G-ACXY (D.42), Gipsy Major, 22.10.34, Percival Aircraft Co. Ltd., Gravesend; fitted with Gipsy Six engine; to France 2.36 as F-AOXY

G-ADGK (D.51), Gipsy Major, 27.5.35, Mrs. E. M. Highfield, Heston; crashed near Baden Baden, Germany 6.6.35

G-ADOE (D.53), Cirrus Major 1, 29.8.35, North Sea Aerial & General Transport Co. Ltd., Brough; Blackburn Aircraft Ltd., Brough 12.36; Air Couriers Ltd., Heston 3.45; fitted with Gipsy Major; G. Chappelle-Knight, Jersey 6.47; ditched in the English Channel off Ferring, Sussex 7.10.47

Percival Gull Six

G-ACUP (D.46), 7.7.34, K. H. Williams, Shoreham; S. K. Davies, Cardiff 5.37; to Australia 5.39 as VH-ACM; re-registered 4.49 as VH-CCM

G-ACYS (D.47), 24.10.34, Maharajah of Patiala; left Croydon on delivery 29.10.34 piloted by A. F. Muir; became VT-AGY; impressed 3.42 as HX794

G-ADEP (D.49), 20.3.35, Percival Aircraft Co. Ltd., Gravesend; Brian Allen Aviation Ltd., Croydon 1.36; sold abroad 8.36

G-ADEU (D.48), 26.3.35, Percival Aircraft Co. Ltd., Gravesend; to Marquis d'Aulan 2.38 as F-AQNA; later to Monsieur de Suares, Reims

G-ADFA (D.50), 17.4.35, C. E. Gardner, Warlingham 12.4.35; R. Ince, Gravesend 4.36; Vickers Armstrongs Ltd., Brooklands 7.40; scrapped 11.45

G-ADKX (D.52), 17.7.35, Shell Co. of Egypt Ltd., Almaza, Cairo; Lt. Col. N. A. Blandford-Newson, Cairo 10.40; impressed 11.40 as AX698

G-ADMI (D.54), 19.8.35, W. R. Porter, Hooton; to M. Lejeune Esbly 8.36 as F-APEI

G-ADPR (D.55), 12.9.35, Miss Jean Batten, Gravesend; impressed 7.40 as AX866; rest. 8.46 to Percival Aircraft Ltd., Luton; flown to Old Warden 25.4.61

G-ADSG (D.58), 3.10.35, Duchess of Bedford, Woburn Abbey; R. C. Preston, Newtownards 11.37; W. Fairweather, Muzzaffarpur, India 4.39; sold 8.39 as VT-ALT

Once G-ACUP, Percival Gull VH-CCM was winner of the Warana Air Race at Archerfield, Brisbane, on 6 October 1968. Six exhaust stubs proclaim its Gipsy Six engine. (*R. W. Livingstone*)

G-ADSM (D.59), 21.10.35, Asiatic Petroleum Co. Ltd., Croydon; impressed 8.40 as BD165 and flown to Ford where it is believed to have been destroyed by enemy bombing 8.40 before being taken on R.A.F. charge

G-ADZO (D.63), 17.12.35, Percival Aircraft Co. Ltd., Gravesend; H. L. Brook, Sherburn-in-Elmet 12.36; scrapped after C. of A. expiry 8.2.38

Percival Mew Gull

G-ACND (E.20), prototype, 11.7.34, Percival Aircraft Co. Ltd., Gravesend; believed crashed near Angoulême, France 10.35

G-ACND (E.20A), 18.7.35, Percival Aircraft Co. Ltd., Gravesend; transferred to Luton in 1936, burned at Luton 7.7.45

G-AEKL (E.21), 30.6.36, Percival Aircraft Co. Ltd., Gravesend; Air Publicity Ltd., Heston 9.36; damaged at Speke 19.9.36; C. E. Gardner, Warlingham 6.37; Giles Guthrie, Ipswich 5.38; destroyed by enemy bombing at Lympne 6.40

G-AEMO (E.23), 15.9.36, S. S. Halse, Johannesburg 'Baragwanath'; registered ZS-AHO for South Africa Race; crashed at Bomoboshawa, Southern Rhodesia 31.9.36

G-AEXF (E.22), ZS-AHM (A. M. Miller 'The Golden City'), 11.9.36, A. Henshaw, Heston; sold in France 7.39; H. E. Scrope, White Waltham 7.50; J. N. Somers, White Waltham 5.53; F. Dunkerley, Barton 9.54; J. E. G. Appleyard, Yeadon 10.62; Northern Air Taxis Ltd., Yeadon 5.65; M. Barraclough and T. Storey, Coolham, Sussex 4.72

G-AFAA (E.24), 2.9.37, Percival Aircraft Co. Ltd., Luton; burned at Luton 7.7.45

Percival Vega Gull

G-AEAB (K.20), 17.2.36, Percival Aircraft Co. Ltd., Gravesend; D. W. Llewellyn, Gravesend 9.36; crashed by Lake Tanganyika in South Africa Race 30.9.36

G-AEAS (K.23), 2.4.36, Percival Aircraft Co. Ltd., Gravesend; Vernon Motion, Gravesend 4.36; registration cancelled 12.36

G-AECF (K.21), 5.3.36, Hon. Drogo Montague, Gravesend; to France 4.37 as F-AQCF

G-AEEM (K.22), 25.3.36, Sir Chas. Rose, Portsmouth; D. W. Llewellyn, Luton 1.37; Bowmaker Ltd., Luton 11.37; to Sweden 5.39 as SE-AHR

G-AEHA (K.24), 29.4.36, Percival Aircraft Co. Ltd., Gravesend; to Guy de Chateaubrun 6.37 as F-AQEA

G-AEIF (K.25), 12.5.36, Col. A. Hamilton Gault, Gravesend; to M. Roger Goldet 4.38 as F-AQMZ

G-AEJJ (K.27), 31.5.36, L. H. G. Ltd., Heston; British American Air Services Ltd., Heston 9.39; impressed 4.40 as X9455; scrapped 10.44

G-AEKD (K.28), 13.6.36, Lt. Patrick Randolph, Gravesend; crashed at Sanganer Aerodrome, between Bombay and Jaipur, India and owner killed 12.10.37

G-AEKE (K.29), 7.6.36, Sir Connop Guthrie, Heston; Mrs. Beryl Urquhart, Gatwick 10.36; crashed 24.1.38

G-AELE (K.26), 19.5.36, W. L. Everard M.P., Ratcliffe; ditched in the Bay of Canche, near le Touquet 26.6.39

G-AELF (K.30) Marquess of Douglas and Clydesdale, Hamble or Renfrew; to India 3.38 as VT-AJZ

G-AELS (K.31), 21.7.36, Sir George Lewis, Gravesend; impressed for Royal Navy use at Lee-on-Solent 3.40 as W9376

G-AELW (K.32), 30.7.36, Anglo American Oil Co. Ltd., Heston; impressed 3.40 as X9349; scrapped at Cardiff 12.40

G-AEMB (K.33), 24.8.36, G. W. Harben, Hatfield; impressed 3.40 as X9371

G-AEPS (K.45), 13.2.37, Percival Aircraft Co. Ltd., Luton; P. G. Aldrich-Blake, Heston 2.37; Airwork Ltd., Almaza 8.38; to Egypt 10.38 as SU-AAX

G-AERH (K.41), 4.12.36, W. R. Porter, Hooton; crashed into house and burned out on take-off from Hanworth in Isle of Man Race 29.5.37

G-AERL (K.42), 8.12.36, Air Service Training Ltd., Hamble; impressed 4.40 as X1033; used by Station Flight, Aboukir; spun in at Aboukir 17.5.41

G-AETD (K.46), 21.2.37, Percival Aircraft Ltd., Luton; Barbara Chateaubrun, Gravesend 3.38; to Belgium 3.39 as OO-ANC

G-AETE (K.47), 26.2.37, I. G. Williamson, Croydon; W. H. Whitbread, Brooklands 9.38; Airwork Ltd., Heston 11.38; to Belgium 2.39 as OO-ATY

G-AETF (K.48), 12.2.37, de Havilland Aircraft Co. Ltd., Hatfield; impressed 3.40 as W9378 for use by the Royal Navy at Hatston; skidded into wall 19.9.40

G-AEWO (K.49), 28.4.37, Percival Aircraft Ltd., Luton; to MM. P. Pedroline and M. Vargi, Switzerland 4.39 as HB-UTU

Alex Henshaw's G-AEXF fitted with Gipsy Six R and de Havilland airscrew, lowered cabin and cut away spats for the 1938 King's Cup Race. (*Aeroplane*)

G-AEWP (K.51), 30.3.37, Percival Aircraft Ltd., Luton; crashed at Johnstone, near Renfrew 3.7.37

G-AEWS (K.52), 15.4.37, European Air Commerce Ltd., Gatwick; C. H. Self, Gatwick 7.38; impressed 4.40 as X9435; crashed near Taunton 10.10.40

G-AEXU (K.56), 20.5.37, W. L. Runciman. Woolsington; impressed 4.40 as X1032 and based at Aboukir in 1943

G-AEXV (K.57), 11.5.37, Air Commerce Ltd., Heston; impressed 3.40 as X9391; rest. 1.46 to Brevet Flying Club, Hanworth; British & Continental Airways Ltd., Southend 12.46; dismantled at Southend 4.50

G-AEYC (K.59), 2.6.37, Percival Aircraft Ltd.; impressed 10.39 as W6464; rest. 6.46 to Lambskin Exports Ltd., Kidlington; d.b.f. at Gatwick 14.8.60

G-AEYD (K.60), 23.5.37, Percival Aircraft Ltd., Luton; to Cairns Aviation Ltd., Salisbury, Southern Rhodesia 5.38 as VP-YBV

G-AEZJ (K.65), 15.7.37, D. Schreiber, Heston; to T. J. Bendien, Almelo, Holland 3.38 as PH-ATH

G-AEZK (K.66), 16.7.37, G. M. Tonge, Hatfield; impressed 3.40 as X9339

G-AEZL (K.67), 23.7.37, F. C. J. Butler, Hamble; impressed 5.40 as X9436

G-AFAU (K.69), 30.7.37, Percival Aircraft Ltd., Luton; impressed 2.40 as X9332; restored to register 9.46 as G-AIIT q.v.

G-AFAV (K.76), 27.8.37, Wrightson Air Hire Ltd., Heston; E. Thomas, Ringway 3.39; impressed 5.40 as X1034; undercarriage collapsed at Lydda 1.2.41

G-AFBC (K.75), 8.9.37, A. R. Coleman, Norwich; impressed 3.40 as X9340; rest. 6.47 to A. J. Muir, Perth; Anglo Continental Air Services Ltd., Luton 7.48; Lady Sherborne; Group Capt. C. M. M. Grece; crashed at Eastleigh 12.7.54

G-AFBD Registration reserved 15.8.37 for Vega Gull but not used

G-AFBO (K.70), 30.8.37, Secretary of State for Air, Berlin; seized by Germans at outbreak of 1939–45 war

G-AFBR (K.79), 30.9.37, Indian Aviation Development Corporation, Bombay; crashed at Luton 1.6.38

G-AFBW (K.82), 15.10.37, R. E. Gardner, Hamsey Green; D. Stewart Clarke, Macmerry 6.39; impressed 1.40 as W9377; used by Royal Navy at Donibristle

G-AFEA (K.84), 20.1.38, A. Henshaw, Trusthorpe, Lincs.; Gloster Aircraft Ltd., Hucclecote 9.39; Universal Flying Services Ltd., Fairoaks 8.46; D. F. Little, Fairoaks 1.47; sold abroad 7.52

D. F. Little's fifteen year old Vega Gull G-AFEA awaiting the start of the South Coast Air Race at Shoreham on 7 August 1951. (*A. J. Jackson*)

G-AFEH (K.100), 22.3.38, H. F. Broadbent, Hanworth; J. M. Barwick, Leeming 1.39; impressed 3.40 as X9315; rest. 6.46 to Lancashire Aircraft Corporation, Squires Gate; scrapped at Squires Gate 4.53

G-AFEK (K.89), 18.2.38, R. D. Craig, Heston; Earl of Amherst, Shoreham 5.39; impressed 3.40 as X9392; scrapped in 1944

G-AFEM (K.91), 26.3.38, Lt. Col. A. Hamilton Gault, Heston; impressed 3.40 as X9368; scrapped in 1943

G-AFGU (K.92), 23.4.38, S. Smith, Woolsington; crashed and burned at Brundholme, Ghyll, Westmoreland 14.5.38

G-AFIE (K.99), 25.7.38, Smith's Aircraft Instruments Ltd., Hatfield; destroyed by German bombing at Hendon 7.10.40

G-AFIM (K.93), 12.7.38, Mrs. H. M. Russell-Cooke, Heston; abandoned at Le Bourget in May 1940

G-AFIT (K.90), 21.7.38, R. E. Gardner, Hamsey Green; impressed for Royal Navy use 9.39 as W9375

G-AFVI (K.109), P5992, 4.6.39, Secretary of State for Air, Lisbon; crashed at Tortosa, Spain, 18.5.44

G-AFWG (K.71), L7272, registered 3.7.39 to Secretary of State for Air, Buenos Aires; registration cancelled as 'lapsed' 12.46

G-AHET (K.105), P5989, 9.7.46, Essex Aero Ltd., Gravesend; M. J. Taylor, Denham 7.56; Tourist Trophy Garage Ltd., Fairoaks 8.57; E. N. Husbands, Fairwood Common 5.59; d.b.r. in forced landing near Liverpool 2.5.60

G-AIIT (K.69), G-AFAU, X9332, 26.11.46, St. Christopher Travel-Ways Ltd., Heston; withdrawn from use at Croydon 11.47; scrapped 12.50

Percival Q.6

G-AEYE (Q.20), 27.1.38, Percival Aircraft Ltd., Luton; impressed 2.40 as X9328; rest. 5.46 to Southern Aircraft (Gatwick) Ltd.; C. G. M. Alington, Gatwick 2.48; W. J. Twitchell, Luton 4.51; J. B. Peak, Cambridge 6.56; w.f.u. 5.59

G-AFFD (Q.21), 6.4.38, Sir Philip Sassoon, Lympne; impressed 4.40 as X9407; rest. 8.46 to Yorkshire Aeroplane Club, Sherburn-in-Elmet; to instructional airframe at College of Aeronautical Engineering, Redhill 8.56

G-AFFE (Q.23), 13.4.38, H. B. Legge & Sons Ltd., Hamsey Green; impressed for the Royal Navy 9.39 as W9374; destroyed by German bombing, Lee-on-Solent 16.7.40

G-AFGX (Q.27), 13.7.38, S. Leigh, (Intava) Heston; impressed 3.40 as X9336

G-AFHG (Q.26), 29.6.38, Lord Londonderry, Newtownards; impressed 2.40 as X9329; believed abandoned in France 6.40

G-AFIW (Q.30), 16.9.38, Vickers Aviation Ltd., Brooklands; J. Brockhouse & Co. Ltd., Castle Bromwich (later Minworth); Lt. Cdr. R. E. Bibby, Hooton 4.47; scrapped at Luton 9.49

G-AFIX (Q.31), 13.12.38, W. A. Burnside, Croydon; A. H. White, Luton 4.39 (used by Western Airways Ltd.); impressed 4.40 as X9406; rest. 5.46 to London and Oxford Steel Co. Ltd.; Freemantle Overseas Radio Ltd. 12.46; Starways Ltd., Speke 5.49; crashed at Broomhall 6.5.49

G-AFKC (Q.33), 30.9.38, Lt. Col. E. T. Peel, Almaza, Cairo; impressed 2.40 as W6085; scrapped at Heliopolis 9.41

G-AFKG (Q.32), 14.10.38, L. A. Hordern, Hatfield; impressed 3.40 as X9363

G-AFMT (Q.25), VH-ABL, 13.12.38, Percival Aircraft Ltd.; Vickers-Armstrongs Ltd., Eastleigh 7.39; impressed 4.40 as X9454; d.b.r. at Castletown 10.9.41

G-AFMV (Q.37), 5.4.39, Viscount Forbes, Croydon; impressed at Heliopolis 12.41 as HK838; still flying in North Africa 9.43

G-AFVC (Q.24), F-AQOK, 15.6.38, Western Airways Ltd., Weston-super-Mare; impressed 5.40 as AX860 and served with the Royal Navy at Lee-on-Solent

G-AHOM (Q.42), P5637, 13.7.46, Western Airways Ltd.; Ductile Steels Ltd., Wolverhampton 6.48; E. W. Percival, Luton 8.53; Central Newbury Motors Ltd., Thruxton 1.58; withdrawn from use 7.58, dismantled at Thruxton in 1961

Delivered to the R.A.F. at Hendon on 18 August 1939 as P5637, G-AHOM is shown here at Croydon in 1956. (*A. J. Jackson*)

G-AHTA (Q.46), P5640, 27.7.46, London and Oxford Steel Co. Ltd., Weston-super-Mare; to COGEA, Brussels 11.46 as OO-PQA

G-AHTB (Q.39), P5634, 25.4.47, London and Oxford Steel Co. Ltd., Weston-super-Mare; S. E. Norman, Southend 9.47; d.b.r. at Almaza, Cairo 2.11.47

Percival Proctor 1 (*Manchester-built)

G-AGWV, P6197, 11.3.46, crashed at Benina, Libya 27.7.52; G-AGYA, P6188, 20.2.46, to Australia 8.51 as VH-BQQ; G-AGYB, P6231, 10.4.46, derelict at Cowes 4.53; G-AGYC, P6182, 19.7.46, scrapped at Croydon 2.52; G-AGZL, P6251, 6.4.46, d.b.f. at Broxbourne 23.6.47; G-AGZM, P6259, 28.9.48, crashed near Stapleford 29.1.57; G-AHAB, P6267, 29.10.47, w.f.u. at Panshanger 8.64; G-AHAZ, P6170, 29.3.46, crashed near Zürich 17.9.46; G-AHBS, P6062, 2.4.46, d.b.r. at Little Snoring, Norfolk 3.3.60; G-AHDH, P6177, not converted, dismantled at Panshanger 12.50; G-AHDI, P6194, 24.5.46, to Australia 6.51 as VH-AUC; G-AHDJ, P6264, 12.12.46, crashed at Great Barford, Beds. 18.6.54; G-AHDK, P6034, to Belgium 5.46 as OO-AVG; G-AHES*, R7490, 26.8.46, scrapped at Thruxton 9.55; G-AHEU*, R7521, 25.4.47, w.f.u. at Gatwick 9.56; G-AHEV*, R7529, 23.8.46, w.f.u. at Cardiff 12.54; G-AHFU, P6187, 28.5.46, w.f.u. 2.51; G-AHFW, P6262, 21.6.46, scrapped at Beirut, Lebanon 6.51; G-AHFX, P6190, 29.6.46, to Australia 10.46 as VH-AYV; G-AHFY, P6200, 21.6.46, w.f.u. at Lympne 2.62; G-AHFZ*, R7492, 10.5.46, to South Africa 11.46 as ZS-BMK

G-AHKW*, R7525, 1.8.46, scrapped at Stansted 6.49; G-AHLW, P6168, 24.5.46, d.b.f. at Broxbourne 23.6.47; G-AHMG, P6269, 20.6.46, to Australia 10.46 as VH-AYU; G-AHMR, P6273, 29.6.46, crashed at South Mimms 30.5.51; G-AHMS, P6189, 26.7.46, crashed at Tonnere, France 14.5.47; G-AHMT*, R7528, 14.8.46, w.f.u. at Prestwick

8.48; G-AHMU*, R7485, to New Zealand 7.46 as ZK-AJY; G-AHMW, P6305, to the Belgian Congo 7.46 as OO-CCZ; G-AHMX, P6226, 26.7.46, crashed near Lausanne 3.3.49; G-AHNA*, R7486, 16.7.46, crashed at Tolleshunt D'Arcy, Essex 27.12.67; G-AHNF*, R7496, registered 9.5.46, ntu, re-allotted 7.47 as G-AKBX; G-AHTG, P6192, 1.10.46, crashed near Saroti, Uganda 28.12.47; G-AHTN, P6245, 12.7.46, to Australia 6.48, became VH-BLC in 1954; G-AHTV, P6271, 25.7.47, to Australia 12.53 as VH-BCX

G-AHUW, P6260, to New Zealand 9.46 as ZK-AKQ; G-AHUX, P6185, 21.8.46, to Australia 5.55 as VH-BGY; G-AHUY, P6195, to Belgium 7.46 as OO-USA; G-AHUZ, P6268, 19.8.46, sold in Australia 7.51; G-AHVA*, R7494, 12.9.46, scrapped at Denham 7.62; G-AHVB, P6258, 1.9.46, to France 9.50 as F-BBSM; G-AHVC, P6315, 12.9.46, scrapped at Redhill 5.51; G-AHVD*, R7491, 17.9.46, to France 11.49 as F-BFPN; G-AHVE*, R7497, 16.6.46, to New Zealand 8.46 as ZK-AKP; G-AHVH, P6183, to Iceland 7.46 as TF-TUK; G-AHVI, P6235, 11.9.46, to Southern Rhodesia 9.47 as VP-YHI; G-AHVJ, P6130, 5.11.46, to Southern Rhodesia 9.47 as VP-YGJ

G-AIEB*, R7493, 28.11.46, to Australia 2.52 as VH-AHY; G-AIEC, P6309, to New Zealand 12.46 as ZK-ALS; G-AIED, P6322, 20.12.46, w.f.u. at Shoreham 10.65; G-AIEE, P6246, 20.12.46, abandoned in France 1.51; G-AIEF, P6316, 24.12.46, to Australia 5.47 as VH-SMS; G-AIEX, P6174, 22.1.47, to Germany 7.56 as D-EFAG; G-AIEY, P6227, 28.3.47, converted to Ju 87 replica 1968; G-AIHE, P6248, 9.1.47, crashed at Maulden, Beds. 18.11.51; G-AIHF*, R7495, 10.3.48, stored at Squires Gate 12.50; G-AIHG*, R7488, 23.12.46, w.f.u. at Booker 4.60; G-AIHH, P6186, 28.3.47, scrapped at Squires Gate 9.56; G-AIIJ, P6319, to Ireland 12.46 as EI-ACX; G-AIIK, P6252, not converted, to spares 4.49; G-AIIP, P6173, 3.4.47, w.f.u. at Elstree 10.52; G-AIIW, P6312, 15.11.46, to Australia 11.54 as VH-BQH; G-AIKG, P6196, 16.1.47, to Spain 7.52 as EC-AGX; G-AIKH, P6172, 19.3.47, crashed at Shoreham 25.7.47; G-AIKI, P6179, 20.6.47, to Ireland 3.57 as EI-AJR, rest. 9.57, w.f.u. 10.57; G-AIKK*, R7489, 2.1.47, d.b.r. at Le Touquet 1.4.54; G-AILN, P6230, 18.10.46, scrapped at Croydon 11.50; G-AILP, P6191, 28.2.47, w.f.u. 3.56; G-AIWA*, R7524, 23.1.47; G-AIXP*, R7499, to New Zealand 2.47 as ZK-AOA; G-AIYG, P6173, registered in error 5.12.46 (already G-AIIP); G-AIYH, P6242, 5.5.47, w.f.u. at Luton 7.52; G-AJGO, P6234, 9.9.47, scrapped at Gatwick 5.51; G-AJLS, P6237, 4.12.47, w.f.u. at Blackbushe 4.64; G-AKBX, R7496, G-AHNF ntu, registered 16.7.47, not converted; G-AKVV, P6233, 13.8.48, w.f.u. at Blackbushe 11.50

Percival Proctor 2 *(Z serials Luton-built)*

G-AHEE, BV649, 18.4.46, w.f.u. at Luton 4.50; G-AHMP, BV631, 19.8.46, w.f.u. at Leavesden 4.63; G-AHMY, BV563, 10.7.46, crashed near Boulogne, 21.1.47; G-AHNB, BV639, 14.8.46, w.f.u. at Lympne 10.48; G-AHRY, BV642, 10.10.46, scrapped at Broxbourne 4.54; G-AHVF, BV643, 15.8.46, crashed in Upper Egypt 23.10.46; G-AHVG, BV658, 3.10.46, to Australia 3.57 as VH-AVG; G-AHVK, BV551, 17.10.46, to France 3.54 as F-BFKB; G-AHVL, BV654, to New Zealand 12.46 as ZK-AHQ

G-AIEG, BV644, 10.4.47, to France 11.51 as F-BFYV; G-AIEH, BV556, 19.11.46, w.f.u. at Baginton 3.63; G-AIEI, BV640, 20.12.46, to South Africa 8.47 as ZS-BPZ; G-AIHB, BV629, 23.7.48, crashed at Benghazi, Libya 1.49; G-AIRF, Z7251, to Ireland 11.46 as EI-ACV; G-AJCV, BV655, 18.10.51, to France 11.51 as F-BFYZ; G-AJCX, BV638, 30.6.49, scrapped at Portsmouth 1958; G-AJDB, Z7218, not converted, to Chessington scrapyard 9.50; G-AJTS, BV538, 5.10.48, to New Zealand 12.49 as ZK-ATW

G-AKAE, BV650, not converted; G-AKWO, BV544, 13.4.49, to Australia 5.55 as VH-SCC; G-AKXI, Z7216, 23.11.48, to Australia 8.51 as VH-BQO; G-AKZN, Z7197, 12.1.49, to R.A.F. Museum, Hendon, as Z7197 in 1972; G-ALGG, BV636, 1.2.49, to Norway 3.49 as LN-TVM; G-ALIS, Z7203, 21.5.49, to Australia 2.52 as VH-BQR; G-ALJF, Z7252, delivered at Croft 3.49, converted at Biggin Hill, C. of A. 6.3.59, w.f.u. 7.64; G-ALMS, Z7194, 20.10.49, w.f.u. at Woolsington 12.51; G-ALTG, Z7238, 2.11.51, to Australia 11.51 as VH-BQP; G-ALUY, BV656, delivered to Blackbushe 8.49, not converted; G-ANWY, Z7212, 25.5.55, to Australia 6.58 as VH-BXU; G-AOGD, Z7214, not converted; G-AOGE, BV651, 23.4.56*

The Air Ministry's Proctor 3 G-AGLJ in wartime camouflage, 1945. (*Aeroplane*)

Percival Proctor 3

G-AGLC, DX198, ntu, became G-ALUJ; G-AGLJ, LZ599, 28.9.44, lost in the English Channel 1.4.51; G-AGOG, HM460, 23.6.45, sold in Egypt 4.50; G-AGTH, LZ715, 6.10.46, to French Morocco 8.51 as F-DAAO; G-AGVE, LZ754, 30.1.46, to New Zealand 5.47 as ZK-APG; G-AGWB, LZ734, 10.5.46, returned to the R.A.F. 11.51 as LZ734, rest. 3.57, d.b.f. at Moulton, near Darlington 5.8.67; G-AHBR, LZ593, 1.5.46, ditched off Paignton 10.11.46; G-AHFK, LZ768, 5.4.46, derelict at Nairobi, Kenya 2.64; G-AHGA, LZ704, 7.6.46, w.f.u. at Elstree 9.63; G-AHGB, LZ799, 24.6.46, to South Africa 1.47 as ZS-BGD; G-AHMV, LZ789, 29.8.46, w.f.u. at Perth 8.51; G-AHTU, LZ798, 25.6.46, crashed 17.9.47; G-AHVM, LZ739, 9.8.46, to spares at Lympne 2.49

G-AIFE, DX200, 30.8.48, to Australia 6.56 as VH-BVW; G-AIHD, DX241, 30.7.48, w.f.u. at Woolsington 9.63; G-AIII, LZ800, 7.10.46, to French Morocco 5.52 as F-DAAS; G-AIIL, LZ790, 26.10.46, to Australia 11.51 as VH-AYQ; G-AIIR, HM315, 25.7.47, w.f.u. at Gravesend 7.48, rest. 7.56, w.f.u. at Elmdon 4.63; G-AIKJ, R7532, 2.12.46, d.b.r. near Tonbridge, Kent 16.11.58; G-AIWB, LZ771, to Switzerland 1.47 as HB-UMI; G-AIYF, LZ792, to New Zealand 2.47 as ZK-ANZ; G-AJCN, HM296, 24.2.50, to Belgium 3.51 as OO-RLD; G-AJCU, HM351, 14.2.49, crashed near Slaidburn, Yorks. 25.6.50; G-AJCW, LZ633, not converted, fuselage to Chingford A.T.C. in 1953; G-AJCY, LZ755, 17.6.49, w.f.u. at Kidlington 1.54; G-AJCZ, LZ764, 18.6.49, sold in Spain 3.52; G-AJDA ('4976'), registered 23.9.48, not converted; G-AJTT, DX184, not converted, scrapped at Gatwick 5.49; G-AJVJ, LZ740, 7.2.48, d.b.f. at Cowes 20.4.49; G-AJWN, HM288, 13.10.47, to Belgium 1.50 as OO-INT

G-AKAF, HM366, not converted; G-AKEX, LZ791, 17.2.50, to Sweden 12.50 as SE-BTR; G-AKWB, HM426, to the Gold Coast 2.53 as VP-AAD; G-AKWC, LZ568, not converted; G-AKWD, LZ574, 22.9.50, to Australia 11.51 as VH-ABN; G-AKWE, HM409, 21.6.48, w.f.u. at Staverton 4.52; G-AKWF, DX217, 2.12.49, to Spain 6.52 as EC-AGL; G-AKWJ, R7539, 10.9.48, to spares at Biggin Hill 1962; G-AKWM, LZ639, not converted at Thame; G-AKWN, LZ636, not converted at Blackbushe; G-AKWP, R7535, 24.5.50, w.f.u. at Denham 2.61; G-AKWR, LZ716, 2.5.52, d.b.r. at Shannon 7.7.63; G-AKWU, LZ767, 10.6.48, sold abroad 11.49; G-AKWV, HM350, 7.7.48, crashed at Sutton, near Southend 20.6.53; G-AKWW, LZ689, 24.7.48, crashed in the Italian Alps 15.11.48

G-AKXJ, HM295, 8.11.48, to Brazil 7.52 as PT-ALZ; G-AKXK, HM342, 6.6.48, crashed at Beirut, Lebanon 19.6.58; G-AKXL, HM417, not converted; G-AKXZ, DX229, 26.11.48, crashed at Kosti, Central Africa 2.8.52; G-AKYG, HM400, not converted at Carlisle; G-AKZD, HM339, not converted; G-AKZE, LZ598, not converted at Squires Gate; G-AKZF, LZ649, not converted at Squires Gate; G-AKZG, LZ760, 29.12.48, to Australia 1.57 as VH-KZG; G-AKZR, DX235, 8.12.48, w.f.u. at Denham 7.53; G-AKZS, HM347, 18.8.48, to Australia 1.54 as VH-BEG

G-ALCE, HM356, sold in Italy 8.48; G-ALCF, LZ684, 7.1.49, to Australia 6.49 as VH-AHR; G-ALCG, LZ561, to Italy 2.49 as I-MARG; G-ALCH, LZ657, 21.4.49, w.f.u. at Squires Gate 5.50; G-ALCI, DX199, not converted at Squires Gate; G-ALCJ, LZ582, 28.5.49, scrapped at Squires Gate 5.50; G-ALCK, LZ766, 3.6.49, w.f.u. at Woolsington 6.63, to Skyfame Museum, Staverton as LZ766; G-ALCL, HM390, 11.5.50, w.f.u. at Newtownards 4.54; G-ALCN, LZ579, 12.9.49, sold in the Lebanon 4.52; G-ALCO, LZ682, 29.5.53, w.f.u. at Croydon 6.55; G-ALCP, LZ688, not converted; G-ALCR, DX228, 14.4.49, to France 5.50 as F-BFPS; G-ALER, LZ673, 28.6.49, w.f.u. at Stapleford 3.55; G-ALES, DX181, 17.4.51, w.f.u. 6.63

G-ALFB, LZ770, 8.4.49, to Algeria 6.51 as F-OAJZ; G-ALFC, LZ690, not converted, scrapped at Croydon 1.51; G-ALFF, R7567, 15.3.49, w.f.u. at Lympne 3.50; G-ALFK, DX182, 20.10.49, to France 11.50 as F-BAVQ; G-ALFS, LZ697, 18.2.49, d.b.f. at Wadi Halfa, Egypt 14.6.49; G-ALFV, HM301, 2.3.51, to French Morocco 3.51 as F-DAAB; G-ALFW, LZ626, 11.1.51, to Algeria 1.51 as F-OAIS; G-ALFX, LZ695, 17.6.49, w.f.u. at Yeadon 8.63; G-ALFY, HM281, not converted at Staverton; G-ALGP, HM310, not converted at Croydon; G-ALGR, HM348, 10.10.50, sold in Belgium 10.50; G-ALGS, LZ796, 24.3.49, sold abroad 8.53; G-ALGY, LZ710, 22.3.51, w.f.u. at Lympne 3.52; G-ALIT, DX240, 18.3.50, d.b.r. at Panshanger 17.5.56; G-ALJG, LZ635, 1.9.49, crashed at Nova Ligure, Italy 5.10.49; G-ALJH, DX194, 8.2.50, to Spain 4.53 as EC-AJA; G-ALJI, HM312, 9.8.51, to France 9.51 as F-BENS; G-ALJK, LZ743, 25.8.49, crashed near Sydney, Australia 27.12.49

G-ALOJ, LZ632, to France 4.50 as F-BBTH; G-ALOK, LZ589, 14.12.49, converted to Ju 87 replica at Henlow 1968; G-ALOL, LZ680, not converted at Croydon; G-ALSM, LZ683, 1.6.50, lost in the Timor Sea 11.5.52; G-ALTF, DX234, not converted at Croydon; G-ALUI, LZ751, not converted at Croft; G-ALUJ, DX198, G-AGLC, 31.12.51, to French Morocco 11.53 as F-DADK, rest. 8.56, crashed at Topping, Yorks. 10.2.60; G-ALUK, DX238, not converted at Croft; G-ALVA, LZ576, to France 4.50 as F-BBCQ; G-ALVE, LZ700, not converted at Blackbushe; G-ALWR, HM343, not converted at Hamble; G-ALYC, DX225, not converted at Blackbushe

G-AMAL, R7559, crashed at Peebles 1.10.50; G-AMAN, LZ763, 15.1.52, d.b.r. at Silverstone 19.7.52; G-AMBS, HM319, 3.1.51, d.b.r. at Woolsington 16.8.59; G-AMCO, LZ681, 21.6.51, to Spain 6.52 as EC-AHB; G-AMGE, LZ570, 16.6.51, d.b.r. at Woolsington 10.5.63; G-AMPL, LZ631, not converted at Croydon; G-ANGB, LZ597, to Australia 5.56 as VH-GGB; G-ANGC, LZ804, 22.8.57, to Australia 5.58 as VH-BXQ; G-ANPP, HM354, 24.6.57, stored at Southend in 1971; G-ANPR, HM431, to Australia

6.55 as VH-BPR; G-ANYO registered 1.55, not converted; G-AOAK, R7566, to Belgium 5.55 as OO-DOC; G-AOBF, LZ694, 6.9.55, w.f.u. at White Waltham 9.56; G-AOCD, LZ603, to Belgium 2.56 as OO-DYM; G-AOEJ, HM358, 4.11.55, crashed at Denham 19.3.63

Note: The H numbers often quoted as Hillson constructors numbers were, in fact, line sequence numbers and are not used in this book.

Percival Proctor 4

G-AGPA, RM161, 31.10.45, d.b.r. at Plympton St. Mary 4.8.47; G-AHFR, RM172, 11.5.46, w.f.u. at Hucknall 5.61; G-AJMH, NP237, 28.7.48, to Australia 11.54 as VH-GBW; G-AJMI, NP189, 14.5.48, scrapped at Sherburn-in-Elmet 10.55; G-AJMJ, NP214, 26.4.48, to Kenya 6.48 as VP-KGB; G-AJMK, NP247, 25.3.49, scrapped at Tollerton 7.50; G-AJML, RM160, 3.1.49, crashed at Ivinghoe, Bucks. 14.1.49; G-AJMM, NP188, 29.11.50. w.f.u. at Tollerton 11.51; G-AJMN, NP386, 15.8.47, to Kenya 6.48 as VP-KGC; G-AJMO, NP194, not converted at Tollerton; G-AJMP, NP383, 1.9.47, dismantled at Squires Gate 1953; G-AJMR, NP175, not converted at Tollerton; G-AJMS, NP390, not converted at Tollerton; G-AJMT, NP254, not converted at Tollerton; G-AJMU, NP353, 16.8.48, crashed at Tok, Alaska 21.11.48; G-AJMV, NP400, 23.5.47, to France 10.50 as F-BEEH; G-AJMW, NP233, 19.6.47, scrapped at Rochester 10.54; G-AJMX, RM170, 17.6.47, d.b.r. at Rochester 13.7.52

The recess for the sliding window distinguished the Proctor 4, shown here, from the Proctor 5. G-AJMX was an air taxi operated by Short Bros. Ltd. at Rochester 1947. (*A. J. Jackson*)

G-AJTP, NP281, 30.7.47, ditched off Singapore 17.9.58; G-AJZA, NP395, not converted at Tollerton; G-AKEF, NP287, 31.10.47, w.f.u. at Wolverhampton 1.53; G-AKLB, NP198, (G-AKFS ntu) 14.5.48, dismantled at Squires Gate 11.50; G-AKLC, NP282, (G-AKFR ntu) 28.5.48, crashed near Shipley, Yorks. 19.8.49; G-AKLD, NP276, (G-AKFT ntu) 14.5.48, to spares at Perth 1954; G-AKWL, NP298, 9.7.48, w.f.u. at Blackbushe 9.56; G-AKYI, NP347, not converted at Squires Gate; G-AKYJ, RM186, 4.9.48, to Germany 1.58 as D-EJUT; G-AKYK, RM225, 23.3.49, dismantled at Squires Gate 11.50; G-ALEO, NP288, 3.4.51, crashed at Nuremburg, Germany 30.8.55; G-ALEX, NP177, not converted; G-ALGL, NP174, not converted at Squires Gate

G-ANGH, NP369, not converted; G-ANGI, NP296, not converted; G-ANGM, NP176, 23.3.54, w.f.u. at Southend 10.57, to Ipswich by road 10.59; G-ANGN, NP180, not converted at Southend; G-ANGO, NP300, not converted, burned at Southend 4.60; G-ANGP, NP305, not converted at Southend; G-ANVJ, NP338, 6.4.55, to France 9.57

as F-BIGR; G-ANVK, NP225, 1.10.55, to France 2.56 as F-BEKN; G-ANVW, NP187, 20.4.55, d.b.r. at Olivares de Jucar, Spain 17.6.56; G-ANVX, RM168, not converted at Gatwick; G-ANVY, RM169, 4.6.56, to Sweden 12.57 as SE-CEA; G-ANVZ, RM194, 7.7.55, w.f.u. at Luqa, Malta 7.56

G-ANWA, NP354, 22.4.58, crashed in Corsica 13.2.62; G-ANWC, NP238, not converted at White Waltham; G-ANWD, NP271, 17.6.57, to Austria 8.58 as OE-ACB; G-ANWE, NP307, not converted at White Waltham; G-ANWF, NP329, to Belgium 4.57 as OO-ARL; G-ANWP, MX451, not converted at White Waltham; G-ANWR, NP157, not converted at Panshanger; G-ANWS, NP173, not converted at Panshanger; G-ANWT, NP228, not converted at Stapleford; G-ANWU, NP246, to Belgium 4.57 as OO-ARJ; G-ANWV, NP325, to Belgium 4.57 as OO-ARK; G-ANXD, NP215, not converted at Exeter; G-ANXE, NP268, not converted, burned at Exeter 24.9.60; G-ANXF, NP335, not converted, burned at Exeter 24.9.60; G-ANXG, NP351, not converted at Exeter; G-ANXH, RM181, not converted at Exeter; G-ANXI, LA589, not converted, burned at Exeter 24.9.60; G-ANXR, RM221, 4.3.55

G-ANYC, RM222, 29.4.55, w.f.u. at Elstree 8.61; G-ANYD, RM185, to Belgium 2.55 as OO-ACL; G-ANYP, NP184, 17.7.56, w.f.u. at Thruxton 4.64, to Brooklands Technical College 5.66, to Torbay Aircraft Museum 1972; G-ANYR, NP185, 13.12.55, w.f.u. at Thruxton 12.56; G-ANYS, NP250, 18.5.56, crashed near Enniskillen, N.I. 3.2.63; G-ANYT, NP324, 8.7.55, sold in Germany 7.55; G-ANYU, NP334, 20.2.56, w.f.u. at Thruxton 5.67; G-ANYV, NP308, 12.10.55, w.f.u. at Portsmouth 6.60, burned 2.11.61; G-ANYW, NP355, not converted at Croydon; G-ANYY, NP368, not converted at Gatwick; G-ANYZ, RM190, 15.6.56, crashed in the English Channel 23.10.58; G-ANZA, NP217, not converted at Eastleigh, to Southampton A.T.C. Sqn. 1958; G-ANZB, NP292, not converted at Portsmouth; G-ANZC, NP309, 23.11.55, w.f.u. at Thruxton 3.60; G-ANZD, NP361, not converted; G-ANZI, NP193, not converted at Rhoose, burned 13.6.59; G-ANZJ, NP303, 18.1.57, w.f.u. 9.70, to Southend Historic Aircraft Museum 1971

G-AOAP, NP178, not converted at Panshanger; G-AOAR, NP181, 8.2.57, w.f.u. at Biggin Hill 10.65; G-AOAS, NP186*; G-AOAT, RM226*; G-AOAU, NP227*; G-AOAV, RM230*; G-AOAW, NP269*; G-AOAX, NP273*; G-AOAY, NP289, not converted, scrapped at Biggin Hill 1960; G-AOAZ, NP326*; G-AOBA, NP327*; G-AOBB, NP342, not converted, scrapped at Squires Gate 1960; G-AOBC, NP363*; G-AOBD, NP385*; G-AOBE, NP403*; G-AOBI, NP358, 6.11.56, w.f.u. at Halfpenny Green 8.64; G-AOBW, NP339, 22.7.55, w.f.u. at Elstree 7.64, to Southend Historic Aircraft Museum 1971

* Not converted, scrapped at Panshanger 1955–57

Percival Proctor 5

G-AGSW (As.1), RM193, 5.11.45, crashed at Porquis, Ontario, Canada 19.7.46; G-AGSX (As.2), RM196, 21.11.45, d.b.r. at Brussels 17.5.47; G-AGSY (Ae.2), RM197, 3.12.45, to Australia 2.46 as VH-ARV; G-AGSZ (As.3), 6.2.46, to Australia 7.51 as VH-ADP; G-AGTA (Ae.10), 19.1.46, reduced to spares in Brazil 12.47; G-AGTB (Ae.8), 29.1.46, to Australia 11.47 as VH-BCM; G-AGTC (Ae.3), 1.1.46, d.b.r. at Malaga, Spain 2.5.69; G-AGTD (Ae.9), 6.2.46, crashed at Carlisle 18.10.48; G-AGTE (Ae.14), 1.3.46, to Tangier 2.53 as F-OAMV; G-AGTF (Ae.16), 12.3.46, w.f.u. at Whatfield, Suffolk 7.64

G-AHBA (Ae.17), 21.3.46, w.f.u. 11.63; G-AHBB (Ae.18), 28.3.46, to the Argentine 10.46 as LV-NEH; G-AHBC (Ae.26), 18.4.46, crashed near Madrid, Spain 21.9.54; G-AHBD (Ae.27), 26.4.46, w.f.u. at Baginton 3.68; G-AHBE (Ae.28), 12.4.46, to India 1.47 as VT-CEP; G-AHBF (Ae.31), 10.5.46, to India 1.47 as VT-CFP; G-AHBG (Ae.32), 16.5.46, to India 1.47 as VT-CFQ; G-AHBH (Ae.37), 14.5.46, d.b.r. at Jersey 4.8.65;

G-AHBI (Ae.38), 10.5.46, to Turkey 5.56 as TC-TUL; G-AHBJ (Ae.39), 3.5.46, w.f.u. at Croydon 12.57; G-AHGJ (Ae.41), 16.5.46, w.f.u. at Cranfield 9.63 for static testing glued joints; G-AHGK (Ae.45), 6.6.46, sold in Egypt 1..48; G-AHGL (Ae.47), 27.6.46, crashed at Jersey 9.9.60; G-AHGM (Ae.48), 24.5.46, scrapped at Croydon 2.52; G-AHGN (Ae.44), 14.6.46, to the U.S.A. 3.50 as N558E; G-AHGO (Ae.23), 8.4.46, to New Zealand 6.48 as ZK-ARA; G-AHGP (Ae.42), 5.6.46, to Southern Rhodesia 11.49, became VP-YKR in 1954; G-AHGR (Ae.56), 27.6.46, d.b.r. at Hamburg, Germany 15.10.61; G-AHGS (Ae.57), 3.7.46, to Iceland 5.54 as TF-HGS; G-AHGT (Ae.25), 29.4.46, to Ethiopia 1.51 as ET-P-4

G-AHTD (Ae.60), 9.7.46, d.b.r. at Flushing, Belgium 20.12.47; G-AHTE (Ae.58), 12.7.46, w.f.u. at Elmdon 8.61; G-AHTF (Ae.59), 12.7.46, to Finland 12.53 as OH-PPB; G-AHTG (Ae.61), 17.7.46, to Australia 1.51 as VH-BDA; G-AHTH (Ae.62), 25.7.46, d.b.r. at Redditch 8.3.48; G-AHTI (Ae.66), 25.7.46, to Spain 1.53 as EC-AHX; G-AHTJ (Ae.67), 17.7.46, to India 5.48 as VT-CTF; G-AHTK (Ae.68), 27.7.46, crashed in sea off Ostend, Belgium 4.8.57; G-AHTL (Ae.70), 9.8.46, to Algeria 2.54 as F-OAOZ; G-AHTM (Ae.71), 27.7.46, to Finland 10.51 as OH-PPA

G-AHWO (Ae.72), 31.7.46, damaged in Ireland 5.59, rebuilt as EI-ALY 11.61; G-AHWP (Ae.69), 3.7.46, lost at sea N.E. of Ramsgate 6.1.48; G-AHWR (Ae.73), 17.8.46, d.b.r. near Baginton 18.6.54; G-AHWS (Ae.74), 30.7.46, to French Cameroons 10.55 as F-OATM; G-AHWT (Ae.75), 17.8.46, w.f.u. at Luton 3.51, burned at Stansted 20.9.52; G-AHWU (Ae.36), 31.5.46, crashed at Elmdon 24.6.54; G-AHWV (Ae.77), 28.8.46, w.f.u. at Biggin Hill 3.63; G-AHWW (Ae.78), 14.8.46, to New Zealand 9.50 as ZK-AVW; G-AHWX (Ae.80), 27.9.46, to Italy 11.48 as I-ADOH; G-AHWY (Ae.81), 23.8.46, crashed at Bembridge, I.O.W. 9.9.48; G-AHWZ (Ae.82), 3.9.46, to Trinidad 4.57 as VP-TBR; G-AHZX (Ae.83), 13.9.46, crashed in the English Channel off Jouin-sur-Mer 16.4.47; G-AHZY (Ae.84), 31.8.46, to Belgium 9.57 as OO-ARM; G-AHZZ (Ae.85), 4.9.46, to South Africa 2.48 as ZS-BUP

G-AIAA (Ae.20), OO-CCD, 13.6.46, d.b.r. at Burnaston 26.11.61; G-AIAB (Ae.43), 15.6.46, crashed at Luton 20.11.47; G-AIAC (Ae.51), 16.8.46, d.b.f. at Broxbourne 23.6.47; G-AIAD (Ae.24), 8.4.46, crashed in Mediterranean Sea off Nice, France 17.5.48; G-AIAE (Ae.86), 25.9.46, converted to Ju 87 replica 1968; G-AIAF (Ae.87), 17.9.46, crashed at Stanton Harcourt, Oxon. 19.11.61; G-AIAG (Ae.88), 23.9.46, crashed at Naples, Italy 1.7.54

Proctor 5 G-AIAE wearing the last two letters of its registration after conversion to flying scale replica of a Junkers Ju 87 for film purposes in 1968. (*Aviation Photo News*)

G-AIEM (Ae.90), 24.10.46, to Kenya 8.48 as VP-KGJ; G-AIEN (Ae.96), 27.2.47, to Australia 3.56 as VH-BSH; G-AIEO (Ae.97), 10.10.46, to New Zealand 11.48 as ZK-ARP; G-AIEP (Ae.98), 4.10.46, w.f.u. at Cambridge 4.59; G-AIER (Ae.99), 21.10.46, to Australia 4.52 as VH-AAH; G-AIES (Ae.102), 26.10.46, w.f.u. at Denham 8.65; G-AIET (Ae.103), 31.10.46, to Ireland 11.62 as EI-AMV; G-AIEU (Ae.105), 18.3.47, to South Africa 12.48 as ZS-DCO; G-AIEV (Ae.106), 19.11.46, to Australia 3.52 as VH-ALR; G-AIEW (Ae.55), 24.7.46, to Transjordan 6.48 as TJ-AAK

G-AIYZ (Ae.108), 21.12.46, to South Africa 3.49 as ZS-DCV; G-AIZA (Ae.122), 14.2.47, w.f.u. at Squires Gate 2.48; G-AIZB (Ae.49), 3.6.46, to Algeria 5.54 as F-OAPR; G-AIZC (Ae.104), 23.4.47, scrapped at Croydon 7.50; G-AIZD (Ae.101), 27.9.46, to Transjordan 10.48 as TJ-AAN

G-AKCY (Ae.121), 28.8.47, crashed at Baghdad, Iraq 24.12.49; G-AKDY (Ae.113), 9.9.47, to Kenya 12.47 as VP-KEW; G-AKDZ (Ae.117), 5.9.47, crashed near Addis Ababa, Ethiopia 14.7.59; G-AKEA (Ae.127), 2.10.47, crashed at Cherbourg, France 25.6.57; G-AKEB (Ae.100), 25.9.47, to France 11.54 as F-BHCM; G-AKIH (Ae.124), 27.12.47, to Turkey 5.52 as TC-PAR; G-AKIT (Ae.128), 20.1.48, sold abroad 8.49; G-AKIU (Ae.129), 26.2.48, w.f.u. 1.65 and taken by road to Edenbridge, Kent; G-AKIV (Ae.139), 13.3.48, to Australia 8.48 as VH-BLU; G-AKIW (Ae.131), 30.4.48, to Australia 10.50 as VH-DIW; G-AKIX (Ae.130), 21.4.48, w.f.u. in Egypt 10.51; G-AKPB (Ae.65), SU-ACH, registered 14.2.48, to Egypt 2.48 as SU-AFG, later F-BESV

G-AKYA (Ae.112), 31.8.48, sold in Jordan 9.62; G-AKYB (Ae.116), 26.8.48, w.f.u. at Biggin Hill 3.64; G-AKYC (Ae.114), 8.12.48, w.f.u. at Lympne 4.55; G-AKYD (Ae.119), crashed in the Scheldt estuary off Flushing, Holland 14.8.58; G-AMCP (Ae.150), 24.7.50, to France 3.55 as F-BEAK; G-AMED (Ae.115), 19.7.51, to Dakar 10.52 as F-OAMF; G-AMKM (Ae.138), 26.7.51, to France 8.51 as F-BFVP; G-AMTI (Ae.151), 15.7.52, to Turkey 7.52 as TC-GUN; G-AMTJ (Ae.152), 15.7.52, dismantled at Boscombe Down 9.61; G-ANAT (Ae.92), VN895, 11.3.54, d.b.r. at Elmdon 30.3.58; G-ANGG (Ae.95), VN898, 3.5.54, to Sweden 7.54 as SE-BZW; G-ANMD (Ae.94), VN897, 30.4.54, to Belgium 5.54 as OO-ADS

Overseas demonstrator G-AKLG at Redhill in 1948 inscribed 'Percival Prentice' in Greek and Arabic. (*E. J. Riding*)

Percival P.40 Prentice 1 *(with date of first flight as civil aircraft)*

G-AKLF VR209, 1.3.48, Percival Aircraft Ltd., Luton; to the R.A.F. 1949 as VR209; to No.2 F.T.S., South Cerney; scrapped at Minworth 1957

G-AKLG VR210, 1.3.48, Percival Aircraft Ltd., Luton; to the R.A.F. 1949

G-AOKF VR284, first flown 19.4.59, C. of A. 22.4.59, Maitland Air Charter Ltd., Biggin Hill; W. B. Wilkinson, Biggin Hill 8.62; sold in Liberia 8.66

G-AOKH VS251, first flown 4.3.60, C. of A. 9.3.60, J. L. Tankard and Co. Ltd., Yeadon; J. R. Batt, Southend 5.67; P. H. Louks, Biggin Hill 11.72

G-AOKL VS610, first flown 16.6.60, C. of A. 20.6.60, A. B. Bryant, Stapleford; Bert Wright Aviation Ltd., Biggin Hill 12.62; J. L. Gullen, Stapleford 7.68; J. R. Batt, Southend 2.72

G-AOKO VS621, 4.6.59, E. F. Allchin, Elmdon; The Proctor Group, Baginton 8.63; Peterborough Aero Club, Sibson 8.67; I. H. Sugden, Fairoaks 1.70; J. F. Coggins, Baginton 9.71

G-AOKT VS382, first flown 25.6.56, test vehicle, scrapped at Southend 11.63

G-AOKZ VS623, not certificated, to instructional airframe at College of Aeronautical Engineering, Redhill

G-AOLK VS618, first flown 28.4.61, C. of A. 28.4.61, A. S. Wright, Stapleford 'Oracle'; A. H. Smith, Biggin Hill 8.64; Hilton Aviation Ltd., Rochester 1.71

G-AOLM VS396, first flown 22.1.60, Aviation Traders Ltd., Stansted; delivered from Stansted to Brussels 7.3.60 as OO-LUC

G-AOLO VS388, first flown 14.10.58, C. of A. 17.10.58, Aviation Traders Ltd., Southend; to E. Defaux, Belgian Congo 10.58 as OO-CIM

G-AOLP VS385, first flown 22.9.58, C. of A. 23.10.58, Hubbard and Kinnear Ltd., Rhoose 'Fonmon Castle'; Torbay Flying Club, Dunkeswell 8.63

G-AOLR VS374, first flown 10.3.59, C. of A. 5.5.60, Aviation Traders Ltd., Southend; Surrey and Kent Flying Club, Biggin Hill 5.60; crashed at Kilsyth, Stirlingshire 30.7.61

G-AOLU VS356, first flown 26.8.59, C. of A. 27.8.59, Maitland Air Charter Ltd., Biggin Hill; W. B. Wilkinson, Biggin Hill 8.64; to Ireland 7.67 as EI-ASP; rest. 10.72; Pilot Properties Ltd., Norwich 3.73

G-AOMF VS316, first flown 6.4.60, C. of A. 12.4.60, Surrey and Kent Flying Club, Biggin Hill; W. B. Wilkinson, Jersey 8.63 who flew it to Australia 3.69 and to New Zealand via Norfolk Island 20.5.69; became ZK-DJC

G-AOMK VR304, 24.7.59, T. D. Keegan Ltd., Steeple Ashton; Steels Aviation Ltd., Lulsgate 4.62; A. F. Jarman, Leicester East 3.63; w.f.u. at Baginton 9.65

G-AONB VR244, first flown 21.2.59, C. of A. 5.3.59, No.600 Sqn. Flying Group, Biggin Hill; Chrisair Ltd., Ramsgate 3.63; w.f.u. at Rochester 3.64

G-AONS VS687, first flown 2.3.58, C. of A. 5.3.58, D. J. Hill, Southend 'Koomela'; flown to Australia 5.3.58 to 29.4.58; became VH-BAO

G-AOPL VS609, first flown 26.4.57, C. of A. 9.9.57, W. G. Pritchard, Rhoose; T. D. Newman, Biggin Hill 10.61; flown to South Africa, arrived at Rand Airport 15.4.67, became ZS-EUS

G-AOPO VS613, first flown 19.3.58, C. of A. 28.3.58, Aviation Traders Ltd., Southend; to Publiceel, Brussels 9.58 as OO-OPO

G-AOPW VS628, first flown 7.5.59, C. of A. 8.5.59, Aviation Traders Ltd., Southend; sales tour of Europe 5.59; fatal crash at Barton 9.8.59

G-AOPY VS633, first flown 21.7.60, Aviation Traders Ltd., Southend; not certificated; given to children's playground at Basildon, Essex 1963

G-AOWT VS397, first flown 10.56, C. of A. 19.12.58, Aviation Traders Ltd., Southend; to the Lebanon 12.58 as OD-ACQ

G-APGT VR313, first flown 15.9.59, C. of A. 21.9.59, Aviation Traders Ltd., Stansted; left on delivery to the Belgian Congo 22.9.59 as OO-CDR

G-APIT VR192, first flown 10.8.58, C. of A. 13.8.58, Airwork Ltd., Perth; Scottish Rural Gas Ltd., Perth 2.61; C.A.V.U. International, Jersey 7.68; withdrawn from use 10.70

G-APIU VR200, first flown 5.5.58, C. of A. 12.5.58, Surrey and Kent Flying Club, Biggin Hill; C. J. d'Oyly, Roborough 4.64; J. F. Coggins, Baginton 9.65; withdrawn from use 3.67

G-APIY VR249, first flown 3.2.58, C. of A. 30.7.58, E. P. Jones, Rhoose 'The Keri Lyn'; Bert Wright Aviation Ltd., Biggin Hill 12.61; A. H. Smith, Biggin Hill 8.64; Laarbruch Flying Club, Germany 5.65; withdrawn from use at Winthorpe 7.67

G-APJB VR259, first flown 11.11.59, C. of A. 6.5.60, Herts and Essex Aero Club, Stapleford; Southend Corporation 3.61; D. P. Golding, Thruxton 12.66, later Hurn; J. F. Coggins, Baginton 3.73

G-APJE VS282, first flown 15.8.58, C. of A. 6.7.59, Aviation Traders Ltd., Southend; E. P. Jones, Rhoose 7.60; Blackpool & Fylde Aero Club, Squires Gate 3.62; Mell Air Ltd., Skegness 9.62; w.f.u. at Skegness 8.64

G-APPL VR189, first flown 22.11.58, C. of A. 2.12.58, F. J. Ibbottson, Jersey; J. F. McClory, Woolsington 6.60; Tyneside Light Alloys Ltd., Woolsington 7.63; J. P. Croft, Biggin Hill 5.65; Miss S. J. Saggers, Biggin Hill 5.72

Percival P.40 Prentice 1 *(scrapped at Southend, Stansted or Minworth* before conversion)*

G-AOKA, VR306; G-AOKB, VR310; G-AOKC, VS732; G-AOKD, VS390; G-AOKE, VR316; G-AOKG, VR301; G-AOKI, VR193; G-AOKJ, VR239; G-AOKK, VR243; G-AOKM, VS741; G-AOKN, VS642; G-AOKP, VS635; G-AOKR, VS649; G-AOKS, VS755, G-AOKU, VS383; G-AOKV, VR321; G-AOKW, VS690; G-AOKX, VS329, G-AOKY, VS630

G-AOLA, VS324; G-AOLB, VS386; G-AOLC, VS395; G-AOLD, VS692; G-AOLE, VS375; G-AOLF, VR322; G-AOLG, VS744; G-AOLH, VS729; G-AOLI, VS695; G-AOLJ, VS644; G-AOLL, VS412; G-AOLN, VS391; G-AOLS, VS365; G-AOLT, VS359; G-AOLV, VS353; G-AOLW, VS327; G-AOLX. VS320; G-AOLY, VS319; G-AOLZ, VS318

G-AOMA, VS286; G-AOMB, VS283; G-AOMC, VS266; G-AOMD, VS255; G-AOME, VS252; G-AOMG, VR268; G-AOMH, VR317; G-AOMI, VR315; G-AOMJ, VR314; G-AOML, VR303; G-AOMM, VR295; G-AOMN, VR294; G-AOMO, VR292; G-AOMP, VR289; G-AOMR, VR288; G-AOMS, VR286; G-AOMT, VR285; G-AOMU, VR276; G-AOMV, VR274; G-AOMW, VR272; G-AOMX, VR270; G-AOMY, VR265; G-AOMZ, VR263

G-AONA, VR245; G-AONC, VR240; G-AOND, VR221; G-AONE, VR220; G-AONF, VR208; G-AONG, VR207; G-AONH, VR196; G-AONI, VS753; G-AONJ, VS751; G-AONK, VS740; G-AONL, VS737; G-AONM, VS733; G-AONN, VS728; G-AONO, VS727; G-AONP, VS726; G-AONR, VS724; G-AONT, VS684; G-AONU, VS681; G-AONV, VS648; G-AONW, VS643; G-AONX, VS639; G-AONY, VS634; G-AONZ, VS242

G-AOOA, VS243; G-AOOB, VS244; G-AOOC, VS246; G-AOOD, VS253; G-AOOE, VS256; G-AOOF, VS257; G-AOOG, VS269; G-AOOH, VS273; G-AOOI, VS276; G-AOOJ, VS277; G-AOOK, VS289; G-AOOL, VS317; G-AOOM, VS321; G-AOON, VS322; G-AOOO, VS323; G-AOOP, VS325; G-AOOR, VS328; G-AOOS, VS332; G-AOOT, VS333; G-AOOU, VS334; G-AOOV, VS338; G-AOOW, VS352; G-AOOX, VS354; G-AOOY, VS355; G-AOOZ, VS357

G-AOPA, VS362; G-AOPB, VS363; G-AOPC, VS364; G-AOPD, VS373; G-AOPE, VS377; G-AOPF, VS378; G-AOPG, VS384; G-AOPH, VS387; G-AOPI, VS392; G-AOPJ, VS393; G-AOPK, VS411; G-AOPM, VS611; G-AOPN, VS612; G-AOPP, VS614; G-AOPR, VS615; G-AOPS, VS616; G-AOPT, VS619; G-AOPU, VS622; G-AOPV, VS625; G-AOPX, VS631

G-AOWA, VR222; G-AOWB, VR267; G-AOWC, VR302; G-AOWD, VR305; G-AOWE, VR312; G-AOWF, VR318; G-AOWG, VR324; G-AOWH, VS241; G-AOWI, VS247; G-AOWJ, VS248; G-AOWK, VS249; G-AOWL, VS272; G-AOWM, VS335; G-AOWN, VS336; G-AOWO, VS371; G-AOWP, VS376; G-AOWR, VS380; G-AOWS, VS389; G-AOWU, VS409; G-AOWV, VS410; G-AOWW, VS646; G-AOWX, VS693; G-AOWY, VS694; G-AOWZ, VS696; G-AOXA, VS697; G-AOXB, VS734; G-AOXC, VS736; G-AOXD, VS739; G-AOXE, VS754

G-APBS, VR248; G-APBT, VR287; G-APBU, VR253; G-APBV, VS381; G-APGA, VR232; G-APGB, VR260; G-APGC, VR261; G-APGD, VR320; G-APGE, VS270; G-APGF, VS281; G-APGG, VS285; G-APGH, VS651; G-APGI, VS686; G-APGJ, VS688; G-APGK, VS730; G-APGN, VR236; G-APGO, VR257; G-APGP, VR271; G-APGR, VR279; G-APGS, VS284; G-APGU, VS337; G-APGV, VS358; G-APGW, VS361; G-APGX, VS414; G-APGY, VS620; G-APGZ, VS637; G-APHA, VS638; G-APHB, VS641; G-APHC, VS647; G-APHD, VS650; G-APHE, VS683; G-APHF, VS685; G-APHG, VS691; G-APHH, VS725; G-APHI, VS723; G-APHJ, VS731; G-APHK, VS735; G-APHL, VS738; G-APHM, VS746; G-APHN, VS747; G-APHO, VS748; G-APHP, VS757; G-APHR, VS756; G-APHS, VS752

G-APIF, VS652*; G-APIV, VR227; G-APIW, VR229; G-APIX, VR235; G-APJA, VR250; G-APJC, VR277; G-APJD, VS278; G-APJF, VS745; G-APJG, VS749; G-APJH, VS682; G-APJI, VS280; G-ARGA, VR211*

Percival P.48 Merganser

G-AHMH (Au.1), first flown 9.5.47 as X-2, Percival Aircraft Ltd., Luton; scrapped at Luton 8.48

Percival P.50 Prince and variants

G-AKYE (P.50/11), 30.4.51, Percival Aircraft Ltd., Luton; to Aeronorte, Brazil 5.51 as PP-NBF; to R. B. Archer, Rio de Janiero 7.54 as PT-ASW

G-ALCM (P.50/1), G-23-1, 18.8.48, first flown 13.5.48, Percival Aircraft Ltd., Luton; dismantled at Luton 7.56

G-ALFZ (P.50/2), 18.1.49, Percival Aircraft Ltd., Luton; to Aeronorte, Brazil via Prestwick 7.8.50 as PP-XEG; became PP-NBA on arrival; d.b.r. 9.3.52

G-ALJA (P.50/3), 31.3.49, Shell Refining & Marketing Co. Ltd.; re-registered in Singapore 7.50 as VR-SDB; later to Borneo as VR-UDB

G-ALRY (P.54/8), 23.1.50, Hunting Aerosurveys Ltd., Luton; to Kenya 5.56 as VP-KNN; to Sté. Protection Aéroportée, Le Bourget 3.59 as F-BJAJ

G-ALWG (P.50/7), 23.3.50, Shell Refining & Marketing Co. Ltd.; re-registered in Venezuela 4.50 as YV-P-AEO 'El Vijeo'

G-ALWH (P.50/10), 23.3.50, Shell Refining & Marketing Co. Ltd.; re-registered in Venezuela 4.50 as YV-P-AEQ; rest. 2.53 to Sperry Gyroscope Co. Ltd.; Decca Navigator Co. Ltd., Biggin Hill 1.61

G-AMKK (P.50/37), 28.3.52, Shell Refining & Marketing Co. Ltd.; re-registered in Singapore 6.52 as VR-SDR; later to Borneo as VR-UDR

G-AMKW (P.50/34), 16.7.52, Ministry of Civil Aviation Civil Flying Unit, Stansted and its successors; w.f.u. 8.70, to Stansted Fire Section 1971

Prince G-ALFZ flying on test as PP-XEG in July 1950 prior to transatlantic delivery to Empresa de Transportes Aereos Norte do Brasil Ltda. (Aeronorte). (*Percival Aircraft Ltd.*)

G-AMKX (P.50/35), 12.12.52, Ministry of Civil Aviation Civil Flying Unit, Stansted and its successors; w.f.u. 12.69, to Stansted Fire Section 1971

G-AMKY (P.50/36), 3.11.52, Ministry of Civil Aviation Civil Flying Unit, Stansted and its successors; w.f.u. 10.70, to Stansted Fire Section 1971

G-AMLW (P.50/43), 26.5.52, Shell Refining & Marketing Co. Ltd.; re-registered in Venezuela 8.52 as YV-P-AEB; to Australia 8.57 as VH-AGF; to Société Protection Aéroportée 3.59 as F-BJAI

G-AMLX (P.50/44), 8.10.52, Shell Refining & Marketing Co. Ltd., re-registered in Borneo 3.55 as VR-UDA

G-AMLY (P.50/45), 22.10.52, Shell Refining & Marketing Co. Ltd.; re-registered in Venezuela 12.52 as YV-P-AEC; later transferred to Borneo as VR-UDC

G-AMLZ (P.50/46), 14.11.52, Shell Refining & Marketing Co. Ltd.; W. F. Martin, Tollerton 8.54; Stewart, Smith & Co. Ltd., Blackbushe 6.56; T. M. Clutterbuck, Leavesden 10.68

G-AMMB (P.50/13), 14.11.52, Percival Aircraft Ltd.; to South Africa 11.52 as ZS-DGX, based at Wonderboom

G-AMNT (P.50/41), 26.3.52, Percival Aircraft Ltd., Luton; to the Thai Air Force 4.52 as Q1-1/98

G-AMOT (P.50/47), 16.7.52, Hunting Aerosurveys Ltd., Luton; d.b.r. in wheels-up landing in the jungle near Mackinnon Road Airfield, Kenya 6.6.58

G-AMPR (P.50/48), 30.9.52, Standard Motor Co. Ltd., Baginton; to the Tanganyika Government 2.56 as VR-TBN; to Polynesian Airlines, Samoa 2.61 as ZK-BYN

Percival P.66 President and variants

G-AOJG (PEM/79), 20.12.56, Hunting Percival Aircraft Ltd., Luton; to the Danish Air Force via Southend 4.7.59 as '697'; later OY-AVA

G-APMO (PRES 2/1031), 29.9.58, Ministry of Transport and Civil Aviation Civil Flying Unit, Stansted and its successors; w.f.u. 7.70, to 1163 Sqn., A.T.C., Earls Colne 1973

G-APNL (PEM/13), WV710, delivered from Empire Test Pilots' School, Farnborough to Air Navigation & Trading Co. Ltd., Squires Gate 29.6.58; scrapped

G-APVJ (PRES 2/114), EC-APC, 4.9.59, Hunting Aircraft Ltd., Luton; delivered to the Sudanese Air Force via Southend 3.3.60, serial number '12'

G-ARCN (PRES 2/1040), EC-APA, Sudanese Air Force '10', 1.9.60, Hunting Aircraft Ltd., Luton; Bristol Aircraft Ltd., Filton 3.62; B.A.C. (Operating) Ltd., Filton 1.64; withdrawn from use 10.70

Piaggio P.166 and P.166B Portofino*

G-APSJ (354), 30.5.59, to Australia 3.64 as VH-ACV; G-APVE (355), 30.5.59, to Australia 8.63 as VH-SMF; G-APWY (362), 11.1.60; G-APXK (364), 12.6.60, to Nigeria 1.70 as 5N-ADQ; G-APYP (365), 19.4.60, to Australia 3.64 as VH-MMP; G-ARUJ (376), 31.1.62; G-ASPC (412)*, 6.7.64, scrapped at Luton 9.72; G-AVSM (416)*, 10.9.69, scrapped at Luton 9.72; G-AWWJ (406), 9L-LAF, 16.2.70, to Nigeria 2.70 as 5N-ADP

Piel CP.301 Emeraude

G-ARDD (549), CP.301-C1, 8.7.60; G-ARIW (112), CP.301B, F-BIRQ, 25.4.61; G-ARRS (226), CP.301A, F-BIMA, 19.7.61; G-ARSJ (581), CP.301-C2, 3.8.61; G-ARUV (PFA.700), CP.301 Series 1, A. to F. 19.8.63; G-ASBS (236), CP.301A, F-BIMJ, 3.8.60; G-ASCZ (233), CP.301A, F-BIMG, 13.12.62; G-ASDW (119), CP.301B, F-BJEY, 18.12.62; G-ASKR (110), CP.301B, F-BIPO, 2.8.63, crashed at Strathaven, Lanarkshire 11.6.64; G-ASLX (292), CP.301A, F-BISV, 21.10.63; G-ASSU (230), CP.301A, F-BIME, 12.8.64; G-ASVG (109), CP.301B, F-BILV, 24.8.64; G-AWXP (565), CP.301C-1, F-BJFZ, 5.1.69, ditched in the English Channel off Dungeness 24.6.71; G-AXXC (117), CP.301B, F-BJAT, 13.5.70; G-AXXM (220), F-BIJT, registered 10.2.70; G-AYCE (530), CP.301C, F-BJFH, 12.6.70; G-AYEC (249), CP.301A, F-BIMV, 8.6.70; G-AYTR (229), CP.301A, F-BIMD, 9.6.71; G-AZGY (122), F-BRAA, 30.8.72; G-AZYS (568), F-BJAY, 19.9.72

Piel CP.1310-C3 Super Emeraude

G-ASMV (919), 17.9.64; G-ASNI (925), 24.5.64

Pierre Robin DR.253 Regent

G-AWCD (113), 8.3.68; G-AWKP (130), 25.7.68; G-AWYL (143), 11.3.69; G-AXDG (147), not imported; G-AXWV (104), F-OCKL, 16.2.70; G-AYUB (185), DR.253B, 21.5.71; G-AZOW (200), 26.4.72

Pierre Robin DR.300/125 and DR.315 Petit Prince*

G-AXDK (378)*, 2.6.69; G-AZJN (642), 4.3.72

Pierre Robin DR.340 Major

G-AXSV (335), F-BRCC, 10.2.70

Pierre Robin DR.360 Chevalier

G-AYCO (362), F-BRFI, 5.6.70; G-AZIJ (634), 8.2.72; G-AZOX (657), 12.5.72, crashed at Biggin Hill 21.7.73

Pierre Robin DR.400/2+2 *(115 h.p. Lycoming O-235-C2A)*

G-BAGS (760), 8.3.73; G-BALI (764), 8.3.73

Pierre Robin DR.400/125 Petit Prince *(125 h.p. Lycoming O-235-F)*

G-BAEM (728), 8.12.72; G-BAGR (753), 19.1.73; G-BAJZ (759), 7.2.73; G-BALF (772), 23.3.73

Pierre Robin DR.400/140 Earl *(140 h.p. Lycoming O-320-E)*

G-BAFX (739), 29.12.72; G-BAGC (737), 29.12.72; G-BAKM (755), 2.2.73; G-BALH (766), 8.3.73

Pierre Robin DR.400/160 Knight *(160 h.p. Lycoming O-320-D)*

G-BAEB (733), 8.12.72; G-BAFP (735), 29.12.72; G-BAHL (704), F-OCSR, 8.12.72; G-BAMS (774), 20.3.73; G-BAMT (775), 26.3.73; G-BAMU (778), 28.3.73; G-BAMV (777), 30.3.73

Pierre Robin DR.400/180 Regent *(180 h.p. Lycoming O-360-A)*

G-BAEN (736), 22.12.72; G-BAJY (758), 23.2.73; G-BALG (771), 15.3.73; G-BALJ (767), 15.5.73

Pierre Robin HR.100/200 and HR.100/210* Royale

G-AZHB (118), 8.2.72; G-AZHK (113), 27.3.72; G-AZKN (122), 21.2.72; G-AZZY* (144), not imported; G-BAEC* (145), 6.3.73

Piper J-2 Cub

G-AEIK (556)*, 5.5.36, scrapped during 1939–45 war; G-AESK (957)*, 25.3.37, w.f.u. 5.38; G-AEXY (971)*, 31.7.37, to Spain 3.53 as EC-ALB; G-AEXZ (997), 21.1.38, based at Fairoaks in 1971; G-AFFH (1166), 25.4.38, to Spain 3.53 as EC-ALA

* Built as Taylor J-2 Cubs by the Taylor Aircraft Company.

Piper J-3 Cub

G-AFFJ (1165), 6.4.38, sold in Germany 1.56; G-AFIO (2348), 13.3.39, scrapped during 1939–45 war; G-AFIY (2425), 25.3.39, dismantled at Bury St. Edmunds 7.41; G-AFIZ (2424), 6.10.38, to Ireland 11.47 as EI-ADR

Piper J3C-65 Cub

G-AKBS (21967), 6.1.48, to Ireland 8.48 as EI-AEB; G-AKBT (21984), 25.11.47, to Portugal 11.48 as CS-AAP; G-AKBU (22021), 25.11.47, to Portugal 12.48 as CS-AAQ; G-AKBV (21962), 25.11.47, to Spain 1.49 as EC-AJI; G-ASPS (22809), N3571N, 21.5.65, based at Booker in 1973

Piper L-4 Cub

G-AIIH (11945), 44-79649, 19.3.47, based at Heyford in 1971; G-AISP (11691), 23.12.46, to the Canary Islands 11.52 as EC-AKD; G-AISV (11810), 23.12.46, to Ireland 10.47 as NC74137; G-AISW (11780), 23.12.46, crashed off the North Foreland 16.2.48; G-AISX (11663), 43-30372, 4.6.47, w.f.u. at Wolverhampton 2.51; G-AIYU (10710), 4.6.47, to Holland 11.57 as PH-NIL; G-AIYV (11295), 12.9.47, to the Mildenhall Aero Club 7.58 as N9829F; G-AIYX (10993), 12.9.47, to Germany 1.56 as D-EHAL; G-AJBE (12109), re-registered 5.48 as G-AKNC; G-AJDS (11658), 9.7.48, to Germany 8.58 as D-EJYD

G-AKAA (10780), 43-29489, 22.8.47, based at Little Snoring in 1973; G-AKNC (12109), to the American Embassy 5.48 as NC6400N; G-ALGH (12156), 44-80545, 29.4.49, to Iceland 7.52 as TF-KAP; G-ALMA (12042), 3.6.49, sold in Germany 2.57; G-ALVR (11535), N73100, 26.5.50, to Germany 9.57 as D-EKYR; G-ANXP (12192), 44-79896, NC79819, 13.10.55, to Germany 10.55 as D-EGUL

P. G. Masefield flying the L-4H Cub G-AIYX, experimentally fitted with a prototype 55 h.p. Coventry Victor Flying Neptune engine in 1955. (*Aeroplane*)

G-ATKI (17545), N70536, 8.11.66; G-ATZM (20868), N2092M, 6.12.66; G-AXDB (10006), 43-1145, F-BFQY, F-BMSJ, 15.4.68; G-AXGP (9542), 43-28251, F-BDTM, F-BGPS, stored at Navestock, Essex in 1971; G-AXHP (12932), 44-80636, F-BETT, 1.8.69; G-AXHR (10892), 43-29601, F-BETI, 6.8.69; G-AXVV (10863), 43-29572, F-BBQB, 17.6.70; G-AYCN (13365), 45-4625, PH-UCM, F-BCPO, 5.6.70; G-AYEN (9696), 43-835, F-BGQD, 12.8.70; G-BAET (11605), 43-30314, OO-AJI, registered 26.9.72

Piper J-4A Cub Coupé

G-AFPP (4-441), 21.2.39, to Germany 6.56 as D-EDED; G-AFSY (4-510), 19.5.39, impressed 5.42 as HM565; G-AFSZ (4-538), 31.5.39, impressed 11.40 as BT440, rest. 1.46, d.b.r. at Fairoaks 30.5.62; G-AFTB (4-541), 15.6.39, impressed 12.40 as BV989, d.b.r. at Larkhill 9.6.42; G-AFTC (4-525), J-4B, 31.5.39, impressed 12.40 as BV990, rest. 1.46, to France 11.49 as F-BFQS; G-AFTD (4-542), 15.6.39, impressed 10.41 as HL531, d.b.r. at Larkhill 10.1.42; G-AFTE (4-537), 16.6.39, crashed at Leicester 8.8.39; G-AFVD and 'VE, reservations only, not imported; G-AFVF (4-586), 14.7.39, impressed 12.40 as BV991, rest. 10.46, crashed at Gatwick 24.6.48; G-AFVG (4-588), 20.7.39, impressed 12.40 as BV987, d.b.r. at Kemble 6.4.41; G-AFVL (4-543), 26.6.39, impressed 11.40 as BT441, crashed at Kimpton, Hants. 30.9.41; G-AFVM (4-554), 29.6.39, impressed 12.40 as BV988, d.b.r. at Shrewton, Wilts. 3.6.42

G-AFWA (4-558), 7.7.39, impressed 3.41 as BV180, d.b.r. at Dunsfold 30.1.43; G-AFWB (4-559), 13.7.39, impressed 3.41 as BV181; G-AFWR (4-589), 24.8.39, impressed 11.40 as BT442, d.b.r. at Winterbourne Stoke, Wilts. 7.7.41; G-AFWS (4-612), 1.8.39, impressed 5.41 as ES923, rest. 1.46, to Finland 7.51 as OH-CPB; G-AFWU (4-619), 11.8.39, scrapped during 1939–45 war; G-AFWV (4-622), 11.8.39, to the R.A.F. as spares 5.41; G-AFWW (4-618), 11.8.39, to the R.A.F. as spares 5.41

G-AFXS (4-647), 28.8.39, impressed 2.41 as DG667, rest. 1.46, to Finland 5.53 as OH-CPF; G-AFXT (4-653), 24.8.39, impressed 3.41 as DP852; G-AFXU, NC24731, impressed 12.40 as BV984; G-AFXV, NC24741, impressed 12.40 as BV986; G-AFXW, NC24751, believed not imported; G-AFXX, NC24761, impressed 12.40 as BV985; G-AFXY, NC24771, believed not imported

Piper PA-12 Supercruiser

G-AJGY (12-1118), 16.5.47, to France 1.53 as F-BGQY; G-AKDM (12-3966), 23.9.47, to South Africa 1.51; G-AKJC (12-3994), 3.10.47, to France 10.47 as F-BCPP; G-ARTH (12-3278), EI-ADO, 24.11.61; G-AWPW (12-3947), N78572, 1.11.68; G-AXUC (12-621), ZS-BIN, VP-KFR, 5Y-KFR, 27.11.70

Piper PA-15 and PA-17 Vagabond

G-ASHU (15-46), N4164H, 20.8.64; G-AWKD (17-192), F-BFMZ, 4.7.68; G-AWOF (15-227), F-BETF, 29.11.68; G-AWOH (17-191), F-BFMY, 26.9.69

Piper PA-18 Super Cub 90

G-APZK (18-7248), 6.5.60; G-ARAO (18-7327), 10.6.60; G-ARBX (18-7355), 18.8.61; G-ARCT (18-7375), 28.9.60, to Ireland 12.72 as EI-AVE; G-AREU (18-7152), N3096Z, 30.9.60, to Ireland 12.65 as EI-ANY

Piper PA-18 Super Cub 135

G-AWDN (18-2151), F-OBKI, 5N-ADS, 10.4.68, destroyed 20.3.69

Piper PA-18 Super Cub 150

G-AOZT (18-5503), 17.4.57, to Jamaica 6.60 as VP-JBQ; G-APKB (18-6250), N8590D, 22.2.58, crashed at Nuthampstead, Herts. 25.5.59; G-APLY (18-6459), 23.5.58, crashed in 1966; G-APPI (18-6575), 31.10.58, crashed near Devizes 13.4.65; G-APUI (18-6670), EI-AKS, 25.5.59, crashed at Good Easter, Essex 25.7.63; G-APUJ (18-6644), N9377D, 25.6.59, crashed at Dunholme, Lincoln 2.8.62; G-APVR (18-7062), N10P, 8.9.59, crashed at Sunk Island, near Hull 1.9.65; G-APYR (18-4466), N2999P, 23.7.60, to Holland 4.66 as PH-AAS; G-APZJ (18-7233), 24.2.60

G-ARAM (18-7312), 25.8.61; G-ARAN (18-7307), 16.5.60; G-AREO (18-7407), 15.9.60; G-ARGU (18-7544), 4.8.61, to Nigeria 8.61 as 5N-AEF; G-ARGV (18-7559), N10P, 24.4.61; G-ARSR (18-7605), 3.8.61, to the Sudan 3.62 as ST-ABM; G-ARSS (18-7606), 3.8.61, to the Sudan 3.62 as ST-ABN; G-ASCU (18-6797), VP-JBL, 22.11.62; G-ATRG (18-7764), N4985Z, 5B-CAB, 18.3.66; G-ATRH (18-7830), 5B-CAD, 18.3.66; G-ATXP (18-7860), 5B-CAE, 15.8.66, sold in South Africa 1.67; G-AVOO (18-8511), 13.6.67; G-AVPT (18-8513), N4267Z, 5.7.67; G-AVPU (18-8533), N4292Z, 3.7.67; G-AWMF (18-8674), N4356Z, 24.7.69; G-AYDN (18-8874), N5204Z, to Kenya 8.70 as 5Y-ANH

Picketing the Piper J-4A Cub Coupé G-AFXS after its impressment in 1941 for A.O.P. duties with D Flight, Larkhill, as DG667. (*Imperial War Museum CH.6118*)

G-BAFS (18-5338), registered 3.8.72; G-BAFT (18-5340), 16.2.73; G-BAKV (18-8993), 22.2.73

Piper PA-19 Super Cub 90 *(surplus military L-18C aircraft)*

G-AWRH (18-1555), 51-15555, French Army F-MBIB, OO-HMI, not imported; G-AXGA (18-2047), 52-2447, Dutch Air Force R-51, PH-NLE, 19.6.69; G-AXLZ (18-2052), 52-2452, Dutch R-45, PH-NLB, 21.4.70; G-AYPM (18-1373), 6.5.71; G-AYPN (18-1600), 6.5.71, crashed near Petersfield, Hants. 28.8.71; G-AYPO (18-1615), 18.8.71; G-AYPP (18-1626), 6.5.71; G-AYPR (18-1631), 8.4.71; G-AYPS (18-2092), registered 13.1.71; G-AYPT (18-1533), 19.11.71; G-AZRL (18-1331), 51-15331, OO-SBR, registered 23.3.72; G-BAFV (18-2045), 52-2445, Dutch R-40, PH-WJK, 2.2.73

Piper PA-22 Tri-Pacer 135

G-AORO (22-2098), VP-KMY, 4.7.57, w.f.u. at Stapleford 10.64; G-APTJ (22-1025), N1207C, 3.4.59, to Southern Rhodesia 8.59 as VP-YRE; G-APXU (22-474), N1723A, 16.3.60; G-APYI (22-2218), N8031C, 18.3.60; G-AWLH (22-977), N1141C, to Israel 5.69 as 4X-ANJ

Piper PA-22 Tri-Pacer 150

G-APTP (22-5009), EI-AJN, 10.4.59; G-APYW (22-4994), N7131D, 1.5.60; G-APZX (22-5181), N7420D, 29.4.60; G-APZY (22-5123), N7334D, 4.5.60, crashed at Cadeby, Leic. 25.7.64; G-ARAE (22-4114), PH-RAC, 26.5.60, crashed near Stapleford 4.3.67; G-ARAX (22-3830), N4523A, 24.5.60; G-ARBT (22-3870), N4559A, 13.9.60; G-ARBU (22-4011), N4855A, 29.6.61, crashed in the Leiza Navarre Mts., Spain 19.5.68; G-ARCC (22-4006), N4853A, 8.7.60; G-ARCF (22-4563), N5902D, 26.10.60; G-ARCG (22-4443), N5743D, 1.7.60, blown over by Britannia at Luton 5.10.69; G-ARDP (22-4254), N7004B, 2.10.60; G-ARDU (22-4950), N7053D, 30.9.60; G-AREM (22-2714), N2303P, 23.9.60, crashed near Shobden 23.9.67; G-AREN (22-6196), N9056D, 4.10.60, lost at sea off Littlehampton 27.5.61; G-ARHO (22-7538), N3643Z, 22.2.62, to Denmark 3.62 as OY-ACW; G-ATWF (22-5216), VP-JBJ, 6Y-JBJ, 13.10.66, d.b.r. at Compton Abbas 3.7.71; G-ATXA (22-3730), N4403A, 27.10.66; G-ATXB (22-5616), N8125D, 9.12.66; G-AVDV (22-3752), N4423A, 4.8.67; G-AWLI (22-5083), N7256D, 23.8.68; G-AZRS (22-5141), XT-AAH, registered 28.3.72

Piper PA-22 Tri-Pacer 160

G-APUR (22-6711), 27.7.59; G-APUT (22-6673), 7.8.59; G-APVA (22-6741), 23.9.59; G-APWR (22-6666), EI-AKP, 18.9.59; G-APXM (22-7055), 26.1.60; G-APXP (22-7111), 29.4.60; G-APXR (22-7172), 5.4.60; G-APXV (22-6411), N9437D, 4.2.60, sold in Ireland 12.72; G-APYN (22-6797), N2804Z, 8.4.60; G-APZL (22-7054), EI-ALF, 24.2.60; G-ARAG (22-7348), 3.5.60, crashed at Kenton Cross, Devon 14.6.70; G-ARAH (22-7423), 29.6.60; G-ARAI (22-7421), 10.9.60; G-ARAJ (22-7393), 6.7.60; G-ARAK (22-7405), 1.6.60, to Liberia 10.62 as EL-ADW; G-ARAL (22-7419), 1.6.60, to Belgium 8.63 as OO-DLH; G-ARBS (22-6858), 31.8.60; G-ARBV (22-5836), N8633D, 18.4.61

G-ARCA (22-7432), 13.8.61, d.b.r. prior to 1.69; G-ARCD (22-7478), 8.7.60, d.b.r. at Squires Gate 1.2.68; G-ARDT (22-6210), N9158D, 7.10.60; G-ARDV (22-7487), 7.6.61, to Ireland 12.65 as EI-APA, rest. 9.68; G-ARET (22-7590), 2.3.61; G-AREV (22-6540), N9628D, 7.11.60; G-ARFD (22-7565), N3667Z, 9.2.61; G-ARGE (22-7606), sold in Portugal 12.61; G-ARGF (22-7615), sold in Portugal 12.61; G-ARGL (22-5898), N8717D, 8.12.60; G-ARGX (22-7616), 29.3.61; G-ARGY (22-7620), 2.3.61; G-ARHP

(22-7549), N3652Z, 2.11.61; G-ARHS (22-7582), N3711Z, 13.4.61, crashed at Ashwood, Worcs. 22.10.67; G-ARHU (22-7602), N3726Z, 23.3.61; G-ARHV (22-7614), N3734Z, 17.8.61; G-ARIB (22-7559), N3661Z, 8.6.61, crashed near Strathallan, Perthshire 17.5.70; G-ARIJ (22-7552), N3655Z, 13.4.61, ditched off Wimereux, France 13.6.65

G-ARLA (22-7200), N3252Z, 20.4.61, d.b.f. at Kirkbymoorside 17.11.68; G-ARSX (22-6712), N2907Z, 29.8.61; G-ARXK (22-6689), EI-AKY, 23.3.62, crashed in sea off Alderney 26.8.66; G-ARYH (22-7039), N3102Z, 4.4.62

Piper PA-22 Caribbean 150

G-APXO (22-7056), 1.2.60, crashed near Burgos, Spain 15.5.70; G-APXS (22-7057), 1.2.60, crashed near Doddington, Kent 8.6.71; G-APXT (22-3854), N4545A, 17.3.60; G-ARCB (22-7470), 1.7.60, to Cyprus 11.68, as 5B-CAQ; G-ARCU (22-7471), 13.8.60; G-ARDS (22-7154), N3214Z, 12.9.60; G-AREL (22-7284), N3344Z, 22.9.60; G-ARES (22-7469), 15.4.61, d.b.r. at Stevenage 1.7.63

G-ARFA (22-7482), N3566Z, 11.10.60, to France 8.63 as F-BLOD; G-ARFB (22-7518), N3625Z, 15.6.61; G-ARFC (22-7531), 8.11.60, crashed at Fairoaks 19.5.64; G-ARFS (22-7322), N3409Z, 23.11.60; G-ARHH (22-7626), 13.5.61, to Denmark 3.63 as OY-AEI; G-ARHN (22-7514), N3622Z; G-ARHR (22-7576), N3707Z, 9.2.61; G-ARHT (22-7583), N3712Z, 23.3.61; G-ARIK (22-7570), N3701Z, 2.11.61; G-ARIL (22-7574), N3705Z, 24.5.62

Piper PA-22 Colt 108

G-ARGO (22-8034), 20.1.61; G-ARIS (22-8102), 9.3.61, crashed at Kidlington 5.11.61; G-ARJC (22-8154), 29.3.61; G-ARJD (22-8262), 24.4.61 d.b.r. at Thruxton 18.11.71; G-ARJE (22-8184), 29.3.61; G-ARJF (22-8199), 23.3.61; G-ARJG (22-8226), 13.4.61; G-ARJH (22-8249), 29.3.61; G-ARJP (22-8129), 29.3.61, to South Africa 8.70, as ZS-IGX; G-ARKK (22-8290), 24.4.61; G-ARKL (22-8297), 13.4.61; G-ARKM (22-8313), 13.4.61; G-ARKN (22-8327), 30.5.61; G-ARKO (22-8347), 1.5.61; G-ARKP (22-8364), 26.5.61; G-ARKR (22-8376), 30.5.61; G-ARKS (22-8422), 20.10.61; G-ARKT (22-8448), 6.7.61

G-ARNC (22-8466), 15.6.61; G-ARND (22-8484), 9.6.61; G-ARNE (22-8502), 29.6.61; G-ARNF (22-8523), 16.11.61, crashed at Woolaston, Glos. 1.9.62; G-ARNG (22-8547), 6.7.61; G-ARNH (22-8558), 13.8.62; G-ARNI (22-8575), 1.8.61; G-ARNJ (22-8587), 10.8.61; G-ARNK (22-8622), 9.8.62; G-ARNL (22-8625), 8.8.61; G-ARNM (22-8643), 16.8.62, to Holland 11.62 as PH-RRL; G-AROL (22-8796), used as spares 7.62; G-AROM (22-8805), 14.12.61; G-ARON (22-8822), 9.3.62; G-ARST (22-8823), 16.8.62, w.f.u. 4.70; G-ARSU (22-8835), to Ireland 5.62 as EI-AMI, rest. 9.70; G-ARSV (22-8844), 16.8.62, d.b.r. at Whitchurch Hill, Berks. 4.3.67; G-ARSW (22-8858), 26.9.62; G-ARUC (22-9175), 30.10.62; G-ASSE (22-9832), N5961Z, 14.7.64; G-ATIH (22-9086), application for C. of A. cancelled

Piper PA-23 Apache 150

G-APCL (23-1159), 18.9.57, to Ireland 12.63 as EI-ANI, rest. 12.64, crash landed at Shoreham 6.7.72; G-APFV (23-1686), EI-ALK, 18.12.59; G-APKO (23-154), ZS-DLD, VP-KOO, 5.4.60, to New Zealand 5.60 as ZK-BWJ; G-AREW (23-250), N1230P, 10.11.60, sold in Switzerland 3.63; G-ARHJ (23-369), 23.3.61, crashed in Elstree Reservoir 27.1.68; G-ARLI (23-120), N1109P, 6.6.61; G-ARLJ (23-127), 14.6.61, crashed at Biggin Hill 10.3.63; G-ATKA (23-596), 5N-ABG, 24.3.66, to Iceland 8.70 as TF-BAR; G-AVDI (23-1111), N223Z, 11.4.67

Piper PA-23 Apache 160

G-APBD (23-1781), EI-ALD, 6.11.59; G-APLJ (23-1366), 16.6.58, to Nigeria 3.60 as VR-NDG, later 5N-ABS, rest. 8.62, to Australia 8.63 as VH-DRR; G-APMY (23-1258), EI-AJT, 19.6.58; G-APVK (23-1719), 23.10.59; G-APZD (23-1869), 23.3.60, crashed at Turnhouse 3.5.68; G-APZE (23-1870), 13.3.60

G-ARBN (23-1385), N3421P, EI-AKI, 11.11.60; G-ARCW (23-796), N2187P, 10.9.60; G-ARED (23-1886), 10.1.61; G-ARJR (23-1966), N4447P, 10.4.61; G-ARJS (23-1977), 12.4.61; G-ARJT (23-1981), 12.4.61; G-ARJU (23-1984), 12.4.61; G-ARJV (23-1985), 12.4.61; G-ARJW (23-1986), 14.4.61; G-ARJX (23-1987), 14.4.61, to Iceland 8.70 as TF-JED; G-ARMA (23-1967), N4448P, 18.5.61; G-ARMI (23-1980), 17.7.61; G-ARTD (23-1530), N4053P, 26.9.61; G-ASDG (23-2044), 2.1.63, to Iceland 6.69 as TF-EGG; G-ASDH (23-2045), 18.1.63, crashed at Hamble 10.1.67; G-ASDI (23-2046), 31.1.63; G-ASHC (23-1319), 5N-ACK, 1.6.63, crashed at Aintree 21.3.64; G-ASMN (23-1989), N4464P, 5N-ADA, 5N-AAT, 9.12.63; G-ASMO(23-1995), N4473P, 5N-ADB, 5N-AAU, 23.1.64; G-ASMY (23-2032), N4309Y, 14.12.63; G-ATFZ (23-1314), OE-FIM, D-GIGI, 19.7.65, crashed near Godalming 1.9.66; G-ATJP (23-1736), VR-NDC, 5N-ADX, 10.6.66; G-ATMU (23-2000), N4478P, 8.2.66; G-ATOA (23-1954), N4437P, 2.3.66; G-AWKZ (23-1708), N4215P, OY-AIV, 4.10.68

Piper PA-24 Comanche 180

G-ARDR (24-1053), N5963P, 16.9.60, crashed near Coupar Angus 12.4.68; G-ARHI (24-2260), 26.1.61; G-ARJI (24-2666), 18.4.61, crashed at Fairoaks 19.1.65; G-ARSC (24-2620), 18.7.61; G-ARUO (24-2427), N7251P, 15.2.62; G-ASFH (24-3239), EI-AMM, 8.3.63; G-ATFS (24-56), N5052P, 16.7.65; G-AWKW (24-1344), N6239P, 4.9.68; G-AXMA (24-3467), N8214P, 14.10.69; G-AZKR (24-2192), N7044P, 18.1.72

Piper PA-24 Comanche 250

G-APUZ (24-1094), 7.7.59; G-APXJ (24-291), VR-NDA, 19.1.60; G-APZF (24-1190), EI-AKV, 4.2.60, d.b.r. at Peniarth, N. Wales 1.6.69; G-APZG (24-1197), EI-AKW, 8.2.60; G-APZH (24-1557), not imported; G-APZI (24-1605), not imported; G-ARBO (24-2117), 15.6.60; G-ARDB (24-2166), 25.8.60, to Holland 6.64 as PH-RON; G-ARDL (24-2161), 6.1.61; G-ARFH (24-2240), N7087P, 31.10.60; G-ARFY (24-2035), N6901P, 16.8.61, crashed at Cork, Ireland 8.8.64; G-ARGS (24-898), N5817P, 23.12.60, d.b.r. at Mayenne, France 19.4.65; G-ARIE (24-1888), ZS-CNL, 29.6.61; G-ARIN (24-1182), N6084P, 22.2.61; G-ARLB (24-2352), 27.4.61; G-ARLK (24-2433), N7257P, to Ireland 6.61 as EI-ALW, rest. 3.64, C. of A. 5.5.64; G-ARLL (24-2463), 24.7.61; G-ARSK (24-2751), 18.8.61; G-ARUW (24-2913), 3.2.62; G-ARXG (24-3154), 4.8.62; G-ARXI (24-2748), N7542P, 6.4.62, to Sweden 8.68 as SE-FFG; G-ARYV (24-2516), N7337P, 17.4.62; G-ASCJ (24-2368), N7197P, 5N-AEB, 30.11.62; G-ASDN (24-3280), N8033P, 17.12.62; G-ASEO (24-3367), 19.3.63; G-ASPE (24-3639), not imported; G-ASRA (24-1285), N6183P, 15.7.64; G-ATAE (24-1322), N6220P, 8.2.65, crashed at Bordesley, Yorks. 12.6.71; G-BAHJ (24-1863), N6375P, PH-RED, 2.5.73

Piper PA-24 Comanche 260

G-ATAO (24-4053), N8634P, 11.2.65; G-ATIA (24-4049), N8650P, 27.8.65; G-ATJL (24-4203), N8752P, 31.10.65; G-ATNV (24-4350), N8896P, 14.2.66; G-ATOY (24-4346), N8893P, 15.4.66; G-AVCL (24-4213), N8763P, to Belgium 9.68 as OO-YET; G-AVCM (24-4520), N9054P, 30.12.66; G-AVGA (24-4489), N9027P, 2.2.67; G-AVGN (24-4514), N9049P, 15.2.67; G-AVJU (24-4657), N9199P, 23.5.67; G-AXTO (24-4900),

N9449P, 9.12.69; G-AYED (24-4923), N9417P, 13.8.70; G-AZSY (24-4438), N8979P, 13.5.72; G-AZWY (24-4806), N9310P, 2.8.72; G-BAHG (24-4306), N8831P, 5Y-AFX, 22.2.73

Pawnee 160 G-ATFR, with tow hook under the tail, was used for glider towing at Lasham from 1964. (*A. J. Jackson*)

Piper PA-25 Pawnee 150 and 160*

G-APVY (25-168), 10.3.61; G-ATFR (25-135)*, OY-ADJ, 30.10.64

Piper PA-25 Pawnee 235

G-ARYT (25-662), 23.2.62, crashed near Downham Market 15.6.64; G-ARZH (25-2026), 10.8.62, crashed near Downham Market 27.7.69; G-ARZY (25-2087), 23.7.62, crashed at Bishop's Itchingham, near Rugby 20.3.63; G-ARZZ (25-2073), N6567Z, 13.8.63, crashed at Quaik, Sudan 28.10.63; G-ASFZ (25-2246), N6672Z, 20.3.63; G-ASIY (25-2446), 10.7.63; G-ASJK (25-2486), 4.9.63; G-ASKF (25-2231), 10.7.63, crashed at Branston, Lincs. 9.7.68; G-ASKV (25-2272), N6700Z, 18.9.63, to the Sudan 10.65 as ST-ACW, rest. 7.69, sold in the Republic of Zaire 2.72; G-ASLA (25-2380), N6802Z, 1.8.63; G-ASLJ (25-2264), 5.9.63, to the Sudan 12.68 as ST-ADS, rest. 10.69, to Holland 11.69 as PH-VBC; G-ASLK (25-2370), N6801Z, 5.9.63, to the Sudan 12.68 as ST-ADT, rest. 10.69, sold in Republic of Zaire 3.72; G-ASOV (25-2657), 17.6.64

G-ASVP (25-2978), 4.9.64; G-ASVR (25-2979), 4.9.64, to the Sudan 9.67, rest. 9.68; G-ASVW (25-2805), 3.9.64, crashed near Wadi Medui, Sudan 25.10.65; G-ASVX (25-2895), N7112Z, 3.9.64; G-ASVY (25-2923), 3.9.64, sold in the Sudan 9.67; G-ASWG (25-2900), 3.9.64, to the Sudan 9.67 as ST-ADM, rest. 7.72; G-ATBM (25-3133), 23.3.65, crashed in Crete 22.7.65; G-ATEC (25-3407), 28.5.65, crashed at Wyberton 1.9.66; G-ATER (25-3405), 17.6.65, crashed near Boston 27.7.69; G-ATFB (25-3155), 24.6.65, to Israel 6.66, as 4X-AIF; G-ATMD (25-2595), SE-EIP, 21.10.65, to South Africa 11.67 as ZS-FEW; G-ATME (25-2802), SE-EMF, 14.1.66, to South Africa 11.67 as ZS-FEV; G-ATPA (25-3720), 15.2.66; G-ATTZ (25-3746), 26.8.66; G-ATUA (25-3738), 26.8.66, G-ATYA (25-2579), N6885Z, 5B CAA, 27.9.66

G-AVDZ (25-3982), 16.2.67; G-AVPY (25-4330), N4636Y, 11.7.67; G-AVXA (25-4244), N4576Y, 26.10.67; G-AWDL (25-4511), 23.2.68; G-AWFS (25-4368), N4648Y, 4.4.68; G-AWMA (25-4682), N4878Y, 17.7.68; G-AXBD (25-4888), 23.6.69; G-AXDF (25-3780), OH-PIC, 23.5.69, crashed near Barton-on-Humber, Lincs. 8.4.72; G-AXED (25-3586), N7540Z, OY-CPY, OH-PIM, 2.6.69; G-AXFD (25-4018), OH-PIK,

6.6.69; G-AXYO (25-5157), N8706L, 12.3.70; G-AYDA (25-4254), 7.8.70; G-AYPG (25-5210), N8756L, 21.7.70; G-AYUD (25-3717), OH-PIH, 30.3.71; G-AZIE (25-5303), 9.2.72; G-AZPA (25-5223), N8797L, 21.3.72; G-AZPB (25-5160), N8709L, 18.4.72

Piper PA-26 Comanche 400

G-ATDV (26-111), N8530P, 29.5.65

G-ATDV, sole British registered Piper PA-26 Comanche 400, showing the three bladed airscrew peculiar to this variant. (*Richard Riding*)

Piper PA-27 Aztec 235

G-ASEP (27-541), N4949P, 11.3.63; G-ASFF (27-556), 8.4.63; G-ASKW (27-576), 19.8.63, ditched 17½ miles off the Suffolk coast 25.2.71; G-ATHA (27-610), N4326Y, 10.8.65

Piper PA-27 Aztec 250

G-APXN (27-119), 17.11.60, to Iceland 7.70 as TF-OBE, rest. 12.70, crashed at Gleneagles, Perthshire 24.6.71; G-APYX (27-105), 4.5.60; G-ARBR (27-170), 28.10.61, to France 9.66 as F-BOES; G-AREE (27-329), 1.3.61; G-AREF (27-285), 28.9.60; G-ARFR (27-5), N4503P, 7.12.60, crashed near Fontanes, Loire, France 16.5.63; G-ARHL (27-402), 24.3.61; G-ARLS (27-431), 14.4.61; G-ARMH (27-443), 14.10.61; G-ARXF (27-2015), 12.3.62; G-ARYF (27-2065), 24.4.62; G-ARYG (27-2093), 27.7.62, crashed near Inverness 22.1.66

G-ASCP (27-2194), not imported; G-ASCR (27-2215), 11.2.63, crashed at Weston-super-Mare 28.4.63; G-ASDX (27-2281), not imported; G-ASER (27-2283), 11.3.63, crashed at Nigg Bay, near Cromarty 14.9.72; G-ASEV (27-2298), 27.8.63; G-ASFG (27-2311), 18.4.63; G-ASHH (27-63), N4557P, N455SL, 29.3.63; G-ASHV (27-2347), 14.5.63; G-ASJP (27-2364), 9.10.64, to Zambia 5.68 as 9J-RIA; G-ASNA (27-2451), 8.5.64; G-ASND (27-134), N4800P, 8.4.64; G-ASNH (27-2486), 17.2.64; G-ASRE (27-2520), 26.6.64; G-ASRI (27-2352), N5287Y, 15.4.64; G-ASTD (27-2549), 5.6.64; G-ASTE (27-2557), 30.5.64, crashed at Yeadon 20.1.69; G-ASYB (27-2641), N5568Y, 1.12.64

G-ATAR (27-2748), N5634Y, 11.2.65, to Belgium 5.68 as OO-MAR, later F-ATAR; G-ATBV (27-2777), N5661Y, 23.3.65; G-ATCM (27-2834), N5712Y, 12.4.65, crashed at Brest, France 26.6.68; G-ATCY (27-2754), N5640Y, 26.4.65; G-ATDC (27-2751), N5668Y, 5.5.65; G-ATFF (27-2898), N5769Y, 29.6.65; G-ATFT (27-2920), N5839Y, 12.8.65, to the Sudan 4.66 as ST-ACY; G-ATHJ (27-2757), N5643Y, 20.8.65; G-ATJR

(27-3033), N5881Y; G-ATJZ (27-2967), N5819Y, 18.10.65; G-ATXG (27-3345), N6133Y, 27.7.66; G-ATZJ (27-3405), N6179Y, 3.11.66

G-AVKZ (27-3658), N6448Y, 18.5.67; G-AVLP (27-3633), N6337Y, 25.5.67; G-AVLV (27-3619), N6352Y, 24.5.67; G-AVNK (27-3355), N6142Y, 30.6.67; G-AVNL (27-3363), N6147Y, 7.7.67; G-AVSO (27-2794), N5679Y, 17.8.67; G-AWPK (27-3947), N6635Y, 17.7.69; G-AWXW (27-4096), N6765Y, 30.1.69; G-AXFA (27-4177), N6837Y, 5.6.69; G-AYDE (27-3807), N6516Y, 22.5.70; G-AYLY (27-3498), N6258Y, 6.11.70; G-AYMO (27-2995), 5Y-ACX, 18.1.71; G-AYSA (27-3799), N6509Y, 9.3.71; G-AYSF (27-3996), N6777Y, 16.2.71; G-AYTC (27-2725), 5Y-ABL, 1.4.71; G-AYTD (27-2850), 5Y-ACA, 6.7.71; G-AYUU (27-3640), N6367Y, 7.4.71; G-AYWF (27-3911), N6606Y, 9.7.71; G-AYWG (27-3926), N6620Y, 16.7.71; G-AYWY (27-4069), EI-ATI, 6.5.71; G-AYZO (27-3321), N6112Y, 4.6.71

G-AZGB (27-4099), N878SH, 11.11.71; G-AZMG (27-3500), 5Y-APA, 18.5.72; G-AZYG (27-2647), 5Y-AAU, 27.4.73; G-BAAJ (27-2569), SE-EIU, 6.10.72; G-BAHC (27-3483), 5Y-ADX, 2.1.73; G-BAJU (27-2546), N5459Y, 2.2.73

Piper PA-27 Aztec E250

G-ATKW (27-2997), N5846Y, 3.12.65; G-ATLC (27-3058), N5903Y, 31.12.65; G-ATPR (27-3082), N5923Y, 4.3.66; G-AVRX (27-3646), N6438Y, 10.8.68; G-AVTS (27-3489), N6251Y, 2.9.67; G-AVVT (27-3486), N6495Y, 9.11.67; G-AWDI (27-3811), N6520Y, 28.3.68; G-AWER (27-3852), N6556Y, 24.4.68; G-AWIY (27-3823), N6599Y, 17.5.68; G-AWVW (27-4054), N6799Y, 19.12.68; G-AXAX (27-4155), N6816Y, 21.3.69; G-AXDC (27-4169), N6829Y, 22.4.69; G-AXIV (27-4166), N6826Y, 7.7.69; G-AXKD (27-4293), N6936Y, 22.7.69; G-AXOG (27-4330), N6965Y, 10.10.69; G-AXOW (27-4306), N6946Y, 10.11.69; G-AXZP (27-4464), N13819, 24.3.70

G-AYBO (27-4510), N13874, 21.4.70; G-AYEM (27-4411), N13762, 12.6.70; G-AYKU (27-4521), N13885, 20.10.70; G-AYTO (27-4568), N14004, 7.5.71; G-AYTP (27-4585), N13970, 8.3.71; G-AYUL (27-4611), N13992, 26.3.71; G-AYVC (27-4607), N13989, 13.4.71; G-AYVJ (27-4020), N6747Y, 21.4.71; G-AYZC (27-4570), N13955, 25.5.71; G-AYZN (27-4220), N6874Y, 28.5.71; G-AZBK (27-4683), N14077, 10.8.71; G-AZFE (27-4577), N13962, 1.10.71; G-AZHA (27-4735), N14172, 25.11.71; G-AZIF (27-4633), N14019, 16.11.71, crashed near Stansted 5.1.72; G-AZJZ (27-4744), N14179, 22.12.71; G-AZMK (27-4715), N14152, 28.3.72; G-AZNY (27-4668), N14058, 8.3.72; G-AZOD (27-4344), N697RC, 8.3.72; G-AZRG (27-4386), N6536Y, 4.4.72; G-AZSZ (27-4194), N6851Y, 3.5.72; G-AZWW (27-4727), N14161, 14.6.72; G-AZXG (27-4328), N6963Y, 30.6.72; G-AZYU (27-4601), N13983, 14.7.72; G-AZZA (27-4016), N6743Y, 18.8.72; G-AZZL (27-4720), N14156, 27.7.72

G-BADD (27-3122), 5Y-ADL, registered 25.7.72, re-registered 1.73 as G-BALU; G-BADE (27-4206), 5Y-AJM, 6.10.72; G-BADI (27-4235), N6885Y, 18.9.72; G-BADJ (27-4841), N14279, 6.10.72; G-BAED (27-3864), N6567Y, 4.11.72; G-BAJX (27-4972), N14346, 23.2.73; G-BAKP (27-4670), N212PB, 9.1.73; G-BALU (27-3122), 5Y-ADL, G-BADD, 2.11.72

Piper PA-28 Cherokee 140

G-ASPK (28-20051), 23.6.64; G-ASSW (28-20055), 5.11.64; G-ASVZ (28-20357), 23.4.65; G-ASWA (28-20349), 4.12.64; G-ATBN (28-20597), 23.4.65; G-ATBO (28-20778), 12.5.65; G-ATEZ (28-21044), 18.10.65; G-ATIV (28-21211), to Holland 2.66 as PH-NLU; G-ATJD (28-21235), 2.2.66; G-ATJE (28-21243), 28.1.66; G-ATJF (28-21283), 13.1.66; G-ATJG (28-21299), 8.2.66; G-ATJH (28-21315), 18.2.66, crashed in the Clwydian Hills, Flint 15.10.66; G-ATMV (28-21465), 1.4.66; G-ATMW (28-21486), 21.4.66; G-ATOI (28-21556), 23.5.66; G-ATOJ (28-21584), 27.5.66; G-ATOK (28-21612), 23.6.66; G-ATOL (28-21626), 23.6.66; G-ATOM (28-21640), 14.7.66; G-ATON (28-21654), 23.6.66; G-ATOO (28-21668), 14.7.66; G-ATOP (28-21682), 4.8.66; G-ATOR (28-21696), 11.8.66; G-ATOS (28-21710), 11.8.66

G-ATPN (28-21899), 25.11.66; G-ATPP (28-21906), 25.11.66; G-ATRO (28-21871), 22.9.66; G-ATRP (18-21885), 25.11.66; G-ATRR (28-21892), 25.11.66; G-ATRS (28-21913), 19.10.67; G-ATRT (28-21920), 29.9.66, d.b.r. at Clacton 15.8.69; G-ATTE (28-21935), 15.9.66; crashed at Royston, Herts. 11.5.67; G-ATTF (28-21939), 2.9.66; G-ATTG (28-21943), 15.9.66; G-ATTH (28-21947), 5.9.66, to Pakistan 4.71 as AP-AWR; G-ATTI (28-21951), 6.10.66; G-ATTJ (28-21955), 1.2.67, to Pakistan 4.71 as AP-AWS; G-ATTK (28-21959), 22.9.66; G-ATTU (28-21987), 28.11.66; G-ATTV (28-21991), 28.11.66; G-ATTW (28-21983), 10.2.67; G-ATUB (28-21971), 19.8.66; G-ATUC (28-21975), 19.8.66; G-ATUD (28-21979), 26.8.66; G-ATVJ (28-21999), to Holland 4.67 as PH-VRH; G-ATVK (28-22006), 11.1.67; G-ATVL (28-22013), 2.12.66; G-ATVO (28-22020), 29.9.66

G-AVBM (28-22527), 7.7.67; G-AVBN (28-22562), 28.7.67, crashed at Sidcup, Kent 30.8.70; G-AVBP (28-22582), 13.4.67; G-AVDD (28-21528), OE-DPD, to Belgium 4.67 as OO-DPY; G-AVFP (28-22652), 13.4.67; G-AVFR (28-22747), 25.5.67; G-AVFX (28-22757), 4.5.67; G-AVFY (28-22762), 27.4.67; G-AVFZ (28-22767), 26.5.67; G-AVGB (28-22772), 19.4.67; G-AVGC (28-22777), 12.5.67; G-AVGD (28-22782), 4.5.67; G-AVGE (28-22787), 19.5.67; G-AVGF (28-22792), 12.5.67; G-AVGG (28-22797), 18.5.67; G-AVGH (28-22802), 25.5.67; G-AVGI (28-22822), 18.5.67; G-AVKV (28-23243), N9759W, not imported; G-AVLA (28-22932), 12.5.67; G-AVLB (28-23158), 11.8.67; G-AVLC (28-23178), 7.9.67; G-AVLD (28-23193), 2.8.67; G-AVLE (28-23223), 21.9.67; G-AVLF (28-23268), 26.10.67; G-AVLG (28-23358), 12.10.67; G-AVLH (28-23368), 7.9.67; G-AVLI (28-23388), 14.9.67; G-AVLJ (28-23393), 31.8.67; G-AVLR (28-23288), 2.11.67; G-AVLS (28-23303), 28.9.67; G-AVLT (28-23328), 21.9.67; G-AVLU (28-23343), 17.9.67

G-AVME (28-21203), N4507R, rebuilt with spare fuselage 28-22700S, 6.7.67; G-AVRP (28-23153), 21.7.67; G-AVRT (28-23143), 8.9.67; G-AVSI (28-23148), 5.4.68; G-AVUP (28-24120), to Ireland 12.68 as EI-ATK; G-AVUR (28-24060), 5.4.68; G-AVUS (28-24065), 19.4.68; G-AVUT (28-24085), 19.4.68; G-AVUU (28-24100), 11.4.68; G-AVWA (28-23660), 9.11.67; G-AVWB (28-23680), 23.11.67; G-AVWD (28-23700), 27.11.67; G-AVWE (28-23720), 18.1.68; G-AVWF (28-23740), to Holland 11.67 as PH-VRK, rest. 2.69, C. of A. 20.5.69; G-AVWG (28-23760), 7.8.68; G-AVWH (28-23780), 18.1.68; G-AVWI (28-23800), 9.5.68; G-AVWJ (28-23940), 4.4.68; G-AVWK (28-23945), 16.5.68, crashed near Morpeth 23.6.68; G-AVWL (28-24000), 21.3.68; G-AVWM (28-24005), 4.4.68; G-AVYO (28-24186), 11.4.68; G-AVYP (28-24211), 1.8.68; G-AVYR (28-24226), 19.12.68

G-AWBD (28-24241), 10.10.68; G-AWBE (28-24266), 2.10.69; G-AWBG (28-24286), 22.8.68; G-AWBH (28-24306), 28.1.69; G-AWBS (28-24331), 28.1.69; G-AWEU (28-24456), 28.8.69; G-AWEV (28-24460), 30.7.69; G-AWEW (28-24468), to Ireland 5.69 as EI-ATN; G-AWEX (28-24472), 20.3.69; G-AWPS (28-20196), 5N-AEK, 6.12.68; G-AWTM (28-25128), 21.8.69; G-AWTN (28-25206), not imported, registered in the U.S.A. as N7299F; G-AWTO (28-25212), not imported, registered in the U.S.A. as N7298F; G-AXAB (28-20238), N6206W, EI-AOA, 7.3.69; G-AYPV (28-25039), 20.1.71; G-AZMX (28-24777), SE-FLL, 24.3.72; G-AZYP (28-25289), LN-MTP, 2.8.72; G-AZZN (28-23674), N3658K, 18.8.72; G-AZZO (28-22887), N4471J, 4.8.72

G-BAFU (28-20759), PH-NLS, 22.1.73; G-BAFW (28-21050), PH-NLT, 13.12.72; G-BAGX (28-23633), N3574K, 19.1.73; G-BAHE (28-26494), N5696U, 19.12.72; G-BAHF (28-25215), N431FL, 3.4.73

Two seat Cherokee 140 trainer G-AXJV, one of a large fleet operated by the Oxford Air Training School, Kidlington. (*Flight Photo 70-1749*)

Piper PA-28 Cherokee 140B

G-AXIO (28-25764), 8.7.69; G-AXIP (28-25790), 11.7.69; G-AXIR (28-25795), 14.7.69; G-AXJV (28-25572), 31.7.69; G-AXJW (28-25656), 22.7.69; G-AXJX (28-25990), 19.9.69; G-AXSZ (28-26188), 11.12.69; G-AXTA (28-26301), 22.1.70; G-AXTB (28-26194), 11.12.69; G-AXTC (28-26265), 16.12.69; G-AXTD (28-26206), 23.12.69; G-AXTE (28-26277), 16.12.69; G-AXTF (28-26224), 22.1.70; G-AXTG (28-26253), 11.12.69; G-AXTH (28-26283), 18.12.69; G-AXTI (28-26259), 11.12.69; G-AXTJ (28-26241), 23.12.69; G-AXTK (28-26235), 15.1.70; G-AXTL (28-26247), 30.12.69; G-AXTM (28-26295), 8.1.70; G-AXTN (28-26307), 22.1.70; G-AZVZ (28-25250), 11.7.72; G-AZWB (28-25244), 1.8.72; G-AZWD (28-25298), 23.6.72; G-AZWE (28-25303), 26.6.72

Piper PA-28 Cherokee 140C

G-AXSH (28-26404), 2.7.70; G-AYDT (28-26558), 22.5.70; G-AYIF (28-26877), 28.8.70; G-AYIG (28-26878), 15.9.70; G-AYIH (28-26910), 25.8.70; G-AYIO (28-26879), N5525U, 18.8.70; G-AYJP (28-26403), 6.10.70; G-AYJR (28-26694), 8.10.70; G-AYJS (28-26916), 15.10.70; G-AYJT (28-26928), 15.10.70; G-AYKV (28-26850), 29.10.70; G-AYKW (28-26931), 10.11.70; G-AYKX (28-26933), 29.10.70; G-AYKY (28-26939), 5.11.70; G-AYMJ (28-26749), 17.12.70; G-AYMK (28-26772), 10.12.70; G-AYML (28-26784), 8.12.70; G-AYMN (28-26754), 25.11.70; G-AYMZ (28-26796), 26.1.71; G-AYNF (28-26778), 12.1.71; G-AYNG (28-26790), 19.1.71; G-AYNJ (28-26810), 7.1.71; G-AYWE (28-26826), N5910U, 2.6.72

Piper PA-28 Cherokee 140D *(1971 model with c/n prefixed 71, e.g. 28-7125049)*

G-AYRM (28-25049), 6.7.71; G-AYUG (28-25139), 29.4.71; G-AZAI (28-25362), 28.6.71; G-AZEG (28-25530), 2.9.71; G-AZFC (28-25486), 10.2.72; G-AZRH (28-25585), 30.3.72; G-BAHR (28-25617), N4227T, 24.11.72; G-BAKH (28-25014), 12.1.73; G-BAKI (28-25015), 9.2.73

Piper PA-28 Cherokee 160 *(160 h.p. Lycoming O-320-B2B)*

G-ARRP (28-52), 12.10.61; G-ARSY (28-103), 19.12.61, d.b.f. at Southend 6.68; G-ARUP (28-127), 14.12.61; G-ARUR (28-133), 17.1.62; G-ARUS (28-159), 18.1.62; G-ARVR (28-280), 20.3.62, crashed at Wolverhampton 26.9.65; G-ARVS (28-339), 13.4.62; G-ARVT (28-379), 2.4.62; G-ARVU (28-410), 9.10.62, to Holland 10.62 as PH-ONY, rest. 4.68; G-ARVV (28-451), 24.10.62; G-ARVW (28-502), 14.3.63; G-ARYO (28-679), not imported; G-ARYP (28-693), not imported; G-ASTC (28-458), N6596D, 16.5.64; G-ATDA (28-206), EI-AME, 6.5.65; G-ATIS (28-2713), 5.11.65; G-AXRL (28-324), D-EFRI, PH-CHE, 6.4.70

Piper PA-28 Cherokee 180 *(180 h.p. Lycoming O-360-A3A)*

G-ARYR (28-770), 6.3.63; G-ASEJ (28-1049), 9.5.63; G-ASEK (28-1082), 24.4.63, crashed at Eskdale, Cumberland 17.9.66; G-ASFL (28-1170), 6.6.63; G-ASHX (28-1266), 9.7.63; G-ASII (28-1264), 9.7.63; G-ASIJ (28-1333), 25.10.63; G-ASIL (28-1350), 16.8.63; G-ASKT (28-1410), 25.3.64; G-ASLM (28-1244), 27.8.63, crashed at Corinth, Greece 21.3.65; G-ASNE (28-1509), 16.3.64; G-ASRW (28-1606), 9.6.64; G-ASUD (28-1654), 11.9.64; G-ASWX (28-1932), 8.1.65; G-ASWY (28-1941), not imported

G-ATAA (28-2055), 1.4.65; G-ATAS (28-2137), 10.5.65; G-ATEM (28-2329), 9.6.65; G-ATHI (28-2525), 19.8.65; G-ATHR (28-2343), EI-AOT, 21.9.65; G-ATHS (28-2800), 21.7.66, sold in the Sudan 2.69; G-ATLW (28-2877), 13.1.66; G-ATNB (28-3057), 6.4.66; G-ATOT (28-3061), 6.5.66; G-ATRU (28-3219), 27.6.66; G-ATTX (28-3390), to Holland 8.66 as PH-VDP; G-ATUL (28-3033), N9007J, 20.5.66; G-ATVS (28-3041), N9014J, 16.6.66; G-ATWO (28-3049), N9021J, 14.7.66; G-ATXM (28-2759), N8809J, 4.8.66; G-ATYS (28-3296), N9226J, 25.8.66; G-ATZK (28-3128), N9090J, 23.9.66

G-AVAX (28-3798), 23.2.67; G-AVAY (28-3793), 16.2.67; G-AVAZ (28-3794), 3.3.67; G-AVBA (28-3795), 10.2.67; G-AVBB (28-3796), 3.3.67; G-AVBC (28-3797), 13.2.67; G-AVBD (28-3799), 23.2.67, destroyed in air collision with Cherokee 180 G-AVBI over Hamble 27.2.70; G-AVBE (28-3800), 23.3.67; G-AVBG (28-3801), 16.3.67; G-AVBH (28-3802), 2.3.67; G-AVBI (28-3803), 13.3.67, destroyed with G-AVBD; G-AVBJ (28-3806), 6.4.67; G-AVBR (28-3931), to France 1.67 as F-BOSO; G-AVBS (28-3938), 1.6.67; G-AVBT (28-3945), 18.5.67; G-AVGK (28-3639), N9516J, 23.2.67

G-AVNM (28-4033), 24.7.67; G-AVNN (28-4049), 3.8.67; G-AVNO (28-4105), 31.8.67; G-AVNP (28-4113), 17.8.67; G-AVNR (28-4121), 3.8.67; G-AVNS (28-4129), 25.8.67; G-AVNT (28-4145), 17.8.67; G-AVNU (28-4153), 25.8.67; G-AVNV (28-4206), 13.9.67; G-AVNW (28-4210), 14.9.67; G-AVOZ (28-3711), N9574J, 15.6.67; G-AVPV (28-2705), 9J-RBP, 8.9.67; G-AVRK (28-4041), 12.7.67; G-AVRU (28-4025), 25.8.67; G-AVRY (28-4089), 15.5.68; G-AVRZ (28-4137), 11.4.68

G-AVSA (28-4184), 15.8.68; G-AVSB (28-4191), 30.3.68; G-AVSC (28-4193), 26.10.67; G-AVSD (28-4195), 19.10.67; G-AVSE (28-4196), 12.10.67; G-AVSF (28-4197), 6.10.67; G-AVSG (28-4377), 15.2.68; G-AVSH (28-4395), 14.3.68; G-AVSP (28-3952), 17.8.67; G-AVVG (28-2909), N7517W, rebuilt with spare fuselage 28-3807S, 15.2.68; G-AVVV (28-2853), rebuilt with spare fuselage 28-3808S, N8880J, 23.3.68; G-AVXZ (28-4340), 11.12.67; G-AVZR (28-4114), 2.2.68; G-AXTP (28-3791), OH-PID, 19.2.70

G-BAAO (28-3980), LN-AEL, 29.9.72; G-BABG (28-2031), N7978W, PH-APU, 26.10.72

Piper PA-28 Cherokee 180D *(1968 model with extra rear cabin window)*

G-AVYL (28-4622), 4.4.68; G-AVYM (28-4638), 11.4.68; G-AVYN (28-4662), 3.5.68, crashed 10 miles west of Ripon, Yorks. 23.9.69; G-AWDP (28-4870), 7.11.68; G-AWET (28-4871), 12.9.68; G-AWIS (28-4979), 9.1.69; G-AWIT (28-4987), 15.10.69; G-AWSL (28-4907), 8.1.69; G-AWTL (28-5068), 13.6.69; G-AWXR (28-5171), 1.5.69; G-AWXS (28-5283), 1.5.69; G-AXIZ (28-5391), 11.7.69, to the Ivory Coast 7.69 as TU-TFB; G-AXMP (28-5436), 8.9.69; G-AXOR (28-5453), 14.10.69

G-AZYF (28-5227), 5Y-AJK, 6.9.72; G-AZZT (28-4604), N5302L, 17.8.72; G-BAJR (28-5008), 15.12.72

Cherokee 180E G-AXXA showing the additional rear window first introduced on the 1968 model 180D. (*Tony Leigh*)

Piper PA-28 Cherokee 180E *(1970 model)*

G-AXSG (28-5605), 16.1.70; G-AXXA (28-5606), 8.5.70; G-AXZC (28-5700), 16.3.70; G-AXZD (28-5609), 16.3.70; G-AXZE (28-5676), 18.3.70; G-AXZF (28-5688), 18.3.70; G-AYAA (28-5799), 26.3.70; G-AYAB (28-5804), 2.4.70; G-AYAP (28-5794), 19.5.70; G-AYAR (28-5797), 7.5.70; G-AYAS (28-5800), 4.6.70; G-AYAT (28-5801), 4.6.70; G-AYAU (28-5802), 11.6.70; G-AYAV (28-5803), 16.6.70; G-AYAW (28-5805), 7.5.70; G-AYBK (28-5806), 4.6.70; G-AYBT (28-5809), 28.5.70; G-AYEE (28-5813), 17.7.70; G-AYEF (28-5815), 21.7.70; G-AYIC (28-5822), 13.8.70, lost at sea between Malta and Sicily 20.12.72; G-AYIE (28-5843), to Italy 9.70 as I-ALPY; G-AYPJ (28-5821), 3.2.71

Piper PA-28 Cherokee 180F *(1971 model with c/n prefixed 71, e.g. 28-715042)*

G-AYUH (28-5042), 6.5.71; G-AYUI (28-5043), not imported, registered in U.S.A. as N8557; G-AZDW (28-5174), 24.9.71; G-AZDX (28-5186), 27.8.71; G-AZLN (28-5210), 11.1.72; G-AZSG (28-5166), 18.5.72

Piper PA-28 Cherokee 180G *(1972 model with c/n prefixed 72)*

G-AZVV (28-5171), 7.6.72

Piper PA-28 Cherokee 235 *(235 h.p. Lycoming O-540-B2B5)*

G-ASLV (28-10048), 9.7.64; G-AWSM (28-11125), 24.12.68; G-BAMM (28-10642), SE-EOA, registered 1.73

Piper PA-28R Cherokee Arrow 180 *(from 1971, c/n prefixed with year of construction)*

G-AVWN (28R-30170), 26.1.68; G-AVWO (28R-30205), 5.3.68; GAVWP (28R-30219), to Ireland 2.68 as EI-ASV; G-AVWR (28R-30242), 7.3.68; G-AVWS (28R-30326), 30.4.68, d.b.r. at Creon, France 14.10.71; G-AVWT (28R-30362), 5.4.68; G-AVWU (28R-30380), 13.5.68; G-AVWV (28R-30404), 20.6.68; G-AVXF (28R-30044), 10.11.67; G-AVYS (28R-30456), 2.5.68, crashed near Cherbourg, France 5.9.71; G-AVYT (28R-30472), 30.5.68

G-AWAY (28R-30496), 5.6.68; G-AWAZ (28R-30512), 27.6.68; G-AWBA (28R-30528), 7.8.68; G-AWBB (28R-30552), 27.2.69; G-AWBC (28R-30572), 15.5.69; G-AWEY (28R-30612), 3.4.69, d.b.r. 6.70; G-AWEZ (28R-30592), 1.5.69; G-AWFA (28R-30691), 12.9.68, to the U.S.A. 7.69 as N23653; G-AWFB (28R-30689), 19.9.69; G-AWFC (28R-30670), 13.6.69; G-AWFD (28R-30669), 26.7.68; G-AWFJ (28R-30688), 8.5.69; G-AWFK (28R-30690), 12.9.69; G-AWIU (28R-30717), 9.12.69, crashed near Conway, North Wales 11.6.71

G-AZGM (28R-30411), N4550J, 18.11.71; G-AZSH (28R-30461), N4612J, 28.4.72; G-AZSM (28R-30684), 5Y-AIQ, 23.5.72; G-AZWS (28R-30749), N4993J, 13.6.72

Piper PA-28R Cherokee Arrow 200

G-AXCA (28R-35053), 9.10.69; G-AXWZ (28R-35605), 2.7.70; G-AYAC (28R-35606), 28.4.70; G-AYHZ (28R-35737), 7.8.70; G-AYII (28R-35736), 11.9.70; G-AYPU (28R-35005), 4.2.71; G-AYPW (28R-35791), 18.2.71, crashed at Halfpenny Green 28.8.72; G-AYRI (28R-35004), 26.1.71; G-AYWW (28R-35049), 29.4.71; G-AYYN (28R-35054), 2.6.71

G-AZAJ (28R-35116), 30.7.71; G-AZDE (28R-35141), 25.8.71; G-AZFI (28R-35160), 29.9.71; G-AZFM (28R-35218), 28.12.71; G-AZNL (28R-35006), 25.3.72; G-AZOG (28R-35009), 29.3.72; G-AZRV (28R-35191), N2309T, 6.4.72; G-AZSF (28R-35048), 5.5.72; G-AZSN (28R-35642), N3083R, 26.6.72; G-AZTT (28R-35205), N2316T, 17.5.72; G-BAAZ (28R-35146), 200B, N2388T, 17.8.72

Piper PA-28R Cherokee Arrow 200-2 *(1972 model with 200 h.p. Lycoming IO-360-CK, increased span and length, and c/n prefixed 72, e.g. 28R-7235044)*

G-AZSE (28R-35044), 12.5.72; G-BAAP (28R-35205), G-AZYO ntu, 10.8.72; G-BAAR (28R-35197), 15.8.72; G-BAHS (28R-35017), N15147, 16.11.72; G-BAHZ (28R-35289), 21.12.72, to Ireland 1.73 as EI-AWL; G-BAIH (28R-35011), 2.1.73; G-BAJT (28R-35294), 21.12.72; G-BALW (28R-35007), 1.3.73; G-BAMY (28R-35015), 13.2.73

Piper PA-30 Twin Comanche 160

G-ASJM (30-33), 9.9.63; G-ASLD (30-58), 14.8.63, to South Africa 8.71, rest. 10.71, crashed at Bembridge, I.O.W. 5.5.72; G-ASLE (30-88), 5.11.63; G-ASMA (30-143), 27.11.63; G-ASMH (30-180), 12.11.63; G-ASMI (30-112), crashed at Gander during delivery 27.11.63; G-ASMR (30-227), 16.1.64; G-ASOA (30-285), 18.2.64, crashed at St. Mary's, Isles of Scilly 10.5.64; G-ASOB (30-279), 13.2.64; G-ASON (30-312), 9.3.64; G-ASOO (30-334), 6.3.64; G-ASOR (30-344), sold in France 10.64; G-ASRH (30-368), 14.6.64; G-ASRN (30-381), 5.5.64, crashed at Newbury, Berks. 18.6.72; G-ASRO (30-395), 24.4.64; G-ASRU (30-376), 13.10.64; G-ASSA (30-421), 19.5.64; G-ASSB (30-432), 24.5.64; G-ASSP (30-458), 9.6.64; G-ASSR (30-467), 9.6.64; G-ASUT (30-347), N7303Y, 30.7.64, to Denmark 8.68 as OY-BKO; G-ASWW (30-556), N7531Y, 2.10.64; G-ASYK (30-573), N7543Y, 11.11.64; G-ASYO (30-570), N7532Y, 4.6.65

The primary role of British registered Twin Comanches was that of air taxi, illustrated here by G-ASON in Gregory colours. (*Alan Hall*)

G-ATEN (30-544), N7483Y, 31.5.65; G-ATET (30-770), N7749Y, 4.6.65; G-ATEW (30-719), N7640Y, 4.6.65; G-ATFK (30-721), N7642Y, 22.7.65; G-ATMT (30-439), N7385Y, 15.2.66, to Cranfield for experimental flying 1.71 as XW938; G-ATSE (30-983), N7896Y, 18.3.66; G-ATSZ (30-1002), N7912Y, 22.4.66; G-ATUO (30-1063), N7965Y, 16.5.66, crashed near Issoire, France 22.3.68; G-ATVA (30-1001), N7911Y, 14.12.67, to the U.S.A. 12.68 as N7126G; G-ATWG (30-1094), N7990Y, 14.7.66; G-ATWR (30-1134), N8025Y, 27.7.66; G-ATXD (30-1166), N8053Y, 14.7.66; G-ATYF (30-1205), N8089Y, 19.8.66; G-ATYR (30-1183), N8069Y, 15.9.66; G-ATZU (30-1271), N8158Y, 20.10.66; G-ATZV (30-1278), N8165Y, 2.11.67

G-AVAO (30-1132), N8023Y, 10.11.66; G-AVAU (30-1328), N8230Y, 7.12.66; G-AVBL (30-1362), N8236Y, 1.2.67; G-AVCP (30-1197), N8082Y, 16.12.66; G-AVCW (30-1375), N8249Y, 2.3.67; G-AVCX (30-1302), N8185Y, 12.1.67; G-AVCY (30-1367), N8241Y, 26.1.67; G-AVFV (30-1404), N8275Y, 23.3.67, crashed into high ground near Snowdon, North Wales 22.10.72; G-AVFW (30-1410), N8278Y, 9.6.67; G-AVGT (30-123), N7105Y, 4.4.67; G-AVHW (30-1414), N8280Y, 29.8.67; G-AVHZ (30-1424), N8287Y, 13.4.67; G-AVJJ (30-1420), N8285Y, 27.4.67; G-AVJT (30-1415), N8281Y, 27.4.68; G-AVKL (30-1418), N8284Y, 3.5.68, to Denmark 11.68 as OY-DHL; G-AVNI (30-1430), N8292Y, 22.6.67; G-AVPF (30-1427), N8289Y, 7.7.67; G-AVPR (30-1511), N8395Y, 21.7.67; G-AVPS (30-1548), N8393Y, 13.7.67; G-AVSJ (30-1327), N8229Y, 31.8.67, crashed near Col du Mont, Verdun, France 23.4.72; G-AVTI (30-1337), N8210Y, 6.12.67; G-AVUD (30-1515), N8422Y, 5.10.67; G-AVUN (30-1329), N8231Y, 22.9.67; G-AWOG (30-1401), N8272Y, 5N-APW, 16.8.68, sold in Japan 8.70; G-AZAB (30-1475), 5H-MNM, 25.6.71

Piper PA-30 Twin Comanche 160B

G-AVVI (30-1613), N8454Y, 6.10.67, to Ireland 6.71 as EI-AVD, rest. 8.71; G-AWBN (30-1472), N8517Y, 29.1.68; G-AWBT (30-1668), N8508Y, 4.4.68; G-AWFI (30-1697), N8536Y, 3.4.69; G-AWIX (30-1704), N8557Y, 10.5.68; G-AWKF (30-1712), N8565Y, 5.6.68; G-AWMB (30-1716), N8569Y, 19.7.68; G-AXRW (30-1774), N8633Y, 5Y-ADM, 29.5.70, crashed at Shipdham, Norfolk 23.1.73

Piper PA-30 Twin Comanche 160C

G-AXAU (30-1753), N8613Y, 22.5.69; G-AXAV (30-1793), N8651Y, 19.6.69; G-AXCO (30-1802), N8660Y, 19.5.69; G-AXDL (30-1856), N8707Y, 21.4.69; G-AXER (30-1820), N8676Y, 22.5.69, to Ireland 12.69 as EI-ANU, rest. 2.71; G-AXMS (30-1974), N8816Y, 2.9.69; G-AXMY (30-1879), N8726Y, 26.8.69; G-AXRO (30-1978), N8820Y, 7.11.69; G-AXSP (30-1982), N8824Y, 31.12.69; G-AYAD (30-1999), N8838Y, 14.4.70; G-AYAF (30-2000), N8842Y, 21.4.70; G-AYSB (30-1916), N8760Y, 25.2.71; G-AZFO (30-1917), N8761Y, PA-39 conversion, 4.1.72; G-BAKJ (30-1232), TJ-AAI, 27.2.73

Piper PA-31 Navajo

G-AVZT (31-86), N9059Y, 15.3.68; G-AWED (31-109), N9076Y, 4.7.68; G-AWOW (31-229), N9172Y, 31.9.68; G-AXAZ (31-245), N9184Y, 11.3.69; G-AXDD (31-376), N9284Y, 3.7.69; G-AXIS (31-466), N6551L, 22.7.69; G-AXMR (31-473), N6558L, 7.10.69; G-AXUH (31-501), N6576L, 30.12.69, sold in Angola 5.70; G-AXXB (31-583), N6645L, 24.2.70; G-AXYA (31-632), N6731L, 24.3.70; G-AXYB (31-641), N6736L, 14.4.70, to Nigeria 10.72 as 5N-AEQ; G-AXYC (31-642), N6737L, 23.4.70

G-AYEI (31-631), N6730L, 18.6.70; G-AYFZ (31-679), N6771L, 3.8.70; G-AYLJ (31-693), N6783L, 3.11.70; G-AYNB (31-688), N6778L, 22.12.70; G-AYSE (31-323), 9Q-CSO, 16.4.71; G-AYUF (31-700), N6790L, 19.5.71; G-AYVM (31-516), N6589L, 8.4.71; G-AZAC (31-701), N6791L, 18.6.71; G-AZBG (31-569), N6633L, 15.7.71; G-AZBP (31-551), N6617L, 19.7.71; G-AZDH (31-728), N7215L, 13.9.71; G-AZHL (31-760), N7238L, 9.12.71; G-AZIM (31-776), N7250L, 2.12.71; G-AZME (31-754), N7232L, 14.1.72; G-AZTL (31-589), N6650L, 28.4.72, crashed near Stapleford 3.1.73; G-AZUH (31-780), N7430L, 30.5.72

G-BACG (31-46), 5Y-AFY, 6.10.72; G-BAEG (31-761), N7239L, 10.10.72

Piper PA-32 Cherokee Six 260

G-ATES (32-20), 27.10.65; G-ATJV (32-103), 3.1.66; G-ATRW (32-360), 27.5.66; G-ATRX (32-390), 28.4.66; G-ATTY (32-460), 3.6.66; G-ATVC (32-99), N3269W, 23.5.66; G-AVBU (32-733), 16.2.67; G-AVBV (32-743), not imported, went to Israel as 4X-ANG; G-AVTJ (32-219), rebuilt with spare fuselage 32-860S, N3373W, 18.8.67; G-AVTK (32-223), rebuilt with spare fuselage 32-856S, N3266W, 25.8.67; G-AWCX (32-206), rebuilt with spare fuselage 32-859S, N3360W, 8.4.71; G-AWCY (32-211), rebuilt with spare fuselage 32-858S, N3365W, 2.4.69; G-AWCZ (32-225), rebuilt with spare fuselage 32-857S, N3294W, 21.5.71; G-AZMO (32-499), SE-EYN, 15.2.72; G-AZYE (32-646), N3732N, 5Y-AEA, 4.8.72

Piper PA-32 Cherokee Six 300 *(c/n prefixed with year of construction from G-AYWK)*

G-AVFS (32-40038), 2.5.67; G-AVFT (32-40108), 22.5.68, to Ireland 6.68 as EI-ASY; G-AVFU (32-40182), 17.8.67; G-AVUY (32-40305), 13.6.68; G-AVUZ (32-40302), 1.2.68; G-AXBC (32-40685), 23.7.69; G-AXZX (32-40182), cancelled (already registered as G-AVFU); G-AYWK (32-40008), N8616N, 6.5.71; G-AZDJ (32-40068), N5273S, 26.8.71; G-AZTD (32-40001), N8611N, 19.5.72

G-BADO (32-40011), N8664N, 19.9.72; G-BAGG (32-40007), 24.11.72; G-BAHV (32-40118), N1400T, 17.12.72, G-BAIA (32-40006), 14.12.72

Piper PA-34 Seneca 200 *(c/n prefixed with year of construction, e.g. 34-7250018)*

G-AZIK (34-50018), N2392T, 15.12.71; G-AZJB (34-50017), N1036U, 9.12.71;

G-AZOL (34-50075), N4348T, 9.3.72; G-AZON (34-50081), N4381T, 13.4.72; G-AZOT (34-50073), N4340T, 5.5.72; G-AZTO (34-50141), N4516T, 15.5.72; G-AZVJ (34-50125), N4529T, 19.5.72; G-AZXH (34-50215), N5068T, 12.7.72; G-AZZS (34-50221), N5212T, 10.8.72

G-BABK (34-50219), N5203T, 22.8.72; G-BACB (34-50251), N5354T, 1.9.72; G-BADL (34-50247), N5307T, 25.10.72; G-BAGZ (34-50007), N15067, 16.1.73, to Ireland 6.73 as EI-AWS; G-BAIG (34-50243), N5257T, 7.12.72; G-BAKD (34-50013), N1378T, 22.1.73; G-BAMZ (34-50035), N15209, 15.2.73

Piper PA-39 Twin Comanche *(Lycoming IO-320-B1A port; LIO-320-B1A starboard)*

G-AYFI (39-67), N8911Y, 2.7.70; G-AYFT (39-66), N8922Y, 8.7.70; G-AYIP (39-65), N8910Y, 21.8.70; G-AYKO (39-80), N8921Y, 23.10.70; G-AYLB (39-63), N8908Y, 23.10.70; G-AYWV (39-84), N8927Y, 15.7.71; G-AYWZ (39-85), N8928Y, 3.6.71; G-AYXA (39-86), N8929Y, 6.7.71; G-AYXY (39-87), N8930Y, 20.7.71; G-AYXZ (39-88), N8931Y, 22.7.71; G-AYZE (39-92), N8934Y, 27.5.71; G-AYZP (39-91), N8933Y, 15.6.71; G-AYZY (39-89), N8949Y, 25.6.71; G-AZBC (39-111), N8951Y, 19.8.71; G-AZBD (39-112), N8952Y, 19.8.71; G-AZBF (39-113), N8953Y, 7.10.71; G-AZBW (39-114), N8954Y, 4.8.71; G-AZIA (39-129), N8966Y, 9.12.71; G-AZMW (39-54), D-GMWV, 19.4.72; G-AZNM (39-130), N8967Y, 15.6.72, sold in West Germany 8.72; G-BALP (39-145), N8979Y, 17.1.73

Pitts S-1 Special

G-AXNZ (EB.1/PFA.1383), completed by A. Etheridge and W. Berry at Old Warden in 1973; first flown 6.6.73

G-AYLU (370-H/PFA.1526), under construction by J. Randall at Crowthorne, Berks. in 1973

G-AZCE (373-H/PFA.1527), under construction by R. J. Oulton at Lydney, Glos. in 1973

G-AZPH (S-1S-001-C), N11CB, first flown in the U.S.A. 3.3.70, uncrated at Farnborough 12.4.72, C. of A. 25.5.72, Aerobatics International Ltd., competitor in World Aerobatic Championships, Marseilles 7.72

Robinson Redwing

G-AAUO (1), Mk.I, 26.6.30, Robinson Aircraft Co. Ltd., Croydon; evaluated by the Scarborough Aeroplane Club; crashed at Shoreham 11.3.33

G-ABDO (2), first Mk.II, 6.12.30, Robinson Aircraft Co. Ltd.; Miss E. R. Gerrans, Maylands, Romford 8.34; damaged in hangar fire at Gravesend 7.37

G-ABLA (3), 4.5.31, Redwing Aircraft Ltd.; Wiltshire School of Flying Ltd., High Post 10.31; crashed at Great Durnford, Wilts. 12.10.32

G-ABMF (5), 6.6.31, Will Hay, Brooklands; Wiltshire School of Flying Ltd., High Post 8.34; C. H. Burge, Broxbourne 6.36; W. H. Sparrow, Christchurch 5.38; sold in the Midlands during the 1939–45 war

G-ABMJ (4), 22.5.31, Scarborough Aeroplane Club; Miss D. Reynolds, Gatwick 3.33; Miss R. Norman, Heston 3.34; to Ireland 12.34 as EI-ABC

G-ABMU (6), 1.7.31, Eastern Counties Aeroplane Club, Ipswich or Colchester, crashed at Ipswich 5.1.33

G-ABMV (7), 22.7.31, L.G.O.C. Flying Club, Broxbourne; shipped to H. T. Parry, Hokitika, New Zealand 4.33 as ZK-ADD; to instructional airframe 1942

G-ABNP (8), 20.8.31, Eastern Counties Aeroplane Club, Ipswich or Colchester; damaged beyond repair in forced landing at Frinton, Essex late in 1935

John Pothecary flying his restored Redwing II, G-ABNX. (*Aviation Photo News*)

G-ABNX (9), 12.3.32, C. P. Hunter, Hooton; S. Reid, Macmerry 5.35; Edinburgh Flying Club 3.38; College of Aeronautical Engineering, Redhill 4.51; V. Mitchell, Panshanger 1953; later stored at Heath End near Farnham, Surrey; J. Pothecary and E. H. Gould, Christchurch 12.59; re-issued with A. to F. 30.3.62; based at Slinfold by J. Pothecary in 1973

G-ABOK (10), 19.10.31, Redwing Aircraft Ltd., Gatwick; G. J. Dawson, Gatwick 6.34; destroyed in hangar fire while on overhaul at Gravesend 7.37

G-ABRL (11), Mk.III, first flown 5.33; reconverted to Mk.II; C. of A. 21.12.34, Redwing Aircraft Ltd.; flown to Africa by Mrs. Keith Miller; wrecked in forced landing 10 miles from Kotonu, Dahomey 5.2.35

G-ABRM (12), Mk.II, 22.2.33, Eastern Counties Aeroplane Club, Ipswich; damaged beyond repair in 1935

Rollason D.31 Turbulent *(with special category C. of A., see also Druine, Vol. 2, p. 508)*

G-AJCP (PFA.512), re-allocation of Anson 1 registration (ntu) as owner's initials; A. to F. 20.3.59, G. J. C. Paul, Fairoaks; J. M. Fowler, Fairoaks 8.65; N. H. Kempt, Panshanger 6.66

G-APBZ (PFA.440), first flown 1.1.58, A. to F. 7.2.58, N. H. Jones, Croydon; P. J. Sullivan, Redhill 7.61; F. G. Bennett and partner, Fairoaks 1.62; d.b.r. in forced landing at Berck, France 15.4.63

G-APIZ (PFA.478), first flown 2.4.58, A. to F. 3.4.58, Miss J. H. Short, Cambridge: N. H. Jones, Redhill (Tiger Club) 6.61; crashed at West Clandon, Surrey 25.5.63

G-APKZ (PFA.479), first flown 13.6.58, A. to F. 13.6.58, G. Stewart (Biggin Hill Flying Club); crashed near Biggin Hill 6.12.60

G-APLZ (PFA.480), 20.11.58, N. H. Jones, Redhill; J. B. Griffiths, Redhill 5.61; I. B. Willis, Norwich 3.67; P. S. Bryan, Swanton Morley 6.69; C. Slack and partners, Swanton Morley 5.71

G-APMZ (PFA.481), 16.5.59, N. H. Jones, Redhill (Tiger Club); J. D. Lawther, Newtownards 3.63; crashed at Newtownards 1.2.64

G-APNZ (PFA.482), 25.6.59, N. H. Jones, Redhill (Tiger Club); won King's Cup Race at Baginton 8.7.60, pilot J. de M. Severne

G-APTZ (PFA.508), 7.7.59, Hon. J. C. Baring, Redhill; P. W. F. Sterry, Fairoaks 6.65; J. Mackay, Wick 4.67; G. Edmiston, Thurso 9.72

G-APVZ (PFA.545), 19.2.60, N. H. Jones (Tiger Club), Croydon; J. P. Garood, Cambridge 4.63; W. A. Draper, Alconbury 8.67; E. Gardner, Hemswell 1.70; F. R. Maw, Sibson 10.72

G-APYZ (PFA.546), 11.6.59, C. W. Carver, Fairoaks; D. J. Lovell, Redhill 4.62; P. G. Russell, Lincoln 5.68; J. N. Gladish, Sherburn 7.69; P. J. Crediton, Sherburn 4.72; A. R. Lee, Little Snoring 5.73

G-APZZ (PFA.552), 12.5.60, N. H. Nones (Tiger Club), Redhill; R. G. d'Erlanger, Redhill 8.62; ditched in the English Channel 10.7.64

G-ARBZ (PFA.553), 16.1.61, Mrs. J. H. Waugh, Pocklington; M. B. Lucking, High Easter 6.67; C. Y. Lee, Biggin Hill 1.71; D. Hilliard, Bodmin 8.72

G-ARCZ (PFA.554), 14.11.60, N. H. Jones, Redhill (Tiger Club); G. R. Janney, Redhill 4.65; A. H. Green, Writtle 6.66; R. W. Morgan, Portsmouth 3.69; J. West, Booker 2.71

G-AREZ (PFA.561), 21.11.60, C. M. D. Roberts, Staverton

G-ARGZ (PFA.562), 30.3.61, N. H. Jones, Redhill (Tiger Club); D. S. Crichton, Biggin Hill 5.63; B. G. Pleasance, Stapleford 6.66; R. G. Stock, Rochester 5.69; G. S. Long and partners, Jenkins Farm, Navestock 5.72

G-ARIZ (PFA.563), 28.3.61, N. H. Jones, Redhill (Tiger Club), destroyed in air collision with Taylorcraft Plus D EI-ALJ/G-AHAD, Limerick, Eire 25.8.62

Starting the 40 h.p. Ardem 4CO2 engine of the Tiger Club's Turbulent seaplane G-ARJZ at Lee-on-Solent in 1968. (*Air Pictorial*)

G-ARJZ (PFA.564), 14.4.61, N. H. Jones, Tiger Club seaplane flown at Lee-on-Solent 1967–70 and from the Club's seaplane base at Rye, Sussex from 2.73

G-ARMZ (PFA.565), 4.8.61, N. H. Jones, Redhill (Tiger Club); N. J. Minchin, Fairoaks 6.64; A. Mackintosh, Shobdon 9.66; F. Shepherd, Dunstable 1.73

G-ARNZ (PFA.579), 22.8.61, N. H. Jones, Redhill (Tiger Club); F. Goatcher, Portsmouth 7.66; R. M. Long, Navestock 5.68; R. W. Morris, Stapleford 3.70; J. N. Eccott, Ringway 9.71

G-ARRZ (PFA.580), 17.4.62, N. H. Jones, Redhill (Tiger Club)

G-ARZM (PFA.581), cabin model, 27.4.62, N. H. Jones, Redhill (Tiger Club)

G-ASAM (PFA.595), 24.9.63, N. H. Jones, Redhill (Tiger Club); won King's Cup Race at Rochester 12.7.69, pilot R. G. d'Erlanger

G-ASDB (PFA.1600), 3.11.64, N. H. Jones, Redhill (Tiger Club), crashed at Shoreham during air display 11.8.68

G-ASDE (PFA.1601), 26.9.63, Rollason Aircraft and Engines Ltd., Croydon; left Croydon 22.9.64 crated for shipment to Fort Worth, Texas for M. H. Spinks Jnr.; re-registered N69M on arrival

G-ASHT (PFA.1610), 23.7.63, A. J. Tyrrell, Redhill; H. Beckwith, Yeadon 6.70; crashed at Thornwaite, near Harrogate, Yorks. 1.5.71

G-ASMM (PFA.1611), 9.6.65, Bee-Bee Flying Ltd., Shoreham; K. A. Browne, Redhill 6.69

Rollason D.31A Turbulent *(with full C. of A.)*

G-ARLZ (RAE.578), 9.9.66, N. H. Jones, operated by the Fairoaks Aero Club; Usworth Flying Group 7.73

G-AWPA (RAE.100), 29.1.69, N. H. Jones, leased to Usworth Flying Group

G-AWPB (RAE.101), 16.4.69, J. B. Griffiths and Dick Emery Ltd., Redhill; crashed during an air display at Sleap 25.5.70

The Rollason D.62 Condor prototype in 1965 with all-yellow colour scheme and 90 h.p. Continental engine. (*A. J. Jackson*)

Rollason D.62 Condor *(75 h.p. Continental A75)*

G-ARHZ (PFA.247), 11.8.61, N. H. Jones, Redhill; fitted with 90 h.p. Continental C90-14F in 1964; F. W. Tilley, Rochester 5.67; J. W. Spiers, Lympne 10.71

Note: The sole British home-built Condor was D.62 G-AVJH (PFA.603), commenced at Sidcup, Kent, but moved to Rochester in 1964 for completion by owner J. Norton. Powered by a 90 h.p. Continental C90-8F, it flew at Rochester in 1971. Registration G-ARWG, allotted in advance 12.58 to home-built D.62 Condor PFA.600, embodied the initials of R. Watling-Greenwood who, with G. P. Sykes, began construction but sold it incomplete. H. Garner and J. Fitzgerald were continuing the project in 1972

Rollason D.62A Condor *(100 h.p. Rolls-Royce Continental O-200-A)*

G-ARVZ (RAE.606), 29.8.63, Rollason Aircraft and Engines Ltd.; operated by the Stapleford Flying Club in 1973

G-ASEU (RAE.607), 12.3.64, N. H. Jones, Redhill; operated by the British Women Pilots' Association, Fairoaks; to Brighton Flying Group, Shoreham 1972

Rollason D.62B Condor *(Fuselage four inches shorter; flaps fitted to G-ATOH and subsequent aircraft)*

G-ASRB (RAE.608), 28.1.65, Rollason Aircraft and Engines Ltd.; operated by the West Essex Flying Club, Biggin Hill in 1973

G-ASRC (RAE.609), 4.2.65, N. H. Jones; converted to D.62C in 1970; operated by the Kent Gliding Club, Challock in 1973

G-ATAU (RAE.610), 24.8.65, N. H. Jones; operated by the Rochester Flying Club in 1973

G-ATAV (RAE.611), 8.10.65, N. H. Jones; converted to D.62C in 1969; operated by the Doncaster Gliding Club in 1973

G-ATOH (RAE.612), 18.3.66, N. H. Jones; operated by the Fairoaks Aero Club in 1973

G-ATSK (RAE.613), 5.5.66, N. H. Jones; operated by the Fairoaks Aero Club in 1973; crashed at Fairoaks 20.7.73

G-ATUG (RAE.614), 17.6.66, N. H. Jones; operated by the Blackbushe Aero Club in 1973

G-ATVW (RAE.615), 29.9.66, N. H. Jones; operated by the Armstrong Whitworth Flying Group, Baginton in 1973

G-AVAW (RAE.617), 15.2.67, N. H. Jones; operated by the Dorset Flying Club, Compton Abbas in 1973

G-AVCZ (RAE.618), 3.3.67, N. H. Jones, Redhill; winner of Manx Air Derby 28.4.68 piloted by owner; operated by the Stapleford Flying Club in 1973

G-AVDW (RAE.619), 11.3.67, N. H. Jones; operated by the Fairoaks Aero Club in 1973

G-AVEX (RAE.616), 7.4.67, N. H. Jones, operated by the Rochester Flying Club in 1973

G-AVKM (RAE.620), 6.6.67, N. H. Jones; operated by the Hull Aero Club, Paull in 1973

G-AVMB (RAE.621), 17.7.67, N. H. Jones; operated by the Sherburn Aero Club, Sherburn-in-Elmet in 1973

G-AVOH (RAE.622), 18.8.67, N. H. Jones; operated by the Fairoaks Aero Club in 1973

G-AVRV (RAE.623), 3.11.67, Rollason Aircraft and Engines Ltd.; operated by the Wycombe Air Centre; crashed in the sea off Folkestone 6.7.68 after air collision with Beagle Airedale G-ARZR

G-AVVN (RAE.624), 7.12.67, N. H. Jones; operated by the Scottish Gliding Union, Portmoak, Kinross in 1972; converted to D.62C in 3.73; Norfolk Gliding Club, Tibbenham 3.73

G-AVXW (RAE.625), 5.1.68, N. H. Jones; operated by the Portsmouth Flying School in 1973

G-AVZE (RAE.626), 13.2.68, N. H. Jones; operated by the Sherburn Aero Club, Sherburn-in-Elmet in 1973

G-AWAT (RAE.627), 10.4.68, N. H. Jones; operated by the Lincoln Aero Club, Hemswell in 1973

G-AWFI (RAE.628), 24.5.68, N. H. Jones; operated by the Sherburn Aero Club, Sherburn-in-Elmet in 1973

G-AWFN (RAE.629), 18.8.68, N. H. Jones; operated by the West Essex Flying Club, Biggin Hill in 1973

G-AWFO (RAE.630), 27.8.68, N. H. Jones; operated by the West Essex Flying Club, Biggin Hill in 1973

G-AWFP (RAE.631), 10.12.68, N. H. Jones; operated by the Brighton Flying Group, Shoreham in 1973

G-AWSN (RAE.632), 31.1.69, N. H. Jones; operated by the Rochester Flying Club in 1973

G-AWSO (RAE.633), 1.4.69, N. H. Jones; operated by the Sherburn Aero Club, Sherburn-in-Elmet in 1973

G-AWSP (RAE.634), 29.5.69, N. H. Jones; operated by Nipper Aircraft Ltd., Castle Donington in 1970; later by the Goodwood Flying School

G-AWSR (RAE.635), 4.7.69, N. H. Jones; operated by the South Yorkshire Flying Club, Doncaster; operated by The Rochford Hundred Flying Group, Southend 12.72–3.73; Fenland Aero Club, Holbeach 4.73

G-AWSS (RAE.636), 16.4.69, N. H. Jones, Redhill; converted to D.62C in 1970; later operated by the Coventry Gliding Club, Husbands Bosworth

G-AWST (RAE.637), 23.7.69, N. H. Jones; operated by the South Yorkshire Flying Club, Doncaster; crashed at Old Edlington, Yorks. 1.7.71

G-AXGS (RAE.638), 6.10.69, N. H. Jones, Redhill; long range version entered by owner in London–Sydney Air Race 12.69

G-AXGT (RAE.639), 1.11.69, N. H. Jones; operated by the South Yorkshire Flying Club, Doncaster in 1971

G-AXGU (RAE.640), 5.12.69, N. H. Jones; operated by the Dorset Flying Club, Compton Abbas in 1971

G-AXGV (RAE.641), 26.1.70, N. H. Jones; operated by the Doncaster Aero Club in 1973

G-AXGZ (RAE.643), 27.7.70, N. H. Jones; operated by the Lincoln Aero Club, Hemswell in 1973

G-AYFC (RAE.644), 14.9.70, N. H. Jones; operated by the Stapleford Flying Club in 1973

G-AYFD (RAE.645), 14.12.70, N. H. Jones; operated by the West Lancashire Aero Club, Woodvale in 1972

G-AYFF (RAE.647), 2.2.71, N. H. Jones; operated by the Doncaster Aero Club in 1973

G-AYFH (RAE.649), 4.6.71, N. H. Jones; operated by the Fairoaks Aero Club in 1973

G-AYZS (RAE.650), 26.1.72, N. H. Jones; operated by the Blackbushe Aero Club in 1973

G-AYZT (RAE.651), 10.3.72, N. H. Jones; operated by the Hull Aero Club, Paull in 1973

G-BADM (RAE.653), registered 8.9.72, Rollason Aircraft and Engines Ltd.

Rollason D.62C Condor *(130 h.p. Rolls-Royce Continental O-240-A)*

G-AXGY (RAE.642), 30.6.70, N. H. Jones; operated by the South Yorkshire Flying Club, Doncaster; crashed at Bessacarr, near Doncaster 25.2.71

G-AYFE (RAE.646), 15.2.71, N. H. Jones; operated by the London Gliding Club, Dunstable in 1973

G-AYFG (RAE.648), 16.4.71, N. H. Jones; operated by the Coventry Gliding Club, Husbands Bosworth in 1973

G-AZMV (RAE.652), 30.3.72, N. H. Jones; operated by the Ouse Gliding Club, Rufforth in 1973

Rollason Beta

G-ATEE (PFA.247 reallocated from prototype Condor), the Luton Group's prototype, registered 1967 to D. G. Wiggins but was not completed

G-ATLY (RAE.01), Beta B.1, A. to F. 14.2.68, Rollason Aircraft and Engines Ltd., Redhill 'Forerunner'; converted to B.2; won Manx Air Derby 26.4.69, pilot F. Marsh

G-AWHV (RAE.02), Beta B.2, A. to F. 27.3.69, Rollason Aircraft and Engines Ltd., Redhill 'Blue Chip'; won Goodyear Trophy at Halfpenny Green 1.9.69, pilot D. M. Jones

G-AWHW (RAE.03), Beta B.4, 3.7.69, T. D. Motors Ltd., Tollerton; M. Hennessey, Shobden 'Dandy Dick' 5.70; Rollason Aircraft and Engines Ltd., Redhill 1.72

G-AWHX (RAE.04), Beta B.2, 15.12.71, F. Marsh, Cambridge 'Pie in the Sky'

G-AXYV (PFA.2202/6), registered 1970 to D. G. Wiggins; under construction by the Luanda University Ultra Light Aircraft Construction Group; Angola in 1972

G-BADC (JJF.1/PFA.1384), registered 7.9.72 to J. J. Feeley, and under construction at Ashford, Middlesex in 1973

The prototype Cutty Sark in its ultimate form with amphibian undercarriage and Gipsy II engines. (*Flight Photo 10681*)

Saro A.17 Cutty Sark

G-AAIP (A.17/1), 13.9.29, Saunders-Roe Ltd., East Cowes; N. Holden, Selsey 4.30; S. Kirston and R. Mace, Woolston 5.30; C. Shaw and T. Rose, t/a Isle of Man Air Services 1.32; sold 5.33; scrapped in 1935

G-AAVX (A.17/4), 5.5.30, Saunders-Roe Ltd., East Cowes; Royal Singapore Flying Club 12.30; re-registered in Singapore 10.34 as VR-SAA; scrapped 1935

G-ABBC (A.17/5), 2.7.30, Saunders-Roe Ltd., East Cowes; Francis Francis, Heston 1.31; British Amphibious Air Lines Ltd., Squires Gate 'Progress' 3.32; stored at East Cowes from 4.35 until destroyed by German bombing 4.5.42

G-ABVF (A.17/9), 30.3.32, Saunders-Roe Ltd., East Cowes; sold to the Japanese round-the-world pilot Yoshihara 5.32

G-ACDP (A.17/10), 11.4.33, Air Service Training Ltd., Hamble; scrapped at Hamble at C. of A. expiry 10.4.39

G-ACDR (A.17/11), 24.4.33, Air Service Training Ltd., Hamble; dismantled as spares in 1938

G-ADAF (A.17/12), 4.2.35, R. H. Kulka Ltd., San Domingo, Mexico; sold abroad 12.35

G-AETI (A.17/8), 28.4.32, Far East Aviation Co. Ltd., Hong Kong; not British registered until 2.37 for Air Service Training Ltd., Hamble; scrapped 2.40

Saro Skeeter

G-AMTZ (SR.907), G-AMDC, Mk.5, 180 h.p. Cirrus Bombardier 702, Saunders-Roe Ltd., Eastleigh; temporarily XG303 in 1954; converted to Mk.6, 200 h.p. D.H. Gipsy Major 201, C. of A. 21.5.57; instructional airframe 1959

G-ANMG (SR.904), Mk.6, C. of A. 8.6.55, Saunders-Roe Ltd., Eastleigh; to the Army Air Corps, Middle Wallop 11.55 as XK773

G-ANMH (SR.905), Mk.6, first flown 29.8.54, Saunders-Roe Ltd., Eastleigh; to the Army Air Corps, Middle Wallop 11.55 as XJ355

G-ANMI (SR.906), Mk.6, Saunders-Roe Ltd., Eastleigh; to the Army Air Corps, Middle Wallop 2.56 as XK964; rest. 5.56; registration cancelled 9.58

G-APOI (S2/5081), Mk.8, 215 h.p. Gipsy Major 215, registered 7.58 to Saunders-Roe Ltd., delivered East Cowes-Eastleigh by sea 2.9.58, C. of A. 31.3.60; w.f.u. 3.61; rest. 2.72 to B. G. Heron, Bournemouth

G-APOJ (S2/5091), Mk.8, registered 7.58 to Saunders-Roe Ltd.; registration not taken up; airframe used for military production

G-APOK (S2/5111), Mk.8, details as G-APOJ above

G-AWSV (S2/5107), XM553, Mk.12, 215 h.p. Gipsy Major 215, A. to F. 27.1.69, Maj. M. Somerton-Rayner, Middle Wallop

Saro P.531-1

G-APNU (S2/5267), aerodynamic prototype, first flown 20.7.58, registered to Saunders-Roe Ltd., East Cowes/Eastleigh; withdrawn from use 1960

G-APNV (S2/5268), development prototype with full span tailplane and external hoist; first flown 30.9.58; Royal Navy trials 1959 as XN332; to Fleet Air Arm Museum, Yeovilton 10.71

Saro P.531-2

G-APVL (S2/5311), first prototype of Westland Wasp naval helicopter; first flown 9.8.59; Royal Navy trials 1960 as XP166

G-APVM (S2/5312), second Wasp prototype, first flown with D.H. Gnome 3.5.60; Royal Navy trials 1961 as XR493

Scheibe SF-25 Motorfalke *(see also Slingsby Type 61A Falke)*

G-AVBK, (4544), SF-25A, A. to F. 6.3.67; G-AVIZ (4551), SF-25A, 25.7.67; G-AXEO (4645), SF-25B, D-KEBC, 8.5.69; G-AXIW (4657), 12.8.69; G-AXJR (4652), D-KICD, 29.7.69; G-AYBG (4696), 19.5.70; G-AYIL (46108), D-KMAC, 2.10.70

Scottish Aviation Prestwick Pioneer 1 *(all registered to the manufacturers)*

G-AKBF (101), VL515, first flown 5.11.47; converted to Mk.2 as G-AKBF, f/f 5.5.50 as G-31-1, C. of A. 29.5.52; converted to Pioneer C.C.1. f/f 22.6.53 as XE512 for No.267 Squadron, R.A.F., Malaya

G-ANAZ (103), VL516, first flown 20.12.50; converted to Mk.2 as G-ANAZ, f/f 3.9.53; converted to Pioneer C.C.1, f/f 19.9.53 as XE514 for No.267 Squadron

G-APVL, the Saro P.531-2 or first Wasp prototype, at Eastleigh in August 1959. (*Saunders-Roe Ltd.*)

G-ANRG (105), first flown 24.6.54, C. of A. 26.6.54; temporarily XH469 in September 1954; damaged at Rangoon 23.7.55; f/f at Prestwick after repair 13.5.57; w.f.u. at Prestwick 8.59; reduced to spares 1.62

G-AODZ (115), first flown 31.8.55, C. of A. 2.9.55; w.f.u. at Prestwick 1.59

G-AOGF (118), first flown 18.12.55, C. of A. 19.12.55, to the Iranian Customs Authority 3.58 as EP-AHD

G-AOGK (125), first flown 29.1.56, C. of A. 1.2.56, to No.78 Squadron, R.A.F. Khormaksar, Aden 5.56 as XL517

G-AOUE (119), first flown 24.7.56, C. of A. 26.7.56, damaged beyond repair at Fort Bragg, North Carolina 6.11.56

G-AOXP (120), first flown 21.3.57, C. of A. 25.7.57, to the Iranian Customs Authority 3.58 as EP-AHE

G-APNW (149), first flown 31.7.58, crated without markings 25.8.58; shipped to Katuniyake and allotted Royal Ceylon Air Force serial CC603

G-APNX (150), first flown 22.8.58, career as G-APNW above, became CC604

Scottish Aviation Twin Pioneer *(date of first flight precedes C. of A. date)*

G-ANTP (501), 25.6.55, 9.8.57, Scottish Aviation Ltd.; Prestwick; converted 1959 to Ser.3; crashed on take-off from Jorhat, Assam, India 10.3.60

G-AOEN (502), 28.4.56, 30.8.56, Scottish Aviation Ltd.; converted 1959 to Ser.3; d.b.r. in forced landing on island in the Zambesi, Mozambique 12.12.59

G-AOEO (503), 26.8.56, 28.9.56, Scottish Aviation Ltd., Prestwick; crashed at Tripoli, Libya 8.12.57

G-AOEP (504), 27.12.56, 3.1.57, Scottish Aviation Ltd., to Consolidated Zinc Pty. Ltd., Sydney 5.57 as VH-BHJ; Australian Iron and Steel Pty., Ltd. 11.59; destroyed by hurricane at Cockatoo Island, W.A. 23.12.60

G-AOER (505), 13.12.57, 16.9.59, Rio Tinto Finance and Exploration Co. Ltd.; registered in Mexico 9.62 as XC-CUJ; to Arizona Airmotive, Tucson 1964

G-APHX (507), 10.6.57, 24.10.57, British International Airlines Ltd., Kuwait; to Kuwait Oil Co. 11.62 as 9K-ACB; rest. 5.69; J. F. Airlines Ltd., Portsmouth 4.71; Flight One Ltd., Staverton 4.73

G-APHY (508), 10.7.57, 24.10.57, British International Airlines Ltd., Kuwait; to Kuwait Oil Co. 11.62 as 9K-ACC; rest. 5.69; J. F. Airlines Ltd., Portsmouth 4.71; Flight One Ltd., Staverton 2.73

G-APIR (521), 24.1.58, 2.2.58, Scottish Aviation Ltd.; leased to Iraq Petroleum Transport Co. Ltd., Basra 2.58 to 4.62; converted to Ser.3 in 1961; British Govt. gift to Royal Nepalese Govt., Katmandu 5.65 as 9N-RF6

G-APJT (529), 21.3.58, 30.3.58, Government of Federated Malay States; to Royal Malayan Air Force 4.58 as FM1001 'Lang Rajawali' (King Eagle)

G-APLM (523), 15.4.58, 1.8.58, Fison-Airwork Ltd., Lagos; re-registered 12.60 as VR-NDM, later 5N-ABQ; rest. 4.63 to Bristow Helicopters Ltd., Redhill; re-registered to Bristow in Nigeria 9.63 as 5N-ABQ; d.b.r. at Ugheli, Nigeria 4.4.67

G-APLN (526), 13.4.58, 20.6.58, Fison-Airwork Ltd., Lagos; re-registered 12.60 as VR-NDN, later 5N-ABR; rest. 12.62 to Bristow Helicopters Ltd., Redhill; ditched off the Moroccan coast near the Canary Islands 16.1.63

G-APLW (532), 11.5.58, 23.5.58, Scottish Aviation Ltd.; to Borneo Airways Ltd. 9.59 as VR-OAG; rest. 9.63 to Keegan Aviation Ltd.; to Malaysia-Singapore Airlines 6.64 as 9M-ANO; w.f.u. 6.67

G-APMT (537), 3.6.58, 23.7.58, Scottish Aviation Ltd.; to the Red Lion and Sun Organisation, Iran 7.58 as EP-AGG; converted to Ser.3 in 1961; rest. 5.61 to B.U.A., Dakar; to Sierra Leone Airways Ltd. 8.62 as 9L-LAC 'Freetown'; returned to Prestwick 4.65; to the Nepalese Govt. 6.65 as 9N-RF8

G-APPH (540), 6.11.58, 7.11.58, Iraq Petroleum Transport Co. Ltd., Basra; to the Australian Iron and Steel Co. 2.61 as VH-AIS 'Yampi Pioneer'

G-APPW (533), prototype Ser.2, 31.8.58, Scottish Aviation Ltd., Prestwick; application for C. of A. cancelled 1.60; fuselage to British Army 4.62

G-APRS (561), Ser.3, 13.9.59, 13.9.59, Scottish Aviation Ltd., leased to Deutsche Taxiflug 1960; leased to B.U.A. for Sierra Leone Airways 3.61; returned to makers 1.62; to the Empire Test Pilots School, Farnborough 3.65 as XT610

G-APUM (547), Ser.3 2.9.59, 3.9.59, Iraq Petroleum Transport Co. Ltd., Basra; British Govt. gift to the Nepalese Govt., Katmandu 5.65 as 9N-RF7

G-APXL (566), Ser.2, PI-C433, C. of A. 13.11.59, first flown 24.12.59 as 'XL, leased to Iraq Petroleum Transport Co. Ltd., Basra 12.59 to 9.60; to Philippine Air Lines 10.60 as PI-C433; later to Bird Bros., Bangkok as XW-PBO

G-ARBA (548), Ser.3, 23.2.61, 24.2.61, Iraq Petroleum Transport Co. Ltd., Basra; temporarily to Iraqi Airways Ltd. 4.62; w.f.u. at Prestwick 8.71

G-ASAL (599), registration reserved 5.62 for undisclosed variant by Scottish Aviation Ltd.; registration not taken up; cancelled 3.69; fuselage in store 1971

G-ASHN (513), EP-AGB, first flown 12.11.57, registered 3.63 to Keegan Aviation Ltd.; C. of A. 11.6.63; to Aero Taxis Ecuadorianos, Quito 6.63 as HC-AHT

G-ASJS (515), EP-AGC, first flown 20.11.57, registered 6.63 to Keegan Aviation Ltd.; to Fjellfly, Skien, Norway 9.63 as LN-BFK

G-AYFA (538), Ser.3, XM285, first flown 16.7.58, ferried Shawbury–Prestwick 29.11.69 as G-31-15; C. of A. 1.7.70, Scottish Aviation Ltd.; Flight One Ltd. 3.72, first flown at Staverton 8.3.72 after survey conversion

G-AZHJ (577), Ser.3, XP295, first flown 5.10.60, ferried Shawbury–Prestwick 25.8.70 as G-31-16; Flight One Ltd., first flown at Staverton 11.8.72 after survey conversion, C. of A. 1.9.72

Scottish Aviation Bulldog Series 101

Registered to Scottish Aviation (Bulldog) Ltd. for ferrying to Sweden for the Royal Swedish Air Force. First flight/C. of A. dates are followed by the airport of outbound Customs clearance, date of delivery and subsequent military serial.

G-AYWN (101), 22.6.71/5.7.71, Southend 26.7.71, Fv.61001; G-AYWO (102), 14.7.71/19.7.71, Southend 26.7.71, Fv.61002; G-AYWP (103), 1.8.71/2.8.71, Luton 6.8.71, Fv.61003; G-AYZL (104), 18.8.71/23.8.71, Luton 25.8.71, Fv.61004; G-AYZM (105), 24.8.71/30.8.71, Luton 31.8.71, Fv.61005; G-AZAK (106), 10.9.71/14.9.71, Luton 15.9.71, Fv.61006; G-AZAL (107), 21.9.71/23.9.71, Gatwick 24.9.71, Fv.61007; G-AZAM (108), 28.9.71/30.9.71, Gatwick 2.10.71, Fv.61008; G-AZAN (109), 6.10.71/8.10.71, Gatwick 8.10.71, Fv.61009; G-AZAO (110), 12.10.71/14.10.71, Gatwick 15.10.71, Fv.61010; G-AZAP (111), 19.10.71/21.10.71, Gatwick 29.10.71, Fv.61011; G-AZAR (112), 1.11.71/4.11.71, Gatwick 5.11.71, Fv.61012; G-AZAS (113), 5.11.71/10.11.71, Gatwick 15.11.71, Fv.61013; G-AZAT (114), 29.10.71/1.11.71, Luton 3.11.71, Fv.61014

G-AZEN (117); 9.11.71/10.11.71, Gatwick 11.11.71, Fv.61015; G-AZEO (118), 15.11.71/17.11.71, Luton 18.11.71, Fv.61016; G-AZEP (119), 19.11.71/24.11.71, Gatwick 25.11.71, Fv.61017; G-AZES (121), 22.11.71/23.11.71, Gatwick 25.11.71, Fv.61018; G-AZET (122), 29.11.71/1.12.71, Gatwick 2.12.71, Fv.61019; G-AZHV (124), 2.12.71/8.12.71, Luton 9.12.71, Fv.61020; G-AZHW (125), 9.12.71/13.12.71, Gatwick 16.12.71, Fv.61021; G-AZHX (126), 16.12.71/22.12.71, Gatwick 27.12.71, Fv.61022; G-AZHY (128), 21.12.71/22.12.71, Gatwick 27.12.71, Fv.61023; G-AZHZ (129), 24.12.71/1.1.72, Yeadon 11.1.72, Fv.61024; G-AZIS (130), 28.12.71/1.1.72, Yeadon 11.1.72, Fv.61025; G-AZIT (132), 11.1.72/13.1.72, Gatwick 20.1.72, Fv.61026; G-AZIU (133), 14.1.72/19.1.72, Gatwick 21.1.72, Fv.61027; G-AZIV (134), 20.1.72/26.1.72, Gatwick 27.1.72, Fv.61028; G-AZIW (135), 25.1.72/26.1.72, Luton 27.1.72, Fv.61029

G-AZJO (137), 28.1.72/2.2.72, Luton 3.2.72, Fv.61030; G-AZJP (138), 4.2.72/7.2.72, Gatwick 9.2.72, Fv.61031; G-AZJR (139), 8.2.72/9.2.72, Gatwick 17.2.72, Fv.61032; G-AZJS (141), 19.2.72/23.2.72, Gatwick 24.2.72, Fv.61033; G-AZJT (142), 19.2.72/25.2.72, Gatwick 1.3.72, Fv.61034; G-AZJU (143), 28.2.72/1.3.72, Gatwick 3.3.72, Fv.61035; G-AZMP (145), 3.3.72/8.3.72, Gatwick 12.3.72, Fv.61036; G-AZMR (146), 8.3.72/15.3.72, Gatwick 16.3.72, Fv.61037; G-AZMS (148), 14.3.72/15.3.72, Manston 16.3.72, Fv.61038; G-AZMT (149), 17.3.72/22.3.72, Gatwick 23.3.72, Fv.61039; G-AZMU (151), 21.3.72/22.3.72, Gatwick 23.3.72, Fv.61040

G-AZPI (152), 28.3.72/12.4.72, Gatwick 13.4.72, Fv.61041; G-AZPJ (154), 31.3.72/12.4.72, Gatwick 13.4.72, Fv.61042; G-AZPK (155), 18.4.72/19.4.72, Gatwick 20.4.72, Fv.61043; G-AZPL (156), 20.4.72/26.4.72, Gatwick 27.4.72, Fv.61044; G-AZPM (157), 27.4.72/3.5.72, Lympne 4.5.72, Fv.61045; G-AZPN (158), 4.5.72/10.5.72, Lympne 11.5.72, Fv.61046; G-AZPO (162), 10.5.72/18.5.72, Lympne 19.5.72, Fv.61047; G-AZPP (163), 16.5.72/18.5.72, Gatwick 19.5.72, Fv.61048; G-AZPR (164), 23.5.72/24.5.72, Gatwick 6.6.72, Fv.61049; G-AZPS (165), 7.6.72/8.6.72, Gatwick 12.6.72, Fv.61050

G-AZTX (166), 13.6.72/15.6.72, Lympne 16.6.72, Fv.61051; G-AZTY (167), 21.6.72/22.6.72, Gatwick 23.6.72, Fv.61052; G-AZTZ (171), 5.7.72/12.7.72, Norwich 16.7.72, Fv.61053; G-AZUA (172), 30.6.72/1.7.72, Manston 7.7.72, Fv.61054; G-AZUB (173), 11.7.72/21.7.72, Speke 23.7.72, Fv.61055; G-AZUC (174), 20.7.72/27.7.72, Norwich 9.8.72, Fv.61056; G-AZUD (175), 21.7.72/27.7.72, Speke 30.7.72, Fv.61057; G-AZUE (176), 14.8.72/16.8.72, Speke 20.8.72, Fv.61058

Bulldog G-AZPP at Biggin Hill in natural metal finish during its ferry flight from Prestwick to Sweden via Gatwick in May 1972. (*M. D. N. Fisher*)

Scottish Aviation Bulldog Series 101

Registered to Scottish Aviation (Bulldog) Ltd. for ferrying to Sweden for the Swedish Army.

G-AZWH (179), 16.8.72/24.8.72, Speke 27.8.72, Fv.61061; G-AZWI (180), 22.8.72/29.8.72, Norwich 9.9.72, Fv.61062; G-AZWJ (181), 25.8.72/29.8.72, Speke 4.9.72, Fv.61063; G-AZWK (182), 30.8.72/5.9.72, Speke 16.9.72, Fv.61064; G-AZWL (183), 20.9.72/21.9.72, Norwich 24.9.72, Fv.61065; G-AZWM (184), 25.9.72/27.9.72, Norwich 6.10.72, Fv.61066, rest. 12.72 to manufacturers; G-AZWN (185), 10.10.72/11.10.72, Speke 14.10.72, Fv.61067; G-AZWO (186), 12.10.72/13.10.72, Speke-Norwich 14–18.10.72, Fv.61068; G-AZWP (187), 12.10.72/18.1.73, Stapleford 26.1.73, Fv.61069; G-AZWR (188), 13.10.72/19.10.72, Norwich 15.11.72, Fv.61070

G-BACR (189), 18.10.72/27.10.72, Norwich 17.11.72, Fv.61071; G-BACS (190), 7.11.72/15.12.72, Norwich 9.1.73, Fv.61072; G-BACT (191), 14.11.72/8.12.72, Norwich 14.12.72, Fv.61073; G-BACU (192), 8.12.72/18.12.72, Norwich 17.1.73, Fv.61074; G-BACV (193), 15.11.72/12.1.73, Norwich 22.1.73, Fv.61075; G-BACX (194), 26.12.72/4.1.73, Norwich 17.1.73, Fv.61076; G-BACY (195), 4.1.73/12.1.73, Norwich 22.1.73, Fv.61077; G-BACZ (196), 12.1.73/18.1.73, Norwich 26.1.73, Fv.61078; G-BADA (197), 21.2.73/15.3.73, Norwich 5.4.73, Fv.61079; G-BADB (198), last for Sweden, 23.1.73/29.1.73, Norwich 31.1.73, Fv.61080

Other Bulldog production *(continued from Volume 1, page 197)*

Bulldog Series 102 for Malaysia: (c/n 136) FM1226; (140) FM1227; (147) FM1228; (150) FM1229; (159) FM1230; (160) FM1231; (168) FM1232; (169) FM1233; (174) FM1234

Bulldog Series 103 for Kenya: (c/n 144) '701'; (153) '702'; (161) '703'; (170) '704'; (178) '705'. These aircraft were airfreighted Prestwick–Nairobi 25.7.72 in a Canadair CL-44J of Cargolux Airlines, Luxembourg

Bulldog T.Mk.1 for the R.A.F.: (c/n 199) XX513, first aircraft of 130 ordered, first flown at Prestwick 29.1.73

S.E.5A *(Aircraft Disposal Company stock)*

Where known, the key to the manufacturer (see page 136) is given first.

G-EATE F9022, 25.5.20, Handley Page Ltd., Cricklewood; Maj. J. C. Savage, Hendon 11.21; smoke writing demonstration at Hendon 30.5.22; scrapped 1922

G-EAXQ 4, F5249, 14.7.21, Aircraft Disposal Co. Ltd.; 5th in University Air Race, Hendon 16.7.21 flown by N. Pring, New College, Oxford; scrapped 11.22

G-EAXR 4, F5303, 9.7.21, Aircraft Disposal Co. Ltd., Croydon; scrapped 7.22

G-EAXS 4, F5285, 8.7.21, Aircraft Disposal Co. Ltd., Croydon; scrapped 7.22

G-EAXT 4, F5258, 9.7.21, Aircraft Disposal Co. Ltd.; 2nd in University Air Race at Hendon 16.7.21 flown by R. K. Muir, St. Catherine's College, Cambridge

G-EAXU 4, F5333, 14.7.21, Aircraft Disposal Co. Ltd.; won the University Air Race, Hendon 16.7.21 flown by W. S. Philcox, Caius College, Cambridge; destroyed at Croydon 17.4.22 in ground collision with Martinsyde G-EAXB

G-EAXV 4, F5253, 9.7.21, Aircraft Disposal Co. Ltd.; 3rd in University Air Race 16.7.21 flown by A. R. Boeree, Oriel College, Oxford; scrapped 7.22

G-EAXW 4, F5259, 8.7.21, Aircraft Disposal Co. Ltd., Croydon; scrapped 11.22

G-EAXX 4, F5257, 14.7.21, Aircraft Disposal Co. Ltd., Croydon; 4th in University Air Race 16.7.21 flown by H. A. Francis, Caius College, Cambridge

G-EAYL 4, F5300, 9.1.22, C. C. Turner, Hendon; Maj. J. C. Savage, Hendon 1.22; written off 8.2.25

G-EAZT 3, E6013, registered 30.11.21 to G. Wigglesworth, Bekesbourne; Dr. E. D. Whitehead Reid, Bekesbourne 8.22; beyond repair after taxying accident 1922

G-EBCA 3, E5956, 2.8.23, G. Wigglesworth, Bekesbourne; Dr. E. D. Whitehead Reid, Bekesbourne 10.22; scrapped in 1930

G-EBCE 2, C9208, 26.5.22, Maj. J. C. Savage, Hendon; sold abroad 4.27

G-EBOG Previous identity not recorded, C. of A. 23.12.26, D. A. N. Watt, Brooklands; rebuilt for racing purposes as the D.W.1; burned at Whitchurch 1932

G-EBPA D7016, 12.4.27, Mrs. S. C. Elliott-Lynn, Stag Lane; F. G. Miles, Shoreham 2.29; scrapped 3.32, unserviceable after C. of A. expiry 11.4.28

G-EBPD D7022, 12.9.26, F/O H. R. D. Waghorn, R.A.F. Upavon; crashed 27.4.27

G-EBQK F9130, 13.5.27, K. Hunter, Brooklands; Maj. J. C. Savage, Hendon 9.29, C. of A. expiry 31.7.29, scrapped at Hendon 2.32

G-EBQM 1, D7020, 14.4.27, F/O A. H. Wheeler; K. G. Murray, Brooklands 1.30; withdrawn from use and dismantled at C. of A. expiry 4.11.30

G-EBQQ 1, C1091, 21.9.28, Lt. G. H. B. Maddocks, Brooklands; fatal crash at Brooklands 9.11.28

G-EBTK Previous identity not recorded, registered 9.8.27 to L. R. Oldmeadows, Brooklands; Kent Aircraft Services, Kingsdown, Kent, 7.30; C. B. Field, Kingswood, Surrey 8.32; scrapped at Kingswood Knoll 11.34

G-EBTO Previous identity not recorded, C. of A. 22.9.27, W. L. Hay, Shoreham; W. L. Handley, Castle Bromwich 1.29; withdrawn from use 12.29

S.E.5A *(New aircraft converted by the Savage Skywriting Co. Ltd.)*

G-EBDS 5, Previous identity not recorded, C. of A. 4.10.22, Maj. J. C. Savage, Hendon; scrapped at Hendon after C. of A. expiry 22.11.24

G-EBDT 5, (606), 15.2.23, Maj. J. C. Savage, Hendon; to Düsseldorf, Germany 5.29 as D-1636, later D-EVIS; to Holland 4.34 as PH-ATA; to D-EATA 1.36

G-EBDU Previous identity not recorded, C. of A. 10.10.22, Maj. J. C. Savage, Hendon 'The Sweep'; scrapped at Hendon after C. of A. expiry 9.10.23

G-EBDV 2, (1699), F7997, 17.10.22, Maj. J. C. Savage, Hendon; scrapped at Hendon after C. of A. expiry 16.10.23

Walley Handley's S.E.5A G-EBTO with 120 h.p. Airdisco air-cooled engine.

G-EBDW	2, (717), C8675, 4.10.22, Maj. J. C. Savage, Hendon; scrapped at Hendon after C. of A. expiry 29.9.24
G-EBDX	2, (1693), F7991, 25.10.22, Maj. J. C. Savage, Hendon; sold in the U.S.A. 4.27
G-EBDY	2, (1071), C9029, 8.1.23, Maj. J. C. Savage, Hendon 'Smokestream'; scrapped at Hendon after C. of A. expiry 7.1.24
G-EBDZ	2, (744), C8702, 8.1.23, Maj. J. C. Savage, Hendon; sold in the U.S.A. 4.27
G-EBFF	6, (646), F896, 17.3.23, Maj. J. C. Savage, Hendon; sold in the U.S.A. 4.27
G-EBFG	6, (682), F932, 7.5.23, Maj. J. C. Savage, Hendon; sold in the U.S.A. 4.27
G-EBFH	6, (685), F935, 25.5.23, Maj. J. C. Savage, Hendon; crashed in the United States 17.10.23 while operating with the Skywriting Corp. of America
G-EBFI	2, (1680), F7978, 25.5.23, Maj. J. C. Savage, Hendon; sold in the U.S.A. 4.27
G-EBGJ	2, (716), 30.5.23, Maj. J. C. Savage, Hendon; sold in the U.S.A. 4.27
G-EBGK	2, (1062), 12.6.23, Maj. J. C. Savage, Hendon; sold in the U.S.A. 4.27
G-EBGL	2, (1662), 19.6.23, Maj. J. C. Savage, Hendon; sold in the U.S.A. 4.27
G-EBGM	2, (1678), 7.7.23, Maj. J. C. Savage, Hendon; dismantled for spares in the United States 6.24
G-EBIA	6, (654), F904, 15.1.24, Maj. J. C. Savage, Hendon; w.f.u. 2.28; stored at Whitley 1928–56; rebuilt at Farnborough 1957 as D7000; airworthy as F904 in 1973, based at Farnborough for the Shuttleworth Trust
G-EBIB*	6, (688), F938, 28.4.24, Maj. J. C. Savage, Hendon; w.f.u. at C. of A. expiry 6.8.35; presented to the Science Museum for permanent exhibition at South Kensington with R.A.F. serial F937
G-EBIC*	6, (687), F937, 17.4.24, Maj. J. C. Savage, Hendon; w.f.u. 9.30; stored at Brooklands by R. G. J. Nash; restored at Colerne 1950 with spurious serial B4563; later repainted as F937, changed to F938 in 1968 and stored at Henlow; transferred to the R.A.F. Museum, Hendon in 1972

* True c/n and identities as shown initially but airframes were inadvertently switched in their skywriting days.

G-EBID 6, (326), C6376, 11.7.24, Maj. J. C. Savage, Hendon; withdrawn from use at C. of A. expiry 9.6.28; scrapped by Coley & Atkinson at Hounslow in 1932

G-EBIE 6, (328), C6378, 25.7.24, Maj. J. C. Savage, Hendon; withdrawn from use at C. of A. expiry 9.6.28; scrapped by Coley & Atkinson at Hounslow in 1932

G-EBIF 2, (1398), 21.8.24, Maj. J. C. Savage, Hendon; to Düsseldorf, Germany 5.29 as D-1632; to Holland 4.34 as PH-IMI; to Germany 1.36 as D-EIMI

G-EBQA Previous identity not recorded, C. of A. 8.2.27, Maj. J. C. Savage, Hendon, 'Virgini'; to Australia 1928; w.f.u. 1.29; scrapped at Hounslow in 1932

G-EBQB Previous identity not recorded, C. of A. 31.3.27, Maj. J. C. Savage, Hendon; scrapped at Hendon after C. of A. expiry 10.6.30

G-EBQC Previous identity not recorded, C. of A. 6.5.27, Maj. J. C. Savage, Hendon; sold in Germany 6.31 as D-2081

G-EBTM Previous identity not recorded, C. of A. 13.9.27, Maj. J. C. Savage, Hendon; to Düsseldorf, Germany 5.29 as D-1634

G-EBVB Previous identity not recorded, C. of A. 19.1.28, Maj. J. C. Savage, Hendon; to Australia 1928; scrapped at Hendon after C. of A. expiry 14.4.34

G-EBXC (1347) Previous identity not recorded, C. of A. 31.3.28, Maj. J. C. Savage, Hendon; to Düsseldorf, Germany 5.29 as D-1635

G-EBXL (1206) Previous identity not recorded, C. of A. 23.4.28, Maj. J. C. Savage, Hendon; to Düsseldorf, Germany 5.29 as D-1632

S.E.5A *(replica aircraft built 1965 by Miles Marine and Structural Plastics Ltd.)*

G-ATGV (SEM.7282), P. to F. 1.5.65, Twentieth Century Fox Productions Ltd.; re-registered in Ireland 6.67 as EI-ARA; crashed at Weston 15.9.70

G-ATGW (SEM.7283), P. to F. 11.8.65, Twentieth Century Fox Productions Ltd.; re-registered in Ireland 6.67 as EI-ARB; destroyed in air collision with Alouette II helicopter G-AWEE during filming off Wicklow Head 18.8.70

Short Shrimp *(dihedral on lower mainplane only)*

G-EAPZ (S.540), first flown by J. Lankester Parker 10.12.19; re-engined with 240 h.p. Puma and shipped to Sydney for L. Hordern 3.21 as G-AUPZ; made two surveys of New Guinea coast piloted by F. Hurley; crashed in Sydney Harbour 1.23

Short Sporting Type *(Shrimp with dihedral on both mainplanes)*

G-EAUA (S.541), first flown by J. L. Parker 28.7.20; first flown with 300 h.p. Hispano-Suiza by R. W. Kenworthy 10.12.21; last flown 28.3.23

G-EAUB (S.542), first flown by J. L. Parker 21.1.21; dismantled and stored at Rochester with G-EAUA until both were scrapped in 1924

Short S.8 Calcutta and S.8/8 Rangoon*

G-EBVG (S.712), first flown 14.2.28, C. of A. 25.7.28, Imperial Airways Ltd. 'City of Alexandria'; Air Pilots Training Ltd., Hamble 3.36; reverted to I.A.L. 9.36; capsized by storm at Mirabella, Crete 28.12.36

G-EBVH (S.713), first flown 3.5.28, C. of A. 13.9.28, Imperial Airways Ltd. 'City of Athens', later 'City of Stonehaven'; Air Pilots Training Ltd., Hamble 6.37, dismantled for spares later in 1937

G-AADN (S.748), first flown 6.4.29, C. of A. 11.4.29, Imperial Airways Ltd. 'City of Rome'; forced down off Spezia and foundered with all hands 26.10.29

G-AASJ (S.752), first flown 10.1.30, C. of A. 13.1.30, Imperial Airways Ltd. 'City of Khartoum'; crashed in the sea off Alexandria, out of fuel, 31.12.35

G-AATZ (S.754), first flown 28.5.30, C. of A. 3.6.30, Imperial Airways Ltd. 'City of Salonika', later 'City of Swanage'; Air Pilots Training Ltd., Hamble 10.37; scrapped at Hamble in 1939

G-AEIM* (S.757), first flown 24.9.30 as S1433, civil C. of A. 26.9.36, Air Pilots Training Ltd., Hamble; scrapped at Hamble in 1938

Short S.16 Scion 1

G-ACJI (S.766), first flown 18.8.33, C. of A. 14.2.34, Short Bros. Ltd.; Yorkshire Airways Ltd., Yeadon 4.37; impressed 3.40 as X9375, later 2725M

G-ACUV (S.774), 19.7.34, Aberdeen Airways Ltd., Dyce; Nash Aircraft Sales and Hire Ltd., Brooklands 6.39; probably used as spares during 1939–45 war

G-ACUW (S.775), 23.8.34, Short Bros. Ltd.; Atlantic Coast Air Services Ltd., Barnstaple 4.35; Lundy and Atlantic Coast Air Lines Ltd. 11.38; impressed 5.40 as AV981; spun in on approach to Ringway 1.11.40

G-ACUX (S.776), seaplane launched 5.10.34, C. of A. 1.2.35, Papuan Concessions Ltd., Port Moresby; re-registered 2.38 as VH-UUP; withdrawn from use 12.47; preserved by Marshall Airways Ltd., at Bankstown, Sydney in 1973

G-ACUY (S.777), 26.2.35, Short Bros. Ltd., Rochester; impressed 4.40 as AV974

Short S.16 Scion 2

G-ACUZ (S.778), first flown 13.2.35, C. of A. 21.3.35, Airwork Ltd., Tollerton; Nottingham Airport Ltd. 5.38; impressed 3.40 as W7419; scrapped 4.44

G-ADDN (S.785), first flown 9.6.35, C. of A. 13.6.35, Southend-on-Sea Flying Services Ltd.; Aircraft & Allied Enterprises Ltd. 3.40; impressed as X9364

G-ADDO (S.786), first flown 10.7.35, C. of A. 11.7.35, Earl of Amherst, Heston; Olley Air Service Ltd., Shoreham 7.36; Great Western & Southern Air Lines Ltd., Shoreham 8.39; impressed 7.40 as AX864; scrapped 4.44

G-ADDP (S.787), first flown 10.7.35, C. of A. 12.7.35, West of Scotland Air Services Ltd., Renfrew; H. G. Thyne, Lympne 4.38; Williams and Co., Squires Gate 5.39; impressed 3.40 as X9374; scrapped 4.41

Rangoon G-AEIM at Rochester in January 1936 after being converted into an instructional aircraft for Air Pilots Training Ltd., Hamble. (*Short Bros. Ltd.*)

G-ADDR (S.788), first flown 6.8.35, flown with Gouge flaps as M-3, Short Bros. Ltd., Rochester; fitted with standard wing 4.36; C. of A. 14.4.36; impressed 3.40 as X9366; to Bury St. Edmunds A.T.C. Sqn. 9.41 as 2724M

The experimental Scion 2 G-ADDR with tapered wing, Gouge flaps and Class B marking M-3 in November 1935. (*Short Bros. Ltd.*)

G-ADDS (S.789), first flown 23.8.35 as VH-UUT, C. of A. 26.8.35, Adelaide Airways Ltd.; crashed at Meadows, S.A. 22.1.36; rebuilt at Rochester as G-AEOY

G-ADDT (S.790), 20.1.36, Pobjoy Airmotors and Aircraft Ltd., Rochester; crashed at Porthcawl, South Wales 26.7.36

G-ADDV (S.792), 22.5.36, R. J. B. Seaman, Ramsgate; Ramsgate Airport Ltd. 11.36; Southern Airways Ltd., Ipswich 4.39; impressed 4.40 as X9456, later 2726M

G-ADDX (S.794), 15.5.36, R. J. B. Seaman, Ramsgate; Plymouth Airport Ltd. 11.36; Southern Airways Ltd., Roborough 4.39; impressed 4.40 as X9430

G-AEOY (S.789), G-ADDS, VH-UUT, C. of A. 26.8.35, Pobjoy Airmotors and Aircraft Ltd., Rochester; Arabian Airways, Aden 11.37; crashed 17.12.37

Short S.16/1 Scion 2 *(Pobjoy-built)*

G-AEIL (PA.1003), 27.6.36, R. J. B. Seaman, Roborough; reverted to Pobjoys 6.36; Arabian Airways Ltd., Aden 3.38; crashed at Mukerius 25.4.40

G-AEJN (PA.1004), 5.9.36, Pobjoy Airmotors and Aircraft Ltd., Rochester; C. G. M. Alington, Gatwick 3.38, E. D. Spratt, Gatwick 1.39; impressed 5.40 as AV990; to Kemble as instructional airframe 9.41 as 2722M

G-AETT (PA.1005), 15.4.37, Pobjoy Airmotors and Aircraft Ltd.; leased to Lundy and Atlantic Coast Air Lines Ltd. 11.39; crashed at Barnstaple 13.2.40

G-AEZF (PA.1008), seaplane first flown 9.12.37, Elders Colonial Airways Ltd., Freetown, Sierra Leone; converted to landplane at Rochester 11.41 and flown as M-5 at Barton-in-the-Clay; C. of A. 10.9.42; Air Couriers Ltd., Gatwick 3.47; Golden Eagle Marine & Air Transport Ltd., Woolsington 8.47; S. S. Caro, Elmdon 4.48; F. J. Parsons, Exeter 10.50, w.f.u. 5.54

Short S.17 Kent

G-ABFA (S.758), first flown 24.2.31, C. of A. 18.4.31, Imperial Airways Ltd. 'Scipio'; sank after heavy landing at Mirabella, Crete 22.8.36

G-ABFB (S.759), first flown 31.3.31, C. of A. 21.5.31, Imperial Airways Ltd., 'Sylvanus'; set on fire and burned out at Brindisi 9.11.35

G-ABFC (S.760), first flown 2.5.31, C. of A. 12.5.31, Imperial Airways Ltd. 'Satyrus'; scrapped at Hythe 6.38

Short S.22 Scion Senior

G-ACZG (S.779), seaplane first flown 22.10.35 as VT-AGU, C. of A. 11.1.36, Irrawaddy Flotilla Co. Ltd.; crated and shipped to Rangoon 1.36

G-ADIP (S.810), seaplane first flown 10.8.36 as VT-AHI, C. of A. 19.8.36, Irrawaddy Flotilla Co. Ltd.; shipped to Rangoon 8.36; later to Palestine Airways Ltd. as VQ-PAD; impressed at Lydda 8.40 as Z7187

G-AECU (S.834), landplane first flown 15.6.36, C. of A. 27.8.36, Short Bros. Ltd., Rochester; Iraq Petroleum Transport Co. Ltd., Haifa 12.38; impressed for Iraq and Persia Com. Flt. 2.42 as HK868

G-AENX (S.835), landplane first flown 22.6.37, converted to seaplane and first flown 14.8.37, C. of A. 11.9.37, West of Scotland Air Services Ltd., Greenock; Elders Colonial Airways Ltd., Freetown, Sierra Leone 2.38; sunk at moorings, Bathurst, Gambia 8.39

G-AETH (S.836), reserved for Short Bros. Ltd. 2.37, marks not used; first flown by J. L. Parker at Rochester 18.10.39 as single float seaplane L9786; to M.A.E.E., Felixstowe 1.40; transferred to Helensburgh; sunk at sea in 1944

Short S.23 Empire Flying Boat

G-ADHL (S.795), first flown 4.7.36, C. of A. 20.10.36, Imperial Airways Ltd. 'Canopus'; first service 31.10.36; scrapped at Hythe in 1947

G-ADHM (S.804), first flown 11.9.36, C. of A. 4.12.36, Imperial Airways Ltd. 'Caledonia'; first service 18.12.36; scrapped at Hythe in 1947

G-ADUT (S.811), 28.10.36, Imperial Airways Ltd. 'Centaurus'; first service 12.12.36; impressed by R.A.A.F. 9.39 as A18-10; sunk at moorings in Japanese air raid on Broome, Western Australia 3.3.42

G-ADUU (S.812), launched 21.11.36, C. of A. 25.11.36, Imperial Airways Ltd. 'Cavalier'; sank in Atlantic between New York and Bermuda 21.1.39

G-ADUV (S.813), first flown 11.1.37, C. of A. 15.1.37, Imperial Airways Ltd. 'Cambria'; first service 21.2.37; scrapped at Hythe in 1947

G-ADUW (S.814), launched 15.12.36, C. of A. 23.12.36, Imperial Airways Ltd. 'Castor'; first service 4.1.37; scrapped at Hythe in 1947

G-ADUX (S.815), launched 23.1.37, C. of A. 25.1.37, Imperial Airways Ltd. 'Cassiopeia'; first service 26.1.37; crashed at Sabang, Sumatra 29.12.41

G-ADUY (S.816), launched 11.2.37, C. of A. 16.2.37, Imperial Airways Ltd. 'Capella'; first service 27.2.37; wrecked at Batavia, Java 12.3.39

G-ADUZ (S.817), 1.3.37, Imperial Airways Ltd. 'Cygnus'; first service 8.3.37; wrecked on take-off at Brindisi, Italy 5.12.37

G-ADVA (S.818), 14.3.37, Imperial Airways Ltd. 'Capricornus'; crashed in the Beaujolais Mountains near Ouroux, France, in snowstorm 24.3.37

G-ADVB (S.819), 3.4.37, Imperial Airways Ltd. 'Corsair'; first service 9.4.37; B.O.A.C. 4.40; scrapped at Hythe in 1947

G-ADVC (S.820), 21.4.37, Imperial Airways Ltd. 'Courtier'; first service 28.4.37; crashed on landing in Phaleron Bay, Athens 1.10.37

G-ADVD (S.821), 8.5.37, Imperial Airways Ltd. 'Challenger'; first service 15.5.37; crashed in Mozambique Harbour 1.5.39

G-ADVE (S.822), 29.5.37, Imperial Airways Ltd. 'Centurion'; first service 5.6.37; capsized by gust and sank in River Hooghly on landing at Calcutta 12.6.39

G-AETV (S.838), 17.6.37, Imperial Airways Ltd. 'Coriolanus'; first service 20.6.37; to QANTAS 9.42 as VH-ABG; dismantled at Rose Bay, Sydney 1948

G-AETW (S.839), 28.6.37, Imperial Airways Ltd. 'Calpurnia'; first service 1.7.37; crashed in Lake Habbaniyah during sandstorm at night 27.11.38

G-AETX (S.840), 16.7.37, Imperial Airways Ltd. 'Ceres'; first service 20.7.37; wrecked by explosion at moorings, Durban, South Africa 1.12.42

G-AETY (S.841), 26.7.37, Imperial Airways Ltd., 'Clio'; first service 1.8.37; impressed 7.40 as AX659; crashed into high ground near Bowmore, Loch Indaal, Scotland 22.8.41

G-AETZ (S.842), 16.8.37, Imperial Airways Ltd. 'Circe'; first service 1.9.37; shot down by Japanese fighter between Java and Broome, W.A. 28.2.42

G-AEUA (S.843), 26.8.37, Imperial Airways Ltd. 'Calypso'; first service 4.9.37; to QANTAS 9.39 as G-AEUA; impressed by R.A.A.F. immediately as A18-11; crashed near Daru, New Guinea 8.8.42

G-AEUB (S.844), 13.9.37, Imperial Airways Ltd. 'Camilla'; B.O.A.C. 4.40; to QANTAS 2.42 as VH-ADU; lost at sea off Port Moresby, New Guinea 22.4.43

G-AEUC (S.845), 25.9.37, Imperial Airways Ltd. 'Corinna'; B.O.A.C. 4.40; destroyed by Japanese air raid on Broome, Western Australia 3.3.42

G-AEUD (S.846), 9.10.37, Imperial Airways Ltd. 'Cordelia'; impressed 7.40 as AX660; rest. to B.O.A.C. 12.41; scrapped at Hythe in 1947

G-AEUE (S.847), 23.10.37, Imperial Airways Ltd., 'Cameronian'; B.O.A.C. 4.40; scrapped at Hythe in 1947

G-AEUF (S.848), 9.11.37, Imperial Airways Ltd. 'Corinthian'; B.O.A.C. 4.40; crashed landing at Port Darwin, N.T., Australia 22.3.42

G-AEUG (S.849), 8.1.38, Imperial Airways Ltd. 'Coogee'; to QANTAS 7.38 as VH-ABC; impressed by R.A.A.F. 9.39 as A18-12; crashed at Townsville, Q. 28.2.42

G-AEUH (S.850), 10.2.38, Imperial Airways Ltd. 'Corio'; to QANTAS 7.38 as VH-ABD; rest. to Imperial Airways Ltd. 9.39; shot down by Japanese off Timor 30.1.42

G-AEUI (S.851), 26.2.38, Imperial Airways Ltd. 'Coorong'; to QANTAS 3.38 as VH-ABE; rest. to Imperial Airways Ltd. 9.39; scrapped at Hythe in 1947

G-AFBJ (S.876), 25.11.37, Imperial Airways Ltd. 'Carpentaria'; to QANTAS 11.37 as VH-ABA; rest. to B.O.A.C. 7.42; scrapped at Hythe in 1947

G-AFBK (S.877), 18.12.37, Imperial Airways Ltd. 'Coolangatta'; to QANTAS 12.37 as VH-ABB; impressed by R.A.A.F. 9.39 as A18-13; crashed at Rose Bay, Sydney 11.10.44

G-AFBL (S.878), 30.3.38, Imperial Airways Ltd. 'Cooee'; to QANTAS 3.38 as VH-ABF; rest. to B.O.A.C. 8.42; scrapped at Hythe in 1947

Short S.26

G-AFCI (S.871), 'Golden Hind', reg'n. reserved for Imperial Airways Ltd. 10.37; first flown 21.7.39 and transferred to Air Ministry ownership; impressed 7.40 as X8275; rest. to B.O.A.C. 12.41; C. of A. 11.1.42; last service 11.8.47; flown to Rochester 14.4.48; moored there until towed to Harty Ferry on the River Swale and damaged beyond repair, March 1954

G-AFCJ (S.872), 'Golden Fleece', reserved as above; first flown 8.7.40 as X8274; delivered to Stranraer 26.11.40; sank off Cape Finisterre, Spain 20.6.41

The erstwhile G-AFCJ 'Golden Fleece' after launching at Rochester in June 1940 as X8274 with rear and mid-upper turrets.

G-AFCK (S.873), 'Golden Horn', reserved as above; first flown 24.2.40; impressed 7.40 as X8273; rest. to B.O.A.C. 12.41; crashed in the River Tagus at Lisbon, Portugal 9.1.43

Short S.30 Empire Flying Boat

G-AFCT (S.879), first flown 28.9.38, C. of A. 27.10.38, Imperial Airways Ltd. 'Champion'; B.O.A.C. 4.40; scrapped at Hythe in 1947

G-AFCU (S.880), first flown 27.11.38, C. of A. 8.3.39, Imperial Airways Ltd. 'Cabot'; impressed 3.30 as V3137; destroyed by German air attack while moored at Bodϕ, Norway 6.5.40

G-AFCV (S.881), first flown 6.12.38, C. of A. 7.7.39, Imperial Airways Ltd. 'Caribou'; impressed 3.30 as V3138; destroyed by German air attack while moored at Bodϕ, Norway 5.5.40

G-AFCW (S.882), first flown 12.38, C. of A. 25.3.39, Imperial Airways Ltd. 'Connemara'; burned out on the water at Hythe 19.6.39

G-AFCX (S.883), 29.3.39, Imperial Airways Ltd. 'Clyde'; sunk by hurricane while at moorings on the River Tagus at Lisbon, Portugal 15.2.41

G-AFCY (S.884), first flown 18.4.39, C. of A. 24.4.39, Imperial Airways Ltd. 'Awarua'; to Tasman Empire Airways Ltd. 3.40 as ZK-AMC; w.f.u. 11.47

G-AFCZ (S.885), first flown 4.4.39, C. of A. 6.4.39, Imperial Airways Ltd. 'Australia', renamed 'Clare' 10.39; lost at sea off West Africa 24.9.42

G-AFDA (S.886), first flown 9.5.39, C. of A. 12.5.39, Imperial Airways Ltd. 'Aotearoa'; to T.E.A.L. 5.39 as ZK-AMA; w.f.u. at Auckland 11.47

G-AFKZ (S.1003), first flown 21.2.40, C. of A. 26.2.40, Imperial Airways Ltd. 'Cathay'; B.O.A.C. 4.40; scrapped at Hythe in 1947

Short S.33 Empire Flying Boat

G-AFPZ (S.1025), 20.4.40, B.O.A.C. 'Clifton'; to the R.A.A.F. as A18-14; to QANTAS 7.42 as VH-ACD; crashed at Rose Bay, Sydney 18.11.44

G-AFRA (S.1026), 8.5.40, B.O.A.C. 'Cleopatra'; scrapped at Hythe 11.46

G-AFRB (S.1027), construction abandoned 5.40

Short S.25 Sunderland 3 *(with R.A.F. Transport Command codings)*

G-AGER JM660/OQZR, 26.1.43, B.O.A.C. 'Hadfield'; Aquila Airways Ltd., Hamble 12.48; scrapped at Hamble 7.56

G-AGES JM661/OQZS, 19.1.43, B.O.A.C. unnamed; crashed in fog at 2,000 ft. on Slieveglass, near Brandon Head, Co. Kerry, Ireland 28.7.43 and d.b.f.

G-AGET JM662/OQZT, 5.2.43, B.O.A.C. unnamed; burned out on the River Hooghly at Calcutta while refuelling 15.2.46

G-AGEU JM663/OQZU, 15.2.43, B.O.A.C. 'Hampshire'; Aquila Airways Ltd., Hamble 1.49; withdrawn from use at Hamble 3.53 and scrapped there 8.53

G-AGEV JM664/OQZV, 10.2.43, B.O.A.C. 'Hailsham'; beyond repair after heavy landing in Poole Harbour 4.3.46

G-AGEW JM665/OQZW, 8.3.43, B.O.A.C. 'Hanwell'; damaged on take-off at Sourabaya, Java and sank 5.9.48

G-AGHV JM722/OQZB, 31.8.43, B.O.A.C. 'Hamble'; broke moorings and capsized during sandstorm at Rod-el-Farag during the night of 9–10.3.46

G-AGHW ML725/OQZC, 4.9.43, B.O.A.C. 'Hamilton'; crashed into high ground at Brighstone Down, Isle of Wight 19.11.47

G-AGHX ML726/OQZX, 11.9.43, B.O.A.C. 'Harlequin'; scrapped at Hythe 10.48

G-AGHZ ML727/OQZZ, 14.9.43, B.O.A.C. 'Hawkesbury'; Aquila Airways Ltd., Hamble 1.49; withdrawn from use in 1949 and scrapped at Hamble 1.52

G-AGIA ML728/OQZA, B.O.A.C. 'Haslemere'; Aquila Airways Ltd., Hamble 7.48; dismantled for spares at Hamble 7.52

G-AGIB ML729, B.O.A.C. unnamed; crashed in the desert 130 miles south of Tobruk, Libya during the night of 5–6.11.43

G-AGJJ ML751/OQZJ, 21.1.44, B.O.A.C. 'Henley'; Aquila Airways Ltd., Hamble 2.49; scrapped at Hamble 1.52

G-AGJK ML752/OQZK, 5.2.44, B.O.A.C. 'Howard'; Aquila Airways Ltd., Hamble 3.49; scrapped at Hamble 1.52

G-AGJL ML753/OQZL, 19.4.44, B.O.A.C. 'Hobart'; Aquila Airways Ltd., Hamble 3.49; scrapped at Hamble 1.52

G-AGJM ML754/OQZM, 16.2.44, B.O.A.C. 'Hythe'; Aquila Airways Ltd., Hamble 2.49; scrapped at Hamble 1.52

G-AGJN ML755/OQZN, 10.3.44, B.O.A.C. 'Hudson'; Aquila Airways Ltd., Hamble 2.49; damaged beyond repair at Madeira 21.1.53

G-AGJO ML756/OQZO, 21.2.44, B.O.A.C. 'Honduras'; struck by unknown vessel, broke away from moorings and was damaged beyond repair at Hythe 21.2.49

G-AGKV ML786/OQZD, 31.10.44, B.O.A.C. 'Huntingdon'; Short Bros. and Harland Ltd., Belfast 12.48; withdrawn from use 5.51

G-AGKW ML787/OQZE, 28.7.44, B.O.A.C. 'Hotspur'; Short Bros. and Harland Ltd., Belfast 12.48; withdrawn from use 5.51

G-AGKX ML788/OQZF, 23.8.44, B.O.A.C.; converted to Sandringham 1 as 'Himalaya' at Rochester with C. of A. 2.1.46; Aquila Airways Ltd., Hamble 5.49; withdrawn from use 3.53; scrapped at Hamble 8.53

G-AGKY ML789/OQZG, 17.8.44, B.O.A.C. 'Hungerford'; Aquila Airways Ltd., Hamble 1.49; sank off Calshot 28.1.53; salvaged and scrapped 5.53

G-AGKZ ML790/OQZH, 1.9.44, B.O.A.C. 'Harwich'; scrapped at Hythe 5.49

G-AGLA ML791/OQZI, 7.9.44, B.O.A.C. 'Hunter'; Aquila Airways Ltd., Hamble 1.49; scrapped at Hamble 8.49

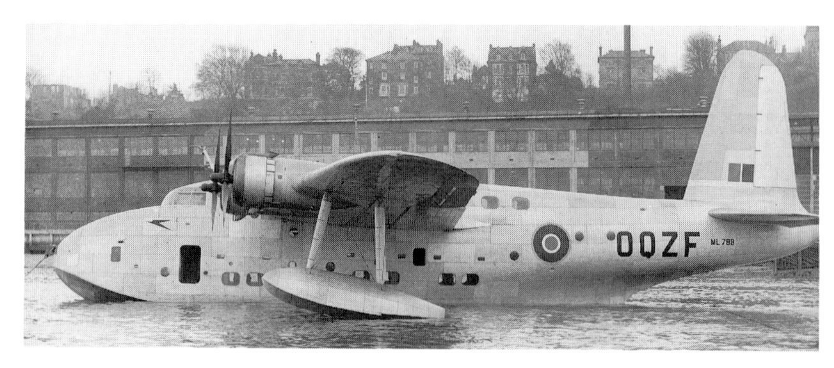

Sandringham 1 ML788/OQZF (later G-AGKX 'Himalaya') at Rochester in November 1945.

G-AGWW (SH.5C), EJ156, 14.3.46, Short Bros. (Rochester and Bedford) Ltd., Belfast; to Cia Aeronáutica Uruguayana S.A. (CAUSA) 5.46 as CX-AFA

G-AGWX (SH.6C), ML876, 29.3.46, Short Bros. (Rochester and Bedford) Ltd., Belfast; ordered for Dodero subsidiary ALFA as LV-AAS but transferred before delivery to CAUSA as CX-AKF

G-AHEO JM716, 24.2.47, B.O.A.C. 'Halstead'; Aquila Airways Ltd., Hamble 7.48; scrapped at Hamble 11.49

G-AHEP DD860, not certificated, B.O.A.C. 'Hanbury'; returned to R.A.F. 9.47 as DD860; rest. 11.48 to Allen Aircraft Services Ltd.; cancelled 9.52

G-AHER PP142, 17.4.46, B.O.A.C. 'Helmsdale'; Aquila Airways Ltd., Hamble 10.49; scrapped at Hamble 1.52

Short S.25 Sunderland 5

G-AHJR (SH.1552), SZ584, 16.7.46, B.O.A.C., Hythe (on loan from the R.A.F. for freight flights); returned to R.A.F. 4.48; derelict at Belfast 10.52

G-ANAK PP162, Blackburn-built, registered 7.53 to Aquila Airways Ltd.; not converted; damaged beyond repair by severe gale at Hamble 27.11.54

Short S.25 Sandringham 2 *(with Short and Harland civil conversion numbers)*

G-AGPT (SH.2C), DD834, 5.12.45, Short Bros. (Rochester and Bedford) Ltd., Belfast; to Dodero 5.46 as LV-AAP 'Uruguay'; crashed at Buenos Aires 29.7.48

G-AGPZ (SH.1C), DV964, 17.11.45, Short Bros. (Rochester and Bedford) Ltd., Belfast; to Dodero 4.46 as LV-AAO 'Argentina'

G-AHRE (SH.43C), ML843, 12.11.46, Short Bros. (Rochester and Bedford) Ltd., Belfast; to Dodero 12.46 as LV-ACT 'Paraguay'

Short S.25 Sandringham 3

G-AGPY (SH.3C), DD841, 21.1.46, Short Bros. (Rochester and Bedford) Ltd., Belfast; to Dodero 8.46 as LV-AAR 'Brazil'; 1947 overhaul allotted SH.54C

G-AGTZ (SH.4C), EJ170, 26.2.46, Short Bros. (Rochester and Bedford) Ltd., Belfast; to Dodero 5.46 as LV-AAQ 'Inglaterra'; 1947 overhaul allotted SH.53C

Short S.25 Sandringham 5

G-AHYY (SH.31C), ML838, 4.3.47, B.O.A.C. 'Portsmouth'; scrapped at Hamworthy, Dorset 3.59

G-AHYZ (SH.35C), ML784, B.O.A.C.; burned out while undergoing civil conversion at Belfast 18.1.47

G-AHZA (SH.34C), ML783, 22.4.47, B.O.A.C. 'Penzance'; scrapped at Hamworthy, Dorset 3.59

G-AHZB (SH.38C), NJ171, 25.4.47, B.O.A.C. 'Portland'; crashed at Bahrein 22.8.47

G-AHZC (SH.39C), NJ253, 17.5.47, B.O.A.C. 'Pembroke'; scrapped at Hamworthy, Dorset 3.59

G-AHZD (SH.40C), NJ257, 28.5.47, B.O.A.C. 'Portmarnock'; to QANTAS 7.51 as VH-EBV; withdrawn from use at Rose Bay, Sydney 8.55

G-AHZE (SH.36C), ML818, 16.6.47, B.O.A.C. 'Portsea'; scrapped at Hamworthy, Dorset 3.59

G-AHZF (SH.41C), NJ188, 11.7.47, B.O.A.C. 'Poole'; to QANTAS 7.51 as VH-EBY; withdrawn from use at Rose Bay, Sydney 8.55

G-AHZG (SH.37C), ML828, 23.9.47, B.O.A.C. 'Pevensey'; to QANTAS 7.51 as VH-EBZ; withdrawn from use at Rose Bay, Sydney 8.55

G-AJMZ (SH.56C), JM681, 18.12.47, B.O.A.C. 'Perth'; scrapped at Hamworthy, Dorset 3.59

Short S.25 Sandringham 7

G-AKCO (SH.57C), JM719, 18.3.48, B.O.A.C. 'St. George'; to Capt. Sir Gordon Taylor 10.54 as VH-APG; to Tahiti 5.58 as F-OBIP

G-AKCP (SH.58C), EJ172, 15.4.48, B.O.A.C. 'St. David'; to CAUSA 3.51 as CX-ANI

G-AKCR (SH.59C), ML840, 1.5.48, B.O.A.C. 'St. Andrew'; to CAUSA 12.50 as CX-ANA

Short S.45 Seaford 1

G-AGWU (S.1293), NJ201/OZZA, registered 12.45 to Ministry of Supply and Aircraft Production; reverted to the R.A.F. 2.46 as NJ201

G-ALIJ (S.1292), NJ200, registered 17.2.49 to R. L. Whyham; not collected from Felixstowe

Short S.45 Solent 2

G-AHIL (S.1300), 16.6.48, B.O.A.C. 'Salisbury'; converted to Solent 3 in 1950 as 'City of Salisbury'; w.f.u. 9.51; scrapped at Hamworthy in 1954

G-AHIM (S.1301), 24.5.48, B.O.A.C. 'Scarborough'; withdrawn from use 6.50; scrapped at Belfast in 1952

G-AHIN (S.1302), 22.4.48, B.O.A.C. 'Southampton'; converted to Solent 3 in 1950 as 'City of Southampton'; scrapped at Hamworthy near Poole in 1954

G-AHIO (S.1303), 27.1.49, B.O.A.C. 'Somerset'; to Trans-Oceanic Airways Pty. Ltd., Sydney 11.51 as VH-TOD; to Oakland, California 6.56 as N9945F

G-AHIR (S.1304), 4.5.48, B.O.A.C. 'Sark'; withdrawn from use 5.50; scrapped at Belfast in 1952

G-AHIS (S.1305), 8.7.48, B.O.A.C. 'Scapa'; converted to Solent 3 in 1950 as 'City of York'; withdrawn from use 9.51; scrapped at Belfast in 1952

G-AHIT (S.1306), 10.11.47, B.O.A.C. 'Severn'; withdrawn from use 12.49; scrapped at Belfast in 1952

G-AHIU (S.1307), 2.3.48, B.O.A.C. 'Solway'; withdrawn from use 2.50; scrapped at Hamworthy, near Poole in 1954

G-AHIV (S.1308), 18.2.48, B.O.A.C. 'Salcombe'; to Trans-Oceanic Airways Pty. Ltd., Sydney 1.51 as VH-TOC 'Star of Papua'

G-AHIW (S.1309), 25.3.48, B.O.A.C. 'Stornoway'; withdrawn from use 3.50; scrapped at Belfast in 1952

G-AHIX (S.1310), 20.10.48, B.O.A.C. 'Sussex'; converted to Solent 3 in 1949 as 'City of Edinburgh'; crashed landing in Southampton Water in gale 1.2.50

G-AHIY (S.1311), 25.11.48, B.O.A.C. 'Southsea'; converted to Solent 3 in 1950; withdrawn from use 9.51; scrapped at Belfast in 1952

Solent 3 G-AKNP 'City of Cardiff' at Belfast before delivery to Trans Oceanic Airways for the Sydney–Hobart service in 1951. (*Short Bros. and Harland Ltd.*)

Short S.45 Solent 3

G-AKNO (S.1294), NJ202, 1.4.49, B.O.A.C. 'City of London'; to Trans Oceanic Airways Pty. Ltd., Sydney as VH-TOA; sank off Malta during delivery 28.1.51

G-AKNP (S.1295), NJ203, 19.3.49, B.O.A.C. 'City of Cardiff'; to Trans-Oceanic Airways Pty. Ltd., Sydney 1.51 as VH-TOB; to U.S.A. 6.56 as N9946F

G-AKNR (S.1296), NJ204, 27.4.49, B.O.A.C. 'City of Belfast'; to Tasman Empire Airways Ltd. 11.51 as ZK-AMQ 'Aparimu'; scrapped at Auckland in 1957

G-AKNS (S.1297), NJ205, 24.6.49, B.O.A.C. 'City of Liverpool'; temporarily to M.A.E.E. 1951 as WM759; w.f.u. 7.51; scrapped at Hamworthy in 1954

G-AKNT (S.1298), NJ206, Ministry of Transport and Civil Aviation 'Singapore'; to South Pacific Airlines, Oakland, California 11.55 as N9947F

G-AKNU (S.1299), NJ207, 12.12.51, Aquila Airways Ltd. 'Sydney', later 'City of Sydney'; crashed at Chessell Down, Isle of Wight 15.11.57

G-ANAJ (S.1293), NJ201 (temporarily registered G-AGWU from 12.45 to 2.46), 30.4.54, Aquila Airways Ltd., Hamble 'City of Funchal'; wrecked by gale and driven ashore at Santa Margherita, Italy 26.9.56

Short S.45 Solent 4

G-ANYI (SH.1558), ZK-AMN, 16.1.55, Aquila Airways Ltd., Hamble 'Awateri'; sold in Portugal 10.58, abandoned in the Tagus estuary, scrapped 8.71

G-AOBL (SH.1556), ZK-AML, 5.5.55, Aquila Airways Ltd., Hamble 'Aotearoa II'; sold in Portugal 10.58, abandoned in the Tagus estuary, scrapped 5.71

Short S.A.6 Sealand 1

G-AIVX (SH.1555), first flown 22.1.48, 6.6.52, Short Bros. and Harland Ltd., Belfast; S.B.A.C. Show 9.52; Paris Air Show 6.53; scrapped at Belfast 4.55

G-AKLM (SH.1562), 28.7.49, Short Bros. and Harland Ltd., Belfast; crashed into mountainside and burned out at Lindesnes, Norway 15.10.49

G-AKLN (SH.1563), Short Bros. and Harland Ltd.; to Vestlandske Luftfartselskap, Bergen via Rochester 3.6.52 as LN-SUF; converted to Sealand 3 on arrival

G-AKLO (SH.1564), 5.5.50, Short Bros. and Harland Ltd., Belfast; to Shell Refining Co. Ltd., Balik Papaan 10.52 as VR-SDS; returned as VR-UDS in 1954

G-AKLP (SH.1565), VP-TBA, 11.11.49, Short Bros. and Harland Ltd., Belfast; to Shell, Balik Papaan 9.54 as VR-SDV; delivered ex Blackbushe as VR-UDV

G-AKLR (SH.1566), Short Bros. and Harland Ltd., Belfast; to Jugoslovenski Aerotransport, Belgrade 9.51 as YU-CFJ; flown out by T. Brooke-Smith

G-AKLS (SH.1567), Short Bros. and Harland Ltd., Belfast; to Jugoslovenski Aerotransport, Belgrade 9.51 as YU-CFK; flown out by J. Eassie

G-AKLT (SH.1568), Short Bros. and Harland Ltd., Belfast; to the Christian and Missionary Alliance, Djakarta 1.51 as PK-CMA

G-AKLU (SH.1569), 6.6.50, Short Bros. and Harland Ltd.; to Vestlandske Luftfartselskap, Bergen 5.51 as LN-SUH; converted to Sealand 3 on arrival

G-AKLV (SH.1570), 16.4.52, Short Bros. and Harland Ltd.; to Ralli Bros. Ltd., Dacca, East Pakistan 6.52 as AP-AFM 'Pegasus'; returned to Shorts crated via Tilbury Docks 27.10.57 and scrapped soon afterwards

G-AKLW (SH.1571), Short Bros. and Harland Ltd., Belfast; to H. E. Ahmed Abboud Pasha, Cairo 9.51 as SU-AHY and delivered ex Croydon, via Corsica 23.2.52

G-AKLX (SH.1572), Short Bros. and Harland Ltd., Belfast; to the East Bengal Transport Commission 12.52 as AP-AGB

G-AKLY (SH.1573), Short Bros. and Harland Ltd., Belfast; to the East Bengal Transport Commission 12.52 as AP-AGC

G-AKLZ (SH.1574), Short Bros. and Harland Ltd., Belfast; to the Indian Navy, Cochin via Rochester–Jersey 13.1.53 as INS-101

G-AKMA (SH.1575), Short Bros. and Harland Ltd., Belfast; to the Indian Navy, Cochin 1.53 as INS-102

The former Sealand 1 VP-TBA 'St. Vincent' at Blackbushe in Shell Borneo colours as VR-SDV in August 1954.

Short S.C.7 Skyvan 1

G-ASCN (SH.1828), first flown 17.1.63; converted to Skyvan 1A, first flown 2.10.63; C. of A. 15.4.64, Short Bros. and Harland Ltd.; last flown 15.8.66

Short S.C.7 Skyvan 2

G-ASCO (SH.1829), first flown 29.10.65, C. of A. 7.4.66, Short Bros. and Harland Ltd.; demonstrated in Ansett-MAL colours; to ground trial installations airframe at Belfast factory 5.68

G-ASZI (SH.1830), first flown 28.1.66, C. of A. 11.2.66, Short Bros. and Harland Ltd.; converted to Skyvan 3, first flown 15.12.67; to Skyliner mock-up 1970

G-ASZJ (SH.1831), first flown 3.3.66; converted to Skyvan 3, first flown 20.1.68; C. of A. 22.5.68; converted to Skyliner 8.70

G-ATPF (SH.1833), first flown 19.6.66, C. of A. 14.7.66, Scott (Toombridge) Ltd. for Emerald Airways Ltd.; Short Bros. and Harland Ltd. 1.67; leased to South West Aviation Ltd., Exeter 2.68; scrapped at Belfast 1970

G-ATPG (SH.1835), first flown 30.8.66, C. of A. 13.10.66, Scott (Toombridge) Ltd. for Emerald Airways Ltd.; Short Bros. and Harland Ltd. 1.67; to Remmert Werner, St. Louis, Michigan 4.67 as N731R; leased Atlas Cargo, Boston

G-AVGO (SH.1837), N4906, first flown 5.11.66, C. of A. 22.2.67, Short Bros. and Harland Ltd.; delivered to Northern Consolidated Airlines Inc., Anchorage, Alaska 4.67 as N4906

G-AVJX (SH.1838), VH-EJR, first flown 13.1.67, C. of A. 11.5.67, Short Bros. and Harland Ltd.; conv. to Skyvan 3; to Australia 9.68 as VH-FSG; to U.S.A. 10.72 as N10TC

G-AXCS (SH.1834), I-CESA, first flown 24.7.66 for Aeralpi; returned to Belfast 3.69 and scrapped

Short S.C.7 Skyvan 3

G-AWCS (SH.1839), VH-EJS, first flown 21.5.68, C. of A. 29.5.68, Short Bros. and Harland Ltd.; South West Aviation Ltd., Exeter 7.68

G-AWCT (SH.1842), VH-EJT, first flown 8.8.68, C. of A. 13.9.68, Short Bros. and Harland Ltd.; to Cia dos Diamantes de Angola 10.68 as CR-LJF

G-AWJM (SH.1853), first flown 13.12.68, C. of A. 2.1.69, Short Bros. and Harland Ltd.; to Forrester Stephen, Melbourne 3.69 as VH-FSH; rest. 11.72 to Short Bros. and Harland Ltd.

G-AWKV (SH.1847), N735R, first flown 6.6.68, C. of A. 4.7.68, Short Bros. and Harland Ltd.; to Remmert Werner 12.68 as N735R; to Cherokee as N3419

G-AWSG (SH.1851), G-14-1, first flown 22.10.68, C. of A. 7.11.68, Short Bros and Harland Ltd.; to P. T. Suryadirnow, Hong Kong 3.71

G-AWVM (SH.1852), first flown 8.11.68, C. of A. 3.2.69, Short Bros. and Harland Ltd.; leased to Sadia 1969 as PP-SDO; later to Caribair as N33BB; rest. to Shorts 6.70; sold in the U.S.A. 4.73

G-AWWS (SH.1854), G-14-2, first flown 3.1.69, C. of A. 22.1.69, Short Bros. and Harland Ltd.; to Canada 3.70 as CF-VAN; to Pan Alaskan A/L as N7978

G-AWYG (SH.1856), G-14-28, first flown 25.1.69, C. of A. 25.2.69, Loganair Ltd., Abbotsinch

G-AXAD (SH.1857), G-14-29, first flown 5.2.69, C. of A. 15.4.69, Short Bros. and Harland Ltd.; to Cherokee Airlines, Los Angeles 6.69 as N20CK

G-AXAE (SH.1858), G-14-30, first flown 24.2.69, C. of A. 21.3.69, Short Bros. and Harland Ltd.; to U.S.A. 3.69 as N3748; to Cherokee Airlines, Los Angeles 4.69 as N21CK

G-AXAF (SH.1859), G-14-31, first flown 14.3.69, C. of A. 2.5.69, Short Bros. and Harland Ltd.; to Cherokee Airlines, Los Angeles 6.69 as N22CK

G-AXAG (SH.1861), G-14-33, first flown 4.4.69, C. of A. 27.5.69, Short Bros. and Harland Ltd.; flown in Sadia colours; to Pan Alaskan A/L 9.69 as N123PA

Skyvan 3 CF-YQY, formerly G-AXCT, acquired by Selkirk Air in 1969 to support motorised sledging operations of the parent company, Sigfusson Transportation, in Northern Manitoba. (*Short Bros. and Harland Ltd.*)

G-AXCT (SH.1862), G-14-34, first flown 22.4.69, C. of A. 28.5.69, Short Bros. and Harland Ltd.; to Selkirk Air, Winnipeg 6.69 as CF-YQY

G-AXCU (SH.1863), G-14-35, first flown 8.5.69, registered 28.3.69 to Short Bros. and Harland Ltd.; to Alaska Leasing 10.69 as N100LV

G-AXFI (SH.1865), first flown 3.6.69, registered 14.5.69 to Short Bros. and Harland Ltd.; to Alaska Leasing 11.69 as N200LV; rest. 3.70 to Shorts; C. of A. 17.3.70; Gulf Aviation Ltd., Bahrein 3.71

G-AXLB (SH.1869), G-14-41, first flown 13.8.69, C. of A. 11.3.70, Short Bros. and Harland Ltd.; to Olympic Airways SA., Athens 6.70 as SX-BBN

G-AXLC (SH.1870), G-14-42, first flown 1.9.69, C. of A. 25.5.70, Short Bros. and Harland Ltd.; to Olympic Airways SA., Athens 6.70 as SX-BBO

G-AXLD (SH.1872), G-14-44, first flown 25.9.69, registered 23.7.69 to Short Bros. and Harland Ltd.; to Nordair Ltd., Montreal 10.69 as CF-NAS

G-AXLE (SH.1873), G-14-45, first flown 7.10.69, registered 23.7.69 to Short Bros. and Harland Ltd.; to Delaware Air Freight (Del-Air) 1.70 as N10DA

G-AXNV (SH.1868), G-14-40, first flown 10.7.69, registered 8.9.69 to Short Bros. and Harland Ltd.; conv. to Skyvan 3M; to Ecuador Army Air Service 4.71 as SAE-T-100

G-AXWU (SH.1866), first flown 27.6.69, C. of A. 4.2.70, Short Bros. and Harland Ltd.; to Nigeria via Gatwick 13.2.70 for United Nations; leased to Olympic Airways SA., Athens 8.72 to 10.72 as SX-BBT

G-AYDO (SH.1874), G-14-46, first flown 17.10.69, registered 13.5.70 to Short Bros. and Harland Ltd.; to Indonesian National Oil Co. 9.71 as PK-PSA

G-AYIX (SH.1884), G-14-56, first flown 23.9.70, C. of A. 17.11.70, Short Bros. and Harland Ltd.; to Royal Flight of Nepal 11.70 as 9N-RAA

G-AYJN (SH.1885), G-14-57, first flown 11.11.70, C. of A. 25.11.70, Short Bros. and Harland Ltd.; Gulf Aviation Ltd., Bahrein 11.70

G-AYJO (SH.1886), G-14-58, first flown 17.11.70, C. of A. 14.9.70, Short Bros. and Harland Ltd.; Gulf Aviation Ltd., Bahrein 11.70

G-AYYR (SH.1864), G-14-36, CF-TAI, first flown 14.5.69, registered 12.5.71 to Short Bros. and Harland Ltd.; to Malaysia Air Charters Ltd., Kuala Lumpur as all-passenger conversion 8.71 as 9M-AQG

G-AYZA (SH.1892), C. of A. 21.5.71, Short Bros. and Harland Ltd.; to Hong Kong 9.71 for Indonesian National Oil Co. as PK-PSC

G-AYZB (SH.1893), C. of A. 28.6.71, Short Bros. and Harland Ltd.; to Hong Kong 9.71 for Indonesian National Oil Co. as PK-PSD

G-AZRY (SH.1901), G-14-71, 19.5.72, Short Bros. and Harland Ltd., company demonstrator

G-AZSR (SH.1902), G-14-72, 22.6.72, Short Bros. and Harland Ltd.; to Royal Thai Police via Gatwick–Nice 23.6.72

G-AZWX (SH.1906), 29.9.72, Short Bros. and Harland Ltd.; delivered to Thai Highways via Gatwick–Nice 30.9.72, adopted serial U-01 on arrival

G-AZYW (SH.1903), Skyliner, 2.9.72, Short Bros. and Harland Ltd.; B.E.A., Abbotsinch 1.73

G-BAHK (SH.1907), Skyliner, 1.2.73, Short Bros. and Harland Ltd.; delivered to Gulf Aviation Ltd., Bahrein 2.73

G-BAID (SH.1909), 19.2.73, Short Bros. and Harland Ltd.; d/d to Mexico via Reykjavik 21.2.73

G-BAIE (SH.1911), 5.4.73, Short Bros. and Harland Ltd.; sold in Mexico 6.73

G-BAIT (SH.1908), Skyliner, 20.4.73, Short Bros. and Harland Ltd.; B.E.A., Abbotsinch 4.73

Short S.C.7 Skyvan 3M

G-AXMO (SH.1871), G-14-43, first flown 8.9.69, registered 15.8.69 to Short Bros. and Harland Ltd.; to the Indonesian Air Force 8.69 as T-701

G-AXPT (SH.1867), first flown 30.6.69, C. of A. 5.2.70, Short Bros. and Harland Ltd., company demonstrator

G-AYCS (SH.1876), G-14-48, first flown 6.5.70, C. of A. 10.5.70, Short Bros. and Harland Ltd.; to Muscat and Oman Air Force 5.70 as '903'

G-AYDP (SH.1879), G-14-51, first flown 22.5.70, registered 13.5.70 to Short Bros. and Harland Ltd.; to Muscat and Oman Air Force 11.70 as '901'

G-AYZD (SH.1894), registered 20.5.71 to Short Bros. and Harland Ltd.; to Royal Nepalese Army via Heathrow 26.8.71 as RA-N14

G-AZHP (SH.1898), 26.11.71, Short Bros. and Harland Ltd.; to Royal Nepalese Army 1.72 as RA-N15

G-AZKL (SH.1897), 30.5.72, Short Bros. and Harland Ltd.; to Royal Thai Police via Gatwick–Nicosia 9.6.72; became '1897' on arrival

SIAI-Marchetti SF.260

G-AXAH (103), OO-HAY, 3.4.69; G-AXKA (122), OO-HEI, 23.7.69, to Australia 2.70 as VH-SFN; G-AXVY (2-27), OO-HEV, 26.1.70; G-AYDD (2-28), OO-HEL, 12.5.70; G-AYFK (2-39), OO-HEZ, 26.6.70, to Belgium 9.71 as OO-CNL; G-AZMY (2-50), OO-HOA, 11.2.72; G-BAGB (107), LN-BIV, 8.12.72

Sikorsky S-51

G-AJHW (5117), first flown at Yeovil 18.4.47, C. of A. 24.4.47, temporarily WB220 in 1948–49 for Navy trials, B.E.A. 'Sir Baudwin' 5.49, to Canada 6.57 as CF-JTO; G-AJOO (5121), first flown at Yeovil 6.6.47, C. of A. 6.6.47, wrecked at Fawar, Sudan 16.10.49; G-AJOP (5126), first flown at Yeovil 28.7.47, to A.F.E.E., Beaulieu 8.47 as VW209; G-AJOR (5132), first flown at Yeovil 14.8.47 as G-28-1, C. of A. 19.8.47, B.E.A. 'Sir Owen', to Canada 6.57 as CF-JTP; G-AJOV (5135), first flown at Yeovil 3.10.47, C. of A. 13.10.47, B.E.A. 'Sir Lamorah', to Canada 6.57 as CF-JTQ; G-AKCU (5128), first flown at Yeovil 24.11.47, C. of A. 28.11.47, crashed at Croesor Dam, Caernarvonshire 24.5.49

Sikorsky S-61N

G-ASNL (61220), N4604G, 14.3.64, to Holland 8.68 as PH-SBH, rest. 10.69; G-ASNM (61221), N4605G, 1.3.64, to Holland 12.68 as PH-SBC, rest. 10.69, ditched in the North Sea 50 miles east of Aberdeen 15.11.70; G-ATBJ (61269), 21.4.65; G-ATFM (61270), CF-OKY 'Morning Star', 9.8.65; G-ATYU* (61393), registered 23.8.66, to military marks 1.67 as XV370; G-AWFX (61216), AP-AOB, 15.9.68; G-AYOM (61143), N94565, JA-9506, N4585, 3.4.71; G-AYOY (61476), 22.4.71; G-AZCF (61488), 16.9.71; G-AZDC (61424), I-EVMA, 28.1.72; G-AZNE (61467), VR-BDU, 14.2.72; G-AZRF (61473), PK-HBT, 22.6.72

G-BAKA (61493), 30.4.73; G-BAKB (61702), 'Montrose', 9.2.73; G-BAKC (61703), 'Forties', 30.3.73

* Sikorsky S-61D-2

Simmonds Spartan *(two seaters)*

G-EBYU	(1), 18.7.28, O. E. Simmonds, Hamble; Simmonds Aircraft Ltd., Hamble 11.28; beyond repair in forced landing at Bury St. Edmunds 10.3.29
G-AAFP	(11), 17.4.29, Simmonds Aircraft Ltd., Hamble; d.b.r. 3.30
G-AAFR	(12), 27.4.29, Simmonds Aircraft Ltd., Hamble; Hampshire Aeroplane Club Ltd., Hamble 5.29; crashed at Bursledon, Hants. 27.3.30
G-AAGN	(14), 27.4.29, Simmonds Aircraft Ltd., Hamble; d.b.r. in 1930 and rear fuselage used in construction of unregistered Blake Bluetit at Winchester
G-AAGO	(29), 26.6.30, Simmonds Aircraft Ltd., Hamble; Spartan Aircraft Ltd., Cowes 5.31; withdrawn from use 12.33
G-AAGY	(15), 7.5.29, Simmonds Aircraft Ltd., Hamble; B. S. Thynne, Hendon 9.29; F/O J. F. X. McKenna 5.31; Phillips and Powis Aircraft Ltd. Woodley 1.33; Eastern Flying Club, Warley 8.38; scrapped at South Nutfield in 1947
G-AAHA	(23), 27.6.29, C. Coombes, Shanklin; F. G. Gibbons, Heston 6.31; Spartan Aircraft Ltd., Cowes 8.31; sold abroad 3.32, believed as ZS-ADC
G-AAMA	(17), 15.7.29, National Flying Services Ltd., Hanworth; w.f.u. 12.32
G-AAMB	(21), 31.7.29, National Flying Services Ltd., Hanworth; Alexander Duckham and Co. Ltd. 11.30; Wiltshire School of Flying Ltd., High Post 2.33; F. S. Davies and S. A. Kew, Maylands 5.38; ditched off Southend 26.2.39
G-AAMC	(20), 28.6.29, National Flying Services Ltd., Hanworth; crashed at Hanworth 28.7.29
G-AAMD	(24), registered 19.7.29 to National Flying Services Ltd.; not delivered; certificated in December 1930 as G-ABHH
G-AAME	(26), 3.8.29, National Flying Services Ltd., Hanworth; w.f.u. 12.31
G-AAMF	(33), registered 19.7.29 to National Flying Services Ltd.; not delivered; registration cancelled 12.30

G-AAMG (34), registered 19.7.29 to National Flying Services Ltd.; not delivered; C. of A. 19.6.30, Spartan Aircraft Ltd., Cowes; to Felixstowe as seaplane; reverted to landplane; crashed near Ratcliffe, Leicester 6.9.30

G-AAMH (22), 19.8.29, National Flying Services Ltd.; Flg. Off. T. P. Gleave, Tangmere 11.32; crashed in forest, 12 miles from Kutahya, Turkey 19.10.33

G-AAMI (35), registered 2.8.29 to National Flying Services Ltd.; not delivered; C. of A. 13.2.30, Wilhelm Omsted; to Norway 4.30 as N-43, later LN-ABG

G-AAMJ (36), registered 2.8.29 to National Flying Services Ltd.; not delivered; registration cancelled 12.30

G-AAMK (37), registered 2.8.29 to National Flying Services Ltd.; not delivered; registration cancelled 12.30

G-AAML (38), 11.4.30, National Flying Services Ltd., Hanworth; Lt. C. R. V. Pugh R.N. 3.31; crashed at Croydon 3.10.31

G-AAWM (10), 8.4.29, Brooklands School of Flying Ltd., Brooklands; damaged beyond repair after accident 12.30

G-ABHH (24), G-AAMD, 16.12.30, Lt. Finch White, Hanworth; crashed at Tunis 3.2.31; sold abroad 3.32, believed as ZS-ADI

G-ABNU (25), 21.9.31, College of Aeronautical Engineering Ltd., Brooklands; scrapped at Brooklands in 1948

Simmonds Spartan three seater G-AAHV 'Silver Wings II' at Brooklands in 1936. (*R. P. Howard*)

Simmonds Spartan *(three seaters)*

G-AAGV (27), 17.5.29, Pleasure Flying Services Ltd., Cramlington; Cramlington Aircraft Ltd. 11.29; damaged 9.30 and rebuilt 1934 as G-ABXO

G-AAHV (44), 15.8.29, Simmonds Aircraft Ltd., Hamble; Pleasure Flying Services Ltd., Cramlington 8.29, Rev. C. D. C. Boulton, Clacton 1937; stored in a barn in Hertfordshire during 1939–45 war, scrapped at White Waltham 1953

G-AAJB (19), 25.6.29, Simmonds Aircraft Ltd., Hamble; sold abroad 11.29

G-ABXO (27), G-AAGV, 5.1.35, Cramlington Aircraft Ltd.; H. G. Hubbard, Cambridge 8.38; registration cancelled 1.12.46

SIPA S.901* and S.903

G-ASXC* (8), F-BEYK, A. to F. 8.10.64; G-ATVI (89), F-BGHN, 27.5.66; G-ATWD (74), F-BGBY, 16.1.57, crashed in the Humber estuary off Cleethorpes 20.8.67; G-ATXO (41), F-BGAP, 22.7.66; G-AWLG (82), 1.8.68

Slingsby Type 61* and Type 61A Falke *(Starke Stamo MS1500/1, manual cockpit starting)*

G-AYPY (1723), first flown at Wombleton 8.2.71, C. of A. 10.3.71, Vickers Ltd., Kirkbymoorside; operated by the Lakes Gliding Club, Walney; fitted with Rollason R.S.1 engine in 1972

G-AYSD (1726), 29.3.71, L. Hill, Sutton Bank; operated by the Yorkshire Gliding Club

G-AYUM (1730), 26.3.71, Vickers Ltd., Kirkbymoorside; operated by the Doncaster Gliding Club

G-AYUN (1731), 8.4.71, Vickers Ltd., Kirkbymoorside; operated by the Norfolk Gliding Club, Tibenham 3.73

G-AYUO (1732), 29.4.71, Vickers Ltd., Kirkbymoorside; Airways Aero Associations Ltd., Booker 6.71; crashed at Booker 12.2.73

G-AYUP (1735), 21.5.71, Vickers Ltd.; to the A. and A.E.E., Boscombe Down 5.71 as XW983 for evaluation; to No.2 Gliding Centre, Spittlegate 8.71

G-AYUR (1736), 28.5.71, Vickers Ltd.; Pentland Flying Group, Penicuik, Midlothian 8.71

G-AYYJ (1733), 4.6.71, Vickers Ltd., Kirkbymoorside; sold in Sweden 7.71

G-AYYK (1737), 14.6.71, Vickers Ltd.; Scout Association, Lasham 8.71

G-AYYL (1738), 25.6.71, Vickers Ltd.; Ulster and Shorts Gliding Club 10.7

G-AYZU (1740), 25.8.71, Vickers Ltd.; Lasham Gliding Society Ltd. 12.71

G-AYZV (1741), 10.9.71, Vickers Ltd.; Worcestershire Gliding Club Ltd., Bickmarsh 1.72; sold in Denmark 4.73

G-AYZW (1743), 24.9.71, Vickers Ltd.; Portmoak Falke Syndicate, Portmoak 1.72

G-AZHD (1753), 2.12.71, Vickers Ltd.; West Wales Gliding Co. Ltd., Haverfordwest 2.72

G-AZHE (1755), experimental installation of American two cylinder Franklin 2A-120-A engine as Type 61B; C. of A. 20.5.73, Vickers Ltd.

G-AZIL (1756), 17.12.71, Vickers Ltd.; I. Jamieson, Aboyne 2.72; based with the Deeside Gliding Club

G-AZMC (1757), 18.2.72, Vickers Ltd.; W. J. Dyer and P. O. Trubshawe, Roborough 4.72

G-AZOK (1766), 24.3.72, Vickers Ltd.; Scottish Gliding Union Ltd., Portmoak 5.72

G-AZYY (1770), 24.8.72, Vickers Ltd., Kirkbymoorside; J. A. Towers, Tees-side 10.72

G-BADH (1774), 29.9.72, Vickers Ltd., Kirkbymoorside; Southern Soaring Centre, Inkpen 5.73

G-BAIZ (1776), 16.1.73, Vickers Ltd., Kirkbymoorside; Lasham Gliding Society 3.73

Production also included the following for export: (a) Type 61 (c/n 1744) 9V-BEJ; (1747) 9V-BEL; (1750) 9V-BEN; (1751) 9V-BEP; (1768) OH-416. (b) Type 61A (c/n 1742) VH-GZO; (1754) OH-415

Slingsby Type 61C Falke *(Stark Stamo MS1500/2 with electric starter)*

G-AZMD (1758), 17.3.72, Vickers Ltd., Kirkbymoorside; H. R. Dimock, Lasham 4.72

G-AZPC (1767), 28.4.72, Vickers Ltd., Kirkbymoorside; Hon. P. R. Smith and S. H. C. Marriott, Ballykelly 7.72

G-BAKY (1777), 2.2.72, Vickers Ltd. Kirkbymoorside; Sir L. and Lady J. Redshaw, Askam-in-Furness, Lancs. 5.73

G-BAMB (1778), 16.3.73, Vickers Ltd., Kirkbymoorside; J. R. Milford and P. G. Purdie, Reading 5.73

Production also included the following for export: (c/n 1752) to Australia, believed as VH-GSS; (1769) Australia; (1775) New Zealand

S.N.I.A. SA-315B Llama *(see also Sud-Aviation SE-3130 Alouette II)*

G-AZNI (06), delivered to British Executive Air Services Ltd., Kidlington via Le Touquet–Lympne 17.5.72, C. of A. 5.6.72

Sopwith Pup *(none was issued with C. of A.)*

G-EAVF Registered 20.8.20 to M. E. Tanner with two airframe numbers, 3210 and 764 quoted; scrapped in 1921

G-EAVV C440, registered 4.11.20 to Handley Page Ltd.; transferred to the Aircraft Disposal Co. Ltd. and scrapped

G-EAVW C312, registered 27.10.20 to Flt. Lt. T. Gran, R.A.F. Abingdon; scrapped in 1921

G-EAVX B1807, registered 2.11.20 to A. R. M. Rickards, Fairford, Glos.; damaged beyond repair in nose-over at Hendon 16.7.21 while being piloted in the Aerial Derby by D. L. Forestier-Walker

G-EAVY C438, registered 4.11.20 to Handley Page Ltd.; transferred to the Aircraft Disposal Co. Ltd. and scrapped

G-EAVZ C540, registered 22.11.20 to Handley Page Transport Ltd., Cricklewood; transferred to the Aircraft Disposal Co. Ltd. and scrapped

G-EBAZ* C1524, first flown 10.8.18, registered 9.1.22 to H. Sykes, Erith; P. T. Capon, Hendon 6.23; scrapped in 1924

G-EBFJ C242, first flown 27.12.18, registered 22.2.23 to J. T. Norquay; scrapped in 1924

G-EBKY** (W/O 3004/14), converted from Sopwith Dove, q.v., by R. O. Shuttleworth 1937–38; first flown as Pup 26.2.38; preserved in airworthy condition by the Shuttleworth Trust as N5184, later N5180

All built by the Standard Motor Co. Ltd. except *Whitehead and **Sopwith

Note: One Pup, C476, ex R.A.A.F. stock, civilianised 6.21 by C. D. Pratt, Geelong, Vic. as G-AUCK, later fitted with 80 h.p. Genet II; burned 9.45

Sopwith Pup *(other aircraft)*

G-APUP (N5182), registered 2.59 to K. C. D. St. Cyrien, Horley; a rebuild using the engine of N5182, and original parts from N5182 and the prototype; first C. of A. flight at Fairoaks 8.73

G-AVPA (CJW.1), registered 6.67 to C. J. Warrilow; a replica under construction at High Wycombe in 1974

Sopwith Dove

G-EACM (W/O 2714), K-122, 11.6.19, Sopwith Aviation Co., Brooklands; used by Maj. Barker VC to fly H.R.H. Prince of Wales at Hounslow 10.5.19; sold abroad 5.20, almost certainly to Bishop-Barker Aeroplanes Ltd., Toronto, registration G-CAAY issued 23.6.20

G-EACU (W/O 2769/1), K-133, 7.8.19, Sopwith Aviation Co., Brooklands; to Maj. Olof Enderlein of the Royal Swedish Air Force 1.23 as S-AFAA

Sopwith Dove G-AUKH, formerly G-EAKH, on the Larkin stand at the 1922 Melbourne Motor exhibition. (*via Keith Meggs*)

G-EAFI (W/O 2769/2), K-148, 30.6.19, Sopwith Aviation Co., Brooklands; sold in Norway 7.21; believed to Oscar Bladh, Stockholm 8.24 as S-AYAA

G-EAGA (W/O 3004/1), K-157, 14.8.19, Sopwith Aviation Co., Brooklands; sold abroad 9.19

G-EAHP (W/O 3004/2), K-168, 11.9.19, Sopwith Aviation Co., Brooklands; sold abroad 9.19

G-EAJI (W/O 3004/3), 30.9.19, Sopwith Aviation and Engineering Co. Ltd., Brooklands; sold abroad 8.20, believed to E. O. Cudmore, Melbourne as G-AUDN

G-EAJJ (W/O 3004/4), 26.4.20, Sopwith Aviation and Engineering Co. Ltd., Brooklands; to Larkin Supply Co., Melbourne 3.20 as G-AUJJ; scrapped 6.25

G-EAKH (W/O 3004/5), 17.4.20, Sopwith Aviation Co., Brooklands; to Larkin Supply Co., Melbourne 3.20 as G-AUKH; scrapped 6.28

G-EAKT (W/O 3004/6), 17.4.20, Sopwith Aviation Co., Brooklands; sold abroad 3.20, believed to A. L. Long, Hobart, Tasmania as G-AUDP; crashed before reg'n.

G-EBKY (W/O 3004/14), registered 27.3.25 to D. L. Hollis Williams; C. of A. 12.4.27; C. H. Lowe-Wylde, West Malling 9.30; w.f.u. 12.33; rest. 7.37 to R. O. Shuttleworth, Old Warden and converted to Sopwith Pup q.v.

Sopwith Gnu

G-EAAH (A.16), K-101, not certificated, Sopwith Aviation Co., Brooklands and Southport, Lancs.; crashed at Southport 10.6.19

G-EADB (W/O 2976/1), K-136, 7.7.19, Sopwith Aviation Co.; E. A. D. Eldridge, Brooklands 5.23; J. R. King, Brooklands 6.25; Southern Counties Aviation Co., Shoreham 8.25; Lloyds Commercial Aircraft Co., Brooklands 2.26; crashed at Horley, Surrey 2.3.26

G-EAEP (W/O 2976/2), K-140, 7.7.19, Sopwith Aviation Co., Brooklands; unsold, withdrawn from sale and dismantled, Brooklands 7.20

G-EAFR (W/O 3005/1), K-156, 3.10.19, Sopwith Aviation Co., Brooklands; unsold, withdrawn from use at C. of A. expiry 10.20

G-EAGP (W/O 2976/3), K-163, 7.8.19, Sopwith Aviation Co., Brooklands; Lt. Col. F. K. McClean 6.23; Maj. S. A. Packman, Cramlington 11.24; Southern Counties Aviation Co., Shoreham 7.25; crashed at King's Lynn 2.5.26

G-EAGQ (W/O 2976/4), K-164, 7.8.19, Sopwith Aviation Co., Brooklands; unsold, withdrawn from sale and dismantled at Brooklands 8.20

G-EAHQ (W/O 2976/5), K-169, 27.4.20, Sopwith Aviation Co., Brooklands; to Larkin-Sopwith Aviation Co., Melbourne 5.20 as G-AUBX; used by Fulham Air Transport, Melbourne; registration cancelled 3.22

G-EAIL (W/O 2976/6), 27.4.20, Sopwith Aviation Co., Brooklands; to Larkin-Sopwith, Melbourne 3.20 as G-AUBY; used by K. R. Farmer, Melbourne; destroyed on ground by freak storm, Essendon Airport 19.4.46

G-EAIM (W/O 3005/2), 27.10.19, Sopwith Aviation Co., Brooklands; sold to Larkin-Sopwith Aviation Co., Melbourne 11.19, believed as spares

G-EAME (W/O 3005/4), registered 3.9.19 to the Sopwith Aviation and Engineering Co. Ltd., Brooklands; remained unsold; registration cancelled 9.21

G-EAMF (W/O 3005/6), details as G-EAME above

G-EAMG (W/O 3005/5), 15.1.21, Sopwith Aviation and Engineering Co. Ltd., Brooklands; remained unsold, registration cancelled 9.21

G-EAMH (W/O 3005/3), details as G-EAME above

Southern Martlet

G-AAII (2SH), 3.10.29, L. E. R. Bellairs, Shoreham; Southern Aircraft Ltd. 4.33; A. H. Tweddle, Hanworth 11.34; to Ireland 12.35 as EI-ABG

G-AAVD (201), 23.6.30, Southern Aircraft Ltd.; W. R. Westhead, Heston 2.32; A. R. Ramsey, Woodley 10.33; H. M. Goodwin, Walsall 2.36; M. N. Mavrogordato, Witney 11.38; derelict at Turnhouse in 1944

G-AAYX (202), 14.7.31, L. E. R. Bellairs, Shoreham; Southern Aircraft Ltd. 7.32; W. K. Vinson, West Malling 1.38; Butlins Ltd., Pwllheli 6.47; acquired by the Shuttleworth Trust for preservation in 1955 and stored

G-AAYZ (203), 27.6.30, Rt. Hon. F. E. Guest, Hanworth; E. C. T. Edwards 10.31; M. Maxwell, Croydon 10.35; scrapped in 1937

G-ABBN (204), 8.8.30, Marquess of Douglas and Clydesdale, Hamble; H. H. Leech, Farnborough 5.31; National Aviation Day, Hanworth 1.32; scrapped 1935

G-ABIF (205), 30.5.31, Mrs. M. Freeman-Thomas; T. C. Sanders 7.32; Air Travel Ltd., Gatwick 10.35; G. D. Tucker, Hatfield 10.38; given to A.T.C. 1940

G-ABJW Metal Martlet (31/1), registered 19.3.31 to Viscountess Ratendone, Shoreham; scrapped 11.32

G-ABMM Metal Martlet (31/2), registered 19.5.31 to W. R. Westhead, Heston; not completed; registration cancelled 12.32

Spartan Arrow

G-AAWY (51), 26.6.30, Gipsy I, Sandown and Shanklin Flying Services Ltd.; Isle of Wight Flying Club 8.34; fitted with Hermes II; dismantled in 1940

G-AAWZ (52), 27.6.30, Gipsy I, Spartan Aircraft Ltd., Cowes; W. C. Mycroft, Elstree 2.39; Yapton Aero Club, Ford 8.39; scrapped during 1939–45 war

G-ABBE (75), 27.6.30, Gipsy II, Capt. H. H. Balfour, Ramsgate; evaluated as seaplane; Spartan Aircraft Ltd. 2.31; to New Zealand 5.31 as ZK-ACQ

G-ABGW (77), 10.12.30, Gipsy II, B. S. Thynne, Hamble; crashed 10.34

The second Spartan Arrow at Hanworth for the 1930 King's Cup Race, with four ailerons and link struts. Early production aircraft were converted later to have ailerons on the bottom wing only. (*Flight Photo 8779*)

G-ABHD (80), 19.1.31, Gipsy II, G. P. Fairbairn, Melbourne; re-registered to owner in Australia 2.32 as VH-UQD; crashed at Essendon 11.6.35

G-ABHR (81), 7.1.31, Gipsy II, Household Brigade Flying Club, Heston; A. W. A. Whitehead, Hamble 2.33; withdrawn from use 3.39

G-ABKL (76), 4.4.31, Gipsy I, Bristol and Wessex Aeroplane Club, Whitchurch; Capt. W. H. Amory, Hamble 10.32; E. D. Ward, Hooton 12.36; burned out in hangar fire at Hooton 8.7.40

G-ABMK (82), S-1, 26.6.31, Hermes II floatplane, O. S. Baker (for Hon. A. E. Guinness); G. Duller, Woodley 2.33; to Norway 7.35 as LN-BAS

G-ABOB (83), 28.7.31, Gipsy II, Spartan Aircraft Ltd., Cowes; A. L. Maffery, Hendon 11.36; Exeter Aero Club 5.38; Thanet Aero Club 4.39; crashed 1939

G-ABST (87), 21.4.32, Javelin III, D. Napier and Son Ltd., Heston; dism. 1936.

G-ABWP (78), 23.7.32, Hermes II, Henlys Ltd., Heston; R. O. Shuttleworth, Old Warden 12.36; rest. 1953 to Spartan Group, Croydon, later Denham; R. E. Blain 8.64; stored at Baginton in 1971

G-ABWR (79), 24.9.32, Hermes II, R. V. L'Estrange Malone, Heston; Flying Hire Ltd., Chilworth 8.35; W. J. Gunther, Gravesend 7.36; to Denmark 8.38 as OY-DOO

G-ACHE (84), 16.6.33, Hermes II, Spartan Aircraft Ltd., Cowes; F. H. C. Cornell, Croydon 12.34; crashed at Horsham, Sussex 28.4.35

G-ACHF (85), 7.7.33, Gipsy II, Lady D. Clayton East Clayton, Brooklands; Marquess of Kildare, Lympne 8.35; T. A. S. Webb, Lympne 7.36; Romford Flying Club Ltd. 3.39; burned out in hangar fire at Maylands, Romford 6.2.40

G-ACHG (86), 19.6.33, Spartan Aircraft Ltd., Cowes; to Denmark 10.35 as OY-DUK; to C. Peyron, Stockholm 4.37 as SE-AFR; Östersunds Flygklubb in 1951

Spartan Three Seater I *(Hermes II engines unless otherwise stated)*

G-ABAZ (53), 26.6.30, Gipsy II, C. Coombes, Sandown; Sandown and Shanklin Flying Services Ltd. 4.31 (used by Isle of Wight F/C); reg'n. canc. 12.46

G-ABET (54), 7.11.30, Gipsy II, Capt. L. Wigham Hall, Brooklands; Nottingham Airport Ltd. 5.36; Kennings Ltd., Skegness 5.39; registration canc. 12.46

G-ABJS (56), 31.3.31, Spartan Aircraft Ltd., Cowes; Air Trips Ltd., Croydon 3.32; to Australia 12.35 as VH-UUU; VH registration cancelled 7.36

G-ABKJ (55), 24.4.31, Gipsy II, Spartan Aircraft Ltd., Cowes; W. L. Gordon, Hamble 1.32; Kennings Ltd., Skegness 5.39; registration cancelled 12.46

G-ABKK (58), 1.5.31, Spartan Aircraft Ltd., Cowes; Dorothy Spicer, Stag Lane 2.32; Air Trips Ltd., Croydon 5.35; crashed at Coventry 10.5.36

G-ABKT (57), 10.4.31, L. S. Tindall; Lincolnshire Aero Club, Skegness 1.33; Peterborough Flying Club, Horsey Toll 3.39; T. H. Ward, Sheffield 3.41; stored during 1939–45 war; registration cancelled 12.46

G-ABLJ (59), 22.7.31, Gipsy II, Portsmouth, Southsea and I.O.W. Aviation Ltd.; Yapton Aero Club, Ford 9.38; A. C. Douglas, Tangmere 2.39; C. J. Rice, Leicester 1943; given to the Air Training Corps 1944

G-ABPZ (60), 7.10.31, Oscar Garden, trading as Skywork Ltd., Cape Town; re-registered in South Africa 11.32 as ZS-ADP; crashed 12.12.33

G-ABRA (61), 6.10.31, Oscar Garden, Cape Town; J. Stark, Allhallows, Kent 10.32; E. A. Rance, Stag Lane 3.33; to Ireland 6.34 as EI-AAT

G-ABRB (62), 9.10.31, Oscar Garden, Cape Town; re-registered in Tanganyika 11.32 as VR-TAJ; crashed at Ladysmith, Natal 26.5.34

G-ABTT (64), 20.2.32, Gipsy II, Spartan Aircraft Ltd., Cowes; crashed at Stanton, Suffolk during *Morning Post* Race 21.5.32

G-ABTU (65), 13.5.32, British Air Transport Ltd., Croydon; scrapped in 1936

G-ABWO (66), 26.5.32, Spartan Aircraft Ltd., Cowes; W. Westoby, Banbury 5.36; Romford Flying Club 3.39; burned out in hangar fire, Maylands 6.2.40

G-ABWU (67), 3.6.32, Spartan Aircraft Ltd., Cowes; Southend Flying Services Ltd. 1.33; H. V. Armstrong, Hooton 9.35; burned out in hangar fire 8.7.40

G-ABWV (68), 15.6.32, Spartan Aircraft Ltd., Cowes; Rollason Aviation Co. Ltd., Croydon 6.32; crashed and burned at Grantham, Lincs. 26.9.33

G-ABWX (69), 25.6.32; Spartan Aircraft Ltd., Cowes; J. Miskelly, Dumfries 8.32; crashed at Dumfries 12.9.32

G-ABYG (70), 27.7.32, Scarborough Aero Club; Miss Joan Hughes and N. M. Browning, Abridge 5.35; W. Catton, Abridge 9.37, registration cancelled 12.46

G-ABYH (71), 19.11.32, Henlys Ltd., Heston; F. G. Barnard, Hayling Island 7.33; looped too low and crashed at Hayling Island 20.7.35

Malling Aviation Ltd.'s immaculate white and brown, last production, Spartan Three Seater II at Ramsgate on 21 August 1937. (*A. J. Jackson*)

Spartan Three Seater II *(Hermes IV engines unless otherwise stated)*

G-ABTR (101), 2.6.32, Hermes IIB, Spartan Aircraft Ltd., Cowes; British Airways Ltd., Eastleigh 5.36; F. G. Barnard, Hayling Island 9.37; burned with other derelict aircraft at Gatwick in 1947

G-ABYN (102), 14.9.32, Spartan Aircraft Ltd., Cowes; E. G. Croskin, Hedon 7.35; to Ireland 10.38 as EI-ABU; stored at Cloughjordan in 1971

G-ABZH (103), 4.10.32, Spartan Aircraft Ltd., Cowes; Henlys Ltd., Heston 3.33; Aerofilms Ltd., Stag Lane 7.33; withdrawn from use 10.33

G-ABZI (104), 31.12.32, Spartan Aircraft Ltd., Cowes; to Iraq Airwork Ltd. 1.33 as YI-AAB; rest. 7.35 to No.601 Sqn. Flying Club, Hendon; crashed and burned in take-off accident at Farnborough 7.8.36

G-ACAD (105), 10.2.33, Lady D. Clayton East Clayton, Brooklands; R. O. Shuttleworth, Old Warden 6.36; D. B. Prentice, Ford 6.38; reg'n. canc. 12.46

G-ACAF (106), 31.3.33, Hill and Phillips, St. Austell; Air Publicity Ltd., Heston 9.36; L. C. G. M. Le Champion, Leamington 6.38; reg'n. canc. 1.39

G-ACEF (107), 27.10.36, H. Pritchett, Christchurch; Malling Aviation Ltd., West Malling 3.37; scrapped during 1939–45 war

The Saro-Percival Mailplane at Hamble in June 1932, named 'Blackpool' and equipped with small cabin and twin rudders for the India flight.

Spartan A.24 Mailplane and Cruiser I

G-ABLI (A.24/1), conversion of Saro-Percival Mailplane, 24.2.32, Spartan Aircraft Ltd., Cowes; fitted with twin rudders and small cabin and named 'Blackpool'; scrapped in 1933

G-ABTY (24M), Cruiser I, 16.8.32, Spartan Aircraft Ltd.; Spartan Air Lines Ltd., Heston 5.34; Hon. Mrs. V. Bruce, Croydon 2.35; lost in Channel 11.5.35

Spartan Cruiser II

G-ACBM (2), 21.2.33, Airwork Ltd., Heston; to Iraq Airwork Ltd. 2.33 as YI-AAA; rest. 6.34 to Spartan Air Lines Ltd.; British Airways Ltd., Eastleigh 3.36; Straight Corporation Ltd., Exeter; scrapped 11.37

G-ACDW (3), 12.5.33, Spartan Air Lines Ltd. 'Faithful City'; to Misr Airwork Ltd., Almaza 4.34 as SU-ABL and used on daily Cairo–Jerusalem–Haifa route

G-ACDX (4), 19.6.33, Spartan Air Lines Ltd., Heston; British Airways Ltd., Eastleigh 4.34; beyond repair in forced landing at Gosport, Hants. 9.10.35

G-ACJO (5), 7.9.33, Spartan Aircraft Ltd., Cowes; to Aeroput, Belgrade 9.33 as YU-SAN

G-ACKG (7), 14.11.33, Spartan Aircraft Ltd., Cowes; to Maharajah of Patiala 11.33 as VT-AER; returned to Heston for overhaul 29.9.35

G-ACMW (6), 28.3.34, Spartan Aircraft Ltd., Cowes; left Heston 5.4.34 on delivery to Aeroput, Belgrade as YU-SAO piloted by Vladimir Strizewski

G-ACNO (8), 26.2.34, Spartan Aircraft Ltd., Cowes; to the Bata Shoe Company, Zlin, Czechoslovakia 5.34 as OK-ATQ 'Cape of Good Hope'

G-ACOU (9), Spartan Aircraft Ltd., Cowes; left Heston 5.34 on delivery to the Bata Shoe Co., Zlin, Czechoslovakia, piloted by L. A. Strange; C. of A. 14.7.34; sold abroad 8.34

G-ACSM (10), 13.6.34, Spartan Air Lines Ltd.; British Airways Ltd., Eastleigh 2.36; Northern and Scottish Airways Ltd., Renfrew 8.36; Scottish Airways Ltd., Renfrew 6.38; impressed 4.40 as X9433, scrapped 7.40

G-ACVT (11), 2.8.34, Spartan Air Lines Ltd.; British Airways Ltd. 2.36; crashed at Ronaldsway, Isle of Man 23.3.36

G-ACYL (12), 24.10.34, United Airways Ltd., Blackpool; British Airways Ltd. 12.35; Scottish Airways Ltd., Renfrew 6.38; impressed 4.40 as X9431

G-ACZM (14), 13.12.34, Spartan Air Lines Ltd.; British Airways Ltd. 1.36; Northern and Scottish Airways Ltd., Renfrew 8.36; Scottish Airways Ltd., Renfrew 6.38; withdrawn from use at Renfrew 1.40; scrapped 4.42

Spartan Cruiser III

G-ACYK (101), 16.4.35, Spartan Air Lines Ltd.; British Airways Ltd. 4.36; Northern and Scottish Airways Ltd. 8.36; crash landed at Largs, Ayr 14.1.38

G-ADEL (102), 18.4.35, Spartan Air Lines Ltd.; British Airways Ltd. 10.36; Northern and Scottish Airways Ltd., Renfrew 1.37; Scottish Airways Ltd. 6.38; impressed 4.40 as X9432; scrapped 7.40

G-ADEM (103), 3.6.35, Spartan Air Lines Ltd.; British Airways Ltd. 3.36; Northern and Scottish Airways Ltd. 8.36; crashed at Blackpool 20.11.36

Stampe et Vertongen SV-4A *(120 h.p. Renault 4PO5)*

G-AZCB (140), F-BBCR, converted to SV-4C, C. of A. 26.10.72; G-AZNK (290), F-BCGZ, F-BKXF, 16.3.72

Stampe et Vertongen SV-4B *(Rollason conversions, 145 h.p. Gipsy Major Mk.10-1)*

G-AROZ (508), F-BDGQ, 7.6.62, Tiger Club 'Léon Biancotto', crashed at Biggin Hill 15.5.65; G-ASHS (265), F-BCFN, 20.5.63; G-ATKC (1081), F-BFRK, 12.5.66; G-AVCO (1040), F-BBGN, 31.12.67, G-AVKW (561), F-BDDG, 6.7.67, crashed near Godstone, Surrey 29.10.67; G-AWEF (549), F-BDGT, 2.7.68; G-AWIW (532), F-BDCC, 6.2.69: G-AXYW (163), F-BBPF, 27.4.70; G-AYIJ (376), F-BCOM, 25.2.72; G-AZSA (1206), F-BFZM, Belgian Air Force V-64, 4.5.72, repainted 5.73 as 'MX457'; G-AZUL, Belgian Air Force V-27, 15.6.72

Stampe et Vertongen SV-4C *(140 h.p. Renault 4Pei or 4PO3)*

G-ATIR (1047), F-BCDM, F-BMKQ, 27.10.69; G-AVES (476), F-BDBM, 16.6.67, to the U.S.A. 10.70 as N3956; G-AVYG (537), F-BDCH, 17.1.68, to the U.S.A. 8.70 as N14SV; G-AVYY (548), F-BDCS, 6.12.67, to Canada 3.70 as CF-AYF; G-AWWR (1073), F-BAUT, 5.9.69; G-AWXZ (360), F-BHMZ, 26.6.70

G-AXAC (616), F-BDFL, 10.4.69, sold in the U.S.A. 6.72; G-AXCZ (186), F-BCFG, 23.4.69, d.b.r. in forced landing at Wareside, Herts. 12.5.71; G-AXHC (293), F-BCFU, 13.6.69; G-AXHD (522), F-BDIK, to the U.S.A. 5.70 as N527R; G-AXIJ (1077), F-BJDV, 28.8.69, sold in the U.S.A. 8.70; G-AXJT (418), F-BCTB, to the U.S.A. 10.70 as N12SV; G-AXMC (278), F-BBHA, registered 5.8.69; G-AXME (545), F-BDCP, 31.12.70; G-AXNH (185), F-BCFF, 10.10.69, ditched in the English Channel off Hythe 10.4.72; G-AXNW (381), F-BFZX, 7.4.71; G-AXOK (232), F-BCGG, 14.1.70, crashed at Sibson 18.6.72; G-AXPK (266), F-BCLY, 3.12.69, crashed at Leicester East 15.6.71; G-AXPW (1098), F-BFUI, 9.3.70; G-AXRP (554), F-BDCZ, 3.12.69

G-AYCG (59), F-BBAE, 15.5.70; G-AYCK (1139), F-BANE, 15.5.70; G-AYDR (307), F-BCLG, 21.9.70; G-AYGE (242), F-BCGM, 31.12.70; G-AYGR (641), F-BMMI, 7.9.70, destroyed in air collision with Tiger Moth G-ANMO at Weston-super-Mare 30.7.72; G-AYHV (609), F-BDFE, registered 23.7.70; G-AYJB (560), F-BDDF, 26.3.71; G-AYLK (673), F-BDNR, 1.3.71; G-AYWT (1111), F-BLEY, 26.5.71; G-AYZI (15), F-BBAA, registered 24.5.71

G-AZGC (120), F-BCGE, 15.10.71; G-AZGD (413), F-BGRL, 12.7.72; G-AZGE (576), F-BDDV, 9.12.71; G-AZIO (389), F-BACB, registered 24.11.71; G-AZIR (452), F-BCXR, registered 24.11.71; G-AZNF (1101), F-BGJM, 30.6.72; G-AZTP (90), F-BENH, to Canada 9.72 as CF-DJQ; G-AZTR (596), F-BDEQ, 8.6.72

G-BAKN (348), F-BCOY, 6.4.73; G-BALA (1096), F-BKOF, 21.2.73; G-BALK (387), F-BBAN, registered 3.1.73

Robert Blackburn's private Stinson SR-9D Reliant, running up at Brough in 1937, was also used for communications by Blackburn Aircraft Ltd. until impressed for similar duties with No.51 Group in 1939.

Stinson SR-9 Reliant

G-AEVX (5156), SR-9B, 13.5.37, impressed 2.40 as W7980; G-AEVY (5253), SR-9D, 13.5.37, impressed 2.40 as W7984; G-AEXW (5262), SR-9D, 6.7.37, impressed 2.40 as W7982; G-AEYZ (5265), SR-9D, 11.8.37, impressed 2.40 as X8521; G-AFBI (5400), SR-9D, 9.11.37, impressed 12.39 as W5791; G-AFTM (5160), SR-9C, NC2217, 26.7.39, impressed 2.40 as W7983

Stinson SR-10 Reliant

G-AFHB (5819), 28.7.38, impressed 2.40 as W7981, rest. 8.45, converted to SR-10J, to Kenya 1.47 as VP-KDK; G-AFRS (5904), 14.7.39, impressed 2.40 as W7978; G-AFVT (5911), 25.1.40, sold in U.S.A. 6.68; G-AGZV (5902), NC21133, BS803, 6.5.46, to Kenya 10.47 as VP-KDV, to New Zealand 6.54 as ZK-BDV

Sud-Aviation SO-1221 Djinn

G-AXBX (1043FR93), F-BIUA, 13.3.69, sold in France 4.70; G-AXFO (1001FR7), F-BHOI, 13.6.69, to France 4.70 as F-BSES; G-AXFP (1041FR91), F-BIFP, 13.6.69, to France 4.70 as F-BSEX; G-AXFR (1042FR92), F-BIFQ, 13.6.69, sold in France 4.70; G-AXFS (1015FR51), ex West German Army, F-BIEU, 13.6.69, to France 4.70 as F-BSEU; G-AXFT (1105FR72), F-BMLH, sold in France 4.70; G-AXFU (1106FR18), F-BMLO, 13.6.69, sold in France 4.70

Sud Aviation SE-3130, SE-318B and SE-318C Alouette II *(see also S.N.I.A. SA-315B)*

G-ATDT (1901), SE-318B, not imported; G-AVEE (1203), SE-3130, F-BNKZ, 3.2.67; G-AWAP (1966), SE-318B, F-BOSD, 6.1.68; G-AWEE (1971), SE-318B, 13.3.68, destroyed in air collision with S.E.5A replica G-ATGW/EI-ARB off Wicklow Head while filming 18.8.70; G-AWFL (1997), SE-318C, 17.4.68; G-AWFY (2007), SE-318C, 7.5.68; G-AWLC (2014), SE-318C, 1.8.68, w.f.u. 2.72; G-BANR (1648), EI-AUI, 16.2.73

Supermarine Channel Mk.I

G-EAED (978), N1529, 23.7.19, Supermarine Aviation Works Ltd., Woolston; written off 6.21; probably withdrawn from use at C. of A. expiry 22.7.20

G-EAEE (977), N1710, 23.7.19, Supermarine Aviation Works Ltd., Woolston; overturned and sank during a pleasure flight at Bournemouth 15.8.19

G-EAEF (976), N2452, 7.8.19, Supermarine Aviation Works Ltd., Woolston; Bermuda and Western Atlantic Aviation Co. Ltd. 11.20; scrapped 7.21

G-EAEG (975), N2451, 28.5.20, Supermarine Aviation Works Ltd., Woolston; Bermuda and Western Atlantic Aviation Co. Ltd. 5.20; to Trinidad 3.21; scrapped

G-EAEH (974), N1716, 5.6.20, Supermarine Aviation Co. Ltd., Woolston; to Norske Luftreideri 5.20 as N-9

G-EAEI (973), N1715, 28.5.20, Supermarine Aviation Works Ltd., Woolston; to Norske Luftreideri 5.20 as N-10

G-EAEJ (972), N1714, 14.8.19, Supermarine Aviation Works Ltd., Woolston; Bermuda and Western Atlantic Aviation Co. Ltd. 5.20; crashed 5.21

G-EAEK (971), N1711, 23.7.19, Supermarine Aviation Works Ltd., Woolston; in service until dismantled at Woolston 2.21

G-EAEL (970), N1528, 28.5.20, Supermarine Aviation Works Ltd., Woolston; to Norske Luftreideri 5.20 as N-11; seriously damaged due engine failure at Tregenes, near Stavanger 20.9.20; rebuilt with Mercedes by S. Bredal

G-EAEM (969), N1526, 17.7.20, Supermarine Aviation Works Ltd., Woolston; delivered 5.20 to Royal Norwegian Navy at Horten

Supermarine Channel Mk.II

G-EAWC (1141), 29.12.20, Supermarine Aviation Works Ltd., Woolston; shipped to Bermuda 3.21 en route to Venezuela and British Guiana

G-EAWP (1146), 25.7.21, Supermarine Aviation Works Ltd., Woolston; believed to have been the armed version with modified planing bottom supplied to the Chilian Navy in 1922; registration cancelled as sold abroad 1.23.

A Supermarine Channel Mk.I N-9, formerly G-EAEH, moored in Bergen Harbour while in service with Norske Luftreideri in 1920.

Taylor J.T.1 Monoplane

G-APRT (PFA.537), built by designer John Taylor at Ilford 1958–59, first flown at White Waltham 4.7.59, P. to F. 24.8.60; P. J. Houston, Redhill 10.61; M. Slazenger, Newtownards 4.64; J. E. Cull, Shobden 4.68

G-AVPX (A.J.P.1/PFA.1410), 1,500 cc. Volkswagen, P. to F. 19.9.68, A. J. Perkins, Rush Green

G-AVTX (PFA.1408), registered 25.8.67 to P. Lockwood, under construction at Huddersfield 1971; sold to P. J. Houston and re-allocated as PFA.1442

G-AWGZ (M.1/PFA.1406), Ardem 4CO2 Mk.1, P. to F. 12.5.69, J. Morris, Weston-super-Mare

G-AXYK (PFA.1409), 1,600 cc. Volkswagen, first flown at Biggin Hill 24.5.71, C. of A. 15.11.71, C. Oakins, Biggin Hill

G-AYSH (PFA.1413), registered 10.2.71, to C. J. Lodge, built at Broomfield, Chelmsford, Essex; first flown at Tolleshunt d'Arcy 19.6.73

G-AYUS (PFA.1412), registered 19.3.71 to D. G. Barker, under construction at Lancing, Sussex in 1973

G-AYWL (PFA.1435), registered 20.4.71 to D. G. Wiggins, under construction at the University of Luanda, Angola, in 1971

G-AYYC (PFA.1421), registered 7.5.71 and constructed by J. B. Sharp and the Kirby Flying Group, Leicester East; C. of A. 11.10.72

G-AZSK (PFA.1436), registered 12.4.72 to R. R. Lockwood, under construction at Eye, Suffolk, in 1973

Taylor J.T.2 Titch

G-ATYO (JFT.1), P. to F. 12.10.66, first flown at Southend 4.1.67, J. F. Taylor, crashed at Southend 16.5.67

G-AXWY (PFA.3212), registered 30.1.70 to S. E. Tomlinson, under construction at Stevenage, Herts. in 1973

G-AXZR (PFA.1503), registered 17.3.70 to A. J. Fowler and D. E. Evans, under construction at Wrexham in 1973

G-AYZH (PFA.1316), registered 21.5.71 to K. J. Munro, under construction at Dartford, Kent in 1973

G-AZLA (PFA.3218), registered 23.12.71 to J. Chappell, under construction at Huddersfield in 1973

G-BABE (PEB.01/PFA.1394), registered 3.8.72 to P. E. Barker, under construction at Great Barford, Beds. in 1973

G-BABY (JRB.2), registered 21.8.72 to J. R. Bygraves, under construction at Old Warden in 1973

Taylorcraft Model A and Model B*

G-AFDN (406), 14.3.38, impressed 7.41 but found unsuitable for R.A.F. use and no serial was issued; G-AFEX ntu, reservation only for Malcolm and Farquharson Ltd., Heston; G-AFHF (458), 9.5.38, w.f.u. 5.39; G-AFJO (568), 10.9.38, w.f.u. 3.43, rest. 2.46, crashed at Staverton 15.6.52; G-AFJP (585), 10.9.38, w.f.u. 9.39, rest. 5.47, crashed at Woodbridge 3.10.53; G-AFJW (619), 10.9.38, crashed at Rearsby in 1939; G-AFKN (628), 31.10.38, crashed at Bury St. Edmunds 11.3.39; G-AFKO* (1091), 5.1.39, converted to Taylorcraft Model H three-seat glider 1943, first flown thus at Rearsby 6.7.43

Taylorcraft Plus C

G-AFNW (100), 9.5.39, County Flying Club, Rearsby; impressed 7.41 as ES956; crashed at Garth, near Builth Wells 14.3.42

G-AFTN (102), 17.5.39, Wiltshire S. of F., High Post; impressed 9.41 as HL535; rest. 5.46 to B. Arden, Exeter; stored near Exeter since 1957

G-AFTO (103), 22.5.39, Coventry (Civil) Aviation Ltd., Whitley; impressed 9.41 as HL533; destroyed in fatal crash 23.11.42

G-AFTP (104), 26.5.39, West Suffolk Aero Club, Bury St. Edmunds; impressed 7.41, found unsuitable for R.A.F. use and no serial issued

G-AFTT (101), 16.5.39, West Suffolk Aero Club, Bury St. Edmunds; impressed 7.41 but found unsuitable for R.A.F. use and no serial issued

G-AFTY (105), 7.6.39, Malling Aviation Ltd., West Malling; Wiltshire S. of F., High Post 8.39; impressed 9.41 as HL536; burned out at Lydd 3.5.42

G-AFTZ (106), 15.6.39, West Suffolk Aero Club, Bury St. Edmunds; Luton Flying Club 8.39; impressed 8.41 as HH987; rest. 5.46 as G-AHLJ q.v.

G-AFUA (107), 20.6.39, Malling Aviation Ltd., West Malling; A. Harrison, Castle Bromwich 7.39; stored until rest. 9.47 to R. M. Smith, Walsall; beyond repair in forced landing at Northaw, Herts. 18.10.48

G-AFUB (108), 24.6.39, Coventry (Civil) Aviation Ltd., Whitley; impressed 9.41 as HL534; rest. 1.46 to J. L. Brockhouse, Walsall; eight subsequent owners ending with W. A. Rollason Ltd., Croydon 6.52; to Ireland 6.53 as EI-AGD

G-AFUD (109), 29.6.39, Luton Flying Club; impressed 8.41 as HH986; rest. 2.46 as Taylorcraft Plus C.2 G-AHBO q.v.

G-AFUX (111), 30.6.39, J. W. W. Hurndell, Odiham; impressed 8.41 as HH988; crashed at R.A.F. Westley 7.10.42

G-AFUY (112), 5.7.39, S. Lawrence, Alfreton, Derbyshire; impressed 7.41 as ES957; spun in at Tilshead, Wilts. 9.12.41

G-AFUZ (113), 10.7.39, County Flying Club, Rearsby; impressed 7.41 as ES960; crashed at Buntingford, Herts. 29.1.41

G-AFVA (114), 13.7.39, Grimsby Aviation Ltd., Waltham; impressed 8.41 as HH982; rest. 1.46 as Taylorcraft Plus C.2 G-AHAE q.v.

G-AFVB (115), 14.7.39, Luton Flying Club; impressed 8.41 as HH985; beyond repair in flying accident 25.9.42

G-AFVU (116), 22.7.39, Romford Flying Club, Maylands; destroyed in hangar fire at Maylands 6.2.40

G-AFVW (117), 22.7.39, Coventry (Civil) Aviation Ltd., Whitley; impressed 9.41 as HL532; beyond repair in flying accident 21.11.42

G-AFVX (118), 1.8.39, Taylorcraft Aeroplanes (England) Ltd., Rearsby; impressed 10.41 as HM501; to instructional airframe 5.43 as 3775M

G-AFVY (119), 4.8.39, Derby Aero Club, Burnaston; impressed 8.41 as HH984; forced landed on fire at Old Sarum and burned out 17.5.42

G-AFVZ (120), 5.8.39, Derby Aero Club, Burnaston; impressed 8.41 as HH983; flew into high ground at Newport, Isle of Wight 11.11.41

G-AFWK (121), 22.8.39, W. G. Turnbull, Rearsby; impressed 7.41 as ES958; beyond repair in flying accident 13.2.43

G-AFWL (122), 31.8.39, Taylorcraft Aeroplanes (England) Ltd., Rearsby; dismantled at Rearsby 5.40

G-AFWM (123), 25.8.39, County Flying Club, Rearsby; impressed 7.41 as ES959; rest. 5.46 to the Earl of Cardigan, Marlborough; four later owners; scrapped at Portsmouth in 1960

Taylorcraft Plus C.2

G-AHAE (114), G-AFVA, HH982, 13.3.47, Wiltshire S. of F., Thruxton; Newcastle Aero Club 2.50; D. Sturgeon, Newtownards 9.52; scrapped at Panshanger 1957

G-AHAF (110), T9120, 19.6.46, Wiltshire School of Flying Ltd., Thruxton; destroyed at Thruxton 29.5.48 when Taylorcraft Plus D G-AHUG landed on it.

G-AHBO (109), G-AFUD, HH986, Air Training (Oxford) Ltd., Kidlington; last owner Wycombe Flying Club, Booker 2.51; d.b.r. near Northampton 24.5.52

G-AHLJ (106), G-AFTZ, HH987, Vickers-Armstrongs Ltd., Chilbolton; Universal Flying Services Ltd., Fairoaks 6.57; Fairoaks Aero Club 7.59; to Ireland 4.60 as EI-ALH

Taylorcraft Plus D *(pre-war production)*

G-AFWN (124), 31.8.39, Taylorcraft Aeroplanes (England) Ltd., Rearsby; damaged in 1942; stored until rebuilt as the prototype Auster J-1 in 1945

G-AFWO (125), 17.4.40, Taylorcraft Aeroplanes (England) Ltd., Rearsby; impressed 8.40 as X7534; rest. 12.46 to Aircraft (Hereford) Ltd.; last of seven subsequent owners was the Stapleford Flying Group 6.62; fitted with Cirrus Minor 2A engine 1963; crashed into building at Willesden Lane, N.W.2 on 29.5.63

G-AFZH (126), 15.7.40, Taylorcraft Aeroplanes (England) Ltd., Rearsby; impressed 8.40 as W5740; rest. 3.46 as G-AHEI q.v.

G-AFZI (127), 15.7.40, Taylorcraft Aeroplanes (England) Ltd., Rearsby; impressed 8.40 as W5741; rest. 1.46 to H. J. Curtis, Kidlington; Crewsair Flying Club, Southend 12.51; Alouette Flying Club, Biggin Hill 7.59; crashed on take-off at Bembridge 21.10.63

G-AFZJ (128), Taylorcraft Aeroplanes (England) Ltd., Rearsby; to School of Army Co-Operation, Old Sarum 12.39; flown as '128' in camouflage in France 4.40–5.40; C. of A. 18.7.40; scrapped at Rearsby 7.41

Taylorcraft Plus D G-AFZI in service with No.1424 Flight, Larkhill in 1942, after impressment as W5741. (*Aeroplane*)

G-AFZK	(129), registration not taken up, aircraft not constructed
G-AFZL	(130), registration not taken up, aircraft not constructed
G-AGBF	(131), 17.7.40, Taylorcraft Aeroplanes (England) Ltd.; impressed 8.40 as X7533; beyond repair in forced landing at Alford, Lincs. 17.1.41
G-AGDB	(132), Taylorcraft Aeroplanes (England) Ltd., Rearsby; flown in camouflage with civil markings 1941; converted to Auster I (c/n 137) LB267
G-AHEI	(126), G-AFZH, W5740, 31.5.46, Newman Aircraft Ltd., Panshanger; R.A.F. Flying Club, Panshanger 7.48; N. D. Norman, Staverton 3.50; Lt. Col. D. H. Tapp, Staverton 2.51; to Algeria 3.54 as F-OAQP

Taylorcraft Plus D *(post-war conversions)*

G-AGZN (178), LB319, 19.7.46, crashed at Loughborough 1.2.48; G-AHAD (154), LB283, 17.5.46, to Ireland 5.60 as EI-ALJ; G-AHAH (199), LB340, 8.3.46, crashed at Musbury, Devon 10.7.47; G-AHAI (202), LB343, 21.3.46, crashed at Doncourt les Conflans, France 8.11.59; G-AHAJ (221), LB374, 8.3.46, crashed at Cranleigh, Surrey 30.11.47; G-AHAK (177), LB318, 13.3.46, crashed landing at Speke 16.6.57; G-AHCG (206), LB347, 12.4.46, to Ireland 7.63 as EI-ANA; G-AHCH (164), LB293, 4.5.46, d.b.r. at Rearsby 16.3.47; G-AHCI (159) LB288, 29.4.46, burned out at Shoreham 18.9.51; G-AHCR (211), LB352, 17.9.46, d.b.r. at Exeter 20.4.68; G-AHGW (222), LB375, 4.10.46; G-AHGX (162), LB291, 7.9.46, to Finland 2.52 as OH-AUG; G-AHGY (204), LB345, 8.5.46, w.f.u. at Booker 7.48; G-AHGZ (214), LB367, 13.5.46

G-AHHA (160), LB289, 6.6.46, to Switzerland 6.46 as HB-EOR, later D-EMOV; G-AHHB (156), LB285, 12.7.46, to Belgium 8.59 as OO-DCL; G-AHHC (136), LB266, 7.9.46, to Finland 11.51 as OH-AUD; G-AHHX (173), LB314, 16.7.46, to Germany 1.57 as D-ELUS, later D-ELUV; G-AHHY (216), LB369, 19.7.46, to Southern Rhodesia 12.58 as VP-YPX; G-AHHZ (229), LB382, 21.6.46, crashed at Snarford 15.10.50; G-AHKN (180), LB321, 11.5.46, burned out at High Post 26.2.47; G-AHKO (228), LB381, 22.5.46, to Germany 3.56 as D-ECOD; G-AHNG (200), LB341, 15.8.46; G-AHNZ (208), LB349, 4.6.46, to France 10.50 as F-BAVU

G-AHSB (174), LB315, 13.7.46, wrecked by gale at Gatwick 6.11.52; G-AHSC (192), LB333, 13.7.46, to Ireland 7.46 as EI-ACP; G-AHSD (182), LB323, 12.7.46, w.f.u. at Skegness 9.62; G-AHSE (212), LB365, registered 24.8.46 to Auster Aircraft Ltd., not converted, dismantled at Rearsby 10.47; G-AHSF (224), LB377, 7.9.46, d.b.r. at Rearsby 2.9.47; G-AHSG (217), LB370, 16.7.46, damaged at Newtownards in 1952, scrapped at Stapleford 1959; G-AHSJ (172), LB313, 2.8.46, d.b.r. in forced landing at Chingford 25.8.56; G-AHSK (213), LB366, 10.9.46, w.f.u. at Perth 8.50 and scrapped; G-AHSL (189), LB330, 30.9.46, crashed at Macmerry 23.7.48

G-AHUA (193), LB334, 9.8.46, to Finland 3.50 as OH-AUB; G-AHUG (153), LB282, 6.7.46; G-AHUH (150), LB279, 18.11.46, crashed at Swanage 17.7.49; G-AHUM (157), LB286, 10.7.46, w.f.u. at Fairoaks 6.55; G-AHVP (146), LB276, 1.8.46, crashed at Elmdon 15.4.51; G-AHVR (170), LB311, 23.1.47, crashed at Heanton, Devon 24.4.60; G-AHVS (201), LB342, 3.10.46, crashed and burned at Sleap 12.8.61; G-AHWD (230), LB383, 18.2.49, w.f.u. at Elstree 4.52; G-AHWI (166), LB296, 7.2.47, destroyed in ground collision with Spitfire at Gatwick 8.5.53; G-AHWJ (165), LB294, 7.8.46; G-AHWK (220), LB373, 25.10.46, w.f.u. at Lulsgate 9.52; G-AHXE (171), LB312, 18.10.46; G-AHXF (184), LB325, 27.6.47, to Finland 11.52 as OH-AUH; G-AHXG (181), LB322, 1.10.46, wrecked by gale at Sleap 12.2.61

G-AIIU (196), LB337, 3.12.46, d.b.r. at Denham 28.12.58; G-AIRE (223), LB376, 27.2.47, w.f.u. at Hemswell 6.66; G-AIXA (134), LB264, 20.2.47; G-AIXB (225), LB378, 4.7.47, to Southern Rhodesia 2.56 as VP-YNM, later ZS-DVV; G-ARRK (built from spares, c/n given as 157 belonging to one of the contributing aircraft), 6.10.61, to Ireland 4.62 as EI-AMF

Thruxton Jackaroo *(with R.A.F. serial of the Tiger Moth used)*

G-ANFY	NL906, 13.2.58, Wiltshire School of Flying, Thruxton; M. F. Ogilvie-Forbes, Thruxton 3.65; withdrawn from use 5.68
G-ANZT	T7798, 22.11.57, N. H. Jones, Croydon; M. F. Ogilvie-Forbes, Thruxton 3.65; withdrawn from use 3.68
G-AOEX	NM175, 11.7.57, Wiltshire School of Flying, Thruxton; M. F. Ogilvie-Forbes, Thruxton 3.65; withdrawn from use at Thruxton 2.68
G-AOEY	DF150, 11.7.57, Wiltshire School of Flying, Thruxton; flown to Nigeria 9.58 by F. J. Ibbotson and re-registered VR-NCY; derelict at Lagos in 1968
G-AOIO	N6907, 15.7.58, Blackpool and Fylde Aero Club, Squires Gate; J. Bower, Doncaster 6.63; Air Navigation & Trading Co. Ltd., Squires Gate 6.64; P. R. Harris, Booker 1.71; P. A. Gliddon, Booker 12.72
G-AOIR	R4972, 12.12.57, Wiltshire School of Flying, Thruxton; J. Horlock, Swansea 6.67; P. Martin, Barton 6.68; Stevenage Flying Club, Old Warden 7.70
G-AOIT	T5465, 14.11.58, Wiltshire School of Flying, Thruxton; Caledonian Flying Services Ltd., Renfrew 1.60; withdrawn from use at Renfrew 7.65
G-AOIV	T6917, 27.10.58, Wiltshire School of Flying, Thruxton; sold in Argentina 8.59; retained British marks; scrapped at Don Torcuate Airport
G-AOIW	T6918, 23.4.59, Wiltshire School of Flying, Thruxton; crashed at Thruxton 23.4.64
G-AOIX	T7087, 20.3.58, Wiltshire School of Flying, Thruxton; M. F. Ogilvie-Forbes, Thruxton 3.65; C. Boddington, Sywell 3.68; used as spares 1968
G-APAI	DE978, 30.12.57, Wiltshire School of Flying, Thruxton; M. F. Ogilvie-Forbes, Thruxton 3.65; beyond repair landing at Chilbolton 8.4.64
G-APAJ	T5616, 5.6.58, Wiltshire School of Flying, Thruxton; M. F. Ogilvie-Forbes, Thruxton 3.65; J. T. Hayes, Hemswell 6.68; R. V. Snook, Hemswell 9.69
G-APAK	T7922, conversion to Jackaroo abandoned

Jackaroo G-APHZ at Oakville, Ontario as CF-QOT in 1971. *(J. F. McNulty)*

G-APAL N6847, 15.5.59, Wiltshire School of Flying, Thruxton; C. R. Watson, White Waltham 4.60; Stevenage Flying Group, Old Warden 6.65; crash landed at Wilhamstead, Beds. 5.7.68

G-APAM N6850, 29.10.59, Miss Sheila Scott, Thruxton; British Skydiving Ltd., Blackbushe 6.64; R. Jones, Thruxton 4.68

G-APAO R4922, 1.5.59, J. S. Read, Thruxton; P. G. Barber, Thruxton 6.62; Wiltshire School of Flying 6.66; R. W. Biggs, Thruxton 3.68

G-APAP R5136, 11.9.59, Wiltshire School of Flying, Thruxton; M. F. Ogilvie-Forbes, Thruxton 3.65; H. D. V. Leach, Hannington strip, Hants. 6.68

G-APHZ N6924, 8.7.58, Airspray (Colchester) Ltd., Boxted; Air Ulster Ltd., Nutts Corner 5.60; Wiltshire School of Flying 7.64; M. F. Ogilvie-Forbes, Thruxton 3.65; B. H Witty, Dunkeswell 9.70; to Canada 5.71 as CF-QOT

G-APJV N7446, 30.1.59, Glamorgan Aviation Ltd., Rhoose; w.f.u. at Rhoose 2.61

G-APOV* R5130, 7.4.60, Rollason Aircraft and Engines Ltd., Croydon (used by the Tiger Club, Redhill); crash landed at Staplehurst, Kent 3.7.61

Note: Registrations G-APRB, 'RC, 'SU and 'SV, reserved for Jackaroo conversion of Tiger Moths N6667, T8197, N6585 and DE636, were not taken up

* Converted by Rollasons at Croydon in 1960

Tipsy S.2 *(Belgian-built)*

G-AENF (28), OO-ASA, 29.10.36, burned in 1948; G-AFFN (36), OO-ASJ, 9.3.38, scrapped at Blackbushe 2.53; G-AFVH (29), OO-ASB, 8.7.39, to Belgium 7.49 for preservation as 'OO-TIP'

Tipsy S.2 *(British-built, three only received Authorisations to Fly)*

G-AEOB (T.51, later 101), 14.1.37, Tipsy Light Aircraft Ltd., Hanworth; later based at Whitchurch, Bristol; scrapped at Hanworth 12.37

G-AESU (102), 22.4.37, Fairey Aviation Co. Ltd., Harmondsworth; crashed 9.37

G-AEWJ (103), Tipsy Light Aircraft Ltd., Hanworth; crashed at Broadstairs 6.6.37

G-AEXK (104), 29.6.37 Tipsy Light Aircraft Ltd., Hanworth; E. D. Ward, Hooton; scrapped at Hooton 8.37

G-AEXL (105), Tipsy Light Aircraft Ltd., Hanworth; withdrawn from flying 1937

G-AEYG (106), Tipsy Light Aircraft Ltd., Hanworth; withdrawn from flying 1937

Note: Registrations G-AEYH, G-AEZV and G-AEZW allotted to airframes 107 to 109, were not taken up

Tipsy B and BC* *(Belgian-built)*

G-AFCM (503), OO-DOS, 1.5.38, burned at Slough in 1952; G-AFEI (506), OO-DOV, 18.1.38, burned in grandstand fire at Hooton Racecourse 8.7.40; G-AGBM* (502), registered 29.1.40, flown by the Fairey Aviation Co. Ltd. as F-0222, impressed 6.41 as HM494, rest. 1.46, to Belgium 1.47 as OO-DOP

Tipsy Trainer 1 *(British-built)*

G-AFGF (1), 26.7.38, Brian Allen Aviation Ltd., Heston; Airwork Flying Club, Heston 12.38; Brian Allen, Heston 4.39; burned at Slough in 1952

G-AFJR (2), 6.10.38, R. E. Bibby, Hooton; Yorkshire Aeroplane Club, Sherburn 2.39; Tattersall's Garages Ltd., Squires Gate 9.49; converted to Belfair in 1957; based at Jenkin's Farm, Navestock, Essex by R. M. Long in 1973

G-AFJS (3), 22.10.38, Yorkshire Aeroplane Club, Sherburn; Cardiff Ultra Light Aeroplane Club, Cardiff 1.49; crashed at St. Mellons 3.7.55

G-AFJT (4), 21.11.38, Maj. J. E. D. Shaw, Kirkbymoorside; Sir Arthur Longmore, Grantham 9.39; K. C. Millican, Woolsington 7.49; to Finland 8.50 as OH-SVA

G-AFKP (5), 9.12.38, Duke of Richmond and Gordon, Goodwood; used by Fairey in 1941 as F-0222 in succession to G-AGBM; F. Ellam, Thame 6.46; H. C. Oulton, Almaza 8.49; W. C. Jelliss, Khartoum 11.50; crashed at Gedaref, Sudan 4.6.52

G-AFMN (6), 27.1.39, E. D. Ward, Hooton; destroyed by fire at Hooton 8.7.40 while stored under the racecourse grandstand used as a hangar

G-AFRT (8), 1.5.39, Air Sales and Service Ltd., Bekesbourne (used by Kent Flying Club); burned at Slough in 1952

G-AFRU (9), 17.7.39, Airtraining (Oxford) Ltd., Kidlington; Moss Bros. Aircraft Ltd., Chorley 1.46; L. D. Birkett, Barton 10.48; scrapped at Redhill 1954

G-AFRV (10), 22.7.39, Airtraining (Oxford) Ltd., Kidlington; Moss Bros. Aircraft Ltd., Chorley 1.46; J. H. Reed, Woolsington 6.48; D. G. Walling, Fairford 6.69; I. B. Willis, Enstone 12.72; R. C. Bailey, Shoreham 2.73

Belgian-built Tipsy S.2 G-AFFN alongside the Sopwith Pup G-EBKY at the R.Ae.S. Garden Party, Heathrow, on 8 May 1938. *(A. J. Jackson)*

G-AFSC (11), 18.7.39, Airwork Flying Club Ltd., Heston; J. C. Rice, Leicester 9.45; Cardiff Ultra Light Flying Club 6.50; Armstrong Siddeley Flying Club, Baginton 8.53; based at Tees-side by F. H. Greenwell in 1973

G-AFVN (12), 21.7.39, Airtraining (Oxford) Ltd., Kidlington; I. H. Cameron, Perth 3.49; Montgomery Ultra Light Flying Club, Welshpool 3.52; based at Wickenby by W. Callow and partners in 1973

G-AFVO (15), 29.6.39, Maj. J. E. D. Shaw, Kirkbymoorside; Fairey Aviation Co. Ltd., White Waltham 1.46; sold in Belgium 9.46 as OO-DAU

G-AFVP (14), 29.8.39, Airsales and Service Ltd., Bekesbourne for the Kent Flying Club; used by the R.A.F. 20.5.40 to 9.6.40; scrapped during 1939–45 war

G-AFWT (13), 5.8.39, W. R. Trounson, White Waltham; West London Aero Services Ltd., White Waltham 7.51; Home Counties Flying Group 10.53; based at Old Warden by A. G. Thelwall and partners in 1973

G-AISA (17), 27.6.47, Tipsy Aircraft Co. Ltd., Hanworth; Royal Naval Flying Club, Gosport 7.49; based at Coleford by A. Liddiard and partner in 1973

G-AISB (18), 29.9.47, Tipsy Aircraft Co. Ltd., Hanworth; Royal Naval Flying Club, Gosport 7.49; owned by the Cranfield Flying Group in 1973

G-AISC (19), 16.4.48, Tipsy Aircraft Co. Ltd., Hanworth; Fairey Aviation Co. Ltd., White Waltham 1.49; based at Compton Abbas by the Wagtail Flying Group in 1973

Tipsy Belfair

G-AOXO (537), OO-TIG, 21.11.58; G-APIE (535), OO-TIE, 25.7.58; G-APOD (536), OO-TIF, 1.11.62

Tipsy Nipper Mk.II *(Belgian-built)*

G-APYB (T66/39), Stamo 1400A, 2.3.60; G-ARBG (T66/18), Stamo 1400A, 30.3.61; G-ARBP (T66/54), Ardem 4CO2 Mk.2, 20.6.60; G-ARDY (T66/55), Martlet VW, 19.9.60; G-ARFV (T66/44), Stamo 1400A, 20.12.60, d.b.r. at Halfpenny Green 29.8.71; G-ARXN (T66/77), Stamo 1400A, 25.3.65; G-ASRY (T66/25), OY-AEK, registration not taken up; G-ASXI (T66/56), VH-CGH, Stamo 1400A, 30.10.64; G-ASZV (T66/45), 5N-ADE, Stamo 1400A, 15.7.65; G-ATBW (T66/52), OO-MAG, Stamo 1400A, 8.6.65; G-ATKZ (T66/72), Stamo 1400A, 1.3.66; G-ATUH (T66/6), OO-NIF, HEPU 40-3500, 25.8.66; G-AVDK (T66/9), OO-NIK, HEPU 40-3500, 9.6.67, w.f.u. 5.68; G-AVKT (T66/70), OO-HEL, Ardem 4CO2 Mk.X, 13.6.67, converted to Mk.III as specimen aircraft for Nipper Aircraft Ltd., q.v., crashed at Paull, Yorks, 19.8.72

Vickers F.B.27 Vimy

Unreg. (13), possibly F8608, Vickers Ltd., Brooklands; damaged at Clifden, Ireland after first transatlantic flight 14.6.19; permanently exhibited at the Science Museum, London

G-EAAR (C-105), B9952, registered 1.5.19 to Vickers Ltd., Brooklands; flown to Amsterdam for ELTA Exhibition 8.19; registration cancelled 5.20

G-EAOL F8625, first flown 20.9.19, registered 16.10.19 to Vickers Ltd., Brooklands; flown to Madrid for demonstrations 10.19; sold to the Spanish Government in 1920

G-EAOU F8630, 3.11.19, Vickers Ltd., Brooklands; flown to Australia November–December 1919; preserved for all time at Adelaide Airport, S.A.

G-AWAU (VAFA.02), replica, first flown at Wisley 3.6.69, C. of A. 4.6.69, Vintage Aircraft Flying Ltd., Wisley; repainted 7.69 as H651; damaged by fire at Ringway 16.7.69; rebuilt as F8614 and placed in the R.A.F. Museum, Hendon in 1972

Vickers F.B.27 Vimy replica G-AWAU at the Paris Air Show in June 1969. (*Brian Service*)

The prototype Viking Mk.I at Brooklands in October 1919. (Vickers Ltd.)

Vickers Vimy Commercial

G-EAAV K-107, first flown 13.4.19, C. of A. 20.7.19, Vickers Ltd., Brooklands; crashed at Tabora, Tanganyika 27.2.20

G-EASI (41), 13.5.20, S. Instone and Co. Ltd., Croydon 'City of London'; Imperial Airways Ltd., Croydon 6.24; scrapped in 1926

G-EAUL (40), 18.8.20, Vickers Ltd., Brooklands; sold in China 8.21

G-EAUY (39), registered 31.7.20 to Vickers Ltd., Brooklands; sold in China 2.21

Vickers Viking amphibians

G-EAOV (Viking I), registered 21.10.19 to Vickers Ltd., Brooklands; crashed near Rouen, France 18.12.19

G-EASC (Viking II), registered 26.3.20 to Vickers Ltd., Brooklands; withdrawn from use late in 1920

Viking Mk. IV G-EBED during the Vickers sales tour of Spain in 1923.

G-EAUK (Viking III), registered 10.7.20 to Vickers Ltd., Brooklands; to the Air Council 19.1.21 as N147; delivered to Gosport 5.21

G-EBBZ Viking Mk.IV Type 60 (15), registered 14.3.22 to Sir Ross Smith for proposed round-the-world flight; crashed at Brooklands 13.4.22

G-EBED Viking MK.IV Type 60 (17), C. of A. 6.10.22, Vickers Ltd., Brooklands; L. Hamilton, St. Moritz 7.26 as Type 67; withdrawn from use 7.27

Vickers Vulcan

G-EBBL (1), Type 61, 23.6.22, Instone Air Line Ltd., Croydon 'City of Antwerp'; Imperial Airways Ltd., Croydon 3.24 'City of Brussels'; scrapped at Croydon 5.24

G-EBDH (2), Type 61, 28.8.22, Instone Air Line Ltd., Croydon; accident at Oxted, Surrey in 1922; Vickers Ltd., Brooklands 6.23; w.f.u. 7.23

G-EBEA (3), Type 61, 28.8.22, Instone Air Line Ltd., Croydon 'City of Brussels'; Vickers Ltd., Brooklands 6.23; withdrawn from use 7.23

G-EBEK (4), Type 63 freighter, 6.11.22, Air Council, Martlesham, converted to Type 61 for the Empire Exhibition, Wembley in 1925; scrapped 1926

G-EBEM (5), Type 61, 15.9.22, Douglas Vickers M.P., Brooklands; L. Hamilton, Brooklands 1.26; lost at sea off the Italian coast 7.5.26

G-EBES (6), Type 61, registered 11.8.22 to Queensland and Northern Territory Aerial Services Ltd.; aircraft not completed

G-EBET (7), Type 61, 27.11.22, Queensland and Northern Territory Aerial Services Ltd., Longreach; sent back to England as specification not met

G-EBFC (8), Type 74, registered 25.1.23 to Vickers Ltd., Brooklands; Douglas Vickers 6.23; C. of A. 23.12.24; Imperial Airways Ltd., Croydon 1.25; withdrawn from use 12.25 and stored at Croydon until dismantled and burned in 1927

G-EBLB (9), Type 74, 11.5.25, Imperial Airways Ltd., Croydon; crashed and burned at Purley after take-off from Croydon 13.7.28

Vickers Viastra

G-AAUB (1), Type 160, registered 29.1.30 to Vickers (Aviation) Ltd., Brooklands; converted to Type 199 Viastra III in 1930 and Type 220 Viastra VIII in 1931; dismantled at Brooklands in 1933

G-ABVM (1), Type 203, VH-UON, N-1, O-6, registered 23.3.32 to Vickers (Aviation) Ltd., Brooklands; frustrated export dismantled at Brooklands 12.32

G-ACCC (1), Type 259, 16.5.33, Flt. Lt. E. H. Fielden, Hendon (Royal Flight); Secretary of State for Air, Croydon 5.35; scrapped at Croydon in 1937

Vickers Viking prototypes

G-AGOK (1, later 101), Type 491, TT194, registered 18.5.45 to Vickers Aviation Ltd., Wisley; d.b.r. in forced landing at Effingham, Surrey 23.4.46; scrapped at the Shoebury, Essex, gunnery ranges in 1947

G-AGOL (2, later 102), Type 495, TT197, registered 4.7.45 to Ministry of Supply and Aircraft Production; to the R.A.F. 2.50 as VX238, later 7215M

G-AGOM (3, later 103), Type 496, 24.4.46, B.O.A.C. (B.E.A. Division), Northolt; to R.A.F. 12.47 as VX141 for Blind Landing Experimental Unit, Bedford

Vickers Type 498 Viking 1A *(many later upgraded to Viking 1, see page 216)*

G-AGON (4, later 104), 10.5.46, B.E.A., to R.A.F. 8.47 as VW214, rest. 7.54 to Eagle, B.K.S. 2.55, to spares at Southend 1956; G-AGRM (5, later 105), 17.5.46, B.E.A., to R.A.F. 8.47 as VW215; G-AGRN (6, later 106), 17.5.46, B.E.A., to R.A.F. 8.47 as VW216; G-AGRO (7, later 107), 12.6.46, B.E.A., James Stuart Travel 7.48, scrapped at Tollerton 2.49; G-AGRP (8, later 108), 18.6.46, B.E.A., Hunting 6.51, Overseas Aviation 2.59, scrapped 6.62; G-AGRR (9, later 109), 5.7.46, B.E.A., Britavia 3.51, Mexico 10.52 as XB-QEX, rest. 3.56 to Eagle as 'Lord Charles Beresford', to Germany 4.57 as D-AIDA, later D-BETA, OE-FAT and OE-HAT; G-AGRS (110), 9.7.46, B.E.A., B.S.A.A.C. 2.48, to B.W.I.A. 1.49 as VP-TAV 'Jamaica', rest. 6.57 to Independent Air Travel, later Eagle, Orion and Air Safaris, scrapped at Southend 5.63; G-AGRT (111), 17.7.46, B.E.A., B.S.A.A.C. 2.48, to B.W.I.A. 6.48 as VP-TAW 'Grenada', rest. 5.57 to Independent Air Travel, later Eagle, burned out at El Adem, Libya 26.2.58; G-AGRU (112), 3.8.46, B.E.A. 'Vagrant', B.S.A.A.C. 2.48, to B.W.I.A. 4.49 as VP-TAX 'Barbados', rest. 3.55 to British International Airlines, Channel Airways 1.59, to Soesterberg, Holland 1.64 as coffee stall; G-AGRV (114), 5.10.46, B.E.A. 'Value', James Stuart Travel 7.48, Hunting 5.51, Tradair 8.59, w.f.u. at Southend 8.60; G-AGRW (115), 3.8.46, B.E.A. 'Vagabond', James Stuart Travel 7.48, Hunting 5.51, later Overseas and Autair, w.f.u. 7.68, to Soesterberg, Holland as coffee stall

G-AHON (116), 15.8.46, B.E.A. 'Valentine', Trans World Charter 1.48, trooping 1952 as WZ973, d.b.r. at Malta 27.5.52; G-AHOP (117), 16.8.46, B.E.A. 'Valerie', Crewsair 'Crew Monarch' 5.51, Airwork 5.52, trooping as WZ972, scrapped at Hurn 8.67; G-AHOR (118), 26.8.46, B.E.A. 'Valet', Airwork 4.53, trooping 1952–56 as XD637, to Trek Airways 11.55 as ZS-DNU 'Piet Retief', rest. 4.58 to Air Safaris, d.b.r. at Tarbes, France 29.5.60; G-AHOS (119), 3.9.46, B.E.A. 'Valiant', B.S.A.A.C. 2.48, to B.W.I.A. 12.48 as VP-TAT 'Trinidad', rest. 6.57 to Independent Air Travel, later Eagle 'Sir John Warren' and Orion 'Sirius', w.f.u. at Southend 5.62; G-AHOT (121), 7.9.46, B.E.A. 'Valkyrie', Trans World Charter 1.48, Crewsair 'Empire Trader' 8.52, Airwork 3.53, trooping 1953 as XD635, to Trek Airways 10.54 as ZS-DKH; G-AHOU (122), 20.9.46, B.E.A. 'Valley', B.S.A.A.C. 2.48, to B.W.I.A. 6.48 as VP-TAU 'Antigua', rest. 6.57 to Independent Air Travel, later Overseas Aviation and Universal Air Charter, w.f.u. at Southend 5.62; G-AHOV (123), 30.9.46, B.E.A. 'Valour', James Stuart Travel 7.48,

British West Indian Airways' Viking 1A VP-TAX 'Barbados', formerly British European Airways' G-AGRU. (*P. R. Keating*)

Crewsair 6.51, scrapped at Southend 1952; G-AHOW (124), 11.10.46, B.E.A. 'Vanessa', James Stuart Travel 7.48, Crewsair 'Africa Trader' 8.52, Airwork 4.53, trooping 1953 as XD636, to Trek Airways 10.54 as ZS-DKI, rest. 1.56 to Air Safaris, later Eros, Air Ferry and Invicta, w.f.u. at Manston 9.67

Vickers Type 610 Viking 1B *(for British European Airways)*

G-AHPK (148), 14.4.47, 'Veracity', crashed at Ruislip, Middlesex 6.1.48; G-AHPL (149), 14.4.47, 'Verdant', later 'Lord Anson', to C.A.A. 6.53 as VP-YKK 'Lundi', rest. 12.58 to Pegasus Airways, later Autair and Invicta, w.f.u. at Manston 2.69; G-AHPM (152), 21.4.47, 'Verderer', later 'Lord Rodney', Eagle 4.53, trooping 1953 as XF632, later XG349, crashed at Stavanger, Norway 9.8.61; G-AHPN (155), 24.3.47, 'Ventnor', later 'Lord St. Vincent', crashed at Heathrow 31.10.50; G-AHPO (157), 12.3.47, 'Venture', later 'Lord Dundonald', Eagle 4.53, trooping 1953 as XF631, to spares at Blackbushe 12.55; G-AHPP (160), 15.4.47, 'Venus', later 'Sir Charles Saunders', Eagle 3.56, to Goa 4.56 as CR-IAC; G-AHPR (164), 28.4.47, 'Verily', later 'Prince Rupert', Independent Air Travel 6.56, Maitland Drewery 3.60, to spares at Hurn 3.62; G-AHPS (167), 14.5.47, 'Verity', later 'Sir Doveton Sturdee', B.K.S. 7.55, to Germany 4.56 as D-ABOM, later D-BORA, rest. 5.64 to Autair and used as spares at Luton

G-AIVB (215), 16.5.47, 'Vernal', later 'Robert Blake', Eagle 6.54, to T.A.I.P., Goa 4.56 as CR-IAD; G-AIVC (216), 16.5.47, 'Vernon', later 'Lord Collingwood', Eagle 9.54, trooping 1955 as WZ353, to Germany 3.57 as D-AGAD, later D-BEPO, later F-BJER; G-AIVD (217), 16.5.47, 'Veteran', later 'Lord Duncan', to Germany 3.56 as D-ADAM, later HB-AAR, rest. 2.63 to Air Ferry, w.f.u. at Manston 4.66; G-AIVE (218), 22.5.47, 'Vestal', crashed at Largs, Ayrshire 21.4.48; G-AIVF (219), 30.5.47, 'Vibrant', later 'Sir James Somerville', to Germany 4.56 as D-AGIL, later D-BARI and HB-AAN, rest. 2.63 to Air Ferry, later Invicta, w.f.u. at Manston 4.66; G-AIVG (220), 30.5.47, 'Viceroy', later 'Sir George Rooke', d.b.r. at Le Bourget 12.8.53; G-AIVH (221), 30.5.47, 'Vicinity', later 'Lord Howe', Eagle 10.54, trooping 1955 as XG896, to spares at Blackbushe 2.60; G-AIVI (222), 4.6.47, 'Victor', later 'Viking', to Germany 3.56 as D-ABEL, later D-BALI; G-AIVJ (223), 18.7.47, 'Victoria', later 'Lord Jellicoe', Overseas Aviation 12.55, to Germany 3.56 as D-ABIR, later D-BONA and OO-EEN 'Sinjoor'; G-AIVK (224), 23.6.47, 'Victory', later 'Lord Keyes', British International Airlines 5.55, Overseas Aviation 11.59, scrapped at Gatwick 1962; G-AIVL (225), 25.6.47, 'Vigilant', later 'Lord Hawke', Eagle 6.55, to spares at Heathrow 6.61; G-AIVM (226), 8.7.47, 'Vigorous', later 'George Monck', to Germany 12.55 as D-CADA, later D-ADEL;

G-AIVN (227), 27.6.47, 'Violet', later 'Edward Boscawen', to C.A.A. 9.54 as VP-YMO 'Rukuru'; G-AIVO (228), 18.8.47, 'Villain', later 'Edward Vernon', Eagle 6.53, trooping 1954 as XF630 and XG568, to Airnautic, France as spares in 1962; G-AIVP (229), 7.8.47, 'Vimy', air collision with Russian Yak fighter, crashed near Gatow, Berlin 5.4.48

G-AJBM (239), 7.8.47, 'Vincent', later 'Charles Watson', to the Argentine Air Force 1.56 as T-92; G-AJBN (240), 11.9.47, 'Vindictive', later 'Lord Nelson', Eagle 10.54, to spares at Blackbushe 9.60; G-AJBO (241), 12.9.47, 'Vintage', later 'John Benbow', Eagle 10.54, trooping 1955 as XF629, later XG895, crashed at Blackbushe 1.5.57; G-AJBP (242), 16.9.47, 'Vintner', later 'Sir Edward Spragge', Eagle 6.54, renamed 1958 as 'Sir Edward Hughes', to France 12.58 as F-BJAH; G-AJBR (243), 24.9.47, 'Virginia', later 'Sir Bertram Ramsey', B.K.S. 3.55, to Germany 1.57 as D-AHAF, later D-BONE; G-AJBS (244), 25.9.47, 'Virgo', later 'Sir Cloudesley Shovell', to the Argentine Air Force 1.56 as T-93; G-AJBT (245), 19.9.47, 'Viper', later 'Sir Thomas Troubridge', to C.A.A. 4.55 as VP-YNF 'Mazoe', rest. 12.58 to Pegasus Airlines, Autair 1.60, scrapped at Luton 2.62

G-AJBU (246), 16.1.48, 'Virtue', later 'Lord Bridport', Fieldair 1.56, Independent Air Travel 1.57, w.f.u. at Hurn 3.60; G-AJBV (247), 23.1.48, 'Viscount', later 'Sir Henry Morgan', Eagle 2.53, to Iraqi Airways 5.53 as YI-ACJ; G-AJBW (248), 21.1.48, 'Vista', later 'Sir William Cornwallis', Eagle 6.55, to France 6.58 as F-BFDN; G-AJBX (249), 27.1.48, 'Vital', later 'Sir Edward Hughes', Eagle 6.53, to Germany 1.56 as D-AFIX, later D-BABA, rest. 1.60 to Continental Air Services, Maitland Drewery 8.60, later Air Safaris, Eros and Air Ferry, w.f.u. at Manston 5.65; G-AJBY (250), 8.1.48, 'Vitality', later 'Lord Torrington', to Germany 3.56 as D-AFUS, later D-BELA; G-AJCA (252), 1.2.49, 'Vixen', later 'Sir John Leake', to Misrair 7.54 as SU-AIF, rest. 5.60 to Air Safaris, to spares at Hurn 1962

G-AJCD (255), 17.2.49, 'Vizor', later 'Lord Barham', Eagle 10.54, trooping 1955 as XF633, later XG350, to Airnautic, France as spares in 1962; G-AJCE (256), 24.3.48, 'Vivacious', later 'Lord Exmouth', Eagle 3.55, later Independent Air Travel, Continental Air Services and Overseas Aviation, d.b.r. at Lyons, France 14.8.61; G-AJDI (258), 25.2.49, 'Volatile', later 'Lord Keith', to the Argentine Air Force 1.56 as T-91; G-AJDJ (259), 1.3.49, 'Volley', later 'Lord Beatty', to Misrair 6.54 as SU-AIG; G-AJDK (260), 22.3.49, 'Volunteer', later 'Richard Kempenfelt', to the Arab Legion Air Force 11.53 as VK500; G-AJDL (262), 30.3.49, 'Vortex', later 'Lord St. Vincent', crashed near Nutts Corner, Belfast 5.1.53; G-AKBG (263), 25.4.49, 'Votary', later 'Sir Thomas Hardy', Hunting-Clan 10.54, later Air Safaris, to spares at Hurn in 1962; G-AKBH (264), 25.4.49, 'Voyager', later 'Lord Hood', Eagle 'Sir Henry Morgan' 3.55, trooping 1955 as XG567, to France 4.61 as F-BJRS

Vickers Type 614 Viking 1A

G-AHOX (125), 26.10.46, B.E.A. 'Vanguard', to the R.A.F. 8.47 as VW218; G-AHOY (128), 5.11.46, B.E.A. 'Vanity', James Stuart Travel 7.48, Hunting 7.49, Pegasus Airlines 4.58, later Autair and Invicta, w.f.u. at Manston 1969; G-AHOZ (129), 11.11.46, B.E.A. 'Vantage', Aviation Traders 12.48, to B.W.I.A. 1.49 as VP-TAZ 'British Honduras', to C.A.A. 9.51 as VP-YJA 'Hunyani', rest. 9.57 to Eagle, Channel Airways 6.62, w.f.u. at Southend 1.63

G-AHPA (130), 14.11.46, B.E.A. 'Varlet', to the R.A.F. 8.47 as VW217; G-AHPB (132), 13.11.46, B.E.A. 'Variety', Hunting 1.49, later Tradair, Overseas and Autair, w.f.u. 1968, to Soesterberg, Holland as coffee stall; G-AHPC (133), 18.11.46, B.E.A. 'Vassal', Hunting 1.49, later Tradair and Air Safaris, to spares at Hurn 7.62; G-AHPD (134), 20.11.46, B.E.A. 'Vampire', Hunting 1.49, d.b.r. landing at Bordeaux, France

8.5.51; G-AHPE (137), 5.12.46, B.E.A. 'Vandal', Aviation Traders 12.48, to B.W.I.A. 1.49 as VP-TBB 'Bahamas', rest. 6.57 to Independent Air Travel, later Continental Air Services and Overseas Aviation, to spares at Gatwick 6.61; G-AHPF (138), 5.12.46, B.E.A. 'Vedette', Aviation Traders 12.48, to B.W.I.A. 1.49 as VP-TBC 'British Guiana', to C.A.A. 12.51 as VP-YJB, rest. 9.57 to Eagle, to Austria 4.58 as OE-FAE, later OE-HAE

The much-reregistered Viking 1A G-AHPF in its final role as OE-HAE with Aero Transport, Vienna. (*Aviation Photo News*)

Vickers Type 616 Viking 1B

G-AIHA (146), registered 10.9.46 to Vickers-Armstrongs Ltd., Wisley; to C.A.A. 9.46 as VP-YEW 'Zambesi', converted to Viking 3B, rest. 8.56 to Eagle as 'Sir Richard Kempenfelt', reduced to spares at Heathrow 8.60

G-AJCF (257), registered 17.9.47 to Ministry of Civil Aviation; to C.A.A. 2.48 as VP-YHT 'Shire'; to West Deutsche Fluglinie 7.57 as D-ALYK, later D-BLYK 'Düsseldorf'; to Airnautic, Perpignan 12.59 as F-BJES, based at Nice 1973 by Transports Aériens Reunis

Vickers Type 618 Nene Viking

G-AJPH (207), VX856, first flown 6.4.48, Ministry of Supply; to Eagle Aviation Ltd. as Viking 1B, later Viking 3B 'Lord Dundonald', C. of A. 10.9.54; trooping 1955 as XJ804, dismantled for spares at Blackbushe 9.62

Vickers Type 621 Viking C.Mk.2 *(civilianised as Viking 1, 1A, 2 or 3)*

G-AIJE (127), 20.9.46, Vickers-Armstrongs Ltd., Wisley, to R.A.F. 9.46 as VL226, rest. 1.48 to Ministry of Supply, to Boscombe Down as VL226 three more times by 9.57, rest. to Independent Air Travel, crashed at Southall 2.9.58; G-AIKN (131), 19.10.46, Vickers-Armstrongs Ltd., to R.A.F. 1.47 as VL227, rest. 11.55 to Ministry of Supply, B.K.S. Air Transport 3.57, Continental Air Services 1.58, scrapped at Southend 1969; G-ANZK (145), VL230, registered 3.55 to Field, dismantled for spares at Bovingdon; G-AOCH (150), VL231, A82-1, VL231, 1.6.56, Dragon Airways, to Germany 2.57 as D-AMOR, later D-BABY, rest. 5.63 to Air Ferry, Invicta 4.66, w.f.u. at Manston 7.68; G-APAT (153), VL232, 17.5.57, Eagle 'Lord Hood', later Orion and Air Safaris, w.f.u. at Hurn 5.61; G-APOO (156), VL233, 8.12.58, Tradair, Channel Airways 12.62, w.f.u. at Southend 4.65; G-APWS (140), VL229, delivered to Tradair, Ringway–Southend 10.10.59 and reduced to spares

Vickers Type 623 and Type 626 Viking C.Mk.2 *(civilianised as Viking 2B)*

G-AOBY (179), VL248, Type 626, registered 6.55 to Air Couriers (Transport) Ltd., Biggin Hill; to Mexico 6.55 as XB-FIP 'Jorge'

G-APOP (177), VL246, Type 623, 8.12.58, Tradair Ltd., Southend; Channel Airways Ltd. 12.62; withdrawn from use at Southend 4.65

G-APOR (178), VL247, Type 623, 12.6.59, Tradair Ltd., Southend; Channel Airways Ltd. 12.62; withdrawn from use at Southend 3.65

Viking 1B G-AIXR in service with Tradair Ltd. at Southend in 1959. (*W. L. Lewis*)

Vickers Type 627 Viking 1B

G-AIXR (233), 29.4.47, Airwork Ltd., Blackbushe; trooping 1952 as WZ355; Tradair Ltd. 4.59; Channel Airways Ltd., Southend 12.62; w.f.u. at Southend 9.63

G-AIXS (234), 5.5.47, Airwork Ltd., Blackbushe; trooping 1952 as WZ354; crashed at Blackbushe 15.8.54

G-AJFP (235), 12.6.47, Airwork Ltd., Blackbushe; to Indian National Airways 12.48 as VT-DAP; scrapped in 1962

G-AJFR (236), 25.7.47, Airwork Ltd., Blackbushe; Tradair Ltd., Southend 4.58; Channel Airways Ltd. 12.62; dismantled for spares at Southend 1966

G-AJFS (237), 1.9.47, Airwork Ltd., Blackbushe; trooping 1952 as WZ311; Tradair Ltd., Southend 2.58; Channel Airways Ltd. 12.62; w.f.u. at Southend 4.64

G-AJFT (238), 6.10.47, Airwork Ltd., Blackbushe; trooping 1952 as WZ306; Air Safaris Ltd., Hurn 9.61; Eros Airline (U.K.) Ltd. 3.62; w.f.u. at Gatwick 9.63

Vickers Type 632 Viking 1B

G-AJBZ, 'CB and 'CC (c/n 251, 253 and 254), registered 17.9.47 to Ministry of Civil Aviation but markings not used; delivered to Air-India 2.48 as VT-CRB, VT-CRC and VT-CSP respectively

Vickers Type 634 Viking 1B

G-AKTU (211), EI-ADI, 10.7.47, Airwork Ltd., Blackbushe; trooping 1954 as WZ356; Air Safaris Ltd. 6.61; dismantled for spares at Hurn 6.62

G-AKTV (208), EI-ADF, 5.6.47, Airwork Ltd., Blackbushe; trooping 1954 as WZ357; Tradair Ltd. 7.59; Channel Airways Ltd., Southend 1.63; w.f.u. 9.63

G-AMNK (210), EI-ADH, SU-AFM, 15.7.55, Hunting Air Transport Ltd.; Don Everall Aviation Ltd., Elmdon 6.60; ditched off Heraklion, Crete 24.8.60

G-ASBE (214), EI-ADL, SU-AFL, delivery flight to Autair (Luton) Ltd. 28.6.62; dismantled for spares at Luton 4.63

Vickers Type 635 Viking 1B

G-AMGG (290), ZS-BNE, 20.3.51, B.E.A. 'Sir Robert Calder', Eagle Aviation Ltd. 8.55, crashed at Agadir, Morocco 12.12.59; G-AMGH (293), ZS-BNH, 22.3.51, B.E.A. 'Sir John Duckworth', Eagle 8.55, to Germany 4.57 as D-CEDO, later D-AEDO and D-BOBY, rest. 10.59 to Continental Air Services, later Kay Rings Ltd. and Trans World Leasing, to spares at Southend 7.61; G-AMGI (297), ZS-BNL, 17.4.51, B.E.A. 'Sir Henry Harwood', Eagle 8.55, w.f.u. at Heathrow 6.60; G-AMGJ (295), ZS-BNJ, 5.4.51, B.E.A. 'Sir John Warren', First Air Trading Co. Ltd. 1.56, to Germany 4.57 as D-AHUF, later D-BASE, F-BIUX and I-RASC; G-AMNJ (296), ZS-BNK, 27.5.52, B.E.A. 'Lord Fisher', to Germany 12.55 as D-CEDA, later D-AEDA, D-BACU and F-BIPT; G-AMNR (291), ZS-BNF, 8.8.52, B.E.A. 'Lord Charles Beresford', Eagle 6.55, Independent Air Travel 2.56, later Overseas Aviation, w.f.u. 4.61; G-AMNS (294), 1.8.52, B.E.A. 'Sir Dudley Pound', to the Argentine Air Force 1.56 as T-90; G-AMNX (292), ZS-BNG, 17.7.52, B.E.A. 'Sir Philip Brooke', Eagle 6.55, dismantled for spares at Heathrow 10.61

Vickers Type 636 Viking 1B

G-AJJN (289), 10.4.47, Vickers-Armstrongs Ltd., Wisley (demonstrator); B.E.A. 'Vulcan' 3.50, later 'Sir Charles Napier'; B.K.S. Air Transport Ltd. 'Jim Mollison' 1.55; Continental Air Services Ltd. 10.57; Channel Airways Ltd. 8.59; withdrawn from use at Southend 6.63

Vickers Type 639, 641 and 643 Viking 1

G-AHPG (139), 3.3.47 B.E.A. 'Velocity', to C.A.A. 3.47 as Type 641 VP-YHJ 'Sabi', to Suidair International 12.49 as ZS-DDO, rest. 5.57 to Independent Air Travel, later Falcon Airways and Lux International, to coffee stall at Blantyre, Malawi 1.62; G-AHPH (141), 4.5.47, B.E.A. 'Velox', to Suidair International 5.47 as Type 643 ZS-BSB 'Rex', to C.A.A. 6.50 as VP-YIR 'Luangwa', rest. 9.57 to Eagle, Channel Airways 6.58, d.b.r. Southend 28.7.59; G-AHPI (142), 10.7.47, B.E.A. 'Velvet', to Hunting 7.47 as Type 639 'A.C. Greta', crashed in Sicily 16.2.52; G-AHPJ (147), 30.4.47, B.E.A. 'Vengeance', to Hunting 5.48 as Type 639 'A. C. Speke', Overseas Aviation 12.49, Autair 1.62, to Aero Sahara 6.65 as F-OCEU, later F-BMEU

Vickers Type 644 Viking 1B

G-AIVR, 'VS and 'VT (c/n 230–232), registered 18.11.46 to Ministry of Civil Aviation but markings not used; delivered to Iraqi Airways via Bovingdon 10.47 as YI-ABP 'Al Mahfouthah', YI-ABQ 'Al Mamounah' and YI-ABR 'Al Mahroosa' respectively

Vickers Type 637 and Type 651 Valetta C.Mk.1

G-APII VL275, Type 651, delivered Wisley–Ringway 9.12.57 for Eagle Aviation Ltd. and dismantled for spares

G-APIJ WD162, Type 651, delivered to Eagle and dismantled as G-APII above

G-APKR VW802, Type 651, 19.1.59, Decca Navigator Co. Ltd., Biggin Hill; d.b.r. landing at Gatwick 21.9.63 due to undercarriage collapse

G-APKS VL263, (165), Type 637, Decca Navigator Co. Ltd., Biggin Hill; dismantled for spares at Biggin Hill 1.59

Vickers Type 668 Varsity T.Mk.1

G-APAZ (561), WF415, 1.5.59, Ministry of Supply, Cranfield (later Staverton); used for research by Kelvin and Hughes Ltd., Staverton; crashed at Tuffley, Gloucester 27.3.63

G-ARFP (546), WF387, 16.5.63, Ministry of Civil Aviation; returned to the R.A.F. 5.68 as WF387; to the College of Aeronautics, Cranfield; later to Short Bros. and Harland Ltd., West Malling

Vickers Viscount Prototypes

G-AHRF (1), 630, f/f 16.7.48 as VX211, C. of A. 19.8.49, M.o.S., d.b.r. at Khartoum 27.8.52; G-AHRG (2), 663, registered 23.5.46 to Vickers, f/f 15.3.50 as VX217; G-AJZW (3), 640, registered 25.6.47 to Vickers, construction abandoned; G-AMAV (3), 700, f/f 19.4.50, C. of A. 3.10.51, Vickers 'Enterprise', scrapped at Wisley 1961

Vickers V.701 Viscount *(for British European Airways)*

G-ALWE (4), 20.11.52, 'Discovery', crashed at Ringway 14.3.57; G-ALWF, (5), first flown 3.12.52, C. of A. 9.2.53, 'Sir John Franklin', Channel Airways 8.63, leased to British Eagle 11.64 to 5.65 as 'City of Exeter', Cambrian Airways 1.66, w.f.u. 12.71 and preserved at Speke; G-AMNY (6), first flown 7.1.53, C. of A. 16.2.53, 'Sir Ernest Shackleton', d.b.r. landing at Malta 5.1.60; G-AMNZ (20), first flown 10.2.53, C. of A. 24.9.53, 'James Cook', Cambrian Airways 12.62, w.f.u. at Rhoose 11.71; G-AMOA (9), 16.4.53, 'George Vancouver', Channel Airways 12.63, Cambrian Airways 1.66; G-AMOB (11), 22.4.53, 'William Baffin', to VASP, Brazil 8.62 as PP-SRI; G-AMOC (13), 29.5.53, 'Richard Chancellor', Channel Airways 12.63, leased to British Eagle 1964–65 as 'City of Glasgow', leased to Bahamas Airways 12.65 to 3.66 as VP-BCH, Cambrian Airways 1.67, scrapped at Rhoose 10.70; G-AMOD (15), 24.6.53, 'John Davis', to VASP, Brazil 8.62 as PP-SRJ; G-AMOE (17), 8.7.53, 'Sir Edward Parry', Channel Airways 12.63, leased to British Eagle 1964–65 as 'City of Manchester', Cambrian Airways 2.65; G-AMOF (19), 5.8.53, 'Sir Martin Frobisher', to VASP, Brazil 8.62 as PP-SRM; G-AMOG (7), 2.4.53, 'Robert Falcon Scott', Cambrian Airways 12.62

G-AMOH (21), 12.10.53, 'Henry Hudson', Channel Airways 12.63, leased to British Eagle 1964–65 as 'City of Liverpool', Cambrian Airways 10.65, w.f.u. at Rhoose 9.72; G-AMOI (22), 30.10.53, 'Sir Hugh Willoughby', to VASP, Brazil 8.62 as PP-SRL; G-AMOJ (23), 25.11.53, 'Sir James Ross', Cambrian Airways 11.66; G-AMOK (24), 8.12.53, 'Sir Humphrey Gilbert', to LAV, Venezuela 2.63 as YV-C-AMB; G-AMOL (25), 31.12.53, 'David Livingstone', Cambrian Airways 12.62, crashed at Speke 20.7.65; G-AMOM (26), 25.1.54, 'James Bruce', d.b.f. on take-off at Blackbushe 21.1.56; G-AMON (27), 3.3.54, 'Thomas Cavendish', Cambrian Airways 12.62; G-AMOO (28), 11.12.53, 'John Oxenham', Channel Airways 12.63, leased to British Eagle 1964–66 as 'City of Birmingham', Cambrian Airways 11.66; G-AMOP (29), 13.2.54, 'Mungo Park', Cambrian Airways 12.62, w.f.u. at Rhoose 2.72

G-ANHA (61), 19.10.54, 'Anthony Jenkinson', to VASP, Brazil 12.62 as PP-SRP; G-ANHB (62), 20.11.54, 'Sir Henry Stanley', to VASP, Brazil 8.62 as PP-SRN; G-ANHC (63), 19.12.54, 'Sir Leopold McClintock', destroyed in air collision with Italian F-86 fighter at 23,500 ft. above Anzio, Italy 22.10.58; G-ANHD (64), 4.5.55, 'William Dampier', to VASP, Brazil 8.62 as PP-SRO; G-ANHE (65), 28.6.55, 'Gino Watkins', to VASP 8.62 as PP-SRQ; G-ANHF (66), 11.7.55, 'Matthew Flinders', to VASP 8.62 as PP-SRR; G-AOFX (182), 25.7.56, 'Sir Joseph Banks', to VASP 8.62 as PP-SRS

Vickers Viscount *(other 700 series)*

G-ANRR (74), 732, 11.5.55, Hunting-Clan, leased to M.E.A. 9.55 to 9.57 as OD-ACF, crashed at Frimley, Surrey 2.12.58; G-ANRS (75), 732, 14.6.55, Hunting-Clan, leased to M.E.A. 10.55 to 9.57 as OD-ACH, to Misrair/United Arab 8.59 as SU-AKY, British Eagle 'City of Newcastle' 3.65, leased B.E.A. as 'George Bass', to spares 7.69; G-ANRT (76), 732, 12.7.55, Hunting-Clan, leased to M.E.A. 10.55 to 9.57 as OD-ACG, leased to Iraqi Airways 2.58 to 2.59 as YI-ADM, to Misrair/United Arab 7.59 as SU-AKX; G-ANXV (97), 747, registered 1.55 to Butler Air Transport, d/d in Australia 9.55 as VH-BAT 'Warrel', later MacRobertson Millar VH-RMO; G-ANYH (145), 747, registered 1.55 to Butler Air Transport, d/d in Australia 9.55 as VH-BUT 'Warrawee II', later MacRobertson Millar VH-RMP

G-AOCA (91), 755, registered 5.55 to Airwork Ltd., to Cubana 5.56 as CU-T603; G-AOCB (92), 755, registered 5.55 to Airwork Ltd., to Cubana 5.56 as CU-T604, to Cunard Eagle, Bermuda 1961 as VR-BBL, rest. 10.62 to Cunard Eagle, C. of A. 12.10.62, British Eagle 'City of Edinburgh' 10.63, Invicta Airways 1.68, British Midland Airways 1.69, scrapped 1970; G-AOCC (93), 755, registered 5.55 to Airwork Ltd., to Cubana 6.56 as CU-T605, to Cunard Eagle, Bermuda 1961 as VR-BBM, rest. 9.62 to Cunard Eagle, C. of A. 12.9.62, British Eagle 'City of Belfast' 10.63, Invicta Airways 2.68, to spares 1.69; G-AODG (77), 736, LN-FOF, 11.11.55, B.E.A. 'Fridtjof Nansen', leased to M.E.A. 3.57 as OD-ACR, rest. 11.57 to Airwork Ltd., British Midland Airways 6.67, d.b.r. landing at Castle Donington 20.2.69; G-AODH (78), 736, LN-FOL, 5.12.55, B.E.A. 'Roald Amundsen', leased to British West Indian Airways 4.57 as VP-TBY, rest. 11.57 to Airwork Ltd., later B.U.A., d.b.r. landing at Frankfurt, Germany 30.10.61; G-AOGG (140), 759, 12.11.56, Hunting-Clan, to Icelandair 4.57 as TF-ISN 'Gullfaxi'; G-AOGH (149), 759, 19.12.56, Hunting-Clan, to Icelandair 4.57 as TF-ISU 'Hrinfaxi'

G-APBH (226), 798, 15.5.57, Vickers, to Northeast Airlines 2.59 as N6599C, to Essex International 10.63 as N1298; G-APCD (243), 754, registered 4.57 to Cyprus Airways, d/d instead to M.E.A. 11.57 as OD-ADD, later to Royal Jordanian Airlines as JY-ACK; G-APCE (244), 754, registered 4.57 to Cyprus Airways, d/d instead to M.E.A. 12.57 as OD-ADE, crashed at Ankara 1.2.63; G-APFR (229), 797, N7467, registered 8.57 to Vickers, to Canadian Dept. of Transport 10.58 as CF-DTA; G-APKJ (88), 744, N7402, 29.1.57, registered 1.58 to Vickers, to All Nippon Airways, 7.60, d.b.r. landing

Kuwait Airways' Viscount 776 9K-ACD at Heathrow in February 1967 before restoration to B.K.S. Air Transport Ltd. as G-APNF. *(Aviation Photo News)*

Aerolineas TAO Colombia's Viscount 745 HK-1057, bought from Alitalia in 1968, was previously N7420, G-ARHY, PI-C773, N745HA and I-LIRT. (*Aviation Photo News*)

at Itami, Japan 12.6.61; G-APKK (89), 744, N7403, 3.2.57, registered 1.58 to Vickers, leased to All Nippon Airways, Japan 7.60 to 9.61, to Empire Test Pilots' School, Farnborough 1.62 as XR801, to spares at Baginton 5.72; G-APLX (230), 798, G-16-6, N7468, 23.4.58, Vickers, to Northeast Airlines 10.58 as N6595C, later to J. W. Mecom as N776M; G-APNF (225), 776, G-16-4, N7463, EI-AJW, 3.4.58, B.E.A. 'Phillip Carteret', Kuwait Oil Co. 10.58, later Kuwait Airways 9K-ACD, rest. 2.67 to B.K.S. Air Transport, burned out at Woolsington 22.9.70; G-APNG (228), 793, G-16-3, N7466, EI-AJV, 27.4.58, B.E.A. 'James Lancaster', to Royal Bank of Canada 4.59 as CF-RBC, later N505W and N24V

G-APOW (72), 702, VP-TBL, 16.9.59, B.O.A.C. for Kuwait Airways, to Bahamas Airways 11.63 as VP-BCD, rest. 12.68 to Field Aircraft Services Ltd., Wymeswold, scrapped 4.70; G-APPX (73), 702, VP-TBM, 15.11.58, B.O.A.C. for Kuwait Airways, to Bahamas Airways 4.61 as VP-BBV, rest. 12.68 to Field, leased to British Midland Airways 6.69, Air International, Stansted 7.71; G-APTA (71), 702, VP-TBK, 21.3.59, B.O.A.C. for Kuwait Airways, leased to Bahamas Airways 1961 as VP-BBW, rest. 1.65 to Channel Airways, leased to Bahamas Airways 1965–67 as VP-BBW, leased to B.K.S. 7.67 to 10.67, scrapped 1969; G-APZB (30), 707, EI-AFV, 1.2.60, registered 10.64 to Tradair Ltd., Southend, Starways Ltd., Speke 11.62, British Eagle 'City of Newcastle' 1965, Channel Airways 6.65, scrapped at Southend 2.70; G-APZC (34), 707, EI-AGI, 29.1.60, Tradair, leased Kuwait Airways 6.60 to 7.61, Channel Airways 1.63, scrapped at Southend 12.69; G-APZN (190), 761, XY-ADH, 5.4.60, B.O.A.C. for Kuwait Airways, leased to M.E.A. 1963–64, returned to Union of Burma Airways 11.64 as XY-ADH; G-APZP (250), 779, LN-FOH, OE-LAB, 1.4.60, B.E.A., to Indian Airlines Corp. 1.62 as VT-DOE

G-ARBW (247), 779, LN-FOM, OE-LAE, 25.6.60, B.E.A., to Indian Airlines Corp. 1.62 as VT-DOD; G-ARBY (10), 708, F-BGNL, 17.8.60, Maitland Drewery Ltd., Biggin Hill, Silver City Airways 12.61, later B.U.A., to Air Inter 2.67 as F-BOEC; G-ARER (12), 708, F-BGNM, 21.9.60, Maitland Drewery, Silver City Airways 12.61, later B.U.A., to Air Inter 7.66 as F-BOEA; G-ARGR (14), 708, F-BGNN, 20.6.61, Maitland Drewery, Silver City Airways 12.61, later B.U.A., to Air Inter 7.66 as F-BOEB; G-ARHY (118), 745, N7420, registered 1.61 to Vickers, to Philippine Air Lines 5.61 as PI-C773, later to Hawaiian Airlines as N745HA, to Alitalia 3.65 as I-LIRT, to Aerolineas TAO 11.68 as HK-1057; G-ARIR (36), 708, F-BGNS, 3.5.61, Starways Ltd., Speke, to Air Inter 11.63

as F-BLHI; G-ARKH (31), 707, EI-AFW, VR-BBJ, 6.4.61, Cunard Eagle, to Cunard Eagle (Bermuda) 7.62 as VR-BBJ, later to Bahamas Airways as VP-BCF; G-ARKI (32), 707, EI-AFY, VR-BBH, 28.5.61, Cunard Eagle, to Cunard Eagle (Bermuda) 1.62 as VR-BBH, later to Bahamas Airways as VP-BCE; G-ARUU (198), 745, N7442, registered 6.61 to Vickers, to Empire Test Pilots' School, Farnborough 1962 as XR802, to spares at Baginton 5.72

G-ATDR (393), 739, SU-AKN, 18.6.65, British Eagle 'City of Glasgow', scrapped 1969; G-ATDU (87), 739, SU-AIE, 26.6.65, British Eagle 'City of Liverpool', scrapped 4.69; G-ATFN (394), 739, SU-AKO, 25.10.66, British Eagle 'City of Truro', crashed at Pfaffenhofen, near Munich, Germany 9.8.68; G-ATTA (124), 745, N7426, 10.5.66, B.K.S. Air Transport Ltd., scrapped 1970; G-AVED (286), 798, N6593C, N746HA, YS-07C, 17.2.67, B.K.S. Air Transport Ltd., scrapped at Woolsington 11.70; G-AVIY (333), 786, HK-946X, AN-AKP, YS-011C, 17.4.67, B.K.S. Air Transport Ltd., scrapped 10.69; G-AWCV (186), 760, VR-HFI, 9M-ALY, VR-AAU later VR-AAW, 5.4.68, British Midland Airways, scrapped 5.70; G-AWGV (116), 745, N7418, I-LIRE, 26.4.68, British Midland Airways, scrapped 5.70

Vickers V.802 Viscount *(for British European Airways)*

G-AOHG (156), 18.2.57, 'Richard Hakluyt'; G-AOHH (157), 1.3.57, 'Sir Robert McClure'; G-AOHI (158), 8.3.57, 'Charles Montague Doughty', crashed on Ben More, Perthshire 19.1.73; G-AOHJ (159), 27.3.57, 'Sir John Mandeville'; G-AOHK (160), 1.4.57, 'John Hanning Speke'; G-AOHL (161), 11.4.57, 'Charles Sturt'; G-AOHM (162), 26.6.57, 'Robert Machin'; G-AOHN (163), 29.4.57, 'Alexander Gordon Laing'; G-AOHO (164), 30.4.57, 'Samuel Wallis'; G-AOHP (165), 14.5.57, 'James Weddel', d.b.r. in forced landing near Copenhagen, Denmark 17.11.57; G-AOHR (166), 30.5.57, 'Sir Richard Burton'; G-AOHS (167), 21.6.57, 'Robert Thorne'; G-AOHT (168), 1.7.57, 'Ralph Fitch'; G-AOHU (169), 9.7.57, 'Sir George Strong Nares', d.b.f. landing at Heathrow 7.1.60; G-AOHV (170), 23.7.57, 'Sir John Barrow'; G-AOHW (253), 26.7.57, 'Sir Francis Younghusband'

G-AOJA (150), 11.2.57, 'Sir Samuel White Baker', crashed at Nutts Corner, Belfast 23.10.57; G-AOJB (151), 4.2.57, 'Stephen Borough'; G-AOJC (152), 15.1.57, 'Robert O'Hara Burke'; G-AOJD (153), 10.1.57, 'Sebastian Cabot'; G-AOJE (154), 24.1.57, 'Sir Alexander Mackenzie'; G-AOJF (155), 4.2.57, 'Sir George Somers'; G-AORC (254), 9.8.52, 'Richard Lauder', crashed at Craigie, Ayrshire 28.4.58; G-AORD (171), 4.9.57, 'Arthur Phillip'

Vickers V.806 Viscount *(for British European Airways)*

G-AOYF (255), prototype, f/f 9.8.57, C. of A. 9.9.57, 'Michael Faraday', d.b.r. landing at Johannesburg 20.10.57; G-AOYG (256), 9.10.57, 'Charles Darwin', Cambrian Airways 10.70; G-AOYH (311), 13.12.57, 'William Harvey', B.K.S. Air Transport 7.68, later Northeast Airlines; G-AOYI (257), 27.11.57, 'Sir Humphry Davy', Cambrian Airways 9.70; G-AOYJ (259), 8.1.58, 'Edward Jenner', leased to Cyprus Airways 1965; G-AOYK (260), 10.2.58, 'Edmund Cartwright', leased to Cyprus Airways 1965–69, to Mandala Airways, Indonesia 5.70 as PK-RVK; G-AOYL (261), 13.2.58, 'Lord Joseph Lister', B.K.S. Air Transport 6.68, later Northeast Airlines; G-AOYM (262), 19.3.58, 'John Loudon McAdam', to Cambrian Airways 1.72; G-AOYN (263), 24.3.58, 'Sir Isaac Newton', to Cambrian Airways 1.72; G-AOYO (264), 3.4.58, 'Adam Smith', B.K.S. Air Transport 5.68, later Northeast Airlines; G-AOYP (265), 15.5.58, 'John Napier', Cambrian Airways 11.70; G-AOYR (266), 10.4.58, 'Sir Richard Arkwright', B.K.S. Air Transport 2.70, later Northeast Airlines; G-AOYS (267), 11.6.58, 'George Stephenson'; G-AOYT (268), 1.5.58, 'James Watt', to Winner Airways, Formosa 4.69 as B-3001

G-APEX (381), 20.6.59, 'John Harrison', B.K.S. Air Transport 2.70, later Northeast Airlines; G-APEY (382), 17.7.59, 'William Murdoch', B.K.S. Air Transport 5.68, later Northeast Airlines; G-APIM (412), 20.6.59, 'Robert Boyle', to Cambrian Airways 1.72; G-APJU (413), 30.7.59, 'Sir Gilbert Blane', to Mandala Airways, Indonesia 8.70 as PK-RVM; G-APKF (396), 11.7.59, 'Michael Faraday', to Lao Airlines, Laos 9.69 as XW-TDN; G-APOX (418), 9.4.59, 'Isambard Brunel', to Mandala Airways, Indonesia 6.70 as PK-RVL

Vickers V.812 Viscount *(Continental Airlines/Channel Airways)*

G-APPC (362), 7.10.58, Vickers, to Continental 10.58 as N250V, rest. to Channel Airways 5.67, w.f.u. at Southend 9.68, scrapped 7.72; G-APPU (364), 12.11.58, to Continental 11.58 as N252V, rest. 5.67, crashed at Southend 4.5.68; G-ATUE (357), N244V, 12.5.66, Alidair Cargo Ltd., Baginton 6.72; G-ATVE (366), N254V, 27.5.66, leased to Treffield International Airways 4.67 to 6.67, scrapped at Southend 7.72; G-ATVR (365), N253V, 10.6.66, leased to Treffield International Airways 4.67 to 6.67, to Stansted Fire School 8.72

G-AVHE (363), N251V, 14.3.67, leased to Air Ferry 1.68 to 10.68, w.f.u. at Southend 4.70, scrapped 7.72; G-AVHK (359), N246V, 22.3.67, w.f.u. 5.70, scrapped at Southend 7.72; G-AVIW (358), N245V, 31.3.67, Alidair Cargo Ltd., Baginton 6.72; G-AVJL (389), N247V, 21.4.67, Alidair Cargo Ltd., Baginton 6.72; G-AVJZ (360), N248V, crashed at Southend during test flight 3.5.67; G-AVNJ (361), N249V, 9.8.67, leased to Air Ferry 1.68 to 10.68, w.f.u. at Southend 10.69, scrapped 7.72

Vickers V.828 Viscount *(for All Nippon Airways)*

G-ARKX (443), 21.7.61, Vickers, d/d to Japan 7.61 as JA-8201, to Merpati Nusantara 1970 as PK-MVT; G-ARKY (444), 16.6.61, d/d to Japan 7.61 as JA-8202, crashed at Aichi, Nagoya 19.11.62; G-ARKZ (445), f/f 24.8.61, C. of A. 2.9.61, d/d to Japan 9.61 as JA-8203, to Merpati Nusantara 1970 as PK-MVU; G-ARWT (448), f/f 7.3.62, C. of A. 24.3.62, d/d to Japan 4.62 as JA-8205, to Merpati Nusantara 1970 as PK-MVS; G-ARWU (449), f/f 12.4.62, C. of A. 26.4.62, d/d to Japan 5.62 as JA-8206; G-ARWV (450), f/f 21.5.62, C. of A. 4.6.62, d/d to Japan as JA-8207

G-ASBM (457), f/f 18.9.62, C. of A. 2.10.62, d/d to Japan 10.62 as JA-8208, to SAETA, Ecuador 1971 as HC-ASP; G-ASBO (458), f/f 22.10.62, C. of A. 2.11.62, d/d to Japan 11.62 as JA-8209, to SAETA, Ecuador 1971 as HC-AST; G-ASBR (459), f/f 19.12.62, C. of A. 1.2.63, d/d to Japan 2.63 as JA-8210, to Merpati Nusantara 1970 as PK-MVM

Vickers V.843 Viscount *(Civil Air Administration, People's Republic of China)*

G-ASDP (451), f/f 14.3.63, C. of A. 26.6.63, d/d via Hong Kong 6.7.63, became '402'; G-ASDR (452), 19.7.63, d/d via Hong Kong 4.8.63, became '404'; G-ASDS (453), 27.8.63, became '406'; G-ASDT (454), f/f 1.10.63, C. of A. 18.10.63, became '408'; G-ASDU (455), f/f 14.11.63, C. of A. 15.1.64, became '410'; G-ASDV (456), 27.2.64, became '412'

Vickers Viscount *(other 800 series)*

G-AOXU (248), 804, 13.9.57, Transair Ltd., later B.U.A., to LOT 12.62 as SP-LVC, to N.Z.N.A.C. 3.67 as ZK-NAI; G-AOXV (249), 804, 24.9.57, Transair Ltd., later B.U.A., to LOT 11.62 as SP-LVA, crashed at St. Trond, Belgium 20.8.65; G-AOYV (316), registered 1.57 to Vickers as 810 prototype, to VASP, Brazil 10.60 as PP-SRH

The Viscount 810 demonstration prototype G-AOYV rigged for de-icing trials with the Vanguard fin. (*B.A.C. Ltd.*)

G-APDW (258), 808, 19.12.57, Eagle Aviation Ltd., Blackbushe, to Eagle (Bermuda) 3.58 as VR-BAX 'Enterprise', to Maritime Central Airways 1959 as CF-MCJ, to Aer Lingus 4.62 as EI-AMA; G-APDX (312), 808, 27.2.58, Eagle, to Eagle (Bermuda) 2.59 as VR-BAY 'Good Fortune', to Aer Lingus 2.60 as EI-ALG; G-APKG (395), 804, 23.4.58, Transair Ltd., later B.U.A., to LOT 11.62 as SP-LVB, crashed at Warsaw 19.12.62; G-APND (402), 831, 23.2.59, Airwork Ltd., later B.U.A., leased to Alia, Jordan 1966–67 as JY-ADB, British Midland Airways 1.69; G-APNE (403), 831, 17.3.59, Airwork Ltd., later B.U.A., leased to Alia, Jordan 1966–67 as JY-ADA, British Midland Airways 4.67, to Arkia, Israel 9.72 as 4X-AVE; G-APTB (424), 833, 18.6.59, Hunting-Clan, later Transair Ltd. and B.U.A., to Arkia, Israel 12.69 as 4X-AVB; G-APTC (425), 833, 29.6.59, Hunting-Clan, later Transair and B.U.A., to Arkia, Israel 10.69 as 4X-AVC; G-APTD (426), 20.7.59, Hunting-Clan, later Transair and B.U.A., leased to Alia, Jordan 1967 as JY-ADC, leased to British Midland Airways 1969, to Arkia, Israel 2.70 as 4X-AVD

G-ASED (419), 831, ST-AAN, 4.6.63, Air Charter Ltd., Gatwick, leased to Aviaco 1965 as EC-AZK, British Midland Airways 2.67, to Alidair Air Cargo 5.72; G-AVJA (336), 815, AP-AJD, 2.6.67, Hawker Siddeley Aviation Ltd., leased to British Midland Airways 6.67, crashed at Ringway 20.3.69; G-AVJB (375), 815, AP-AJF, 12.5.67, Hawker Siddeley Aviation Ltd., leased to British Midland Airways 7.67, leased to Nigeria Airways 1968–69, sold to British Midland 5.69, Kestrel Aviation Ltd. 4.72; British Midland Airways 1.73

G-AWXI (339), 814, D-ANOL, 21.3.69, British Midland Airways, crashed at Heathrow 22.1.70; G-AYOX (370), 814, D-ANAC, 7.4.71, Universal Aviation and Supply Co., Castle Donington, to Arkia, Israel 4.71 as 4X-AVA; G-AYTW (175), 803, PH-VID, EI-AOL, 1.4.71, Progressive Airways Ltd., Norwich, not delivered, remained at Dublin

G-AZLP (346), 813, ZS-CDT, 4.3.72, British Midland Airways Ltd.; G-AZLR (347), 813, ZS-CDU, 10.3.72, British Midland Airways Ltd.; G-AZLS (348), 813, ZS-CDV, 29.3.72, British Midland Airways Ltd.; G-AZLT (349), 813, 5.4.72, British Midland Airways Ltd.; G-AZNA (350), ZS-CDX, 19.4.72, British Midland Airways Ltd.;

G-AZNB (351), 813, ZS-CDY, 9.5.72, British Midland Airways Ltd.; G-AZNC (352), 813, ZS-CDZ, 19.5.72, British Midland Airways Ltd.; G-AZNH (342), 814, D-ANUE, registered 18.2.72 to Airwork Services Ltd., Hurn, to Muscat and Oman Air Force 2.72 as '503'; G-AZNP (343), 814, D-ANEF, registered 18.2.72 to Airwork Services Ltd., d.b.r. landing at Hurn 28.1.72, used as spares; G-AZOV (439), 837, OE-LAH, registered 7.3.72 to W. S. Shackleton Ltd., Baginton, sold in Taiwan 12.72

Progressive Airways' former Aer Lingus Viscount 803 G-ASTW, shown at Dublin in 1971, remained undelivered when the Norwich-based airline ceased operation. *(Ian Macfarlane)*

South African Airways' Viscount 813 ZS-CDT at Southend in 1972 after purchase by British Midland Airways Ltd. as G-AZLP. (*W. L. Lewis*)

Vickers Type 950 Vanguard

G-AOYW (703), prototype, first flown 20.1.59, Vickers-Armstrongs Ltd., Wisley; redesignated 11.60 as Type 951; scrapped at Wisley in 1964

Note: c/n 701 and 702 were allotted to test fuselages

Vickers Type 951 Vanguard *(for British European Airways)*

G-APEA (704), first flown 22.4.59, C. of A. 4.5.59, 'Vanguard', delivered 27.3.61, w.f.u. 12.72; G-APEB (705), f/f 23.7.59, C. of A. 19.10.59, d/d 17.3.61; G-APEC (706), f/f 17.10.59, C. of A. 11.1.61, d/d 14.1.61, crashed near Arselle, Belgium 2.10.71; G-APED (707), f/f 24.12.59, C. of A. 25.2.60, d/d 30.1.61; G-APEE (708), f/f 1.2.60, C. of A. 2.12.60, d/d 3.12.60, crashed landing in fog at Heathrow 27.10.65; G-APEF (709), f/f 5.4.60, C. of A. 9.12.60, d/d 13.12.60, to Merpati Nusantara Airlines, Jakarta 5.72 as PK-MVJ

Vickers Type 953 Vanguard *(for British European Airways)*

G-APEG (710), f/f 1.5.61, C. of A. 19.5.61, d/d 19.5.61, converted to Type 953C Merchantman and redelivered 7.71; G-APEH (711), f/f 1.6.61, C. of A. and d/d 21.6.61; G-APEI (712), 20.7.61, d/d 20.7.61; G-APEJ (713), 16.8.61, d/d 17.8.61; G-APEK (714), 15.9.61, d/d 16.9.61, converted to Type 953C Merchantman and redelivered 2.70; G-APEL (715), 5.10.61, d/d 7.10.61, converted to Type 953C Merchantman and redelivered 10.70; G-APEM (716), 2.11.61, d/d 3.11.61, converted to Type 953C Merchantman and redelivered 11.69; G-APEN (717), 14.11.61, d/d 14.11.61; G-APEO (718), 27.11.61, d/d 27.11.61, converted to Type 953C Merchantman and redelivered 2.70; G-APEP (719), 13.12.61, d/d 13.12.61, converted to Type 953C Merchantman and redelivered 2.71; G-APER (720), 16.1.62, d/d 16.1.62; G-APES (721), 24.1.62, d/d 24.1.62, converted to Type 953C Merchantman and redelivered 3.70; G-APET (722), 21.2.62, d/d 21.2.62, converted to Type 953C Merchantman and redelivered 10.72; G-APEU (723), 30.3.62, d/d 30.3.62

The former Air Canada Vanguard CF-TKG at Southend in August 1971 as Type 952F, G-AYLD, with freight door designed and installed by Aviation Traders Ltd. who also converted B.E.A. aircraft to Type 953C Merchantmen.

Vickers Type 952 Vanguard *(former Trans-Canada/Air Canada aircraft)*

G-AXNT (737), CF-TKN, first d/d 1.5.61, C. of A. 22.12.69 for Air Holdings (Sales) Ltd., Southend; leased Lebanese Air Transport 3.70 to 8.70; leased to Invicta Air Cargo Ltd., Manston 9.70

G-AXOO (733), CF-TKJ, first d/d 5.5.61, C. of A. 1.3.70 for Air Holdings (Sales) Ltd., Southend; leased to Indonesia Angkasa Civil Air Transport 3.70 to 4.70 as PK-ICC; rest. 6.70 to Air Holdings (Sales) Ltd.; Invicta International Airlines Ltd., Manston 3.73

G-AXOP (745), CF-TKV, first d/d 7.7.62, C. of A. 7.5.71 for Air Holdings (Sales) Ltd., Southend; leased to Invicta International Airlines Ltd. 5.71; crashed near Basle, Switzerland 10.4.73

G-AXOY (727), CF-TKD, first d/d 7.12.60, d/d to Stansted 8.7.69, registered 6.10.69 to Air Holdings (Sales) Ltd., C. of A. 2.5.70; leased to Air Viking, Reykjavik 6.70 to 1.71 as TF-AVA; leased to Thor Cargo Iceland 2.71 to 6.71 as TF-JEJ; rest. 11.71, d/d to Invicta International Airlines Ltd., Manston 5.5.72

G-AYFN (725), CF-TKB, first d/d 15.4.61, d/d to Stansted 13.8.69, registered 23.6.70 to Air Holdings (Sales) Ltd., Southend; leased to Thor Cargo Iceland 3.71 to 8.71 as TF-JES; test flown 15.5.72 as G-41-172; d/d to Air Trader, Malmö 21.7.72 as SE-FTK; rest. 4.73 to Air Holdings (Sales) Ltd.

G-AYLD (730), CF-TKG, first d/d 19.1.61, registered 14.10.70 to Air Holdings (Sales) Ltd., Southend; converted to Type 952F, f/f 19.7.71, C. of A. 11.8.71; d/d to Air Trader, Malmö 22.1.72 as SE-FTH; returned to Southend 24.11.72 at termination of lease; Silver City Airways Ltd. 2.73

G-AZNG (744), CF-TKU, first d/d 7.11.62, d/d to Stansted 14.11.69, registered 10.2.72 to Air Holdings (Sales) Ltd., Southend; to Air Trader, Malmö 13.4.72 as SE-FTI; rest. 4.73, to Merpati Nusantara Airlines, Jakarta 8.73 as PK-MVC

G-AZRE (729), CF-TKF, first d/d 7.1.61; registered 23.3.72 to Air Holdings (Sales) Ltd., Southend; C. of A. 27.3.72; d/d to Invicta International Airlines Ltd., Manston 27.3.72

G-AZUI (740), CF-TKQ, first d/d 12.8.61, d/d Gander–Southend 3.4.72, registered 9.5.72 to Air Holdings (Sales) Ltd, Southend; to Merpati Nusantara Airlines, Jakarta 6.72 as spares

G-BAFK (739), CF-TKP, first d/d 16.6.61, d/d Cambridge–Southend 28.8.72, C. of A. 22.11.72, Air Holdings (Sales) Ltd., Southend; left on delivery to Merpati Nusantara Airlines, Jakarta 23.11.72

G-BAMX (728), CF-TKE, first delivered 1.2.61, PK-MVW, registered 1.73 to Air Holdings (Sales) Ltd., see reference to CF-TKE below

Note: The complete batch of Vanguard 952 aircraft built for Trans-Canada Air Lines 1960–61 comprised (c/n 724–746) CF-TKA to CF-TKW, including CF-TKQ. When replaced by Douglas DC-9s, the majority returned to Europe but the following were not British registered: (c/n 726) CF-TKC to Europe Aéro Service, Perpignan 6.72 as F-BTOX; (728) CF-TKE to Merpati Nusantara Airlines, Jakarta 3.72 to 12.72 as PK-MVW 'Widjajakusuma', see G-BAMX above; (731) CF-TKH to Europe Aéro Service, Perpignan 4.72 as F-BTOU; (732) CF-TKI d/d Goose Bay–Stansted 16.2.69, dismantled at Cambridge 4.72; (734) CF-TKK to Europe Aéro Service, Perpignan 10.72 as F-BTYB; (735) CF-TKL to Europe Aéro Service, Perpignan 6.73 as F-OCUA; (738) CF-TKO to Air Trader, Malmö 5.72 as spares; (741) CF-TKR d/d Goose Bay–Stansted 6.11.69, to Europe Aéro Service, Perpignan 7.73 as F-OCUB; (743) CF-TKT to Europe Aéro Service, Perpignan 11.72 as F-BTYC; (746) CF-TKW to Europe Aéro Service, Perpignan 5.72 as F-BTOV

Vickers VC10 Type 1100 prototype

G-ARTA (803), f/f 29.6.62, Vickers Aviation Ltd., Wisley; converted to Type 1109 for Laker Airways Ltd., Gatwick 1968; leased to M.E.A. 1968–69 as OD-AFA; rest. 4.69 to B.U.A. Ltd., Gatwick; C. of A. 18.4.69; British Caledonian 'Loch Ness' 1971

Vickers VC10 Type 1101 *(for B.O.A.C.)*

G-ARVA (804), f/f 8.11.62, C. of A. 9.8.63, d/d 8.12.64, to Nigeria Airways 9.69 as 5N-ABD, crashed near Lagos 20.11.69; G-ARVB (805), f/f 21.12.62, C. of A. 8.8.63, d/d 6.2.65; G-ARVC (806), f/f 21.2.63, C. of A. 6.6.63, d/d 1.12.64, leased to Nigeria Airways 1967–69; G-ARVE (807), f/f 15.4.63, C. of A. 1.10.64, d/d 1.10.64; G-ARVF (808), f/f 6.7.63, C. of A. 27.8.63, d/d 4.9.64; G-ARVG (809), f/f 17.10.63, C. of A. 4.12.63, d/d 18.12.63, leased to Air Ceylon 1967–69; G-ARVH (810), f/f 22.11.63, C. of A. 10.1.64, d/d 2.7.64, leased to Air Ceylon 1967–69; G-ARVI (811), f/f 20.12.63, C. of A. 22.4.64, d/d 22.4.64; G-ARVJ (812), f/f 25.3.64, C. of A. 22.4.64, d/d 23.4.64; G-ARVK (813), f/f 28.2.64, C. of A. 2.5.64, d/d 2.5.64; G-ARVL (814), f/f 2.6.64, C. of A. 15.6.64, d/d 16.6.64; G-ARVM (815), f/f 8.7.64, C. of A. 22.7.64, d/d 22.7.64

The VC10 test bed G-AXLR flying near Hucknall in 1970 with one Rolls-Royce RB.211 prototype engine replacing the two port Conways.

Vickers VC10 Type 1103 *(for British United Airways Ltd.)*

G-ASIW (819), f/f 30.7.64, C. of A. 27.8.64, d/d to Gatwick 30.9.64; to British Caledonian Airways Ltd. 1971 as 'Loch Lomond'

G-ASIX (820), f/f 17.10.64, C. of A. 30.10.64, d/d to Gatwick 2.11.64; to British Caledonian Airways Ltd. 1971 as 'Loch Maree'

G-ATDJ (825), f/f 18.6.65, C. of A. 28.6.65, d/d to Gatwick 29.6.65; to British Caledonian Airways Ltd. 1971 as 'Loch Fyne'

Vickers VC10 Type 1106 *(RB.211 test bed)*

G-AXLR (829), XR809 'Hugh Malcolm V.C.', first d/d to the R.A.F. 31.8.66, registered 30.7.69 to Rolls-Royce Ltd., Hucknall; f/f 6.3.70 with RB.211 test engine; to Rolls-Royce (1971) Ltd., Filton 7.72

Vickers Super VC10 Type 1151 *(for B.O.A.C.)*

G-ASGA (851), f/f 7.5.64, C. of A. 31.12.65, d/d 3.1.66; G-ASGB (852), f/f 29.9.64, C. of A. 29.4.65, d/d 30.4.65; G-ASGC (853), f/f 1.1.65, C. of A. 29.1.65, d/d 1.2.65; G-ASGD (854), f/f 11.2.65, C. of A. 26.2.65, d/d 3.3.65; G-ASGE (855), f/f 6.3.65, C. of A. 24.3.65, d/d 27.3.65; G-ASGF (856), f/f 24.3.65, C. of A. 2.4.65, d/d 2.4.65; G-ASGG (857), f/f 17.9.65, C. of A. 22.10.65, to Autoflare development trials until 6.67, d/d 21.6.67; G-ASGH (858), f/f 2.10.65, C. of A. 22.10.65, d/d 4.11.65; G-ASGI (859), f/f 28.1.66, C. of A. 11.2.66, d/d 12.2.66; G-ASGJ (860), f/f 22.2.67, C. of A. 3.3.67, d/d 3.3.67; G-ASGK (861), f/f 1.9.67, C. of A. 27.10.67, d/d 27.10.67; G-ASGL (862), f/f 22.12.67, C. of A. 23.1.68, d/d 25.1.68; G-ASGM (863), f/f 26.2.68, C. of A. 9.4.68, d/d 6.3.68; G-ASGN (864), f/f 1.5.68, C. of A. 4.5.68, d/d 7.5.68, blown up at Dawsons Field, Jordan 12.9.70; G-ASGO (865), f/f 11.9.68, C. of A. 27.9.68, d/d 27.9.68; G-ASGP (866), f/f 20.11.68, C. of A. 6.12.68, d/d 6.12.68; G-ASGR (867), f/f 17.2.69, C. of A. 11.3.69, d/d 31.5.69

Note: Registrations G-ASGS to G-ASGZ, reserved for Super VC10s, although not used, were not cancelled until 7.72

Vickers-Supermarine Type 236 Walrus I *(Supermarine-built, metal hulls)*

G-AHFL L2246, 2.8.46, United Whalers Ltd., Cowes 'Boojum'; to Vestlandske Luftfartselskap 7.48 as LN-TAK; sank at Soerfjorten, near Bergen 31.8.49

G-AHFM W3070, 25.7.46, United Whalers Ltd., Cowes 'Moby Dick'; scrapped at Cowes 7.50

G-AHFN (6S/35698), L2336, 27.8.46, United Whalers Ltd.; Charles Mauritzen Ltd., Leith 10.49; stored at Prestwick until taxied to Loch Ryan by C. Fulford 6.55, driven ashore by storm at Stranraer and wrecked 3.7.55

G-AHFO L2282, 8.7.46, United Whalers Ltd., Cowes 'Snark'; scrapped at Cowes 7.50

G-AHTO W2688 } registered 3.6.46 to United Whalers Ltd., Cowes;
G-AHTP Z1763 } not converted, scrapped at Cowes 7.50

G-AIIB X9467, registered 10.9.46 to Messrs. A. C. Brown and L. C. S. Odstone; wrecked by gale at Weston-super-Mare airport in 1947

G-AIZG (6S/21840), L2301, Irish Air Corps N-18, EI-ACC, registered 20.12.46 to Wg. Cdr. R. G. Kellett who flew it Dublin–Biggin Hill 3.47, partially scrapped at Thame 1949, rebuilt at R.N.A.S. Arbroath 1964 for permanent exhibition in Service colours at R.N.A.S. Museum, Yeovilton

G-AMCS '4501', registered 6.50 to F. C. Bettison, not converted, dismantled for spares 11.50

Vickers-Supermarine Walrus II *(Saro-built, wooden hulls)*

G-AIEJ (S2/10761), HD903, 6.11.47, Western Airways Ltd., Weston-super-Mare; scrapped at Weston-super-Mare 12.48

G-AIKL (S2/12325), HD915, registered 23.9.46 to Western Airways Ltd.; scrapped at Weston-super-Mare 10.47

G-AIWU HD867, 15.8.47, A. J. Payne, Cowes; Sir C. A. C. Hampson, Tangier 12.47; withdrawn from use and scrapped 7.50

G-AJJC (S2/8474), HD917, 25.5.48, Essex Aero Ltd., Gravesend; to Vestlandske Luftfartselskap 9.49 as LN-SUK

G-AJJD HD916, registered 18.2.47 to Essex Aero Ltd., Gravesend; not converted, registration cancelled 3.49

Scottish Airlines' Walrus Mk.II G-AJNO at Prestwick in 1949 with locally designed crew door. (*Aviation Photo News*)

G-AJNO	(S2/23642), registered 10.4.47 to Scottish Aviation Ltd., Prestwick; fully converted in Scottish Airlines colours 1949 but never used; scrapped in 1959
G-AJNP	(S2/8757), registered 10.4.47 to Scottish Aviation Ltd., Prestwick, not converted.
G-AKIA	HD929, registered 9.9.47 to Ciro's Aviation Ltd., not converted.
G-AKJE	HD925, registered 9.9.47 to Ciro's Aviation Ltd.; not converted, scrapped at Redhill in 1952

Vickers-Supermarine Type 309 Sea Otter I

G-AIDM	(014352), 23.4.47, Vickers-Armstrongs Ltd., Eastleigh; sold in Venezuela 11.47
G-AJFU	JM747, registered 3.2.47 to British Aviation Services Ltd., Blackbushe; scrapped at Blackbushe in 1950
G-AJFV	JM959, 21.4.49, British Aviation Services Ltd., Blackbushe; ferried to Burma 4.49 as XY-ABT
G-AJFW	JM957, registered 3.2.47 to British Aviation Services Ltd., Blackbushe; converted but not used; scrapped at Blackbushe in 1950
G-AJLT	(181716) } registered 3.47 to British South American Airways Corporation
G-AJLU	(129893) } Ltd.; not converted, scrapped at Langley in 1949
G-AJVR	JM966, registered 4.6.47 to J. M. McEwan Gibb; not converted, registration cancelled 6.48; converted at Squires Gate as G-AKYH q.v.
G-AKIC	JM826 } registered 9.9.47 to Ciro's Aviation Ltd.; not converted,
G-AKID	JM764 } dismantled at Redhill 3.50 as spares for the Dutch Navy
G-AKPN	JN139 }
G-AKPO	JN114 }
G-AKPP	JM989 }
G-AKPR	JN197 } registered 10.1.48 to J. Patient for sale to Egypt
G-AKPS	JN187 }
G-AKPT	JN138 }
G-AKPU	JN137 }
G-AKPV	JN194 }
G-AKRF	(S2/04991), JM977, registered 14.1.48 to R. L. Whyham, Squires Gate; left Gravesend on delivery to the Dutch Navy 6.49; became '18-1', later '12-1'
G-AKRG	JN134, registered 14.1.48 to R. L. Whyham, Squires Gate; scrapped at Burnaston in 1957 after some years in storage fully converted
G-AKRX	(1806/C/206), JM968, registered 20.1.48 to British South American Airways Corporation Ltd., not converted, scrapped at Langley in 1949
G-AKWA	JM739, registered 2.7.48 to British South American Airways Corporation Ltd.; not converted, scrapped at Langley in 1949
G-AKYH	JM966, registered 16.4.48 to R. L. Whyham; converted at Squires Gate but not used locally; sold to the Dutch Navy 10.49 as '18-3', later '12-3'
G-ALTX	(S2/0802), JM827, registered 21.6.49 to Autocars (Worcester) Ltd., sold to the Dutch Navy 3.50
G-ALVB	(S2/0807), JM818, registered 22.8.49 to Essex Aero Ltd., Gravesend; sold to the Dutch Navy 10.49 as '18-2', later '12-2'

Vickers-Supermarine Type 361 Spitfire IX

G-ASJV MH434, Belgian Air Force SM-41, OO-ARA, 22.8.63, T. A. Davies, Elstree; Grp. Capt. T. G. Mahaddie, Henlow 1.68, used in Battle of Britain film 1968

G-ASSD SM-43, OO-ARB, 12.11.63, Film Aviation Services Ltd.; J. Crewdson, Cambridge 6.66; G. A. Rich, Henlow 10.66, used in Battle of Britain film 1968, to Confederate Air Force, U.S.A. 5.69 as N1882

G-AVDJ (CBAF.5542), MH415, SM-40, OO-ARD, 1.3.67, Grp. Capt. T. G. Mahaddie, Elstree; to Confederate Air Force, U.S.A. 11.68

Vickers-Supermarine Type 502 Spitfire Trainer 8 *(retractable tail wheel)*

G-AIDN (6S/729058), MT818, N-32, 7.1.47, Vickers-Armstrongs Ltd., Eastleigh; V. H. Bellamy, Eastleigh 9.56; J. S. Fairey, Andover 9.63

G-AKBD (6S/730847), registered 14.7.47 to Vickers-Armstrongs Ltd., but not proceeded with, registration cancelled 5.48

Vickers-Supermarine Type 509 Spitfire Trainer 9 *(fixed tail wheel)*

G-ALJM (6S/735189), 21.7.49, Vickers-Armstrongs Ltd., Eastleigh; to the Egyptian Air Force 3.50

G-ASOZ (CBAF.1722), MJ627, Irish Air Corps 158, registered 2.64 to Film Aviation Services Ltd., Elstree; dismantled for spares 12.64

G-AVAV (CBAF.7269), MJ772, Irish Air Corps 159, N. A. Samuelson, Elstree; used in Battle of Britain film 1968; W. J. Roberts, Shoreham 7.70

G-AWGB (CBAF.4494), TE308, Irish Air Corps 163, N. A. Samuelson, Elstree, later Henlow; used in Battle of Britain film 1968; to Canada 8.70 as CF-RAF

Victa Airtourer 100 *(see also Glos Airtourer)*

G-ASYZ (78), first flown 29.1.65, C. of A. 5.2.65, Victa (U.K.) Ltd., Goodwood; Elliott Flying School, Swansea 1.66; Ulster F/C, Newtownards 8.67; Rednall Polishing & Spraying Co. Ltd., Elmdon 5.72

G-ASZA (83), 3.3.65, Glamorgan Flying Club, Rhoose; crashed at Caerphilly 26.5.66

G-ATCI (91), 30.4.65, G. A. Bambrough Ltd. (Sunderland Flying Club), Usworth

G-ATCK (92), 5.5.65, G. Stewart, Biggin Hill; Biggin Hill Flying Club 8.69

G-ATCL (93), 13.4.65, G. A. Bambrough Ltd. (Sunderland Flying Club), Usworth

G-ATEX (110), 18.6.65, J. F. Williams-Wynne, Rhoose; Glamorgan Flying Club, Rhoose 7.66

G-ATGC (115), first flown 11.8.65, C. of A. 14.8.65, Ulster Flying Club, Newtownards

G-ATJB (122), 23.12.65, P. G. Bartlett, Tollerton; Rogers Aviation Ltd., Cranfield 9.69; W. C. Smeaton, Blackbushe 8.71; E. Wilkinson, Southend 6.72

G-ATJC (125), 14.1.66, Victa (U.K.) Ltd., Goodwood; Midland Air Touring Group, Castle Donington 1.67

Victa Airtourer 115 *(see also Glos Airtourer)*

G-ATHT (120), 7.9.65, Victa (U.K.) Ltd., Goodwood; P. A. Dalton, Thruxton 5.66; Eagle Aircraft Services Ltd., Leavesden 9.70; G. C. Goddard, Goodwood 1.71

G-ATUP (152), ZK-CMF, 22.12.66, Victa (U.K.) Ltd., Goodwood; crashed on St. Catherine's Down, Isle of Wight 24.6.68

Wg. Cdr. K. H. Wallis airborne with passenger in the Wallis WA-116-T two seat autogyro G-AXAS. (*Wallis Autogyros Ltd.*)

Wallis WA-116 Agile

G-ARRT	(2), WA-116 prototype, first flown at Boscombe Down 2.8.61, P. to F. 11.8.61, K. H. Wallis, Shoreham (later Reymerston Hall, Norfolk); reached 15,220 ft. and broke World's Class E3 height record 11.5.68 and 3 km. speed record 12.5.69
Unreg.	(B.201), Beagle-built, first flown at Shoreham 10.5.62; damaged beyond repair due to nosewheel fork failure on take-off 12.5.62
G-ARZA	(B.202), Beagle-built, first flown at Shoreham 6.7.62, P. to F. 30.8.62; to Army Air Corps, Middle Wallop as XR942; rest. 1.66 to Norfolk and Norwich Aero Club, Swanton Morley; N. D. Ferranti, Deiniolen, Carm. 10.68
G-ARZB	(B.203), Beagle-built, P. to F. 30.10.62, Beagle Aircraft Ltd.; Army evaluation as XR943; rest. 12.64 to Wallis Autogyros Ltd.; modified and fitted with a variety of armament for James Bond film in 1966
G-ARZC	(B.205), Beagle-built, C. of A. 23.6.65, Norfolk and Norwich Aero Club, Swanton Morley; d.b.r. on take-off at Swanton Morley 7.11.65
G-ASDY	(B.204), Beagle-built, first flown at Shoreham 8.62, P. to F. 30.10.62, Army evaluation as XR944; rest. 9.64 to Wallis Autogyros Ltd. and flown later as Wallis WA-119 with 990 cc. Hillman Imp engine; fitted 1972 with 60 h.p. two cylinder Franklin 2A-120-A as test vehicle
G-ATHL	(212), 14.6.66, Wallis Autogyros Ltd., Reymerston Hall; later re-engined with Franklin 2A-120-A; to G. V. Wallis, Coton Court, Cambridge
G-ATHM	(211), registered 11.65 to Wallis Autogyros Ltd.; to Ceylon 6.66 as 4R-ACK; returned to Reymerston Hall in 1971; rest. 4.71
G-ATTB	(214), 24.6.66, J. Pickering, Hinckley, Leicestershire; returned to Reymerston Hall 1972
G-AVDG	(215), registered 28.12.66 to Wallis Autogyros Ltd.; stand-by machine for film work
G-AVDH	(216), registered 28.12.66 to Wallis Autogyros Ltd; test flown with metal rotor; components used in the construction of G-AXAS

G-AXAS (217), WA-116T two seater, 13.3.69, Wallis Autogyros Ltd.; established World A.U.W. to Tare Wt. record for any type of aircraft at R.A.E., Bedford 30.6.71 with a ratio of 3.14 to 1

Wallis WA-117 *(100 h.p. Rolls-Royce Continental O-200-B)*

G-ATCV (301), first flown 3.66, C. of A. 16.5.66, Wallis Autogyros Ltd.; withdrawn from use 5.67 and parts used in the construction of G-AVJV

G-AVJV (K/402/X), first flown 5.67, C. of A. 23.6.67, K. H. Wallis; evaluated by Hawker Siddeley Dynamics Ltd. at Hatfield with Linescan 212 infra red sensor; later fitted with special silencing for Loch Ness investigation

G-AXAR (G/403/X), registered 25.2.69 to G. V. Wallis, Coton Court, Cambridge; to Airmark Ltd., Storrington, Sussex 1970; crashed at Farnborough during S.B.A.C. Show 11.9.70

Wallis WA-118 Meteorite *(120 h.p. Wallis-modified Meteor Alfa)*

G-ATPW (401), WA-118 Series 1, first flown 6.5.66, C. of A. 16.5.66, Wallis Autogyros Ltd.; withdrawn from use 5.67 and parts used in the construction of G-AVJW

G-AVJW (K/502/X), WA-118 Series 2, C. of A. 12.7.67, K. H. Wallis, Reymerston Hall; first flown with modified Alfa 9.8.69

Wallis WA-120 *(130 h.p. Rolls-Royce Continental O-240-A)*

G-AYVO (K/602/X), registered 6.5.71 to K. H. Wallis, first flown 13.6.71 with enclosed cockpit for high speed and long range research

Wallis WA-121

G-BAHH (K/701/X), 21.12.72, K. H. Wallis, first flown 28.12.72

Wassmer WA.41 Super IV Baladou

G-ATSY (117), 14.7.66; G-ATZS (128), 28.2.67; G-AVEU (136), 23.3.67; G-AVHJ (138), 14.4.67; G-AVKU (144), registered 1.5.67, believed not imported; G-BAGM (164), F-BCDF, F-OCOF, 14.12.72

Wallis autogyros at Reymerston Hall, Norfolk, in 1968 with the WA-118 Meteorite nearest the camera. Those with ring insignia were G-ASDY, G-AVDH and 'DG flown in the James Bond films. (*Wallis Autogyros Ltd.*)

Westland Limousine I

G-EAFO (W.A.C.1), K-126, 21.8.19, Westland Aircraft Works, Yeovil; destroyed in ground collision with Fairey Fawn at Netheravon 3.9.25

Westland Limousine II

G-EAJL (W.A.C.2), 16.10.19, Westland Aircraft Works, Yeovil; Aerial Survey Company (Newfoundland) Ltd., St. John's 8.22; registration lapsed

G-EAMV (W.A.C.3), 27.4.20, Westland Aircraft Works, Yeovil; Aerial Survey Company (Newfoundland) Ltd., St. John's 8.22; registration lapsed

G-EARE (W.A.C.4)*, 7.10.20, Westland Aircraft Works, Yeovil; Instone Air Line Ltd., Croydon 6.22; scrapped at C. of A. expiry 19.6.23

G-EARF (W.A.C.5)*, 21.10.20, Westland Aircraft works, Yeovil; Instone Air Line Ltd., Croydon 6.22; scrapped after C. of A. expiry 16.5.23

G-EARG (W.A.C.6), 29.9.22, Westland Aircraft Works, Yeovil; Aerial Survey Company (Newfoundland) Ltd., St. John's 11.22; scrapped 9.23

G-EARH (W.A.C.7), construction abandoned, rear fuselage used to accelerate the completion of Limousine III G-EARV for Martlesham Competition 1920

* With 300 h.p. Hispano-Suiza

Westland Limousine III

G-EARV (W.A.C.8), 7.8.20, Westland Aircraft Works, Yeovil; Aerial Survey Company (Newfoundland) Ltd., St. John's 1.21; to Laurentide Air Service Ltd. 1924 as G-CAET ntu; scrapped at Lac à la Tortue, Quebec in 1924

G-EAWF (W.A.C.9), J6851 ntu, Air Council, Croydon; leased to Instone Air Line Ltd., Croydon; scrapped at C. of A. expiry 12.4.22

Westland Widgeon I to III

G-EBJT (WA.1671), Widgeon II, initially Widgeon I, c/n W.1, C. of A. 16.9.26, Westland Aircraft Works, Yeovil; Dr. E. D. Whitehead Reid, Bekesbourne 1.28; fatal crash near Detling, Kent 19.10.30

G-EBPW (WA.1677), 12.4.27, Westland Aircraft Works; R. A. Bruce, Yeovil 5.27; crashed after air collision with Blackburn Bluebird G-EBKD over Ensbury Park Racecourse, Bournemouth 6.6.27

G-EBRL (WA.1679), 14.7.27, R. A. Bruce, Yeovil; crashed at Yeovil 3.6.31

G-EBRM (WA.1680), 13.9.27, R. G. Cazalet, Wexford; converted to Widgeon IIIA in 1929

G-EBRN (WA.1724), 28.3.28, Wg. Cdr. E. R. Manning, Croydon; H. R. Law, Croydon 11.29; Flt. Lt. A. H. Wheeler, Northolt 11.33, later Andover; N. C. Alderson, Stranraer 2.48; burned at Stranraer in 1951

G-EBRO (WA.1682), 27.8.27, Westland Aircraft Works; Sqn. Ldr. Hon. J. Cochrane, Andover 4.31; J. G. Ormston, Broxbourne 7.31; I. P. Tidman, Walsall 3.36; A. O. Humble Smith, Portsmouth 8.37; scrapped during 1939–45 war

G-EBRP (WA.1694), 20.1.28, Westland Aircraft Works, Yeovil; to the French Motor Car Co. Ltd., Delhi, India 1.28 as G-IAAW, later VT-AAM

G-EBRQ (WA.1684), 26.7.27, Sqn. Ldr. H. M. Probyn, Old Sarum; Wg. Cdr. E. L. Howard Williams, Hinaidi, Iraq 7.32; withdrawn from use 1.36

G-EBUB (WA.1695), 19.3.28, Westland Aircraft Works; to Australia 8.28 as G-AUHU; airworthy as VH-UHU in 1972 at Boort, Victoria

G-EBUC (WA.1696), registration reserved 3.28 for Westland Aircraft Works, Yeovil but never used; spare airframe, probably for Australia

Westland Widgeon III VH-UHU, built in 1928 as the prospective G-EBUB, was still airworthy in Australia 44 years later. (*P. J. Ricketts*)

Widgeon IIIA CF-AIQ, formerly G-AALB, after modernisation by A. S. Carson at Flin Flon, Manitoba in 1939. It also acquired a coupé top to the front seat. (*H. W. Francis via J. R. Griffin*)

G-EBUD (WA.1697), 1.8.28, Brockway Motors Ltd., Sydney; to Australia 8.28 as G-AUIN; crashed at Grenfell, N.S.W. 30.11.29 as VH-UIN

G-EBUE (WA.1698), registration reserved 3.28 for Westland Aircraft Works, Yeovil but never used; spare airframe, probably for Australia

G-AADE (WA.1778), 6.3.29, C. S. Napier, Yeovil; crashed at Beaulieu, Hants, 10.7.32

Westland Widgeon IIIA

G-EBRM (WA.1680), 13.9.27, R. G. Cazalet, Wexford; Widgeon III converted to IIIA in 1929; Brooklands Aviation Ltd. 11.30; scrapped at Brooklands 1931

G-AAFD (WA.1782), 25.3.29, Anglo American Oil Co. Ltd., Heston 'Miss Ethyl'; J. Turner, Heston 3.32; ditched in the Channel off Boulogne 6.6.33

G-AAFN (WA.1779), 26.3.29, Westland Aircraft Works, Yeovil; crashed 1.30

G-AAGH (WA.1866), 18.9.30, Westland Aircraft Works, Yeovil; Westland Aircraft Ltd., Yeovil 11.46; crashed and burned at Merryfield, Som. 27.7.48

G-AAJF (WA.1776), 2.7.29, Westland Aircraft Works; Miss C. R. Leathart, Cramlington 10.30; crashed on take-off at Munich, Germany 17.5.31

G-AALB (WA.1783), 1.8.29, W. J. McDonough, Winnipeg, Manitoba; re-registered in Canada 5.30 as CF-AIQ; coupé top 1939; converted to snowmobile 1946

Westland Wessex

G-EBXK (WA.1771), 21.3.29, Westland Aircraft Works; converted from Westland IV; National Aviation Day Displays Ltd., Ford 7.35; w.f.u. 5.36

G-AAGW (WA.1876), 21.10.29, Imperial Airways Ltd., Croydon; converted from Westland IV; Air Pilots Training Ltd., Hamble 3.36; used by No.11 A.O.N.S. from 11.39; withdrawn from use at Watchfield 8.40

G-AAJI (WA.1897), intended for Wilson Airways Ltd., Nairobi as VP-KAD; order cancelled and marks reallotted to Avro Five; aircraft completed as G-ABAJ

G-ABAJ (WA.1897), G-AAJI ntu, P-1, 27.5.30, Westland Aircraft Works; to SABENA 6.30 as OO-AGC; rest. 3.35 to Sir Alan Cobham, Ford; Flight Refuelling Ltd., Ford 2.36; Trafalgar Advertising Co. Ltd., Gatwick 1.37; scrapped 1938

G-ABEG (WA.1901), 2.10.30, Westland Aircraft Works; Imperial Airways Ltd., Croydon 5.33; d.b.r. at Chirindu, Northern Rhodesia in 1936

G-ABVB (WA.2156), 6.5.32, Portsmouth, Southsea and Isle of Wight Aviation Co. Ltd., Portsmouth; damaged beyond repair at Ryde, I.O.W. 30.5.36

G-ACHI (WA.2151), 23.6.33, Imperial Airways Ltd., Croydon; Air Pilots Training Ltd., Hamble 3.36; withdrawn from use at C. of A. expiry, Hamble 5.40

G-ACIJ (WA.2152), 27.9.33, Westland Aircraft Works, Yeovil; to the Egyptian Air Force 5.34 as W202

G-ADEW (WA.1899), OO-AGE, 6.8.30, registered 3.35 to Sir Alan Cobham, Ford; used by Cobham Air Routes Ltd.; ditched in the English Channel 3.7.35

G-ADFZ (WA.1900), OO-AGF, 30.8.30, registered 3.35 to Sir Alan Cobham, Ford; used by Cobham Air Routes Ltd.; Trafalgar Advertising Co. Ltd., Gatwick 2.37; registration cancelled 1.12.46

Westland Sikorsky S-51 Mk.1A

G-AKTW (WA/H/1), first flown 5.10.48, C. of A. 24.7.51, Westland Aircraft Ltd.; evaluated by R.A.F. as XD649; converted to S-51 Series 2 Widgeon 1955

G-ALEG (WA/H/2), first flown 19.12.48, C. of A. 26.4.49, Westland Aircraft Ltd., Yeovil; to the Ministry of Supply 1951 as WZ749

G-ALEI (WA/H/4), 12.5.49, Pest Control Ltd., Bourn; crashed at Sion, Switzerland 4.5.50; returned to Westland, Yeovil for use as rotor test rig

G-ALIK (WA/H/3), first flown 30.3.49, C. of A. 25.4.49, Westland Aircraft Ltd., Yeovil; converted to S-51 Series 2 Widgeon 1955

G-ALIL (WA/H/5), Westland Aircraft Ltd., Yeovil; to the R.A.F. 3.49 as WB810

G-ALMB (WA/H/6), first flown 29.9.49, C. of A. 31.3.50, Westland Aircraft Ltd., Yeovil; to Italy 4.51 as I-MCOM

G-ALMC (WA/H/7), Westland Aircraft Ltd., Yeovil; to the R.A.F. 11.50 as WF308

G-AMAK (WA/H/20), Westland Aircraft Ltd.; first flown in Class B markings 4.50 as G-17-1 and crashed at Yeovil in this condition 7.6.50

G-AMAS (WA/H/26), Westland Aircraft Ltd., Yeovil; first flown 21.7.50 as G-17-2 before despatch to the Thai Air Force 8.50

G-AMAT (WA/H/27), Westland Aircraft Ltd., Yeovil; first flown 25.7.50 as G-17-3 before despatch to the Thai Air Force 8.50

G-AMJW (WA/H/120), first flown 29.4.53 as G-17-2, C. of A. 22.5.53, Westland Aircraft Ltd.; to the Thai Air Force 5.53; displayed in museum at Don Muang in 1969 as '305/53'

G-AMOW (WA/H/122), first flown 5.2.53 as G-17-3, Westland Aircraft Ltd., Yeovil; delivered to the Italian Air Force by air 26.2.53, became MM80038

G-AMOX (WA/H/123), first flown 6.2.53 as G-17-6, Westland Aircraft Ltd., Yeovil; delivered to the Italian Air Force by air 27.2.53; became MM80040

G-AMRE (WA/H/121), 26.9.52, Westland Aircraft Ltd., Yeovil; to Norway 10.52 as LN-ORG; rest. 2.54 to Westland; crashed at Yeovil 29.4.57

G-ANAL (WA/H/90), 3.7.53, Evening Standard Newspapers Ltd., Blackbushe; re-registered 3.55 as G-ANZL

G-ANAM (WA/H/91), Westland Aircraft Ltd., Yeovil; to Japan 6.53 as JA-7014; crashed in the sea off Sendai, Miyagi Prefecture 15.5.67

G-ANGR (WA/H/130), 18.1.54, Westland Aircraft Ltd.; sold in Japan 2.54 for military rescue work

G-ANGS (WA/H/131), 18.1.54, Westland Aircraft Ltd.; sold in Japan 2.54 for military rescue work

G-ANLV (WA/H/132), 8.7.54, Silver City Airways Ltd., Lydd; crashed at Montfort L'Armory, France 14.6.57

G-ANLW (WA/H/133), 6.7.54, Westland Aircraft Ltd., Yeovil; converted to S-51 Series 2 Widgeon in 1958

G-ANZL (WA/H/90), G-ANAL, 3.7.53, Fairey Aviation Co. Ltd., White Waltham; crashed near Netheravon, Wilts. while flying from Old Sarum 2.10.59

G-AOAJ (WA/H/134), G-17-1, first flown 14.4.55, C. of A. 22.4.55, Westland Aircraft Ltd., Yeovil; crashed at Yeovil 25.10.56

G-AOHX (WA/H/139), Westland Aircraft Ltd., Yeovil; to Japan 5.56 as JA-7025; crashed at Fukushima 17.7.60

Westland Sikorsky S-51 Mk.1B

G-ALKL (WA/H/11), first flown 15.9.49 as G-17-1, Westland Aircraft Ltd.; to the Egyptian Air Force 11.49

G-ALMD (WA/H/12), first flown 21.11.49, Westland Aircraft Ltd.; to the Egyptian Air Force 11.49

G-AMHB (WA/H/30), 15.3.51, Westland Aircraft Ltd., Yeovil; to the Belgian Congo 5.51 as OO-CWA; to Mexico 4.55 as XB-JUQ

G-AMHC (WA/H/29), 16.10.51, Westland Aircraft Ltd., Yeovil; to the Belgian Congo 1.52 as OO-CWB; to Mexico 4.55 as XB-MAF

G-AMHD (WA/H/48), 19.10.51, Westland Aircraft Ltd., Yeovil; to the Belgian Congo 2.52 as OO-CWC; to Mexico 4.55 as XB-JUN

Westland Sikorsky S-51 Series 2 Widgeon

G-AKTW (WA/H/1), first flown 3.1.56, C. of A. 30.8.56, Westland Aircraft Ltd.; re-registered 10.58 to Bristow Helicopters Ltd. as G-APPR

G-ALIK (WA/H/3), first flown 23.8.55, C. of A. 7.1.57, Westland Aircraft Ltd.; re-registered 10.58 to Bristow Helicopters Ltd. as G-APPS

G-ANLW (WA/H/133), 22.12.58, Westland Aircraft Ltd., Yeovil

G-AOZD (WA/H/140), 12.8.57, Westland Aircraft Ltd., Yeovil; Bristow Helicopters Ltd., Redhill 12.60; re-registered in Nigeria 12.66 as 5N-AGL

The Hong Kong Police Widgeon helicopter G-APBK/VR-HFL with 'skyshouting' equipment at Yeovil in December 1957. (*Westland Aircraft Ltd.*)

G-AOZE (WA/H/141), 12.8.57, Westland Aircraft Ltd., Yeovil; Bristow Helicopters Ltd., Redhill 12.60; re-registered in Nigeria 6.62 as 5N-ABW

G-APBK (WA/H/145), 11.12.57, Westland Aircraft Ltd., Yeovil; to the Hong Kong Police Force 12.57 as VR-HFL; later 9M-AOP

G-APBL (WA/H/146), 13.12.57, Westland Aircraft Ltd., Yeovil; to the Hong Kong Police Force 10.57 as VR-HFM

G-APPR (WA/H/1), G-AKTW, 28.11.58, Bristow Helicopters Ltd., Redhill; re-registered in Nigeria 6.62 as 5N-ABV; seized by the Biafrans circa 1969

G-APPS (WA/H/3), G-ALIK, 28.11.58, Bristow Helicopters Ltd., Redhill; re-registered in Nigeria 1.63 as 5N-AGA

G-APTE (WA/H/149), 22.4.59, Westland Aircraft Ltd.; leased to Bristow Helicopters Ltd. 4.59; leased to Shamrock Helicopters Ltd., Dublin 7.60; re-registered in Nigeria 12.66 as 5N-AGM; rest. 7.68 to Bristow; w.f.u. 10.70

G-APTW (WA/H/150), 1.6.59, Westland Aircraft Ltd.; leased to Executair Ltd., Elstree 7.59; Westland communications aircraft in 1972

G-APVD (WA/H/151), 9.7.59, Westland Aircraft Ltd.; Ferranti Ltd., Hollinwood, Lancs. 6.63; Miss G. V. Aldam, Upminster, Essex 4.72

G-APWK (WA/H/152), 8.9.59, Westland Aircraft Ltd.

Westland Sikorsky S-55 Series 1

G-AMHK (55016), American built, registered 1.51 to Westland Aircraft Ltd. for trials; R.A.F. evaluation 1952 as WW339; to Norway 9.53 as LN-ORK

G-AMJT (WA/A/1), registered 5.51 to Westland Aircraft Ltd., Yeovil; to the R.A.F. 3.53 as XA862

G-AMYN (WA/A/4), registered 2.53 to Westland Aircraft Ltd.; test flown as G-17-3; to the French Navy 4.54

G-ANFH (WA.15), first flown 15.10.54, C. of A. 2.11.54, British European Airways Corporation 'Sir Ector'; B.E.A. Helicopters Ltd. 4.64; Bristow Helicopters Ltd. 5.69

G-ANJS (WA.18), first flown 15.6.54, C. of A. 15.7.54, The South Georgia Co. Ltd.; lost at sea off the Brazilian coast while operating from whaling factory ship 'Southern Harvester'

G-ANJT (WA.19), first flown 30.6.54, C. of A. 16.7.54, The South Georgia Co. Ltd.; ditched in Antarctic waters 29.1.58 while attempting to land on whaling factory ship 'Southern Venturer'

G-ANJU (WA.23), first flown 26.8.54, C. of A. 17.9.54, The South Georgia Co. Ltd.; ditched in the South Atlantic 20.12.56 while operating from 'Southern Harvester'

G-ANJV (WA.24), first flown 4.9.54, C. of A. 30.9.54, The South Georgia Co. Ltd.; Bristow Helicopters Ltd. 8.61; converted to Series 3 in 1963; based at Abu Dhabi 4.70

G-ANUK (WA.39), 4.5.55, The South Georgia Co. Ltd.; Bristow Helicopters Ltd. 8.61; converted to Series 3 in 1963; crashed 4.8.72

G-ANZN (WA.54), 9.6.55, Westland Aircraft Ltd., Yeovil; to Bahamas Airways Ltd. 7.55 as VP-BAF

G-ANZO (WA.55), 9.6.55, Westland Aircraft Ltd., Yeovil; to Bahamas Airways Ltd. 7.55 as VP-BAG

G-AOCF (WA.56), first flown 8.7.55, C. of A. 29.8.55, British European Airways Corporation, Gatwick; B.E.A. Helicopters Ltd. 4.64; to Libya 10.65 as 5A-DBA; rest. 4.66 to Autair Ltd., Luton; Bristow Helicopters Ltd. 12.67; converted to Series 3 in 1968; to Bermuda 12.68 as VR-BDB

G-AODA (WA.113), first flown 4.8.55, C. of A. 9.9.55, Shell Refining Co. Ltd., Bahrein; World Wide Helicopters (U.K.) Ltd., Doha, Qatar 11.61; to Iran 9.65 as EP-HAC, later 9Y-TDA

G-AODB (WA.114), 13.9.55, Shell Refining Co. Ltd., Bahrein; World Wide Helicopters (U.K.) Ltd., Doha, Qatar 11.61; to Bermuda 1.69 as VR-BDH

G-AODO (WA.116), 20.2.56, Fison-Airwork Ltd., Lagos; Bristow Helicopters Ltd., Redhill 12.61; converted to Series 3 in 1963; to Bermuda 6.63 as VR-BBZ

G-AODP (WA.117), 30.4.56, Fison-Airwork Ltd., Lagos; re-registered in Nigeria 8.61 as VR-NDL, later 5N-ABP; rest. 3.63 to Bristow Helicopters Ltd.; to Trinidad 5.63 as VP-TCN; rest. 3.65 to Bristow; converted to Series 3 in 1965; re-registered in Nigeria 1.69 as 5N-ABP

G-AOHE (WA.126), 5.10.56, The South Georgia Co. Ltd.; Bristow Helicopters Ltd. 8.61; converted to Series 3 in 1965; cancelled as destroyed 6.69

G-AMHK, the American-built Sikorsky S-55 imported by Westland Aircraft Ltd. for inspection and trials in 1951 before embarking on large scale production. (*Westland Aircraft Ltd.*)

G-AORT (WA.173), first flown 16.10.56, C. of A. 20.11.56, Westland Aircraft Ltd., Yeovil; to Saudi Arabian Airlines 12.56 as HZ-ABE

G-AOYB (WA.191), 11.4.57, Fison-Airwork Ltd., Nairobi; Airwork (Helicopters) Ltd., Redhill 10.60; to Bermuda 12.60 as VR-BBN; rest. 6.63 to Bristow Helicopters Ltd., Redhill; to Germany 12.64 as D-HOBI, later VR-BBN

G-AOZK (WA.240), first flown 30.12.57, C. of A. 10.1.58, Fison Airwork Ltd., Nairobi; Airwork (Helicopters) Ltd., Redhill 10.60; re-registered in Nigeria 8.61 as VR-NDK, later 5N-ABO; rest. 3.63 to Bristow Helicopters Ltd., Redhill; converted to Series 3 in 1963; named 'Kestrel' 1972

G-APKC (WA.250), 7.2.58, Fison-Airwork Ltd., Bourn; Airwork (Helicopters) Ltd., Redhill 10.60; to Trinidad 8.62 as VP-TCG

G-APRV (WA.295), 7.4.59, Westland Aircraft Ltd.; to Bermuda 4.59 as VR-BBE; later to Iran as EP-HAA

G-APRW (WA.296), 7.4.59, Westland Aircraft Ltd.; to Bermuda 4.59 as VR-BBF; to Germany as D-HODA; rest. 8.64 to Bristow Helicopters Ltd.

G-APWM (WA.297), 23.10.59, H. H. Shaikh Abdullah Mubarak al Sabah C.I.E., Kuwait; re-registered in Kuwait 8.60 as 9K-BHD

G-APWN (WA.298), 20.10.59, Westland Aircraft Ltd.; Bristow Helicopters Ltd., Redhill 3.63; converted to Series 3 in 1964; re-registered in Nigeria 12.65 as 5N-AGI; rest. 12.67 to Bristow

G-APWO (WA.299), 20.10.59, Westland Aircraft Ltd.; Bristow Helicopters Ltd., Redhill 3.63; converted to Series 3 in 1966; to Iran 4.66 as EP-HAG

G-APXA (WA.318), 12.12.59
G-APXB (WA.319), 1.1.60
G-APXF (WA.320), 20.2.60
} Westland Aircraft Ltd., Yeovil; H. H. Shaikh Abdullah Mubarak al Sabah C.I.E. 1.60; re-registered in Kuwait 8.60 as 9K-BHA, 'HB and 'HC

G-APXI (WA.321), registered 12.59 to Westland Aircraft Ltd.; not taken up

Westland Sikorsky S-55 Series 2

G-AOCZ (WA.115), 28.6.55, Westland Aircraft Ltd., Yeovil; to Iran 9.65 as EP-HAE; converted to Series 3 in 1957; rest. 8.67 to Bristow Helicopters Ltd., Redhill; to Bermuda 2.69 as VR-BDF, later to Nigeria as 5N-AIM

G-AOYY (WA.192), 16.7.57, Westland Aircraft Ltd., Yeovil; to Wheeler Airlines Ltd., Montreal 7.57 as CF-KAD

G-AOYZ (WA.193), 16.7.57, Westland Aircraft Ltd., Yeovil; to Wheeler Airlines Ltd., Montreal 7.57 as CF-KAE

G-APDY (WA.241), first flown 25.8.57, C. of A. 13.11.57, Westland Aircraft Ltd., Yeovil; converted to Series 3 in 1961; Bristow Helicopters Ltd. 12.66; sold in Nigeria 9.67

G-APPY (WA.268), 22.4.59, Westland Aircraft Ltd.; to Iran 4.59 as EP-BSK

G-APPZ (WA.269), 16.7.59, Westland Aircraft Ltd.; to Iran 4.59 as EP-CSK

G-AYXT (WA.154), XK940, registered 28.4.71 to Autair Helicopter Services Ltd., Luton

G-AYZJ (WA.263), XM685, registered 24.5.71 to Autair Helicopter Services Ltd., Luton

Westland Sikorsky S-55 Series 3

G-ASOU (WA.402), 9.4.64, Westland Aircraft Ltd.; to Germany 4.64 as D-HODE; rest. 5.66 to Bristow Helicopters Ltd.; re-registered in Nigeria 8.66 as 5N-AGK; rest. 9.67 to Bristow; to Bermuda 2.69 as VR-BDG, later 5N-AIN

G-ATIU	(WA.412), 7.10.65, Westland Aircraft Ltd.; Bristow Helicopters Ltd. 1.66; to Iran 2.66 as EP-HAF; rest. 8.71; to Nigeria 8.71 as 5N-AIV
G-ATKV	(WA.493), 7.1.66, Westland Aircraft Ltd.; Bristow Helicopters Ltd. 9.67; to Iran 11.67 as EP-HAN; rest. 4.68 to Bristow
G-ATLZ	(WA.125), ex French Air Force, 1.10.66, Bristow Helicopters Ltd.; to Iran 1.67 as EP-HAK; rest. 10.71; to Nigeria 11.71 as 5N-AJH
G-AWWA	(WA.397), 16.12.68, Westland Aircraft Ltd.; to Bermuda 12.68 as VR-BDD; rest. 8.71 to Bristow Helicopters Ltd.; to Nigeria 10.71 as 5N-AJG
G-AXZS	(WA.492), Brunei AMDB-102, VR-BDM, 12.5.70, Bristow Helicopters Ltd.; re-registered in Trinidad 6.70 as 9Y-TDJ
G-AYNP	(WA.71), XG576, 19.1.71, Bristow Helicopters Ltd., Redhill or Manston
G-AYTK	(WA.65), XJ401, 28.4.71, Bristow Helicopters Ltd., Redhill or Manston
G-AYYI	(WA.82), XG587, 30.6.71, Bristow Helicopters Ltd.; re-registered in Nigeria 8.71 as 5N-AIS
G-BAGD	(WA.78), XG583, 24.11.72 Bristow Helicopters Ltd., Redhill
G-BAMH	(WA.83), XG588, registered 1.73 to Bristow Helicopters Ltd., Redhill

Westland Wessex 60 Series 1

G-APLF	(WA.53), Wessex 1, registered 2.58 to Westland Aircraft Ltd., Yeovil; registration not taken up
G-ASWI	(WA.199), 17.9.65, Westland Aircraft Ltd.; to Bermuda 3.70 as VR-BDS; rest. 12.70 to Bristow Helicopters Ltd., North Denes; temporarily VR-BDS in 1971
G-ATBY	(WA.460), 15.10.65, Westland Charters Ltd.; to Bermuda 3.70 as VR-BDT; rest. 12.70 to Bristow Helicopters Ltd., North Denes
G-ATBZ	(WA.461), 5.11.65, Westland Charters Ltd.; Bristow Helicopters Ltd., North Denes 3.71
G-ATCA	(WA.462), 23.12.65, Westland Charters Ltd.; Bristow Helicopters Ltd., North Denes 3.71; crashed and burned on test flight at Rhoose 9.9.72
G-ATCB	(WA.463), 6.5.66, Westland Charters Ltd.; Bristow Helicopters Ltd., Cork 3.71

Bristow Helicopters Ltd.'s Wessex 60 G-AZBY at the company's maintenance base at Redhill in 1972. (*P. J. Bish*)

G-ATSC (WA.544), 18.8.66, Bristow Helicopters Ltd.; to Ecuador 3.70 as HC-ASD; rest. 8.72 to Bristow Helicopters Ltd., Redhill

G-AVEW (WA.562), 13.3.67, Bristow Helicopters Ltd.; to Australia 5.68 as VH-BHL

G-AVMC (WA.561), re-registered G-AVNE to avoid confusion with the standard radio message 'Visual Meteorological Conditions' or VMC

G-AVNE (WA.561), 3.6.67, Westland Helicopters Ltd., Yeovil; to Indonesia 8.70 as PK-HBQ

G-AWOX (WA.686), G-17-1, 12.9.68, Westland Aircraft Ltd.; to Bermuda 10.68 as VR-BCV; rest. 12.69 to Bristow Helicopters Ltd., North Denes; sold in Australia 4.72

G-AWXX (WA.694), 15.4.69, Westland Helicopters Ltd., Yeovil; to Australia 7.69 as VH-BHX

G-AXPJ (WA.696), 25.11.69, Bristow Helicopters Ltd.; to Indonesia 8.70 as PK-HBR; crashed in sea off Kalimantan Coast 8.6.71

G-AXXL (WA.732), 25.6.70, Bristow Helicopters Ltd.; re-registered in Nigeria 12.70 as 5N-AIR

G-AYNC (WA.739), 25.2.71, Bristow Helicopters Ltd.; to Australia 4.71 as VH-SJD

G-AZBY (WA.740), 17.9.71, Bristow Helicopters Ltd.

G-AZBZ (WA.741), 29.10.71, Bristow Helicopters Ltd.; re-registered in Nigeria 12.71 as 5N-AJI

G-AZCA (WA.742), 31.12.71, Bristow Helicopters Ltd.

Zlin 226/326/526

G-ASIM (838), 326, OK-SNA, 25.6.63, N. M. Browning, Stanford Rivers strip, Essex, crashed at Seething 22.8.71; G-ATDZ (304), 326, OK-LHC, 6.6.65, M. D. Popoff, North Thoresby strip, Lincs.; G-ATMZ (136), 226, OK-LLT, OE-CKW, OO-MDB, 15.3.66, crashed at Redhill 8.4.67; G-AVPZ (1015), 526, OK-VRE, 24.7.68, crashed at Kidlington 5.5.68; G-AWAR (1036), 526A, 11.2.68, crashed at Hullavington 3.6.70; G-AWJX (1049), 526, 7.6.68, Imperial Tobacco Group Ltd. Fairoaks; G-AWJY (1050), 526, 18.7.68, C.S.E. (Aircraft Services) Ltd., Kidlington; G-AWPG (1061), 526, 30.6.69, H. Foulds, Rochester; G-AWSH (1052), 526, 1.12.68, International Aerobatics Ltd., Farnborough

APPENDIX F

Airships and Free Balloons

As in the case of gliders (Volume 2, Appendix F), a special Lighter-than-Air Register was also created which remained in force until 1928. The first entries were made in 1920 when five spherical balloons, G-FAAA to G-FAAE, were registered—four to C. G. Spencer and Co. Ltd. and the last to R. F. Dagnall. Then in 1920–21 came the rigid airships R.36/G-FAAF and R.33/G-FAAG and three privately owned Short-built balloons G-FAAH to G-FAAJ; in 1922 two moored kite balloons G-FAAK and G-FAAL; and between 1923 and 1926 eight free balloons G-FAAM to G-FAAS and G-FAAU for C. G. Spencer and Co. Ltd. G-FAAT was a reservation for a projected K.S.R.1 semi-rigid airship, while G-FAAV and G-FAAW were the famous rigid airships R.100 and R.101 respectively. The last special registration, G-FAAX, was issued to the non-rigid A.D.1 airship in 1927

It was later decided to register all future balloons and airships in the same sequence as heavier-than-air machines but the requirement did not arise until 1951 when Lord Ventry's non-rigid airship 'Bournemouth' received the marks G-AMJH. Since then a marked revival in ballooning, due mainly to the development of hot air balloons with propane gas burners, has resulted in the considerable list given below:

G-APOB	Free Balloon, 'The Small World'
G-ATDK	Warm-Air Airship
G-ATGN	Thorn Coal Gas Balloon
G-ATLU	Turner Hot Air Balloon
G-ATTN	Piccard Hot Air Balloon
G-ATWM	Montgolfier Balloon
G-ATXR	A.F.B.1 Free Balloon
G-ATZG	A.F.B.2 Free Balloon
G-AVAT	Free Balloon 'Jambo'
G-AVJR	A.F.B.3 Free Balloon
G-AVKO	Gloster Non-Rigid Airship
G-AVSL	Lebaudy Replica Airship
G-AVTL	HAG.1/4 Free Balloon
G-AVUE	Free Balloon 8828
G-AWCR	Piccard AX-6
G-AWGF	Free Balloon 8879
G-AWJB	Brighton Hot Air Balloon
G-AWJC	Brighton Gas Balloon
G-AWMO	Omega O-80
G-AWOK	Gas Balloon
G-AWVR	Non-Rigid Airship
G-AXAO	Omega O-56
G-AXDT	Omega O-84
G-AXGH	Piccard Hot Air Balloon
G-AXJA	Omega O-56
G-AXJB	Omega O-84
G-AXMD	Omega O-20
G-AXVU	Cameron O-84
G-AXWB	Cameron O-65
G-AXXP	Hot Air Balloon
G-AYAJ	Cameron O-84
G-AYAL	Cameron O-56
G-AYAM	Cameron O-84
G-AYBU	Omega O-84
G-AYDB	Brighton Balloon
G-AYJZ	Cameron O-84
G-AYMV	Western O-20
G-AYTL	Gray Hot Air Balloon
G-AYTN	Cameron O-65
G-AYUK	Western MB-65
G-AYVA	Cameron O-84
G-AYVU	Cameron O-56
G-AYZF	Western O-65
G-AYZG	Cameron O-84
G-AZAA	Cameron O-84
G-AZBH	Cameron O-84
G-AZBT	Western O-65

G-AZBX	Western O-65
G-AZDF	Cameron O-84
G-AZER	Cameron O-42
G-AZFH	Western O-65
G-AZFN	Cameron O-56
G-AZHR	Piccard AX-6
G-AZIP	Cameron O-65
G-AZJF	Cameron O-65
G-AZJG	Western O-65
G-AZJI	Western O-65
G-AZKK	Cameron O-56
G-AZLB	Western O-65
G-AZLX	Western O-65
G-AZNR	Cameron O-56
G-AZNS	Cameron O-84
G-AZNT	Cameron O-84
G-AZNU	Cameron O-84
G-AZNV	Cameron O-65
G-AZNW	Cameron O-84
G-AZOO	Western O-65
G-AZPX	Western O-31
G-AZRI	Payne Hot Air Balloon
G-AZRN	Cameron O-84
G-AZSP	Cameron O-84
G-AZST	Western O-65
G-AZUP	Cameron O-65
G-AZUV	Cameron O-65
G-AZUW	Cameron A-140
G-AZUX	Western O-56
G-AZVO	Cameron O-84
G-AZVT	Cameron O-84
G-AZXB	Cameron O-65
G-AZYH	Cameron O-84
G-AZYL	Portslade Mk.17 Free Balloon
G-AZYV	Burns Free Balloon
G-BAAX	Cameron O-84
G-BADG	Cameron O-84
G-BADU	Cameron O-56
G-BAEK	Cameron O-65
G-BAGH	Cameron O-84
G-BAGI	Cameron O-31
G-BAGY	Cameron O-84
G-BAIF	Western O-65
G-BAIR	Thunder O-56
G-BAIY	Cameron O-65
G-BAKO	Cameron O-84
G-BALD	Cameron O-84
G-BAMA	Cameron O-77
G-BAMK	Cameron D-96 Airship

APPENDIX G

Miscellaneous Craft

Between the years 1960 and 1968 a one-man rotorcycle (prototype of a proposed infantry vehicle); three experimental hovercraft; and seven unpowered gyro-gliders were issued with aircraft registrations as follows.

G-APYF	(S2/7592)	Saro XROE-1 Rotorcycle
G-APYH		Britten-Norman CC-1 Cushioncraft
G-ARRJ		Saucer P.45 Series 2
G-ARSM		Britten-Norman CC-2 Cushioncraft
G-ATLH	(FT.5)	Tigercraft Tiger Mk.1 Gyro-Glider
G-AVDE	(1)	Turner Gyro-Glider Mk.1
G-AWJN	(FT.6)	Tigercraft Tiger Mk.2 Gyro-Glider
G-AWJP	(FT.8)	Tigercraft Tiger Mk.3 Gyro-Glider
G-AWJR	(FT.9)	Tigercraft Tiger Mk.1 Gyro-Glider
G-AWJS	(FT.10)	Tigercraft Tiger Mk.1 Gyro-Glider
G-AWJT	(FT.11)	Tigercraft Tiger Mk.1 Gyro-Glider

INDEX OF AEROPLANES

All aircraft mentioned in this book are listed in the index, including those outside the British civil E to Z range. Listing is arranged alphabetically by manufacturers and then in order of type numbers. Where these were not allotted, an alphabetical or chronological list of type names is used. Where aircraft are mentioned in the main narrative, only the first page of that narrative is listed. Pages allotted to each manufacturer in the main narrative and appendixes will be found on pages 9 to 10.